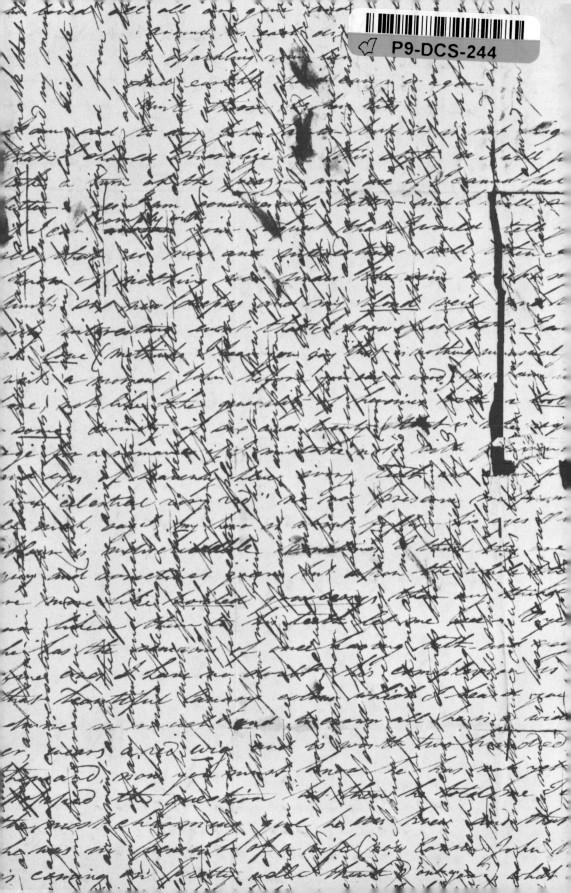

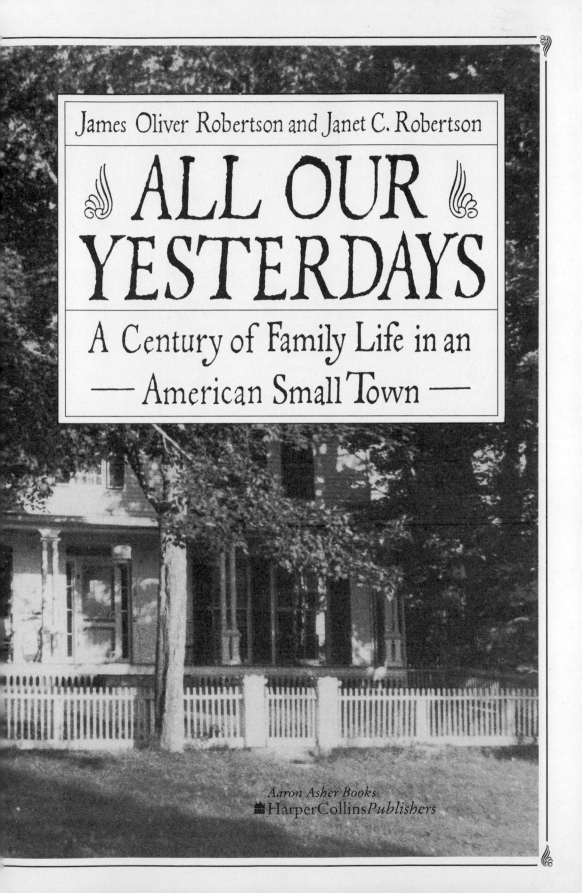

James Oliver Robertson and Janet C. Robertson

ALL OUR YESTERDAYS

A Century of Family Life in an
— American Small Town —

Aaron Asher Books
HarperCollins*Publishers*

FIRST EDITION

DESIGNED BY JOEL AVIROM
Map on page xiv by Paul Pugliese

LIBRARY OF CONGRESS CATALOGING-IN-PUBLICATION DATA
Robertson, James Oliver.
All our yesterdays : a century of family life in an American small town / James
Oliver Robertson, Janet C. Robertson.–1st ed.
p.   cm.
"Aaron Asher books."
Includes bibliographical references and index.
ISBN 0-06-019017-5 (cloth)
1. Hampton (Conn.)–Social life and customs.   I. Robertson, Janet C., 1933– .
II. Title.
F104.H24R63 1993
974.6'45–dc20   91-58350

93 94 95 96 97 ❖/CW 10 9 8 7 6 5 4 3 2 1

—————————— FOR ——————————
THE PEOPLE OF HAMPTON, CONNECTICUT,
THE LIVING AND THE DEAD,
WITH OUR THANKS

❧ CONTENTS ❧

Authors' Note

Many people of widely differing education wrote the documents quoted in this book. They often did not spell the way we spell in the twentieth century. In order to make their prose and their voices more accessible without distorting their eloquence, we have made a few changes. We have rarely changed their spelling, but we have occasionally added punctuation, and sometimes we have added a word or two where clarity required. In general, we have expanded abbreviations and ellipses. However, we have tried to keep our interference to a minimum.

For instance, one carpenter wrote letter after letter from the West without ever using a period or a capital. We put in the periods to separate his sentences, but did not find it necessary to capitalize even his first-person-singular pronouns. And his orthography for "bare ast" frontier children would have suffered by modernization. On the other hand, when a well-educated late-nineteenth-century letter writer used "principal" when she meant "principle," we silently corrected her.

We did not wish to distract by calling attention to any of our emendations. However, the reader may feel confident that nothing has been done which alters meaning.

Preface

৶৶

It is our hope that this book gives significant voice to ordinary people who are now dead, and who can therefore not tell their own stories. The memory of human beings is never dependable. We all forget the horrors and pleasures, the accomplishments and failures of our own lives. How much more do we forget about people who lived and died in other times and places? Without some memory, some record, and some stories told, we are all deprived of pasts that not only belong to us, but that shape us, our beliefs and ideals, and our acts.

In what follows, we have tried to honor the aspirations, fears, hopes, orneriness, endurance, and even the despair of the many members of the Taintor, Bulkeley, Davis, and other families of Hampton, Connecticut, whose stories we have come to know. We have written in admiration and respect for hundreds whose lives have touched ours profoundly, over separating distances of three, four, five, or six generations.

J.O.R./J.C.R.
Hampton, Connecticut

ALL OUR YESTERDAYS

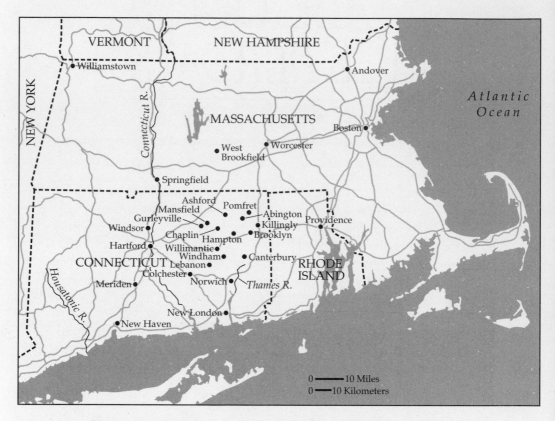

Southern New England, showing towns the Taintors and Bulkeleys frequented.

PROLOGUE
RELICS OF THE PAST

❧

Wherever one goes in New England—in farm country, suburbs, or really deep woods—there are stone walls. People ask about them. Tourists speculate about them, sometimes wonder whether they were built by Indians. The stone walls are, in fact, the boundaries of fields first created by settlers.

Those fields were cleared of trees, often plowed and planted, and certainly "rock-picked." (Rock picking is every New England farmer's springtime misery. During the winter as the earth freezes and thaws, rocks rise to the surface of the fields; they must be removed before plowing can proceed. Stacked at the edges of the fields, they are the raw material for all those stone walls.) Wherever there is a wall, there was once a field, even in what is now forest. Those walls stand as evidence that in the days settlers built them many more people lived off the produce of New England's rocky soil than do today.[1]

Such relics of the past—along with old houses, churches, and fences where there are no walls—stand mutely insistent that all America started out rural and agricultural. Even Manhattan and Chicago were farmed at one time, and Los Angeles was ranch country. Only in the twentieth century has the United States become an urban nation. The small-town world of stone walls, old houses and churches and fences, has been left far behind. The life that produced them is totally gone. What follows is an excursion into one of America's old towns, an old house still standing there, and through that house into the lives of people and families who lived in the world where they built those stone walls.

The hill-country northeastern-Connecticut town of Hampton was settled early in the eighteenth century and incorporated in 1786. It lies thirty-six miles east of Hartford, and about the same distance west of Providence, Rhode Island. Hampton's tiny village still is two long rows of large old houses facing each other on the Main Street, balancing the centrally located Congregational church. The church comes complete with Greek Revival columned porch and pointed spire. Its signboard proclaims it the second oldest Congregational church building surviving in Connecticut. The village itself, which might have been lifted from a Norman Rockwell painting, is on the National Register of Historic Places.

In New England a village is not the same thing as a town. A New England town is a geopolitical unit that was intended, when New England towns were first established, to be an agriculturally self-supporting community. The 25.3 square-mile *town* of Hampton is a rough oval of swamp-topped hills around the valley of a southward-flowing stream appropriately called Little River. The *village* is on a ridge west of and high above the river. The arable soil in the town today seems most easily to grow rocks, but there are still a few farms. Once cleared of trees, as was all of New England, most of Hampton today is reforested. Its hillsides and swamps, according to one native, are "only good for holding the world together."

The whole town of Hampton seems to have survived from a forgotten time. It is still very rural. Its only businesses are its three or four farms, a general store, a garage, an insurance agency, a gas distributor, and assorted small manufacturers and cottage industries. It is still governed by the direct democracy of a town meeting. And, simply by its size, Hampton is out of the past. Historically, the majority of the whole American population lived in rural places of fewer than 2,500 people until 1920. Hampton is still such a place. It achieved its highest population of 1,379 people in the year 1800. The 1990 census for the first time showed a population greater than that; the whole town now has only about 1,500 people.

We had been house-hunting for years. One day in 1965 a real-estate agent showed us a big white house with green wooden shutters on its (more than thirty) windows, in the middle of a dead-looking village. The house had a deep porch on the front and one side. Huge old maple trees fronted it and surrounded its yard stretching north of the church on the Main Street of Hampton.

We walked into a time warp. No one had lived in the house for years, but it was filled with worn furniture and the leftover trappings of many people's lives. In the biggest room there was a dining table with about twenty Hitchcock chairs crowded around it. There was a summer kitchen whose only water source was a cast-iron hand pump in a soapstone sink. There were four bathrooms, all of whose fixtures looked late Victorian, with tubs standing on ball-and-claw feet. There was a rusted-out coal-fired furnace in the basement, but only one heat duct to the upstairs with its six

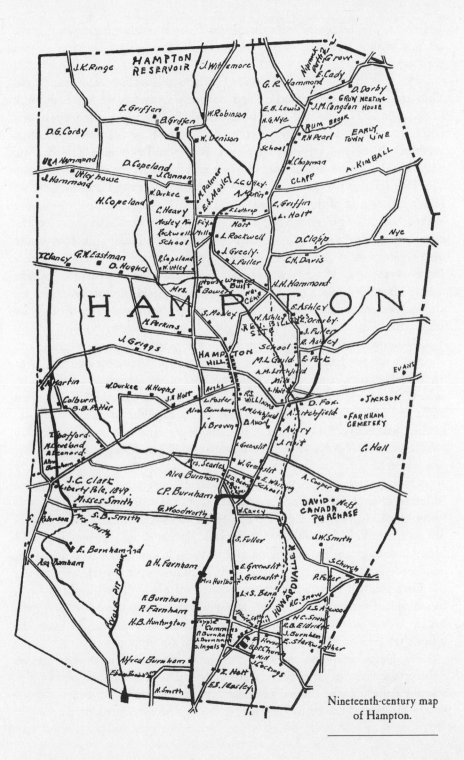

Nineteenth-century map
of Hampton.

bedrooms. There seemed to be fireplaces everywhere, including one in the kitchen with a swinging iron crane to hold pots and a bake oven in the wall next to it.

We bought the house from three brothers whose last name was Davis. They told us their family had owned it since shortly after it had been built in the 1790s. The day we took possession, the Davises turned over their family's original deed. Handwritten, dated 1804, it was from Thomas Stedman, Jr., to the Davises' ancestors, Roger and Solomon Taintor. We put the old deed in our safe-deposit box and did not give it much thought. The Davises also handed us a copy of their aunt Dorothy Davis Goodwin's historical account of the "ancestral home." She described the way the house looked when Roger and Solomon Taintor bought it: "Like most of the houses of that period it was a squarish, clapboarded building painted white on a foundation of field stone . . . two stories and an attic in height, with a slight overhang in the gables and plain pitch shingled roof. It had a plane paneled front door with plain glass lights on either side and above the door, and on the front four windows downstairs & five upstairs each with 24 small panes. There has never been anything fancy about the house."[2]

When we moved in, we did not have the money to fix up a house, and we really did not have the time either. What little money we had we spent on a kitchen with running water and an ill-conceived but essential heating system. We took off old wallpaper, built bookshelves, scraped and painted walls and trim to make the place livable, and began what we now recognize as the lifelong process of decorating, remodeling, and not quite keeping up with a very old, big house that could most kindly be described as a handy-man's special.

Over the years, we have realized that the house was "modernized" and added to several times before we started work on it. In the nearly two centuries since it was built, there have been many repairs, changes, and "make-do" efforts to keep it livable. We found old doors, molding, trim, joists, and beams reused in the backs of closets, on walls, in ceilings. There was even handmade paneling lining the attic stairs. Gradually, after years of learning the do-it-yourself necessities of survival in an old wooden house with a two-hundred-year-old "dug" (not artesian) well for a water supply, we began to feel we knew the frugal Yankees who had constantly made do while they lived in the spaces we now occupy.

The Davis family did not leave the house empty. Although they moved most of the furniture out, there were many relics of their long occupation scattered through the rooms, in closets, and in the attic. They left a sleigh bed, a cushioned chaise longue, a first edition of the *Encyclopaedia Ameri-*

cana, a photograph of Yale's first football team. There were a spinning wheel and barrels full of unidentified junk in the attic. There was a box full of carefully folded early nineteenth-century newspapers. And there was a child's penmanship exercise book that had belonged to Henry G. Taintor. In a scattered, disjointed way, all this made us aware that real people had preceded us in the house, that they had changed it when they lived there–just as we were changing it to suit our lives.

After nearly twenty years in our Hampton house we had gotten to know about as much as anyone ever knows about the previous owners. We became friends with Wendell and Alison Davis, the only members of the family who still lived in Hampton. Every time something went wrong in the house–like our basement filling with several feet of water in a spring runoff–Wendell cheerfully assured us that whatever had happened "wasn't covered by the guarantee."

One day after the two of us–an historian and a novelist–had evinced particular interest in early Hampton people, Wendell Davis arrived at our door with a big cardboard box filled with dusty old pamphlets, prints, and ribbon-tied packets of letters in his arms. "Would you be interested in these?" he asked in a tentative voice. It turned out that for more than 150 years, his ancestors–Taintors and Davises–had saved nearly every piece of paper that came in their door. We'd had no idea that hundreds of their let-ters, stacks of deeds, packets of their receipts and accounts, inventories, pamphlets, books, pictures, and business documents even existed, because the family had taken "all that junk" with them when they moved out.

It was a wonderful serendipity that connected us to such a treasure trove of love letters, reports of travels, news of kin, advice from parents, agonies of children, newspapers still folded back to the page being read when they were put down 150 years ago, and the business records of an ordinary small-town family from the 1790s to the 1920s.[3]

The Davises brought us, piecemeal, a collection that now fills twenty-five large file boxes. Along with the hundreds of letters, books, and pam-phlets, there are visiting cards, invitations to dances, college catalogues, and programs of plays. There are class-day speeches and course notes. Nothing was stored in any particular order. Early nineteenth-century letters had no envelopes. There were no stamps on them. They were just folded sheets of paper, sealed with sealing wax, hand-marked with a postage amount, some-times stamped with a postmark that invariably did not tell a year. The handwritings were old-fashioned and some of them nearly impossible to read. Some of the letters were "crossed"–the writer first wrote horizontally

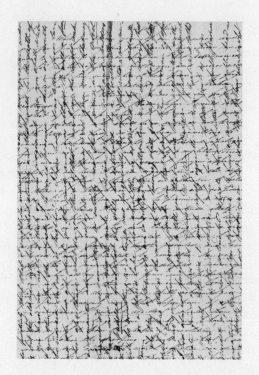

A crossed letter. The writer wrote horizontally on all the pages, turned them ninety degrees, and then wrote across them.

on all the pages, then wrote vertically across the horizontal writing, usually in the same page order. A magnifying glass and very bright light sometimes helped in reading them.

People who had lived in our rooms—in our house, in this same town—had read these letters. We looked out the same windows they looked out as they wrote. We were in the same spaces. Out of those carefully folded pages came realities of their lives, private lives in a world that no longer existed. These relics from a long-ago past were not so mute as the house itself, or the stone walls and fields in the town. We found ourselves rejoicing over the family's successes, amused at their peculiarities, weeping over their tragedies.

We began to imagine we could hear their voices. A Hampton minister in the 1820s wrote about "plausible, deceitful, licentious, especially *lascivious* members"[4] of his church. A father wrote to his son in 1835, "I would Informe you that . . . your mother has ben very much out of helth," but reassured him that the doctor "thinks that the Cancer tumer is thurily Subdued."[5] A servant girl from Hampton wrote of her voyage to San

Francisco in the Gold Rush, "Picked up a beau & of course had a very pleasant time."[6] A mother in the early 1860s sitting with her feet up against the
oven in our kitchen wrote to her lovelorn son, "There are better fishes in
the sea than were ever caught, and who knows but your hook may draw
them out?"[7] A distraught father wrote in the 1870s that "little Carrie died
last night. . . . Susie is quite heartbroken and . . . has not yet recovered her
strength since the baby's birth."[8] Reading these letters, we were plunged
into the midst of a family's life as by a time machine. So we have written,
from the Taintor-Davis Collection, a saga of nineteenth-century small-town
family life as it was lived and as it looked from within.[9]

The Taintors and Hampton's people were neither typical nor unusual in the
nineteenth century. Some of them succeeded, some of them failed, some of
them moved on; none became famous. Some built themselves comfortable
lives. Many did not. Some left Hampton for the cities, but most left to start
or live in some other small town, west of Hampton. When the first
Taintors moved to Hampton, they already had some capital to buy land and
put themselves into business—but that was not unusual for Americans on
the move. The element in their lives that puts them at the center of the
experience of their contemporaries is where they lived: in a family group in
an agrarian small town. Precisely the particularities of Hampton's life and
the Taintors' experience illuminate the history of nineteenth-century
Americans. "The shapes of knowledge are ineluctably local," as anthropolo-
gist Clifford Geertz recently wrote, and history is best explained "in local
frames of awareness."[10]

Today's mainstream values about family and community life come out
of the past of small towns like Hampton because, throughout the nineteenth century, the great majority of the population lived in small towns
with fewer than 2,500 people. We still pay homage to nuclear families,
direct democracy, and the small entrepreneur in our machine-dominated,
electronic, citified world. The belief that family life—ideally in a single-family home—should be at the center of morality, religion, education, and work
comes from small-town America. So does the idea that political participation is the duty of every responsible adult. Even our more abstract beliefs—
about the roles of women and men, the separation of domestic and public
life, the importance of work, and the place of God and the church—all come
from small-town America.

Early nineteenth-century Connecticut towns supplied an unusually
large number of the people who settled the rest of the country. Alexis de
Tocqueville wrote in *Democracy in America* that in 1830 thirty-six members
of the House of Representatives (sixteen percent) were born in Conn-

ecticut, although the state itself sent only five members to Congress (it had only about two percent of the population). In the 1860s, the Speaker of the House, a representative from Pennsylvania who sponsored the Homestead Act, was Galusha Grow—who had been born on what is now known as Grow Hill on the northern edge of Hampton, Connecticut. New England towns like Hampton have been the model for small-town life throughout American history; they have bred other small towns across the country.

Nostalgia is strong in nearly all that has been written of small towns and nineteenth-century families. But if we look through the window provided by the Taintors and Hampton, we will not see our modern selves. Rather, by listening to the voices of people who lived then, we will understand that our world is utterly changed, that the assumptions and values we have thoughtlessly accepted from the small-town experience do not fit our own times. In L. P. Hartley's phrase, "the past is a foreign country." People thought and behaved differently there.[11]

The lives of small towns underwent subtle, often imperceptible changes over the more than a century before the 1920s. The consequences of the changes people welcomed into their lives then were no more visible to them than the consequences of changes in our lives today are visible to us. Only now has it become clear that those changes added up to the permanent abandonment of the foundations and values of the agrarian small-town world.

As we have come to know it in the past twenty-five years, Hampton itself has seemed a relic of the past. We quickly discovered that it made a difference to live in such a small place. Everybody knew everybody else's business. We, who had read Sinclair Lewis's *Main Street,* Shirley Jackson's "The Lottery," and even Grace Metalious's *Peyton Place,*[12] were frightened by what we thought we knew from their works—that small towns were small-minded and oppressive. Only gradually did we begin to understand, with the gentle help of our new neighbors, that Hampton was like an extended family. People actually cared about each other. Most consciously tried not to be too judgmental, perhaps on the principle—they mentioned it often enough—of "Judge not that ye be not judged." On the other hand, they frequently, publicly, and often intemperately expressed their anger at each other.

The institutions in town did what they were supposed to do. The elementary school taught our children reading, writing, arithmetic, and some music and art. The churches rang their bells on Sunday and drew congregations which they cared for, and which represented a majority of the town's population. The fire company and ambulance corps, made up entirely of volunteers, served competently in emergencies. The annual Memorial Day parade brought nearly everyone out, either marching or on the sidelines, and all the children in town got free ice cream at the end of the speeches. Volunteers who worked to serve the town's needs staffed every board and committee of government. This old-fashioned, dead-seeming town was still alive and functioning.

We came to Hampton's town meeting (no representatives, just personal responsibility) from a world in which town meetings themselves were subjects of nostalgia. We had grown up with a radio program called "Town Meeting of the Air," we had seen Thornton Wilder's play *Our Town,* and town meetings had been held up to us by teachers and politicians as the models of American democracy. Here in Hampton, in all its prickly reality, was the thing itself. We even discovered, after we had lived in town for a few years, that a once-popular book on the subject, *Town Meeting Country,* by Clarence Webster, had been written in Hampton, about Hampton.

At least once a year, all adults are entitled to come to town meeting—no more than a third ever do. They discuss the budget (including the schools and other town services), discuss any other issues the town wants to take up, vote to decide those issues, and lay the taxes on their property to pay for what they have decided. In town meeting, people say things about principles in public, and they discover what they have in common—and what they do not. It is one of the places where people work openly and publicly, as they have since the first Hampton town meeting in 1786, to build and maintain community. But it is not all sweetness and light.

Of course there are fears, feuds, angers, frustrations, poverty, and misery in an extended family of over a thousand people. That is the human condition; no community, whatever its size, is immune. What was surprising to our urban eyes when we came to Hampton was that the town seemed to know and many wanted to help when someone local was suffering or in trouble.

All the families of old-timers seem to be related to each other. Some claim descent from original settlers. And all the established families have character which lasts over generations. Distinctive character sometimes sticks to houses. People have always said we live in "the Davis house," which they often called "Maple Terrace" because early-twentieth-century Davises had named it that. The field in back was "Roger Davis's field" even after we had owned it for many years. After more than twenty years in Hampton now, we are still "new people," outsiders, yet at the same time we have been taken into the community. The community is a shifting cast of characters set in the scenery of a particular place. How long does outsider status last? Maybe for generations.

John Taintor (1725–1798) of Colchester, Connecticut
  m. (1751) (1) Esther Clark (1729–1756)
  m. (1758) (2) Sarah Bulkeley (1735–1806), sister of Captain John
    Bulkeley

JOHN TAINTOR'S CHILDREN

- John 1760–1825 (m. Sarah Hosford), lived in Windham, Connecticut, then in New York City
- Charles 1762–1854 (m. Mary Abbe), lived in Windham, Connecticut
- Gershom
- Roger 1767–1831 (m. *Abigail-Nabby-Bulkeley*)
- Solomon 1769–1827 (m. *Judith Bulkeley*)
- Sarah (m. Joshua Robbins Bulkeley), lived in Williamstown, Massachusetts
- Polly (m. Gilbert Grosvenor of Pomfret, Connecticut)

(Capt.) John Bulkeley (brother of Sarah Bulkeley Taintor) m. (1757) Judith Worthington

---

CAPTAIN JOHN BULKELEY'S CHILDREN

- John, whose daughter Roxana married James Mather Goodwin
- William (m. Mary Champion), who had twin sons, Henry and Epaphroditus
- Gershom, who moved to Williamstown, Massachusetts
- Elijah
- *Abigail* (Nabby) 1768–1831 (m. *Roger Taintor*)
- Joshua Robbins (m. Sarah Taintor–sister of Roger and Solomon), lived in Williamstown
- Mary
- *Judith* 1775–1849 (m. *Solomon Taintor*)
- Gurdon
- Gad (m. Orra Barstow), had four children
- Lydia (m. (1) John Worthington, (2) Dr. William Mason)
- *Dan* 1784–1842 (m. Phebe Burnett in Hampton)
- Harriet 1787–1878 (m. Samuel S. Moseley 1787–1866), had seven children

Our story begins when Hampton was settled at the beginning of the eighteenth century. It focuses on Roger and Solomon Taintor, two brothers born in the late 1760s in the prosperous town of Colchester, Connecticut, who moved to Hampton in the 1790s. By that time Hampton, like nearly every town and settlement in America in the years after the Revolution, was an agricultural community on the make.

Roger and Solomon were sons of John Taintor, the innkeeper in Colchester, and his wife, Sarah Bulkeley. They had gone into business when they were quite young with their two older brothers, John and Charles Taintor, in the town of Windham, buying and selling land and goods. Their move to Hampton established them as independent merchants in a village which had just recently itself become independent of the town of Windham.

Roger, the elder brother by two years, had married Nabby (Abigail) Bulkeley, one of his first cousins, in Colchester in 1789. Their first child died, and they were childless when they moved to Hampton. Solomon Taintor, the younger brother, married Judith Bulkeley, Nabby's younger sister, just after the brothers located in Hampton. In the spring of 1800, each couple had a son.

On June 8, 1804, Roger and Solomon Taintor paid two thousand dollars to Thomas Stedman, Jr., for eleven acres and the house north of the Meeting House in Hampton. According to the deed, they actually became owners of the house and garden the next April (planting time). Local tradition says Thomas Stedman had built the house at least ten years earlier for his nephew and namesake, the young lawyer Thomas Stedman, Jr., from whom the Taintors bought it.[13]

Dorothy Davis Goodwin's story of the ancestral home tells that "the two families owned everything in common, in the house, the farm and in a store that was built at the south side of the lot. Nabby kept house one month and Judith the next. One brother ran the farm, the other conducted an extensive export business in wool, in the store, which brought traders from all the surrounding towns. A sideboard in the house has a shelf which pulls out over the central drawer and there, after a successful deal, decanters were set out and the trader was invited to partake of hospitality."

The Davis family wanted to leave that sideboard in the house when we moved in. We took an instant dislike to each articulated hair carved on its claw feet and we had a sideboard of our own, so we asked them to take it with them. They did. Now we have reconstructed the story of four generations of Taintor descendants who lived out their lives in that house in Hampton which Roger and Solomon bought in 1804.

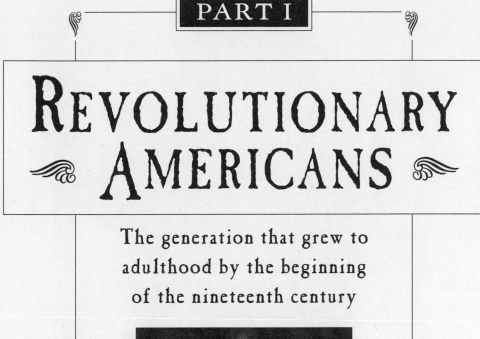

PART I

REVOLUTIONARY AMERICANS

The generation that grew to
adulthood by the beginning
of the nineteenth century

Dr. and Mrs. John Brewster
(neighbors of the first Taintors in Hampton),
painted by John Brewster, Jr., about 1798.

CHAPTER 1

BRED IN
HAMPTON'S BONES

&

"Little children, too young to join in the procession,
remembered vividly through life the long train, reaching from
Gallows Hill to [the] Jail ..."[1]

E very beginning has a past. The Taintors started their lives in
Hampton in the 1790s. By that time people in the town already told
stories about nearly a hundred years of carving out frontier farms
and building a new community. Their stories described gathering
people into churches, religious schisms and fights, tough-minded ministers
and their tough-minded flocks. They told of the heroism and hardships of
Hampton men and women who had recently fought a War for
Independence. In the 1790s the Taintors and Hampton were part of a new
nation–of former traitors and revolutionaries–trying to be independent and
self-governing. The town already had a past. As the Taintors gradually
became part of its life, they learned its stories.

Religion at the Core

When you drive into Hampton today, what you see in the center of the village is the Congregational church. Big and white, with a columned Greek
porch on its narrow front facing the street and a tall, classical steeple, it
looks the quintessence of the New England Colonial church.

But it is not what the Taintors saw when they moved to Hampton in
the 1790s. Then, what they called the Meeting House was a building that
looked like a very large house. Its long side faced the road in those days,
the way the rest of the houses in the village did. Its doorway was in the

 15

center, the way house doorways were. There might have been a porch and a bell-tower, but not the ones we see today. To the people who lived in Hampton then, that big building was part of the assumed furniture of life—important but ordinary, certainly not picturesque. It was not set aside for Sundays, not sanctified, not even reserved exclusively for religious meetings. It was simply the place where the community came together. And it had not been there forever, only for about forty years.

Religion, like the Meeting House, was an inseparable part of the fabric of everyday life. It was at the center of people's assumptions—about business, about farming, about family relationships, about government, about public and private behavior. The early Puritans who had founded New England had established their Congregational church as the only church. Everyone paid taxes to support the established church, whether or not they were members.

Membership in the church was based on an individual-community covenant. Thirty-five families banded together to make the original covenant of the Hampton church in 1723. They had just ordained the first minister of their congregation (which was then the second parish of the town of Windham):

> We do this day . . . humbly and heartily avouch the Lord . . . to be our God and the God of our seed, entirely and everlastingly dedicating both ourselves and ours unto his holy fear and service according to his word promising and covenanting to walk with God, and love one another as God's chosen people and a particular church of Christ ought to do complying with the whole will of God so far as he hath been pleased . . . to discover his mind to us by his Spirit, word and providence acknowledging . . . the Lord Jesus . . . as head of the church . . . looking for acceptation only in Christ both of our persons and services.[2]

To participate in this congregational covenant was to be a member of the church. In order to become a member, one had to live a Godly life in the eyes of the members, one had publicly to avow faith and defend it in detailed cross-examination by the members, and one had to experience "conversion" in a way that was convincing to oneself and to the members of the congregation. Achieving membership was no easy matter. The children of members of the Hampton congregation were accepted as members. But at no time were all the inhabitants of Hampton members of the church, although everyone was subject to "the laws of Christ's kingdom." In each town the church recorded who was born, who was baptized, who was married, who died, and who was a member of the "Religious Society," as the congregation was called. Because the records are spotty at best, we don't know Hampton's exact population in the early eighteenth century, or exactly how many were members of the church. In Hampton as in all other Puritan congregations, debate over membership and the qualifications for it would go on until the middle of the nineteenth century at least.

William Billings (Yale, 1720) was Hampton's first minister. He preached in private houses because the congregation did not, during his tenure, raise sufficient money to build a meeting house. Not everyone in the congregation found him to their taste. On September 11, 1729, Jeremiah Utley acknowledged "before God & this Congregation that my Saying I had Rather hear my dog bark than hear Mr Billings preach was a vile and Scandalous expression. . . . I do hereby declare to God and this Church my sorrow & repentance for it."[3]

Brought to bed of a fever on May 20, 1733, "Reverend William Billings Departed this Life about five of the clock in the afternoon in the thirty sixth year of his age." Billings had brought 172 new members into the church in the decade of his ministry. He left a widow and four young children.[4]

The minister who loomed large in Hampton memories when the Taintors came to town was Samuel Moseley (Harvard, 1729), who succeeded Billings and remained minister for fifty-seven years. He came to town in 1734, married Billings's widow, and finished building his predecessor's house. That house still dominates one end of Hampton's main street, and it is the only house that looks down the length of the village.

Moseley's long ministry spanned the important religious and political movements of the eighteenth century. He was a central figure in Hampton's response to the enthusiasm, the revivals, the itinerant ministers, and the separatisms of the Great Awakening in the middle of the century. Moseley used these upheavals to strengthen his own power as minister. He fought vigorously but not always successfully to prevent the splintering of his congregation as separatists split off to follow popular preachers or form congregations based on less orthodox theologies.[5]

At no time was the population of Hampton as homogeneous as the popular myth of the New England small town would have it. We know this because the church records show that Moseley baptized many local Indians and Negroes (as African-Americans were then called) and made them church members. The Indians were families of Pequots or Nipmucks who had remained in the Hampton area after the white invasion, and Moseley's taking them into the church was part of the general effort to Christianize and detribalize them. The African-Americans were slaves in a few of the more well-to-do Hampton families. By the end of Moseley's ministry, "Indians" disappeared from the baptismal records and their family names were gone from Hampton's records, but "negroes" continued to be a recognized part of the community.

Samuel Moseley's family took an important place in town life. His eldest son, Ebenezer, who graduated from Yale in 1763, began life as a preacher, in Brookfield, Massachusetts, in 1765. Two years later, Ebenezer was ordained to the Indian mission to the Six Nations at Onohoquaga on the Susquehanna. His Indian parishioners offered him a bride, and he avoided marrying her without offending the Iroquois only by telling them he needed his father's permission to marry. He left the mission not long after—whether because of that incident or not is not known—and returned to Hampton. In 1773 he married and took the unusual step of leaving the ministry. He became a merchant-storekeeper in Hampton. He fought in the Revolution and became the colonel of a regiment of Connecticut militia. When the Taintors moved to Hampton, Ebenezer Moseley was Town Clerk and one of Hampton's most influential men.[6]

Sarah, the youngest of Samuel Moseley's children, married Joseph Steward, a young minister who was also a portrait painter. They lived with Moseley and took care of him in the years just before his death. Steward painted portraits in Hampton in those years and he taught John Brewster, Jr., the deaf and dumb son of Dr. John Brewster, to paint. The Stewards moved to Hartford shortly after Samuel Moseley died and for many years thereafter operated an art gallery in the upstairs northeast room of the State House.[7]

Samuel Moseley had been unable to prevent a group of Hampton families—most of whom lived in the north end of town near the Pomfret town line and the village of Abington—from breaking away from his congregation in 1770. They formed a Baptist Society and hired a preacher. They were more tolerant of enthusiastic preaching and based membership on the Grace of Baptism. Their numbers increased in the course of the Revolution under the influence of important Baptist leaders and preachers from Rhode Island. Then Hampton families—the Grows, the Dodges, the Lyons—gave land and money for the construction of a Baptist meeting house on what is now called Grow Hill. William and James Grow were the first ministers to preach in that building, just when the Taintors moved to Hampton in the 1790s.[8]

When the Taintors came to Hampton the shadow of Samuel Moseley still loomed in the congregation. His stories were still told. The gravestone of his second wife, Mary, was quite new—she had died in 1794. The Taintors could read the epitaph that reminded the whole town of her qualities: "She was benevolent, sincere, And unaffectedly pious; A fond and tender parent, Fervently devoted to domestic duties, and care of her household."[9]

Rev. Ludovicus Weld, who was ordained Hampton's third Congregational minister in 1792, lived at some distance from the church and the main street of the village because the Moseley family owned the house Samuel had lived in, and house lots near the meeting house were not available. Weld was presiding over important shifts in the status of the church as the Second Great Awakening began in the 1790s. New members–the great majority of them women–joined the church, and in order to make membership easier, the Hampton congregation even decided "that this Church will not in future exact confessions of persons guilty of adultery or fornication as a term of admission to the Church." Little Puritan exclusivity remained in Hampton as the nineteenth century began. There were, however, continuing conflicts about who belonged to what church.[10]

Revolution as the Frame

On the morning of April 20, 1775, Captain James Stedman and his company of militiamen marched north from Hampton to Pomfret. A messenger had brought news to Colonel Israel Putnam (in Brooklyn, the town east of Hampton) of the battle at Lexington and Concord, Massachusetts, where valiant "minutemen" fired on and drove back the British army. Putnam is said to have dropped his plow as did the ancient Roman hero, Cincinnatus, and set out for Concord; in fact, he called the militia to rally in Pomfret. Captain Stedman's Hampton company was well-trained, and therefore one of those picked to march immediately to help the minutemen in Massachusetts.

Hampton's revolutionary stories, as the new patriotic citizenry told them in the 1790s and after, began thirty years earlier. They told of how, when the British and Americans together won the terrible French and Indian War in 1763–in which many Hampton men fought–the new King George III and his government started deliberately to oppress the war-weary Americans. The royal government imposed a stamp tax and a tax on tea, used the royal navy to regulate American commerce, and quartered a standing army in America to take away the rights of the Colonists to tax and govern themselves.

In the 1770s, many communities formed extra-legal Committees of Correspondence to keep in touch with other towns, organize mutual resistance against the British, and suppress identified loyalists. Secret organizations of protesters–"Sons of Liberty"–orchestrated demonstrations against the British and tried to prevent the sale of British goods. Citizens of Hampton, prepared with tar and feathers, searched the wagons of merchant Jeremiah Clark because they suspected him of smuggling tea into town.[11] Windham's Committee of Correspondence had four members from Hampton, including Ebenezer Moseley, Joseph Ginnings, William Durkee, and John Howard. In 1774 it collected and sent 258 sheep to Boston to help feed the city, because the British government had closed the port of Boston to supplies from the sea and the British army was quartered there.[12] In small towns like Hampton, after the Revolution was won, people told of early incidents as if local patriots' acts had meshed purposefully with the large-scale Boston Tea Party and with the burning of the royal navy ship Gaspée in Rhode Island.

Like every small community, Hampton had long had a militia that trained and paraded in the center of the village. Militia drills were social occasions accompanied by drinking, dining, and dancing. Young men sought uniforms and brightly painted weaponry to attract the girls in town. Rank or an officer's commission marked a man's status in the hierarchy of the community. Captain James Stedman led the best trained of Hampton's militia out of the village in April 1775 to go to battle. Hampton militiamen fought at Bunker Hill under Israel Putnam's command in June. Samuel Moseley's son Samuel died at Bunker Hill.[13]

Hampton men fought throughout the long years of the Revolution. Whole families of men went to the war. Seventeen cousins named Fuller served. Sergeant Abijah Fuller was a big man, but his friend Ralph Farnham was bigger, "the heaviest man in the Connecticut line," according to the stories. In the bloody battle at White Plains, Farnham was wounded, and Sgt. Fuller threw him over his back and carried him off the field with "bullets falling like hail around them."[14] Nathaniel F. Martin, who was a Hampton artisan, housepainter, and furniture maker by the 1790s, was the only survivor of his company at that battle of White Plains when he was sixteen.

Hampton men campaigned with Benedict Arnold (a brilliant militia leader from Norwich and New Haven) at Quebec, before Arnold became the arch-traitor of the Revolution. Ebenezer Moseley raised and commanded an entire new militia regiment in 1776 to help relieve Providence from British occupation. There were Hampton members of the new Continental Army at Valley Forge. The terrible stories of freezing and starving there were part of Hampton lore.[15] Men in Hampton long remembered with pride that they had fought with Washington.

The Continental Congress ran the war. Eliphalet Dyer and Samuel Huntington from Windham (of which Hampton was the second parish) were members from Connecticut. Huntington was one of the traitors to the king whom we now revere as signers of the Declaration of Independence. In the latter part of the war he was the President of Congress (which made him President of the United States). The long, bloody, and discouraging years of war were marked by few American victories.

Hampton was affected not only by the deaths of the men who fought in militia regiments, but by the brutal frontier warfare that went on as well. People from Windham and Hampton had formed the Susquehannah Company in 1753 for the settlement of the Wyoming and Susquehanna valleys in Pennsylvania. Many men and young families had left Hampton to settle there in the succeeding twenty-five years. In 1778, during the Revolution, Indians and British attacked and killed settlers in the Wyoming valley. According to the stories told in Hampton after the War, men named Durkee, Dorrance, Fuller, Abbott, and Williams from Hampton were among those "barbarously tortured and butchered." Their homes were burned, their "farms ravaged," their "families taken prisoners, or driven out naked and starving into the wilderness." The wives of John Abbott and Thomas Fuller, "each with nine children, and utterly destitute, begged their way back as best they could" to their family homes in Hampton.[16]

On the "home front" women kept the farms producing while the men were fighting. They worked the fields themselves. They took over making cloth and clothes from weavers and tailors who were now soldiers. In order to clothe a soldier in Hampton, the story ran, some women made a suit of clothes in less than two days, starting with the wool on a sheep's back. "The son came home in rags, and the sheep was sheared and bundled away in the cellar, while its wool was spun, woven, and made up into a substantial suit of clothes in time for the young soldier to wear back to the camp in triumph."[17] During the war, the women of Hampton, with the help of the one lame carpenter left in town, framed, raised, and finished a whole

The house built by the women of Hampton during the Revolutionary War
(now privately owned).

two-story house. It still stands, and is still pointed out as "the house the women built."

When the Taintors moved to Hampton in the 1790s, they brought their own family's heroic stories of the Revolution with them. Roger and Solomon's oldest brothers, John and Charles, had gone to war from the family home in Colchester. Nabby and Judith's eldest brother, John Bulkeley, served as a lieutenant. Another of their brothers, William Bulkeley, was visiting at the Henry Champion house in Colchester when he was sixteen "when a special messenger dispatched by Gen. Washington arrived, bringing the news of the distress of the American Army. He at once yoked up his oxen and joined the relief train which set out under the command of Col. Henry Champion. This was said to have been the first assistance which reached Valley Forge."[18] William Bulkeley later married the colonel's daughter Mary. Two of her brothers had been generals in the war.

Almost every town and family had direct connections to the Revolution and vivid stories of its part in their lives. By the 1790s the stories told were almost uniformly heroic. The growing myth of the Revolution suggested a level of voluntary enthusiasm and patriotism that did not reflect the realities of a long and dreadful war. While the first year, 1775, was generally one of enthusiasm, thereafter farmers frequently held back livestock and provisions from the soldiers. Money depreciated and inflation grew. Soldiers ate bad food and wore tattered clothes. They were infrequently paid. Some were even executed for desertion. Connecticut soldiers, like those from New Jersey and Pennsylvania, mutinied—and some men from Hampton may have been involved. The ultimate American victory, however, gave memories of the war an enthusiastic shine of patriotism.[19]

Confirming Independence

Hampton people—led by Col. Ebenezer Moseley, with Capt. James Stedman and Deacon Isaac Bennet—petitioned the new state of Connecticut for independence from the town of Windham three years after the Treaty of Paris formally ended the War for Independence. Hampton's village had become the central focus of more than a thousand people. That dense population and the ten-mile separation from Windham Center seemed to justify political independence. On October 2, 1786, the Connecticut Assembly granted their petition, carving the town mostly from Windham, with some land from the surrounding towns of Mansfield, Pomfret, Brooklyn, and Canterbury. Hampton held its first recorded Town Meeting on November 13, 1786. The townspeople chose Capt. James Stedman moderator (to chair the meeting), a post he often held until he died two years later. They made Thomas Stedman, his brother, first Town Clerk, and

Capt. Stedman, Deacon Isaac Bennet, and Jeduthan Rogers Hampton's first Selectmen (the town's executive).[20]

In the first two years after Hampton became a town, people gathered often in Town Meeting. An independent town needed to elect officials to carry out all its new tasks. Bridges had to be built and tended, highways needed constant work, schools had to be kept and provided for, the weights and measures used by everybody in the exchange of food and other produce of their farms had to be supervised for accuracy, deeds and other documents concerning property had to be recorded, fences had to be inspected so that people's animals stayed where they belonged and did not destroy their neighbors' food and property, stray animals had to be impounded, chimneys had to be inspected for fire hazards, inns and other public businesses had to be supervised.

At a Town Meeting held on November 12, 1787, Hampton took a vital step: "Amos Utley was chose a Deligate to meet in a Convention" in Hartford to consider ratifying a Constitution "reported by the deligates from the United States lately assembled in the City of Philadepha." The Town Meeting also chose "a Committee to consult on matters concerning the Constitution and draw instructions for our Deligates and make Report to the Adjourned Town Meeting." Thomas Fuller, Elijah Walcutt, Philip Pearl, Ebenezer Hovey, Abner Ashley, James Stedman, James Howard, David Martin, Andrew Durkee, Benjamin Durkee, Thomas Stedman, and John Brewster were the members of that committee.[21] There is no record of the instructions they drew up.

For the first time in the history of the world common people "consulted" and decided how to govern their nation. The men Hampton chose for the committee had helped make a revolution. Now they were trying to make it permanent. There is no record of how the Hampton delegation voted at the ratifying convention. The federal constitution and the arguments over it and over how democratic government should function were very much part of the context of the small town into which the Taintors moved.

The Revolution's emphasis on independence, as it was worked out in individual and family life, changed the way people lived. The traditional care and security which families ideally had provided all members were part of the pre-Revolutionary—perhaps mythical—past. Grown children now sought independence in important new ways. Some moved out of town, but that had happened in the past; now it accelerated. Heads of families used public records in new ways to enforce family obligations. For the first generation after the Revolution, families recorded in deeds and leases the provisions they made for the security of their members.[22]

In 1798, for example, Ebenezer Griffin, a solid and respected Hampton farmer, deeded "one half of all the lands and buildings" he owned in Hampton to Ebenezer Junior "for the consideration of the love and good will I have for my son."[23] Two and a half years later he gave his daughters "Hannah Mun, Artemissa Burnham, Ellewissa Edwards, Olive Lummiss, Betsey Griffin, Lucy Forbs" half of his land "in the Ohio purchase . . . being and lying on or near the confluence of the rivers Ohio and Muskinggum." Finally, Griffin sold all the rest of his land in Hampton to his son, Ebenezer, Jr.,

> reserving for myself and my wife Elizabeth the use of the House we now live in, so far as that the said Ebenezer Junior shall not put another Famely (except his own natural Famely) into the house during our natural lives. . . . Also reserving house room and fire wood for my daughter Olive So long as she lives without a husband, and also for my daughter Betsey so long as she remains Single. And also on condition that the said Ebenezer Junior shall keep and support two horses for me and my Wife during our natural lives.[24]

By turning over his property to his son, Griffin assured him a home and a good working farm. Perhaps he also kept his son from migrating west to seek land and independence. And he assured himself, his wife, and his dependent daughters that none of them would end up among the elderly poor to be publicly discussed and cared for by the town.

One of the most important responsibilities Hampton as a town took over was the care of the poor within its borders. Previously, the Second Parish of Windham Religious Society (the members of the Congregational church in Hampton) had been responsible for the poor. There were people in the town who, because of circumstances, illness, or old age, could not support themselves, and whose immediate families could not support them. An early Town Meeting chose a committee "to make preparations for the Support of the Poor and Render an Account to the Town of their Expenditures." The town "voted that the poor be kept by those persons who will keep them cheapest." Five poor people were "bid off" at that early meeting: Mr. Zachariah Manard to be kept by Jonathan Hovey for five shillings, nine pence per week; Mrs. Mary Holt to be kept by Samuel Ashley, Jr., for two shillings per week; Mrs. Ormsby to be kept by Captain James Stedman; Mr. Nathaniel Fuller and wife to be kept by Amos Utley at five shillings per week.[25]

The town "bid off" the poor several times a year. It paid the lowest bidder to feed, clothe, and house the poor person or couple he had bid for. In 1787 the town went a step further when it "voted that the house belonging to the widow Sarah Molton be hired for the use of the Town . . . and that those persons who shall bid off the Poor Shall have liberty to Keep them at the House that is to be Hired for the Use of the Town or keep them at their own House at their option."[26] This experiment of a town poor house did not last. Perhaps it was too expensive to maintain; perhaps people preferred to keep the services of the poor available close at hand in their own houses.

The town let "those that keep the poor . . . have the Benefit of all their Labour,"[27] making the poor in essence the servants of those who cared for them. The work they did in the household or on the farm went to their masters, but people viewed it as an exchange for their being housed and fed and clothed. The town made every effort to be sure both the poor and those who bid to care for them carried out their obligations in that exchange.[28]

In the matter of health care the town tried to behave as a family was expected to behave. It gradually became more humane. The "doctoring" of the poor was bid off separately from their care for the first time in 1792: "Royal Brewster [himself a doctor] bid off the Doctoring of the Poor at two pounds and Sixteen Shillings for one year." Thereafter, the cost of doc-toring the poor was bid off every year. Later it was voted "that the poor of the Town be gratified with the choice of a Physician to be employed for them in case of Sickness," and the town cautioned that "the person bydding off the doctoring Shall employ a Skilful physician, such as the Select Men Shall approve."[29] In the same year, the town voted to "procure a herse at the expence of the Town to convey Corps to the grave."[30]

The town sometimes funded aid and welfare. At Town Meeting on April 17, 1792, the citizenry "voted to allow Doctor John Brewster [the elderly father of Royal Brewster] four pounds on account of his Doctoring Richard Ringe at the time that he lost his leg. . . ." Also they "voted to give Amos Ford five Shillings it being for fixing out his Son in the time of the war."[31] Hampton agreed with the neighboring town of Pomfret to share the care of "William Stone and his Idiot Son Benjamin."[32] It provided foster care for children: "Voted that the Select Men have the care of the Family of Josiah Rogers to put out the two oldest children and provide for the rest at their Discretion."[33]

When family members failed in their responsibilities, the Town Meeting did more than nudge. On December 7, 1795, "Thomas Stedman Junr. was Chose Agent for the Town of Hampton to apply to Benjamin Holt of Windham to support his mother Mary Holt and if Necessary to institute a suit against sd. Benjamin to Compell him to Support his Mother and Releave Sd. Town of Hampton from the Burden of Supporting her."[34]

Nine years later, however, the town saw its duty as helping a town resident with family support when it "agreed to give Thomas Farnam nine shillings per week for him to take his Father."[35]

Indians were not part of the town's extended family—there were few left in Hampton by the end of the eighteenth century and they lived isolated lives, ignored by the rest of the population. Whether the Connecticut state government or the federal government was responsible for their welfare was a matter of controversy. But Hampton insisted that it was not when on April 8, 1799, the Town Meeting ordered the Selectmen to "apply to the State for a reimbursement of the expence accrued by the Sickness and death of an Indian woman lately in this Town."[36]

Sometimes the people in Hampton could see trouble coming for them and tried to head it off by fobbing it onto Windham. In 1788 Clement Neff returned after "long captivity in Algiers," and was established as a resident of the town—after some debate between Windham and Hampton as to who was responsible for him. Then the *Windham Herald* carried a notice:

> MARRIED, last week, in the Episcopalian form by Timothy Larrabee, Esq., Mr. CLEMENT NEFF of Hampton, to Miss PATIENCE DEAN of this town. N. B.–Mr. Neff has been a prisoner in Algiers 24 years, in 12 of which he never saw the sun. He is now in the youthful bloom of 65, and has lost an eye–his bride a blushing maid of 28.

Four years after the wedding, Patience Neff was being cared for as one of the poor of Hampton. The town "voted that Patience Neff be under the care of Select Men, and that they procure a place for her if she needs help."[37]

Hampton provided for the young, as well as for the poor and elderly. The whole community shared parental responsibility for education. Children were taught to read and write and cipher in small one-room schools. The town was divided into eight school districts so that children could walk (the standard means of transportation) the distance to school. Town Meeting fixed "the places where the School Houses Shall Stand."[38] For example, William Martin and "Naomy his wife" leased some land in a corner of one of their "plow fields . . . big enough to Set a School house on, that is 25 feet long and 20 feet wide" to the school committee of the "Goshen School District." The Committee agreed "that we will make as much Stone wall as we take Down for the bigness of the . . . School House on the opisit Side of the Road where the old School house now stands," and also agreed "that know family Shall have liberty to live in Said house without the leave of both parties." School houses were not used all year long, and people in Hampton did not let possible dwellings stand empty.[39]

School districts themselves changed as the populations of the families in them changed. In 1790, the town "voted that John Fuller and Benjamin Fuller be a School District by them Selves." Either they had very large families, enough to fill a school house between them, or they sent their children to school in neighboring Canterbury.[40]

The committees in each school district hired teachers and collected taxes to pay for the educational system. The school committees examined the young men and women who applied to be teachers to be sure they were literate and could do elementary arithmetic. These teachers were usually young, unmarried people with some education beyond the earliest years. Typically, they came from Hampton or neighboring towns. The committees also occasionally examined the pupils, and the town bought public securities to support the schools and provided "the several districts" with the interest income.[41]

Roads were another important community concern. Roads connected people to each other. Children walked on them to school, families walked or rode on them to church, to stores, to visit each other. They were essential for the movement of food and goods inside the town as well as between Hampton and other towns. The town built bridges to carry the roads over frequent streams.

At its very first Town Meeting in 1786 Hampton elected surveyors of highways to build and improve roads. The town established as many as eighteen highway districts and constantly changed their number, boundaries, and responsibilities. People argued about public rights-of-way across their property, even about roads and paths already in use.[42] When the town elected Solomon Taintor a surveyor of highways shortly after he moved to Hampton it spelled out what highway surveyors were supposed to do, and what the responsibilities of every resident were:

Voted that whenever the town shall lay a tax for repairing highways, it shall be the duty of the surveyors to warn out the inhabitants of their respective Districts to remove all nuisances in the highways; and in Case the publick highways should be blocked up in the winter Season with Snow So as to impede the publick travel it shall be the duty of the surveyors to warn out the inhabitants of their respective Districts to open the paths in their several districts as Soon as may be after such nuisance hath happened; And the rule of compensation for such Service Shall be four cents pr. hour for a Man while in actual Service and eight cents pr. hour for a yoke of oxen, Boys and Steers in proportion to their service; and the Surveyors are directed not to Lay out more than one-quarter of their taxes in the winter Season; and if any person shall refuse to let his oxen go on such occasions, the Surveyor in whose District Such Person so refusing lives Shall forthwith collect one fourth part of such persons tax in money to pay for hired oxen.[43]

Hampton people taxed themselves in several different ways in order to pay for all the town services. Tithingmen collected the tax to support the church, school district committees collected a school tax within each district, highway surveyors collected a highway tax in each district, and constables collected the general town tax. Most people paid their taxes by working or giving services or goods to the town. They did not usually pay cash because there was very little currency in circulation.

People also paid state taxes, and frequently the elected town constables were used as tax collectors for both state and town taxes. Roger Taintor, for example, was elected a "Constable and Collector of State Taxes" in 1800, and Solomon was so elected in 1801–but he refused to serve, the first time the town records show such a refusal by an elected officer.[44] We do not know why Solomon would not serve, but the fact of his and his brother's elections shows that in crucial ways the Taintors had been accepted in their new home.

The Bustle of the Place

Families go on for generations in small towns. Hampton's first white settlers came mostly from Massachusetts in 1709. Some of their descendants–named Canada, Shaw, Moulton, Colburn, and Howard–were still there when the Taintors came to town. And so were descendants of nearly every other family of the first generation of Hampton's settlers: Hoveys, Pearls, Durkees, Holts, and Fullers. By the time the Taintors established themselves in Hampton, the town had four households of Fords and four of Hoveys, five households each of Jenningses and Smiths, six of Burnhams, Durkees, Moseleys, and Utleys, ten households of Holts and ten of Martins, eleven of Fullers, and twelve separate households of Clarks. And nearly three hundred years after the first settlers came, there are still members of many of their families in Hampton.

Everyone in Hampton farmed, because each person and each family had to produce at least some of its own food. Most of those who farmed thought of their work as "improvement"–of their own lives, of their time on earth, and of the land. And all who farmed believed there were "rules of good husbandry," established from time immemorial, possibly of divine origin, which they must try to observe. The distinctions invented by historians between "subsistence" and "commercial" or "market" farming had no meaning for the farmers of Hampton. They farmed because they needed and wanted the fruits of the soil both for food and for exchange.

People originally moved to Hampton—as to most American rural places—because land was available. The land was fresh to intensive farming. Farmers cleared the fields by cutting the trees and brush. As soon as they had done that, they grazed animals in them or planted corn around the stumps. Later they removed the stumps and picked out the surface rocks so they could plant more. They pastured animals in fields after harvests, in woodlands, and in the most rocky areas. It took nearly a century to progress from these rough beginnings to the bustling agricultural community the Taintors found—of farms with fenced and cultivated fields, orchards, pastures, and woodlots.

Because everyone's life depended on the crops grown in town, everyone in town was concerned about keeping the necessary animals of the community out of the crops, and away from the possibility of doing damage. Hampton voted in 1794 "that Swine may go at larg in the Highway well ringed," which meant that pigs could roam in the roads provided they had nose rings which prevented their rooting and making holes. Neighbors took each other to court over damage done by animals. Thomas Farnam and Abner Ashley, Jr., had to post a bond to Andrew Durkee that they would "at all times hereafter erect and maintain a good, lawful fence and sufficiently tight to Stop geese and Pigs throughout," the penalty for which was fifty pounds per year "for each and every succeeding year said fence shall remain unrepaired and for every successive failure and neglect."[45] The large amount of the penalty is some measure of the seriousness of the damage that wandering animals could do.

Fences kept animals in as well as out. When they got out, they were put in the town pound, which was periodically rebuilt. Very carefully. The Town Meeting on September 14, 1790,

> Proposed to build a Pound with Stone in the following Manner (viz) to build a wall 4 feet thick at the bottom 2 feet thick at the top 6 feet high Sd. wall to be Bound across three feet from the ground with a tier of flat Stones and also Bound on the top with a tier of flat Stones across with four Stiks of hewed timber 10 inches thick locked together laid on top of Sd. Wall with a good Sufficient gate 4 feet wide. the above Sd. Pound to be 30 feet Square Sd. Sticks of timber to be of Chesnut and laid Setting 4 inches within Sd. wall. . . . Voted to Set the Pound where the old one now Stands. . . .[46]

The same Amos Utley who had represented Hampton in the convention to ratify the United States Constitution three years later built the new town pound for five pounds sixteen shillings.

People with skills other than farming were necessary to the life of the town. There had to be mills to grind grains and saw lumber. Farmers with streams on their land for water power often built and operated such mills. Artisans, people with specially trained skills, made the things from iron, wood, clay, leather, and fibers that farmers needed in their fields and houses. Hampton could not support any artisan fully, so all artisans farmed as well as worked their trade. Merchants collected produce from farms and artisans and sold it "abroad," and imported and sold goods in Hampton.

By the 1790s, when the Taintors came, there were several operating mills with their necessary dams. There were at least seven sawmills—most on the Little River, but also on the Natchaug, on "Seder Swamp Brook," and on Merrits Brook. There were at least three gristmills for grinding corn or wheat. One of them had been leased to Thomas Stedman, Jr., "for one barrel of Cyder or one bushel of Indian Corn or the value of either of them in money to be paid yearly." Joseph Fuller owned a fulling mill (a mill in which cloth is fulled or milled by being beaten with wooden mallets run by machinery and cleansed with soap or fuller's earth in order to clean and thicken it) on a brook near the Little River. Two families in town—the Howards in the southern part of Hampton now called Howard's Valley and the Stedmans along the Little River at what was called "Bigelow"—owned dams, mill ponds, and complexes of grist-, saw-, and fullers mills that they operated themselves or leased to others.[47]

Hampton artisans' shops included at least five blacksmiths' shops—Abraham Ford's, John Hovey's on the road to Scotland, Amasa Martin's, and Captain Abner Robinson's. Elijah Simons was both a smith and a tool-maker, with a shop and a store. Shubael Martin ran a cooper's shop which he leased from his father for "so long as he . . . Shall improve it for a Coopershop and no longer" for the rent of "one Kernel of corn annually." There were at least two other coopers in town. Coopers made the barrels that were the essential packaging for most goods being sent in and out of town as well as for liquids like cider and rum. Nathaniel F. Martin was a furniture maker, woodworker, and tailor.[48]

While "shops" sold the products of the artisans who ran them, "stores" were places where merchants kept goods that they bought and sold but did not make. Hampton contained several stores concentrated near the Meeting House in the village. Ebenezer Moseley had opened one some time after the Revolution. And Roger and Solomon Taintor occupied another by 1803.[49]

A Cautionary Tale

All communities and all families have secrets. They are the stories every-one knows but nobody talks about. Ellen Larned, the great nineteenth-century historian of Windham County, persuaded Hampton residents to tell her one of those family secrets (perhaps because she was of a local family herself). Eighty years after the Taintors moved to Hampton, she reconstructed the terrible story of Elizabeth Shaw, a story the Taintors must have known because it had already survived half a century by the time they moved to town.

In the 1740s, Elizabeth Shaw—perhaps a descendant of the William Shaw who bought land on Little River in 1709—lived with her parents in the southern part of Hampton. As Larned heard the story, Elizabeth was

> represented as a weak, simple girl, deficient in mental capacity. Her father was stern and rigid. . . . After giving birth secretly to a living child, the poor bewildered girl, fearful of exposure and punishment, stole away to a ledge of rocks near by, hid the babe in some nook or crevice, and left it to perish. Her father suspected and watched her, and—unable, perhaps, to force her to confession—himself, it is said, made accusation against her. She was arrested and examined. Search was made, and the poor little body found in the grim Cowatick Rocks.[50]

Elizabeth Shaw was tried on September 17, 1745, at the Superior Court session in Windham. Roger Wolcott was the chief of the five judges and a large number attended the trial. The grand jury's charge was "That one Elizabeth Shaw, Jun., of Windham [Hampton was then still part of Windham], a single woman, was on the 29th of June, 1745, delivered of a living male bastard child, in Windham, and did secretly hide and dispose of the same in the woods in said Windham, and there left it until it perished for want of relief, and did endeavor to conceal the birth and death thereof, so that it should not come to light, whether said child were born alive or not, and did cause to perish said child." Elizabeth pled not guilty, and she was sentenced to be hanged on December 18, 1745. (Connecticut was still a colony, and the English legal system was, essentially, what prevailed.)

Larned reported what she called "a doubtful tradition that Elizabeth Shaw's father . . . went to Hartford and procured a reprieve from the Governor, but . . . on his way home was met by a sudden storm, the rivers became impassable, and his return was delayed until after the execution." Instead, according to Larned:

> On the fatal day, a gallows was erected on a hill a mile southwest from Windham Green. An immense concourse of people from all the adjacent country witnessed the mournful spectacle. Little children, too young to join in the procession, remembered vividly through life the long train, reaching from Gallows Hill to Windham Jail, following the cart which bore the hapless Elizabeth, sitting on her coffin, crying

continuously, "Oh, Jesus! have mercy upon my soul!" through the dreadful death-march and the last harrowing ceremonies.

One hundred thirty years later, Larned interviewed descendants of those "little children, too young to join in the procession" who had told the story "remembered vividly through life" to their own children. The cautionary tale was told to each Hampton generation, including the Taintors'. It was told to us when we moved to town.

CHAPTER 2

CHANGING LIVES IN A CHANGING WORLD

૭

*"Two brother and sister couples (Solomon & Judith a bride &
groom) moved to Hampton and took the Thomas Stedman
place in 1797."* [1]

W e cannot go back and ask the Taintors why they moved to
Hampton, or how their lives were changed in their new home, or
how they meant to change them. We have gone to Hampton's
South Burying Ground and stared at their graves, wishing we
could talk to them. We have their great-granddaughter's story that Roger
and Nabby, Solomon and Judith Taintor bought their house and moved in
together and shared the housework and were in business together. It is a

The twin Taintor grave monuments in Hampton's South Burying Ground.

story she wrote much later than the facts–a hundred and forty years later. So, in order to tell the stories of the changes in the Taintors' lives and in Hampton's immediately after the nineteenth century began, we have had to become detectives, trying to find eyewitnesses from the past, trying to piece together bits of evidence.

The Taintors and Their House

We start with the physical evidence and the oral traditions–what people tell even now. There is the actual town of Hampton and its village on the hill above the Little River. There is the house we bought in the village.

Even the simplest facts are hard to find. We have not been able to find out when the house was built. A long tradition, reported a hundred years ago by Ellen Larned in her *History of Windham County* and repeated to us by the Taintors' descendants, is that the Thomas Stedman who built the Meeting House also built our house for his nephew, Thomas Stedman, Jr. But we have found no record that would verify the story.

The documentary evidence, from deeds, is that in July 1790, Thomas Stedman, Jr., bought sixty square rods of land (a rod is sixteen and one-half feet long) located "ten rods north of the meeting house on the west side of the highway." Our house sits a little more than ten rods north of the Meeting House on the west side of the highway. Thomas Stedman's new piece of land abutted to the north on land belonging to Marcy Martin, which she sold in 1791 to Daniel Fuller, and we have been told that Daniel Fuller lived in the house just north of our house. Thomas Stedman's deed mentions no buildings on his lot. Three years later, in March 1793, he bought ten more acres "adjoining Hampton Meeting House . . . beginning at the east end of a Stone wall between the . . . Meeting House and *Said Stedmans House.* . . ." So by 1793 Stedman had a house on his sixty square rods of land, which is where our house is.[2] We do not know when that house was built.

People who wrote deeds in the early nineteenth century (usually the sellers themselves) wanted to record land boundaries of property which anyone in their day could find. They mentioned oak trees, piles of stones, or stone walls, many of which are not there now. For the purposes of a deed it was rarely a matter of interest whether there was a house or other building on a piece of land. No one made official records of the building of houses; only very recently have building permits come to Hampton. So what we can verify is that the house into which the Taintors moved is still standing, it was built by 1793, and it was lived in by Thomas Stedman, Jr., in that year.

The evidence is also elusive about exactly when the Taintor families came to town. We do know when they bought the house: 1804. And tied to the house is the family tradition that the "two brother and sister couples ([when] Solomon & Judith [were just] a bride & groom) moved to Hampton and took the Thomas Stedman place in 1797."[3] That is, Solomon and Judith, Roger and Nabby are supposed to have rented the house and lived in it seven years before they bought it.

We turned to Hampton's vital statistics records. The ones for the early nineteenth century were copied by Town Clerk Jonathan Clark from church records long after the events themselves. We found Solomon Taintor's marriage to Judith Bulkeley recorded on December 13, 1797, which indicates a distinct probability that they were in residence in Hampton at the time because people were then usually married at home, not in church. The birth of Solomon and Judith's first son, Edwin Bulkeley Taintor, on May 18, 1800, is also in the Hampton records, as is the birth of Roger and Nabby's son John Adams Taintor (possibly named for the President, who was a New Englander) a month before, on April 22, 1800. It seems likely that those boys were born in our house.[4]

The earliest clear record we have found of a Taintor in Hampton is of Roger Taintor witnessing a deed on October 15, 1796, and another on April 27, 1797. He was obviously in town on those days and present wherever those deeds were being written and signed, perhaps in Ebenezer Moseley's store, since Moseley was a justice of the peace who signed the deeds. And on March 12, 1798, a Hampton Town Meeting elected Solomon Taintor a surveyor of highways. He must have been living in town by then because the town did not elect nonresidents to such offices, and a surveyor usually lived along one of the roads for which he was responsible.

The Hampton deed records show that on August 16, 1799, Roger and Solomon bought nine acres of land in Hampton Village (but not the lot on which our house stands). On January 24, 1800 (before the boy babies were born), the Taintors registered the settlement of a disagreement between them and Dr. John Brewster and Thomas Stedman, Jr., about the boundaries between all of their lands. There is no evidence that there was a house on that first piece of Taintor land. There is no evidence there was not a house on it.[5] So we can be certain that the Taintors were living in town by 1798, maybe as early as 1796. But where they lived is only indicated by their family's oral tradition.

The town records show that both Roger and Solomon Taintor were elected to town offices before 1804.[6] The records show them collecting debts in court and doing business in a "Store occupied by Messrs. Roger & Solomon Taintor" near the Meeting House.[7] And the earliest documents in the Taintors' own records show them buying goods from their older brothers John and Charles, who were active merchants in Windham, being parties to one of the first mortgages in Hampton, and keeping accounts of goods sold to some eminent Hampton families.[8]

We have found what the Taintors did to their house when they bought it—in the account book of the man who painted it for them. In October and November 1804, Nathaniel F. Martin and two other men—a journeyman (day-worker) and an apprentice—spent a total of fifty man-days painting for the Taintors. Martin provided paints of "White lead," "Red led," and "Ston yallow," as well as about sixteen and a half pounds of putty for the job. The following January (1805), Martin did four more days of painting. From the size of the job it would seem that he painted the outside of the Taintors' new house—and white lead was the predominant color (twenty-six and one half pounds of it). The house is still white outside, but without the red and yellow (trim?) colors Martin's account indicates it had in 1804. It is not possible to tell, from Martin's account, whether there was inside painting done as well that winter. Certainly there was a lot of woodwork in the house that would have required painting—particularly paneling (which was always painted) in the downstairs rooms on the chimney walls of each room.

In the fall of 1805, Martin and his crew did more painting for the Taintors. This time it took a total of twenty-one man-days, and Martin used different colors, "Spanish White" (fourteen pounds) and "Spanish Brown" (more than seventeen pounds), as well as varnish and turpentine, all of which makes this sound like an inside job. Martin also charged the Taintors for "putting on Carpits Cloth & tacks" in 1805, and he repaired some furniture and made them a "winsor Rocking Chair" and "2 Cherry Crickets" (low wooden stools or footstools). Whether or not they had been housekeeping in it before, the Taintors marked their new status as homeowners with painting the house inside and out as well as adding to its furnishings.

In February 1807, Martin charged the Taintors for "painting Little house" ("4 lb. white led, 1 lb. Spanish White, and 4 lb. Spanish Brown"). This was probably their store. Confusion about what is a "house" and what is a "store" is a result of modern distinctions and modern, specialized architecture. At the beginning of the nineteenth century, the only architecture, the only building type people in Hampton were familiar with was *domestic*. Houses were all they knew for human activity. Barns were for animals and crops. Houses housed families, and meetinghouses housed the community in its public aspect. The "shops" of most artisans were not separate from their houses, and the "chambers" in which lawyers conducted business, doctors studied and met patients, and merchants stored their goods were normally rooms in houses. School was kept in schoolhouses (which people could live in when school was out). Storehouses were not unknown as separate buildings, but they were thought of–as in Martin's account with the Taintors–simply as some other form of house, a "little house" in that case, probably to distinguish it from the "great house" the Taintors lived in.

Villages, such as Hampton's, were more or less orderly collections of houses, some larger and some smaller, but with almost no visible ways to distinguish dwelling places from more public houses. There were, in the life of ordinary rural and small-town people, no distinctions drawn between home and work and family life. Families lived and did their work in the same places. As the meetinghouses only gradually began to acquire architectural features that visibly distinguished them from other houses, so stores only gradually developed characteristic "fronts" with windows, porches, and signs that signaled their function to the public. The houses which were called and thought of as public houses–inns and taverns–had developed a practice by the eighteenth century of putting colored signs out, often with pictures, to direct those unfamiliar with the village. But it was only as domestic life and the life of work began slowly to separate in nineteenth-century America that architecture began to reflect that separation. When the first textile mills were built, they, too, looked like houses, and even when their size distinguished them from ordinary houses, their builders and designers continued to make them in the same style and with the same materials as large houses and meeting houses.

One of the first specialized buildings in Hampton was built by order of the Town Meeting in 1808 "to cover the Herse." It was "to be Set on Doc'r. Hoveys land, between his dwelling house & the School house," and the town specified "good chestnut timber with white oak studs," for its framing, "good white pine clapboards" for its sheathing, and roofing of "oak bords & chestnut shingles," using ten-penny nails throughout.[9] As is true of much of the physical evidence in any old community, the building to house the hearse has disappeared. The changes wrought by the Taintors in their house and store when they first bought them have also disappeared. But they are evidence that the Taintors and the town were actively changing their world as they changed the architecture of Hampton.

The Evidence from Account Books

Hampton's was a handmade world in the early nineteenth century. The word "manufacture" meant "to make by hand." The skills that could be trained into people so they could make all the things essential to household and farm were vital skills. Machines that could do the skilled work of manufacturing had just begun to be invented, and it would be decades–in some cases more than a century–before such machines produced the goods needed in agriculture and in small-town life.

Account books are rich sources of information about how people worked and lived in small towns in the decades following the Revolution. Nathaniel F. Martin, the man who painted the Taintors' house, kept an account book of his work as a farmer and artisan–woodworker, furniture maker, painter, and tailor–for sixty-three years, from 1784 to his death in 1847.[10]

By the 1780s, when Martin started his account book, American producers, artisans and farmers alike, were operating in a money-and-market economy. There was so little cash in circulation, however, that it was essential to keep accounts of what one sold (goods, labor, services) and what one received (also goods, labor, services). A money value was assigned to each transaction, debits were recorded in the book on the left leaf of each person's account, and credits on the right. The transactions in Martin's book–like those in most contemporary accounts–were not barter transactions. There was no direct exchange of goods or work or services. Even when there was agreement in advance that goods or services would be rendered in payment, every transaction was recorded as a money transaction, and only in unusual circumstances was the mode of payment–cash or goods or services–specified.

Artisans and merchants often carried accounts over several years since it took time for either creditor or debtor to produce goods, render services, or work for the other in order to balance an account. Occasionally, both would get together to "reckon up" and balance the account, and both would sign the book when they did. Such "book accounts" were substitutes for a money supply as well as creators of credit in the developing American economy, which was desperately short of both.

The opening leaf of Martin's book is dated "Windham, January 3rd 1784" (it was still two years before Hampton became independent of Windham). And an old newspaper obituary is inside announcing the death of "Nathaniel F. Martin, Esq., aged 87 years," on September 26, 1847.

> The deceased was one of the small band of patriots who served their country faithfully, in its struggle for liberty and independence. . . . [Martin] entered the army at an early period of the revolutionary war, and was in the sanguinary battle of Long Island on the 27th of August, 1776, in which the Americans were defeated with great loss, and was the only man of the company to which he belonged, who escaped captivity or death. . . . He was . . . through life, a good citizen, an inflexible republican, a disinterested patriot, a man of great firmness and energy of purpose, and of unblemished reputation. He ardently loved his country and its institutions, and was ever ready to do whatever he could to promote the welfare of the one, and secure the perpetuity of the other.

Out of the account book records there gradually emerges something of "a man of great firmness and energy of purpose," a man of considerable skill who spoke with a strong Yankee accent (often recorded in his spelling). He engaged in his work and life in Hampton with enthusiasm.

Nathaniel F. Martin was a normal jack-of-all-trades farmer. And as an artisan he was not a specialist either. He cut and sewed clothes. He painted sashes, houses, and wagons. He plastered. He made paints. He made leather goods, including shoes and harness. He made and repaired innumerable bellows for forges and fireplaces. He repaired and rebuilt clocks. He made wall (those New England stone walls). He repaired tools and made replacement handles for the many ordinary wooden-handled implements used in farm and household work. He may have built houses; he certainly put roofs on them. He constantly repaired and sometimes made plows, "shays," "sleys," wagons, carriages, and the other vehicles and machines used on every farm. In the nineteenth century he made and patented washing machines. He patented and sold an improved water wheel for mills. He built saw- and gristmills. In his later career he became a mechanic—one of the new breed of artisans fascinated by machines. He made all kinds of furniture. And he seems to have worked for nearly every family in Hampton.[11]

His account book gives a picture of the dailiness of small-town life. In March 1786, Martin made a candle stand for Joseph Fuller, the first recorded candle stand of many he made in his lifetime. The making of such stands—relatively small pieces of furniture—required a lathe (part of the special equipment of a furniture maker which Martin possessed) for turning their principal support. The growing demand for candle stands in Martin's lifetime shows a generally increasing affluence in the population of Hampton. People were using more candles.

Among the many things Martin made for the well-to-do family of Captain James Stedman was a pair of trousers and a pair of "breeks [boy's trousers] for Tommey" (Thomas Stedman, Jr.), who grew up to sell his house to the Taintors. Martin also made eight and one-half rods of wall (about 140 feet) for Captain Stedman. Stedman, and later his widow, paid Martin in milk, veal, and other foodstuffs from their farm.

Martin's account book tells us something about what other people did, not only what he did. For years, Martin did a great deal of work for Ebenezer Griffin—and for Ebenezer, Jr.—making clothes and tools, plowing, and mending tools. Griffin paid in molasses, wine, codfish, "bords," tallow, veal, rum, cider, and pork. The frequency of imported goods in what Griffin paid Martin shows Griffin traded outside of town; he did not just farm. Local merchants often hired Griffin to cart goods for them between Hampton and the port towns of Norwich and Providence.

Abraham Ford, a blacksmith, sharpened picks for Martin, and "shoed hors" at least once for him. In return, among other things, Martin turned a "handel to tooth drawer" for Ford, which makes it appear that Ford was the local dentist. At least he was equipped to pull teeth–but maybe only of horses.

Over the years, Martin made coats and trousers for John Clark. He charged Clark for "cradleing 1 Acor oats" and for pulleys for a loom (a large machine which required trained skill to operate, not an ordinary household possession). Was Clark a weaver, or were his wife and daughters? Women in artisan and farm households produced goods for exchange in a family economy. The accounts were almost invariably kept in men's names. Clark paid Martin in milk and cheese (both of which were probably produced by the women of his household).

In 1787, Martin made his first recorded "Sley," for which he charged one pound sixteen shillings, and six shillings more for painting it. This was evidently a "bare bones" sleigh, because later he charged Dr. John Brewster seven pounds for what must have been a fancier one.

Heavy sleighs were essential to farm work in New England, since the transportation of most heavy and bulky goods to and from farms was more easily accomplished, given the very crude state of road surfaces, in winter when the ground was solid, using nonwheeled, skidded vehicles. Lighter, more graceful sleighs were also becoming the early-nineteenth-century version of today's recreational vehicles. They were status symbols. We can tell from the cost of painting a sleigh in Martin's account book, as well as the occasional detailing of colors and decorations, that people took pride in the public display of their sleighs. For forty years, Nathaniel F. Martin was a major sleigh maker in Hampton.

At about the same time Martin started making and painting fancy sleighs, he also began to make larger and more elaborate furniture, the sort of furniture that served as the outward sign of higher social status. The first time Martin listed making two Great (the word meant "large" but might have indicated a particular style) Chairs, he charged Richard Martin two shillings six pence for one, and a "Mr. Huntington" six shillings six pence for the other. Mr. Huntington's style, being addressed as "mister," indicates high social status as the price indicates a better, fancier chair.

Clothing, including hats, was another sign of social position. Martin made twenty-nine high hat blocks, nine round hat blocks, and some other hat block items for Abel Avery. In return, he received a girl's hat, the making of a hat, a hat for Nancy Martin, cash, five hundred tacks, a "dressing hat," "Almanacks & a ballad," and a subscription. Abel Avery was certainly a hatter, and he might also have been a bookseller, considering the "Almanacks & a ballad" as well as the subscription. Later, Martin bought a fur hat from Nathan Eastman, "to be paid in chair." One April he bought a boy's hat from Eastman to be paid in chairs, and in May, he bought a man's hat "to be paid in Appel trees in the faul."

Drilling with the militia was a way for the men in a family to shine in front of their neighbors. Hampton's militia units continued training, parading, wining, dining, and dancing from the end of the Revolution until the Civil War. The village on Hampton Hill became famous for "great regimental musterings" which drew crowds from out of town.[12] Martin's accounts show that Hampton's militiamen kept their drums, spontoons (lancelike large-bladed spears that were carried by militiamen on parade–and sometimes used as weapons in close combat), and other equipment in repair and brightly painted.

Martin's skills as a painter of sleighs and houses and furniture did not extend to portrait painting, although there was a strong tradition that allied decorative and portrait painting. Portraits were an important indicator of the achievement of high status. And there were at least two portrait painters in Hampton in Martin's lifetime: Joseph Steward, the Reverend Samuel Moseley's son-in-law, who left in the 1790s, and John Brewster, Jr., the deaf-mute son of Dr. John Brewster. Nathaniel F. Martin had extensive accounts with Dr. Brewster that had to do with painting. The small quantities of colors, and some of the items–a "frame for painting," for example– lead to the conclusion that these accounts are for materials used by John Brewster, Jr. But his noting "½ point [pint] oil pr John" is the only purchase that can positively be identified with John Jr. That was in 1803, about the time that John Brewster, Jr., painted the portrait of his little half-sister, Betsey Avery Brewster, that we saw in the Boston Museum of Fine Arts. Brewster left Hampton to become a successful itinerant portraitist in Maine and Massachusetts. He visited Hampton frequently in the first decades of the nineteenth century, and in 1817 he became one of the first students at the new Hartford Asylum for the Deaf. His surviving portraits are valued today as outstanding examples of early American artistic accomplishment.[13]

Small-town artisans manufactured everyday necessities as well as the expensive symbols of changing status and increasing aspirations. "Capt. Abnor Robinson" paid Martin for work, furniture, and a new "Sley" in ironwork. He was an ironmonger and blacksmith, doing the kind of manufacturing that every community required in order to have the necessary ironwork on plows, looms, carts, sleighs, tools, hinges, and all the other implements of modern civilized life.

Martin once made a very expensive "pr Bellows" costing three pounds ten shillings for Elijah Simons, another ironworker in town, and charged

Simons one shilling six pence more for "hanging pr bellows." Such a large, hanging bellows could only have been for Simons's forge.

Martin made a habit, throughout his career, of issuing promissory notes payable in chairs, usually Windsor chairs, which he made the winter following. Like most small-town artisans, he seems to have expected to do his skilled work when farm work was not pressing. Cyporan Parish delivered forty-nine and a half pounds of maple sugar to Martin one April after "sugaring off" season was over. (Maple sugar, made from sap tapped from maple trees in February and March, and boiled down on special iron "trays," was the only locally produced substitute other than honey for expensive imported sugar.) Martin promised to pay Parish for the sugar "in Chairs next winter."

Martin slowly expanded his furniture-making repertoire throughout his career in response to Hampton's increasing population and affluence. He made "3-back" and "4-back" chairs (perhaps what we now called "ladder-back" chairs, with reference to the number of lateral slats in the back), "Great Chairs with Rocker," "trundel beds," "bedsteds," sometimes painted, and at least once, a "Green Chist" (a chest painted green, but whether a boxlike chest or a chest of drawers is not specified). He made many Windsor chairs, many "cherry tables," as well as dining tables and dining chairs.

Martin also turned his hand to special tasks his neighbors needed. He once mended spectacles for Joshua Holt. He made a "tap and fasset [faucet]" for Benjamin Fuller, perhaps to tap a barrel of cider. He took five days to make a Clock case for Fuller, and charged him a bit extra for "painting Clock Case." He mended gun stocks. He mended wheels. And he made clothes, furniture, and toys for children. He recorded making a squirrel trap for Benjamin Fuller's son, James, and a "Chist" for another son, Elisha.

There is no record that Nathaniel F. Martin ever had a formal apprentice, but he did have a series of young men who worked for him. By tradition, anyone who wanted to become a skilled manufacturer, a master craftsman or artisan like Martin, had to spend many years in apprenticeship to a master. But education and the training of artisans was changing. Independent Americans, even children, were unwilling to commit to years in the service of someone else. And, as more and more machines with "built-in skills" were being designed and made, the careful acquisition of proficiency in a craft seemed impractical, a waste of time for young men on the make.

Youngsters did not go into traditional apprenticeships of their own free will; they were put there by their parents. The agreements made were similar to those for indentured servants or bond servants. A man named Hugh

Gill, for instance, made such a contract about his son, and the record found its way into Taintor family papers:

> . . . Hugh Gill of his voluntary and free will lets his Son John Gill to [Stephen] Long for the Term of Four years and Seven Months. . . . Long Engages . . . to provide Sufficient Victuals drink & Lodging for . . . John Gill in Sickness & Health and at the Expiration of Said Term . . . Long Engages to give . . . John Sixteen Pounds [sterling] in Merchantable–Neat–Stock at or Equivalent to Beef in the fall of the year of Sixteen Shillings and Eight pence per Hundred and to Learn him to read write & Cypher what is Commonly called the five Common Rules in Arithmetick–and give . . . John two Suits of Clothes from head to feet–one Suit Suitable for Lords days, the Other for Week days.[14]

Martin's apprentices spent considerably less time with him. From 1793 to 1795, Jonathan Clark, Jr. (who later became an eminent figure in Hampton), worked for him. According to Martin's account, Clark's "work towards first two months" was "to be paid in tools." Clark learned the carpenter's skills from Martin which he practiced the rest of his life in Hampton. Later, David Porter worked five months for Martin, and received "Jointer Jack & Smooth Plain" and a "Grovin plow" (three woodworking tools) as part of his pay. And later still, Benjamin Young worked for Martin, perhaps for as long as six months. Martin noted that Young "lost one Day at Thanksgiving," and fifteen days "going hom."

These young men worked for Martin for short periods in order to acquire some of the skills and "secrets" of the carpenter-furniture maker's trade or the tailoring trade, and some of the tools and equipment. They were learning just enough to increase the skills and products they could market as independent adult farmers in the fast-changing, rapidly mechanizing early-nineteenth-century world.

Young women, too, worked for Martin. Women were not limited to inheritance or marriage for means of support. Nor were they limited to farm work. Some were skilled spinners and weavers. They could hire themselves out to work in households. Abigail Smith worked twenty-two weeks for Nathaniel F. Martin for three pounds six shillings' worth of store goods and two shillings for "a horse to Ashford," where her family lived. She may have worked in Martin's household to earn a trousseau (most of the store goods she was credited with were cloth, thread, buttons, and ribbons) or to contribute to her own independence.

Nancy Martin worked in Nathaniel F. Martin's household for twenty-nine weeks one year, thirty-three weeks the next, and thirty-seven weeks the next. She was paid approximately half of the weekly pay Martin recorded for a hired man, Cyrus Utley, in the same year Nancy started work. She took her pay in "callicow," lawn, "sattin," a fur hat, cloth, "shoes made," buttons, a great coat, "Chist with 2 drawers," "Baze," "Chints," shoes mended, a hat, "shaul," apron cloth, "calicoe," another "shaul," shirt cloth, and "woven bed tickin."

Some women were in the marketplace themselves. Those who ran farms of course were, and so were those who were shopkeepers and artisans. When Nathaniel F. Martin sold Betsy Coburn "508 feet Chesnut Seeling boards" for $4.23, she was credited by eight yards of cloth at twenty-five cents per yard (which she probably wove herself), and by "her work." She also sold Martin large quantities of wood "to be taken out for sawing" from her wood lot. Perhaps Martin used some of those boards to build mills, the houses that held the new machinery.

As the use of machines that were both symbols and realities in the industrial revolution spread, many turned their hands to invention. The federal Constitution gave Congress power "to promote the progress of science and useful arts" and a Patent Office in the State Department gave people a place to register their ideas and secure their rights to them. Martin invented and patented an improvement on the water wheel that provided motive power for sawmills, gristmills, spinning mills, weaving mills, and the other kinds of mills that were becoming necessary to nineteenth-century community life. He sometimes sold licenses to use his patent.

His accounts show that he himself built mill wheels and the mills for which they provided power. Martin built "two grist mills one grand the other not grand" for James Howard in Howard's valley. He worked on Howard's fulling mill and on the "Floom" which carried the water to the water wheel. Martin made a sawmill wheel for Thomas Williams and worked at "bresting" the sawmill saw. He also did repair work on William Fuller's sawmill and a gristmill in Hampton. While a skilled worker was ordinarily provided meals when on the job, Martin carefully noted, in recording the bargain he made with Fuller "on the mill," that he was to "Eat Breakfast & supper at hom."

Martin's reputation as a mill builder and expert on water wheels involved him in industrial development outside of Hampton. He charged Capt. Artemas Gurley, a mill owner and one of the developers of a cotton-spinning mill in Mansfield, for consultations on two separate occasions in 1812 and 1813. Each consultation cost Capt. Gurley two dollars, once for "my time & hors ride to view grist mill one Day and advice," and the other occasion for "my time & hors ride to view Cotton Factory and advice." Shortly thereafter, Martin charged the Mansfield Cotton Factory

Co. for hauling laths to Mansfield, and for hauling cast iron from Stafford and more iron from Hartford, and charged them $12.50 for the "use of my pattent right on A wheele to operate factory." (Part of Mansfield today is still known as "Gurleyville," and is the site of some of Artemas Gurley's mills.)

Martin tried everything. In 1821 he turned a part on his lathe for Dr. Charles Moulton's "Electirifing Masheen." Galvanometry and static electricity were very popular scientific pursuits in the 1820s. Perhaps Dr. Moulton had some medical applications of electricity.

Two other Hampton artisans–William C. Young and Ebenezer Jewett, both contemporaries of Nathaniel F. Martin–have left account books. Both men were blacksmiths, manufacturers of the metal items essential to community life. Young made the iron or steel parts of axes, hammers, knives, shovels, hoes, and wedges; he made bolts, nails, and spikes; he made the iron parts of churns; and he made spindles, irons, hinges, hooks and eyes, hoops, and "linch pins." He also shod horses and oxen, mended ironwork on carts, and sharpened knives, axes, and scythes.[15]

Jewett specialized by repairing plows and other farm tools. He shod horses and oxen, summer and winter. He also drove teams, carted, plowed, and did all manner of farm work for a very large part of Hampton's population.[16] His activity, constantly "shuin" and repairing and "sharpin" tools of all kinds, is vivid from his account book. His language and the sheer number of the transactions he recorded make it possible to envision the bustling activity of people in the small prospering town of Hampton–farming, running mills, spinning, weaving, buying and selling.

Jewett's ordinary smith's work for farmer William Alworth, for example, included (in Jewett's spelling which, if pronounced, reproduces his accent):

~ mendin Skimer [mending a skimmer, to skim cream off milk],
~ Shuin & docterin mair [shoeing and doctoring a mare],
~ 5 lb 7 oz Bass [a sizeable fish for Little River],
~ pintin & Sharpin Share [pointing and sharpening a plowshare],
~ 2 Shad [more fishing],
~ Rufus to ride horse to plow 2 Spels [Rufus could have been Jewett's son or hired man–it was common to have someone on a plow horse],
~ mendin chain [chains were handmade, of course, and links could be repaired or replaced],
~ the use of my cart 30 days,
~ makein betel ring & 5 weags [wedges] [a beetle was a heavy wood implement with a handle used for driving wedges],

~ makein buckit Ear [the "ear" on a bucket held the bale or handle],
~ Sundaries [sundries],
~ mendin colter [an iron blade fixed in front of the share of a plow, which makes a vertical cut in the soil],
~ fixin colter,
~ makein 38 cart Nails & fixin 65 old ones,
~ fixing 2 carts Streeks & Setin tine [a cart strake or streak is a section of the iron rim of the wheel],
~ mendin chain & Ear to plow,
~ kee [key] to youk [yoke] [used to fasten the yoke around the neck of the ox or horse],
~ Sharpin 7 harrow teeth,
~ mendin Nipers [nippers] & clasp,
~ mendin Bridle bits,
~ makein 190 floor Nailes,
~ makein Laderhook & Sharpin 3 old ones,
~ 15 lb 6 oz Veal.

William Alworth gave Jewett in return many "galons of Scolded Sider" (scalded to keep it from fermenting), multiple "Barils of New Sider" and of "Sweet Sider," and apples; he also made Jewett "Sider" of his own "apels." He paid him with bushels of rye and corn, as well as "Bushels of tators."

Abiah Farnham, who was a shoemaker, shows up rather differently in Jewett's account book. Farnham's "side" of the ledger was principally about shoemaking, "Tapin [putting taps on] my Shoes, tapin Betsy & Ebenezer Shoes, tapin Rufus Shoes, makein Polly shoes, healin [heeling] my Brothers Shoes," but it included other kinds of work, such as "helpin digin a grave," "half the four non [forenoon] to plant, half a day to plant tators," and "makein a plaid cap."

On January 26, 1813, Jewett and Farnham got together in order to settle their accounts. Jewett recorded that he had "this Day [reckoned] with mr Abial Farnham on all acompts from the Begining of time to this Day and found Due to me the Sum of twelve Shillings and four pence." Both men signed the account book.

The account then continued, and three years later, the two men again reckoned and "balanced all books to this day." No money ever changed hands. Both of these men, like Nathaniel F. Martin and many others, took their goods and labor into the Hampton marketplace, they haggled over their transactions, they sought gain, and they operated in a money economy—without moving from their small agricultural community in which very little money circulated, and where profit was having work to do, food to eat, and gradual "increase" in one's estate. Theirs was a capitalist economy, although its values differed from those of modern capitalism.

The Spice of Life

The Taintors left no written evidence of what they ate or how they expected to live their daily lives when they moved to Hampton. Two remarkable sets of Hampton public documents from the 1790s, however, give an unusually detailed insight into expectations of daily life in the town. From them we can establish a baseline for the turn of the century from which to measure later change.

In 1795, John and Hannah Curtis deeded to their son Ebenezer their farm and house. They called it a "mansion" when they registered the deed in the town records. The Curtis house still stands—although it has been moved from its original site—and Hampton still considers it a mansion. Four years later, in 1799, Ezekiel Holt executed a deed and a lease between himself and John Hovey "for the sole purpose of Securing for himself and his wife Abiah a comfortable support during their natural lives."

Both the Curtis and the Holt-Hovey transactions had the same purpose. They formalized the welfare and security measures of aging couples. They differed because the Curtises' house was larger and more elegant than the Holts', and the Curtises had correspondingly more elaborate expectations for "a comfortable support." Each document specifies each family's housekeeping requirements and lists in remarkable detail the provisions required for a year's support.

By the terms of their deed the Curtises continued to "occupy and enjoy" their house and farm for the rest of their lives. They maintained the farm "according to the Rules of good husbandry and suffer no Waste to be done on [the] premises and the buildings . . . Excepting the necessary decays thereof." They continued to live in the same two-thirds of the house they already occupied (their son Ebenezer probably lived in the rest), and they continued to have "the garden adjoining said House . . . and the Hogpen Staning therein East of said house."

The Holts had smaller quarters. They continued to live in the "west room" of their house "extending from the celler to the garret with the privelege of Setting a bed in the bedroom chamber & using the well when needfull." The Hoveys, who lived in the rest of the house, had "liberty to use the oven and to do their great work in the west room." It sounds like the west room was the kitchen with its big fireplace, the center of the household where the women cooked and sewed and both the Holts and Hoveys ate. Hovey agreed to plow and manure "one acre of ploughland" every year for Ezekiel Holt's use but only so long as Holt "was able and willing to improve it with his own hand."

The Curtises, on the other hand, continued to have the use of all their farm to work as they wished.[17] Ebenezer Curtis agreed to provide his parents "two good Milk Cows for their sole use and . . . good keeping of Said cows both Summer and Winter and in such manner as they may be handy for use . . . and . . . one good riding Horse for their sole use and also find and provide Suitable Keeping . . . both Summer and Winter and also keep Said Horse well Shod fit for business . . . and the privilige to keep some Poltry."

If the Curtis parents "shall fall Sick and have need of Physick and nursing during their joint lives or the longest liver of them," then Ebenezer would "be at the Sole Expence of Doctring and nursing and all necessary work that they Shall stand in need of when they are unable to do it."

Finally, Ebenezer Curtis provided his parents "Annually and in each year . . . as much firewood as they . . . Shall need delivered at [their] Dwelling House cut and fitted to use for fireing in the House." He also provided for "a certain Negrow Girl Named Violet," a slave whom his father had inherited, "Suitable Clothing meat Drink washing Loging and Doctering and nurceing . . . During her Natural life."[18]

In the Holts' deed, John Hovey agreed to do less for the Holts. He provided "houseroom firewood, washing, lodging, nursing Cloathing . . . and every thing that is necessary & convenient, for their Support & comfort in Sickness and health and also pay all the Just debts . . . Holt now owes . . . also provide a Horse for him and Abiah his wife to ride when they want." The Holts got no cows, and no right to keep poultry. They had no servant. Hovey insisted that if the Holts did not themselves use all he provided them, they had no right to sell it; any excess reverted to him. Finally, Hovey agreed to provide the Holts "a decent monument at their graves in memory of them."[19]

Both transactions contained specific lists of the food each family expected to consume in a year. Ebenezer Curtis would "find and provide and deliver" to his parents at the mansion every year by the end of March:

> Five Barrels [a barrel of liquid contained about thirty-one gallons] of good Cyder . . . Sixteen Bushels [a bushel contained thirty-two dry quarts] Indian Corn Six Bushels of Wheat Six Bushels of Rye Two Hundred Pounds of well fatted Pork Two Hundred Pounds of Well fatted Beef twenty five Pound of good brown Sugar four gallons of Melasses four gallons of good west India Rum Two Bushels of Malt four Cakes of Chocolot twelve Pounds of Rice two pounds of Raisens half a pound of Allspice one quarter Pound of Peper one

pound of Ginger Eight Bushels of Appels half a Bushels onnions twenty-five Pounds of good flax ten pounds of good Sheeps wool Twelve pounds of Tallow three pounds of good Bohee Tea two pair of good Mens shoes made of Calf Skin and two pair of Womens made as aforesd. two bushels of Rock Salt.

John Hovey agreed to provide the Holts:

eight barrels Cider eight bushel Indian Corn, Six bushels rye, Six Score pork Seventy pound well fatted beef & the various kinds of sausage, eighty pounds cheese So much butter as they want, twelve Pounds tallow, three Gallons of ardent spirits, Six quarts Molasses, Six pounds Sugar, 12 lb tobacco Tea, chocolate . . . fresh meat when convenient.

It is apparent from both lists that the Holts expected to consume much less than the Curtises. Perhaps the Curtises expected to entertain guests.

Cider was the principal source of fruit and its nutrients for everyone in Hampton. Some people also ate fresh berries and apples in the summer and fall. Farmers fermented and stored cider in barrels. The Holts expected to consume significantly more cider than the Curtises. The more affluent Curtises ate raisins, apples, and onions as well.

The Holts expected to eat their eight bushels of Indian corn and six bushels of rye (ground in local gristmills) as bread, johnnycake, and por-ridge, and as thickening in soups and stews. The Curtises ate much more grain than the Holts (thirty bushels as against fourteen), and they con-sumed wheat flour and malt in addition to corn and rye; they ate rice as well, which had to be imported from the South (the only grain on either list not grown in Hampton).

The Curtises ate 400 pounds of meat, half pork and half beef, as com-pared to a total of 190 pounds for the Holts, two-thirds of it pork. Farmers preserved most pork and beef, the pork usually by curing and smoking, the beef by "corning" or pickling in brine. Fresh meat was available only when animals were slaughtered, usually in the fall and in the late winter. If some-one went hunting, there was venison—which is why the Holts specified "fresh meat when convenient." Farmers made sausages (included on the Holt list) at slaughtering time from organ meats and otherwise trimmed or wasted parts of the animal, treated with spices or salt in order to preserve them.

Poultry was usually a game food: ducks, pigeons, turkeys, geese, quail, and pheasants shot for the pot. Farmers raised chickens and geese (the domestic poultry to which only the Curtises were entitled) for eggs and down and feathers; people killed and ate them only when they ceased to be useful producers.

Fresh fish from Hampton's streams and ponds, particularly shad in spring and fall, were at best a supplement to the staple diet. Nathaniel F. Martin was one of those who "went fishin'." He caught shad out of the Little River, the stream that runs through the middle of Hampton, and sold them for between three and nine pence each. On one occasion he sold Benjamin Fuller 36 shad at once. Ocean fish came to Hampton salted or dried. Shellfish and other seafoods were not available.

The Holts required eighty pounds of cheese a year and "so much butter as they want." Early-nineteenth-century Americans only drank milk fresh out of the cow. Cheese and butter were the dairy products that were part of normal diets. The Curtises made their cheese and butter from the milk of their two cows; their servant, Violet, did the milking, churning, and cheese making. The elderly Holts, who did not have a servant, required the final products from the Hoveys. It was easier to store butter and cheese than milk and cream. They were important forms of marketable farm goods: they figure largely in the exports from Hampton.

Both the Curtises and the Holts required "twelve pounds tallow." Tallow was beef fat. It was rendered and used to make candles and soap. That each family needed the same twelve pounds maybe indicates a traditional household requirement of a pound a month. It also shows that most households used little soap and few candles. People tended to live with the sun, so they were up and working for the summer's long hours (the longest day of the year in Hampton sees slightly more than sixteen hours of sunlight) and sleeping in their warm beds for the many hours of darkness in the winter (the shortest day of the year in Hampton is about nine hours long).

Both the Holts and the Curtises consumed rum or "ardent spirits," molasses, and sugar. Rum was the most popular of ardent spirits in New England. It was produced by the fermentation and distillation of molasses, itself a product of sugar refining. Hampton farmers also distilled cider to make applejack or apple brandy. The consumption of such "spirits" was high and increasing at the beginning of the nineteenth century. While drunkenness was discouraged, temperance and prohibition movements were just beginning.

New England imported its molasses and some of its sugar from the Caribbean. It is remarkable how much more of all the sugar products the Curtises required as compared to the Holts (twenty-five pounds of sugar as opposed to six, four gallons of molasses as opposed to six quarts, four gallons of rum as opposed to three of spirits), and more refined (good brown sugar requires a refining process, as does good West Indian rum). Sugar, molasses, and rum had to be bought in Hampton.

Other stimulants on both lists were tea and chocolate. America was a nation of tea drinkers, even more than it had been in the 1770s at the time of the Boston Tea Party. The China trade–based on tea–was swiftly becoming a large part of overseas commerce. Every Hampton merchant imported tea. Chocolate, a product of the Western Hemisphere, was the other source of caffeine in the Holts' and Curtises' diets.

Only the Holts included tobacco on their list, twelve pounds of it. People did not grow tobacco in Hampton, although some was produced in the Connecticut River valley. Merchants imported it in the form of "twist," dried and cured tobacco leaves twisted tightly together, braided, and packed in barrels. They sold it powdered (snuff) for sniffing, or by the pound or the twist. Users of both sexes cut off chunks and shredded it to smoke or chew.

The Curtises expected to continue much of the processing and manufacturing which was normal to most households. Their requirement of twenty-five pounds of flax and ten pounds of "sheeps wool" indicates the women of the household expected to continue to prepare fibers of linen and wool and spin them into thread (possibly combining them in threads used to make a common fabric known as linsey-woolsey). The Holts required "Cloathing," so they did not intend to continue the laborious processes of making thread or clothes.

The Curtises' requirement of two bushels of rock salt indicates their intention to process and preserve meats and vegetables. Finally, the Curtises' short list of exotic spices–allspice, pepper, and ginger, all of them imported from the Indies (roughly today's Indonesia)–reveals the flavor of the differences greater wealth afforded people in Hampton at the beginning of the nineteenth century.

We do not know exactly where the Taintors fitted on the Holt-Curtis continuum when they moved to Hampton. They were never as poor as the Holts, nor did they start out as well off as the Curtises. But they, like nearly every other family in Hampton, quickly changed their expectations, as the records of Hampton merchants show. Within two decades, nearly every family in town ate food as diverse and as well flavored as the Curtises did at the beginning of the nineteenth century.

Women Leave Their Mark

We have found it difficult to learn much about Hampton women's lives at the beginning of the nineteenth century. There are no contemporary diaries or letters, so far as we can discover. We know that women did most of the housework, the cooking and serving, the cleaning, and the doctoring and nursing of families. Wives were an essential and important part of the work and production of every household. And there is *some* direct evidence in the public records and in men's account books that the lives of Nabby and Judith Taintor as well as those of their contemporaries were changing.[20]

We have found Nabby's and Judith's signatures on deeds,[21] and on one short note written by one of them, so we know they were literate. When they moved to town, that was not true of all women in Hampton. At least not all could write. In the 1790s, for instance, seven heirs of Nathaniel Farnam sold the land they inherited. None of the four women involved could sign her name, however, so each made a mark instead. That same deed was witnessed by four men and two women, and both women witnesses were able to sign their names.[22] Often the wives of justices of the peace signed as witnesses to the deeds their husbands notarized. By the 1820s, thirty years later, on the other hand, there are no women in Hampton public records who could not sign their names.

Considering the literacy of Nabby and Judith Taintor, it is interesting that their family saved only one note from them—but maybe there were no others. Nabby and Judith had sisters in Hampton—their sister Harriet, who married a Moseley, and their sister Mary, who eventually moved in with Harriet. Their brother Dan also lived in town. Visiting each other was possible for all these Bulkeley relatives. The first generation of Taintors born in Hampton communicated with their fathers—in contrast to the next generation, who wrote to the women in the family as well as the men.

Women in Hampton inherited land and sold it. Single women, especially, must have hoped for such inheritances. In one deed, Susannah Ashley, "A Single woman," sold the land that came to her "by inheritance out of the Estate of my honoured Father Joseph Ashley."[23] If single women did not inherit land (land holdings in Hampton were getting small enough so that farmers often left their land to one son), they were provided for otherwise. As we have seen, Ebenezer Griffin provided for his daughters.[24] In a deed in which Aaron Fuller leased his land to his son Rufus in return for support for himself and his wife, Sarah, the lease required Rufus "to provide house room" for his sister Eunice "so long as she shall remain in a Single State." If Eunice married, Rufus must "pay her two hundred & Sixty seven dollars." Even if she did not marry, she was to get the $267.00 (it is not clear when) "in consideration for her past Services in her fathers famely & her portion in his Estate."[25] And in a similar deed, Joseph Moseley gave his daughters Esther and Anna one-third of the farm profits if they outlived him as well as "houseroom and firewood sufficient for their comfort and convenience," and their brother was "to help them to Meeting on the Sabbath as much as half the time."[26] The fact that fathers made such provisions for their single daughters speaks to the subservient status of single women in their families, and to their precarious independent economic position.

Even though Nabby and Judith Taintor were married when their father died, they inherited shares equal to those of their brothers and sisters in his large property in Colchester. But husbands were the legal owners of their wives' property. When Roger and Solomon bought up much of the rest of their father-in-law's estate, they did not have to buy the shares that had come to their wives; those shares were legally theirs. And when James M. Goodwin and Roxana, his wife, sold the Taintor brothers the share which had come to Roxana, Goodwin was a necessary party to the deed.[27]

After 1800, the Hampton public records occasionally show women acting to protect their financial independence before they married. A "Jointure" was registered among the Hampton deeds, for example, between Captain John Serjeant and Widow Martha Clark because there was "a purpose of marriage between the parties." John agreed with Martha "that she shall have and enjoy free and clear from every demand from him . . . all the Estate now belonging to" her and all the profits from it. Martha's property was to be "intirely at her dispose at her decease, without the least claim or contract made by" John. That is, Martha could will her property to anyone she wished, as any male property-owner could. And if Martha survived John she was to have "right to all his Estate during the term of her life."[28] Maybe the widow Martha Clark had learned bitter lessons in her first marriage, and so determined to protect herself.

In an 1809 premarital agreement, Love Ashley not only required her husband to "provide a comfortable and decent Support for her both in Sickness and in health for and during my natural life," but she also made him agree to give back, when he died "all the estate both real and personal" which belonged to her that came into his "possession in consequence of our intermarriage."[29] In this agreement, Ashley gave up whatever dower rights she might have had in her husband's estate in order to retain her own property and the independence it symbolized.

If women did not protect themselves as Clark and Ashley did, their rights were indeed small. Widows with dowers did not own the property they lived on. Roger and Solomon Taintor gave a mortgage to Asa Smith, for example, on his mother's widow's dower because he–not she–was the legal owner.[30] When the heirs of Benjamin Martin sold part of his farm to Roger and Solomon Taintor, the deed left a picture of a widow's lot: she merely retained "liberty . . . to pass [and] repass in the most convenient place and doing the least damage to get firewood from the ceder Swamp."[31]

Property was not an income for a woman by itself. But it could be exchanged for a livelihood. Abigail Hammond and her daughter Mercy

Hammond, for instance, deeded to John Holt all the land in Hampton they inherited in return for "a comfortable, decent, and honorable support" for their lifetimes, "in Sickness, and in health, in Victuals, and Drink, Washing, Lodging, House room, firewood, and Cloathing, entertainment for friends, according to ancient custom, Nursing," and even "Horses to ride when necessary." On the other hand, when Tabitha and Esther Moulton were deeded a small farm by their mother, they worked it themselves.[32]

Despite increasing possibilities for women to acquire greater independence, the specter of poverty remained. If a woman lost everything, the town took over her support. Such poor women were sometimes forced into the households of the more prosperous. In 1816, for instance, Nabby and Judith Taintor had "the widow Scott" for a short time when Roger bid her off for one dollar a week from among the town's poor.[33] No matter how kind the more prosperous families might have tried to be, it is difficult to imagine that impoverished women were anything but miserable. They could only see a bleak future of dependence.

By 1816, women were called upon by the town for the care of the elderly poor. The elderly Stephen Comins, in one case, had deeded "certain land which I am entitled to as bounty lands, granted to me by the King of Great Britain for services by me performed as a private soldier in the old French war So called which commenced in 1755 . . ." to Stephen Jr. and Betsey Comins in 1816. (He signed with a mark.)[34] Three months later the Town Meeting "Voted That Select Men contract with Betsey Comins for the boarding of Stephen Comins & wife at $2.34 per week & use of their house & garden."[35] So Betsey took on the care of her in-laws.

The lives of small-town women and their families were indeed changing by the first decades of the nineteenth century. One of the most obvious of those changes for Nabby and Judith Taintor was in the size of their own families. The Taintor husbands and the Taintor wives both came from large families—there were nine Taintor brothers and sisters and thirteen Bulkeley brothers and sisters. But in their married lives, Nabby and Roger had two children, Judith and Solomon had three. It seems clear that knowledge and practice of birth control techniques (perhaps *coitus interruptus* or abstinence—the use of contraceptive devices was not widespread) were available to the Taintors. Many of their contemporaries also had smaller families, but the pattern was by no means universal.

But one aspect of life had not changed for women. The deaths of children were still an ordinary part of every family's experience. Nabby Taintor had a daughter Clarissa who died at age four. Judith's daughter Caroline died at two. When Hezekiah Hammond was credited two shillings for "Diging grave for Infant" for Nathaniel F. Martin, he was participating in a common task. And Martin made a lot of coffins around the times he made "cradels."

Nabby and Judith Taintor each gave birth to a son in 1800. Judith's second son was not born until 1813. We do not know whether they had midwives to help them in childbirth or whether they helped each other. There were not always midwives to help.[36] For example, Jon Hall paid Nathaniel F. Martin for "a call in the Night & riding six miles in hast[e] To visit his wife when in travel" [in labor, "travail"].[37] Both Taintor women survived childbirth and lived to see their sons grow up and marry in a world vastly changed from that of their own childhoods.

CHAPTER 3

MERCHANTS ASPIRING TO BE GENTLEMEN

❧

"Please to pay Roger and Solomon Taintor one hundred and thirty gallons of good molasses of the first quality in part payment of a Black horse bought of them and cash...."[1]

R oger and Solomon Taintor were merchants together all their lives in Hampton from the 1790s until 1827 when Solomon died. Roger continued their joint affairs until his death in 1831. In their thirty years of working together they farmed, bought and sold land, raised, bought, and sold livestock (principally sheep), sold wool, imported goods to Hampton and retailed them there, bought and exported farm products from Hampton, gave credit to their customers, mortgaged land, lent money, invested in new banks and insurance companies and manufacturing concerns, and went into partnerships (always together) with other men in the Hampton vicinity who were similarly in business. They did not specialize. Men on the make in small-town America were jacks-of-all-trades, willing to put their minds and labor to whatever opportunities for increase their world and their occupations offered.

The Taintors were not in business to maximize profits in order to buy consumer goods. The word the Taintors used for their economic goal was "increase," meaning long-term growth of their estate in order to achieve at least a "competency." They did not use the word "profit" as we do to mean the intent to achieve measurable gain in a transaction.[2]

They were in business to become gentlemen, to achieve a place in the leading class in their world, to leap over "the one great horizontal division" in their society between ordinary people and gentlefolk. They, like their fellow Americans, recognized steps that could be taken to achieve the gentle status they sought. It was unnecessary to be born gentle in the American social hierarchy, although it had traditionally been necessary in Europe. One could acquire the attributes of gentle status, and one could gain a reputation as a leading citizen. In the eyes of the community a gentleman had a substantial estate, a network of kin and connections, some education, knowledge and experience of the wider world, a household of which he was the head, and a substantial and suitably furnished dwelling. He was actively engaged in town affairs and government and was generally acknowledged as a leader.[3]

Along the way toward their goal the Taintors carefully put away in boxes or trunks the records, papers, and books that were the evidence of their business: promissory notes, deeds, letters, memoranda, daybooks (journals), account books, ledgers, and even scrap paper covered with calculations of compounded interest. Much of that evidence has disappeared. The leather-bound ledgers with their tough rag-paper pages became scrapbooks into which their grandchildren carefully glued columns of edifying poems, articles, and stories cut from late nineteenth-century newspapers—obliterating the dusty ancient accounts. Many of the other papers have gone the way of 150 years of attic storage: into mouse nests, mold, dust, scraps used to start stove and fireplace fires, or simply "out."

It is from the scattered bits that remain that we have reconstructed how, in their effort to become gentlemen, these two small-town merchants helped create American capitalism. The Taintors' wealth started in farming. As their agricultural assets increased, they gradually transferred the surplus thus acquired into investments out of town and out of farming. And they gradually took leading roles in governing their town.

Merchant Farmers

Small-town merchants like Roger and Solomon Taintor had to manipulate and market what was available—principally land and the products of the land—in order to acquire and increase their capital. Land, buildings, transportable farm products, and the credit that could be realized from them were the only forms of capital available to them. Working their own land or hiring work done on it produced for the Taintors what is comparable to today's "cash flow" (with very little cash involved). It made the rest of their merchant activities possible.

Roger and Solomon concentrated their farm production on marketable animals. They sold wool from their flocks as well as the animals themselves. The earliest letter to Roger Taintor in the Collection, from 1810, discusses the sale of a valuable ram to a breeder in New Haven and mentions Roger and Solomon going to New Haven and Hartford to breed their sheep. Roger Taintor scribbled a memorandum on the letter that he paid "$100 in Providence for the sheep." The prices of "full Blood Sheep" mentioned in the letter—eight dollars for a ram and fifteen dollars for a ewe with lamb—are prices for valuable breeding stock of high-quality, wool-producing sheep.[4]

The Taintors invested ever more carefully in these products of their farm in order to realize the highest possible cash flow for their mercantile activities. By the 1820s they were successful large-scale wool producers and wool brokers. In one year in that decade they sold at least 1,434½ pounds of wool in the Brighton Market near Boston, Massachusetts. They produced about a third of that from their own sheep and were brokers for the rest.[5] Their annual cash income from wool and the sale of sheep, lamb, mutton, sheepskins, and ram stud services amounted to several hundred dollars. They provided food, shelter, and space for the sheep on their own land. The costs of hiring men to work the farms, keep them and their walls in repair, produce the fodder, and care for the sheep were considerable.[6] Nevertheless, those operations provided an increasing flow of cash for capital investment.

Roger and Solomon Taintor bought up farm produce in Hampton and exported it along with their own produce. Their earliest accounts, with Jesse Brown & Son, of Norwich, and with Samuel Dorrance, of Hampton, show them selling animals and provisions valued at well over a total of $3,000 between 1804 and 1808 to those two firms.[7] They delivered fifty-four oxen, seven mules, and seven horses to the Browns. They also sold them 138 "Neat Tounges" (a half barrel—they paid eighty-three cents for the half barrel itself), sixty-five firkins of lard (they paid twenty-one cents each for the firkins, small casks each equal to one-fourth of a barrel) which totaled 2,267 pounds, and 2,560 pounds of "skim cheese" in 149 "butter firkins." And they shipped the Browns 293 pounds "Smoak'd hams." They sold only animals to Dorrance, and did not have to pay for "droving" the animals since he drove them from Hampton to market himself.

Over their years as merchant farmers the Taintors processed some products to make them easier to store and transport. They bought a small piece of land in Hampton with water rights "for a distillery," and Nathaniel F. Martin recorded that he mended "worm to Still" and "rivited" the Taintors' still. They made cider and distilled it into applejack or apple brandy. Martin also worked on the Taintors' cheese press; they exported cheese on a large scale. It may be that their wives made the cheeses.[8]

In 1807, ten years after they moved to Hampton, the Taintors began a major expansion of their land holdings. When they started buying, they owned about twenty acres in contiguous lots and fields on Hampton hill. In four purchases over two years, they bought up sixty acres of a working farm next door to their own. They had to track down the heirs of Benjamin Martin, who had owned the farm, in order to buy it, which took them to upper New York State and to Vermont, and cost them $757.38. Much of the new acreage was swampy, perhaps not good for more than "holding the world together"; but it was part of a working farm, useful for animal pas-turage and firewood, and some of it undoubtedly grew feed crops and hay.[9]

Later, the Taintors bought twenty-four and a quarter acres lying across the Hampton-Mansfield town line which Mary Perkins of Becket, Mass-achusetts, had inherited from her father, Benjamin Chaplin.[10] They also joined Ebenezer Moseley and John Brewster in a complex mortgage deal to William Alworth, which resulted in Roger and Solomon acquiring fifty-two acres of Alworth's farm for $811.71.[11] They incorporated that land into their own farming operations. They paid Eliezer Baker "for all work that I did in clearing a certain Piece of land for them on their Alworth Lot So Call'd in the sum-mer 1811."[12] They used the lot for sheep-raising, and in 1817 young William Alworth—the son of the man from whom they had acquired it—paid them ten dollars for "our ram has broke into the sheep of the Taintors and done damage and whatever . . . damage shall appear to be we promise to pay."[13]

When Solomon Taintor died in 1827, the two brothers farmed over three hundred acres in Hampton and neighboring towns. Like most Hamp-ton farmers then, as now, the land they farmed was not in one contiguous plot. It included about twenty acres in their "home lot and the south mow-ing," forty-three more acres which they called "the Moseley lots" and "the Leach lot," about eighty-five acres on "Allworth hill," twenty acres in "the Perkins lot in Chaplin," seventeen acres on "Ragged Hill in Abington," and the 127.5-acre farm called "the Cunningham lot" in Abington. They had become among the largest farmers in town.

The family tradition that Solomon ran the farm while Roger was the mer-chant is not directly borne out by any of the written evidence. Both men were merchant farmers as well as farmer merchants. And they passed on the dual tradition to their children. Solomon's elder son Edwin (who was always called Bulkeley) was a small-town farmer all his life, but also was a merchant and a storekeeper when he was young. Solomon's younger son, Henry, became a merchant and investor who listed himself everywhere all his life as "a farmer." Roger's son, John, insisted for his entire life that he was a merchant, and he lived in cities (Springfield and Hartford), but he gained a national reputation as a stock breeder and improver of breeds of sheep and cattle.

Merchant-Storekeepers

The Taintors had a store, the "small house" Nathaniel Martin had painted in 1807. In it they stored all the goods they imported to Hampton—which came from Norwich, New London, Providence, Hartford, Boston, and New York. The brothers retailed some of those goods from their store. We know something of the variety of what they sold because of a very early bill they presented to James Howard, an eminent Hampton resident. In the winter and spring of 1803 Howard or someone from his family visited the Taintors' store on several occasions and made some purchases:

> Jan. 26. 1 yard Towcloth, 250 nails, 1½ yards webbing, ³⁄₁₆ yard Casimer, a Skein of silk, 5 buckles, 1 quart Rum.
> Jan. 28. 4 yards flannel, silk
> Feb. 5. 7 pounds Coperas.
> Apr. 21. ⅛ yard Scarlet Broad Cloth.
> Apr. 23. 1 yard Nankeen, 1 vest pattern, 1 pair Stockings, 1 pocket handkerchief, 4 yards holland.

Towcloth was short-staple flax ("tow") made into cloth—as opposed to the long-staple "line" which produced linen. Webbing was the strong wide band of woven material used by upholsterers. "Casimer" is another word for cashmere, "a thin fine twilled woolen cloth used for men's clothes." A skein was a certain length of thread or yarn wound upon a reel, and usually put up in a kind of loose knot. A skein of cotton was eighty turns of thread on a fifty-four-inch reel—but we do not know what the measure of a skein of silk was in 1803. Nankeen was a kind of cotton cloth, originally from Nanking, China, from a yellow variety of cotton; the term came to mean an ordinary, very durable cotton cloth dyed yellow. Holland was a linen fabric "from the province of Holland." "Coperas," usually "green copperas," was ferrous sulphate, also called green vitriol, used in dyeing, tanning, and making ink.[14] Over several years, the Taintors sold the Howards more of the same goods, as well as velvet, buttons, files, scythes, white lead (for paint), pine boards, molasses, gin, gunpowder, and twist tobacco.[15]

The Taintors "bought" their store goods by accepting them in payment for goods they exported. For instance, Jesse Brown & Son in Norwich shipped the Taintors fifty bushels of salt, 114 gallons of rum, two barrels of sugar, and two tuns (a kind of barrel) of molasses containing 110 gallons. They also sent drafts and bills on merchants in New York, all in payment for the livestock, meat, lard, and butter the Taintors sent them. Samuel Dorrance paid for the animals he bought from the Taintors (including fifty-one sheep in 1806 alone) by delivering molasses, tobacco, flour, rum, and powder. He also paid in sizable drafts on merchants and important farmers in northeastern Connecticut. The Taintors also bought store goods by exchanging such drafts and notes for goods from merchants. Sometimes, if they had any, they even paid cash to their suppliers.

There was little currency in circulation, so money rarely changed hands in the Taintors' store transactions. The money supply in the United States had been short since the original British Colonies were founded. There were no easily available precious metals. Most of the gold and silver coins which did circulate were not American in origin, but were Spanish gold reales and Austrian silver thallers. As late as 1812, the Taintors were party to a bond which specified that it be paid as "five hundred silver dollars of American or Spanish coinage, or American Gold equivalent."[16]

The new federal government had created the Bank of the United States in 1791 to provide an expanding national credit supply. But the Bank's operations rarely affected small towns. And states were cautious about chartering banks. As a result, when the Taintors started business in Hampton, few bank notes, no stock shares, few bonds, and few instruments of credit issued or guaranteed by governments were circulating in small towns. The creation of most of the credit needed in the country was left to whatever efforts local merchants chose to make.

The Taintors' efforts to create credit show up in their earliest extant accounts. They sold their goods and services on credit on their account books. Furthermore, they bought goods and services in Hampton and in the mercantile centers of Norwich, Providence, Boston, and New York by issuing promissory notes. And they accepted promissory notes that originated either with the person paying them or with third parties whose notes the payee happened to hold.[17]

When they accepted third- and fourth-party notes, they had to know something about the originators of the notes. One note, for example, a part of the Taintors' Samuel Dorrance account, was drawn on Dorrance by Parrum Palmer, a Hampton farmer, in the following form: "Please to pay Roger and Solomon Taintor one hundred and thirty gallons of good molasses of the first quality in part payment of a Black horse bought of them and cash $5.74." One of the Taintors wrote calculations on the note listing the value of the molasses at $67.60, making the total note worth $73.34. The Taintors also calculated $4.20 of interest for twenty-one months on the note, so we know Dorrance did not pay immediately. In order to accept such a note, the Taintors had to know both Parrum Palmer and Samuel Dorrance well enough to know how likely it was that they would get the 130 gallons of molasses–or its current market value–and the cash, or its equivalent, for the black horse.

Palmer's note is evidence that the Taintors did not think of themselves as operating in a strictly cash market. Nevertheless, they were aware of the current dollar value of all the goods they bought and sold. Their accounts were always kept in money. But they could not insist that every transaction be a cash transaction, since there was so little cash in circulation.

Merchants like the Taintors cultivated sources of knowledge and information about operators in more distant markets in order to acquire corresponding relationships with merchant firms in those markets. Markets in which they could safely operate were limited by their direct acquaintance with some party in every negotiation. Later in the nineteenth century Dun & Bradstreet started in New England as a firm devoted to searching out market and credit information in order to provide local merchants with the kind of information the Taintors had to acquire by themselves.

A merchant's credit system, especially one as elaborate as the Taintors' became, required extensive record keeping. Modern accounting practices had not yet been invented. By our standards, the bookkeeping of these particular canny Yankee merchants was rudimentary.[18] Nevertheless, they managed a complicated mercantile business that included what we would consider wholesaling and retailing.

The Taintors' elaborate credit network required their calculating and collecting interest, chasing people whose notes they held, taking people to court if they did not pay, making sure that sheriffs executed orders of the court against their debtors, and keeping track of notes, due dates, interest due, and goods collected in payment. One of the earliest evidences of the Taintors' mercantile activity in Hampton is the public record of their collection of a debt in 1801. For a $14.85 debt and $3.20 costs, they forced "Elijah Cheney and Bulah his wife" to "set off 4 and ⅓ acres to the said Taintors use for the term of one year."[19]

By 1810, the Taintors began to use lawyers to collect on their notes. That year, they sold seven notes to J. Baldwin, a prominent Windham attorney. He collected the notes with interest. They preserved a receipt from Stephen Abott in Brookfield, Massachusetts, for a "note of hand against William Flint of Braintree for $13.58 on demand with Interest . . . received to collect and account for." On the reverse is an endorsement dated four years later, "Received on the Within Receipt fifteen dollars."[20] They also used Andrew T. Judson of Canterbury, an eminent lawyer and political leader, to collect on notes they held from Canterbury.

By the mid-teens, they began to use their new neighbor, lawyer Joseph Prentis, as a note collector. Their circulation of notes had grown so large that the list they gave him to collect took ten notebook pages.[21] In 1829, Roger Taintor kept another notebook which listed ninety-six separate notes (the interest calculated on each). He gave them to Chauncey F. Cleveland, another neighbor who was a rising politician and lawyer, for collection. The largest amount owing was $34.10, and the smallest debt

Attorney Cleveland was to collect was for twenty cents.[22] Throughout their careers the Taintors took recalcitrant debtors to court and paid the necessary costs. In September 1826, for example, they paid $21.21 just to board their witnesses in Brooklyn for suits before the court there.[23] These sharp practices are reminiscent of Dickens's and Trollope's descriptions of creditors and debt collectors harrying those to whom they had given credit.

Keeping track of promissory notes was not always a matter of collecting. It also meant paying on notes issued, sometimes long after the notes were written. For example, on September 6, 1815, the Taintors paid John Day of Williamstown, Massachusetts, "90 gals Rum in full payment of a certain note ... for 3 mules they bought of Day Ten Years since said note being mislaid & cannot be found."[24] Even when there was not a paper record, the Taintors, ambitious to be recognized as gentlemen, acknowledged their debts.

Promissory notes in the early nineteenth century, unlike modern checks, had no standard form. They were frequently written on small slips of paper and were simple dated acknowledgments of amounts owed. They were often idiosyncratic. For instance, in June 1809, Nathan Huntington acknowledged receiving from Roger and Solomon Taintor "one Cherry dining Table worth four dollars one good feather bed worth ten dollars–& one barrow hog worth two dollars and fifty Cents which I promise to deliver to said Taintors when demanded." That was a note for $16.50. Figuring out who received what from whom, though, is further complicated by an endorsement on the reverse of the note which acknowledges receipt of "1 hog [it weighed sixty-two pounds, at four cents a pound] the one mentioned within $2.48."[25] So it seems the Taintors did demand the hog. But they left no record of what else happened.

One particular transaction perhaps sums up the way the Taintors' credit system worked. When James Howard died in 1810, Roger and Solomon Taintor figured his outstanding debt to them at about one hundred dollars. When they had still not collected it from Howard's estate after three years, they tried to realize what they could on it by selling the debt to a merchant in Ashford who gave them a piece of paper:

> This certifies that I have this day sold to Roger and Solomon Taintor seventy-five gallons of cider brandy at six shillings per gallon and one yoke of steers at $45 and have taken a note on David Avery for $25 and seven cents which is now due on the note, also a note against James Howards Estate Decd. which is now due on the note $40.81 and also said Taintors order on the Commissioners or the administrators on James Howards Estate for $54 which notes and order I take at my own risk and for Such sums as may be paid on the Dollar on Sd Howards Estate.[26]

Roger and Solomon Taintor's interest in storekeeping was primarily because it provided active exchange and some cash flow. They gave up active retailing in the teens because their other merchant activities provided more than enough business. They continued to store stocks of cloth, which they occasionally retailed. People in Hampton bought miscellaneous other items from them. And they sold rum and molasses out of their store until they died.

Merchant Families

The Taintors' success as merchants, and their accumulation of capital, depended in large part—as did everything else in their lives—on their families. The people we call either "kin" or "relatives" they called interchangeably their "friends" or their "connections." Throughout their careers Roger and Solomon had business relations with brothers, sisters, wives, brothers-in-law, uncles and aunts, first cousins, and other close relatives. Their location in Hampton brought several relatives to live there. And the two of them never operated in business, so far as the evidence shows, without each other. They showed a distinct preference throughout their lives for being in business with family.

On September 13, 1809, Roger and Solomon made a partnership agreement with young Samuel S. Moseley (the son of Col. Ebenezer Moseley), who was shortly to become kin. By 1811, Moseley was part of their family as well as a business connection when he married Harriet Bulkeley, Nabby and Judith's youngest sister. Roger and Solomon entered partnerships many times in the course of their business careers, often with family, and always with men who had themselves important kin connections in town. Partnership was the preferred organizational form of business among merchants in their day. We include the agreement they made with Moseley because its actual language conveys something of the flavor of their dealings:

> Know all men by these presents that we Roger & Solomon Taintor & Samuel S. Moseley all of Hampton in the County of Windham do agree to Form ourselves into a Company to carry on the Mercantile business in . . . Hampton for the Term of Three Years. . . .
>
> The Taintors are to put into the Company as Capital the sum of Two Thousand Dollars and Moseley is to put into the Company the sum of Two Thousand Dollars which Two sums are to be considered the Capital of the Company and if either of the parties shall advance more than the above mentioned sums the company are to allow him the interest on the overplus advanced—
>
> And Samuel S. Moseley with the advice of the Taintors shall Transact the Business of the Company according to his best skill and

judgement and render an account yearly of the profits & loss to the Company (if requested)

And Moseley for his Services and for his Capital . . . shall receive Two thirds of the neat ["net"] profits . . . and the Taintors shall Receive one third part of the profits. . . .

And the Company are to pay all the expense of carrying on the Company Business together with the Board of Moseley during the term above mentioned

And what Goods that shall remain on hand at the expiration of the . . . term shall be divided to each one according to the profits he shall receive . . . and Moseley shall faithfully settle all the accounts of the Company and make a collection of the Company's property and account with each one of the partners as soon as possible after dissolution of the Company

And the Firm is to be known by the name of Samuel S. Moseley. . . .[27]

The Taintors intended to be "silent" partners in this firm, in the sense that they would not visibly participate in the store's operations and the firm name did not include Taintor. They did, however, intend to be consulted. They sought, as all investors at the time did, to have active direction of their investment, although Moseley managed this firm.

When they had moved to Hampton, Roger and Solomon were in a partnership with their older brothers and a cousin–brother-in-law (John and Charles Taintor, and Gad Bulkeley) in Windham; John and Charles Taintor themselves had a large retail store in Windham. In 1809 Taintors & Bulkeley dissolved the partnership. As a result, Roger and Solomon received more than $2,600 of their capital in the form of more than seventy promissory notes and a mortgage on a farm in Canterbury that had been held by the business.[28] They promptly invested that capital in other ventures, perhaps in the partnership with Samuel Moseley.

They were later involved in another partnership with their brothers John and Charles, which included a man named Solomon Gilbert. When "the concerns of the late Company of Sol. Gilbert & Co.," which had operated a store in Windham, were settled in 1813, Roger and Solomon received notes, book debt, cash, and goods including "one silver watch worth $10.25" totaling nearly $3,900.[29] That capital, too, was reinvested.

Roger and Solomon's business dealings with their Bulkeley connections included their buying up a large part of the estate of their uncle and father-in-law, John Bulkeley, Sr., in Colchester. Gad Bulkeley (who had been the Bulkeley in Taintors & Bulkeley) first sold one hundred acres from his father's estate to them in 1809 in order to pay estate debts and to prepare for the complex division of property among John Bulkeley's twelve surviving children and their heirs. The next year, Roger and Solomon bought more than one-half of their late father-in-law's land. In this complicated transaction, they paid Gad Bulkeley for his share, Roxana Goodwin (a granddaughter) for hers, their brother-in-law Dan Bulkeley for his, and their sister-in-law Harriet Bulkeley for hers.[30] They laid out a total of $3,530, which, with their wives' shares, gave them a more than two-hundred-acre farm with a dwelling house and barns in Colchester. They kept that family farm for twelve years as one of their income-producing properties.

From the early teens to their deaths Roger and Solomon had business connections with Nabby and Judith's younger brother, Dan Bulkeley. Dan moved from Colchester to Hampton, married a Hampton woman, Phoebe Burnett, the daughter of an important Hampton family and kin group. He became the postmaster and quite possibly the central and most important storekeeper in Hampton in the 1820s and 1830s. Until his death in 1844, Dan Bulkeley had business connections with two generations of Taintors and Taintor kin.

Moseley's and Bulkeley's stores were located in the village in Hampton, just as the Taintors' store was. But there was little question of what we would think of as competition among the stores in town. In the early decades of the century stores were still places where merchants stored their goods. The goods in any store were limited by the liquid capital of the merchant, by the necessity of bulk import (which limited the variety any merchant could stock), and by the slowness (by modern standards) of getting goods bought and delivered from distant markets. No one store in a small town was likely to duplicate the goods of any other at any one time. Customers went to the store run by their kin or by storekeepers on whose books they were carried.

While the Taintor brothers' dealings with their numerous kin may have been frequent and amicable, kinship did not imply special treatment in business. They preserved a receipt for a note that a man in Williamstown, Massachusetts, was to collect, which serves as illustration. Their brother-in-law Gurdon Bulkeley had delivered the note. It was for a debt of $104 that Roger and Solomon had lent Gurdon's brother, Joshua Robbins Bulkeley (who was also their sister Sarah's husband and their wives' brother).[31] They chased a relative who "hired money" and used a collector as they did with any other delinquent debtor. Merchants expected to gain, not lose, through family connections.

Merchant Investors

In their search for increase, the Taintors went beyond the limits of farming and storekeeping. They moved their capital to new ventures as frequently as they realized it in any one enterprise.

Land was the most obvious investment. Before 1800, there were only two mortgages registered in all of Hampton's Deeds. After that year, mortgages begin to appear with increasing frequency in the town records. By mortgaging their land, farmers could command credit and then use it to acquire goods or to invest in more land, buildings, equipment, or animals. The Taintors provided mortgage money. In economic terms, they enabled the realization of the value of agriculture. In the more practical terms they used and understood, they hired out their capital at low risk for secured gain.

The earliest mortgage the Taintors took (they carefully preserved the document) was dated January 11, 1802. In it, Nathan Deans put up one and one-half acres in Brooklyn, Connecticut, as security for eighty dollars he owed the Taintors.[32] Perhaps they lent him the money in the form of a promissory note or as advance credit for a purchase he wished to make from them. Perhaps they took the mortgage in order to secure a debt he had already run up at their store.

The Taintors' acquisitions of mortgages started slowly. In 1808 they took three small mortgages in Ashford and as many in Hampton. They took a mortgage on a small piece of land near the Hampton meeting house for $125 which Guy Cummins owed them (they sold it eight years later for $200 after Cummins died). And they took a mortgage on a small piece of land in Hampton "between Abner Allins House and Thomas Fuller's."[33]

From 1809 on, Roger and Solomon engaged in increased numbers of mortgages because they had more liquid capital available to them. And they began to sell mortgages for the first time. Their view, as reflected in these transactions, was that mortgages were best held for short term. They took a mortgage on Abner Allen's four acres on Bigelow road in January 1809, and sold it in August 1810 for nineteen dollars more than its face value. A March 1809 mortgage on thirty acres adjoining their own land they sold in February 1810 for twenty-two dollars more than its face value. An April 1809 mortgage they took from Amasa Martin he paid off in February 1810, a very short term indeed. And four months was too long in one instance. In August 1809, they foreclosed on an April mortgage to Roswell Culver (who had had a shop and garden on their new house lot in 1804), and received "all the lands" Culver inherited from his father in Norwich–a total of six and one-half acres. Given this kind of credit activity, it is not surprising that Roger Taintor was twice in 1809 a court-appointed appraiser on executions of judgments against debtors in Hampton.[34] He was becoming a trusted man of property.

The Taintors' mortgage activity increased throughout the rest of their lives. They gradually extended their range from Hampton into neighboring towns and into more distant regions. Migration out of Hampton–and out of the rest of Connecticut–increased after the War of 1812 ended, and regions of upper New York, along with Pennsylvania, Ohio, and parts even farther west, attracted many of the migrants. Land was available there, in quantity, for agricultural development. And the Taintors provided some of the capital needed for that development. Their investments in land, through mortgages, brought them a very satisfying increase of their own capital. They also made it possible for established farmers and for younger people who inherited land to realize some of the value of that land and invest in their own future increase.[35]

In order to get the cash needed for mortgage investments, the Taintors continued to invest in silent partnerships with active merchants and retailers. In 1810, they put together a partnership with Rufus Pearl, an Ashford merchant, and until his death in 1821 were involved in the widespread mercantile and mortgage business of Rufus Pearl & Company.[36] The company's operations enabled them to take sizable chunks of capital out of it periodically for use in other undertakings. By 1818, Rufus Pearl & Company had grown so much that the Taintors received nearly thirteen thousand dollars' worth of notes as payment for "the debt the R. Pearl & Co. owes them."[37]

The records of the company's operations show the same kind of importing and exporting the Taintors did in Hampton. They also show increasing use of local banks: the company accepted banknotes drawn, for example, upon the Phoenix Bank in Hartford (from which the Phoenix Insurance Company grew) and the Hartford Bank.[38] And Rufus Pearl & Co. participated in mortgages in many of the towns of northeastern Connecticut as well as of upper New York State.

The Taintors participated in other partnerships through Rufus Pearl & Co. They became partners in Moses White & Co. in the town of Union, Connecticut, to which they provided mortgage money.[39] They participated in Pearl, Rider & Taintors, which terminated in 1817.[40] And, as partners in Rufus Pearl & Co., they became participants in the Loomises & Barker Co. of Westford Society, Ashford. Loomises & Barker had been formed "to Carry on the Gun Making Business" during the war with the British that started in 1812.

This was the first war in which the United States participated after the Revolution, and it was fought against the same enemy. The Taintors were among the party–the Republicans–which supported the war (as opposed to the Federalists, who did not), and the war was very unpopular. It brought the call-up of militia, and Roger and Solomon had relatives who served. The threat of the invasion of Connecticut was real, both from the sea and overland through New York or northern New England from Canada.

During the war, the United States fought land and sea battles against the British on the Great Lakes on both sides of the Canadian border, in Virginia (where the British did invade and where they captured and burned Washington, D.C.), and in Louisiana. The memorable victories of the war came at Put-in Bay on Lake Erie, where Commodore Oliver Hazard Perry defeated a British fleet; at Baltimore, where Francis Scott Key wrote a poem about "the star-spangled banner" yet waving; and at New Orleans, where Tennessee militia general Andrew Jackson defeated Wellington's veterans. The war ended in 1815.[41]

Loomises & Barker Co. (many of the documents spell William Loomis's name "Lummis") was a gun-making business in a building in Ashford owned by William Loomis. John Loomis, William Loomis, and Calvin Barker were the essential artisans and mechanics in the company, so important that they agreed "to pay the Company one Dollar Per Day for Every Day they shall be Absent from the Business of said Company excepting ten days for Each in Each Year they are to have Reserved for their own use." Each of them contributed $800 as his share of the capital, much of it in the value of the building and of their tools. Rufus Pearl & Company's share was $1,500.

There is no evidence of the kind of guns–muskets or cannons–the company made. At one time, the company bought ninety-six bars of "Swedes Iron" in Boston, so their operations required high-grade iron. They also contracted for 8,500 "quarters of Good Merchantable Screw Augers free from flaws," for which the Taintors agreed to pay in goods. Since these were ordinary screws, it seems likely they were making muskets. And financial conditions during the war in at least one case made them stipulate "silver money on demand" for a debt owed them. (When they collected that debt four years later, however, they did not get silver money, but rather cotton yarn worth less than the debt's face value.)

The Loomises & Barker partnership was dissolved at the end of 1817, and Roger and Solomon Taintor and Rufus Pearl took over all the movable property and debts of the company. They also acquired from William Loomis the buildings the gun company used, which they intended to sell as a place suitable for manufacturing. The agreement they made with Loomis shows some of the equipment and buildings of this early factory: Loomis agreed "to put the Gun factory So Called in Good Repair," by repairing "the trip hammer in Such a manner as to Draw Iron [stretch it out by hammering] in the Best manner into large and Small Drafts," and repairing "the Bellows Wheel in Such a manner as to answer the Purpose for which it was made," and also by repairing the floor "to Make it as Strong and Durable as when New." Furthermore Loomis agreed "to hang the Door to the Coal house & fill up holes Made by the Water Near the Water or filing Shop, and to under pin the Water Shop where it is needed, and to Make a Sufficient Dam to Prevent the Water from Running between the filing and Water shop."[42] At the end of 1818, the Taintors were still trying to sell off the remains of the company. They sold three thousand augers to Henry S. Catten of Savannah–a connection possibly made by their oldest brother, John Taintor, who had business dealings with Savannah and eventually made a family connection to that southern mercantile center.[43]

The Taintors diversified their investments more and more in the period after the War of 1812. They began to bank their cash (and thereby invest) in the Windham County Bank in Brooklyn. They deposited several thousand dollars in cash per year in the bank, which they drew upon by checks, and the bank's cashier, Adams White, Jr., began to figure in their affairs as a source of financial information.[44]

The Taintors made the only stock investment of which they left a record in October 1824. They bought twenty shares of stock in the Hartford Bank for $107 per share (seven dollars over par value). They bought the stock from a Hartford broker who was a friend of Roger's grown son John–practically a family connection–purely for its dividend income. There is no evidence anywhere in their papers that they speculated on a rise in the value of capital assets. Indeed, the whole tenor of the Taintor brothers' records indicates that they considered investment for capital gain to be speculation, which they regarded as morally reprehensible, on a par with gambling. They eventually left their Hartford Bank stock to provide dividend income for their heirs.[45]

They also very cautiously lent money to manufacturing concerns as "portfolio" investments that did not require their active participation in management of the companies. When, however, a company in which they had invested was threatened with bankruptcy, they immediately took a more active role. Their involvement with the Willimantic Cotton Manufacturing Company grew from such necessity. It was a cotton textile firm in the town of Mansfield that had been incorporated by the Connecticut legislature in 1814. The company owned "a quantity of land in . . . Mansfield with several dwelling houses, together with a large and commodious building and machinery for manufacturing cotton, and a store, and necessary out buildings." The factory village consisted of five houses, a blacksmith shop, a machine shop, a barn, and a shed, besides the factory building itself. The company owned nearly three hundred acres of farmland because its dam on the Willimantic river flooded so much land. The company spun cotton yarn, "put out" the yarn to local hand weavers, and then sold the resulting cloth.

Debts gradually increased to a point early in the 1820s when the company owed nearly twice the value of its assets and was unable to pay. In November 1822, the principal stockholders and officers petitioned the state court in Brooklyn to supervise the sale of assets and the dissolution of the company.[46] Among other of the company's creditors, Roger and Solomon Taintor brought suit to try to protect the more than two thousand dollars they had lent the company, and early in 1824, Roger was made trustee in the bankruptcy dissolution.[47]

Roger's first effort was to keep the factory going, and to put it into good repair and appearance for sale. His first charge against the company was on March 1, 1824, for three dollars for "1 day attending the Company business at Factory" and two dollars for Solomon doing the same. Perhaps they consulted with each other about what needed to be done to the fabric of the factory and its village, or perhaps they went over the company's books together, but Solomon thereafter left the matter entirely in Roger's hands.

Roger immediately traveled to Windham "after money and notes" of one of the company directors, and to Mansfield later "to Let out the farm and attend . . . to the factory business," to Windham again, and to Brooklyn to do some company business at the court there. In April, he journeyed to "the factory to meet with the Carpenters and Mr. Hopkins the machine maker," and later traveled to North Mansfield to get deeds and do other factory business. He paid out thirty dollars for spools and bobbins—an indication that the mill was still spinning yarn.

In May, he went to Norwich "to see Mr. Hopkins and others about the factory," and later paid $46.80 to Joseph and O. O. Hopkins & Co. for repairing machinery (a roller, a spreader, and replacing seventy-two brass teeth). He went "to the factory to employ men to paint the factory and buildings" and to buy seventy-five panes of glass. He later paid for lamp black used for painting the factory's doors, and for "Spanish brown and white lead" paint pigments, and a "Bill of work" for ten days repairing "Cards, belts, Drums etc. @ 83 Cts." a day. He paid Daniel Burnam & Co. for repairs, J. H. Strong for oil and paints, and Amos Ford fifty dollars for forty-nine and one-half days painting the factory building and carting the paints and oil. He hired L. Woodworth & Co. of North Coventry to put the mill wheel in good repair—it was broken, and required carpentry, blacksmithing, new bolts, washers, and wedges. Woodworth apologized for charging $41.38 for the work, and left it in Roger Taintor's hands whether he would judge the whole bill reasonable or pay whatever less he thought right. Roger paid Woodworth the full amount.[48]

In July, Roger journeyed "to the factory to hire it to Smith and others" for fifty dollars. In September, Roger traveled to "Coventry to settle accounts and get a Load yarn from the Factory," perhaps to put out to weavers. In November, Roger went to Norwich and Lebanon "to Settle accounts and hire the factory [rent it out] or sell it." And on December 22, his birthday, he journeyed again "to the Factory after yarn." While doing the company's business he consulted attorneys in Mansfield, Norwich, and Brooklyn, and paid one dollar for each consultation—regardless, presumably, of the number of what modern lawyers call billable hours he spent with them.

In January 1825, Roger wrote nineteen advertisements and ten letters to newspaper publishers in Boston, Providence, Norwich, Hartford, and local newspapers to advertise the factory for sale. And he began to make partial payments to the company's creditors, including sizable sums to "R & S Taintor," from money that he had collected. In the spring he had to make several small payments for damage done to farmers' land by "flowing"—water backed up by the company's dam.

Roger spent two days in February 1825 in Willimantic "to sell Factory." And in April, he finally made a special trip to Mansfield to deed the factory and its other buildings to Joseph Hutchins of Canterbury, Joseph Breed of Norwich, and Edmund Smith of Mansfield for eight thousand dollars—it had been valued in the bankruptcy documents at twelve thousand dollars. He also sold pieces of land belonging to the company. And in 1825 he made significant payments—always called "dividends"—to the creditors. A first payment of ten percent was followed by one of fifteen percent. That in turn was followed by one of thirty-three percent as the money from land and factory sales came in.

In February 1826, Roger spent two and a half days (still at the rate of three dollars per day) in Mansfield selling the "Factory farm" and attending to other business of his trust. By the end of the year he had sold "the Willimantic farm," the last piece of the company's property. And in July 1827, he closed his accounts of the company's affairs. One of his last transactions was the sale of some "damaged steelyards [scales]" to Bulkeley & Grosvenor, his brother-in-law Dan Bulkeley's store in Hampton.

The Willimantic Cotton Manufacturing Company had owed more than $33,000 in 1822 when it went bankrupt, with assets worth little more than $17,000. Roger Taintor collected $25,839.60 by selling those assets, collecting the receivables, and carefully nurturing the assets and money he held. The expenses of the company in trusteeship were considerable, but the creditors nevertheless received approximately seventy percent by the time he ended his trusteeship.

By the end of their lives, Roger and Solomon Taintor had successfully transferred their accumulated capital from farming and retailing to investments that produced cash income. They rarely any longer accepted goods (however carefully valued in cash equivalents) in exchange for land or goods. After the Willimantic Cotton Manufacturing Company sale, the active management of any particular investment was remote from their daily lives. They had started their careers as ex-Colonial small-town merchants and ended them as independent capitalist investors still in the same small town. Along the way they, like many of their contemporary small-town businesspeople, had helped create, out of farming and agriculture, the capital for investment in banks, machine manufacturing, and railroads.

Merchant Politicians

Throughout Roger and Solomon Taintor's lives they were active in the political life of Hampton. Early on they identified with the Republicans, thus carrying the status, in their politics, of "new men," antiestablishment outsiders. By the end of their first decade in Hampton, however, they had become established public figures.

In the 1790s, all over America, the men who had supported the federal Constitution and the administrations of Washington and Adams were called Federalists. In Connecticut they were identified both in state and local governments as the supporters of the established order and of the men and families who traditionally held office. At the end of the eighteenth century Thomas Jefferson and James Madison organized opposition to the Federalists and the establishment. They and their followers called themselves Republicans and supported democracy and the expansion of the franchise. In Connecticut Republicans like the Taintors were opposed to the continuation of an established church, and they sought to broaden the group of men who held public office. They inclined more to popular rule than their Federalist opponents who had controlled the state government since the Revolution.[49]

Both Roger and Solomon entered town politics when they started in business. Solomon was more successful earlier than Roger.[50] Perhaps Solomon was the farmer; Hampton still elects farmers. He was elected First Constable and collector of state taxes in 1801. He was elected one of the Selectmen in 1802 and in 1803. He was elected a surveyor of highways in 1798, 1804, 1805, 1806, 1807, 1810, 1813, 1814, 1815, and 1816. In 1815, he was made a member of a special committee to deal with highway problems in the midst of controversy about roads and highways as a result of inflation at the end of the War of 1812.

Solomon held other local offices. In 1804, he was a grand juror, and in 1811, he was a member of the First School Society Committee. His and Roger's sons were pupils in the school.

Roger Taintor was not so popular with Hampton's town meeting as his brother. In 1800, he was elected constable and collector of state taxes, and he was a surveyor of highways. In 1802, he was made a member of the committee to try to get the Windham County Court House located in Hampton, and in 1808, he was made member of a special committee "to raise Money by Subscription to mend the old road or purchase a new road between Hez'h Hammond's & Col. Eben'r Moseley's" after heavy August rains (possibly a hurricane) had damaged several roads in town. Roger Taintor was made a surveyor of highways in Town Meeting in 1809, perhaps because he had done a good job raising funds for the road repairs after the 1808 rains. It was one of the few years his brother was not elected to that job.

The town records provide some glimpses of the concerns the Taintor brothers dealt with in the early years of the century. In the fall of 1808 the Town Meeting took time to deal with—in this case get rid of—a man who had been a long-standing problem, Josiah Rogers. Rogers's family had been among the poor supported by the town for some years. Now the Town Meeting gave "Josiah Rogers 50 dollars to enable him to remove with his Family to Susquehanna." Rogers left. But in October the Town Meeting heard that Thomas Stedman had sent after Rogers to collect a debt. The town was clearly horrified at the possibility that Rogers might be forced to return in order to pay Stedman. "Whereupon the town Voted to pay . . . Stedman 20 dollars for . . . Rogers Debt and the Cost arisen" and the Town Meeting sent someone immediately "to prevent . . . Rogers being Stoped on his journey."[51] The Hampton Town Meeting had proved itself capable of swift and determined action.

In May 1809, Hampton elected Solomon Taintor its representative to the Connecticut State Assembly, the first time he was elected to that high office. He was elected again for both sessions of the Assembly (the Connecticut Assembly met alternately in Hartford and New Haven) in 1811 and in 1812. Eighteen-twelve marks a high point in Solomon's political career. Not only was he elected to the State Assembly, but he was also elected Hampton's First Selectman (the local equivalent of mayor) in November of that year, with a fresh slate of selectmen, which makes it sound like a Republican sweep of Hampton's offices. Solomon also became a member of a three-man committee to draft a series of town ordinances about impounding animals—a matter of direct concern to stock-raising farmers like the Taintors. Solomon was also appointed a justice of the peace by the state legislature in 1811, an indication that Republicans were strong in the legislature as well as in Hampton just before the War of 1812 started. Combining the positions of state representative, First Selectman, and justice of the peace was rare among Hampton political leaders and, in Solomon Taintor's case, it lasted no more than a year.

Rapid disillusionment in New England about the war set back the Republican cause everywhere, and it lost Solomon all his offices by the end of 1812. The war was regarded as a "Republican War" because it was championed by Republican leaders from the West like Henry Clay of Kentucky and John Calhoun of South Carolina, leaders who had made their support of James Madison's renomination for a second term in 1812 conditional on his asking for a declaration of war against Great Britain. The Federalists, still strong in New England and Connecticut, who opposed Republican measures leading up to the war as well as the conduct of the war itself, finally called a convention in Hartford in 1815 that threatened secession from the Union if "Mr. Madison's war" was not brought to an end. The war ended in 1815 with a treaty of peace negotiated and signed even before the Federalists could bring effective pressure on the government.

The end of the war, combined with Andrew Jackson's victory at the Battle of New Orleans (after the treaty was signed) and the obstructionism of the Hartford Convention, brought discredit on the Federalists everywhere. In Connecticut it gave impetus to political activism by new leaders and it gave new energy to the Republicans.[52] Hampton elected Solomon Taintor again to the State Assembly in 1816 after the war was over. He was reelected in 1817, and the Hampton Town Meeting voted, "that our Representative be instructed to use his influence in the next General Assembly . . . to obtain a Convention for the purpose of framing a written Constitution for this state." Connecticut was governed under a continuation of the seventeenth-century "Fundamental Orders" and the Republicans were eager for a new, written constitution.

While the Federalist Party was swept away at the end of the war, some of the issues that had divided Federalists and Republicans in Connecticut still counted. The Taintors found themselves among the "democratic" Republicans who wanted elective office to be open to ambitious farmers and coming businessmen. They opposed those who called themselves "national" Republicans and who had joined with many old Federalists to support the established order, restricted voting, and the families who traditionally held office in town. At the center of what became an acrimonious fight in every town in Connecticut was the question of whether or not to continue the established church, which was both symbol and real center of the established social and political order. A "Toleration Party" (predominantly Republicans) won control of the state constitutional convention called in 1818, and they wrote a constitution that disestablished the church. No longer would every citizen be taxed to support a church.

That new constitution came to a Hampton vote on October 5, 1818. There is no record of the debate, merely of the vote: "The house was divided & the names of the yeas & nays taken & counted, when it appeared that there were 89 in favor of its adoption & 120 against it." Roger and Solomon Taintor both voted *for* the new constitution and disestablishment, as did Dan Bulkeley, their brother-in-law, the entire extensive Burnham family (all thirteen Burnhams at the Town Meeting), half of the Clark clan, both of the leading Baptists in town (Thomas Grow and Thomas Grow, Jr.), the Pearl family, the Hovey family, and Nathaniel F. Martin, Ebenezer Jewett, and several other leading artisans. On the other side, of course, were Rev. Ludovicus Weld, the minister, and many of the faithful of his church, including all the Moseleys (among them the Taintors' brother-in-law and business partner Samuel), Joseph Prentis, Amos Ford, the Brewsters (including John, the painter), and most of the Fullers.

Democratic Republicans like the Taintors and those willing to vote in public to disestablish the church were not the majority in Hampton even if they were in the state. Most Connecticut towns voted to ratify the new constitution. It went into effect and disestablished the state church in 1819. In Hampton, however, twelve of the thirteen town officials elected after the vote against the constitution had voted with the majority. The Taintors and their democratic Republican friends were swept out of office.

It was 1820 before either of the Taintors was again elected. That year Roger became the town's representative to the Connecticut Assembly. Solomon was made town agent, member of the Board of (Tax) Relief, and surveyor of highways. In 1821 he was sent to the Assembly in Roger's place. He was also moderator of Town Meeting, and again was a member of the Board of Tax Relief, town agent, and surveyor of highways. Roger was elected a selectman and made a justice of the peace. In 1822, Solomon again moderated Town Meeting and was elected tax assessor. Roger became First Selectman (Nathaniel F. Martin was a selectman that year as well), and Roger was also made state representative. Solomon's son, Edwin Bulkeley Taintor, was elected First Constable and collector of taxes. Among its other business that year, in a combined effort to deal with a paternity question and a single mother "on welfare," the Town Meeting voted "that a suit be commenced against Jesse Fuller to compel him to indemnify the Town against any expense on account of Clara Neff's bastard child."[53]

The Republicans in Hampton had clearly come on stream again, and with greater influence than ever before. In 1823 Roger Taintor was again made a selectman and a justice of the peace. Solomon was elected an assessor and made a surveyor of highways. And in that year the Reverend

Ludovicus Weld was forced to resign his ministry and move out of town. He had been the leader of the old establishment, and his departure marked its downfall in Hampton.

Roger and Solomon continued to seek and be elected to offices of local importance for the rest of their lives. Solomon was a highway surveyor, town auditor, moderator, and member of several special town committees until his death in 1827. Roger continued as a justice of the peace as well as town officeholder until he died in 1831. They did not create a new establishment to succeed the old, but they and their contemporaries, eager to participate in local government, were active and competitive office-seekers. Their aspirations, like those of their whole generation that came of age in the years following the War for Independence, had been revolutionary, and their achievements had gone far to change their personal and their political worlds. Their ambitions as farmers and merchants had been social and political as well as economic, in fact all three inseparably. They had defined the status and role of "republican gentleman" in the thirty years in which they had made themselves into republican gentlemen.

CHAPTER 4

BRINGING UP GENTLEMEN

❧

"To be sure your Father and myself ... once aspired to be
at the tip, top, of Gentility; but we are so-so...."[1]

John and Bulkeley Taintor grew up nearly as twins, born within a few
weeks of each other in 1800. Their parents, Roger and Nabby, Solomon
and Judith, lived out their lives together in the Hampton house in which
John and Bulkeley grew up. The sons spent their first twenty
years together at home and in school. Their parents educated the children for a world beyond their own.

Education for a New Century

John and Bulkeley probably learned to read and write from their parents at
home. The law required that they attend the common school in their district in Hampton—it was in the center of the village but we do not know
exactly where—and they acquired more skills in literacy and arithmetic in
school. Hampton maintained its one-room primary schools from the 1780s
to the 1940s.[2]

John and Bulkeley's school curriculum focused on American Revolutionary heroes. John's parents saved a small piece of paper, boldly if
ungrammatically signed "John A Taintor,s Hampton," that has a poem
copied in a childish hand:

> But we must all forbare to sigh
> Since Washington was born to die
> He ever was his countrys friend
> But Washington must have an end.[3]

Death was part of the little boys' education for life. George Washington's death in 1799 had been the occasion of widespread mourning. And when the boys were ten, in 1810, Bulkeley's little two-year-old sister Caroline died at home. John's poem goes on to laud Jefferson as Washington's successor and to emphasize the continuation of life.

From a later year in school John Taintor kept a "Moral and Pleasing Collection of Pieces" called *The Rose,* published in 1812. It included a piece on Benjamin Franklin, another Founding Father, who was "a journeyman printer" from which "condition he arose to be a principle conducter in the revolution of a great nation." Franklin was "nearly the inventer of electricity, a most useful branch of science," and "he was stiled the American Newton. In Europe his name was great, and America venerates him forever."[4]

When the boys were fourteen the Taintor parents did something not every family did: they sent John and Bulkeley away for further schooling, first to Phillips Academy in Massachusetts, then to Plainfield Academy in Connecticut, and finally to Bacon Academy in their parents' hometown of Colchester. Boys who were sent away to academies were preparing for college. Obviously, the Taintor parents had already decided by 1814 that the boys should go to college. If they did, their status as gentlemen would be assured.

In 1814, John and Bulkeley went to Phillips Academy in Andover, Massachusetts.[5] It was wartime, and the threat of an invasion of Connecticut may have influenced the Taintor parents in sending the children out of state to school. It was also a year after the birth of Bulkeley's little brother Henry in the house in Hampton. Besides, the family had connections to a young man attending the Andover Theological Seminary, Jesse Flint, who became the boys' tutor. They (and several other boys) lived with him at the Andover Seminary while they attended the Academy.

The Taintors kept one long letter from Flint, who clearly liked both of the boys. He wrote in August 1814, telling why he was sending them home to Hampton for a vacation:

> . . . The Boys have studied very hard, & their health demands it. They see the other Boys all going, and they would be lonesome. They are strongly bent (especially Bulkeley) to be here next Term; & it may be dangerous to check them. Bulkeley has had a bad & dangerous tooth, as the Doctor says, & I wish to see it extracted before it swells to break again. I have done for him, with the best counsel, all I could, . . . I rejoice that the Boys are so much engaged, & have so high an opinion of the Academy. Allthough they may be enthusiastic [used here in the obsolete sense of "filled with God"] in their opinion, yet it may be unsafe to correct it. . . .

This was during the Second Great Awakening, a time of widespread religious revival and growing controversy. The Taintors, as Republicans who were antiestablishment, may have developed misgivings about their children's education at Andover when they heard about their enthusiasm from Flint. The school was a bastion of orthodox congregationalism oriented toward Harvard. Flint's letter also described the boys' studies and what may have appeared as other shortcomings in their education to the Taintor parents:

> We have not devoted any time to speaking [rhetoric] as you wished. This is my reason. Too many strings at once, are not favorable to business; especially when so large a string as the Latin must be pulled [both rhetoric and Latin were central to academic work]. I should like to spend 3 or 4 weeks, exclusively to speaking, with the Boys. Because that would be the way to effect the object of it successfully. They have made proficiency in composition by Letter writing, with some assistance from me.

Frugality was a virtue as well understood by a teacher as by ambitious parents like the Taintors. Flint was eager to justify the costs of the boys' education:

> . . . With regard to the Boys expenses, since they came on, you may think we have been extravagant. But I think not. . . . They spent two Dollars apiece coming on here. We went to Boston, Salem & Nahant at two different times, which took considerable of a sum. However, I meant to be as frugal as though it had been my own case, or very nearly so. The Boys have not bought many things without asking my advice; & I requested them to keep an account of every outgo. . . .

Flint included in his letter news of some of the boys' friends, particularly Isaac Clark from Hampton and George Cowles of New Hartford, Connecticut, who was "very lonely" after the Taintor boys had left. He concluded by saying that his room was "desolate" since the students had departed: "Tell your Son's that I had a prosperous journey from Boston in the Stage, & that I have an anxiety to hear the same of them. I hope the robbers have not hurt John, as he seemed somewhat to apprehend. . . . Do let me know how the Boys got home."[6] (The highway robbers of childhood folklore had apparently impressed John.)

Academies like Andover, with its close relationship to a theological seminary and its tradition as a training ground for young men going to college to prepare for the ministry, emphasized morality and religious instruction. John kept a booklet called "Constitution for the Society for Promoting Good

Morals in Phillips Academy, Andover." Another copy the family kept may have been Bulkeley's. The Taintor Collection includes many religious pamphlets and tracts dating from John and Bulkeley's years in academies.[7]

Although there is no clear evidence that the Taintor parents were full members of the church in Hampton at this time, they nevertheless wanted their sons to have a moral and religious education. Gentility required a deep and active commitment to Christian doctrine and behavior. Schools and parents expected pupils to be very much involved in the religious movements of the day and to participate in the sometimes bitter and always serious debates and discussions about the role of the church in society, politics, and everyday life, and about the changing nature of Christian doctrine.

The young Taintors and their friends were much impressed by and involved in the religious ferment of the Second Great Awakening. No letters survive from John or Bulkeley while they were at Andover, but there is a letter from Isaac Clark, one of their friends, who wrote from Andover to his maternal grandfather, Isaac Bennet, a deacon of the Hampton church. It is couched in terms utterly different from those a grandson would use today—not only in its language but in its discussion of moral conduct and its author's willingness to mention the inevitability of his grandfather's death:

> Honored Grandfather,
> ... I now attempt to write to a Grandparent, whom I have always tenderly loved. And although I, who am, as it were, but a youth, am writing to one of grey hairs, yet I trust a few lines will be greatfully received from one, for whose welfare you have always manifested the tenderest regard. ...
> Oh! Sir, my religious advantages in this place, are very great. I cannot sufficiently estimate them. It is a solemn as well as happy thing, to live in the enjoyment of such exalted privileges. I cannot *sin* at so cheap a rate as the heathen, who never saw a *bible,* or heard of a Saviour. As showers produce vegitation & give a character either to the wheat or the tares, so we, in this place, must be fast ripening for happiness or misery. Our characters are rapidly forming. This, Sir, appears to be an important era of the world. Much is doing for the promulgation of the gospel. Unquestionably such a missionary zeal never before inflamed the breasts of Christians as at the present day.
> Missionary, tract & bible societies, together with charitable societies for the purpose of educating pious, indigent young men for the gospel ministry, have been formed & are forming through out our land:—there is a society of the last description formed in this vicinity. The Students of the Academy & Institution, coming from different parts ... are made acquainted with the religious state of society in almost every quarter. Much religious intelligence has been lately

received. Revivals are very numerous, & in many places quite power-ful. In several towns in the western part of *Conn,* there have been great revivals. Also in New York City, likewise in Albany, Troy, Buffeloe & Sackets Harbour. Very many places in this State have recently experienced a wonderful outpouring of the Holy-Spirit.

... The number of Scholars is not far from Seventy. Among this number are about twenty hopefully pious:–three religious meetings are held each week by the scholars. Mr. Adams [the principal] attended on Sabbath evenings, while his health would permit. ... The season is cold and backward. March & April have not been so pleas-ant as was Febr. ... A letter from my *Grandfather* would rejoice me very much. I must now close, after requesting ever to be remembered in your prayers, and wishing that the remainder of your days may be pleasant, & your death happy. Believe these to be the sincere desires of your affectionate and beloved Grandson Isaac Clark. ...[8]

We know that in 1815 John studied Greek at Plainfield Academy, nearer to home than Andover.[9] In 1816 and 1817, both John and Bulkeley attended Bacon Academy in Colchester, Connecticut. Connecticut acade-mies prepared their students to enter Yale College, although the several cat-alogues of different colleges (large single sheets listing faculty and students at Harvard, Williams, Yale, and Middlebury) among the Taintors' papers make clear that the boys, if not their parents, were thinking of more than Yale. They would choose a college on the basis of its general theological position, not–as students and parents do today–because of any compar-isons about academic excellence.

Only one letter survives from either of the boys in school. It is from John in Colchester to his father, Roger, written in the formal style he used throughout his life when addressing his parent:

Sir   According to your request I now attempt to write a few lines to inform you of the death of Epaphroditus Bulkeley [John's twenty-six-year-old first cousin, a twin, who had served as a sergeant in the War of 1812, and whose father, William, had gone in the first train of sup-plies to Valley Forge in the Revolution]. He expired last night about twelve Oclock. his funeral will be attended tomorrow at 2 Oclock P.M. I am in good health. No news to write. In great haste I remain yours &c   J. A. Taintor

Epaphroditus Bulkeley died unmarried, of causes here unspecified, and left the large sum of $600 (in a will young John Taintor witnessed) "to my beloved Cynthia Selden," the daughter of a minister in Chatham, Connecticut.[10]

Among the papers John Taintor saved from his terms at Bacon Academy (there are receipts for three terms, ending September 4, 1816, January 1, 1817, and September 3, 1817) are penmanship and calligraphy exercises; beautifully executed diagrams and charts of calculations for finding the new moon and calculating a predicted eclipse of the sun that would happen long after he died, on August 27, 1891; a brief notebook of General Principals of Syntax in Latin (several of which are incorrect); and handwritten copies of speeches and play parts. There is a handwritten "Scheme of the Exhibition" dated Bacon Academy, September 3, 1816, which scheduled thirty performances of speeches, parts of Shakespeare plays, poems, essays, songs and declamations in the morning, and ten more in the afternoon! It lists the names of thirty-six scholars, some who gave multiple performances, including "E. [Bulkeley] Taintor" who acted a part in a scene from *Henry IV* and gave a declamation on "Importance of Union to the U. States," and "J. Taintor" who acted a scene from *Merchant of Venice* and spoke on "Patriotism."[11] John Taintor became a theater buff as he grew older; the first evidence of his interest in drama is from his Bacon Academy days. He kept notebooks with handwritten parts for several plays.

On July 6, 1817, John gave a patriotic declamation at Bacon Academy on the War of 1812, which had ended two summers before. The seventeen-year-old John Taintor had learned his lessons in rhetoric (as well as patriotism) well:

> Had it not been for the merciful interposition of Heaven in our behalf instead of being privileged to assemble here today on this joyfull religious occasion, we might have been sitting in sackloth lamenting the dire effects of a dismembered union. We might have been flying to extinguish the flames of civil discord, or while the plains of New England were smoking with the blood of her dearest sons, we might have been compelld to bow to the dictates of a British army, while its licentious soldiery were committing those outrages and abominations which their brutal countersign promised them at New Orleanes. . . . There was a time during the period of this war when a dark cloud overspread the land . . . our enemies with augmented forces on every side were spreading their vandal war along the shores of the Chesepeak and other places, plundering private property, pillaging and burning defenseless villages, insulting the living and rifling even the mansions of the dead.
>
> Great God! Are there Americans to be found who have advocated their cause, who have palliated their crimes? Tell it not to our descendents, publish it not to the ears of a reproaching world! . . . When the genius of America sat morning in solitude, and liberty stood weeping over her bleeding altars many of the friends of their country were

almost ready to despair of the republick, but Heaven did not abandon her cause. . . . Hope soon began to brighten through the gloom! Victory on victory by sea and land. . . . At the moment of the greatest publick triumph, when the mantle of Washington had descended on the illustrious Jackson, we received the joyfull news of Peace. . . .

The Republick is the worlds last hope of liberty! the fast-anchored land of a nation's rights! It has stood the test! . . . But he who once spake to the raging seas has commanded Peace. And the billows of war and the winds of faction have obeyed him! . . . The tempest of war has subsided into the delightfull charms of peace. To him, whose Omnipotent arm poises the scale of Empires and guides the destinies of nations, who puts down and builds up at his pleasure, to His name be all the Praise.[12]

In December of the same year, after he had started at Yale, John Taintor's patriotism continued unabated. He replied to a toast at a dinner: "The mention of America . . . has never failed but to fill me with the liveliest emotions. In my earlyest infancy . . . the story of her then recent struggle raised a throb in every breast that loved liberty. . . . I saw her spurning alike the luxeries that would enervate and the legions that would intimidate . . . and displaying a magnanimity that defied misfortune and a moderation that ornamented victory. It was the first vision of my childhood, it will decend with me to the grave. . . ."[13]

Young Gentlemen at Yale

John and Bulkeley Taintor entered Yale College in October 1817. Young gentlemen no longer went there simply to study for the ministry, although Yale's recent president, the Reverend Timothy Dwight, had been a major force in the Second Great Awakening. The college prepared young gentlemen for roles of leadership in business, the professions, and politics.

The set courses of instruction in 1817 included a strong emphasis on science and the "useful arts" along with more traditional courses. In the first year scholars studied arithmetic, algebra, geography, and Roman antiquities. In the second year, they studied English grammar, "the Elements of Chronology and History," logarithms, geometry, plane trigonometry, "Mensuration," surveying, navigation, conic sections, spherical geometry, and trigonometry. In the third year they studied "Fluxions," natural philosophy (physical science), astronomy, chemistry, and "History of Civil Society," and in the final year they studied chemistry and natural philosophy again, logic, metaphysics, ethics, and theology. Each year the students also studied the "Learned Languages" (Hebrew, Greek, and Latin), as well as rhetoric and oratory.[14] College courses consisted almost entirely of lectures, and classroom recitations required oral reproduction of lessons from books and lectures.

John and Bulkeley lived in a private boardinghouse in New Haven during their first term. At the beginning of their second term, in February 1818, John wrote his father: "We have obtain'd a room with John Adams of Andover in Middle College [a new dormitory] south entry second story back-side middle room. A Sophomore room. We arrived here on Thursday at 6 P. M. all safe, and bought our Cloaks the next day."[15]

The "cloaks" John mentioned were what we would call black academic gowns, which the faculty (fellows) wore and that all students were required to wear to classes, lectures, meals, and official college functions. They were very expensive (John's cost sixteen dollars, more than the cost of a term's tuition). They provided instant identification of their wearers as scholars and gentlemen deserving of deference and consideration.

The idea that "clothes make the man" was close to social and political reality in early-nineteenth-century America, where appearance of dress (and hair) were the most important visible clues to status. All clothes were made by hand; in ordinary households they were made at home. Anyone aspiring to high status outside home and village would need to be dressed like a gentleman, and that required the services of professional gentlemen's outfitters. John's tailor bills (none of Bulkeley's survive) were sizable throughout his college years. In March, John reported that

> we . . . have got a new room-mate. . . . He is John S. Peyton from Virginia who has lately enter'd our Class. He is about 17 years old and has the appearance of a Gentleman and a Schollar, not fond of Company but very studious. . . .–I here send you an account of money paid out this term.

LAST TERM BILLS	THIS TERM
$27.50 Board	$16.00 Cloak
12.25 Tuition	2.00 Wood
9.50 Room & washing	1.00 taxes
2.00 a Trunk	2.00 wood
1.75 at Tailors	1.00 curtains,
	moving etc.
1.00 for Waiters	
	$22.00 Total
$54.00 Total	54.00
	76. ·
	4.00 necessarily spent
	$80.00 and I have 8 dollars
	remaining

John ended his accounting by writing, "If you feel disposed to send on more money . . . (which will be absolutely necessary before the term is out) it will be gratefully received and carefully expended."[16] John's estimate of expenses, like his accounting, was informal and rather inaccurate. The receipted bills for all his college expenses consistently add up to rather more than he reported.

Like all college freshmen, John complained about food. In March of his first year he wrote, "I am now well, but have been rather unwell for one or two days on account of eating bad oysters in the hall."[17] In August 1818, he wrote: "The board in the hall is miserable, many have gone home sick. It is but a few days since every individual of the lower Classes left the hall and informed the President that they would not go back again until there was a reform. the President said there should be a reform, but it has not come yet."[18] The college required all students to eat in the hall and forbade them food in their rooms.

Early September was the end of the college year. There was a hierarchy at Yale, and in September of 1818 John and Bulkeley got off the bottom rung. "We expect pretty jolly times in a few weeks when the next freshman class enters. . . ."

Yale's faculty required that "in order to preserve a due subordination among the Students, the classes shall give and receive, in the course of their collegiate life, those tokens of respect and subjection, which from common and approved usage belong to their standing in the College."[19] Yale did not teach democracy. It deliberately reinforced hierarchical relationships appropriate to a class-structured society.

John and Bulkeley Taintor's college years were a time of tension between older notions of the importance of hierarchy and newer democratic ways. The political and religious controversies about participation in public life were part of the boys' Yale experience. Everywhere people argued that there was something distinctly undemocratic about college education itself. Republican newspapers—to which John Taintor subscribed while he was still in college—had frequent articles challenging the usefulness and practicality of the education he was getting. "The old absurd plan of holding up the *dead languages,*" according to an article attacking Harvard's education in one of John's copies of the *Independent Chronicle & Boston Patriot,* "is powerfully operating to erect in this country *a combined monkish aristocracy.* . . . The people of this state have been taxed a great amount to support our Colleges [Yale was supported by Connecticut taxes]. Whose sons are educated . . . in these colleges? Are they not almost exclusively the sons of the wealthy . . . ? And all the Hebrew and Greek they learn are not one penny's service to the public." This article, like others, advocated college education based on modern languages, science, and literature, so that people of the "middling interest" would no longer be compelled to support the education of rich young men who would go forth "to deceive, demoralize and oppress the community."[20]

John Taintor's interest in these matters came, perhaps, from the family's Republican bent. His freshman year had been the year of the controversies over the new Connecticut state constitution, in which his father and Uncle Solomon figured prominently on the Republican side in Hampton. The democratic arguments for modernizing college education appealed to men who had argued for democratizing state government and disestablishing the Church.

In February 1819, a few months after the new constitution passed, John wrote his father: "it is reported by Charles Weld that there is not a democratic justice in Hampton who can draw a writ or write his name. He is carefull to tell this to strangers and his own party."[21]

Charles Weld's father was Rev. Ludovicus Weld, who had led the faction in Hampton opposed to the new constitution. Roger and Solomon Taintor were among the Republicans now being called "democrats," and Roger Taintor was one of the democratic justices of the peace about whom Charles Weld was circulating the typical antidemocratic rumor that democrats were illiterate bumpkins.

From 1819 on, John sent his father his copies of the two semi-weekly newspapers to which he subscribed at Yale. One was from New York, The American (For The Country), and one from Boston, the Independent Chronicle & Boston Patriot. Both were partisan democratic papers (there were no shibboleths about "nonpartisan" or "objective" reporting in newspapers then: the intent of newspapers was the advocacy of party). John's correspondence thereafter with his father included political news and discussion. He wrote in April 1819: "The Freemen met [this was the town election meeting–there were no secret ballots] here yesterday and if I should wright over two sheets I could not describe the meanness and deceit practiced by the Federalists. They endeavored to divide the republicans by supporting . . . a democrat and . . . a churchman. They brought forward the sick, lame, blind, and even got two from the poor house, the President of Yale, every Professor, Tutor, Minister and in fact every thing they could get. . . . a great many republicans left the house disgusted."[22]

Republican support of disestablishment so incensed some Congregationalists that they were still fighting on that issue two years after the constitution passed. John wrote in June 1820: "The committees of the two brick churches have refused to admit the republicans on the Fourth of July and on this account about forty from the North and a large number from the Middle churches have left their societies and joined the Episcopalians. In this number are some of the first republicans in town."[23] After he left Yale, John Taintor himself became an Episcopalian. In Connecticut, there was often a connection between being a Republican and being an Episco-palian because of the disestablishment issue.

By March 1821, John was praising the democrats of New York State for initiating what their opponents called "the spoils system," whereby a newly elected majority party removed the civil servants belonging to their opposition and replaced them with their own supporters. "I sincerely wish we could have a similar measure adopted in our own state, not only for removing those called Federalists, but for removing that selfish, unprinci-pled, suspicious vain class, at present headed by Elisha Tracy and seconded by the famous Mr. Huntington, who, as all agree is supported only by the rabble in Norwich. They are a burlesque upon any party however low. I might go on loading them with epithets which they richly deserve, but am prevented by the reflection that you are better acquainted with them than myself and consequently more heartily despise that low, narrow minded policy which is evident in their every action. Superior must be the mind of him, who can be influenced and led about by the devices and intrigues of these self sufficient men. . . ."[24] Tracy and Huntington were leaders of a Republican faction with which all the Taintors were at odds.

But John and Bulkeley's lives at Yale were only peripherally taken up by political issues. Mostly, like all college students, they were interested in the day-to-day doings of their small world. And they only reluctantly reported to their parents about some of the events in which they partici-pated. John wrote in his sophomore year:

29 November 1818

Sir.   I received your letter of the 22d inst yesterday in which I find . . . the report of a great riot in College which in some respects is true.–I had calculated to pass this affair over in silence, but since it is your request I will endeavor to give you a short account. On Sunday the 15, on account of some difficulty previous about 200 sailors and people from town came up to the College to whip the students. The faculty (who were then present) threatened to dismiss any student who should leave the College yard. The civil authority came among the sailors and took a number of them to jail and ordered the remain-der home but as soon as the authority had gone; about 50 of our stoutest fellows, armed with clubs, stones and anything they could get, rushed among the sailors which soon obliged them to run in every direction but not without some sore heads The next day four of the leaders viz. Livingston, M. R. Strong, Hill and Little were complained of, and bound over to the county Court now sitting in this city. They will probably be fined for which the whole College [student body] stands ready to pay. The faculty suspended Livingston & Strong (who have since been restored) and gave warnings to about 30 more. Thus the affray has ended–

I have no news to write, except we are well. I wish you to write again soon. Yours &c.   J. A. Taintor

N. B. *I would just inform you that we shall not have more than enough money to pay for our expenses this term.*[25]

Money brought out sibling rivalry between John and his cousin Bulkeley, who was so nearly his twin. John wrote his father in July 1819, complaining that Bulkeley had received money "which he says is to pay him for staying here last vacation. now, it is not right that he should receive more than myself, since it cost me more to go home than it did him to stay here. But he says he is out of money, and there is a very good reason for it; he sold his old books last term and took the money. I kept my books this term and then sold them, besides he has bought more new books then I have." He followed his complaint with a small boast: "This College has chosen 18 Commencement Speakers of which number I have the misfor-tune to be one. We received our first lecture on oratory Saturday."[26]

Junior year saw changes at Yale as well as for the Taintor scholars there. There was a new hall, "a very fine stone building 40. ft by 80. ft and 31 ft in height." And the Taintor boys saw a great sight, of which John wrote in October 1819: "The Cittizens of this place were highly pleased on Wednesday last by the appearance of a Balloon prepared in this place by a Frenchman. It ascended from the green at 5. P. M. It rose to a great height and fell near the mouth of the harbour. The Balloon was 30 ft. long about 60. ft. in circumfirence with a paper boat 8 ft. long attached to it. We shall probably see another soon."[27]

The October 30, 1819, issue of John's *Independent Chronicle & Boston Patriot* gave an account of a balloon launched by a man with a French-sounding name. It may have been the same balloon John saw in New Haven, but this time it flew much closer to home in Hampton. The article said, "The balloon lately sent up from New-York by Mr. Guille, landed at Bozrah in Connecticut, about two hours and a half after its ascension. Bozrah is about 113 miles from N. York in a straight line; the balloon, therefore, must have traveled at the rate of 45 miles an hour. Mr. Guille has set out in pursuit of it."

The paper printed a letter from Norwich, Connecticut, following the account, written in the rhetoric of "Yankee Doodle," the popular Revolutionary War song, and lampooning the "hicks" in a back-country Connecticut small town:

News! If you have not heard it—so brush up your ears. The balloon that left you on Wednesday, landed last evening at 9 o'clock in good health and spirits, in Bozrah, 4 miles from this. *All the world* have been, or are going, to see it—Jonathan, Tabitha, Mehitabel, Debby, Ozias, Father, David, &c.c. all are on the go to get a peep at the strange thing. It seems the parachute is with it, though I have not been to see it myself. It is chained to Luke's ox cart to keep it down, for it has an inclination to escape, or get back to Vauxhall, being full of the stuff. There were a bottle of wine, some crackers, and a [illegible] in it—all very comfortable. P. S. Father and I have just returned from the balloon—all nature was there and more too. The parachute, basket, and all are safe; and they are to be carried down to New-York. It frightened some people half to death; and it would amaze you to see the people.

In his final year at Yale, John Taintor's formality with his father became more pompous. He was aware, in his increasingly democratic, revolutionary milieu, that he did not have to follow in his father's footsteps, and that birth and inheritance did not give him a position in life. He began to wonder what he should do and what profession, if any, he should enter. As an educated gentleman his choices were different from those of his father. A letter he wrote at the end of 1820 conveys the tone of his attempts to break away from his family at the same time that he remained a dutiful son:

—December 16, 1820

Sir   I was surprised to find in your letter of last week a censure for my not writing, when you had not written me but once this term. I should have written before but I deemed it unnecessary as I was sending papers to you weekly. The case with me is simply this, and I think it would be well could all think so; if I receive a letter from my friends [relatives], I am glad to hear they are well and happy, but if I do not receive one I am equally satisfied, knowing that I should be immediately informed in case of sickness or distress. The subject of writing letters is doubtless useful when attentively pursued by absent friends in communicating information and improving in composition, but situated as I am, but a few hours ride from the place of my nativity, it loses half its effect. . . .

I have never enjoyed better health or been more contented than at present. Could I always live in the same manner, I should think myself happy, but I do not expect it. There is a busy world in which each in our time must take a part and however well he may be acquainted with classical learning he will make a poor figure unless he is familiar with "men and manners."

Permit me then to apply this to my own case. I am soon to fix upon a pursuit which will engage my whole attention, but prior to this, and after spending four years in College it is proper that I should see beyond the bounds of my native state. I have long had a desire to visit the Capitol and some of the first cities of our country. I have therefore a request to make which I will express in few words, and if granted, will I think fully justify the expense incurred. My object is to visit Washington and the places through which I should pass. . . . I have directed my papers to you which I think you will find interesting. I wish you to keep them safe as they will hereafter be valuable. . . .

I am respectfully, yours   J. A. Taintor[28]

John expressed ambivalence about the value of his education, echoing the powerful ambivalence in the Republic generally about gentility, aristocracy, and traditional values in a revolutionary nation. Perhaps John's approaching twenty-first birthday was the reason for the following yet further evidence of "senioritis":

–March 24, 1821

Sir   I sit myself down to consult you upon a subject which, though I have never mentioned before, has been the cause of frequent and unpleasant considerations. Twenty one years have passed away without one serious conclusion, where or in what employment I am to spend the remainder of my life. It is now time to awake and attend to it in earnest. I cannot but think, had I been differently advised five years ago, I might have been prosperously settled in an employment which although laborious is a sure means of support. Consider the expense I have incurred in College, all which is necessary to make one respectable in such a situation. And where am I now? . . .

I can 'tis true read some of the Languages and make some calculations in Mathematics, which I should not have required in business. But can these purchace me a support and I should wish, wealth? It will not be pretended. I might I confess study a profession or keep a private school. With regard to the former I shall only ask you to look at the Attorneys and Physicians who literally fill every Town and village in our Country, and are scarce able to gain their daily bread. And should I ever undertake the latter, it will be as the last resort from all my endeavours. I am now speaking of matter of fact and not indulging in idle speculation.

The truth is, I am astonished that I have remained here until this present time. I have passed my time pleasantly in College, yet it has been a painful thought that when I leave, I am to commence as it were a new life, new habits are to be formed, new manners required, new principles learned and a support to be gained depending (for aught I know) upon my own individual exertions. What then at this late hour should I do? I ask this advice of you, not because I am undecided myself, but that I may obtain your opinion before I express my own.

Strange is the idea some men have, that a College education makes the man. The truth is it neither increases his happiness or wealth, but on the contrary constantly harrows up his domestic quiet and is usually the companion of poverty. The professional man does not perhaps hassard his property in the undertaking, but he risks that, the want of which, makes life not worth possessing, I mean his health and happiness.

Do you doubt this? Look for a moment at those who have attended strictly to their profession. Think you theirs is the lot of health or prosperity? Their very countenances refute the former and your own observation the latter. It is doubtless a subject of extreme regret to some that . . . they have chosen their profession or employment without mature deliberation. It is then highly important to one just entering the world not only that he should consider his ability to perform the design, but also the natural tendency of his feelings and disposition. Life is a scene of constant trouble and disappointment, a round of sickening trifles, and little does it matter where we live and die, provided the great end of our creation is answered.

But to conclude. Since I anticipate your answer in part, I must say again, that no consideration however great or valuable would induce me to the study of a profession and that one of three employments shall engage my whole attention. As it is a private thing I wish your individual opinion and not of those who judge from probabilities and have nothing to lose by the undertaking. Respectfully yours   J. A. Taintor[29]

The "three employments" John actively sought after college were retail merchandising, stock breeding, and foreign service for the United States government. Perhaps he already had them in mind. There is no direct evidence of what Roger thought about John's plans or career, except that it was he who had originally insisted upon college for his son.

At the beginning of his very last term John wrote to his father about his concern about the year-end examinations, and for the first time mentioned a professor whose teaching influenced his life.[30] Professor Benjamin Silliman lectured on chemistry to each junior and senior class. Silliman devoted his life to spreading knowledge of science, but he insisted on the harmony between science and religion. When John and Bulkeley studied with him, Professor Silliman was about forty years old. He continued teaching at Yale and lecturing about science all over the United States until he retired in 1853, having been a professor for fifty-one years and one of the most famous scientists of his time.[31]

All students were enjoined to "take notes of the several heads of the instruction" in all lectures because they would "be examined by the

Professors concerning the knowledge . . . gained from the preceding Lecture." John's notes on Silliman's lectures had started in September 1819. He sustained some interest and understanding, although with evident difficulty, up to the thirteenth lecture in that year's series. His notes then stop, except to include one more lecture which he labeled the twentieth. In 1821, perhaps to be better prepared for the final college examination, he took far more comprehensive and understanding notes on Silliman's lectures. His interest in science, obvious from his lifelong work on the improvement of breeds of sheep and cattle, is evident in his preservation of these notes–the only college notes he kept. His cousin Bulkeley took and kept comprehensive notes on an unbroken series of sixty-four lectures by Professor Silliman.[32]

Ordinary Americans, not just students at Yale College, were excited about science in these years. People associated science and the new technologies that grew from it with the Revolution and Benjamin Franklin, indeed with the nation itself. Everywhere organizations for promoting science were forming. In 1820, for example, the Connecticut legislature chartered the Windham County Agricultural Society. Roger and Solomon Taintor were members. (They kept their copy of its constitution.) The Society's purpose was "the encouragement of Agriculture and domestic manufactures" and its more than one hundred members sponsored annual cattle shows and distributed premiums of $100 per year for improvements in scientific breeding and for inventions. John and Bulkeley's college careers prepared them for a new scientific America.

Young Men on the Road

Roger and Solomon Taintor frequently visited nearby towns on horseback, by wagon, and by horse-drawn sleigh. They went further afield–to New York City, Philadelphia, upstate New York, Boston, and Providence–by regularly scheduled stagecoach and by boat. They left no record that they considered travel difficult.

Their sons learned early to travel with ease. John and Bulkeley Taintor's correspondence relates details of some of their trips. The earliest of those letters came from their Hampton friend Isaac Clark, who wrote in 1817: "I have lived in hope that you would call and see me before you returned to N.Haven. . . . If you go to Ashford to take the stage and pass by my father's, do call and see me.[33]

Ashford, the town on Hampton's northwestern border, was the nearest stop for a scheduled stagecoach to Hartford, where a connecting stage to New Haven could be found. The distance to New Haven was about eighty miles, and might take the best part of two days. The young men also took the steamboat to New Haven from the busy port of Norwich on the Thames River, about eighteen miles south of Hampton. They ordinarily traveled from Hampton to Ashford or Norwich by hitching a ride with someone driving a wagon, cart, or carriage there. On rare occasions some-one made a special trip to take them. They did not (so far as we can dis-cover) ever walk the distance to the stage or steamboat, as more ordinary folk might have.[34]

While he was in college John traveled to New York City to the the-ater, because Yale discouraged students from going to plays. There was a rule that "if any Student shall, any where in New-Haven, act a part in, or be present at the acting of any comedy or tragedy, he shall be fined not exceeding eighty cents."[35] Nevertheless, John's interest in drama increased. He kept copies of several plays published in New York during and just after his college years. They included *The Students of Salamanca; A Comedy, in Five Acts*, by Robert Francis Jameson;[36] *Brutus; Or, The Fall of Tarquin. An Historical Tragedy in Five Acts*, by John Howard Payne;[37] *The Broken Sword. A Grand Melo-Drama, Interspersed with Songs, Choruses, etc.;*[38] *The Point of Honor, A Play, in Three Acts, Taken from the French*, by Charles Kemble;[39] *The Wheel of Fortune; A Comedy*, by R. Cumberland;[40] *She Would Be a Soldier, Or The Plains of Chippewa; An Historical Drama, in Three Acts*, by M. M. Noah;[41] *Marion; Or, The Hero of Lake George: A Drama, in Three Acts, Founded on Events of The Revolutionary War*, by M. M. Noah;[42] *Percy's Masque, A Drama, in Five Acts;*[43] and *Monsieur Tonson, A Farce, in Two Acts*, by William T. Moncrieff.[44]

John preserved a particularly enticing playbill from a New York theater performance on Saturday evening, May 1, 1819, possibly his first experi-ence of the theater in "the great world." It describes an evening with spe-cial effects akin to those of modern movies. The bill for the evening included a great melodramatic spectacle which had "A Grand Procession of Persians . . . The Interior of a Vast Cavern . . . A Characteristic Dance by a Troop of Amazons . . . A Dagger Fight between the Sentinels . . . Dungeons of the Fortress," a "Secret Mine" into which actors were lowered and raised, "Cannon which they fired," mines which exploded, a "Grand Combat of Hindoos and Persians," a "Flying Bridge" which fell "crowded with combatants," and the piece concluded "with the total Defeat of the Persians."[45] As we read the playbills John kept and found his play scripts we thought it an odd coincidence to be so connected to a man who had taken such pleasure in the theater, because it is one of the chief pleasures of our own lives. We, too, go to the theater more than most people. We, too, keep playbills. We, too, act in amateur productions. We envy John some of those spectacular evenings.

UNION LINE

FOR PHILADELPHIA,
AND
BALTIMORE,
At 11 o'clock, A. M.

25 Miles Land Carriage.

Steam-Boat BELLONA—*Capt. Vanderbilt*,
Steam-Boat PHILADELPHIA—*Capt. Jenkins*.

The only Steam-Boat Line,
Via New-Brunswick, Princeton & Trenton,

FARE THROUGH $3.

The Passengers will leave the city, at the foot of Courtlandt-street, every day, (Sundays excepted) at 11 O' CLOCK, A. M. in the POWLES-HOOK Steam boats, for Jersey City, where they will meet the Bellona, and proceed direct to New-Brunswick, where they will take Post Coaches to Trenton, and lodge, and arrive at Philadelphia in the Steam-boat, by 10 o'clock, in time to take the Baltimore Union Line Steam-Boat which leaves Philadelphia at 12 o'clock (noon) daily.

For Seats, apply at the YORK-HOUSE, No. 5, COURT-LANDT-STREET, SECOND OFFICE FROM THE CORNER OF BROADWAY, and at the Steam Boat Hotel, (up stairs) foot of Marketfield-street.

WM. B. JAQUES, AGENT,
FOR LETSON, BAYLES & SHUFF,
PROPRIETORS.

NEW-YORK, AUGUST 13, 1821.
*** All Baggage at its owner's risk.

John Taintor's boat and coach route from New York to Philadelphia, 1821.

John kept two hotel bills from his college years that are evidence of yet more travel. One was from the Norwalk Hotel, in Norwalk, Connecticut, and one from Lawton's Hotel, 81 Benefit Street, in Providence, Rhode Island. Several years later, John stayed at that same hotel in Providence while visiting his bride-to-be.[46] We gasped when we found the Providence bills. Our daughter and son-in-law lived at 83 Benefit Street when we first started going through John Taintor's papers. Visiting them we had often walked by the old house that was number 81.

John and Bulkeley traveled to see the countryside, often with college friends. John wrote to his father of one proposed trip, and the complications of travel arrangements:

> . . . You mentioned in your letter concerning our going to Dartmouth [Massachusetts]. Bulkeley and myself had previously concluded to go together in a waggon to Dartmouth, Boston, and on to Newburyport and perhaps to be gone 10 or 12 days. Our object was to see the country and some students who would be in Boston at that time. But to accomodate all, we have thought of assenting to your proposal provided we can have chaises and return through Boston & perhaps Salem. If I should go to Dartmouth I don't wish to race down there and back full speed, but rather take proper time. After a confinement

of four months this warm weather, I think we shall want some exercise. If you think proper for us to go to Massachusetts in the waggon
I would suggest, having a cloth top put on before we come home, as
we wish to start the monday after Commencement.[47]

In the summer of 1821, before his graduation, John went on a long tour
of New York State, all the way (more than four hundred miles) to Niagara
Falls and into the foreign land of Canada. His letters home are filled with
the excitement of such an extended trip. He wrote from Utica, "Our party
arrived here last evening from Saratoga Springs by the way of Sche-
nectady." Because "of the extreme heat" John's party "thought best to visit
the Springs on our outward passage. There are about five hundred visitors
at Saratoga and many at Ballstown. Among the distinguished characters are
Joseph Bonaparte," who was Napoleon's brother and former King of Spain.
John wrote: "The country through which we travelled yesterday is delightful and far exceeds my expectation. Our road was upon the left bank of the
Mohawk and afforded a fine view of the Erie canal which is fast progress-
ing."[48] It would be four more years before the Erie Canal was completed all
the way from Albany to Buffalo.

Six days later John wrote from the Canadian side of Niagara Falls:

Sir   It is with pleasure that I have to inform you of my safe arrival at
the possessions of *His Most Gracious Majesty*. I arrived here yesterday
from Black Rock, distant twenty miles. Our road was over a level
country on the bank of the river and frequently showed the ravages
of war. I remained two days at Buffalo, visited the battle ground at
Fort Erie and saw the effects of the explosions which buried two
companies of British Infantry in one common grave. The ground is
very interesting and I left it with reluctance.

But the interest of Erie fades when compared with that of
Chippewa. I have visited these plains since my arrival here. The plain
on which the British army was paraded is now covered by fields of
grain with nothing to mark their graves but the unusual growth of
wheat which covers them. I have some relics of these battles which I
shall preserve.

We leave here tomorrow for Bridgewater and Fort George, shall
return to Lewiston and from thence to Rochester and Canadagua.
Our journey has been very pleasant and I think I shall recur to these
days with pleasure and improvement when months of a College life
shall appear like a dream which leaves not a trace behind. In my great
haste I have neglected to mention the Falls which are now in full view
from my window, but for want of time I must defer it until another
opportunity. I cannot determine what day I shall arrive in N. Haven,
since I return through New York. I shall leave this at the first Post

Office I meet with on the other side. Fruit of every variety is in great abundance and I suspect Bulkley will judge of the quality next fall.
In haste Yours &c   J. A. Taintor[49]

The War of 1812 had seen land battles on the Canadian border. In 1821 these were still recent events which fired John Taintor's imagination. That "there was nothing to mark [the British] graves but the unusual growth of wheat which covers them" is the patriotic remark of a man who grew up in an agricultural world and knew the worth of organic fertilizer. And John's sneer about "His Most Gracious Majesty" comes from a republican descendant of the American Revolution who despised kings and all that royalty implied.

John kept a little penciled diary of his tour, made on a folded-up single sheet of paper that could be tucked into a vest pocket. He recorded his expenses (totaling $35.84) and the mileage between towns from Buffalo across New York State and a bit of Pennsylvania to Newburgh, New York, on the Hudson River. The trip ended with a boat ride down the Hudson, into Long Island Sound, and back to New Haven.

On his return to New Haven, John wrote to Bulkeley, who was at home in Hampton: "I was very much fatigued when I arrived here both by the length of the journey and the extreme heat of summer. But I shall never regret the troubles in prosecuting this journey. I am delighted with the country, instead of that wilderness which I had in some places expected, I found flourishing villages and highly cultivated farms. . . ."[50] It is an early view of the West from an easterner. And this was the beginning of a pattern: throughout their lives John traveled much farther from home than Bulkeley ever did. They were no longer twins.

CHAPTER 5

LIVING AND DYING

ॐ

"The furniture ... will be quite too crude and antiquated
for Aunt Taintors new and elegant house."[1]

B y the middle of the 1820s, the trained tastes of the college-educated sons, John and Bulkeley Taintor, informed the lives of their parents. In his twenties, John helped his parents buy horses, carriages, and furniture appropriate to the whole family's rising status. And in the mid-1820s, the Taintors completely remodeled and modernized their house in Hampton. When they finished, it was no longer a simple, center-chimney farm house, but now visibly—inside and out—the residence of gentlefolk.

The House of Gentlefolk

The physical evidence of that remodeling is still obvious in the house today. It was a very big job. Local workmen with only ordinary farm skills in the handling of stone and wood, as well as local skilled artisans like Nathaniel F. Martin and Jonathan Clark, did it all. They took down and entirely removed the huge stone center chimney that had been the core of the house's structure and that had at least three fireplaces on the first floor, and perhaps as many on the second. They hauled away the tons of stone that had been its foundation. The only direct proof in the house today that the center chimney ever existed is the rectangular, framed space in the rafters where it went through the roof. The workmen removed the main front staircase and tore down all the walls and wood paneling that had surrounded the chimney on both floors.

Quantities of dirt and soot had accumulated in the thirty-five years or so since the house had been built. Dust from hammered mortar, pulverized plaster, and chipped or broken stone was thick in the house while the work went on. The remodeling project did not end with the removal of the center chimney. The several downstairs and upstairs rooms (they generally called them "chambers") still required heat. The workmen tore away more walls to construct two new brick chimneys—much more modern and elegant than old-fashioned fieldstone chimneys—each large enough for two fireplaces on the first floor and a modern stove or two on the second.

The brick chimneys presented some problems, and the builders' solutions are still visible. The cellar was subject to annual and unpredictable water flow (Hampton's hilltop, like many others in New England, had been scooped out by glaciers and was a swampy water collector). Early-nineteenth-century brick might rapidly decay when subject to the combination of great weight (the chimneys were to be nearly forty feet high) and intermittent water flow. So they built the two new chimneys on huge oak platforms held four feet above the surface of the cellar floor by massive oak pilings.

Elegance demanded that the new chimneys be symmetrically positioned on the roof. However, the internal structure of the house as it already existed would not permit precise symmetry. They achieved it by sloping each chimney in the attic (the brick courses were corbeled).

The Taintors and the workmen were all frugal New Englanders. They reused the wood paneling that had surrounded the old stone center chimney inside new closets and on the (hidden from ordinary view) walls of the new back and attic stairways. (One of those paneled walls, in the attic stairway, is still painted the "Spanish brown" color that Nathaniel F. Martin applied to it in 1805.) They made a new front staircase and plastered and papered the downstairs and upstairs front halls. They closed up old doorways and made new ones. They took out chair rails, installed new woodwork, and patched the flooring of several rooms.

The house was occupied by two families. The mantels on the new north chimney still have their Greek Revival panels, pilasters, and dentils. The mantels on the new south chimney have the characteristic curves of Empire furniture. It seems likely that Roger and Nabby's family used one front and one back room with the same mantel design, and Solomon and Judith used the two downstairs rooms with the other mantel design. But it took us years of piecing together clues from the Taintors' correspondence before we could guess that Solomon and Judith occupied the north side, Roger and Nabby the south.

The new kitchen for both families was a small, one-story ell at the back of the house into which they built a much lower chimney with fireplace and bake oven. The room was built over the twenty-foot-deep, stone-lined well that still supplies water for the house.

Such massive rebuilding, of course, required redecorating and new furniture. The workmen applied papers to the walls of the new halls and

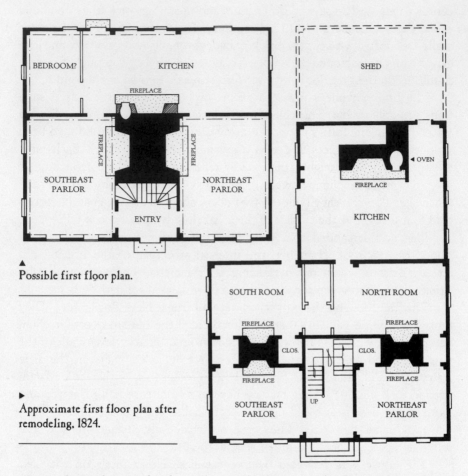

Possible first floor plan.

Approximate first floor plan after remodeling, 1824.

rooms. According to family tradition, the paper in the front stairway and hall when we bought the house in 1967 was the "original" paper–put on in the remodeling of the 1820s. And, since Mary Taintor remembered it from her youth (she was born in 1860), it was certainly a century old. But when we removed it, there was clear evidence that there had been an earlier paper on those walls. So we have seen none of the paper which Roger, Nabby, Solomon, and Judith decided to put up in their elegant "new" house.

In 1825, in a letter to his father from New York City, John wrote, "Mahogany Side Boards can be had for $30."[2] John mentioned the price of mahogany sideboards either because Roger wanted to buy one or because John thought he should; the elaborate sideboard the family removed from the house in 1967 (and subsequently sold) was traditionally the one owned by the early Taintor families.

The remodeled house and its new furnishings were signs not only to the world at large but to the Taintors' family that they had risen in the world. Roger and Solomon's niece and her mother, their sister Sarah (who was married to Nabby and Judith's brother, Joshua Robbins Bulkeley), had written in 1824 from Williamstown, Massachusetts:

March 13th.

Dear Uncle [Roger]

The first of May I expect to remove to Sheffield, and I feel not a little mortified and chagrin'd at the idea of living amongst strangers entirely destitute of furniture &c–I hope dear Sir you will not deem me ungrateful or impertinent, when I ask you to lend me the furniture or a part of it, which you have at Uncle Bulkeley's [another Bulkeley brother who lived in Williamstown]. My husband-to-be is but recently establish'd in business and in no situation at present to pro-vide for me in this respect. The furniture is an encumbrance which Uncle Bulkeley's family would gladly be freed from–I will assure you that I will exert myself that it may not be injured–unless you design to remove it to Connectticut–but I conclude it will be quite too crude and antiquated for Aunt Taintors new and elegant house.

I regret that I have no friends [closer relations] who are able to assist me and that necessity compels me to make this request of you who have performed so many acts of kindness for our family–and manifested so great a degree of compassion in their afflicted condition. Should you have made any arrangements to dispose of this furniture, I hope you will not hesitate merely in consideration of this request. Will you have the kindness to write me soon on this subject. Make if you please my respects to my connections at Hampton. I hope Cousin John will be disposed to visit me when I am within one day's ride of him.

Yours respectfully Mary A. Bulkeley

Sarah Bulkeley's letter, attached to her daughter's, is much less literate as well as less stylized (a sign that education for young women was not only improved but more elaborate in the new generation). But she, too, rec-ognized her brothers' higher status:

Dear Brother

I received your letter & was verry glad to hear from you & your Family. I verry seldom hear from you as none of my brothers except yourself will take the trouble to write me a line. my being poor does not lessen my Affection for my Brothers & sisters.

do tell Brother Solomon I wish he would take his wife & make us a visit. as she is unwell I think it would be for her health. I should be so rejoiced to see them. were I in your situation i would come & see you once a year. I know you have a great deal of business to attend to but I think it would be for your health. I think Dear Brother it is verry nesesary that some of my Brothers should come to williamstown. there can be nothing done About the pasturing untill some of you come here [her four brothers—John, Charles, Roger, and Solomon—owned the land Sarah and her husband worked]. we have considerable stock we cannot hire any pasturing. . . . I cannot write what I wish to say to you could I see you.

yours Affectionately Sarah Bulkeley[3]

Illness, Old Age, and Death

Only a few years remained to most of the older generation of Taintors after they remodeled their house. But illness and death were not strangers in their world. Roger and Nabby's first child had died when she was barely four years old, before John and Bulkeley were born. Solomon and Judith's two-year-old daughter Caroline died in 1810, when the boys were ten. When he was sixteen, John had been at the deathbed of his cousin Epaphroditus Bulkeley. During John and Bulkeley's college years, classmates had died.

And in August 1822, John Taintor was clerking for a Mr. Scarborough in Hartford, from whom he was learning the retailing business. John wrote to his father that "Mr. Scarborough has been sick for some weeks and is now at his fathers, . . . it is very doubtful whether he will be able to do any thing this fall. . . . It is the general opinion here that Mr. S. has the consumption [tuberculosis, a much-feared, insidious killer] and will not recover, but it is not best to have his friends [family and relatives] hear of it. I am fully of that opinion."[4]

A month later, John reported

Mr. Scarborough has returned, but he is no better and unable to attend to business, he will leave here on Tuesday for the Springs [Saratoga Springs] and expects to be gone untill cold weather. I think he will not live through winter. He wishes me to remain with him this winter if I can. . . . His health will not allow him to make any arrangements in business at present, but he wishes to keep his Store open and a run of custom, until he shall be able to attend to it himself. He like all others in his situation, expects to recover this fall, but no one thinks he will. . . .[5]

That letter crossed one from his father written the same day, also on the subject of illness. In Hampton, an epidemic was raging. "The sickness

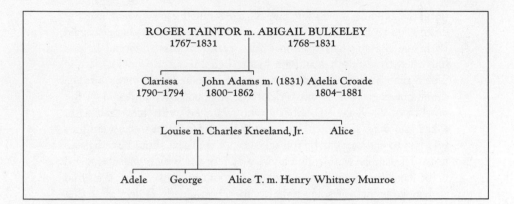

ROGER TAINTOR m. ABIGAIL BULKELEY
1767–1831   1768–1831

Clarissa   John Adams m. (1831) Adelia Croade
1790–1794   1800–1862   1804–1881

Louise m. Charles Kneeland, Jr.   Alice

Adele   George   Alice T. m. Henry Whitney Munroe

increases in this place to an alarming degree. Six died Last week . . . including Fullers wife and Child, Hammond child, Betsey Reed, Bela Searls Son . . . Last night Harriet Nye age 20 died. all of the dissintary–Mr. Hodgkins, Ziba Phelps and a child of A. Washburn are extreem sick besides nearly thirty more–"[6]

Ten days later, Bulkeley reported that Roger himself had contracted the disease. He wrote John, "Your Father has requested me to write to you that he had expected to have started for Hartford this Morning, but is detained by sickness. he having last night been attacked with the simptoms of the Dissentary. But he expects to be able to come in a few days. . . . The rest of us are all well."[7] In the event, Roger did not die that year.

Dysentery was a common disease "characterized by inflammation of the . . . large intestine, accompanied with griping pains, and mucous and bloody evacuations." A form of cholera called *cholera morbus* was similar, although it was "attended with bilious diarrhea and vomiting." It was common in late summer and early fall and was rarely fatal. It would not be until 1832 that the first epidemic of the deadly form of cholera occurred in America.[8]

As John had expected, Mr. Scarborough did die a few months later. John was in Hampton when it happened, and his friend and fellow clerk, T. D. Stewart, wrote him the details of the death, as was the custom. People who were close to someone dying hoped to be at the deathbed, and if they could not, they wanted to know in detail what happened:

> . . . You undoubtedly have heard of Mr. S. death but not the circumstances. He had raised a considerable quantity of blood about 10 days before he died which had an astonishing effect on him. completely exhausted him and from that time he failed rapidly, but at no time so weak but that he could set up and walk about his room.–he continued in one state to all appearances untill the day before he died and even

untill the evening, after I left him. That evening he grew weak fast but did not go to bed until 11 oclock when the gentleman that watched with him (having had watchers for several nights previous) helped him off with his clothes and got him to bed. About 2 o'clock A. M. at which time he called for drink which was immediately given him, he drank but one swallow when desired to be laid down and said he felt much worse. Walter D. Smith who watched with him that night asked him if he should call the family he said no. But in two minutes told him to call them as he himself did not think he should live half an hour. The family were called and I was sent for which was about 4. I went immediately and on entering the room he took me by the hand and spoke to me for some time his speech gradually failing. after that spoke to Mr. Hawes [a Congregational minister] and prayed to himself but by this time his words could scarcely be made out so discon-nected. from 6 to ½ past 6 he lay perfectly senseless and so choaked with phlegm that it was with difficulty he could breathe. at ½ past 6 he writhed with pain 3 times when we supposed he had breathed his last but it was 20 minutes before seven before he drew his last breath and that could with difficulty be heard. He was buried on Saturday afternoon. . . . He left no will that I know of. he doubtless expected to live until spring and would have sufficient time to do all the little things that he left undone but he was mistaken poor fellow.[9]

In March 1825, John made a hurried trip to New York City because his uncle John Taintor, the oldest brother of Roger and Solomon, was there and ill. He wrote his father:

I arrived here this morning from New Haven in the ship United States, & agreeable to your request immediately enquired respecting Uncle Taintor [the eldest uncle was customarily called by the family name, others by their first names, as "Uncle Charles" is below] & it is with pain I must say to you that his life is wholly despaired of. This is the opinion of Mr. Foote [his son-in-law] & his physicians It seems he is so far reduced, that he rarely speaks, and then with difficulty. His stomach is so very weak that he can take scarcely any thing. . . . Uncle Charles is expected here tomorrow morning. I go to Mr. Foote's this evening & should there be any alteration in Uncle T. I shall write. . . .[10]

A few days later, John wrote that his uncle Charles had indeed arrived and had seen to it that the dying man's will was made (people ordinarily made their wills on their death beds). In the letter, John, obviously dis-tressed, dropped the formal "Uncle Taintor" and reported that "Uncle John has been gradually loosing strength, particularly within 2 days." Young John had seen him, but "he was only able to offer his hand, indeed he rarely speaks. He has taken nothing but a little porter for the last two days. He is at times very faint and life seems almost exhausted. He has been perfectly rational, at all times but this afternoon his mind appears different, & although sensible he seems stupid & indifferent to the objects, which surround him. This is doubtless the twilight which precedes the evening of his days. He will be buried here."[11]

John did not feel it inappropriate then in the same letter to tell his father the latest business news from New Haven, and to tell of his own plans for an expedition to Flushing to look at a flock of sheep with a "superior" reputation. And he reported of himself that "I am fine health and spirits and enjoy myself well. Tis like coming into life again to get away from Hampton." In fact this seems to have been the time when he went to an art exhibition at the American Academy from which he saved a catalogue.[12]

A week later, he was still in New York City and wrote that "Uncle Taintor . . . has been constantly failing since I wrote you last."[13] And two days later he wrote, "I can only say Uncle Taintor is yet alive."[14] Finally, on April 1, 1825, John wrote to his father:

It has become my duty to inform you that your brother is no more. He breathed his last Monday night at 12 Oclock. For the last two days he had declined taking anything, in consequence of the distress it gave him. He . . . therefore declined fast, and was perfectly sensible of his situation, even to the last. Monday he was very restless and wished to be moved every hour. He would then be very stupid and much fatigued. After he was moved the last time he was almost gone and after lying 10 minutes he asked to be turned on his other side, and gradually fainted away, 'till life became extinct. He died so quietly that it was scarcely possible to observe the change. He was buried at 4 P. M. Wednesday in a grave-yard in the Bowery. His (mahogany) coffin was enclosed in a box of pine, that he may be removed if desirable [i.e., if the family wishes to reinter him in Windham]. The bearers were J. B. Murray, Benj. Strong, D. S. Hubbard, Nevins, Col. Loomis, Levi Coit, Jos. Otis, J. R. Wheaton. Although it rained very hard all day, many attended the funeral, 20 or 30 hacks went to the grave. . . .[15]

As death was accepted as a part of life, so grief was not expected to overwhelm, especially not the young. John wrote to his father four days later, after he had returned to Hartford, to reassure him, "lest you should have some apprehension for my health, I can say that I never enjoyed myself better than the last month. . . . I have found from experience that one's health depends much on the mind, at least it does with me. I am boarding at Mrs. Whitings directly west of the State House & have every thing I could wish. She has 12 boarders one half ladies. I live plain and am in every respect careful." He told his father that the New York mourners were coming to Windham, and did say of them, "I will give you early notice that you may go to Windham to see them, as they are much depressed."[16]

Bulkeley Taintor wrote to John in 1828 about another cause of death: "Of the circumstances of Daniel Burnhams puting an end to his existence, you will learn from your father, with more of the particulars, than I could write you. To me it is quite misterious, what could have induced, a man of his easy turn of mind, and apparent contentedness with his situation, to make way with himself, probably some secret cause, but which eventually will be brought to light." There is no more in the correspondence about Burnham's suicide, and we cannot say more than Bulkeley could about it.[17]

It was a time when most illnesses were life-threatening. People did not know the causes of most diseases, infections, and epidemics. There were few medical or surgical cures. Death was not unusual. George Sisson, a former neighbor of the Taintors who had moved away from Hampton, in a letter to his son, Rodman, made vivid the way ordinary people dealt with infection, cancer, surgery, and the threat of death:

> . . . I would Informe you that we are all well as Common except Ruth has a bad Cold and your mother has ben very much out of helth. after She Came home from the Doctor, hir Sore healed for Something like a week or ten Days and looked very promising to git well soon, and then there Came out humers in and round the Sore and Did not Do so well and the Doctor Came to Se hir in about four weeks after She came home and apperated on it again with his eating Drops and gave Directions how to proceed with it and then it healed again . . . for some time and then the humers Came again and it pained hir and Sweld and effected hir right arme and hand and was so bad that I went after the Doctor and he Came again and Came on Sunday and went home on thirsday and appurated on it again untill he got a very larg hole in her Brest and made hir a Turrip to Clens hir blood and last Sunday he came again and Says he thinks that the Cancer tumer is thurily Subdued and thinks that it will git well now and She is Better in helth and hir Sore Does not pain hir So bad as it Dit and we feel Incouraged again . . . . It is a time of helth in this place Some few cases crupe. . . .[18]

A late-eighteenth-century medical book left in the Taintor house (it has no remaining cover, title page, or available title) tells of the surgical treatment of abscesses that "the best application" to encourage "the suppuration" for a tumor was "a soft poultice." The "turrip" may have been a turnip poultice. The book also recommends that "when the abscess is ripe or fit for opening" it could be done with a lancet "or by means of caustic," which could well be the "eating drops" George Sisson described.[19]

The End of the First Generation

Solomon, the younger of the brothers, was the first to die in Hampton. He fell ill—there is no record of the nature of his illness—and died on April 25, 1827, when he was fifty-seven years old. The day before, Roger, Dr. William A. Brewster, and Joseph Palmer (a neighbor) witnessed his will:

> I give to my wife one half of the House and garden which I now live in & all of the furniture belonging to me. the same to be at her disposal and four Hundred Dollars a year out of my Property. During her natural life and then to be equally divided between my Sons Edwin Bulkeley and Henry G. Taintor. Also I give Two Thousand Dollars to Henry to make him up equal to Bulkeley on account of his education and the one half of my Property that I own in Williamstown Massachusetts I Give the use and improvement to my Sister Sally B. Bulkeley During her natural life and the remaining part of my property I give to my two sons Edwin B. & Henry G. Taintor to be divided equally between them—the property that Edwin B. Taintor has rec'd is to be considered as part of his portion.[20]

Henry, who was sixteen when his father died, never went to college. Solomon's widow, Judith, survived him more than twenty years, living in the house in Hampton—first with her sister and brother-in-law as well as her son, then with Henry after he married. She was fifty-two when her

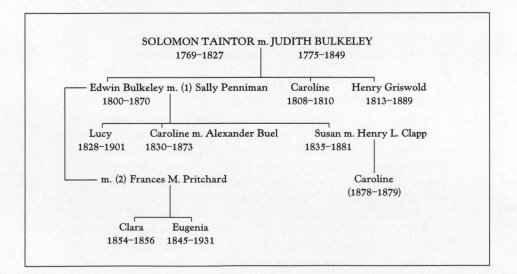

husband died. But even three years later she was not considered too old for possible marriage. Edmund Badger wrote to her brother, "You will remember me affectionately to . . . the Widow. Tell her to marry if she can get a good Husband and take all the pleasure She can for soon old age will prevent all of us from that enjoyment which is designed for Us. . . ."[21] Badger and the elder Taintors had grown up in the eighteenth century without the inhibitions about the pleasures of this world that would haunt their Victorian children or grandchildren.

Roger's old age without his brother must have been lonely. He kept the letters he received from Ludovicus Weld, the former minister with whom he had so thoroughly disagreed ten years before. Weld had retired to New York State. He wrote of his own condition and his memories of Hampton:

> The moment . . . that news arrived, through the medium of public papers, that your brother Solomon was dead, I resolved to inform you that my own life was yet protracted. Yes, Mr. Taintor, I am yet in the land of the living, a monument of mercy, and to say the best of myself that fact will warrant I am the same sinful unfaithful man as formerly. My progress towards the grave is rapid, but O how slowly do I advance in the path to heaven. Tho my health at present is tolerable, yet my constitution, shocked by asthma and adverse winds, is breaking down. I do not expect, neither do I desire, to continue much longer a pilgrim on the earth. . . .
>
> Death has indeed made distressing ravages and materially changed the condition of families, if not of society, in Hampton, in the course of three years. I often visit the place in imagination, and O what changes and desolations do I behold! Some have sold their possessions and strangers now occupy them; some have withdrawn from the Society who were once among the pillars by which it was supported. Some are shaken in property who once, to appearance, were approaching independence. Some have sunk into insignificance and contempt, who once were respectable. Some who merit detestation still hold a decent standing through the criminal partiality of friends, and their own duplicity and hypocritical pretensions. And some, O yes, many have passed the great change and gone to their loving home. . . .
>
> Two of your brothers, Sir, have exchanged worlds since I saw you, and a brother's daughter; and your brother Charles, I learn, has been dangerously sick. The sorrows of the world do not often come singly; they commonly come in clusters. The same is often true of the common blessings of Providence. With respect to this world, you and your family connexions have been remarkably prospered. Your enterprises have succeeded—wind and tide have been in your favor. But recently you have been called to drink bitter cups.

The death of brothers must have deeply affected yourself and family, particularly the death of Solomon; with whom you had been intimately associated not only in professional but in domestic concerns for a long course of years. It is my desire and prayer that you and yours, particularly the deeply affected widow and her children may find it good to be afflicted. How does his widow support her affliction? Is she calm and submissive? Has she given her heart to God? Tell her from me, if you please, that she can find consolation only in him who is touched with the feelings of our infirmities, who died upon the cross, and "ever liveth to make intercession." If she rely upon children, friends, property or any earthly source for support, she will find occasion to say with Job, "Miserable comforters are ye all."

Your brother, Sir, was a discerning man; a man of business, and, if I mistake not, was more disposed in the last years of my acquaintance with him, than previously, to encourage and promote religious institutions. I find it difficult, very difficult to realize that he has finished his course, closed his eyes upon this world, and entered the world of spirits. What was the state of his mind in view of death? Was he rational? Was he apprehensive that the disease would prove fatal? Did he express an hope of an interest in Christ, and of an inheritance incorruptible?–

You and I, Mr. Taintor are about of an age. We are old men. The blossoms of the grave are on our heads. We must soon follow brothers and other friends into eternity and meet them at the Judgment. This is a solemn thought! O are we prepared? . . .[22]

Roger Taintor's account book entry, showing his purchase of maple trees from Anson Fox in 1829.

Roger corresponded along much the same lines with the long-winded Weld for several years after this letter.

The rhythm of Roger Taintor's last years continued to be the rhythm of the life of a farmer. He made note inside the front cover of his final account book—he started it when his brother died, and it ends with his son John's accounting for his estate after his death—that he "sowed the Turnips 7th of August at night." He hired men to plant and hay and shear his sheep each year. He paid his regular hired man, Anson Burnham, $132 a year and "found" (room and board). He carefully oversaw the property and affairs of his young nephew, Henry, and of his brother's widow, with whom he shared the costs of maintaining their house. He noted, one April Saturday, "This day I have seen young Robins in their nest on the apple trees in the Lane." His own last entry in the book was to credit Warren Abbot twenty-five cents for "work on woodhouse."[23]

One act of Roger Taintor's in the last years of his life left a lasting imprint. In June of 1829 he bought fifteen sugar-maple trees from Anson Fox, for which he paid two and one-half gallons of molasses. He planted twelve of the trees in a row across the front of the house lot, a landscaping compliment to a gentleman's house. Three he planted between the house and his store and barn. All fifteen towered over the house when we bought it in 1967. Two have since been lost to hurricanes. Thirteen of the original fifteen maples Roger Taintor planted before he died still stand.

Roger Taintor died on April 2, 1831, less than six weeks before his son John married. Nabby followed Roger to the grave in November that year. Jonathan Clark rendered an account to "Roger Taintor Esqr" on April 4, 1831 for "Coffin clear stuff large" for five dollars (and fifty cents additional to "take measure, carry up"). Clark's breakdown of charges for making a coffin was:

Bords 2 ft 2 in wide	$1·50
Screws 30	·15
Butts	· 5
Handles	·16
Stain	·25
Varnish	·36
Nails	· 6
Cotton Stuffing	· 6
	2·59
Work	2·41
	$5·00[24]

In September 1832, John Adams Taintor paid Jonathan Clark for his mother's coffin and James Holt for "Laying foundations to Monuments." The marble monument for Roger and Abigail Taintor cost $150. It was made by Nathaniel Hodgkins, who was paid $145 cash and "one vest, one pr. pantaloons, and one coat"–perhaps Roger's.

PART II

❦ BORN ❦
REPUBLICAN

The adult lives,
from the 1820s to the 1840s,
of the generation born
after the American Revolution

Portrait painted by John Brewster, Jr.,
about 1810, when his neighbors John and Bulkeley Taintor
were ten years old.

CHAPTER 6

THE WIDER WORLD

ᏗᎢᎢ

*"You have performed a pilgrimage that I trust has made
a wiser, a better, and a happier man; and . . . you have acquired
a juster estimate of your own Country."*[1]

In the 1820s a wider world beckoned John Adams Taintor and Edwin
Bulkeley Taintor, and their college education freed them to taste more
of its variety than their fathers had. They no longer felt they must live
in Hampton.

After college Bulkeley began visiting Brookfield, a small town in
Worcester County, Massachusetts. The Taintors and their Hampton connections had ties to the place. Bulkeley reported to John how he explored
the town's "possibilities":

> . . . I called on Mr Phelps the Clergyman of the Place [Brookfield], Mr
> Bond the merchant who by the way has a very pretty daughter of fif-
> teen, Elisha Hammond, and what you may esteem of greater impor-
> tance, the Miss Uphams. They live in very genteel state. Their house
> is furnished with the greatest splendour and their dress such as would
> not suffer in comparison with the greatest bells of our Country.
> When I first called I saw only the youngest Miss Susan, she is about
> seventeen, very tall of a delicate skin and a form extremely beautiful.
> Her mother presently honoured us with her company and we spent
> some time very pleasantly in conversing upon New Haven where
> they had spent the last winter. They informed me that Miss Harriet
> Upham the eldest sister was unwell that morning with the head-ache,
> and I began to almost despair of seeing her when attracted I suppose
> by our conversation respecting New-Haven, she entered the room.
> And I must tell you that she is a d–m fine girl and were I disposed to

make a visit I think I should spend my *Providence Commencement* [this is a joking reference to John's pursuit of a girl, Adelia Croade, from North Providence, Rhode Island] at Brookfield.

Their Brother who was at Andover while we were . . . is studying Law. . . . I presume however that he will not fill his fathers place nor accumulate in so short a period the property that he did. He [the father] was a young man when he died and left Fifty Thousand Dollars to be divided as the law directs between his wife and three Children, so that if you are a little versed in figures you may easily calculate what the young Ladies will each of them have.

Brookfield is a very pleasant place and the Society is very interesting. You would I presume be very much pleased to make a visit to that place, and were it not that your face seems to be set to the East [the girl in Providence] you might make some acquaintances that you would never regret.[2]

Young gentlemen like Bulkeley and John saw the enjoyable beginning tasks of their adult lives as finding "useful" work and marrying to form the nucleus of a family. Work and family required a place and a household in order for a gentleman to establish himself in the adult world.

Young Men on the Make

John and Bulkeley went to work soon after they graduated from college. In order to learn how to be a merchant, Bulkeley clerked for Solomon and Roger in Hampton. John clerked for Mr. Scarborough in Hartford. Both young men also began to look for wives.

John Taintor saved some of his invitations to the balls and parties he attended in his search for a wife. The earliest solicits his company "at C. C. Button's Hall" in Hampton (Charles C. Button kept an inn and livery stable in the village) on February 23, 1816, at 3:00 P.M. John was fifteen at the time—and the occasion was perhaps a celebration of Washington's birthday. On February 22, 1822, after he was out of college, he received an invitation to a Washington's Birthday celebration in the evening at Bennet's Hotel in Hartford, managed by several of his friends.

Young men in small and large towns arranged dances and organized their own and their friends' social lives in order to meet young women; it was not the young women who did the public organizing and arranging. John kept several urgent invitations from his friend John Cleveland, for instance, to dances and "social times" in the village of Scotland.[3] One letter from Cleveland reported that "nothing has taken place . . . in the vicinity worthy of notice except the appointment of Balls and one Solitary wedding. Mason Cleveland has a Wife, a big word indeed."[4] John saved two

Washington's Birthday.

The company of _Mr J. A. Taintor_

is requested at BENNET'S HOTEL, at half past 6 o'clock, this Evening.

DANIEL BUCK,
JAMES WARD,
DAVID WATKINSON,
JAMES H. WELLS,
} _Managers_ {
CHARLES MUNN,
HENRY W. TERRY,
ISAAC TOUSEY,
O. E. WILLIAMS.

Friday, February 22, 1822.

Invitation to John Taintor for a Washington's birthday party in 1822.

invitations to cotillions in Springfield, Massachusetts—which is all the direct evidence we have that he lived for a time in Springfield during the first years after he graduated from Yale.[5]

Among the first letters we came upon in the Taintor-Davis Collection were a number from John Taintor's friends in a bantering style. They were decidedly ribald, and included many sexual references we had not expected to find. They may have escaped destruction simply because no one read or understood them for nearly 170 years after they were first read by John Taintor. We found them a delight and often laughed out loud as we read. These young men had not acquired the inhibitions we usually associate with the nineteenth century and the Victorian world. They seem to have enjoyed life in a manner still connected to an earlier time.

John's group of friends included his fellow clerk in Mr. Scarborough's store, T. D. Stewart, who came from a small town in New York State, "Rose" (we never learned Rose's first name), Henry Terry, and Oliver Ellsworth Williams of Hartford, among others. Most of the letters were written in the 1820s, after John had graduated from Yale and while he and his friends were beginning to make their way in the world and were seeking wives. They show young men enjoying a sense of freedom far different from the formal obligation of the dutiful son who wrote to his father, Roger.

The earliest of the letters came from T. D. Stewart after he had gone home when Scarborough had died. He addressed John, who had helped him measure cloth many times as "Brother Knight of the Yard stick" and reminisced, "Often times do I call to mind the many many happy hours we have spent together—how the old prison house once appeared—the taste that used to be displayed in arranging the old shop– . . . *& the Smiles &c* bestowed upon the fair sex." He had recently been ill, and told John how "The old woman pronounced sentence of death upon me, others took their last look of me as they supposed, sure that the consumption had a mortgage on me and would soon foreclose it. But they are all mistaken. I am yet spared to torment them."

He offered a description of himself:

T. D. Stewart setting by a table, in one hand holding a pen, on the other leaning his head, in a despondent attitude, very like *Patience on a monument.* His countenance assumes a darker and darker tinge of *Solemncholy* till at length he breaks out in the following Strain. . . .

> *What's this dull town to me?*
> *Taintor's not here.*
> *What is it I wish to see?*
> *What wish to hear?*
> *Where's all the joy and mirth,*
> *Made the old shop a heaven on earth?*
> *Oh! they'r all far away*
> *with Taintor J. A.*

Stewart concluded his letter with an urgent invitation to John: "I want to see you, I want to spend a week with someone who can recall the time passed bye and I know of no one with whom I could enjoy myself as I could with you."[6]

ABIGAIL ELLSWORTH m. (1794) EZEKIAL WILLIAMS
1774–1860   1765–1843
(dau. Oliver Ellsworth)

Oliver Ellsworth Williams m. Elizabeth Baker Croade
1796–1870   1800–1875

Ellen m. Cornelius J. Vanderbilt   Elizabeth Channing   Mary H.   Augusta H.

Just a few days later in July 1823, while John was still at home in Hampton, his friend Rose wrote from Hartford that Adelia Croade, the young woman from Providence, Rhode Island, in whom John was very interested, had come to Hartford. "She's here, *by all that's lovely!*–Yes she *is* here, and has been since Tuesday last–but I knew it not 'till the morning after her arrival, and . . . of course I could not communicate the happy tidings sooner.–The old lady her mother has come along also.–I suppose She and the young lady are the only parties to be consulted in this business." Adelia's father was dead, so John needed permission to marry Adelia only from herself and her mother. Rose assumed John would ask, and consent would be forthcoming: "What a glorious opportunity to have this *agreeable* matter Settled."

Rose went on to imagine his friend enjoying a full sexual conquest:

How pleasant it must be, to be spar'd all the trouble and anxiety, the hopes and fears of a regular siege, and at once to *enter the fortress, sword in hand,* in all the pride and pomp of victory.–No perseverance, no *sweet oil* necessary–all the honor, all the glory of conquest–without any of its attendant toils and dangers.–Methinks I see you, *booted* and *spurred,* mounted on your lovely Pegasus, and performing that short, transporting, delightful journey of *six inches,* two three or four times a day. . . . That croade–oh! heaven! I long to see you bucking her out.– But perhaps I shall offend you.–Give my best respects to your family & friends. . . .[7]

A month later, Stewart replied to a letter from John. He reviewed John's missive, laughing so hard, he wrote, "I thought I should shit. . . . I see you *mounted* on *your lovely Pegasus* and *performing* that *short, transporting, extatic, Journey of six inches* as *often* as *you can raise the steam.* I roared out, stamped, read it over, and laughed till I thought my sides would split." Stewart assured John that "You mistake when you imagine me at Troy *bucking* out with the Seminary [an academy for girls that Emma Willard had founded in 1821[8]] youth; I have never been there. the old woman [Emma Willard] is too d–nd close for me, I want full scope when I go. The citizens of Troy are allowed to visit there but once during a fortnight and then she holds a levee [a formal reception]."

John and his friends were not immune to romanticism, as Stewart made clear:

You ask me what I have been about this summer? Answer The same that you have, indulging my natural laziness, doing nothing but eat, drink, sleep, and ride, and often do I set in the door and cast my eye upon the green spots, the clusters of trees, on the opposite side of the Hudson and exclaim: Taintor is perhaps at this moment lounging in the same manner as myself, I wish he was here and we would take possession of those fields and groves set down undisturbed by human foot steps, charmed with the notes of the tenants of the boughs above us, and relate to each other all the changes that had taken place since our parting. . . .

He concluded his letter with another invitation: "Taintor do come on and spend a few days and we will ride *Pegasus* as often as you wish without spurs but with a riding whip of 6 *inches*. I have been idle in that business 4 months and the one that saddles me first must look out for breakers."[9]

In the fall after he received his friends' letters, John was parading with the militia in Hampton.[10] This gave an opportunity to wear an attractive uniform for the benefit of young ladies and to party with his friends. In September 1823, John wrote to Bulkeley—who was already settled in Brookfield, Massachusetts—about the festivities. Bulkeley replied that he, too, was in the militia, and planning to go to "a splendid Ball in the Evening" and "the day following there is to be a grand Military Review of all the Important Military Companies in the County by the Governor."[11]

Apparently, John did not limit himself to the pursuit of Adelia Croade. His irrepressible friend Rose wrote in November 1823, "What the devil have you been doing all this time?—playing with your tap I suppose,—or with some girl's in connexion with your own—pretty business to spend a year in." John had complained of competition in his romances from a minister, and Rose recommended a remedy: "Methinks if I were a man of elegant leisure, and a *soldier,* I would order out the militia, and take not a moments rest, 'till these destroyers of peace and seducers of innocence, were hunted from society.

> . . . I must also ask you to speak out in plain terms, and tell me who is the lovely being in your vicinity, whose heart is ensnared by one of these crafty creeping canonical catechising corn-doctoring c..t-scratching crop-eared calvinistick sons-of-bitches with whom you visited. Selah. Tell me who he is, and . . . his house shall be pulled down, and his barn shall be set fire to, yea, even his Sh.t-house shall be destroyed from off the face of the earth, and there shall not one cob be left upon another—and this, because he hath taken captive the sweet heart of the Gentile, and hath defiled a virgin of my people.—He shall be slain with the sword when there is none to help and no man shall deliver him out of the hand of the Gentile—Selah! . . ."

Rose went on to review plans for the coming winter and their friends' progress in the wife-hunting line. "Geo. Spalding is engaged to Helen Cowles.—Hen Tracy is . . . to be married in the Spring, lead his dear Ann to the new habitation, and settle down a farmer. . . . Bassett has gone to New York for the winter.—It is positively asserted he is to marry the youngest Miss Mills—so they have dispos'd of him you see." He reported to John that "About eight or ten of us choice spirits, have formed an oyster-club which is a very agreeable association.—Our meetings are weekly—The eating department is confined exclusively, to bread & butter and oysters;–and the drinking, to brandy and whiskey-punch," and he was sure John would enjoy it. He concluded his "report" to John by saying, "The boys are all comfortable, and generally manifest a strong aversion to sleeping alone, these long cold winter nights.–It is our opinion that (unless we have your company) we shall shortly be the only man left of our once happy number, that can boast the life-inspiring joyous name of batchelor."[12]

Within a month, Rose replied to a letter from John reporting on his own and their friends' efforts to marry. "Really, one would suppose from your remark, that I was in the last stages of courtship, and about to launch into that abyss, 'from whose bourne few travellers return'–But I am not so nearly lost as you would have me–and candidly believe I shall not be married, before Sept. or Oct. next." He assured John he would be best man if "that happy event should take place." He further said that "the story you have heard, respecting Mr. Wheaton and Miss Tracy, is pretty generally credited" and that he "should not be surpris'd if he put the screws to hir when he returns."

Rose ended that report, "Henry is to be married christmas eve–He is in ecstacies in anticipation of the raptures of the bridal night, and I hope he will be spur'd (as all good folks say) to f..k her 'till they are both tired of it."[13] Before the year ended, Rose wrote, "We got Henry safely married on tuesday eve of last week, & am sorry to say his back is weak already.–The last week has been past in dissipation & pleasure so called–I can only say I am comfortable as can be expected after it."[14]

John Taintor did not marry as early as most of his friends. He pursued Adelia Croade for many years. In the summer of 1825, Rose wrote him of what only John seemed to consider any longer a romance, "*You lazy rascal–*You have been chasing that *fat-ass'd Rhode-Island broad,* 'till I suppose there is hardly an ounce of flesh upon your bones;–and probably got reduced so low you could not sustain the weight of a quill pen."[15] In another letter, he suggested that John meet a Miss Julia King, "the *young lady . . .* is a beautiful flushing girl of sixteen, modest, delicate, and timid,–with the sweetest figure and face in New York."[16] But John was never permanently distracted from Adelia.

Rose was working in New York City in 1825, and John's friend Henry Huntington, Jr., kept him up to date about social life in Hartford. Huntington enjoyed ribbing John about the country life John did not enjoy. In October 1825, he wrote, "I now take my pen in hand, to write you these few lines, to tell you, that I am well and hope you enjoy the same blessin. Your uncles and aunts are all enjoyin good health except aunt Tabby who hit her head againt the barn tother day in goin over to Uncle Mikes. . . .

The galls here say they want to see you most darnationaly and want to know when you are coming."[17] He later reported from Boston that another of their friends had married:

> We spliced Sam last monday morning at 10 o'clock, and since have been very busy night and day, that is he has–the rest of us have only been busy during the day. I wish you was here, for I want some one to play the devil with, after ten oclock at night I have nothing to do and no Lady to help me. I have been to a party every night this week and there is three more to come yet–as the boy told his mother when she fired off the gun and it Kickd her into the ditch, lie still mother, there's nine more to come yet.[18]

Running after women was not the only pleasure in young John Taintor's life. He went to see the sights of the wider world as often as he could arrange to do so. He always wanted to get away from Hampton. He looked for work in Hartford and New York City.

In November 1825, the Erie Canal opened for its entire length from Buffalo to Albany. The state of New York had started the huge engineering and construction project–the most extensive project yet completed in the United States, and the longest canal in the world–in 1817. Its construction generated great excitement throughout the United States. Thousands worked on digging the ditch and building the locks. Other states and private companies of investors enthusiastically organized their own companies and started canals. As it grew, the Erie Canal provided access to markets for upper New York State farmers–increasing the value of their farms as well as their produce. The Canal made it easy to move migrating people and bulk products to and from New York City, Buffalo, and the vast land areas of the upper midwest via the Great Lakes waterways. And New York City had access, by steam and sail, to the populated and productive markets of all the coast from Maine to the Gulf of Mexico and, by way of the Atlantic, to the rich markets and resources of Europe, the West Indies, the Mediterranean, Africa, and the Far East.

To celebrate the Canal's opening, a procession of boats and barges loaded with dignitaries, and carrying water from all the great rivers of the world as well as from the Great Lakes, started from Buffalo and made its way through salutes and celebrations the length of the canal to Albany, and down the Hudson past New York to Sandy Hook where all the representative waters were poured into the sea to signal the connection of the Great Lakes with the waters and the commerce of the great oceans. John Taintor went to New York for the celebration. New York City was about to explode as the largest port and city in the United States, and as the financial and mercantile center of the nation—because of the Erie Canal. On November 5, 1825, the family at home received a description:

> . . . After pitching about in the Sound two days we had the good fortune to arrive in the East river just as the grand procession of Steam Boats started for the Navy Yard. And it was grand indeed, twenty two boats in a row with three canal boats in tow, two from Buffalo & one from Black Rock, all fitted up in the most splendid manner, and the steam boats filled with passengers. As they came round the Battery the firing commenced from the long row of Cannon extended through it, from all the Forts & the great guns of the Navy Yard. The earth trembled & shook at every discharge. The firing continued for 20 minutes, when the whole fleet went down to Sandy Hook. The Celebration exceeded all I ever saw. The Stores were closed & the whole City joined in the Celebration. I am fully paid for my visit had I no further object.[19]

Where to Go and What to Do

Bulkeley had been, from the time of their graduation from Yale, more committed to small-town life than John. At first, he had gone back to Hampton to live and to begin training for business. As a resident member of the Taintor family, Bulkeley had immediately become involved in Hampton's public life. He was elected constable and collector of taxes, and served on the committee that examined "Miss Woods School."[20] He reported to John that "the appearance of the Scholl was extremely good and the examination particularly interesting. They were examined in History, Chemistry, Geography, Rhetoric &c and on many of the subjects of their examination they appeared much better than we do at New Haven. They had as might have been expected some very learned remarks from me, and no doubt were listened to with the profoundest attention." Bulkeley thought the school would be "of great benefit to this Town and will I hope in time make some alteration in the Society in this Town. For you know that at present it is at a pretty low ebb, and will always continue so unless some pains are taken to improve their minds."[21]

In the event, Bulkeley, having looked very little at the world, chose to live in a small town, albeit not his native Hampton. He settled in West Brookfield, Massachusetts, in 1823, where he became a merchant in partnership with a Mr. Newell. He married Sally Penniman of North Braintree in 1826. He lived on his farm in West Brookfield for the rest of his life.

John, on the other hand, chose city life. He sought ways to get into the mercantile business on his own wherever it might be most advantageous. He enlisted his friends, acquaintances, and family connections in the search for a store, for a location, for partners and capital. He had written to his father in September 1822:

> I am persuaded more and more that business is better here in Hartford than in other places. . . . But, it so happens that there is but one Store in the centre of the town which can be rented, where a stock of goods could be kept and that is Mr. Hill's, situated on a corner in front of the State House and in the most advantageous place to show goods, which is of great consequence. . . . I think there can be no safer business done than here, one that is subject to less risks. Your pay is cash and your books if kept by double entry will show the situation of business at any time. As for waiting for the chance to commence with some experienced man I think it ten chances to one that I should get a broken merchant or some indolent fellow, who would not attend to business, but if you take a young man he will be industrious & ambitious to excell in business. But after all you [Roger was backing the enterprise] must be the judge of a proper person.[22]

E. H. Clark was eager to go into business with John. He and John searched the Hartford area for a store and for stock in the event they found one. They did not, and the partnership was never formed. John also nearly bought a "stock of goods" which had belonged to Daniel Crowell, and a store to go with it, but it was sold before he made the decision.[23] Although he did not in the end start a store in Hartford, he came very close.

He also thought of moving to New York City. His friend Oliver Ellsworth Williams worried that in such an eventuality "you must expose yourself to a world of temptations—which even the firmest nerves—are not always adequate to resist—and which might, for aught we know, bring upon one of the finest fellows that ever I saw—mortification and regret. Thus much by way of hint—from a man who stands more in need of advice & caution, than 10,000 such fellows as you." Williams himself had become a broker in Hartford, and he suggested that if John did not become a storekeeper, he might invest his capital in loans or perhaps stocks.[24]

John's friend Rose dissolved a partnership in Hartford in 1823, and he and John met several times to discuss forming one together in Hartford, Boston, or New York. In 1824, he wrote John:

> . . . think our choice had better be fix'd on Boston. . . . I learn . . . that there are a great many new-comers in Newyork, inquiring and advertising for leases of stores in Pearl and the adjacent streets.—These gentlemen are from Boston, Philadelphia, Baltimore, Richmond, Petersburg, &c. who, under the impression that business is better in Newyork than elsewhere, have simultaneously agreed to "pull up stakes," and try the issue.

NYork it is well known, has been gradually attaining the ascendency in the jobbing business, over our other markets; and many individuals in the above-mention'd towns, after making every effort to retain their customers without success, seem to have determined, (altho' doubtless without unity of design,) that as business wont come to them, they must e'en go to that.[25]

John never became a storekeeper or a merchant. Rather, his long-term interest was in stock breeding and the improvement of domestic livestock, particularly sheep and cattle. His friendship with Peter Hall, of Pomfret, as well as his later friendship with Frank Rotch (the son of a very wealthy whaling and shipping family of Nantucket and New Bedford), was partly based on their mutual interests in these subjects. By the end of 1826, John was selling breeding stock animals, and had become friends with wealthy stock breeders who even had portraits done of their prize animals. Peter Hall wrote him in December 1826:

> Dear John
>   I rec'd your letter . . . in which you wish to know the fate of the Saxony buck "*Lectorial*" left in my care—I offerd him at $30. but have not found one willing to purchase even at this low price—you are aware of the depreciated value of sheep in this quarter. therefore if you have more on hand keep them—they will command a better price ere long—I will keep him without expence till you call for him—
>   I think of going to N.York soon and shall go through Hartford—where shall I find you—my object is to see Watsons bull Comet—for I am told he is a fine animal. The portrait of him you mention as being good and well executed—Mr Fisher has been here and has taken a beautiful portrait of my bull Albion. it is a splendid picture and a capital likeness of the animal.[26]

In 1827 John Taintor was elected a delegate to a convention in Harrisburg, Pennsylvania, sponsored by the Pennsylvania Society for the Promotion of Manufactures and the Mechanic Arts, about protective tariffs "To Encourage Domestic Industry And National Independence." There he met William Hare Powel, the famous stock breeder, with whom he continued to correspond. Among the other eighteen Connecticut delegates to that convention were Gideon Welles (later Abraham Lincoln's Secretary of the Navy), Jonathan Rose (perhaps John's friend "Rose"), Henry L. Ellsworth (later head of the U.S. Patent Office and a land commissioner for western lands), and James M. L. Scovill (founder of a large and enduring Connecticut manufacturing concern). These were the people in the wider world who became John Taintor's acquaintances. It was after meeting them that he went to Europe.[27]

An American on Tour

John Taintor had inscribed his name in *Mathews' Trip to Paris; Or, The Dramatic Tourist,* a play published in New York in 1822. A chorus from it begins:

> *When a man travels, he mustn't look queer,*
> *If he gets a few rubs that he doesn't get here.*
> *To gain all the knowledge, to Paris he goes,*
> *To glean from the wits, and to quiz all the beaus.*[28]

Making a European tour was one of the things a gentleman ought to do. John understood he could make important contacts and purchase fancy European breeding stock while he gleaned "from the wits" and quizzed "all the beaus." He also tried to get a diplomatic job, which would send him abroad. He wrote several times to Ralph I. Ingersoll (a Republican Connecticut congressman known to his father and uncles) in Washington, D.C. Ingersoll replied in January 1827 that he was "not aware at present of any situation abroad that would be desireable for you, that could be obtained. . . . Should I hear of any such opening, you may rely upon my active exertions in your behalf."[29] More than a year later, Ingersoll wrote that he "saw Mr Henry Clay [Secretary of State] last evening. He says that he will entrust dispatches to your care, either for France or England as you shall prefer. . . . Should you be pleased with this arrangement, it will not be necessary for you to come here, but the dispatches will be forwarded to you at New York, or wherever else you may embark."[30]

At the same time, his friend Henry Huntington encouraged John to try for a diplomatic post as secretary to a legation. Huntington wrote from Paris in 1828:

> Mr. Henry Sheldon, son of Dr. Sheldon of Litchfield & secretary of the American Legation in Paris died a few days since at Marseilles where he had gone for the recovery of his health. Mr. S. was a valuable man and excellent sec: and is really a great loss to the country as he understood the affairs of our country with France extremely well. . . .
>
> I have thought that this would suit you exactly, if you could get it, although my wife says she don't want you to get it, because you would quit Hartford, but I am not so selfish, and am willing to make some sacrifice. I think it is one of the most desirable situations for a young man of any that I know of—you are at once, as a matter of course, introduced into the best society in Paris. besides the duties of the office are trifling, and very easily learned, and you have leisure to pursue any other studies you plan, and no city affords so many facilities for a young man to spend time to advantage as Paris does.[31]

John may not have received Huntington's letter before he left for Europe himself, but he tried to get an appointment in London similar to the one Huntington suggested in Paris. He was not successful. Ralph Ingersoll wrote from Washington: "Mr. Albert Gallatin [who had been Jefferson's and Madison's Secretary of the Treasury] who goes to England as Minister, is not now, in this city, and may not be, before the Session of Congress closes. It is probable, however . . . that he will take out one of his sons with him as private Secretary; and it is probable the present Secretary of legation will remain out." Ingersoll could "see no chance" for John as Gallatin's secretary.[32]

John asked Edmund Badger, his father's old friend in Philadelphia, for letters of introduction to English cattle and sheep breeders from William Hare Powel, whom Badger knew, and whom John had met. Badger replied:

> I sincerely hope Your contemplated trip may be beneficial & profitable. You are aware that a young Gentleman in these days can not pass as an accomplished Gentn. without one (at least) crossing the Atlantic. To be sure your Father and myself for instance (by the by We have seen an Englishman) have Acquired a reputation (of some sort) We once aspired to be at the tip, top, of Gentility; but we are so-so—and we never have, as yet, crossed the Briny Ocean—perhaps we yet may. However John go to England—Study Man in Europe, get all their good, shun all their vices and God grant you may return with a fund of usefull knowledge and be the means of benefiting your Country as well as yourself. . . .[33]

John left New York for England at the beginning of May 1828 on the ship *York*. He had the lower berth in the stateroom next to the captain's and his passage cost $140.[34]

No one in the family kept a letter from John describing the voyage, but he himself kept one from Benjamin Rodman, his friend Frank Rotch's brother-in-law, who wrote about his own passage to England at about the same time in another ship:

> . . . You are mistaken about its being a dull time . . . it seems like nothing to go to Europe in a conveyance that is as agreeable as ones own parlour. You may judge that I was not particularly fatigued when I tell you I never could get to bed—that is never could "turn in," till past midnight. The passengers were a jolly set and they had days a plenty. . . .[35]

The cities John Taintor went to see in Europe were world capitals, among the largest cities in the world. London's population was 1.5 million. The Paris population was nearly 900,000. New York, from which he sailed, was the largest city in America, with 200,000 people. The contrasts must have been staggering, particularly for a young man who grew up in a town of fewer than 1,500 people and who had been residing in Hartford, a city of 7,000.[36]

John's bills, receipts, calling cards, business cards, and theater programs saved from his European trip make it possible to piece together where he went, and when. He saw a performance at the Theatre Royal, Drury Lane, London on June 5, 1828, of "The Taming of the Shrew . . . including Songs, Duets, Glees, and Chorusses, selected entirely from the Plays, Poems, and Sonnets of Shakspeare, the overture by Rossini." The evening concluded with "Weber's romantic opera of Der Freischutz." The next day, he bought a "fine brown coat" and "silk waist coat" in Bloomsbury Square.

He crossed the English Channel to Calais by June 8, because he traveled from Calais to Paris that day on a coach run by the French Administration de l'Exploitation Générale des Messageries Royales. In Paris, he stayed at the Hôtel de Montmorency, rue St. Marc 12, from June 10 to 13. His breakfasts that warm early June included two eggs and strawberries with sugar. One morning he had to pay for a sheet of paper. He also paid for "2 Plates broken."

He returned to Calais on June 13 by post coach from Paris. In Calais, he stayed at the Hotel Guillacq, rue Neuve, which offered *"Bains chauds et froids à toute heure. Table d'hôte à 4 heures. Voitures de toute espèce à vendre et à louer à des prix avantageux."* John kept a card with a description of the hotel:

> Quillacq's Hotel late The Silver Lion, Calais. This grand and commodious Establishment has been carried on under the direction and management of Mr. Quillacq, from the time of his quitting the hotel Dessin, in the year 1820, who by the extent and convenience of his arrangements, his unremitted care and attention, and his reasonable charges, has rendered it worthy the patronage of Nobility, Gentry and Travellers who may visit Calais. A Table d'Hôte every day. A large Garden belongs to the Hotel. Warm & cold Baths. Carriages of every description to let, sell or exchanged.

He tore himself away to get back to London by June 16. He stayed at Harrison's New Furnival's Inn Hotel, 9 Furnival's Inn Square, Holborn, London, until the nineteenth, and again from August 6 to 15, spending £6/6/10. (This is the inn where Dickens started writing *Pickwick Papers* a few years later.[37]) During this second London stay John went to the Ascot Heath races, "Second Meeting, Knight's Royal Windsor List, First Day," Tuesday, June 17, 1828. He also went to several theatrical performances, including one at the Theatre Royal, Drury Lane on Tuesday, June 24, to see "the opera Artaxerxes, the composition 'Mild as the Moonbeams,' Colman's three act comedy, 'Ways and Means; or, A Trip to Dover,'" and "Midas." On Friday, June 27, John saw "A comic piece" about Americans called "Jonathan in England" at the same theater. Another day in late June, he went to Vauxhall Gardens to see a reenactment of the Battle of Waterloo with "large bodies of soldiers, horse and foot."

In July 1828, John Taintor crossed to the Continent again. He kept a list of "New and interesting works for travellers on the continent" published by Samuel Leigh of London. He also kept a schedule of the General Steam Navigation Company for July 1828, including London-Calais, London-Ostend, London-Rotterdam, London-Boulogne, London-Hamburg, and London-Newcastle. The steam packets departed from the Custom House or the Tower. And he had a ticket for His Majesty's steam packet *Salamander.*

For the next month he toured the Continent, visiting Belgium, France, and Switzerland. While in Brussels he picked up a pamphlet in French: "Le Nécessaire de l'Étranger dans Bruxelles," which included a chart of exchange between French francs, Belgian florins, and English pounds. He kept a guide to the monuments in the church of St. Thomas at Strasbourg, featuring a description of the mausoleum of the Maréchal Comte de Saxe. While in Paris he received visiting cards, including one from a Mr. Barnett, Consul Américain, rue Plumet No. 14, Faubourg St. Germain, which show

Left: Furnival's Inn Hotel, London, where John Taintor stayed in 1828.
Right: London playbill from John Taintor's 1828 visit.

that he may have indeed carried dispatches. Like all travelers in the City of Light, he may have run out of money, because he kept the card of a *changeur*. It was all a far cry from rural, small-town America, as Bulkeley described it in a letter John received that summer:

> . . . You probably, as you have so many objects, to occupy your attention in England, and particularly those which are new and not to be seen in this country, will neither be much amused, or interested, in any of the occurences, which take place, in so peaceful and so quiet a vilage, as our own; of course I shall say nothing more, than we are all well, and that we are situated, much as when you was last here. . . .
>
> There was a Sale of Saxony Sheep at Boston on the 10th of this month. It was very thinly attended, and the Sheep were sold at unusually low prices. Had you been there, you would have had a noble time to purchase, and would have realized something handsome in seling again. I have not been to Hampton since I saw you there, but shall go as soon as I am through with my haying. Grass is uncommonly large, twice a common crop. The season has been one of the most singular that I ever knew. It has rained almost continually. . . .
>
> I saw in my New York Paper a list of the passengers with whom you sailed, which I should think quite respectable in names and numbers. Since I saw you, I have thought much of geting an English Cow, and if you should get one for your Father, and could do without the funds till [I] should see you, I should be extremely glad to have you purchase one for me, if the expence should not exceede $150. . . .[38]

By the ninth of August John was back in London. Businesses at which he called included a saddler and capmaker in Cockspur Street, a woolen drapery in High Holborn, hat manufacturers in Gracechurch Street and High Holborn, a hosier, glover, and umbrella manufacturer in the Strand, and booksellers in Cheapside and Corn Hill. He also visited wholesale toy warehousemen, a lace manufacturer, a wine and spirit merchant, several tailors, a manufacturer of musical instruments, engravers and printers, and a picture-frame maker.

He spent considerable time in England looking at animals. He went to a Horse Auction on August 11 near "Hyde-park Corner by Messrs. Tattersall," at which fifty-six horses, several greyhounds, and carriages were sold. He visited several wool brokers in London, and one of them wrote an address on the back of his card directing John to Otley, Yorkshire. At another time the same broker suggested "Mr. Kelly, Blackwall, Please to show the bearer the Saxony sheep."

John traveled out of London to Chester, Sheffield, and Derby. He went to All Saints Church, Derby, on Sunday morning, August 17, 1828, where he heard a sermon by the "Right Rev. Lord Bishop of Lichfield & Coventry" and a chorus by Handel and one by Beethoven. Some of the time he traveled with his friend Frank Rotch, who was living in England at the time, and who shared John's interest in livestock. Rotch brought his wife and children along on the trip to Derby.[39]

In September John attended the Warwick races, and went to Bath and Bristol. He visited both the great university towns of Cambridge and Oxford. And at his hotel in Oxford he had his washing done: "9 shirts, 1 vest, 2 cravats, 1 pr. stockings, 1 cot pocket hdkf, 1 silk ditto."

John returned to America, and briefly to Hampton, in the fall of 1828. Like small-town young men a century later, there was no keeping him down on the farm once he had seen Paree. He received a letter from Frank Rotch (who had also returned), reminiscing about their time together in Europe:

> November 9, 1828, New Bedford
>
> Dear Taintor—I do as sincerely rejoice at your safe return as I was
> pleased when first I heard of your resolution to leave this blessed
> Land—you have performed a pilgrimage that I trust has made a wiser, a
> better, and a happier man; and while you have acquired a juster esti-
> mate of your own Country I feel certain your travels have not made
> you a worse American neither have you prostituted our feeling of
> republicanism at the Shrine of Royalty—but have brought to your fire
> side subjects for present amusement and future reminiscence which
> will not leave you through life—Your parents must indeed rejoice over
> you. . . .

Rotch went on to wish they could live their "English lives over again round a good Yankee fire and talking over our Transatlantic scenes." He said of his own voyage home, "we had a most charming company of gentle-men—our lady would have been better left behind. . . . She was a woman of excessive beauty and equal vanity."[40] In another letter to John a few weeks later he said of his shipboard adventures "under other circumstances and with a less thoroughly genteel class of passengers" there might have been "much unpleasantness for we had a most beautiful but a most indiscreet woman on board whose husband was contemptible jealous & mean despised by all and by none more than by this foolish vain unfortunate woman."[41]

Charming Young Ladies

If John Taintor kept letters from Adelia Croade, he did not keep them in his parents' house, and so they are not part of the family's collection. We looked and we hoped, but we did not find any. The letters from women

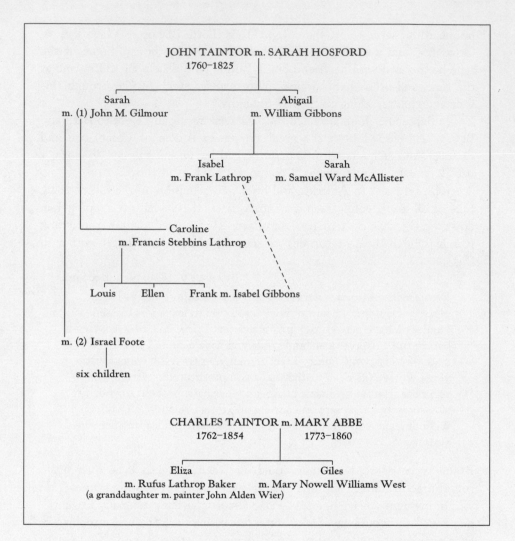

JOHN TAINTOR m. SARAH HOSFORD
1760–1825

Sarah
m. (1) John M. Gilmour

Abigail
m. William Gibbons

Isabel
m. Frank Lathrop

Sarah
m. Samuel Ward McAllister

Caroline
m. Francis Stebbins Lathrop

Louis   Ellen   Frank m. Isabel Gibbons

m. (2) Israel Foote

six children

CHARLES TAINTOR m. MARY ABBE
1762–1854   1773–1860

Eliza
m. Rufus Lathrop Baker
(a granddaughter m. painter John Alden Wier)

Giles
m. Mary Nowell Williams West

that John Taintor did keep were all written in one year–1829, after he came back from Europe. They were all from city women, part of the sophisticated society of which he and his young men friends were a part. These letters were, however, mostly from women with whom John had some family connection: Caroline Gilmour, the daughter of his (considerably older) cousin Sarah's first marriage; and Hannah Gibbons, a niece of his cousin Abigail's husband, William Gibbons (Sarah and Abigail were the daughters of Roger and Solomon's eldest brother John). The first letter came from 2 Greenwich Avenue in New York City. Three people wrote it, Carrie Gilmour, Hannah Gibbons, and John's cousin Giles Taintor. Caroline Gilmour, who was twenty-one, was responsible for the first part:

New York, 2 April 1829

My dear Cousin–From your letter to Mr. Gibbons I understand that
you want a fragment-letter [a letter written by several people], & I
assure you it will give me much pleasure to contribute my mite,–if
everyone finds their own ink it will be like Joseph's coat, of many
colours, for there are no two ink stands in the house containing the
same shade of that valuable liquid ink.

I received a letter from Jane Kirkman [whom John had met on his
way to Europe] yesterday. She inquired about you & says that she
has watched the papers all winter expecting to see your marriage but
she supposes that the lady is not yet 30 years of age before which
you think it highly improper to marry.–I am very much obliged to
Jane for that hint, for it is the first reason good or bad that I have
ever heard assigned for your not becoming a "happy man" long
before now.

Heaven only knows when or where this may find you but I hope it
will be in time to bring you here before we sail for Georgia. That is
Mr. Gibbons & myself–we have been expecting to go every day these
two weeks & we may now sail this week.–it will depend upon the
weather & my Aunt's [William Gibbons' wife's] health which has not
been good for a long time. the complaint is in her head and produces
constant pain.–the Dr has ordered her to confine herself to the house,
principally to her room & do nothing.–

You ought to have been here to the first masquerade given at the
Park. Giles & Lathrop [Francis Stebbins Lathrop, whom Caroline
Gilmour later married] acquitted themselves admirably, they were
quite the nine days wonder of Gotham, particularly Helen McGregor
[Giles in costume] who set all the wise heads there disputing whether
she was male or female. Hannah went as a Nun–I as Carry Gilmour,
the only character I can support. . . .

The letter goes on in a new hand, that of Hannah Gibbons:

Sunday evening "The end of a thing is better than the beginning
thereof" Is one of the Lay Preacher's texts and I will prove the truth
of it in this instance at least, by ending a day which was begun, in bus-
tle and confusion, in the calm tranquility of my Friend's society.

My Uncle and Caroline left us this afternoon. Giles and Lathrop
have been spending the evening with them on board of the ship for
they will not sail till sunrise tomorrow. They have just returned and
left them in very good spirits. Mrs. Gibbons is so much indisposed
that she does not come downstairs and Mrs. Taintor and myself have
come to quite a "realizing sense" of our situation. If you will join *Sister
Hood* it will make us very happy. I will be devoted to you & we will

walk talk visit or any thing you please. we will be objects of envy to the vulgar and astonishment to the great.

I wish I had written this more legibly. did you ever hear the parable of a man looking in a bushel of chaff for a grain of wheat? If yea, in pity do not compare it to my part of this eloquent epistle. the fact is my pen is so very bad and I am so very sleepy that I fear I've scarcely connected sentences.

Present my best regards to your father and tell him that I shall be very much disappointed if he does not visit NewYork this spring for I have not seen anyone that I like to romp with half as well as I do him. and tell your mother that if she does not come to take care of her husband, I shall certainly not let him return so she knows what she may expect–but good night cousin John. you are a marvelous proper man and write soon to your very affectionate friend *Mrs. Dan* [Hannah Gibbons]

Giles Taintor completed the trio of writers:

Dear John   There is about half a page left for me & I suppose you will say I am congratulating myself that there is no more–but I believe I will keep quiet about an excuse for not writing you before, for I never succeed very well in endeavoring to exculpate myself–after what has been said before me, I think I may give up trying to amuse you, for I have been laughing at the perusal of Hannah's letter, till all sense of humour has gone from me–So I will write in plain sober terms– Caroline and Mr. Gibbons after lying in the stream here Sunday night & all day Monday, sailed yesterday (Tuesday)–Lathrop & myself made them two calls on board the ship, by means of a small boat.–

I heard of you in Providence the other day, when I supposed you were in Hartford. I think the lady [Adelia Croade] must visit Providence frequently. . . .

I would give you a description of Our first Masquerade here but I think I can tell it to you better when I see you–I went as Helen McGregor or that was the name they chose to give me. & Lathrop as Rob Roy–I will show you my dress when you come here–

I hope you have allowed your picture to be hung up at home. if you have not, I beg you will be persuaded to do it immediately . . . so goodby Giles Taintor [who was the son of Charles Taintor, Roger and Solomon's older brother].[42]

John Adams Taintor's portrait, the "picture" to which Giles refers, no longer seems to be in the family; we have never seen it.

Among the older ladies who wrote to John was a perhaps somewhat rueful mother, Ellen Kirkman, who had traveled to England on the *York* with him in 1828. On that trip she had been accompanied by her son Hugh and marriageable daughter Jane, who seem to have been a little younger than John. Mrs. Kirkman knew John's cousins and their families, but we do not know how; perhaps she was a Gibbons relative. The tone of her correspondence shows her to have been a practical businesswoman, interested in politics and what was a men's world in the 1820s. She wrote in May 1829 from Nashville:

My Dear Sir   With pleasure and surprise recd yours of 12th March giving us the pleasing information of your Father & being in good health but not one word of your better half. dont you recollect the old saying Procrastination is the thief of time? The Lady if still single must have more love and patience than generally falls to the lot of most Women. I know you of old never to be in a hurry and often ten minutes after the time. You know I never scolded on those occasions. but why remind you of your imperfections? The fact is I charged them to Father & Mother having but one Son—they were excusable—

... We have now determined to travel Eastwardly and will probably leave here in three weeks. I am obliged to visit Frankfurt Kentucky on business which will delay us. Should we visit NYork it would give Jane Hugh and myself much pleasure to meet you, that we might travel over the Old country in conversation and tell our adventures since we parted. ...

Greyhound [a hunting dog brought back from England, named "Whip"] here after much trouble having taken a seat in the Stage for his honour. Hugh a steady hardware Merchant the first assortment being lost in the Marmion that sunk on the French Coast. it was insured to the full amt. Jane still a Spinster. My ladyship a coughing Old Woman as prompt as when you saw me—

... When we visit NYork we will of course see our friends at No 2 [Greenwich Avenue]. I should like to see your Father that we might Tawlk over the new appointments [by recently inaugurated President Andrew Jackson].—

The Jackson fowlks here are much disapointed at the Hickory [Jackson's nickname was "Old Hickory"] measures. ... Now my dear friend have you returned a good republican? I think I perceive a little of the aristocrit feelings in some of your expressions: "a few thorough Gentlemen." There must be difference of rank in all countrys, difference of education and intellect. The honest heart I admire let the outward case be ever so plain. Education and refinement I admire for themselves. I have given up politics.

... Mrs Bacus tells you were at a ball in Providence, that the young Ladies admired you extremely, That you were quite captivating. I am glad they did not see you & Jane in the Roundhouse on board the York.–it is a great sacrifice of time to cross the Atlantic. We have had quite a gay time since our return. . . . believe us your true friends and fellow sufferers, Jane Hugh & Ellen Kirkman

Hugh Kirkman appended a note of his own to his mother's. He wrote, "You say that you think I could hardly of got to Nashville alive with Whip & the rest of the Plunder but I assure you I had a very pleasant time return-ing. . . . I wish you would come out here and see these backwoods people. I think I could show you some rare sport with whip among the Deer & Foxes. by the bye I should like to send you a pup from Whip."[43]

Hannah Gibbons's long letters to John Taintor refer to him as her "friend" (relative) or her "cousin." She wrote each letter on large single sheets of paper, folded to produce four pages. She wrote first horizontally on all pages, then turned the paper ninety degrees and "crossed" her letters by writing on all four pages again, so that the result looks like a plaid. She had a clear, legible hand, but the crossing makes the letters very difficult to read. Hannah's style was a combination of formal and silly, possessed of a wittiness reminiscent of her contemporary, Washington Irving. Her descriptions of New York life are very like those in Irving's *Salmagundi*.[44]

Ere this my friend John Taintor has arrived in Hartford; Ere this he is no doubt laying plans for his amusement during his stay there. In order to reconcile to myself the regret which I feel at the loss of his society–I am determined to commence a correspondence from which I promise myself much amusement and instruction. Every days experience adds strength to an opinion which I have long entertained, that nothing so much tends to improve the taste for epistolary writing as a correspon-dence with a *young* gentleman of understanding. it causes us to write with care and perspicuity–it preserves a purity of language and under the "garb of airy lightness," it enables us to elucidate principles of moral-ity which are indispensibly necessary to the true enjoyment of life.

Having thus premised permit me to offer you my most sincere con-gratulations on your arrival in Hartford; knowing as I do, how long and how constantly it has been your wish and how happy it has made you to see again that one loved face, to hear that sweet voice whis-pering the words of welcome in your ear, to clasp again that hand etcetera etcetera–For my own part I thought I should have died it was so dull after your departure. had I not been consoled by Pylades [Giles Taintor] and Orestes [Frank Lathrop] who always made it a point of popping in their *sweet-faces* just as I was on the point of getting a fit of the *blue devils*. . . . the subject of our correspondence must be general. Our letters must "catch the tune of the times" and relate occurrences which happen under the eye of the visitors.

I have been daily in expectation of receiving a letter from you. . . .

My first impression was that you must be indisposed but I am sure this cannot be or I should have heard of it. The idea of your illness being abandoned, I then sought after some other excuse for you.–"He may have forgotten you" says probability. "It can't be possible" says self love. "I won't believe a word of it" says pride. What then can be the reason? He must–he must–be *dead*.–immediately examined the last week's papers and looked at the obituary, with the fearful apprehension of finding it true. I did not however see your name amongst the list of *deaths*.–

But as you can be excused on no other supposition, and I being unwilling an instant to believe that you could be guilty of a neglect so gross, have come to the conclusion that you must be dead. Alas poor John Taintor! I knew him well. He was a gentleman of infinite goodness. I have passed many pleasant hours in his company. I have always delighted with his conversation. He always selected such *interesting* subjects and discanted with such eloquence upon the merits of Bremer Geese and the beauty of sheep but now alas–O dear–it is particularly affecting–I was going in to write your *Epitaph* but knowing that you would wish to have it done in a proper Style, I determined to stop short, and first read all the Epitaphs, Eulogies, Elegies and funeral orations etc. that my Uncle's Library could produce so that I might be the better prepared for the sad & melancholy office.–And unless I hear from you in a day or two I shall certainly send your Epitaph or Elegy to Mr. Charles King [the editor of the *American,* a New York newspaper]. The "American" shall be encircled with a dark line–The Genius of Hartford [Mrs. Sigourney, a poet] shall burden it with her tears. . . .

Now my good friend if you wish to be thought in the land of the living write me a good long letter sealed with your own seal, signed by your own hand, and delivered to the Servant to convey to the Post Office in presence of Adelia and then I will believe that you are still dear Cousin John.

We have no news whatever since in the city it is as warm as a furnace and the beaux and belles look positively like baked apples.–Went to church last Sunday evening with Pylades and Orestes. we never got there till the sermon was half over, and the first object that met my admiring gaze was Miss Hildreth in all her glory. and wonderful to relate such an effect had the power of her charms on Orestes that he kept awake during the sermon. and what was very polite left *me* to walk home with Pylades while he attended Miss Hildreth. a few weeks since I should have exclaimed against this as being very ill manners but when he has had such an excellent example set him by a gentleman that has made the tour of Europe who can blame him? Not I indeed–so I very composedly walked home with the handsomest cre-

ture in New York and consoled my inward man (as Mr. Snodgrass says) with a piece of cake and some milk punch.

Now, John Taintor who do you think that I have been to see? Why no less a personage than Mrs. Stone and such a visit as I had. O Lord what an addition of airs and graces a two storey house a few chairs and carpets, make in some people. I was ushered into the parlor by one of the *fan-sey* and in about two minutes Mrs. Stone made her appearance. well she curtsied and I bowed until we had positively bound ourselves one to the door and the other to the fireplace. and then we both flounced down on the sofa and she commenced giving me a dissertation of the pleasures of a married life and spoke of "dear Mr. Stone" as being the best of husbands and told me how much happiness she had enjoyed since she had entered the married state. (thinks I to myself that's more than your husband will say I suspect.) "And pray" says the lady "what has become of Mr. J. Taintor–has he left town?" I said "yes." "When he called to see me" said Mrs. Stone "I asked for Miss Gibbons why she had not accompanied him" and he said "he positively did not know where she was. he supposed she was at home" but says Mrs. Stone "he was very excusable for he appeared to think of no one but Miss Hildreth." Well said I did Miss Hildreth appear to be equally smitten. Why said the lady to tell you a secret but remember you must not tell Mr. Taintor I think that she admired Giles Taintor the most and what a fine young man Giles is says Mrs. Stone. I assented to everything that she said and took my leave with the full expectation and determination of telling Orestes [Frank Lathrop] and having a good laugh.

I suppose you will be sorry after what I have told you about Miss Hildreth but it will do no good John.–you were a confounded fool to run after her as you did showing so plainly that you were in love with her. when a woman sees her power she always makes use of it and woe betide the gentleman if he is really in love with her. Now your rival stands guilty in Maiden Lane. his indifference piqued the Ladys pride and she determined to exert herself and play the agreeable to him and that he should admire her and she has an succeeded pretty well. you will have to knack under–to Orestes John. there is no salva-tion for you. However nothing more could be expected from you who are always on some *goose* chase or other–.

But I think that Adelia has now got you under very good disci-pline, for the report in New York now is that when Mr. John Taintor arrived in Hartford a certain lady refused to see him on account of his flirtation in New York, that at last after a great deal of entreaty she was induced to relent and consented to see the gentleman. the result of the interview no one knows but only that Mr. T. has given up a visit to his parents in Hampton to stay and appease the ire of the offended fair-one. Further the deponent sayeth not. . . .

But I have written enough nonsense so adieu my dearest friend and believe me your affectionate sister–.

> When o'er my dark and wayward soul
> The clouds of nameless sorrow roll
> When Hope no more her wreath will twine
> And Mem'ry sits at sorrows shrine
> Nor aught to joy my soul can move
> I muse upon a brother's love
>
> When all the world seems cold and stern
> And bids the bosom vainly yearn
> When those we love are lightly changed
> And friendship weeps o'er looks estranged
> I turn from all the pangs I prove
> To hail a Brother's changeless love
>
> And O at shadowy close of even
> When quiet wings the soul to Heaven
> When the long bits of lingering day
> And all its cares are swept away
> Then while my thoughts are rapt above
> Then most I prize my brothers love.[45]

John also received letters from Adelia's little nieces, Elizabeth and Ellen Williams, the daughters of his friend Oliver Ellsworth Williams, who had married Elizabeth Baker Croade, Adelia's sister. They were put up to the following letter by their "aunty" Adelia. Elizabeth, the younger, wrote most of it:

My dear Mr. Taintor. I should not have written you unless Aunty had reminded me of it–Mother has received her dress from New York, which she likes very much, and so do all of us–You told me to tell you how Auntys foot was [Adelia had broken her foot in a fall from a horse], and I will tell you it is a great deal better, and now I have told, you must not ask her, but I suppose you will. To Day Miss Woodbridge and Miss Russ called–I expect to go to Miss Rechers school. I had rather go there then to Miss Rocknells because Emily, and Hariett Ellsworth go–Mr. Ingersall has been out to our house a number of times, and he wants to be introduced to Miss Parsons. I have written Parsons as bad as I can for I dispise the name Pa son. . . . I hope you will come back very soon for it is dull without you. I think you will have a pleasanter time when you return then you had when you were here for our flowers are all in blossom and if you were here we would give you some of them.

[in Ellen's handwriting:] Nature looks beautifull

From your most affectionate friends Ellen and Elizabeth . . . [in their mother's handwriting:] I dont think Nature looks very beautiful do you? Ellen is getting very sentimental[46]

Hannah Gibbons wrote a very long and funny letter to John again a few weeks after her first letter, in June 1829:

. . . I have just returned from a long walk in Broadway and feel as if I should like to take a "six hours nap" but it will not do to be so lazy so instead of going to bed I mean to *hold commune* with my dear cousin and you are compelled to read my nonsense John Taintor not because I have nothing *else* to do but because I have nothing *better*.

you say I must tell you the *news*. why John Taintor you might as well ask me to jump over the moon. news, indeed. people are all as dull as possible. not a marriage or a death. everything remains in Statu quo from our past.

Poor dear Orestes received a letter yesterday saying that his mother was at the point of death and he went with all speed to Springfield. I hope she may recover for it will be almost a death stroke to Lathrop if she should not. O it will be most melancholy for her to leave four children and all so young. To be sure Frank is capable of taking care of his brothers and he is indeed an uncommonly fine young man and with such an example as he is before them the others can scarecely fail of doing well and that will be some comfort to his mother, but

> "Fairer each friend each object than before
> Just as we leave them ne'er to see them more
> Tis this which makes the bitterness of death
> That else were nothing but the loss of breath"

But of all the sorrows which we are here doomed to endure none is so bitter as that occasioned by the stroke of death which separates us from those dear objects to whom nature or friendship had joined our hearts. . . .

I am sad to say John Taintor—but it is not right that I should moralize in this style so I will just take a turn on the piazza and see if I cannot feel better.

Yes I am considerably better. And I will see if I can comply with your request that I would tell you all that is new and interesting.—well then I know of nothing new under the sun except my Aunt's six new dresses and my *blond veil* and the only interesting event that I know of is that I am in *love*. (Methinks I hear you say "that is nothing unusual." but wait a moment John before you say a word.)

Yes I am in love, not like the generality of heroines with a *toothsome* divinity of six and twenty (that is the right age for a romance if I mistake not, with flaxen hair and eyes of heavenly blue, ivory teeth and lips "celestial rosy red." no no preserve me from all such, say I, *my* hero is about fifty. his eyes O the color is a sublime riddle. sometimes I think they are grey and sometimes green. But upon the whole they are more like *boiled gooseberries* than any thing I can liken them too. his teeth, let me see–O yes he has the semblance of once having teeth– and very fine ones I have no doubt. his complexion is that beautiful Canary color which I heard you admire so much. and to crown all he is a widower, wears a red *wig* and is worth two hundred thousand. now you must know he has not yet posed the question. but then he told me I was the most charming girl he ever knew and that he was in pursuit of a wife. (now cousin John that is coming on pretty well I think don't you?) what do you say to it? Shall I blush and look silly and let out yes? or shall I give up two hundred thousand and the hope of soon being a gay widow and all the dear delights of again having my liberty and say the heart-searching word *no*. Now come advise me upon the subject.

Dr. Chatwood introduced the gentleman and advised me to "set my cap" (as he says) "for him," but I cannot decide till I have seen *Dan* [we have no idea to whom she refers–"Dan" is clearly a nickname]. and if I like *him* then adieu to a marble house in Broadway, to equipage, place, and attendants. Yes all farewell. I will be a "bonnie lassie and go campaigning." but if Dan should not be as refined as I expect–O dear–it will be particularly affecting. and if he should not take a fancy to me, and if he should have one Ebenezer [leg] longer than the other and should squint and have false teeth and his mouth asque and to cap the climax be thirty five O dear–what should I do– John Taintor? Why I do positively think that I might be induced to hide my mortification under a red wig. but the old man will live a short-eternity. and that would be the death of me. but you know how highly I think of your judgement. now you shall write me what you think upon the subject. If he would promise to die in six months I might be induced but as it is, heigho!

I have had a long letter from Caroline and she has got stuck in the mud and was obliged to call a *parson* to her assistance. what do you think of that? Now, I say she ought to make quite a romantic adven- ture out of it. but Carry is not given much that way. I think however it is something so entirely new that I intend in the *novel* which I am now writing to make my heroine–get over–neck and shoulders in a *mud puddle* from which she shall be extricated by a Reverend Divine. now it will be something so entirely new, for generally heroines fall into a mur-mer-ing stream or a placid lake from which they are extri- cated by some gallant cavalier, who they afterwards are so silly as to fall in love with and marry. but my Deborah (for that is the name of my heroine) shall get up, box the *par* son's ears and give him a good punch. now that–I say–is like a woman of spirit.–

O I had almost forgotten to tell you that I have become acquainted with an intimate friend of yours and Pylades–Mr. *William Badger*.– Pylades introduced him to me and told me to make myself agreeable. so down I sat and talked for full two hours without cessation, when lo and behold just as I was in the midst of a very sentimental speech which I intended should produce some sensation Mr. Badger exclaimed "I have a most execrable headache." now that was almost beyond mortal forebearance. but when Mrs. Gibbons came in what does my gentleman do but take a seat by her and I was "not favored" with another look the whole evening. but John Taintor to complete the story, when Pylades asked him how he liked Miss Gibbons, what do you think he had to say in my favor? Why only to think he said he thought me *very Pert.*–did you ever hear the like of that? it was too much and if I ever attempt to play the agreeable again may I be *shot.*–

. . . I feel very much worried about Pylades for he has grown pale and thin, and dreadful to relate is losing his appetite. he came and spent the morning with my Aunt and not withstanding all my persua⁓ sions to induce him to eat he would only be prevailed upon to eat a *pan* of hot-Gingercake, which he did sitting in the rocking chair with his Ebenezers crossed. and every now and then I shared a *look* with the *pan* for which *look* I felt much flattered.

but my dear I have extended this letter beyond the bounds of rea⁓ son and still I feel as if I could write twenty more pages of such non⁓ sense. methinks I hear you say "Defend me from reading them." Pray do not be frightened, Cousin John, for a few words more and I have finished. You must make some allowances for my writing such long letters for you must remember that, living so much secluded from the gay world, writing is so pleasant to me, as to pass an hour in substitut⁓ ing a letter and *an answer* ("mark that, Reader") for an agreeable con⁓ versation with my friends.–

. . . After the best calculation our account stands thus–Counting 90 words to the folio, my letters contain four folios each which being multiplied by three brings you in my debt twelve folio or thereabouts, which I trust you will shortly balance.

but lest you should think from my nonsense and abstruse calcula⁓ tions that I am now stricken mad and exclaim "what a noble mind is here overthrown," I will stop short after having assured you of the lasting attachment of Hannah–Gibbons–

PS–I most sincerely sympathize with you on account of Adelia's three dreadful accidents, namely thrown from her horse, broken one of her Ebenezers, and to cap all climax I hear she has grown *PIOUS*. O Lord what is this world coming to?[47]

That same summer John heard again from the peripatetic Kirkman family. They traveled to New York City by way of Lake Erie and Niagara Falls, and after visiting the Taintor-Gibbons-Gilmour friends they went on to Philadelphia, Saratoga Springs, and Boston. Ellen asked in her letter how John and his father liked "the proceedings of the President? quite dispotic I must say. Not liked by his party in Tennessee."[48] We wish we knew John's reply about his own political opinions. Since a lady kept writing him on the subject, he probably gave them.

Once a Small-Town Boy

After John passed his thirtieth birthday he determined to establish himself on his own. He decided on his way of life and how he would support it, settled away from his parents and Hampton, and at last married Adelia Croade. One result of his permanently leaving Hampton was that none of his correspondence after 1829, except the letters he wrote to his father and to his young cousin Henry, remained in the Taintor house. Before he felt he could marry, he had to settle on his work. He wrote his father from Hartford in November 1830:

Dear Father [the only time John addressed Roger this way in all their correspondence],
    . . . I am greatly in doubt what to do. Mr. Marland the Boston agent for buying wool returned by the last packet, and I think there is but little doubt, of the place if I apply for it. But I do not prefer either the voyage, or a residence across the Atlantic.
    I can at any time get into business in Pearl St. [in New York] and with those who are now considered good. But the business is a very uncertain one, and I might regret ever having formed a connexion in it.
    I very much prefer another course which will be equally more prudent and safe and at the same time give me a vast deal more of comfort. I mean placing my money at interest & living prudently and economically on the income. I have arrived at that period of life, when my habits are formed and I have no fears of dissipation, and as for business I can find employment enough, to keep me out of mischief. One thing is certain, I shall never incur expenses that I cannot readily & conveniently meet. I have no doubt I should manage to your entire satisfaction as well as that of myself–
    If this suggestion shall meet your views and you can give me 10,000 dollars, you can place it wherever you may choose and the principal shall forever remain untouched. . . . Your money and confidence shall not be misplaced in me.

John's letter was unusual for him not only in the familiarity with which he addressed his father, but because in it he volunteered to help his young cousin Henry to find a job, and ended by saying "if Mother wants anything from New York you can say so in your letter & I will get it." He told his father that "Mrs. Croade and Adelia are near me, and send their respects to you and Mother."[49]

Three months later, in February 1831, prior to their marriage which would take place in May, John and his fiancée, Adelia, wrote a joint letter to Roger and Nabby Taintor. (Roger died that April, before the wedding, and Nabby died in November.) John wrote first, "I sent to day by the stage to Windham in charge of Wm Badger of Philad. a ban box containing my Mothers cloak and a cap Adelia has sent her." He went on with news that even distressed us a century and a half later: "Hannah Gibbons is very sick Paterson N. J. with inflammation on the brain, and will not probably recover."

Adelia's appended note to her future mother-in-law is much more formal: "I should have enclosed you a note my dear Mrs. Taintor in your cloak last night, begging your acceptance of the cap which accompanied it. . . . I hope you will like the form of the cap, & will bear in mind, that though the gift is small, it is accompanied with the best wishes of the giver for your welfare."[50]

John Taintor married Adelia Croade and established himself in the city of Hartford. He made the breeding of superior animals for the American market his life's work. His animals–cattle, sheep, and fowl–were always kept in Hampton.

The flavor of as much as we have of John's correspondence and therefore of his business life is redolent of the barnyard despite his residence in Hartford. Typical of Frank Rotch's letters is: "I do not remember whether the Rodman's Heifers had calved when I wrote you last–Dulcibella is perfect symmetry and has a very superior heifer calf but does not give more than 6 quarts in the 24 hours!"[51] Henry Terry writes of game fowls: "The birds all thrive finely and have grown fast since you sent them. I had white fowls before and think them much better on account of the superior size of the eggs."[52] From William Gibbons about a new cow: "Drusa has arrived in fine condition and I have her in my possession all safe–she is a fine Beautiful animal . . . she is as white in every respect as Mr. Hall's Lily."[53] Oliver Ellsworth Williams writes, "Our peaches are in perfection. . . . I shall in all probability have a fine saddle horse before you get here. Now come up and we'll have some cider."[54] John supported his city residence and his life as a stock breeder by investing the money Roger settled on him, as well as the money he inherited from his parents when they died. By the time he himself died, in 1862, he was a very wealthy man.

The relationship between the farms and cities of John Taintor's world was complicated. Experience flowed in both directions. Cities were beacons of opportunity for many, although outside the experience of all but a few. Then as now, there were country people who looked on city life as hell. And the vast majority of all Americans continued to live in rural small towns. John Taintor saw himself as contributing his talents to American agriculture and thus to the improvement of small-town life. But he was very careful to do so from a city.

CHAPTER 7

THE VITAL CENTER

∽

*"If you was agoing to pay Cash I think you may do
as well here as any store in this State."[1]*

The best place to find Dan Bulkeley was his store in the middle of
Hampton village. It was in his home, and it was also the post office.
Throughout the 1820s and 1830s this busy, curious, ingratiating
man–brother and uncle to the Taintors–was at the hub of Hampton's communication with an expanding America. A figure in the town's
changing politics, Dan Bulkeley's trade reached an ever-shifting circle of
suppliers and customers near and far.

Dan Bulkeley was born in Colchester on March 20, 1784, the eleventh
surviving child and youngest son among the thirteen children of Capt. John
Bulkeley and his wife, Judith Worthington. He was five years old when his
sister Nabby married Roger Taintor, a teenager when the Taintors moved
to Hampton and his sister Judith married Solomon. He was twenty-seven
when his only younger sibling, Harriet, married Samuel Moseley in Hampton in 1811. Two years after that Dan married Phoebe Burnett of Hampton–the daughter of James and Chloe Burnett. James Burnett, frequently a
selectman in the early part of the century was, along with Dan's brothers-in-law, a leading figure in the town.

By 1817 (quite possibly before that but there is no evidence), Dan
Bulkeley ran a store in Hampton for a firm called Taintors & Bulkeley
(Roger and Solomon Taintor and Dan Bulkeley were the partners).[2] In 1821
he bought one-half acre and a house on "the east side of the highway by
the meeting house."[3] It is tempting to think this was the same piece of land
on which the Hampton General Store now stands, across the street from
the Congregational church.

We know about Dan's life because when he died in 1842, all his papers went to his executor and nephew, Henry G. Taintor, who lived in the Taintor house next to the church. Henry kept Dan's papers–all the correspondence during his years as postmaster from 1820 to 1836, as well as bills, receipts, and accounts from his multiple enterprises–because Henry hoped (in vain as it turned out) to realize some money for Dan's widow and children. The many facets of Dan Bulkeley's career and much about the life of people who lived in and left Hampton in the third and fourth decades of the nineteenth century are preserved in those papers.

In Dan Bulkeley's Store

Dan's store chamber was dark by today's standards. Perhaps it was stove-heated in the winter. It probably smelled of wood, spices, brine, and alcohol. The customers who came and went could catch a whiff of damp wooden barrels of pickles, rum, molasses, and gin. Dry goods were stored on shelves and in wooden boxes. Those who came into the store spent some time looking, thinking about purchases and sales, and talking with whoever else was there. Dan or his clerk fetched what a customer wanted to see or buy. They conducted business from behind a counter and kept a daybook handy in which to write each transaction.

Dan had several young men as clerk-apprentices at different times, who earned their keep and sometimes a bit more learning how to be storekeepers. His nephew Albert came down from Williamstown and served as a clerk in the late 1820s. There was another clerk named Albert from Coventry in 1830, who had to leave when his father wanted him to "come home as soon as convenient."[4] Solomon Taintor's son Henry worked in the store in 1831. Dan's own son Andrew clerked in the late 1830s and, when he had nothing else to do, scribbled over the outsides of some of his father's letters, doing sums and practicing his signature.

The store was a quiet place; generally, the loudest sounds were people's voices and their shoes on the wooden floor. In the summertime there were a lot of flies and a few mosquitoes buzzing around–there were no screens on doors or windows. Artificial light came from oil lamps used sparingly because oil was expensive. Customers went to the window or out the door if they required more light to match thread, see a calico pattern, or read the normal small print of newspapers.

Dan Bulkeley's post "office" was business he did in his store. He probably had a single box on his counter or a few small boxes on the wall for mail. There were no postage stamps–indeed, the word "stamp" meant what we think of as "rubber stamps" today, not gummed pieces of paper that are stuck onto other pieces of paper. Dan collected fees for mailing letters and he kept track of those fees, at least a portion of which he had to send on to Washington. He wrote the amount paid on each letter–he had no "Hampton" cancellation stamp. People expecting mail or newspapers came in to pick them up. They had no private boxes. When a letter arrived, Dan would try to get word to the addressee through friends, neighbors, or kin who came to the store.

Dan Bulkeley's store dealt in general merchandise. His early accounts show he bought "nankeen, lump sugar, dimity, walnuts . . . , grass seed, and India cotton" from G. Abbe & Co. in New York. He imported reams of paper from Edmund Badger in Philadelphia. He bought hogsheads of molasses. He retailed candles and bought tallow (the raw material for candles) and flax seed to export. He retailed cotton cloth made in nearby towns by the Sprague Manufacturing Company and the Danielson Manufacturing Company. He shipped cranberries by the bushel to Charles Taintor in Windham and he sold Hampton cranberries by the barrel to Norwich and New York merchants.[5]

He retailed hard liquor. A New York merchant firm shipped "1 hogshead St. Croix Rum 107 gals, for $101.65; 2 barrels pure Spirits [pure alcohol] 40 gals + 39 gals, for $37.03. Sent on Sloop Jupiter, Capn. Tyler." The *Jupiter* sailed to Norwich, and Dan sent a wagon to pick up the Bulkeley consignment and cart it to Hampton. The sellers warned that "The pure spirits is as good as could be had, but there is more of it than should be put with the rum which is not so high flavoured as it is some times, but is of very choice quality otherwise."[6]

He also retailed gin. Peregrine Terry, of Enfield, offered to supply "Friend Buckely . . . with from four to Seven Barrels of Gin Manufactured about six or 8 months ago of Our best Kind. the Gin is in our Store at home–and if you Should waunt any and have teams agoing to Springfield this Season I thought it would be handy for them to take." But by the end of 1829 Mr. Terry had "gone temperance," and his clerk wrote to Dan Bulkeley "we do not manufacture any Gin neither do we expect to any more."[7] Dan found other suppliers.

He imported whiskey from the same New York firm from which the rum came.[8] Wine came from Providence, from a supplier who also sold sugar. All the wine and liquors came to the store in barrels but individual customers bought small quantities. Dan inquired of a merchant in nearby Willington about bottles to serve as smaller containers. It took him a while to get them. (Everything took awhile.) Nearly six months elapsed before he heard that "in about four weeks from this they will sell you the bottles. . . ."[9]

Dan Bulkeley also carried candy, imported from New York from R. L. & A. Stuart, Patent Steam Refined Candy Company, who advertised that they had a "Steam Engine and other powerful machinery, for . . . manufacturing Candy, Sugar Plums &c. . . . Also–Superior Double and Treble Refined Loaf Sugar. The Treble is in point of color and quality unequalled in this country or Europe, purified by Steam without the use of Clay or Blood." One Bulkeley store order included "200 Lumps, 400 Lemon Lumps, 200 Barleys, 100 Sugar Candies, 100 Hoarhound. Candies, $5.00."

Delivery of candy, even of such modern manufacture, depended on ships that could be stopped by ice or other natural hazards. And everything ground to a halt in epidemics. In September 1832, Stuart could not send Dan's order on time because "we closed our Store on the 6th of July on account of the Cholera, and reopend our Store day before yesterday, our hands not having all returned yet. . . ."[10] Delivery was never certain. In the winter of 1835, a sugar merchant explained, "I have not one hundred pounds in the world, & do not expect any soon as the [Narragansett] river is Closed [by ice] as far down as Bristol & Sugar is scarce & high, so that I do not think that I shall buy any untill the river opens, which may not be untill the middle or last of February."[11]

Dan Bulkeley carried some patent medicines in his store, items usually sold by traveling salesmen and by medicine shows. He introduced "Doctor Simmons Ointment for ruptures" in 1830. The salesman "was directed to leave it on sale only–as [Doctor Simmons] said it had been proved and was sure to perform a Cure. . . . One or two Credible people in each place try it and if no Cure no pay–but pay if a Cure. where it has been tried in some Cases they would get the breach almost healed and not strong enough. They would fling by [throw away] the truss and it would by a Straine break out again. . . . When using it they must be Careful not lift hard to bring it to a Strain."

Later he wrote, "If you have let any persons take it on trial, your Conditions I presume were that if it Cured they should pay $6 a bottle whether did or did not use an entire Bottle. As soon as you find that it will, or will not Cure please inform me about it. If it will not sell in these parts I must return it this Spring, as it is takeing a great run at the South & West."[12]

The deaths of his brothers-in-law, Solomon and Roger Taintor, and the withdrawal of their capital from his store in 1827 and 1831 changed Dan's business. But he only gradually changed the ways he had learned from his kinfolk. The store stock changed as well. As the years went by, Dan carried more and more household supplies and imported foodstuffs. "Sal aeratus [baking soda], flour, and sal nitre [baking powder]" for cooking, as well as tea and snuff became popular necessities. One shipment from a Providence supplier included one hundred pounds of salt haddock, one hundred pounds of salt codfish, one hundred pounds sal aeratus, a barrel of sugar, and a barrel of flour, forty-five and one-half pounds of soap, boxed, twenty-three pounds of starch, a dozen palm leaf hats, and a large box of tobacco. (Dan would take delivery in Norwich "the dangers of the Seas only excepted."[13])

One of Dan's store accounts shows the beginning of another kind of change when Rufus Burnham bought "2 harness, 4 scythes, 1 horse collar, 1 toaster iron & . . . 2 [skeins] cotton yarn."[14] The horse collar was a relatively new and expensive item, imported into Hampton. Its purchase shows that Rufus Burnham was changing his farm's power equipment from oxen to horses, a shift that made him more dependent on skills and goods not locally available. Wooden ox yokes were manufactured in most small towns, but horse collars required more specialized skills than small communities could support. Using horses also made Rufus Burnham more dependent on merchants like Dan Bulkeley for essential equipment. In his own mind Rufus probably figured that horses were cheaper to feed, faster, and more versatile than oxen.

Rural men and women gradually became more dependent on such products that they did not manufacture. The signs of change were slow to appear—they are much more visible to us who know what resulted. Many were invisible to Dan. By the 1830s, Dan's store began to stock locally made plows and plowshares in standard sizes, an indication that farmers were no longer ordering plows direct from the artisans who made them. Dan's suppliers were becoming specialist manufacturers.

In those same years Dan's records first mention his carrying garden seed in bulk, and retailing it in "papers"—small envelopes not unlike those used today. People usually saved seed from crops the year before. Retailing seed was a new development based on the growth of city nurseries. Large quantities of seed for market crops were also becoming available in small-town stores. For example, Adams White, who ran the Windham County Bank in Brooklyn, Connecticut, but who also farmed, ordered six bushels of blue seed potatoes for planting and six bushels of red top rye seed from Dan in 1840. Twenty years earlier he would have kept back some potatoes for seed, and saved the bushels of rye himself.[15]

Stove pipe was another new product in Bulkeley's store in the 1830s. Cast-iron stoves and kitchen ranges were the modern household appliances of the day. They replaced open hearth cooking, fireplace ovens, and fireplaces themselves. But stoves required pipe connections to chimneys, and Dan Bulkeley, as the local purveyor of this new necessity, had to find specialized suppliers—who were not always dependable. For example, one wrote from Windham, "I have not made enny pipe for two monts or more on the Account of sickness. We shall have pipe of all descriptions in a bout two weeks & shall be abble to supply you & your neighbors. I shall probly be at your plaice soon."[16]

Specialist merchants in large towns retailed the stoves themselves. Coal, just beginning to come from Pennsylvania on the new railroads, was not yet available in Hampton for stove fuel in place of wood.[17]

Butter, along with cheese, had been a major export from Hampton when the Taintors went into business there. Small farmers with a few cows made it, merchants collected it and sold it to city folk. But thirty years later, a Norwich wholesaler warned Dan Bulkeley: "Sir about the Butter if Very Superior is worth about 15 cents but butter Made in May is Very often Not quite No 1 . . . if you Send the butter it must be Very Nice."[18] City merchants by the 1830s could rely on better, more standard-ized, and larger quantities of butter from new, specialized dairy farms.

Dan Bulkeley still bought butter in Hampton, but it was from Hampton farm women who earned "butter and egg" money by selling small quantities to him. Dan retailed the butter, eggs, and cheese to people in town. Families like that of lawyer Joseph Prentis no longer farmed. Their work in town was specialized and they *bought* local farm products to eat. At the same time many of those products no longer found markets out of town.[19]

Another letter signaled one of the most important changes in his busi-ness, one that affected Dan Bulkeley more and more in the years after the Taintors withdrew their capital. He received it in 1831 from a bookseller's clerk who wrote, "if you was agoing to pay Cash I think you may do as well here as any store in this State. I know how you are situated: as you have to take barter for your pay you must pay the same."[20] Large book debts and the exchange reckoning system that had been the commonplaces of Roger and Solomon Taintor's merchant business, of Nathaniel Martin's artisanal accounting—and of commerce everywhere—were beginning to go out of style. In the more complex mercantile and financial world of grow-ing cities and commercial centers, business people demanded cash or its equivalent. Barter and book debt continued in the backwaters of the econ-omy for more than a century, but even there they were used in a new way.

By the mid-1830s, Dan Bulkeley asked for and received cash from many of his retail customers. He also began to treat all barter transactions as cash sales. By then most of his store's business was very small transac-tions and many of his retail customers were women, who brought in items they had made—stockings, socks, silk, and butter, as well as eggs—and who wanted to buy other goods immediately. For example, in a typical transac-tion one day in August 1836, Mrs. Daniel Ashley brought in three pounds of butter, which she "sold" for sixty cents (the clerk credited it to her on the daybook). She then "bought" one pound of raisins for sixteen cents, a quarter-pound of cinnamon for eight cents, a quarter-pound of pepper for eight cents, a quarter-pound of tea for twenty-one cents, and a pint of gin for six cents. That only added up to fifty-nine cents. So she "bought" *one cracker,* valued at one penny, to make up the sixty cents. Because such small-scale barter transactions were the core of his business, Dan accumulated little capital and made no profit as a small-town storekeeper.

In a conscious effort to change small-town business ways, Dan Bulkeley joined with other storekeepers and merchants to stop the long-respectable custom of door-to-door peddling of products like patent medicines. Peddlers were small-time merchants who carried their goods on their backs or in wagons. They had been welcome in the developing economies of newly settled communities, to which they brought much needed manufactured items before there were merchants with the capital to establish stores. But by the beginning of the 1830s, Dan Bulkeley was helping to form the "Windham County Association for the Suppression of Pedlars Hawkers & Petty Chapmen." He was elected to its board of directors.[21]

Merchants all over the state, not only in Windham County, were organizing opposition to peddlers, bringing cases against them into courts, and pressing for laws to prohibit peddling and hawking.[22] An Ashford merchant, for example, who went to court against a peddler asked Dan Bulkeley and Samuel Moseley to attend the trial in order "to show as bold a front as posable on the occasion."[23] Dan Bulkeley circulated an agreement not to trade with peddlers, of which a Brooklyn merchant wrote, "I am of opinion that [merchants] might by proper effort benefit themselves very materially by combining together, in other respects as well as in suppressing peddling. This object alone would be worth much time and effort. If all the merchants would stir themselves I am of opinion that we might get an act prohibiting peddling any kind of goods. This would add very much to our business and increase our profits."[24]

Local chambers of commerce grew out of organizations like the Windham County Association for the Suppression of Pedlars Hawkers & Petty Chapmen. Dan Bulkeley and his fellow merchants were using what were still new rights of self-government to join together and take action in their own interests. It was a step beyond the ways Roger and Solomon Taintor had done business.

Exporting Hampton's Produce

Dan (in partnership with Charles Grosvenor of Pomfret, a family connection) exported some agricultural goods from Hampton, mostly grain and animals. He had a hard time finding and keeping markets because the quality of Hampton produce was declining, and the quantity was inadequate for growing urban markets. But he kept trying, because he needed to bring in money; Hampton, like other small towns, was never completely self-sufficient, and purchasing power for imports was always necessary.

Even barley, a less valuable crop than wheat, was hard to get rid of. In 1828, the Hampden Brewery in Massachusetts asked Dan Bulkeley for four hundred to five hundred bushels of "first quality" barley to make beer. However, four days later they canceled the order: "... since we wrote you ... we have been to New York and have purchased a large quantity. ... We shall therefore not want you to purchase any for us." Here was a new problem. Potential users of Hampton crops, like the brewery, wanted standardized quality that could come, they warned, only from "good substantial Farmers" who produced a single crop.[25] Even if a small-town merchant like Dan Bulkeley could locally put together a sufficient quantity of sufficient quality, buyers like the brewery could not be trusted to wait. They might cancel at any moment because they were now able to get large quantities and good quality from city warehouses.

The small scale of Dan Bulkeley's export business is typified by a transaction one summer in the 1830s. A Coventry man wrote that "Mr. Mitchel wants them fine Cows if he can have them cheap and wants them left with you with the lowest price and he will call and take them soon."[26] And Dan recorded that he "Bot of Jonathan Hovey 100 Bushels Corn, 2 Yokes of Walking Oxen, 100 Bushels Oats, 5 Cowes, 40 Pine Logs on Amasa Clarks Land, 8 head of Young Calfs ... 24 Sheep, Also all the hay [on Hovey's] old farm." The next summer he also bought a one horse wagon, an ox cart, seventy sheep and lambs, and a plow from Hovey.[27] Except for the sheep and cows, there was no longer anything a Hampton farmer like Hovey produced that could be sold outside Hampton.

But as Hampton's commercial agricultural produce declined, the quantity of manufactured products from Hampton's farms began to increase. Dan Bulkeley accumulated hundreds of dozens of hand-knitted socks and stockings, dozens of mittens, and thousands of skeins of silk and other threads from the town's farm women by his store's barter transactions. These became Hampton's major exports in the 1830s and continued until machine-made threads and knitted goods became widely available in the 1850s.

Dan's dealings with Jacob Corlies & Son, Quaker wholesalers in New York City, are a good example. In May 1829, the Corlies firm reported having "182½ doz. Woolen Socks, 4 doz Woolen Stockings, 44½ doz. Childrens Stockings, 72½ doz Woolen Mittins, 30 lb. Woolen Yarn, 3410 Skeins Sewing Silk, 6800 Skeins in a Trunk (all the woolens in 9 boxes)" on hand from Bulkeley & Grosvenor (probably not all from Hampton). Then they reported "Stockings, Socks &c continue verry dull. Some of your merchants sold their Socks this spring at 16/- per doz. . . . Others could not find any body to make them an offer. We shall take such care of yours that there will be no danger of the moth."

By the fall of the next year, 1830, Corlies wrote, "Socks are selling quicker than last year. . . . We have sold one entire box for thee—together with most of the Childrens Stockings. . . . We are in hopes of selling in a few weeks more amount than thee owes us—if thee has any good quality Boys Stockings at home we can sell them immediately—business fore the last month has been verry good better than for several years."

At the end of 1831 the firm wrote Dan Bulkeley that "we can inform thee that our market is quite short of woolen hosiery of every kind. We ourselves have not a single doz. of Stockings, or Socks, on hand. We have orders for over 100 doz. woolen Socks—and should be glad to receive all thee can send us. . . . Hosiery will not be worth within 30 pr cnt. next spring of the prices it now sells for—thee will get from four to six shillings p. doz more for Socks, this month and next, than thee can sell them for next spring. . . . Thee may do well to buy up some from the other merchants provided they do not ask too much advance." New York merchants were gradually developing "seasons" for particular kinds of goods. And they were beginning to tell the manufacturers, in advance, what they would be willing to buy at what seasons. They no longer dealt simply and directly with the haphazard appearance of manufactured goods on their local markets.[28]

In Philadelphia, at least one merchant was already clear by 1831 about controlling the flow of goods on a seasonal basis. "The Hose should now be in this Market in order to have good sales made," he insisted, complaining "the consignors of this description of goods are universally too late in getting them to market—in a few days our season of Sales will be over and they must then remain over liable to moths and other injuries."[29]

Dan's New York sock business expanded. He continued his personal relationship with Corlies, who kept him informed about the New York scene, writing in 1832, "We have continued in town all summer [despite the cholera epidemic]. The health of the city is such at present, that any country merchant would be perfectly safe in coming to it. There are many here at present and every day adds to their number." Later he wrote, "We can sell all thee will send us, and at such prices as will please thee. . . ."

Finally, in 1834, the relationship ended. A Norwich relative wrote to Dan Bulkeley "You are probably aware of the [sudden] death of Jacob Corlies. I saw him well last week in N.York."[30] But Dan still had hopes for exporting Hampton manufactures. He was an indefatigable entrepreneur, and when the sock business did not serve he was ready with another product.

The Silk Business

Women in northeastern Connecticut had been producing small quantities of silk and spinning it into thread since the 1760s. The center of sericulture was the town of Mansfield (next door to Hampton), which produced silk worms, grew mulberry trees to feed the worms, processed cocoons, and spun silk filaments into thread. Production had increased very slowly.

The making of good quality woolen and silk clothing depended on a large supply of silk thread. Dan Bulkeley knew that most clothing was made of wool, and the best sewing thread for wool was silk. And his newspapers told him that millions of dollars' worth of silk goods and thread were imported into the country each year, some of it in the "China trade," but most of it from France and Italy. He was aware that a growing trade deficit was creating economic problems–Europe had reduced its buying of American exports after the end of the Napoleonic Wars, so there was less cash available to pay for European silk. Dan was part of the result in the 1820s, when interest in the possibility of sizable commercial production of American silk spread throughout the country.

At the same time farmers were looking for new and profitable crops, particularly in "older" parts of the country like Hampton, where soil was becoming exhausted and competition was eroding the markets for traditional produce. The domestic production and manufacture of silk seemed to offer the possibility of profit to farmers, employment to many, and reduction of the growing overseas trade deficit. In 1828, silk producers in Windham and Tolland Counties of Connecticut petitioned the Congress of the United States for direct federal government support for the silk industry.[31]

Government committees–in several states as well as in Congress–studied the possibilities of silk production, collected testimony and expert opinion, and published reports, manuals, and guides. Congress ordered the Secretary of the Treasury to collect information about the growth and manufacture of silk in all parts of the United States, and the Secretary published his report in 1828 as a "Manual in relation to the Growth and Manufacture of Silk Adapted to the Different Parts of the Union." Six thousand copies were printed. At the end of the manual, "not received until after this sheet of the Manual was put in type," was a communication on the use of a mill in the manufacture of raw silk "by Daniel Bulkeley, Esq. of Hampton, Windham County, Connecticut."[32]

At least as early as 1826, Dan Bulkeley exported several thousand skeins of silk thread from Hampton.[33] He was instrumental in the growth of silk manufacture in the town, and he played a part in its spread in the United States in the 1830s. Barely had the congressional manual been published when his words were being quoted back at him in letters: "A communication in the Manual published in 1828 from Daniel Bulkeley Esq of Hampton . . . States that We have a small establishment for spinning by Water with a machine similar to a throsttle frame of a Cotton Mill &c, and . . . the silk so spun is much superior to that done by hand."[34] People began to regard him as an authority.

In October that same year a man wrote to him from Philadelphia:

> Will you be good enough on receipt of this to find a woman who is a first rate hand at reeling silk to come to Philadelphia if she be willing to engage for four or six months certain at one to two dollars per week (as you may bargain) besides her travelling Expenses. In case you engage a person please write me when she may be expected to leave home and direct her when she arrives here to call on me at 112 Market St.
>
> The Lady will be employed in a manner altogether pleasant and comfortable to her by the Gentlemen at whose request I trouble you. An effort is making by a few gentlemen here to draw the attention of our Citizens to the general use of American Silk, the which will be materialy promoted by your immediate attention to this request. Will you be kind enough to make an advance if necessary to the person coming in from 10 to 15 Dollars which amount I will immediately remit you. . . .[35]

Reeling the silk from cocoons in near-boiling water was one of the several complex and delicate operations in silk manufacture—the reason the Philadelphia man was willing to pay a premium for someone skilled.

The whole tedious process of reeling, throwing or "throwsting" the silk, dyeing, and spinning it demanded a fine hand and eye. Women often took up silk manufacture because men with more, or other, skills and jobs were unwilling. From childhood, girls were taught fine motor skills involving sewing and the handling of thread not taught to boys. Silk-making offered women the possibility of independent income (as, of course, did much of the new industrial work for similar reasons). Because the production was tedious, a single "manufacturer" produced little, averaging not more than forty to sixty skeins in a year.[36] A merchant in Norwich sent a diploma as a reward to a Miss Black, "the young lady who made the *hundred sks.* of white silk" Dan had sold his firm.[37] Those engaged in the silk business wanted to recognize and encourage such extraordinary achievement.

Dan Bulkeley's advertisement in the *Windham County Advertiser*, November 27, 1832.

If women did most of the manufacturing work, men did the farm work of silk production. One wrote Dan Bulkeley from Philadelphia looking for a market for his agricultural produce, "for the cacoons of Silk worms. . . . I have resided for about 15 Mos. past in Smyrna Del. and having Nothing particular to attend to, I raised a few thousand of the worms. It excited the attention of the farmers generally, and more enquiries were put to me respecting the pecuniary advantage than I could answer, not having that in view. Whatever information you can give respecting this matter will be thankfully received. . . . The Mulberry grows very luxuriently in Delaware and if I thought I could be compensated for my expense & trouble I think I would turn my attention to the Cultivation of the mulberry."[38]

The first step in producing silk was to raise silkworms, whose cocoons were the raw material. But if farmers started producing cocoons and silk, asked a Massachusetts correspondent, "will it be profitable? . . . Or, in other words, is it probable that Filatures [manufacturing concerns] will be estab-lished for the spinning of Silk, & preparing it for exportation?"[39]

Dan Bulkeley and many of his correspondents went into the business of selling silkworms and their eggs: "I acknowledge the receipt of . . . some silk worms, without a day's delay. They hatched . . . and are now feeding vigorously." To grow silk worms the hopeful entrepreneurs needed mul-berry trees—especially the Chinese white mulberry—on which the worms could munch. So Dan went into another agribusiness: the mulberry tree business. But then he had problems.[40]

A customer picked up an order and took it to his upper New York State home:

The trees had been delivered with your directions. But from some cause or other we did not find the trees in that healthy state we had so fondly hoped. We made no stop at N.Y. but put them on board the boat & had them home the next morning. The roots were immediately wet and put under ground. We ploughed our ground and three of us went forthwith to setting them out. They have all been pruned and manured in the best manner we were able. The 3 bundles of smaller trees I believe are generally alive & healthy but from the 7 hundred larger trees our gloomy foreboding have been too truly realized. Many of them I cut to within a foot of the ground & found them dry and black at the pith extending nearly to the bark. . . . I do not think the trees to be of the age and vigour in growth I had expected. Nor were they put up [packaged] in so secure a manner as might have tended more to their safety.[41]

Along with such common problems of the nursery business, Dan also briefly engaged in the speculative boom in a particular type of mulberry tree, the *morus multicaulis*.[42] He grew thousands of seedlings and sold them. The bubble burst shortly after an 1842 auction in North Windham, Connecticut, at which "two trees of one year's growth sold for $106 and $100 each."[43] Such prices were beyond any possibilities for recovery from the sale of finished silk. Dan Bulkeley himself did not ever get more than twenty-five cents each for such trees. Nor did he long stay in the tree business. He soon concentrated on selling mulberry *seed,* and let his customers start from scratch.[44]

Although he was regarded as an authority, Dan himself hoped to improve silk manufacture with help from those who in his view were the real authorities—experienced European silk weavers. He made contact with Charles Dubouchet in Paris, who wrote back, however, with an agenda of his own: "I again repeat to you that I am not a weaver of silk stuffs, but only a spinner and a silk thrower for preparing silk to weave. Being resolved to depart from France . . . and being sollicited to give the preference to the state of Talahassee, where the lands of General Lafayette who makes me an advantage, are situated, I come to beg of you . . . to tell me with the frankness which you already have shown to me in your letter, What are the resources which that state can offer for me and my family in exercising my industrie, favored by a letter from the General."[45]

With silk, as with so many of Dan's enterprises, all was not smooth sailing. His correspondence saves the voices of those who proclaimed the reasons for his failures. "There is returned 24 bunches containing 500 skeins each, one bunch of 450. . . ." wrote Henry Clark. "The reason that the silk dont sell better is that all the merchants buy by the pound, and your silk wont hold out to sell in that way. Another reason is that a good deal of American silk has been sold one cent per skein at auction in NYork. . . . The NYork market strange as it may seem governs the whole western States and even Kentucky and further South."[46]

Strong prejudice against American silk continued to be a problem, especially from the tailors and milliners who made clothes for wealthy city folk and who found a marketable snob appeal in European threads and fabrics. And the colors required were sometimes difficult to dye. At first, Dan could sell only the darks–black, dark blue, dark green, dark "snuff brown," and dark red. White, too, was salable. By the mid-1830s, however, he began to get orders for light green, crimson, scarlet, purple, light blue, pink, and even yellow.

Then Edmund Badger, whose wife ran a millinery shop, warned from Philadelphia about yet another difficulty: "Dr Sir! Mrs Badger wishes to purchase a quantity of very fine Blue, Black, Glossy silk spun over and slack twisted wound in Hanks of ¼lb in each hank. But it must be free from Nots."[47]

And Thomas Gibson wrote in some annoyance from Ohio, "Not long since I bot. a small lot of American Silk to assort up colors which I cannot easily do in Italian without getting a heavier stock than I need & the silk when I bought it appeared well, but it turns out most miserably. Soon as we open and commence retailing from it, we find it gets into an inextricable snarl & we begin to feel that we shall do well if we get our money back that we paid."[48] The "throwsting" and the spinning processes both made knots and snarls possible, and only very skilled manufacturers–or newly invented expensive machinery–eliminated them from American silk.

Dan did have the satisfaction that one of his largest customers, a Providence merchant who took thousands of skeins of silk a year into the late 1830s, wrote, "I would remark that the silk I have had of you is as good as that I get from any where & that there is no one that I should prefer dealings with in the article to yourself."[49] This was, however, the only written praise he received in all his years in the silk business.

The problem he faced–and it was a growing problem for small-town manufacturers in the 1830s and 1840s–was one of scale. Dan's Hampton manufacturers were craftspeople, unable to compete with machine-made standardized goods available from bigger places. But Dan Bulkeley did not see all that; he continued to collect and export silk from Hampton and to sell mulberry trees and seed until the depression of 1839–41 and his own ill health and death in 1842. Raw silk production disappeared from America shortly thereafter when an epidemic blight killed the mulberry trees.

Chasing Debtors

Dan Bulkeley, like Roger and Solomon Taintor, granted credit in order to do business. And like his brothers-in-law, Dan pursued recalcitrant debtors across the country and across the years when they did not pay up. No amount of money was "too small" to forgive or forget.

Unlike the Taintors, Dan rarely made money chasing the people who owed him. In 1824, for example, he had one of his debtors, Schuyler Chamberlin, put into jail in Brooklyn, Connecticut, until he paid. But lawyer Joseph Prentis had to pay on Dan's behalf "eleven dollars for his support . . . a prisoner in gaol at the suit of Taintors & Bulkeley." A month later, Dan paid ten dollars more to support Chamberlin in jail.[50] Chamberlin's whole debt had been for $13.50, with interest, which he had owed for five years. When Dan had him jailed, Chamberlin's revenge was taking the "poor prisoners oath" so Dan had to pay much more to support him in jail than the amount of the debt.

Dan pursued debtors out of Hampton as well as those who stayed in town. He used his franking privilege as a postmaster and his fellowship with other postmasters to collect debts or find out if there was any chance a debtor could pay. Most correspondent postmasters willingly provided this information, and some offered help.[51]

All the debts Dan Bulkeley tried to collect were small, at least from our vantage point. The story of the most complicated of Dan's efforts–to collect $21.58 from James Woodmansee–shows how he went about it. First he had to find the man. He heard he was in Lockport, Pennsylvania, so he wrote to the postmaster there. The very elderly postmaster reported from that remote frontier place that Woodmansee had "a large Family of small Children" on a "small tract of wild Land." He "had a most distressed hard time to begin in the Woods" but now had "a tolerable Stock of young Cattle & Sheep." Although Woodmansee was "infirm" and had an "aged Father" who "now draws a Pension from the UStates [he had been a soldier in the Revolution] of about 96 dol a year or they would not have Survived their great hardships," the postmaster thought that "with an Indulgence . . . they might pay" what Woodmansee owed Dan.

With this hope, Dan made his first effort to collect the eleven-year-old debt. He sent Woodmansee's note to another postmaster to give to a collector. The collector's postmaster replied in turn that "Mr Woodmansee confessd judgment but has not payd as yet and I do not know how soon he will but I trust as soon as he can." Two more years passed, during which Dan sent Jonathan Burnett, one of his wife's kin, to Pennsylvania to check on Woodmansee.[52] Then (it was now at least thirteen years since Woodmansee had contracted the debt) Dan made a second effort with another collector, also without luck. But this second collector had a brother in a neighboring Pennsylvania county who offered to act as Dan's agent in the matter. Another year passed before Dan heard from this agent that Woodmansee had in fact paid "all but a small balance of your demand against him which he thinks you will in consideration of the loss he avers to have sustained in the affair release without further repayment. The balance remaining unpaid is $1.10. . . . Mr W wishes me to say to you he is poor & hopes you will consider him."

Finally, eighteen years after he had contracted the debt, Woodmansee's payment of forty-two dollars (including interest) went not to Dan but to Rapelye & Purdy, New York merchants, who credited it to Dan Bulkeley's account.[53] The finale of this convoluted tale of debt collection came in 1837, when the last agent in the matter wrote Dan Bulkeley for help in collecting a debt of his own.[54]

Dan saved his discouraging letters from debtors; they are not cheerful reading. Among them was one who reported, "It is imposible for me to pay any thing at present the situation of my family is such that I can scarce earn enough to feed them and beside that I am expecting to be Carried to Jail in A few Days on an execution in the Sherifs hands as I have no means to pay any part of it."[55]

Another, a shoemaker, wrote that he was "sorry that you took the trouble and made me the trouble of suing me, making cost does not pay debts." He acknowledged his debt but argued that "the circumstances of my Family have been such that it was imposible for me to do more than suport them," and promised "to do something for you soon." He proposed, since "I dont get any Money . . . I will let you have some shoes. I want you should let it rest as it is a few weeks till I am better able (for I am now confined with the Rheumatism) and then I will make you few pairs and bring over to you." He concluded by warning, "if you press matters I must go to jail which will not be profitable for you or me."[56]

Some few debtors were sufficiently threatening to discourage any possible pursuer, as a Hampton man reported to Dan Bulkeley from Pennsylvania:

Mr Waldo . . . gets the worse for liqueur which he has once. . . . but Tyler [his employer] says if he dont keep steady in futer he will not let him have any of his wages but will send them to his wife. Waldo draws his pay once a month but has bound himself or rather concented to have his money retained in the office in the big iron chest for saftey till his time is out. as circumstances are is no way that his wages can be retained for you. Mr Tyler says he would not presume to do it for two resons, one is he is under bond, an other is for fear of offending him as Tyler says he likes his work and is such a man as he wants that is to say Jack at all trades. under existing circumstances i see no other way for you to get your det only by prosecution. should you take that course i should wish to be excused in doing the business for several reasons: i may get enemyes by it, an another is it will be difficult for me to at tend to it. . . . there is men here that you can confide in to do your business. . . . should Waldo refuse to pay if you should sue him and go to jail he will have the pleasure of going 100 miles to Northumberland. . . .[57]

Bulkeley's Patented Door Guard

In the early 1830s, Dan Bulkeley turned to invention–as did a great many of his contemporaries who tinkered with machines and gadgets for the improvement of life in general and their own pockets in particular. The patent office and the patent laws had been established so that free, independent citizens might exercise their genius to the benefit of others and keep the rewards for themselves. Dan Bulkeley was not alone in patenting an invention and hoping to make money from it: in Hampton, Nathaniel F. Martin had patented at least two inventions before him, and out West another postmaster, young Abraham Lincoln, of New Salem, Illinois, patented an "improvement" to help river steamboats make their way over sandbars.

Dan Bulkeley devised, in 1833 and 1834, what he called a Door Guard. It was a layered metal piece of weatherstripping to be installed on the outside doors of houses to prevent rain from running or being blown in under the door. The entrance doors to most ordinary houses did not have porches, roofs, or eaves to prevent rain running down and under them, and Dan figured that a device to prevent annoying water run-in would be a sure money-maker.

In June 1836, "in conformity to an act of Congress, entitled 'An act to promote the progress of the useful arts,'" Dan Bulkeley received a patent for his Door Guard. (The exact design, along with the patent model required, was lost in a fire at the Patent Office in 1836.) He had already started writing inquiries about advertising in 1833. Now he also wrote to people he knew and talked to people in the store and in Hampton about selling the door guard.

While the response close to home was fairly enthusiastic, Lyman Foster, a Hampton man working in Hiramsville, Pennsylvania, described his frontier town as he pointed out problems with Dan's door guard:

you mentioned in your litter that you had obtained a patent to prevent rain from driving under doors. i think possible it is a good plan and think if i live to return home i shall have them to my doorse. the houses here are built in a plain and cheap manner them that are pretended to be buildings and as i am seven miles from any place as the saying is here and that place has but few good buildings. you would think so if you should see the country here. the buildings with few exceptions are build of logs. Ovens built out doors. Chimneys at one end of the house some made of sticks and clay some of stone toped off with an old whiskey barrel. when that gets burnt out put on another. many people here live in what is called shantees made of bords not so good as hog pens in Connecticut. Do all their cooking out Doors. children in cold wether go barefoot and all most bare ast and whiskey is the cause of it i think. by this time you think that the write of selling would go rather dull here. therefore i think it not worth while to send one [Door Guard].[58]

Dan found several men—almost all originally from Hampton—with whom he made formal agreements to sell Door Guards and to license the rights to manufacture them. Each agent was to keep account of all expenses, and all profits beyond expenses were to be divided fifty-fifty with him. After he had some experience with these agreements, Dan put in a clause that allowed him to take back agencies in case of "mismanagement" or "inattention" on the part of the salesman. He made at least eighteen such agreements between 1834 and 1838, for territories ranging from the next-door town of Ashford, Connecticut, and the nearby cities of Providence and Newport, Rhode Island, to one territory that included Georgia, Alabama, South Carolina, Mississippi, and Louisiana, and another that included Ohio, Indiana, and Illinois.[59]

The reports from outlying districts were soon as discouraging as Foster's from Pennsylvania. Robert W. Robinson wrote about local architecture from Ohio: ". . . am sorry to inform you, that your patent will not take here. the houses are generally made of logs, and very leaky at the top. if you had proposed your patent for the top of the house instead of the door I think it would have been preferable. there is only one place . . . where houses need fixing, that is the County seat . . . but the people have been so imposed upon by the Yankees [New England salesmen] they are very jealous of them."[60]

William Ashley wrote from Portland, Maine, in the spring of 1835, "The price is too high. . . ."[61] There were a great many other excuses from salesmen about why the Door Guards did not sell: George Sisson wrote from Pennsylvania, "It would not be likely that I Should Sell any in Some towns that is new . . . and them living in log houses and . . . my wife is in such a poor State of helth that I cannot leave home long at a time." Robert Robinson reported from Ohio that "Although some like the thing, yet the people are so prejudiced against patents of any description that is almost impossible to give them away." And Jonathan Hovey wrote from Suffield, Connecticut, "I find the people here to be very careful—very prudent, and seem to suppose that if a person travels about with any thing to sell, he is deceiving people."[62]

Dan Bulkeley left no record that he ever made money from his invention. The inventory of his estate when he died in 1842 lists "Letters patent Door Guard with models &c" with a total value of only five dollars.[63]

A Postmaster's Position

The post office's location in Dan Bulkeley's store made it a town center. In 1820, Dan Bulkeley had become Hampton's first postmaster, a political appointment from the Republican administration of James Monroe. Dan's brothers-in-law, Roger and Solomon Taintor, were by then the leading Republicans in town.

Because his postmastership was a political appointment, Dan was the funnel through which the political messages of the Republican Party reached Hampton. He became part of the traditional system in which senators, congressmen, and Presidents used the mails to spread the ideas of their parties. They founded and supported party newspapers and employed the post office to deliver them to as many voters as possible. Mail rates favored newspapers over letters, books, and magazines.

Newspapers were all partisan and political.[64] Postmasters collected and forwarded subscriptions and kept subscribers loyal–both to newspaper and party. Newspapers in opposition to postmasters' parties often found it difficult to get local subscribers and to ensure delivery. A Pomfret man, for instance, wrote Dan, "I did feel rather unpleasant about the paper which was lodg'd in your Office. . . . For I had heard of it and that your Clerk had for some reasons taken it from the rapper, mark'd some pieces, and expos'd it merely for his own sport. This I thought was a very improper thing indeed especially if you had been there yourself."[65] The writer was embarrassed that his newspaper had gone to the wrong post office, been opened, and that the clerk had made fun of him in public. People did not want to be on the wrong subscription list.

In 1824, the bitter battle for the presidency pitted New England's John Quincy Adams, who had been Monroe's Secretary of State, against the western war hero Andrew Jackson. The close election went to the House of Representatives since neither man received a majority of the electoral vote. Adams finally won. In the 1828 campaign four years later, the continuing struggle between Adams and Jackson split Republicans across the country into National (Adams) and Democrat (Jackson) factions. The editor of the *Columbian Register* warned Dan, "The subscriptions . . . seem to break off short this year." He hoped "they do not take offence at my adhering for the most part to the [local] County nominations. I have acted from the full conviction that we shall want to use the republican party in this state after the Presidential contest is over and that therefore it is not advisable to break to pieces on that [national] question." He pointed out that "all [Dan's] subscribers have had the paper one year with the exception of R. Taintor, J. Burnett and P. Pearl, who began only a few weeks ago."[66] It is possible that Roger Taintor, Dan's brother-in-law, and James Burnett, his father-in-law, joined the Adams Republicans in this election. In the event, Jackson won, but the conflict permanently split Republicans everywhere. Jackson's followers became the Democratic Party. Ultimately, their opponents began to call themselves Whigs, and for a while the "Republican" name died out of party politics.[67]

Dan Bulkeley's lists of Hampton newspaper subscribers are a chart of local changes in national party sympathies.[68] But local and state politics, not national politics, were the real centers of party activity. State political parties were made up of changing coalitions of locally powerful and influential men who only periodically focused on adherence to the principles of a "national" party. They tried to elect their own followers to Congress in order to influence federal policies, spending, and appointments in favor of their state political coalitions. Presidential politics did not always reflect local political concerns.

In 1832, Dan received an announcement from the editor of The Globe in Washington of extra issues for the reelection campaign of Andrew Jackson. In its manifesto intended to stir feelings around the country The Globe advertised:

> Extremes have met. The Champion of an unreasonable Tariff [Daniel Webster, senator from Massachusetts] and the Author of Nullification [John C. Calhoun, senator from South Carolina], having no principle in common but a restless ambition, are found united in their efforts to baffle the President [Andrew Jackson] in his foreign negotiations, kindle faction in our halls of legislation, and fill our country with discontent and anarchy. . . .
>
> A band of political managers in Congress are spending sleepless nights and anxious days in devising avaricious, corrupt and corrupting influences which pervade the Republic. With these they hope to vanquish the conqueror of Europe's bravest armies [Jackson, victor at New Orleans in 1815]. . . .
>
> The struggle is for power, for place, for the public treasure. Men who want foreign missions, judgeships and other valuable offices, unable to swerve the stern integrity of Andrew Jackson . . . have united with other aspirants to the Presidency in all sorts of combinations to destroy his popularity and defeat his re-election. . . .
>
> To enable every Freeman to obtain correct information during the impending conflict, we propose to publish thirty numbers of an EXTRA GLOBE. . . . It will be chiefly devoted to a vindication of the

character, fame and principles of ANDREW JACKSON, with a view to his re-election. . . ."[69]

Jacksonians–Democrats–favored widespread political participation. They changed qualifications for voting and officeholding in most states so that by the 1840s every state in the Union had universal white male suffrage, and the only residual property qualifications were for holding office. They also, as their enemies put it, introduced the "spoils system" into American government so that, as they themselves expressed it, all appointed officials of the Executive departments would reflect the will of the people as expressed in presidential elections. The Post Office Department had the largest number of appointive offices in the United States government–several thousand–and the number was growing.

Dan Bulkeley was, throughout his career as Hampton's postmaster, loyal to his party, but with the shifting winds of politics, his party changed names. When he was first appointed, it was not yet an established principle that postmasters should be direct adherents of the presidential faction in power; he was a Republican. After the 1828 election, Dan favored newly elected Jackson. In 1830 he was in enough political favor to be appointed enumerator of the federal census for Windham County.[70] And in 1832, his political object, as his distant cousin Ichabod Bulkeley wrote, "was to sustain the present [Jackson] administration & its principles. To give as large a vote on that ticket as possible."[71] Dan had become a Democrat.

Jacksonians campaigned everywhere against "privilege," "aristocracy," and "monopoly." And part of their attack on the established order was a sporadically virulent opposition to ministers and churches, especially the established tax-supported churches that remained. This was part of the democracy Dan Bulkeley particularly favored. He had voted with his Taintor brothers-in-law in opposition to religious establishment in Hampton in 1818. He subscribed to an antireligious newspaper called *Priestcraft Exposed.*

When Dan's nephew and clerk, Albert, sent some copies to his brother Hiram, an earnest student at evangelical Christian Williams College, Hiram exploded to his uncle Dan:

> I am truly astonished that in this enlightened age and country there could be found so much malice and deadly hostility to true religion as the Editors of this paper manifest, and am still more surprised to learn that their sentiments are yours.
>
> . . . the editors . . . have established this paper filled with the most abominable unscriptural doctrines and the most palpable falsehoods,

without any regard for honour decency or the plain truths of the Bible, in order to fill their purses. . . .

The exposer of priestcraft attacks sabbath-schools, bible and tract societies and even calls in question the right of the Legislature to enact laws to prevent the violation of the Sabbath. . . . I consider the Sabbath as it is now observed by orthodox christians to be a divine institution and an habitual disregard for it as a desprate step towards the abandonment of the Bible and all reverence for its divine Author. . . .

It has long been my intention to go to the heathen and preach the Gospel to such as are perishing for lack of vision, and if I know my own heart, I do not go for the sake of riches or honours, or to bring them a party, but from a desire to do the will of my master and be instrumental in his hands of saving immortal souls. If you are a real universalist you may laugh at what you may think my folly. . . .

Is it possible that the most abandoned, shameless, and impious wretch will receive the reward of the humble follower of Christ at the bar of final retribution? It cannot be. Consider this well I entreat you dear Uncle . . . I have lived among universalists and know the grounds of their arguments and believe them to be such as the terrors of the last day will sweep away.[72]

Edwin Cooley of Lockport, New York, the editor of *Priestcraft Exposed,* was as subject to the enthusiasms of the revivals of the day as he was to the newer transcendental enthusiasms of universalism and atheism. Dan Bulkeley wrote to him in 1832 inquiring because he sensed a "change in [his] sentiments." Cooley replied that "my religious sentiments are different now from what they were a few months since. . . . I think I have experienced a change of heart–that there is a reality in the religion of the Lord Jesus Christ–that every human being 'must be born again' in order to 'inherit eternal life.' I am sorry that being a Christian–a humble follower of the meek and lowly Jesus, should lessen me in the esteem of any man. . . . It is my sincere wish and prayer that you too may be 'converted.'" Less than two years later, Cooley had backslid and reported that he would "recommence the publication of Priestcraft Exposed." "Having had a pretty good Knowledge of the acts of the Clergy for the last two years," he wrote Dan, "I think it a duty I owe to community to expose the rascals."[73]

Dan Bulkeley's antireligious stance was very much a part of the turmoil of reform in the small-town America of the 1830s. So were widespread religious revivals, enthusiastic camp meetings, and increasing missionary activities. Dan's correspondents kept him abreast of the state of their own religious changes. William Ashley wrote from Maine, "The cause of religion is very low here in this region. . . . The enemy is rather upon a vaunting mode, sinners are very bold. . . . we have been as it were

During the winter & spring thus far, as sheep without a shepherd. A Mr Vaill from Connecticut is preaching whose wife hung her self last fall or winter. A good man no doubt—that is the most that you can say about him. . . . I must close by wishing you all the blessings of this life—peace in death, & a glorious immortality."

David Durkee, from Westfield, New York, was more laconic: "I have no Religion to send but we have a plenty Here even Mormanism." Durkee's half-brother, Silas Spencer, on the other hand, wrote to Dan, "Will you please hand this to my mother & tell her that (however strange it may appear to her or to any other of my friends) I have embraced religion as the one thing kneedful; and In the awakening which pervades the western region that God has made my house a house of prayer."[7] On religion as with much else in his life, Dan was not on the winning side.

Welfare Officer

The people who wrote Dan Bulkeley and small-town postmasters like him often needed help. Dan was the means through which many who had moved away from Hampton provided for the kin they had left behind. He became a social welfare worker because he was postmaster. Letters addressed to postmasters traveled free, so people wrote to Dan asking his help and advice in the care of their families.

Silas Spencer, for example, wrote from western New York State that he was "determined" to bring his elderly father "to this country" and asked for Dan's assistance "in arranging his business and enabling to settle of his affairs." Silas's brother John also wrote about their aged parents. The question became more complicated because their mother's son by a previous marriage "is on his crutches. But his leg was so horribly mangled [in an accident] that it will be some time before he will be able to labor such is the want of tone in the limb." The brothers assumed Dan would arbitrate the family disputes about who was responsible for the elderly widow. The sons thought their sister, married to Thomas Rindge, should move west near them and bring their mother. She did take their mother into her home, but she and her husband did not move west.

Silas poured out his complaints about his siblings to Dan Bulkeley, and about a "demand my Father held against me." He insisted, "I considerably over paid the principal, and the note which he held against me is for interest. He & Mother stated when I was in Hampton that they had given [brother] John more than me & perhaps ought not to exact any more from me." He asked Dan to "please hand this to my mother." Finally, when their half-brother David Durkee died in the summer of 1836, Silas wrote a long description of the circumstances to Dan Bulkeley "and *through you* to his and my mother." He concluded, "I would say to my mother that I only wish I could have the privilege to have her reside with me. I would cheerfully and gladly support her while she lives, should my life be spared long enough to do so. I have always felt as tho Thomas Rindge had a very unequal task. I feel it my duty and so does my Brother John to make him a suitable remuneration. we have had conversations to that effect. At all events I desire that in case of her decease, Mr and Mrs Rindge have all the few effects which are in her possesion and for any expenses which may moreover occur, I hope and trust that John and myself will have the manliness and generosity to pay."[75]

Dan Bulkeley seems to have been in charge of much of the care of the elderly left behind by westering Hampton folk. But kinfolk sometimes took the high ground with him, refusing to pay for care, as did Dr. Thomas Fuller, of Cooperstown, New York, about his brother Stephen, who wrote, "the information which you communicate is not unexpected. I have been informed of his habits, and have in former years seen something of them when I visited Hampton. it is painfull to see a good native mind in ruins, especially a brother. (Now Sir) I have the ability to maintain him without injuring my own family, and had he been reduced by unavoidable misfortune, I should have felt it my duty so to do, even to the extent of one or two thousand dollars, if requisite." But, said Fuller, "I at present have some doubts on my mind what is my duty in his case. He has received more then two thousand dollars from my fathers estate, and must have earned somthing himself in early life, but it seems it is all gone out of his hands. where is it. it exists some where. it has only changed hands (and probably lawfully). it must have been spent in Hampton. now if Hampton or individuals of that town possess it, what is justice in such a case. To be plain, I apprehend that the retailers of Poison or in other words ardent spirits, have got the major part of it. am I correct in that opinion. perhaps you are a better judge of it then I am."[76] Dan, who sold gin, rum, and whiskey in his store, was clearly supposed to squirm at this temperance tirade.

Even if family members wished to help, it was not always possible. And since Dan was the "social worker," they wrote him their apologies. Abigail Durkee wrote from Ohio, "I . . . was very glad to hear . . . that you feel interested in the welfare of my parents, and were it in my power to assist them I would gladly do it. I think if I was single I should, but as circumstances now are it is not convenient at present. We are just beginning on a new farm and owing some for building, and calculating to build a barn this spring, which makes us rather destitute of cash." She assured Dan "that I do not feel that you are taking grounds that you have no business with.

neither do I think that you are put up to it by any one, but am sorry that it is not in my power to comply with your proposal" to support her parents.[77]

Another correspondent, David L. Dodge, partner in the New York firm of Phelps, Dodge, thanked Dan Bulkeley "for the interest you take in my Brother & Sister Spragues wellfare & the kind offer of your services in procuring a more comfortable place for them in their decline of life. The farm you mention that can be obtain'd meets my mind, if they should be pleased with the arrangement. If so please to secure it. . . . I have no object but their comfort in the business. . . ."[78] Dan Bulkeley did help the Spragues buy a new place with David Dodge's money and approval.

In his capacity as postmaster Dan also helped, on request, when old soldiers were trying to get pension payments sorted out. Records of service in the Revolution often did not exist, and getting a pension depended on veterans' being able to testify for each other. By 1836, sixty-one years after the beginning of that war, some old Revolutionary veterans were "very much out of health and much Broken down, and did not appear to know much about the Subject of enquiry." One informant wrote Dan Bulkeley from New York after interviewing a veteran, "He says he recollects training Mr Ford to Serve . . . in the Revolution. he knows he went from home, and believes he was in the army but does not know it. he cannot tell what rigement he was in nor Who the Officers ware. Consequently cannot do Mr Ford any good."[79]

Veteran George Dunworth took his case first to attorney Andrew T. Judson of the neighboring town of Canterbury. After Judson became a congressman, he sorted out Dunworth's pension, and sent him a bill for services. Dunworth then wrote to Dan Bulkeley:

> After some Months had passed I calld at the office of Mr Judson again and the following conversation as near as I can recollect passed at the time—I says to Mr Judson I have calld to get an explanation of the bill you presented me. I do not know but it is right—if it is I wish to know it—as I wish no hard feeling to any man—if it is wrong I wish to know it. Says Mr Judson what do you wish to know about it. I says to him the Charge of ten Dollars and the small Charges of Postages &c I am satisfied with, but the Charge of thirty Dollars I do not understand and wish you to explain it to me. [The total pension payment was sixty-nine dollars, of which Judson's bill was for more than forty dollars.]
>
> Mr Judson flew into a passion and says to me get out of my office you old scoundrel get out of my office you old scoundrel I dont want to hear any more of your stuff. get out of my office you old scoundrel. My age and infirmity would not permit me to move quick. Mr Judson

took me by the arm and led me to the door and says, I shall soon go [to Washington] where I will put a Stop to your pension you old scoundrel.

These were the facts as near as I can recollect. and it was done in passion. . . . It has been my aim to live at peace with all men, and among others I lookd upon Mr Judson as one worthy of my confidence and have supported him in all his promotions. . . .[80]

Dunworth asked for Dan Bulkeley's help to find a place to stay in Hampton. Postmaster Bulkeley tried to serve as an intermediary and adviser in the case. We do not know if he helped Dunworth challenge Judson's charges.

Losing the Center

In Hampton, as in other small towns, the personal and the political were joined. Chauncey F. Cleveland, Dan Bulkeley's neighbor, was a rising young lawyer fifteen years Dan's junior. Cleveland went from political strength to strength: Admitted to the bar when he was twenty years old, he was first elected Hampton's representative to the Connecticut legislature when he was twenty-seven and served four years in succession. In 1832 he was reelected to the state legislature and appointed state's attorney. He was thirty-three years old that year. Dan was forty-eight. It is not clear why Dan Bulkeley distrusted and grew to hate Chauncey F. Cleveland. But as the 1830s wore on his personal animosity toward Cleveland became the focus of his political life in Hampton and its post office.

Dan Bulkeley and Chauncey F. Cleveland both started their political lives as Republicans. During the years of their personal conflict the Republican Party splintered and split. The themes of secrecy, conspiracy, and elitism became central to politics everywhere, and they were the themes of Dan Bulkeley's fight with Chauncey F. Cleveland.

Joseph Prentis, Dan's lawyer neighbor, ladled on irony when writing of Cleveland at the beginning of 1835: "You say the Political champion is on a political Excursion to Middletown. What a monstrous weight he must have on his shoulders? Had he not a Giants body & Herculean mind he must most certainly sink under so great a burthen. But it is shocking to human nature to see what men of exalted views, of stern political Integrity, and with minds exclusively devoted to the interests of the Country can endure. The Torture of the rack or even a sacrifice of life would be met with the greatest composure & resignation in such a glorious cause. But enough," Prentis concluded, adding, "If the Country had nothing but such puerile rotten hearted politicians as Cleveland to depend upon to direct the

affairs of State we should all soon sink into worse than brutal servitude &
barbarism."[81]

Thomas Clark penned his opposition to Cleveland from next-door
Mansfield in March 1835: "I don't much like the principle of supporting a
candidate for any office in union with my political opponents, but I have
even thought I would sooner give my support to genuine consistent federalist [the current term for an arch-reactionary] than a one who is as vas-
cilating in his political operations as has been your Mr Cleveland. I never
had any confidence in him as a politician." Clark went on, "I presume by
this time his political mucking [shoveling manure] is in motion and no man
in this section of the state better understands managing mucking of this
kind than he does. . . . I trust you and other old school democrats will once
more rally and put down the man who has for a long time past been in the
habit of, by his duplicity . . . & deceit succeeding in obtaining nearly every
office sought for—and then turns round and shamefully neglects those who
have supported him."[82] The opinions of Dan, Prentis, and Clark presage
those of Dan's cousin Henry G. Taintor thirty years later. Cleveland was
not an easy man to like.

Dan Bulkeley's faction defeated Chauncey F. Cleveland's bid to be
Hampton's representative to the legislature that spring of 1835. But for Dan
this was a Pyrrhic victory; Cleveland's anger now centered on him. The first
warning came from a friend in Hartford: "I learnt last night there was a move
a makeing to place Mason Cleaveland [Chauncey's relative who owned a
store and inn in Hampton] in your shoes as to the Post Office & as it is no
more than fair to be frank I send you this that you may be appries. conjecture
sayes it is to be done in Hartford." And there indeed was a petition being circulated in the state legislature "in the hands of cunning, designing Men or
Man" to have Dan Bulkeley removed from the Hampton post office.

Dan's friend Thomas Clark tried to stop it, and thought he had succeeded. He invoked David Crockett (a former congressman from Tennessee
who had been a Jackson man but became a Whig before he died at the
Alamo in 1836) when he enjoined Dan with Crockett's motto to "'Go a
head' in supporting pure Democracy in Hampton," but he worried and told
Dan to "expect no favors from C.F. Cleveland or those who are controlled
by his influence."[83]

By January 1836, Dan himself feared he might lose the post office.
David Clark wrote him of Cleveland's complicated machinations and deals,
saying he was two-faced. "You speak of Clevelands republicanism. I believe
him one of the worst kind of federalists . . . ,"[84] he warned.

Dan Bulkeley tried to rally support from the newspaper editors whose
subscriptions he had been pushing all the sixteen years of his postmaster-

ship. But their response was at best lukewarm. Meanwhile, Cleveland beat Dan in a Hampton election, becoming representative to the legislature in the spring of 1836.

Then Chauncey F. Cleveland became Speaker of the Connecticut House of Representatives that year. One of the legislature's tasks was to elect U.S. senators, which gave considerable political clout in Washington to men who were powerful in state legislatures. So Chauncey F. Cleveland used that clout to have Dan Bulkeley removed from the post office. We know Dan's side of what happened because he kept the draft of a letter he wrote to Connecticut's Senator Gideon Tomlinson in Washington:

> Sir–Permit me to address you on a subject that very much interests me–and excuse me for the liberty I have taken in so doing–unfortu- nately for me the only acquaintance I have with you is the short intro- duction I had while on a visit to my brothers Mr Taintor in this place some time since, and unfortunately I have no other acquaintance in the City of Washington from Ct. . . .
>
> The subject I would ask your attention is my sudden removal from the P. O.–as P. M.–in this place. On the 27 of April Mr Brown pre- sented to me papers that clearly informed me he was Clothed with authority to conduct the business of the Office in My stead–and demanded the Key and papers belonging to the Office, which in duty bound me to give up to him. I had had no notice of my removal until presented by Mr Brown–
>
> Some weeks since it was intimated to me that there seemed con- spiracy against me for the purpose of removal. . . .
>
> I am not conscious of any error in the discharge of my duty to the department and to the public. if any it is unknown to me. something I am persuaded is wrong–and it would afford me satisfaction to know what. . . .[85]

Senator Tomlinson did not reply, perhaps because he, too, lost his political office that year in an election to the U.S. Senate from Connecticut over which Chauncey Cleveland presided.

There may have been reasons for Dan's removal that were not wholly of Cleveland's making. One man wrote from New York, "I am sorry to hear that you are likely to be hove out of your Office. But if you are not a whole Hog Jackson Man you must expect it."[86] Whether or not Dan was himself a "whole hog Jackson man," he insisted that his enemy, Chauncey F. Cleveland, was not. He wrote to the auditor of the Post Office Department that Cleveland was "a man who up to the last day of the last Election of our late Chief Magistrate [Andrew Jackson] was opposed to him and his Cabinet and the most bitter abuse was heaped upon them and the most bitter epithets were used by him especially on Andrew Jackson and Amos Kendall [the Postmaster General]."[87]

For the next several years Dan tried to make his case to members of the Connecticut delegation in Congress in order to get his postmastership back. At the beginning of 1838, he wrote Congressman Orrin Holt, "the business as near as I can learn was transacted by Mr Judson as principle for the benefit of C F Cleveland to gratify his—Mr C—malicious design towards me."[88] Judson (whom Dan had fought in the veterans' pension case) had been a congressman when Dan was removed from office. Shortly there-after he was appointed a federal district judge. Unlike Dan, Cleveland sup-ported Judson, who had federal connections and could influence federal (post office) appointments. Dan's local connections did not help him with the federal government.

Congressman Holt's reply hid behind a democratic piety. "If the inhabi-tants of your town are dissatisfied with the present incumbent and will so express themselves," he wrote, "I will unhesitatingly cooperate with them. You must be sensible that I could do but little towards effecting a change if the people oppose it."[89] Nor was Dan able to get help from Hampton politi-cos he had supported against Cleveland. Philip Pearl, Jr., the man who with Dan's help had defeated Cleveland in 1835, wrote with cold comfort, "on mature reflection I am of opinion that you had better remain perfectly quiet at present. You cannot expect any aid from any of the Connecticut delega-tion in Congress. . . . I would advise you to keep entirely still . . . & see how the cat jumps."[90]

The rules of politics had changed. In 1820, when Dan Bulkeley was appointed postmaster, it was enough to be a loyal member, with local influ-ence, of the party in national power in order to get the appointment. Dan kept the job because he performed his duties. But by 1836, it was neces-sary to be a direct supporter of the President's faction in the state and local party coalitions in order to *keep* a federal job. What Andrew Jackson's ene-mies called "the spoils system" had kept Dan in office after Jackson's elec-tions in 1828 and 1832. When Dan's enemies took control of the *local* Jackson coalition, he lost the post office.

For sixteen years, Dan Bulkeley's position as postmaster had meshed with his work as an entrepreneur to provide him a locus at the center of Hampton's life. He lived and worked in the middle of the village. He stayed in his home and store for the rest of his life after he lost the postmaster-ship, but without that appointment he was no longer the center of the community.

CHAPTER 8

SEEKING
INDEPENDENCE

ᕙᕗ

*"...he Spred Like a Crow on a perch. He thinks that he Can
not Content Him Self to Stay in Conecticot any More...."*[1]

D an Bulkeley, like many of his contemporaries, considered going
west. His dependence on the Taintors, his dependence on his
political appointment as postmaster, his lack of success in his business enterprises, may all have rankled. Going west–getting out of
town–offered the possibility of escape from the toils, demands, and failures
of family and community.

There were also grand reasons to think about the question of going
west: newspapers and politicians spoke of national destiny, of the manifest
will of God, of the westward course of empire. Churches and burgeoning
missionary societies emphasized the spread of Christian civilization. New
varieties of popular religion stressed the duty of every born-again revived
Christian to extend the Kingdom of God on earth and go west to do it. The
new Church of Jesus Christ of Latter-day Saints–the Mormon Church–set
an example. It gained many adherents in New England and New York State
and was a strong influence to go to a new life "at the West."

There was, furthermore, the tempting possibility of acquiring land of
one's own in the West. From childhood, young men and women who
were part of large farm and small-town families were taught to be independent, hard-working yeomen. Yet they felt they could not achieve those
goals in established communities, where land was expensive, already occupied, and subject to the legitimate claims of many others. Getting out of
town offered the possibility of independence–land of one's own or work
of one's own.

175

Many of the people who left Hampton wanted to keep contact with home and hometown. Who better to write to than the postmaster, especially when letters could travel to him free? Dan Bulkeley received hundreds of letters written by Hampton men and women from other places where they were seeking work or building new homes and new communities. Reading those letters and trying to decipher the usually legible handwriting but wildly erratic spelling, punctuation, and grammar has gradually revealed to us the lives those people made for themselves. Dan may well have read in them substitutes for his own aborted dream.

Westering

There are no letters from people on the far western frontier. There were Connecticut residents in the Texas settlements that declared independence from Mexico in 1836. And there were people from Connecticut on the Oregon Trail in 1837. But for Dan's correspondents the West did not extend so far. Mostly Hampton's West in those years was New York State, western Pennsylvania, and Ohio.

We have met Lyman Foster who went from Hampton with his son Lyman to western Pennsylvania, where they both worked for an early-nineteenth-century developer who was laying out and building a new town. Lyman wrote Dan Bulkeley about what he expected and what he found in 1834:

> . . . i found the sittuation of the place as good as i expected. i did not expect to find a pallace nor the garden of eden here but as the Lord had made it and all very good. i have bin contented since i came here. i have got a good place to bord a good feather bed and some flees but they have not got all my hide yet. the nats which have bin so troblesom here have done nipping.
>
> per haps you have heard many storys about this place. true it is a rough place but healthy. good water as in any other place. . . . i see more people here than i expected. people are here all most every Day to see the place. there is about fifty irishman to work here on railroad.
>
> the hands that bord at the tavern are unesey on account of ther board and i should not think it strange if they should return home as some others. i under stand that some have returned by the way of the wilderness but not heard of any pasing through the red sea. if the hands keep going off as fast as they have done we shall not have many left. but when you see the old solgier quitting the camp you may think that there is war in israel. i have not regreted that i came here as yet. . . .
>
> Lyman and myself have worked to gether most of the time. we have finished off one house and began an other. hour [our] work this

hot weather is inside work. we have a few very hot days here. grass and grain is verry good in this part of the country but no fruit. Mr Neff and James Fuller are both well. . . . tell my familey that i am well and Lyman.

their has bin four bears killed here since i came here and a number seen. some Deer and a few snakes, say rattle snakes, Copperheads. now is the right time of the year for them to bite. a daughter of a Mr Millers was bit by a copperhead last week on the leg. it swelled very bad but she is like to get along. i am not in much danger of snakes whare i go to work is a plain beaten path.

as soon as i finish the house i have began i have got to set out the saw mill fraim. the building is to be 40 ft Long two story high. the bill of timber amounts to 6000 ft. since i began my leter Lyman and others have seen a bear cross the river two miles up the river. and yesterday was seen at the same place four. it is suposed that they are deprived of their natural food making them so plenty.

Mr Penfield has closed his bed and bord whare he is. i no not if he has returned to Hampton. tell him that i am in good health and wide awake and stand to my post as a good soldier and dont mean to leave it as long as i fare as well as i do. . . . wishing you the blessing of God in this life and that which is to come and may we all be so hapy as to meet each other in this world and enjoy each others society once more. . . .[2]

Lyman Foster intended to go back to Hampton. In another letter he told Dan, "Lyman is well and hearty and grows like a weed. . . . we have raised 22 buildings this season and probible 8 or ten more will be. one Dam about Done. two more to build this fall. the Company have about 200 men in their employ. 100 irishmen to work on the railroad this year will but make a beginning as to the work to be done here. . . . tell my wife that we are well and content and i hope they are. . . . it is good times here all peacible and quiet and no nulifiing who will go home."[3]

New communities had quite literally to be built. The Irish immigrants who were pouring into the country provided cheap labor and employers very often treated them with contempt. Letters home were filled with descriptions of the buildings going up and businesses starting. W. B. Moneypenny wrote Dan from Eaton, Pennsylvania, "The mill I calculate to put up will be three run of Stones and to do principally Merchant work and is on a small stream and would be calculated to go with very little water. there is a fall on the stream of fifty or sixty feet so that I can build a wheel of any size I think proper. Lumber is Cheap and there are plenty of stones in the Creek for the building."[4]

Ichabod Thurston wrote from Mount Morris, Pennsylvania. His letter reflected both the aphorisms he had learned in school and the spelling he had not learned. "I am apoligez for so long neglecting to writ to you But as Doct [Benjamin] Franklin remarked that a man that was good at making an excuse was not good for any thing els I will not make many." Thurston was a harness maker who reported, "Buissness is vary good all things considered. I have as much worke as I can do with two apprentices and two Journaman. But one of my Journimen will leve soon. he has done notting for me except make sadles. all the rest of us make at harness–and as much as we can do possibly." He was proud of the prices he could command in his home and wrote Dan, "tell Mr Button [who ran a Hampton inn and stable] that I finished a gig harness yesterday that I have forty dollars for–wheat is worth one Dollar per Bushel, corne and rye is worth thirty eight cents and oats twenty five. we have had a flouring Mill Built here this season with four run of stone. we have one saw mill here and expect to have another soon–the flouering mill is rented five years for twelve thousand dollars."

All who went west were eager to let the folks back home know that they lived in a civilized world of opportunity. Thurston wrote, "we have got a vary good Presbyterian Meeting hous Built here this season and finely. our vilage is improoving smartly. I will give you a little idea how. they had vilage lotts here. I have been a trying to Buy me a place to sitt a shop. I want thirty by thirty five feet and I cannot get it neer the center of Buisness short of an hundred and twenty five dollars and it is a rising evry day."[5]

Small towns wherever they were, new or old, depended on agriculture and on getting the farm products sold "out of the country." Ichabod Thurston's relative Robert wrote from Livonia, New York, "the Wheat crop Is Not so fair this Season as it was Last. . . . thare is a Great Dele of old flouer in the Country that is Sower, the millers is Grinding it over And puting in New Wheat to make it Good, But it Will be out of the Country Soon." He reported of another Hampton man, "E Clarks folks is Well. E has Got as Good a farme as any in Livonia. He is Going to Put in 45 acres of Wheat this fall. he has Got a good Crop of Corne & Grass this Season." At the end of the letter he mentioned his own family, "I have got a Nothe Child. it is a Girl. it is better than 2 months old and Groes well."[6]

A year and a half later, Robert wrote a long letter from Livonia, telling an all-too-typical tale:

We met With Quite a Disaster here thursday Nite. the Large 3 Story Store opsit the Tavern and the Meeting hose Was Consumed to Geather With Most of the Goods. . . . I work in a Shoomakers Shop in the North end of the Store house. It was windy that Nite. the Store & Store house and meeting house Was all doun in 1 hower & 25 minets. the Store Burnt doun first. thare was 2 docters 2 Taylors

In the bilding and a Nother old Store tennet clost Two. the merchant M B Manter, postmaster, Lost about $10,000, $3000 In Sured. he saved His Books & acounts. the docters Lost thare Hole Stock of medason & all of thare Cloths Exsep what thay wor. one had got to Bed.

It Was in the uper part of the bilding. one of the Taylors Staid in the Room til he Had to Jump out of the window. he Saved Just the Close that he had on. Wm Was in the 3 Story and had to Go all most in to the fire to Git doun. but they all escaped. E Clarke Had 4 or 5 hundred bushels of Wheat Stored in the Store house Which Was burnt. Quite a loss for Elisha.

the Lite Shind in the Street in Canandaigua 20 miles away. It was the hotist fire that I Ever Saw & the Quickist. 8 minets from the time it Burst out, at the End 80 feet Long, it Was Covered With flames. But it is Gon & Cant be Recalled.

Robert Thurston's style thrived on disaster. He included in the same letter, "Return to the famealy: Ichabod & Sary is Well. & William H Pierce has buried his Wife. She droped a way Just Like a Candle going out. But She Longed to go. Charles Pierce has got a fine Boy."[7]

Women, too, wrote of small-town ambitions to Dan Bulkeley. Lucy Leach wrote from Cazenovia, New York, on the shores of Lake Erie, "this Village exceeds my expectations. It manifests a spirit of enterprize. blocks of buildings are now going up, when I am in the Principle St. I almost fancy myself in a City. the lake adds much to the beauty of the place."[8] Dan's male correspondents did not mention the beauty.

Lyman Foster wrote again about the town he was helping to build. "i have a good warm shop to work in this winter. Dont work nights. i think i should enjoy myself here if my family was her. tell my wife that i am well. if you write let me know hough [how] my folks git along and wherther they have wood." He especially loved Dan's gossip retailed from home. "you wrote that some of the hampton men had absconded. i think you must have had frosty nights. i wish you would write in par tickular about them and what women they have had to do with if you think propper." Another perennial topic was Hampton politics. Foster mentioned that Dan had written "that Square [Chauncey F.] Cleveland had moved into his castle" and ended with a typical western brag: "if you have any Congressionall men in Hampton that their house is not biggen nough for them to turn round they can be acomidated here we have a building 80 by 90 they can turn round in one story and make nails in the other."[9]

And Silas Spencer wrote from Westfield, New York (on Lake Erie), about a new kind of problem and opportunity small towns began to face after the mid-1830s: "The Great Rail Road from the city of New York to Lake Erie is to terminate Either at Dunkirk or here at Portland Harbor. It will probably fork about 6 miles east of here and go to both. I have real Estate at Portland H. which under present prospects takes a high valuation. So fearful is Dunkirk that P. Harbor will take the termination that the citizens have offered the [Railroad] Co. $500,000 in Land to bring it to Dunkirk."[10] Where railroads already ran, they offered new possibilities for independence. For the rest of the nineteenth century, the coming of a railroad to town was the greatest opportunity possible for any community to grow and its people to prosper.

Finding Work

Anson Howard, Abigail Durkee, and Lester Burnett were among the Hampton farmers who had gone west to new farms in New York, Pennsylvania, Ohio, Illinois, and Michigan and wrote to Dan Bulkeley. Others found work, or moved to work in the building trades, as Lyman Foster did. New towns put a premium on skilled builders.

Starting in the 1820s, people from small towns like Hampton, where populations were pushing the limits of the land's ability to support and provide work, also went off to the new textile mills to work. The first deliberately designed mill *town* in America–Lowell, Massachusetts–started in 1821. The Lowell mill owners recruited young men and women, especially women because they were an obviously underemployed population, to tend the new machines. Some went from Hampton to Lowell. And others went to mills farther afield.

Machines spun cotton thread or wove cotton cloth in the new kinds of mills. Samuel Slater had been instrumental in introducing machine spinning and weaving to the United States from England in the 1790s. By the 1820s, he was the owner and operator of spinning mills and machine shops in Rhode Island, Connecticut, and Massachusetts. And he also had designed and built, in South Oxford, Massachusetts, one of the newfangled "factories" (Francis Cabot Lowell and his Boston Associates built the first in Waltham, Massachusetts, in 1814) in which all of the steps in the making of cotton cloth (carding, spinning, dyeing, and weaving) were accomplished by machines in one building.

Robert Dorrance wrote from South Oxford to Dan Bulkeley, who had asked him to come to Hampton, "I am to work on wages for Mr [Samuel] Slater and it is not conveniant for me to leave my busnis at this time. . . . my health is quite poor and am under the necessity of loosing so much time By reason of sickness, and having the overseeing of the weaving apartment, makes it very inconvenant to leave home."[11]

Work in textile mills large enough to have separate weaving apart-ments (rooms) was new. Overseers like Dorrance, who were responsible for seeing that the machines kept running and that the "operatives" tended their machinery properly, worked for cash wages. A weaving room over-seer was responsible for the quality of the cloth produced by the mill. Robert Dorrance was right to think his business important–he was at work on the cutting edge of technology in a state-of-the-art organization. And that work (for cash wages) made him independent.

Robert Thurston wrote from New York State to Dan Bulkeley about another Hampton man who received cash for his work: "Wm Button Started about the 15 of Jun for Mishegan. I hird [heard] from him at Long Since. he was in Detroit to work. he sends word that he gets good wages. . . . Button has don well Since he Came out here. He Sais that he Dont have to take hiped [hipped] horses & Catten yarrne [cotton yarn] for Pay. the Redy Cash is as good as he wants. . . . he worked in buffalow this Spring a While and the bos was taken sick and button had the management of the bisness. he Spred Like a Crow on a perch. He thinks that he Can not Content Him Self to Stay in Conecticot any More."[12]

For women who wanted to leave Hampton but did not go to the mills, the employment picture was more bleak than for men, but it still held opportunity. Single women could and did leave Hampton. Some went to cities to work in silk manufacture or in millinery trades. By the end of the 1820s some went as far as Philadelphia to work in silk.

Then at the beginning of the next decade there was a new demand, and a possible new occupation. Braiding straw for straw hats was a new form of paid work for women. Edmund Badger (formerly from Hampton) wrote Dan Bulkeley from Philadelphia in 1832, "Ireland is the newest fashion and should you be able to procure Twenty or more of fine Straw of the leghorn plait [braid] We should be glad to buy them at a price that would give you a profit. Mrs. Badger says will you send on a sample Bonnet."[13] Badger fig-ured he had a money making possibility in braided straw bonnets woven by New England women. When they arrived he wrote, "We calculate to make one dollar at least on a Box! We shall pay you what you think you ought to have."[14] The Badgers asked for a "young Lady to come on by Spring"[15] to Philadelphia to help in their millinery shop.

Braiding straw could be done closer to Hampton. Harriet Fuller, who went to Oxford, Massachusetts, to braid straw "with Mrs. Sigourney," wrote however that "the scent of the brimstone effects my lungs very much. I shall be under a necessity of leaving the work at present or I think it will soon destroy my health." But even with her health problem, Harriet preferred not to return to Hampton for her other employment choice, domestic service for the Bulkeleys. She refused on the grounds that their previous helper "better knew how to manage to pleas every member of the family . . . which you know is rather difficult." She hoped "you may proba-bly find som one before my return which do better than me."[16] Perhaps the Bulkeley family found it hard to find domestic help.

When women took domestic work, they did not necessarily receive even the small pay it earned for themselves. David Spencer, Jr., of Pomfret, sent to Dan Bulkeley "$11.00 for Moses Thompson Esqr, for his daughters services for me 13½ week @ 83 cents per week–her wages amount to a tri-fle more than $11.00." He asked Dan to "have the goodness to hand the same to him & take his recpt for it."[17]

Other women went further. Lucy Leach first went to the mill town of Uncasville to find work. She wrote from there that she was trying to "decide our anxiety whether we go to the West or continue in the land of steady habits. . . . It matters but little where I am if I can but find employ-ment. I have passed the Winter very pleasantly in this little out of the way place."[18] She went west to Cherry Valley, New York, where she took up the milliner's trade but did not like her new location. She wrote of her expectation "to leave this place for Youngstown [Ohio] but was disap-pointed. my expectations as to my business was cut short. I delayed too long in making up my mind whether I would go or not therefore annother Lady occupied my place (in the Milinary business). cant say I feel verry sorry. most any other Village I think would be preffered."[19] She noted with some envy that "Miss Dorrance is in the Valley this summer an Assistant teacher in the Female Department in the Academy (a fine Girl)."[20]

Schoolteaching was a possibility for anyone who had more than the minimum education. If one could keep a lesson ahead of the children, one could teach. Jonathan Burnett, kin to Dan's wife, wrote from Pennsylvania, "School teaching is my employment at present. I am in the school I engaged before visiting you–which is at Halseyville in the Town of Ulysses."[21] Robert Robinson wrote, "I am now in Urbana [Ohio] with Mr Edmund Hovey who is manufacturing upon a large scale. I am about taking a school in this place. I have been invited to go in company with a man in an Academy [High School] but think I shall not the first term."[22] Later, accord-ing to Anson Howard, Robinson was "teaching school in Urbana with great eclat."[23]

For women, teaching was an entrée to an independent, better life. Mary B. Eaton was Dan Bulkeley's most prolific correspondent who took to teaching. She left her daughter Cornelia in Hampton, and sought employment, perhaps first in a mill in Douglas, Massachusetts. In her first letter to Dan, she wrote asking for his help "to obtain a school at

Hampton." She explained she had seen a school board member who "observed that they had thought of employing a gentleman to instruct in the new schoolhouse [in Hampton village] this fall, but observed that he should feel willing that I should take it provided that others would give their consent." She felt qualified "to instruct in any branch that you might wish attended to," but warned Dan that "As the good people of Hampton (if I recollect aright) are apt to give extensive lattitude to that unruly member called the tongue I do not care to have any one know that I have written you."[24]

She did not get the Hampton job, and Dan Bulkeley helped her find work in New York City in a milliner's shop. Then she found a position "as instructress in a private family" in New Brunswick, New Jersey. She reported, "My pay is not much. $8 a month board and washing. I did not stay at the shop that you bid me good bye at, but two days. I did not like the idea of my new occupation & thought best to leave. I never was more homesick in my life than I was at times while I was in Newyork although I made many very pleasant acquaintances at my boardinghouse." The shop position had been a step down for Mary, or at least not one suitable to her family's aspirations, so she asked Dan, "If Brother Stephen visits Hampton this fall I do not wish you to mention any thing to him respecting my sewing in the shop I mentioned, as it might not be pleasant to him to know it."[25]

Within a month Mary took the opportunity to start a school of her own and described to Dan how she did it:

> The family that I was instructress in at the time I came here are to leave town in the Spring & I thought I would like to ensure to myself a school against that time; as a favorable opportunity was offering itself. I therefore have taken a chamber, a fine room, in the most central part of the City; give only 29 dollars rent. Had 16 Scholars to commence with. This Week have 18 and have others engaged for the last 6 weeks of the term to make my number 23. The next term I shall probably have a very large school as there is a lady 3 doors above me that has 30 scholars that is to leave here for the South at that time.
>
> . . . I have been at considerable expense commencing my school at this season of the year, for Stove wood &c but I shall be enabled to get through with it all very comfortably and after this term will enable me to lay up something handsome each term.
>
> . . . I am to go to housekeeping [have a home of her own] early in the spring. I shall send for my sister to instruct in French and musick & and it will be much better for us to keep house as we shall have an opportunity of boarding a few young Ladies that will attend my school.

Mary sent along instructions to her daughter in the same letter:

> I wish you my dear daughter to attend Particularly to arithmetic this Winter. I shall need your assistance among the smaller scholars very much next Spring if we live. I do not wish you to give up your geography intirely. Get your geography lesson & cypher at school but do not expose your health by going to school or any where else in very cold or unpleasant Weather and when you go out at school [for recess] put something over you and not stay long. Remember the good instruction I have given you and allow your self in no thing that you know is wrong. I shall send for you to come on early in the spring. . . .[26]

She wrote her next letter several months later from New Brunswick on a day that happened to be Abraham Lincoln's twenty-third birthday out in Illinois, February 12, 1832 (but only he yet celebrated it): "the examination of my School . . . took place last Saturday & . . . gave very good satisfaction, much better than I expected. I have no vacation Untill next August." She sent money to pay for her daughter's schooling in Hampton to Dan. At the same time she tried to excuse not paying a debt she owed him, writing, "I should have enclosed the money I owe you but thought it might be as acceptable when I shall have the pleasure of seeing you face to face. I am purchasing some furniture at present which I will not have to do another term."[27] She was beginning to earn enough money to support a better style of independent living.

The next summer she wrote, after she had seen Dan, complaining, "I have lost $20 this term by my scholars leaving school so much alarmed by the cholera. There is three new cases to day next door but one to me. I am to move this week into one of the handsomest and healthiest streets in town." Again she only enclosed "$2 which must do untill October at which time I will defray the expenses of my daughter's contracting at your Store & my gratitude for the favours confered by your Lordship toward each of us."[28]

Seven months went by before Dan received the last letter he kept from Mary B. Eaton, who wrote of new plans. "I still remain in Newbrunswick and in the same occupation–but am to leave the last of April for home. . . . I wish very much to see my relatives & friends at Hampton. On my return from my journey home I shall locate my school at Newyork or Brooklyn. It is nearer home and I have a better opportunity of frequently seeing my Yanky friends." She hurried on with family gossip: "Sister Harriet is married . . . has a fine husband with a good purse, which is a very convenient article. . . . Please excuse this badly written letter as I am leaving in order to attend lecture."[29] The cosmopolitan tone of a woman rushing to attend a lecture poked fun at the changing small town which from then on she would visit rarely. Mary B. Eaton had made her independent life and moved permanently from Hampton.

Running Away

At least two men in the mid-1830s ran away from their wives and families in Hampton. They wrote to Dan Bulkeley, who must have known their circumstances—at which we can only guess. All we know about what happened comes from the letters he kept. Both were farm workers with a few skills. Their pain and ambivalence about leaving town are vivid.

Asa Martin left in the winter of 1834. He wrote to Dan from the vicinity of Enfield, Connecticut, in the Connecticut River valley close to the Massachusetts border:

> Albany, February 3rd, 1834
>
> . . . I am now in the Town of Long Meadow Massachusetts & Dated my letter at Albany so that you might say if necessary that you Rec'd a letter bareing that Date. I wish you to write me as soon as . . . you Receive this and write as partickular as you can. I wish yout See My Wife and if She inquires after me you may tel hir that you Rec'd a letter dated at Albany. . . .
>
> I wish you to git what potatoes there are that my wife does not kneed. there is my seven inch auger, Shave rasp, one chisel . . . that Hovey has taken. there is a quantity of old iron at the head of the Chamber Stairs together with some tools. I wish you to git them. I have Iron at Deacon Smiths and a broad ax. wish you to get them. I have paint, Stone pots, paterns, and timber, Two Chaise harnesses, and two of waggon harnes—the former belongs to my Father—with some other Effects to numerous to mention. . . . I wish you to Dispose of that as you pleas, to tel my wife that you are authorized By me to Setle my affairs here, and if She does not comply I will send you or Father an Power of Atorney.
>
> Altho my wife has drove me from home in the maner She has I wish hir no harm. my Dear Children I Cannot keep from my mind. if I have done what I am accused of I Could nott have been in my wright mind. Could I Believe it were true I would fall on my knees and Implore the forgivness of Almighty God that he would have compashion on one of the Chiefest of Siners. I would also fall on my knees and ask forgivness of my wife and Children and every other person under Heaven. . . . I am almost Crazy. I Do not no whether you Can Read what I have wrote. I wish you to tel my Father where I am and none else.
>
> I left Hampton Sabath Evening went as far as . . . Chaplin Monday morning. Started and went to the four Corners Mansfield, from there

to willington. fell in Company with John Phelps. went to his house. found he was acquainted with the affair. he proposed my goin back. I told him no, that I had been drove from home and that it would not Do for me to return. . . .[30]

Three weeks later, Martin was working. His tone changed. He bragged, "if I had my tools here I Could make thirty Dollars a month." Of his family he said, "I Should be willing notwithstanding the treatment I have Recd from them that they Should feel as well as I. . . . I pray to God to prosper them in all Lawful pursuits. I wish them no harm. ware it in my power to take the life of my wife or of my Children I Could not do it. I would Sooner Sacrifise my own than inger them. they are what they are and So am I."

He remained bitter about his wife. If she "gits a bill of divorce from me She looses hir best friend, but I think I Cannot Say that I have lost any-thing. She has Stood as a Cipher . . . ever Since I married hir. Accepting runnen me in Debt and playing the game on me [commiting adultery] that perhaps I was gifted at." He wrote Dan that "She told me not the first time that I Caught hir in unlawful acts that if I Exposed hir She would be revenged on me if it Cost her hir life. I told hir that I would pardon hir if She wood reform. She pledged to me hir honor that She would. in lass than one week I Caught hir agin. She then Cried and upeared to feel vary bad. Said she was forced to it, that She had no intention of the kind and wished me to presekute hir for hir Conduct." He said of his wife's lover, "I talked with him Before hir. Proseeded no further."

At last, further down in the letter, we find a hint of the identity of Martin's wife's partner in what he regarded as entirely her crime. "When I left Hampton pounded and bullied by hir Associate I had no boots and there beaing a light snow got my feet wet and took Cold which in Consequence of my lameness as beaing Struck by Hov[e]y all but Occasioned Death. I traveled two Days without my Coat on my arm or great Coat except over Shoulder. my arm now is so that I Can do a fare days work."

The experience left Martin chastened, as he assured Dan that "I have formed a Resolution to let Rum and my Wife alone for the present. . . . I go Sober and Come Sober and If they Catch me they may make they best of me they Can."[31]

Four months passed before Martin's next letter, in the summer of 1834, when he wrote of his past winter's trials, "my health was rather poor. . . . I had a feaver that went rather hard with me but I have got So that I am about, but not able to work. I thinck Some of goin to the Salt water. if I do I shall Come by the way of Hampton."[32] Martin did return to Hampton, but went back to Enfield where times were bad. He wrote Dan that "If I am not able to work Soon I shall be at home. . . . in Consequence of the grate failing here of late I should think the prospect not So good. if I do not return I wish you and Durkee to watch my wife and See that She does not bind my boy out [as an apprentice or contract worker in a mill]. if She attemps the thing pleas to write and I will attend to it Soon."[33]

Martin returned to Hampton again in the beginning of 1835. He wrote to Dan on February 1st:

> . . . when I left Enfield I had fifty Six dollars a part of which I Expected you to Receive. I Recived my Family with a Cordial welcom not Fearing but all was wright. went to Bed. awoke at four in the morning and found my money gone. I must Confess I felt bad. I trid Consealing as far as posible. my health poor. Resolved to go to my friends.
>
> I have one word to Say and then I will forebare. If any man will See his Wife and Child Ravished by the basest of Scoundrels and make no Complaint then I am one of a thousand. my Children are as Dear to me as yours are to you. But my wife and hir Sons they are not.
>
> I ask no mans advice. I was once Capeble of managing my own ConCerns But now it apears I cannot. Dear Sir I wish you to write me in Relation to . . . Wife and Children as near as you Can. . . .
> Respectfully yours A M Martin[34]

This ends the series of Asa Martin's letters. He had left Hampton not for work or land but because his life with his wife and family had become impossible. At least one other man—one of the Hoveys—was involved with his wife. Martin himself was a rum drinker who did not remember what he did under the influence of alcohol. From the evidence of the first letter, he may have committed a crime, but we do not know what. There is no further reference to his situation in any other papers in the Taintor-Davis Collection. We have found no record of Mrs. Martin's views or anyone else's of any of the events alluded to by her husband. Nor have we found any further explanation of the references to "Hovey." Martin's tale shows that manifest destiny and economic betterment were not the only reasons people left small towns.

Anson Fox also ran away from Hampton and wrote to Dan Bulkeley. His letters came from upstate New York, which was "the West"–where a Hampton man could find friends and aquaintances who had gone before him. (A few years before he left town, Anson Fox had delivered to Roger Taintor the maple trees, most of which still stand in the yard of the house near which Roger planted them.) Fox left just ahead of the law in the winter of 1834–5. In the first letter Dan kept, he asked Dan to go with his brother, David Fox, and some other men to "see Browns folks & talk with them & bribe them if possable. I wish you to get it settled so that I can cum holm boaldly in the fall." He did not make clear exactly what "it" was in the letter, because Dan knew. We do not. Anson Fox had been accused of a crime and left town, but was "always . . . sorry that I cum away. you can tell people that I was advised to go from their or else I never should have gon."

Fox seems to have been accused of rape or "cohabitation" with someone named Eliza, who might have been in the Brown household. His in-laws were the Litchfield family, newcomers to Hampton who were well-to-do farmers. His first object was to have Dan find out if he would have any chance in court. "You can tell people how much the Litchfields are against me. you & David can find out near how much might they would have in court. I believe if I had staid their I could settled with Miss Brown & had Eliza tell A diffirant story. & it seams as tho if you could get Eliza to alter her story & have my Wife say. . . ." There is at this crucial point a large mouse-chewed hole in the letter.

The letter continues after the hole: "for the time seams long since I left there altho there is good cumpany here. but I want to see my Children & live with them. I want to cum back & live their. my friends are their & every thing that I have is their." Nevertheless, his troubles seem to have been about more than the rape. There was a legal action "Pope" Chauncey F. Cleveland was bringing against him in the matter of "Backus sythe, the sythe that he & Harvey claims is in the butry." Had he stolen it?

Fox's epistolary style wandered, as did he. "I am to work in Lima now. I went to work in Mendon. I have quit their. it was too solatary place four me. I had as lives [lief] work in A tomb. their was work enough to do. they are putting up two flour mills their, one 50 by 70, one 50 by 65 feet. I did not like the place. one of the men . . . raised last year 5000 bushels of wheat." If true, 5,000 bushels from one farm was a very large crop, far more than any Hampton farm ever produced. Whatever his digressions, Fox always came back to his Hampton troubles. He wanted "David should find out how Litchfield got his news about me . . . he can find out by my Wife, but you must be sly about it for I believe it was she that told Asa [Litchfield] to make this complaint. & if she did, I want to know it. . . . I believe she lied about it."

Fox concluded this first letter by adjuring Dan that "if old Spencer or Miss Litchfield are dead I wish you would write it. I dont want any one to die for me, but when I here that one or both of them are dead, I will have one day of prais & thanksgiving to God if I should out live them."[35]

By the spring of 1835 Fox was already "considerably weand from that place [Hampton]," although he wanted "to cum back & see my friends & see to my affairs a little. . . . I have thought of going to the Ohio where Elisha Farnham is, & I wish you to write where he is & be particular in describing the place where he is. as for Michigan I have no thoughts of going their." Nevertheless, he found himself drawn back by "them children that are as dear to me as the blood that runs in my veins. . . . it is hard to be driven from them as I am. it is wors than death. I have dun wrong I know & who is their in that place but what has? & why should I be used in this way?" He insisted that "as for committing or attempting to commit A rape on that girl I am not guilty. they have tried to get something against me for 3 or 4 years but could not make out anything untill now. now they have driven me from my holm & they are satisfied. but I hope that God will direct my ways & that I may live to see better days. but like Job I have been afflicted of every thing but soar biles & I hope that these afflictions may be all for the best."

Fox instructed his brother David to get "my furnature out of the hands of the Litchfields. . . . now David, dont favor them, as they show me none. get all the property you can before she gets A bill [of divorce] if she gets one. & if she does not get A bill, take the furnature, every thing but that the Law will allow her; that will be onely one bed & A few other things to keep house with." He told his brother not to trust Chauncey Cleveland because "he is deceitful as the very Davel. . . . this I know for I have seen the man myself."

Of his wife he wrote, "if she can live without me let her, or let her friends [her family] help her as they have told her they would if she would leave me. they have got what they wanted, now let them take care of her." And he bragged, "here are girls enough that are glad to get married but I shal not marry here. here is one young widdow that is worth 6 or 7000 dollars. I could have her but I have lived in Hell once & I dont mean to get A cross bitch again if I can help it. . . . Uncle sed I must do as the irishman did by his Wife—get her A cheese & leave her in this wide world to get her bread in. . . . I am not so much cast down but what i can take A glass brandy if I need it & will do it as long as I live. I am A free born man & shall act so as long as I live. . . . I remain your old connecticut friend &c"[36]

Fox settled for a time in western New York State. From there he wrote in the middle of the next winter, "I had rather cum back & live their than here, altho all seam to be very friendly to me here & speak well of me. some have advised me to marry & settle down here. but without some better chance than I have seen I shall not. they call me the old bachelder." He boasted that "I spent the remains of my last year by the side of a good girl &

begun my birth day with her. it was A happy beginning. . . . it seams A little like old times when I used to work out by the month." As a hired hand in Hampton, Fox had many happy times with the girls. He went on boasting, "I can go with any girl I pleas & I take cumfort with them & I will as long as I stay here. . . . I am fat & well & weigh 169 pounds." He asked Dan Bulkeley to "rite me all the news you can & fun if their is any, & how old black prince & Mary Ashley gets along,"[37] apparently referring to Prince Knowles, who was black and Mary Ashley, who was white. Knowles was the head of one of four free African-American households in Hampton, according to the 1830 census. Fox's scurrilous reference to a relationship with a white woman may well be indicative of the ordinary discourse of the hangers-on at Dan Bulkeley's store. There is no evidence that there was any truth to it.

Fox wrote a New Year's letter to Dan at the beginning of 1836, wishing his "trouble" were "so settled that I could cum and go when I pleas & see to my children once in A while." He concluded, "I take A great deal of cumfort in seeing & waiting on the girls here. I went to a newyears dance last knight & we had some sport with some of the girls."[38]

By spring, Anson Fox was hard at work building in the city of Buffalo, the western terminus of the Erie Canal, and wrote a letter that vividly described working-class life in a booming city.

> Buffalo, New York, April 10th, 1836
>
> . . . I am now in Buffalo to work at the carpenters trade for 13/- per day, & pay 20/- per week for board. I expect to stay here about 3 weeks longer. then I shall go back to Bethany & work for A man by the name of Pratt. he is A clever coldwater Presbyterian. he says I must work for him all summer but I dont know what I shall do.
>
> I dont like this place atall. A man has to spend about all he can earn or else be cald A sneak. any man that dresses well & can use a handsaw passes for A carpenter, onley he must not know so much as to show his ignorants. I with two others are planning & leveling the join on A building that is 360 feet long & 90 wide. it is to be four stories high made of brick. their is A great many fine buildings here. they are to begin one this summer that is to be 280 feet square.
>
> their is A great deal of business dun here & of all kinds. it is A low spot of ground & very unhealthy & fild up with all sorts of people, Dutch Irish Swiss negros & Ingens. & the Swiss & Dutch women carry every thing on there head & they look more like the Devel than any thing else.
>
> I with some others went saturday to here the trial of two men for putting another man into A kittle where they were melting off potash. they was cleard. the trial lasted three days. the jineral opinion of people is that they was the means of his death.

the ice on the lake [Erie] is not broke up yet & it is the opinion of people that the lake will not be navagable untill some time in may. when the lake is open business will be lively. Sunday is the time for mecanics [workers] to go from place to place. we are 10 of us going next Sunday to Black Rock & to the [Niagara] falls & cross the river into Canada. he is going with us to show us the girls. but here is every thing carried on that ever was In any place. here is A chaunce for A man to spend as much money as he pleases. the cumpany that I am in are respectable & we mind our own business & let others alone & we have no trouble with the lofers.

. . . if I have any friends give my best respecs to them. if any should be going to the western country let them call at Webster block at the foot of main street, I work on that building in Buffalo. . . .

Anson Fox concluded his last letter to Dan Bulkeley by announcing his intention to return to Hampton by the late summer of 1836. He instructed Dan to tell his wife "that I should be glad to live with her & the children, that I have not been so much against her as have others, & that I think we have both been to blame for hereing [listening] to others. & I should like to live with her again."[39]

Four years later, by the time the 1840 Census was taken, Anson Fox was indeed living in Hampton with his family. He actually came back to the "holm" he had left in such haste. But neither he nor his family was included in the 1850 Census. He had left town again.

Keeping Connected

Seekers for independence wanted to move with kin–siblings, parents, children, and neighbors. They wanted *connections* wherever they were. When they reached a new place, they wrote home to keep connected there as well. Their letters had certain set topics. Crops, the weather, and health were common to all the reports from the West. The letters always included messages "to enquiring friends" and word of Hampton people the writer had seen. Anson Howard wrote from Ohio, for instance, "It is a general time of health with us here; the weather is extreme cold for the season, frequent snow squalls and thunder with them; hay very scarce. it is the season of the year that cattle generally live well on grass, and many have had to live on it this spring for three weeks past, but it is poor living.– My respects to Mr. Taintor and family."[40]

Abigail Farnham Durkee wrote from Salem, Ohio, "We have had a very open winter and no sleighing of any consequence 'til within about three weeks." In her letter to Dan Bulkeley she included a letter to her sister Mary Farnham describing Ohio life: "We are all well yet, and have just returned from meeting [church] about a mile and half from here, myself with several of our neighbors (mostly women) rode on an ox sled, which probably would look rather singular to you but is very common here." Horse-drawn sleighs were standard winter transportation in Hampton in the 1830s. Abigail expressed her pleasure to Mary "that you were doing so well in your line of business." Mary was earning enough money of her own so that Abigail could "hope you will soon be in a situation to visit us," and reminded Mary that "Solomon [Durkee?] remains a bachelor yet, he has a fine farm, and a very pleasant situation."[41] Independent young business people, men or women, expected to marry as part of their entry into the adult world, as Abigail well knew.

Jonathan Burnett, kin to Dan's wife, wrote from Pennsylvania in a teasing mode, "If any of the girls inquire after me—inform them that my health has been on the mend ever since I left the little marshes of the high lands of good old Conn. You will understand Mr Bulkley that frequenting those places often is verry injurious to a persons health. It is apt to bring on the ague &c." He concluded his letter, "Please to direct your letters to Jacksonville town of Ulysses."[42]

Over the edge of their known world, Dan Bulkeley's correspondents wanted letters sent carefully to exact addresses, fearing themselves perhaps lost to civilization. W. B. Moneypenny, for instance, like many who did not want to lose word from home, warned Dan: "When you write please to be particular in the direction . . . Keelers, Northmoreland post office, Luzerne County, Penn."[43] Geography shifted under Dan's correspondents' very feet. In one of her letters Abigail Durkee wrote, "Since I commenced this letter I understand that the township of Salem has changed its name to that of Conneaut, you will henceforth recollect that we live in Conneaut."[44]

People wanted their connections in Hampton to write often, and ladled on irony when they did not, as did Robert Thurston: "tel Buttons folks that I am oblegd to them for Riting So often. I Beleve that I have Not Received a Letter from them this 3 years if Ever . . . and if thay dont Rite Soon I Shal think thay are afrade or that thay are to Lazy or a frade of Paper."[45]

People often asked for technological advice from home. Robert Robinson wanted Dan "to inform me about your water works respecting lead pipes, whether water can be made to run up hill higher than the fountains head, without the aid of a suction pump. . . . it would be an invaluable treasure in this country." He included a political note: "one week from this day the election take place. . . . a man may as well be damned as declare himself in favor of the [Jackson] Administration."[46]

Advice to kin also went home from the emigrants as another way of staying in contact. Elisha Farnham wrote from Cazenovia, New York, for instance, "as to Celinda it seemes to me She ought not to marry a man So much older than herself. I had an Idea She was a pretty nice girl, perhaps She wants Some advice on the Subject. I think She might do better in this Country & much better if she was in Michegan as every thing that leaves this Country & goes to Michagan in the Shape of a woman is married right off."[47]

As movement around the West grew easier, people still stuck to kin and hometown connections. Charles Moulton described his travels in Ohio using those connections:

> Left Conneaut, 10th Decr, going from Elisha Farnham's to the Stage-House in order to take passage. thought I would call at the Post-Office and inquire for a Letter, (not expecting to find any,) but was agreeably surprised to meet with yours and Esqr. Prentis', dated the 4th. I had scarsely time to open it, and not half sufficient to read it, before the Stage was ready, and we were obliged to be off. By the way of Cleveland, Columbus &c (having rested several days at different places on the way,) I arrived here . . . at the house of James Burnham's Esqr where I yet remain, having seen here, his two brothers, Nathan and Leicester, who live in this neighborhood, and Harvey Clark Esqr. living 14 miles west, who happened to call here last evening, as he was going further, on business. They and their families are all in good health and prosperity.[48]

Lucy Leach also used her connections as she moved, explaining to Dan, "I have no permanent home but find one wherever night overtakes me. I am now visiting my Oldest daughter in this section of the Country. I find her very pleasantly situated & has Marryed a fine man. he does great business, goes to N.Y. every month, (Merchant)."[49]

The pull of hometown and family did not stop for many years. People held on to their land in Hampton and like Lyman Foster wrote of the "concolation in antisipating the time when i shall return."[50]

Ebenezer Jewett's family (he was probably the son of the blacksmith) wanted him to leave the West. "My folks are A teasing me to go back to hampton and I have promised them that they might return this season. I am about arranging my affairs here and if nothing happens more than what I know of now I shall land them in hampton betwixt this and the first of July next without fail."[51] Jewett's letters to Dan Bulkeley show the detail with which he kept connected to his Hampton property to which he returned in the summer of 1836: "I wish you to see about haveing my garden plowed and planted. . . . I wish you would get John Pearl to sow it to oats and stock it down to clover and herds grass or some other person. . . . I want you to preserve the buck wheat field . . . or let it out to some boddy to sow.

. . . the mowing out east I wish you would not pasture but run a fence across on the west side of the swales. what rails it lacks you can get south of the house down by the side of the swamp and what it costs deduct out of the rents. and there is a little fence to repair up north to keep the cattle from getting round in to the swales. . . . help me to get Taintors Barn to build."[52] Within a month, Jewett had to borrow money from Dan in order to get his family back to Hampton.[53] He was one of several who came back from the West.

Hopes for a return often receded for others. Abigail Durkee wrote wistfully, "I expect old Hampton and its inhabitants have altered a great deal since I left there. I anticipate much pleasure in again returning to my native country but when it will be I cannot tell."[54] So far as we know, she never came back.

As Hampton migrants fanned out over the continent, each had, perforce, fewer neighbors from home to give aid and comfort. Michigan and Illinois held the farthest western outposts of Hampton in the 1840s. Very gradually and not at all willingly, those emigrants turned from kin and home in Hampton to building their new and independent lives and communities. But no matter how far they turned or where they went, they remained connected to their hometown for a long time. Thousands of moving Americans took to the words and tune of a song introduced in an opera in 1823. As a man in touch with new developments, cosmopolitan Dan Bulkeley promised to send his niece (who had moved to western New York) the words and "notes" to the new song "Home, Sweet Home."[55]

CHAPTER 9

RUNNING IN PLACE

ᏯᎧ

"... To feel that you can tread the ground proudly before them ..."[1]

When we first read the large collection of Dan Bulkeley's letters we found ourselves sympathizing with him in his troubles in business and the post office. Further reading of his correspondence from the West confirmed a perception that he was not a man who ever achieved what he wanted in life. But it was the letters about Dan's family that hit us particularly hard. All too often we found ourselves as parents empathizing with this parent who had lived across the street and had often been in our house, whose children were sources of pain as well as joy to him. We read the letters of Dan's eldest son—who had gone away from home and was writing for money—at a time when we were receiving similar letters from our own son. Perhaps that was why we liked Dan Bulkeley so much. And, as happened more than once as we found our way through the Taintor-Davis collection, we were very sad when we came to Dan Bulkeley's death.

Dan Bulkeley's Daughter

Dan always aspired to the gentility that his Taintor relatives achieved and, like them, his aspirations were vested in his children. His first child was born in 1814, the year after Solomon and Judith produced their second son, Henry Griswold. That first child died, but Dan and his wife had their second baby, Phidelia, in June of 1815. If there was a competition between the families, Dan was very far behind. The older Taintor boys, John and Bulkeley, were already away at an academy, on the road to gentility. It was perhaps at Phidelia's very birth that Dan determined he would some day send her away from Hampton to learn the ways of a gentlewoman.

When Phidelia was fourteen, in 1830, she had not yet gone. Her mother's old friend, Lucy Leach, who may have been Phidelia's godmother, wrote from the West that year to Dan's wife, Phoebe. She teased her about not having a hired girl in the house: "Madam, how do you do & what are you busying yourself about in these days? are you doing house work cooking & such? I conclude you are. I wish you would take a journey out hear next Spring. you would be much pleased with the Western Country. . . . there is quite a number of Yankee Bullfrogs in this place." She then wrote Phidelia that she had not herself settled down so "of course cannot send for you. wait patiently, you may come by & by."[2]

Five years later, when Phidelia was nearly nineteen, her parents sent her to Norwich to an academy. She boarded with her widowed aunt, Orra Barstow Bulkeley, whose husband, Dan's brother Gad, had died some years before. Her situation was nothing like that of Dan's memory of the elder Taintor boys' schooling, but he was trying.

In May, Phidelia wrote her first letter home. It reflected her education and upbringing as well as her full understanding of the family aspirations. Unlike John and Bulkeley Taintor, Phidelia addressed her letter to both her "Dear and much beloved" parents, and wrote in a much less formal and less genteel style, "The ice is broken, I have climed the hill of science and It is a hard one to, I expect the sweat will start in the heat of the summer." Her letter sounds very young. She wrote, "I have not been homesick only In the school house." She was in school with her Norwich cousins and reported "we found the way back alone without getting lost. we have been out a marketing. I purchased me some paper, and a pattern for which I only gave a ninepence. dont you think It was cheap? I wish you to send my bonnet to Harriet as soon as possible for I cannot attend Church until I receive it. I will trim It myself. I should like to have you send me a bunch of quills and a knife. I have been trying to get one. they are so high I cannot affort It, you know. I wish to have my bonnet lined with white satten." She had a clear idea of what would appear genteel.

Phidelia also knew that a young lady's accomplishments would be signs of gentility and eagerly wished to embrace the opportunity offered when "Adeline [a cousin] says she should like to learn music to me. she says she has music books and notes and if you will get the piano when you go to NY and bring It here, she will do all in her power to learn me. I think I shall have plenty of time nights and mornings." She enjoined her mother to "keep up good spirits. you know It is beneficial to health. give my love to the General [her brother Andrew's nickname] and Robert [her youngest brother] and tell them to keep steady. and Mary [her little sister] must be a good girl, and not have her lips cut off."

She tucked in a note to the girl in Hampton who was doing up her bonnet: "Harriet I am In Norwich, and not a hat to wear I should like to have you bleach It and line it with white sattin. I will trim it myself. I have a pattern here for you I gave a nine pence for it you may have It and welcome. Miss Culver says she makes them [the bonnets] very small and the more they stick up the more genteel."[3] If Phidelia could help it, she would go to church in Norwich for the first time in a "more genteel" bonnet.

This was 1835, and Phidelia's father, Dan, had just fought and won his first battle to hang on to his appointment as postmaster. His cousin, with whom Phidelia was staying, wrote that it must have been "very gratifying to you upon your arrival at Hampton to receive the congratulations of your friends . . . to feel that you can tread the ground proudly before them."[4] Gentility seemed nearly within Dan's reach. He went to New York to buy an instrument for Phidelia's musical education.

What he chose was a Seraphine, a keyboard instrument somewhat like a small parlor organ. Phidelia opined that she was "almost tired of waiting"[5] for it. Dan commissioned another relative, George Moseley in New York, to test the instrument. "He pronounced it the best he ever saw it being a good tone & unusually loud sound."[6] At the end of July 1835, George Moseley paid Dan's money for the Seraphine. And the seller was already justifying defects. George had "Enquired respecting those 3 high notes. he says they never did sound, they being so Very high & fine that You never have occasion to use them. . . ." The implication was that Dan should have known as much.

In the event Phidelia did learn to play the Seraphine, a sign of the gentility Dan wished for. But according to his inventory at the time of his death, the instrument belonged to Dan, not to her, when he died in 1842. She had returned to Hampton and was living at home by that time, still unmarried at twenty-seven.

Andrew Jackson Bulkeley

Dan had another ambition beside gentility—to get away from Hampton. His next child, Andrew Jackson Bulkeley, was destined to act that out. But since Dan himself had never managed it, Andrew's life reflected his father's ambivalence. Dan and Phoebe named him for "The General" who was the victor of New Orleans and the symbol of Dan's democratic politics. Andrew's presence is everywhere in the collection of Dan Bulkeley's papers because, perhaps when clerking in his father's store, he practiced and scrawled his name and signature on the outsides (and sometimes the insides) of many of Dan's letters. Long before we understood who he was, we were very much aware that there had been an ANDREW J. BULKELEY.

By the time Andrew was eighteen, Dan was looking for a place to apprentice him. He had not sent him away to an academy. Henry G. Taintor made some inquiries of a firm in Middletown, whose proprietor took note that Andrew "was desirous of obtaining a Situation in a Dry Goods Store." He wrote that "he might suit . . ." if he were "willing to apply himself and . . . can give undoubted references as to moral character and integrity."[7] Perhaps the required references were not forthcoming. At any rate, Andrew did not go to Middletown.

Mr. Stephen A. Johnson, of Winchester & Johnson in Hartford, offered Andrew an apprenticeship, writing to Dan in October that he had "some weeks ago seen Your Son in Hartford. Since which time . . . have written him requesting him . . . to come to Htfd immediately." Johnson said that the "necessary hurry of Business" kept him from detailing the conditions of Andrew's apprenticeship. It was perhaps a fatal omission, but one he promised to rectify when he should see Dan in person.[8]

Andrew took to life in the city. He reported to his father in December (sending his letter "politeness of Mr. Knowles"—that is, carried from Hartford to Hampton by Prince Knowles), "I am enjoying good health. and have business a plenty. three or four acquaintances together with myself gave the Ladies a serenade last evening. and the way they (the Ladies) jumped out of bed want ["wasn't," with a distinct Yankee accent] slow. I have received three or four compliments from them this morning." In this first letter came a request, the forerunner of many: "I am in want of a pair of boots very much and if You conclude to let me have a pair to wear I wish You to have them made on 6½ lasts with thick bottoms and high heels 1½ inches high. if he has some thin handsome cowhide I should like it. if not I should like some thick calf skin. I want them made on the new fashion lasts. they are So much easier. and send them up as soon as You can. for I want them very much." Andrew often wanted things "very much."[9]

By the following February 1839, he was home in Hampton sick. But Winchester & Johnson wanted him back, despite some misgivings on Mr. Johnson's part, who was always waiting to see Dan and voice them in person. "Had I sufficient time to write long I would say more of Andrew. . . . for the last few days I was highly Pleased to see him improve in tact, management, and application. I have many times thought that necessity would compel me to send him home owing to his inattention to Business. I now think very favorable of him hoping that he will eventually make a thorough Merchant."[10]

Andrew was soon back at work, but writing his father that he had problems with his employer. He announced, "I shall not Stay with him, if but one reason, that is, I wish the priviledge of attending Church when I please. I am not allowed to attend the Presbyterian Church and a number of other things which will be of no use to mention. he has not told me what wages he will give me Yet." Andrew concluded with the first of his "Send cash" refrains: "if you have any cash to Spare I wish you would send me a little."[11]

Dan apparently complied, because a month later Andrew wrote he was "very thankful for the money You sent me and when I get able I will return it to You again."[12]

Andrew's monthly report for April contained what must have been news to his parents:

> . . . You must not be astonished when I tell you that I have left Mr Johnsons. I will give you the particulars and I have faith to believe that You will fall on with me. as I have often heard You tell of Clevelands making his boys that have lived with him black his boots, and that is one reason of my leaving. and I think it not only insulting myself but it is a Gross insult upon my parents and I don't think You would uphold me in doing it. if You do, You think different from what You did when I left home. Mr Johnson told Griffin (one other clerk) and Myself that we must take turns about blacking his boots. Griffin declined doing it he says You must Either do it or leave him. . . .
>
> this morning I told him I did not see as we could agree and I might as well leave for we could not agree and I might as well leave. he says if you cannot do everything as he wishes (meaning to black his boots) that I might leave. and as for blacking boots I will not do it. Bulkeley grit cant go that.
>
> I asked Mr Johnson if he had any thing against me otherwise. he says no. I asked him if I had not done every thing as he had Said. he said that I had done every thing as he said. Excepting Blacking his boots. & I told him I should never Black any Mans boots. . . .

The servile status of a bootblack was not for Dan Bulkeley's son. Andrew assured his father, "There are respectable people in Hartford that will assist Me."[13]

Andrew's letter in May of 1839 came from New York City. He had been home for a while and now wrote to his father to explain "the reason of my coming here without Your knowledge." When he left Hampton he intended to go to Albany but was distracted and headed for New York. He became a peddler–a business that would not have cheered his father. He wrote, "I think I can do a good business. the Season is very dull. but I can clear from one to two dollars a day beside my board and washing. I hope by strict attention to business this fall that I shall clear a handsome Sum– last week I carried a quantity of Goods up the Hudson river and Made out very well. Jacob Pratt has cleared 17.–dollars a day in a busy Season. I think I can sell Goods as fast as he can."[14]

Dan immediately wrote his friend William Jones in New York, asking him to see and help Andrew. Jones replied with some reassurance that he had had "conversation with him, & have told him that every thing depends on his getting a character for steadiness & fidelity & that a good season should be his object. that obtained, he may expect to go forward, prosperously."[15] It seems always to have been that elusive "getting a character for steadiness & fidelity" that held Andrew back.

In mid-July Dan received from Charles Curtis & Co. in Hartford the news that Andrew, just after he had left Winchester & Johnson, had borrowed "Cash & Goods to the amount of $14.25" from them "for which he Said you would see it paid; and when he was on his way to New York Said it would be paid the next week, as he expected his Father would send the money. And not hearing from him, or you, since, thought proper to write you about it."[16] A month later, Charles Curtis wrote again, saying he had expected Dan to have paid Andrew's debt.[17] On the same day Dan received a dunning notice from Winchester & Johnson for a debt of Andrew's of $36.47.[18]

By the beginning of September 1839, more grief came from Andrew himself (he was still in New York). First he prepared the way by dwelling on his father's worsening luck, which he wrote was the reason "I did not wish to live at home. I knew You had many Enemies in Hampton. and that they were so bitter towards You that it was flung in my face wherever I went. can you blame a child of Yours for leaving on that account? an affectional father could not." Having played on Dan's sense of guilt, Andrew went on to blame him "for all You have tried to impede the progress of my welfare," but nevertheless promised Dan his "assistance (as far as it goes) at any time." He wrote, "I never should have left You had there been peace and harmony in the family." The letter continues to vacillate between his promises of assistance and refusal to return to Hampton. "I will go in rags and Starve myself before I would see my parents suffer. as for returning to Hampton to live I never can." Then Andrew proffered his unasked-for advice that his family should get out of Hampton:

> if You will obtain a pleasant situation either in this city or some other thriving place we may all live together in peace and harmony. only get out of sight and hearing of Hampton. there are . . . fine hotels on the western Rail Road (and Canal) to be leased. and where a person can get a good living and make a small fortune. and without much labor to Yourself. and annother thing it will be an enjoyment to Yourself to meet with old aqquaintances and also Strangers from all parts of the

country. I think You can amuse Yourself in Your old age in that way. and I always thought I should like to be in a good Hotel. and if You will dispose of your situation [sell your Hampton store] as You think proper and obtain a Situation, I think it will be for the benefit of our family, beneficial to Yourself and You can have my assistance as long as my parents may live.

He concluded with assurances which could hardly have meant much to his father, struggling as he was to avoid paying this errant son's debts in Hartford: "You may think this simple advice. but You may see the child has affection for the parent as well as the parent for the child."[19] Andrew's Hartford creditors were becoming impatient. Charles Curtis "was not a little supprise'd" when Dan refused to pay Andrew's debt. He explained that Andrew had only been hired for a few weeks, and had agreed to work for "nothing but his board." And although Dan had said the debt was entirely without his consent, Curtis insisted he had in fact been a party to it through an intermediary, A. C. Hall. "Mr Hall called to our Store about the Middle of May last, and says to Andrew 'your Father wished me to call on you for the amount of $6.75, and he would Send the money next week.' My oldest clerk paid Andrew the money, and he paid it to Mr Hall on the Spot." At the end of this letter Curtis put in the clincher: "I have Supposed by what I have learned that you was a man of high Standing, and of respectability, and would do the thing that is honest & just."[20]

Winchester & Johnson also informed Dan they would not "reasonably wait much longer" for the payment of Andrew's debt and asked, "Will you send us the amount or shall we leave the Bill [with our lawyers] for Collection?"[21]

Andrew does not seem to have been concerned about his Hartford debts. His letter in October 1839 brought Dan an ultimatum:

. . . I have now taken my pen for the last time to address You. the letter I wrote You has not as Yet received an answer. the ear of a father is deaf to the language of an affectionate Son who would do anything in his power to sustain the peace and happiness of once an affectionate father. . . .

these are my last words. May the smiles of peace, happiness & prosperity, ever Surround You. and when the silver of age has crept up thy Brow You will then think the last words of an affectionate Son are well.

A few days from this time will find me riding upon the waves of a bottomless Ocean. on Saturday I take my departure Island of Madagascar. My love to all. Adieu. Yours Respectfully A.J Bulkeley[22]

Andrew Bulkeley's letter to his father from New York, October 8, 1839.

Dan was sufficiently alarmed by this threat to dash off some money. So Andrew was not on the "bottomless Ocean" a week later. Instead, he wrote as if nothing had happened: "think if I can return home in peace it would be much better for us all and therefore Shall accept of Your request." He casually asked his father to meet him at Curtis's Hotel in New York City and mentioned meeting his well-to-do, genteel cousin Henry Taintor's new father-in-law, Martin Ellsworth.[23] We hesitate to speculate about what Andrew might have said to a man like Martin Ellsworth.

The young man went home to Hampton. But his erstwhile employers, Winchester & Johnson, were not paid, and early in the new year of 1840 the firm brought suit against Dan. Dan employed an attorney in Hartford, who first suggested a settlement and asked Dan "how much" he was "willing to pay." To defend against the suit, he needed a deposition about what Andrew's "services were worth & his ability to perform the duties of

Clerk," and he could find no one in Hartford "who is able to give this proof."[24] It sounds likely that Dan lost the suit.

In March of 1840 Andrew turned twenty-one. Achieving one's majority was an important step toward independence–of one's parents particularly. So Andrew once again left Hampton, this time for the West. He traveled with relatives and acquaintances from Norwich out to Greenville, Illinois, from which he wrote in October, with some surprising news:

[note before the salutation:]
I have leaped through 20 different cities Since I left.
Dear Parents
    Yesterday morning 4 O clock I arrived in this place after about Six weeks hard traveling. and never was A poor soul more happy than me. We were 18 days from Cincinnatti to Saint Louis by Steam Boat. the river was very low and consequently we grounded very often.–I was Sick 10 days on the Ohio River on account of the water but have nearly recovered from it–I am verry much fatigued from my journey but hope I shall soon recover–
    Times are very hard in this part of the country. there is nothing doing Except Saint Louis and not verry thriving there–When I came through Saint Louis I was quite Sick and was unable to find A Situation for myself–but shall return there for that purpose as soon as my health will permit–hoping to find A Situation for the winter certain.
    It has cost me all I could make and Scrape to get here. The River was so low they charged verry high for the passage–and when I arrived in Greenville it took my last cent. and am now destitute of money. and am unable to live on that account. and I can find no employment in this place. and what to do I don't Know and wish You to give me Some advice on the Subject. I wish to get away from this place.
    I think I hate Some of our relatives as bad as You do. What You told me about them I think is verry true. I think You are not far out of the way & Hannah [his girlfriend] wishes to get clear of them as well as myself.
    she says her Uncle Backus [of the Canterbury Backus family] has Several thousand dollars of her property. She don't know the Exact Sum. . . . And now what means must we take to procure the money of Backus. You will best know about that Yourself and wish Your advice on the Subject.
    we have neither of us money to go on with it. and it will be impossible for her to get it without assistance. She certainly can't get it until She is married–which we shall do as soon as we hear from You. We cannot get along without Your assistance and by so doing You shall be well rewarded for it.

Whether it would be best for us to return to the East . . . You will know best. We have nothing to get there with and hope You may fur-nish us with some funds to get along with until we are able to obtain what justice will allow us. . . .

Do send me what money You can possibly spare and I will see that You are paid for it. . . . We shall probably be married as soon as we hear from You and get something to do with–I want to get A Situ-ation to Support us until we can obtain the money from Backus. . . .[25]

Six weeks later, at the end of November 1840, Andrew was over his homesickness and scribbled on the head of his letter "There is A vest at John Bulkeleys belonging to me. that I left on board the boat from Norwich to Albany," the boat he took from home to the head of the Erie Canal to the West. And he also scribbled: "All well. The amount of money Hannah is Entitled to is several thousand dollars. How does the Organ get along?" (a reference to the new organ being installed in the Congregational church across the street from the Bulkeleys' home). His ebullience filled the letter:

Dear Father I recd Your Kind letter last evening. was truly rejoiced on hearing from You. . . .

Since I wrote You there has been A revolution among the Bulkeleys and Fitchs [the relatives with whom Andrew had traveled west]. The Sunday after I wrote You Mrs. Orra Bulkeley [Dan's brother Gad Bulkeley's widow, with whom Phidelia had lived in Norwich five years before], Saml Bulkeley & wife, & Dr. Fitch & wife [Orra Bulkeley's daughter] undertook to break up the friendship that Existed between myself & Hannah (for the purpose of reaping the benefits of her services.) & Supposed they had gratified their own wishes by telling her all the lies They could about me. Mrs. Orra Bulkeley told her I was A low mien contemptible fellow and she said You was A mien good for nothing Bankrupt and that there were some of our family half witted &c–(I am so mad I cant write). Moreover all was Kept Still until Thursday–

before this I became acquainted with Dr. Drake an Eminent Physician and the wealthiest man in Town. He being A Sober candid man I consulted him. he said it was the most rascally piece of Business he Ever heard of–his daughter being an intimate friend of Hannahs–he Knew we were to be Married soon. and Says come to my house and be married. & stay as long as You please.

And now, to go back to My Story. on Tuesday I met Hannah at Dr. Drakes–and agreed to have the Knot tied and accordingly applied for my license. and sent for Mr. Lansing to tie the Knot. Dr. Fitch got wind of it and Sent his Brother and another Gentleman Saying that he wished to receive us into his house. Hannah said no. I dont like to go.

but it was thought by some of them we had better go. we accordingly went and I never Suffered such treatment in my life. Hannah stood by my side. I told Fitch he could not scare me. I should protect her. I said to Lansing if we are to be married in this house let it be done immediately. or we will have it done somewhere Else. we stood up and were Married and immediately left the House. and went to Dr. Drakes and we have not been to the house since. and never wish to Enter it again.

Nearly Every man in Town were in favor of us. and we recd many invitations to make it our home with them as long as we pleased. I remained with Mr. Drake three weeks and commenced [teaching] School three miles west from Greenville. have A very good School—

when I wrote You I had been here but A short time. And had not an opportunity of Knowing the disposition of the people and have formed A favorable opinion of them. they are verry hospitable indeed. A fine country for A Young fellow to make money if he is industrious. . . . I shall probably teach School six months and then go to St. Louis, if You do not wish to have us return to the East again.

Hannah lived with Fitch 17 months and worked like A dog. for which Fitch says he will not pay her a cent. the price for labour is $2.30 per week. the people all advise me to sue him. they say there is no danger but I shall get my case. what must I do about it—

Saml Bulkeley has threatened to shoot me. he says There will A letter come in the [post]office for me soon and he will see what there is in it—Likely!–. At the time of our Election Fitch snapped A pistol at a Man loaded with three balls. The Cap exploded but the pistol did not. he held the muzzle within 6 inches of his breast.

They are saying every thing against us. but to no effect—I have learned a lesson I never shall forget.–It will be of no use for me to borrow money of the friends (as You call them). I dont wish to have anything to do with them in any way. . . .

Mrs. Orra Bulkeley and Fitch are continually talking about You to the people in Greenville. they say You are A vagabond A drunkard and Every thing but A decent man. I will not bear it. Please send the money of Hannah's and Enclose to me all You can spare. . . . tell Henry . . . This state went Whig but I dont know what majority. . . .[26]

Life with family in the West was perhaps not so fraught for other people as it was for Andrew.

Dan managed this time to resist his son's entreaties to send cash. When Andrew wrote at the end of January 1841, he had begun to tire (again) of Illinois:

Dear Father I recd Your letter last Evening. was very much surprised in finding it contained no money. But for all that was very much gratified with the idea of hearing from home and also to hear You were in general health. I find by Your letter, You have recd A letter from Saml Bulkeley, & would like to know the substance of its contents. [So would we! It did not survive in the collection of Dan's letters.] I presume it is filled with infamous slander. and as for making friendship with that Crew I will see them in Bungy Town [Hell] before I will do it. . . . I want nothing more to do with them. they are A remnant of the piece that Chauncey F. Cleveland was cut from.

I wished to know in my last letter whether You wished to have me return home or not? and if so, what inducement You would offer. but I saw nothing in answer to it in Your letter. It is nearly time for me to obtain my . . . Employment and Your silence regarding our returning home Keeps me in suspense. If You wish us to return home, I wish You to send me what money You can. and with what little money I shall obtain by Keeping School we can get along. . . .

My health will hardly admit of my doing any business. this climate does not agree with me. it is too far from the Salt-water. I think if I dont return home (as there is A large number of families going to the Pacific Ocean at the mouth of the Columbia River) I shall go with them. A thousand acres of land Bounty & 2 Years provision for Every person that will go there. It is five thousand miles from this–there are great numbers there from this part of the country now. they say it is A Splendid Country. . . .

If You do not wish to have us return home I wish to have You send me all the money You can spare, and if You cant do that, please send me A shipment of Goods with A good share of Sewing Silk. it sells for 6 dollars per Hundred here. . . . direct them to the care of E & A Tracy, St. Louis, formerly of Norwich Con. . . .

My love to all.–A J Bulkeley[27]

That letter is the last that survives from Andrew in the Taintor-Davis collection. We do not know if Dan wrote to him again.

Dan's Death

Dan Bulkeley died in Hampton on June 10, 1842, in his fifty-ninth year. He did not leave a will–a sign that his final illness was suddenly fatal–and he died a bankrupt. On December 30, 1839, he had written a letter of instruction in case of his death:

Knowing the uncertainty of life and being in bad health–I would recommend for the security of my family should I be sudenly taken away and Knowing that I have very many unsettled accounts which if properly attended too would result justly to their benefit–Should such an occasion arise I should Recommend Henry G Taintor to be appointed Administrator on my Estate & to have him Examine every paper account and paper for many things that are of consequence will be found among them—and when said Estate is Settled it would be my wish after every honest debt is paid to provide properly for my Wife as she is not capable of takeing care of herself—and the Residue if any thing remaining to be distributed to my Children equally and have it placed in form that shall result to their benefit and not squandered. . . .

In September 1840, after Andrew had gone west, Dan added, "I would further Wish that no person by the name of Cleveland nor any one connected with Lester Burnett Should have any thing to do with the Settlement."[28]

The law called on Andrew J. Bulkeley to administer his father's estate. But he—in what was perhaps a last gesture of rebellion—refused. Luckily for posterity, Henry G. Taintor (Dan's nephew across the street in Hampton) was appointed, and he kept all Dan's papers, hoping to find those "many things that are of consequence" among them.

Henry G. Taintor's accounts of Dan's estate show that he paid Robert D. Dorrance five dollars for making Dan's coffin, and that Simeon S. Batterson charged twenty dollars for "Grave Stones erected at the grave of . . . Dan Bulkeley." In another transaction, Hannah D. Clark charged Phoebe Bulkeley $117 to make her "a Hat, crape, Hat Frames, and Ribbon."[29]

After the funeral, there was no way in the Hampton of 1842 to avoid the involvement of the Cleveland family in the settlement of an estate. Mason Cleveland auctioned off the goods—including one "Seraphine" valued at fifty-five dollars—left by Dan which were not "set aside for the widow" along with the land Dan owned. He even bought some of the land himself. Chauncey F. Cleveland, who became governor of Connecticut the year Dan died, bought a pasture and mowing as well as a lot of "old books" that had been Dan's. And in the following years he occasionally rented the "Bulkeley barn" from Henry Taintor. Dan was unsuccessful, even in death, at resisting the effect of the Clevelands.

William Brown, who had taken the postmastership from Dan in 1836, bought Dan's store and himself ran a store in it. The house and house lot next door were sold to Nelson Higgins—who later married Phidelia Bulkeley. But one-third of that house and house lot were "set off to" widow Phoebe Bulkeley. The line of the division ran "through the centre of the front door" and was described and carefully surveyed using degrees, compass directions, chains, and links, and "reserving the privilege to said widow and whoever may own the other part of [the] house of passing & repassing where it shall be necessary to improve their premises . . . and in using the space, stairs, well, oven, &c., always doing as little damage as necessary." Such meticulous measurements and specifications were signs of the poverty of the widow.

Phoebe's sister-in-law, Judith Bulkeley Taintor, the widow of a well-to-do man who had left a will, still lived across the street in a legally undivided house with her son Henry and his wife. Three years later, in 1845, Phoebe's mother, Chloe Burnett, died and left Phoebe some of her clothes, as well as $110 in cash and "one-sixth part of Lester Burnett's note." So Dan had failed once again, from the grave, to control what happened to his estate.

Andrew Jackson Bulkeley returned to Hampton after his father died, and stayed for a time. There is no further letter from Andrew in the collection, but Henry Taintor recorded lending him some money in the early 1840s. After that, there is no record of him in Hampton. According to the family genealogy, which is noticeably sparse on his life, Andrew died in Pensacola, Florida, in 1880.

We found no letters from Dan and Phoebe Bulkeley's two younger children, Robert Worthington Bulkeley, who was five years younger than Andrew, and Mary Buckland Bulkeley, the baby of the family, born in 1825. She grew up to marry A. A. Bennett, a Hampton man who had moved west to Michigan. They were married in 1848 in that state. Robert Worthington Bulkeley lived for several years in Hampton. Henry and John Taintor interested themselves in his life until he became an adult. He did not marry until he was thirty-four, in 1858, when he married Jennie Spicer Dorrance, and not long after that he, too, disappeared from Hampton's records.

No man with the Bulkeley name in Hampton achieved the place or position to which Dan Bulkeley so diligently aspired.

PART III

BECOMING VICTORIAN

The generation born
during and after
the War of 1812 as it matured
in the 1840s and 1850s

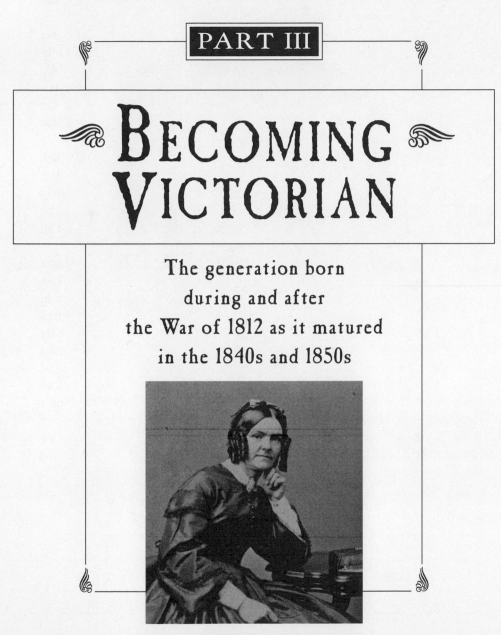

Delia Ellsworth Taintor
in the 1860s.

STARTING A NEW FAMILY

 басу

*"Is not a little baby—one's own baby especially
the neatest thing in the world?..."*[1]

Henry Griswold Taintor married Delia Williams Ellsworth on September 25, 1839, in Windsor, Connecticut. Henry was twenty-six years old, Delia was twenty-one.

The story of how they met is the story of many young couples in the second quarter of the nineteenth century. As we saw in John Taintor's life, the young were encouraged to meet members of the opposite sex because marriage was a necessary step into adulthood. Henry and Delia met through kin in Hartford where both had family. Henry's cousin John lived in the city, and John's sister-in-law was married to Delia Ellsworth's cousin. John and his wife invited Henry to visit. They took him along to dances, arranged invitations for him to people's houses. Delia's kin did the same for her as they "introduced her to society" in Hartford. The two young people came to know each other and fell in love. We have seen none of their early love letters, but the rest of their correspondence and their lives are testimony that it was a lasting love.

What Henry and Delia Brought to Their Marriage

Henry G. Taintor was the grandson of an innkeeper and the son of a leading man of his town. Delia W. Ellsworth was the granddaughter of Oliver Ellsworth, a shaper of the United States Constitution and the third Chief Justice of the Supreme Court (during President John Adams's administration). Her father, Martin Ellsworth, had inherited the elegant family home and land in Windsor, where Delia grew up. It might seem that there was a large social disparity between the two families; however they did not see it that way. No one ever objected to the marriage. The Taintors and the Ellsworths shared republican values that denied the importance of class distinctions.

The shapes of the Taintor and Ellsworth families were very different. Henry was born in 1813, the third child of Solomon and Judith Taintor. He had the unusual experience of growing up in a household with two sets of parents. He had a much older brother, and a sister who had died before he was born, so he was raised as an only child. His older "brothers," Bulkeley and John, were of another generation so far as Henry was concerned; born in 1800, they grew up with eighteenth-century values. Henry was a nine-teenth-century man.

Delia Ellsworth's family was a contrast to the Taintor household. She was the fifth child of six who grew to adulthood in the big house they all called "Elmwood" in Windsor. They were quite a cast of characters. Delia grew up in close contact with two very lively sisters—Abby, who was the elder, sent to Greenfield High School before Delia went, and Ellen, who was six years Delia's junior. Their eldest brother, Oliver, an 1830 graduate of Yale, was "killed by the kick of a horse" in 1841; he never married. Their

The 1792 portrait of Oliver and Abigail Ellsworth, by Ralph Earl, that hung in Elmwood throughout Delia's life.

brother Samuel moved west to Indiana with his family. Frederick, the last brother, stayed at the home place and eventually inherited it.

Henry Taintor's father died when Henry was fourteen, and his uncle and aunt lived only four more years. (His older brother Bulkeley had already married and moved to West Brookfield, Massachusetts.) His mother, Judith Bulkeley Taintor, continued to live in their half of the house in Hampton; Henry lived with her. Henry had a guardian until he came of age in 1834–first his uncle Roger and then his cousin John. John was close to Henry throughout his life in a way that Bulkeley was not. Bulkeley grew more and more distant from both his cousin and his younger brother.

A few of Henry's surviving schoolbooks show how his values and his knowledge took form. When he was just eleven years old he practiced his penmanship at Plainfield Academy by copying such sentences and phrases as "Fortune is inconstant. Sin most commonly brings sorrow. Scorn a mean action. Saint George's Channel between England [and what?]. Renard the virtuous. Olympus a Mountain of Turkey. Beauty soon decays. Make much of time. Teneriffe Peak Canaries Atlantic Ocean. Death is inevitable. Emulation is noble. Isthmus of Panama joins North & South. . . . Wise men commonly measure time. Avoid evil speaking. . . . Good humour pleases. Pyrenean Mountains divide France from Spain. . . . Money makes the mare go. . . . Fear God and keep his commandments. Honor your parents Henry."[2]

Henry was still at Plainfield Academy four years later, when he was fifteen. He wrote a poem in one of his notebooks:

> My boy refused his food forgot to play
> And sickened on the waters day by day
> He smiled more seldom on his mothers smile
> He prattled less in accents void of guile
> Off [of] that wild land beyond the golden wave
> Were [where] I, not he was doomed to be a slave
> Cold o'er his limbs the listless langour grew
> Paleness came o'er his eye of placid blue.
>
> Henry G. Taintor

In his penmanship notebook that year is the affirmation of classlessness that his republican generation learned early: "Honour and shame from no condition rise. . . ." It is followed by another combination of aphorisms and geography (this was in 1828, the year John went to Europe for the first time): "Earth is a tiresome place. The desire of improvement discovers a liberal mind. Hartford New Haven New London Middletown Norwich. Time once past never returns the moment that is lost. . . . Lockport Liverpool London Manchester Middle Haddam. Genuine virtue has a language that speaks to every heart (throughout the world). Forgive your enemies bless them that curse you and pray for. Hail to the day returnin. Raleigh the seat of Government of North-Carolina. Harrisburgh the seat of Government for Philadelphia. Genuine virtue has a language. Geography is a description of the earth, Henry G. Taintor's Book."[3]

Henry did not prepare for college, nor did he follow Bulkeley and John to Yale. His schooling was in preparation for the life of a farmer and businessman. One of his books at Plainfield was *The Scholar's Arithmetic; Or, Federal Accountant,*[4] which contained sections on "Federal Money," "Exchange," "Simple Interest," and "Barter" ("Barter is the exchanging of one commodity for another, and teaches merchants so to proportion their quantities, that neither shall sustain loss"). After he left Plainfield Academy he clerked in a store/post office in Brooklyn, Connecticut, and briefly for his uncle Dan Bulkeley in Hampton.

On September 16, 1830, when he was in his late teens, Henry bought a copy of *The Works of The Late Dr. Ben Franklin; Memoirs of Early Life Written by Himself, and Essays Humorous, Moral, & Literary.* Franklin epitomized the newly popular ideal of the self-made man of business. The acceptance of Franklin's model among small-town capitalists helped create the connection between business entrepreneurship and what later generations thought of as the Puritan work ethic. For Henry, that amalgam replaced the gentlemanly ideal that dominated John and Bulkeley Taintor's lives.

Delia Ellsworth's family valued education for daughters and sons alike. When little Delia was only seven years old (in 1826) she received a letter from the aunt for whom she had been named:

> My dear Delia
>
> I was very much surprised and pleased to find you could write me a letter as I did not know you could write at all. I shall keep it that I may see how much you improve for the year to come. I shall not write you a very long letter because I hope your father will improve the snow [and get out the sleigh] & bring you and Abigail down to see me. . . .
>
> I have just heard by your Mother that you and Abigail have begun to go to your new school. I am glad to hear it is a good one—I send you a work bag to carry your work in, I hope it may be of more use to you than it has been to me—There was a very sad accident happened in Hartford last week, a young man fell from a scaffolding at the South meeting house and was so much hurt that he died in a few days—
>
> As I have company I must close my letter & hope it will not be long before you and Abigail both write a letter to
>
> Aunt Delia
>
> Ask Abigail to accept a thimble which is in your bag.

Little Delia had already learned to read and write at home, so she could read such horrific details as the "sad accident." (Death continued to be a presence in children's lives–Delia's little brother, born the year after this letter was written, died when he was two years old.)

After some years at the local Windsor school, to which she had gone carrying her work bag, Delia's parents sent her away to Greenfield, Massachusetts, High School where they had already sent Abby. Abby's roommate ("chum") wrote to Delia with encouragement, "My dear Chum's sister or the dear sister of my Chum I Love you–I love you and if you will only come away to G[reenfield] H[igh] S[chool] I will do all in *my* power to render you a happy creature. I have just bought some candy . . . and if you will only come 'we will eat together & talk together & do all manners of works together' *Come Come Come.* . . . Your *true & loving friend*–Chum of your Sis."⁵

Once Delia was at the high school she was immersed in difficult studies, including Latin. For the rest of her life she kept Adams's *Latin Grammar,* on the flyleaf of which she had declined her name in appropriate Latin cases: "Delia, ae, ae, am, a, a; Deliae, arum, is, as, is" (apparently she did not feel the need for a vocative plural). For Delia the most important benefit of her education at Greenfield was a deepening personal sense of the meaning of Christianity. Her schoolmates absorbed it with her. Her friend Clarissa wrote to her when they were both fourteen, when Clarissa left school, "With the remembrance of past scenes is & always will be associated yourself with a thousand other recollections which endear us . . . to each other peculiarly. We were both under the same warnings and exhortations brought to see our lost and ruined condition as sinners, and to accept of those offers of salvation tendered to us in the Gospel. We have both joined the Church of Christ, professed ourselves its sincere followers, and each enlisted forever under his banner. If friendship formed under such circumstances is not *strong* and lasting, I know not under what others they could be."⁶

But Christianity was not merely a set of personal beliefs. Delia's teachers made sure she saw her life as a perpetual evangelical mission. One wrote, "I am delighted, my dear, that you enjoy so much from the service of God. . . . We are indeed honoured by being permitted to labour for the dear Saviour, who has died to save us. Oh! if we may be the *instruments* of bringing one soul to know and love him, we shall have cause to spend an eternity in praise. Let us then pray for others, let us strive to interest all around us in the great questions, not discouraged if we do not see the answer to our prayers, nor the fruit of our labours, and remember at the same time, that all will be in vain without the blessing of God."⁷

The lessons Delia learned in Greenfield stuck with her throughout her life. Another teacher wrote after Delia left school, "How should I love to have you so near that you might unite with us [at prayer], a feeble band. But we seem to be much scattered, here & there a friend to Zion who mourns her desolations. But this no doubt is wisely ordered, & did we always exert that christian influence we ought, & prove ourselfs the 'salt of the earth' by being thus scattered, that influence might be more widely extended & more good thus accomplished. Christians are called 'the light of the world' a 'city set upon a hill.' This reflection, *to me* is most striking & humbling. I feel the eyes of the world are upon me, ready to scrutinize my conduct. . . . May our great enquiry be 'Lord what wilt thou have me to do' & when we know our duty be faithful to perform it, & not stand idle in his vineyard."[8]

When Delia married Henry she was certainly "much scattered" from the young ladies with whom she had grown up. Her teacher had evoked the image of the "city set upon a hill" inherited from the early Puritan set-tlers of New England. In the fifty years of her married life on Hampton Hill, Delia saw her duty as the active effort to enlarge the membership and influence of her church, and she did not stand idle in that "vineyard." Always mixed with her humor and her warmth was a sense of her Christian mission.

The personality trait of Henry's at which we can guess was a family tendency toward what the nineteenth century called "melancholy." It is hinted at by the only book with his father Solomon's name in it that stayed in the house: *A Translation of the First Book of Ovid's Tristia, in Heroic English Verse; with the Original Text* by Francis Arden (published in New York in 1821). These are sad poems, written in exile; Solomon had bought the book as he was approaching old age. There are evidences that Solomon periodi-

MARTIN ELLSWORTH m. (1807) SOPHIA WOLCOTT
1783–1857   1786–1870
(son of Oliver Ellsworth)

Oliver	Abigail Wolcott m. David Aiken Hall	Delia Williams m. Henry G. Taintor	Henry

Samuel Wolcott m. Elizabeth Drake	Frederick m. Elizabeth Halsey	Ellen Sophia m. (1) George W. Strong

(2) John Prout

cally withdrew from the world. His sons Bulkeley and Henry were subject to melancholy and withdrawal in their later years. The warm and cheerful young man who married Delia Ellsworth gave little evidence, however, of any sadness within him.

Both Henry and Delia received some counsel in the spring of 1839 when their engagement became firm. Delia's spinster teacher and friend, Elisa Pickett, wrote that although she felt herself "incompetent to counsel," she could reassure Delia that "if after imploring Divine guidance you have come to the decision, and are following the leadings of Providence, what have you to fear? The path of duty is the path of safety. None but the eye of Omniscience & yourself can weigh the secret motives of your heart. Lean on the arm of your almighty friend, & he will uphold you & keep you from sin & danger." Miss Pickett fervently prayed, "May you never have cause to regret the step you have taken, but rather to rejoice. May you be faithful to your Saviour, faithful to the companion of your choice, & yet find in him a help meet to the world of bliss."[9]

At the same time, Henry's mother, Judith, counseled him about the importance of the spiritual in his future married life. He saved only one letter from his mother, written to her nephew Thomas Moseley, the year before Henry married. Perhaps he kept it because in it she used the words she had addressed to him at this crucial juncture in his life. She wrote, "I want you to be happy now, & happy hereafter, & for that purpose will you listen to my entreaties that you will now seek the things that concern your everlasting peace."

Like all mothers at such a time, she remembered his childhood: "It seems to me but a few days since you was a school boy, a child, an infant. Childhood and youth are already surpassed with you & as a man you are endeavouring to prepare yourself to act your part respectably on the drama of life." But, she asked, "Are you equally engaged to be preparing for that life where there is no change of scene, & where joy unspeakable or woe unutterable are to be the eternal portion of the children of men?"

She acknowledged that, as we suspected, the older generation of Taintors had not been churchgoers: "To those who like myself have allowed the best part of life to pass in estrangement from God, & who have now but a trembling hope of forgiveness & acceptance, it seems a duty to warn those in the midst of life not thus by delay to furnish themselves cause for such unavailing regret, & to urge them to come & consecrate to God the freshness & vigor of their lives."

Even as Judith urged religious duty upon her son, she cheered him: "Think not that the religion of Christ is calculated to cast a gloom over the enjoyments of this life. With God's favor every enjoyment of life is heightened." She reminded him that "we shall have an inheritance assured for us when these heavens & this earth shall have passed away."[10]

The emphasis on a spiritual life–mixed with romantic love–was a common element in the counsel both Delia and Henry received. The older generation had recently come to this new sensibility which it considered very modern, and which we tend to relegate to a dusty closet labeled "Victorian." Both of the young people were readers of romantic novels as well as of religious tracts. All their lives they felt no discomfort in the combination of love, romance, and Christianity in their relationship with each other and their world.

Setting Up a Life Together

In November of 1838, when the crops were in in Hampton and the weather turned cold, Henry Taintor went "a-courtin'." Seven times between November 9, 1838, and September 20, 1839 (five days before his marriage in Windsor at Delia Ellsworth's home there), Henry's carefully preserved receipts record that he hired "Horse & Chaise to Windsor," or, on Christmas day 1838, "Horse & Sleigh to Windsor," or "Span [two horses] & Sleigh to Windsor" just after New Year's Day, or "Hack & Span to Springfield" just before his wedding.[11] On the back of one of those receipts, he wrote out a mathematical riddle:

> When first the marriage knot was tied
> Betwixt my wife & me
> My age did hers as much exceed
> As three times three does three.
> But when ten years & half ten years
> We man & wife had been
> Her age came up as near to mine
> As eight is to sixteen.
> What are the ages of each at the time of marriage?[12]

He also copied the solution, which makes the man's age forty-five and his bride's fifteen. It was a joke, not a reference to his own case (he was not quite six years older than Delia). He probably heard a great many jokes about marriage in his uncle Dan's store and from the men with whom he worked in the fields.

Henry and Delia were married by the Reverend S. D. Jewett in Windsor on September 25, 1839, at Elmwood since church weddings were still unusual. Afterward, the young couple came to live in the Taintor house in Hampton. We do not know if they took a wedding trip. It would have been unusual if they had.

As we read their papers we had to keep remembering that the house to which Henry and Delia came did not belong entirely to them. John had moved Roger and Nabby Taintor's furniture out of their half of the house when they died in 1831, and he sold their half to Henry. Judith continued to occupy her half of the house. Henry had recently rebuilt the kitchen ell. In 1838 Andrew Litchfield had sold to "Major Henery G. Taintor" bricks, joists, lath and "bords" (including oak and chestnut) for an extension and enlargement of it. It was finished just before their marriage.[13]

After they started housekeeping the young couple traveled a good deal, often with Judith. They went to Hartford so frequently it did not seem to them to be a journey worthy of much note. Henry's accounts show they made a special trip to New York in May of 1840. In the big city they bought everything from furniture and carpets to hats and gloves and mittens. They indulged in ice cream, cucumbers, and "pine apples." They rode an "omnibus" and went to the theater. They took $439 to spend on that trip, $300 of it "Delia's money." And they also carried $50 from Mrs. William Clark, probably to buy dress goods. Their spending looks profligate when compared to the previous generation's, and even compared to John's.[14]

A few years earlier, when Henry had come of age, among the first things he had done was travel. He had acquired some of the external trappings of his gentlemanly status on those early trips. He bought very elegant clothes in Hartford, including a "Super mulberry box coat for $30.00, a Super Black Coat and pantaloons for $35.00, a black velvet lappell vest, and a Super Bumbazine stock."[15] He traded a gold watch in for a new one, worth $115.[16] He bought a set of ivory-handled cutlery in Boston,[17] staying at the Tremont House and entertaining while he was there.[18] He bought an expensive percussion-cap fowling piece (shotgun) in Springfield, Massachusetts.[19] His travels took him to Washington, D.C., where he called on Samuel Grundy, a Connecticut congressman and early political "boss."[20] He went to the theater in New York and traveled from there to Philadelphia by "Steam Boat."[21] Henry was very musical; when he was at Plainfield Academy he had asked his Uncle Dan to buy him a flute, and in 1836 in Hartford he bought "one pianoforte No. 635 Gilberts make" for $235 from G. K. Hurlburt.[22] By the time he married, he regularly patronized gentlemen's tailors in New York and in Hartford.

Henry's parents had not spent so much. On the other hand, they had brought up their sons not to shrink from the kind of travel and conspicuous consumption associated with gentle status. Delia's family traveled and spent in the same way. Martin Ellsworth, Delia's father, paid for furniture the couple bought in Hartford, which was shipped "via the steam boat

Charter Oak to Norwich, and via the new Norwich and Worcester Railroad Company to Day Ville Depot" in the town of Killingly, twelve miles from Hampton. More than 150 years later, the "mahogany Scroll end French Bedstead" bought at that time is still in the house, as is its hair mattress "weighing 35 pounds."[23]

People in Hampton saw the newlyweds Henry and Delia in their new clothes take up residence in their freshly painted house. Calling on a new couple was polite, and anyway everyone was curious to see the bride and the new acquisitions. Anyone calling saw the elegant mahogany furniture[24] and the pianoforte in the parlor. People saw Henry taking his fancy watch out of his new pocket and no doubt admired Delia's fashionable dresses. Before he married, Henry had bought some expensive vehicles: a one-horse wagon and a "trotting wagon" (a sulky) from New York.[25] The young couple could be seen driving around town in Henry's "Brass Mounted Chaise & harness" drawn by his elegant dapple-gray horse.[26]

When Henry and Delia set themselves up in the house in Hampton they were taking up a leading position in the community, a position the Taintors had already established. Chauncey F. Cleveland was another

Receipt for furniture bought by Martin Ellsworth for Henry and Delia, including their sleigh bed.

(older) leading Hampton gentleman. There were a few others, including Henry's uncle Samuel S. Moseley, but not including his uncle Dan Bulkeley.

In small towns there are always a few people who are exemplars for the place. The rest of the citizenry follows them or rebels against them, loves them or hates them, aspires to their social position or vows never to care about such fripperies. Whatever their feelings, the majority of towns-people are reactors to these few who for various reasons seem to lead the pack. Henry had already established himself as a leader. Like all the other young men in town he had joined the militia. But unlike the majority he had been commissioned as a major and aide-de-camp to General John O. Howard (another Hampton resident) when he was twenty years old.[27]

Henry had inherited more than twenty thousand dollars' worth of property, when he turned twenty-one, most of it in the form of interest-bearing loans that had been made by Roger and John in his name to Hampton people.[28] The incomes and social status of the borrowers ranged from wealthy merchant-farmers like Samuel Moseley, who owed Henry several thousand dollars, to middling farmers like Hezekiah Hammond, who was obligated to pay sixty dollars a year for thirty years,[29] to small farmers on the edge of poverty like Prince Knowles, who owed a total of seventy-three dollars for which he had mortgaged all the land he owned.[30] So Henry's private banking in Hampton (which he continued throughout his life) put him in daily contact with all the conditions of men and women in the town.

All his life Henry called himself a farmer. He thought of himself as fol-lowing his father's footsteps. He did the daily chores of feeding and caring for animals. He worked in the fields and supervised his hired men. The dif-ference between him and his poorer neighbors was that Henry could hire help for the intensive times of farm work, and he usually had a "hired man" who lived and worked in his household throughout the growing sea-son. But during haying season, like all other farmers, he did not leave home. In the summer of 1842, when Delia visited her family in Windsor, Henry wrote to her, "Had I not very urgent business for my hands I know I would see you in less than two weeks, but I am in the midst of haying and cannot leave home. You do not know how much I wish you was here. . . . I get along very well without you when I am in the field or at work out of doors. but when I come in I am very lonesome." He assured her "if I was not in the midst of haying I should take my horse & start for Windsor."[31]

Henry and Delia's married life was not all work and no play. They had a book called *Chess Made Easy*, published in 1837, with a frontispiece show-ing a young couple playing. On the flyleaf was a mathematical riddle, in

Delia's handwriting (we append it for our readers' possible edification and solution, which has been beyond us):

> One hundred & one by fifty divide
> And then if a cipher be added beside
> And your calculation agree with mine
> The result will be one subtracted from nine.

They played backgammon together, and taught their children to play. Over the years they played cards as well–whist was a favorite game–and gambled a little on some of their card games. In later years, they played croquet. They did not feel that games diminished their spiritual credit with an always loving God.

In the second winter of their marriage, Henry and Delia traveled to Washington. Henry recorded that they took along $231 for the trip; they did some business in Baltimore for their neighbor William A. Brewster on the way, and they bought a book for another Hampton neighbor, Dyer Hughes, Jr., in Washington. They probably stayed with Delia's sister Abby, who lived in the Capital with her husband, David Aiken Hall, a lawyer. Abby's first child, Ellen, had been born the previous summer. It is likely that they attended the inauguration of President William Henry Harrison, the "Victor of Tippecanoe" (Tippecanoe had been an important battle against the Indians under Tecumseh in 1811). Harrison caught cold at the ceremonies and died shortly after the Taintors returned home. Henry was a supporter of Harrison. He kept a little book, *Harrison Melodies,* published during the campaign. The refrain of the last song in the book, "The Farmer of Tippecanoe," goes "Hurrah! for the farmer of Tippecanoe, / The honest old farmer of Tippecanoe, / With arm that is strong, and a heart that is true, / The man of the People is Tippecanoe."

The image of the popular born-in-a-log-cabin "man of the people" president had taken hold in Andrew Jackson's day. It had come to characterize the new party politics. Even the opposition espoused it–and in this case defeated the incumbent Jacksonian Democrat, Martin Van Buren, by using it. Henry was a member of William Henry Harrison's new political party, the Whigs.

He returned from Washington to take up his farming like any other "man of the people" and wrote in his account book on April 2nd, 1841, "I have this day sold to Capt. John Lincoln two cows amounting to $45. Mr. L. is to work my highway tax for 95 cts on the dollar the balance is to be paid in money and the cows remain mine until paid for."[32]

But the Taintors were also elegant and well-to-do. On that trip to Washington, they sat for their portraits. Two days after the inauguration, Henry paid Charles Bird King "One Hundred Dollars in full for the por-

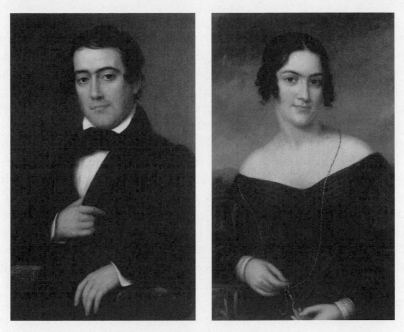

The 1841 portraits of Henry and Delia Taintor, painted by Charles Bird King,
that hung in their south parlor.

trait[s] of himself and lady." King was a well-known portraitist. His like-
nesses of Native American visitors to the Capital were famous and still
hang in world-class museums.[33] Henry and Delia brought the portraits
home to Hampton, and hung them in their front parlor (the southeast room
of the house). They stayed there for more than one hundred years. (Since
the portraits were unsigned, none of Henry and Delia's descendants knew
the identity of the artist until we found King's receipt among the family
papers.)

Changing the Nest

As they established their lives in the house in Hampton, Henry and Delia
made some changes. They had their own quarters painted and papered. The
outside of the whole house was also painted. Plaster was patched and
replaced. When they added modern heating stoves, the pipes ran through
halls and the walls of rooms to better distribute the heat–and that required
further repairs and decoration. Repairs were made to stairways and doors.
Sinks were added.[34] Throughout their lives both Henry and Delia paid
attention to paint, repairs, and decoration, inside and out, in order to keep
the house up as well as to keep it modern.

In the course of time, they made some major changes and additions. In 1844, they had Harvey Smith fence in the "door yard"–a sizable area to the south of the house–with stone posts and wooden rails securely attached to the posts with iron fittings.[35] Neat fencing set the house apart from the road in front, from the old store to the south, and from the outbuildings. And it was an elegant complement to the row of young sugar maples Roger Taintor had set out between the house and the road. Such fences were statements of the developing sense of distinction between the public life of the streets and community, and the private life of the family at home.

Ten years later, after Judith Taintor had died and the entire house had become Henry and Delia's, they took the first fence down and replaced it with a new picket fence. Lewis Fuller cut the wood and charged Henry two dollars for "Picket for Fence & gitting them Out."[36] That same year, 1854, the Taintors built "piazzas" (porches) on the front and on the south side of the house. Some of the wood came from Andrew Litchfield's sawmill on the Little River; some was shipped in by railroad and Litchfield carted it "from Depo."[37] The building of the porches required new siding and some replastering inside the house as well. Susie Taintor, Henry and Delia's niece, wrote to them that year, "I am fancying you now, in the midst of papering, plastering and building. . . . Is it not very tedious?"[38]

Along with the picket fence and the slender Italianate columns on the "piazzas," the Taintors put up outside shutters ("blinds"), to modernize the appearance of the house on new Victorian lines.[39] But it was not modern enough. By 1857, they added the most important element, the one that changed the house irrevocably from its earlier style: they "cut down to the floor"[40] the four front windows and the three south windows onto the piazzas. Workmen from Willimantic, using materials brought in from Norwich, installed large six-over-six windows and replaced all the wood-work in the three downstairs rooms involved. So there was more painting and decorating to be done, this time using "Jappan," "French Yellow," and "Venetian Red" as colors.[41]

The Taintors must have liked bright colors. In 1860, one of the Taintor children wrote to another, "Mr Lathrop has been making a new market-wagon for father. . . . It is painted blue with yellow wheels."[42] That taste was part of being Victorian.

Children Come Along

Henry and Delia's first son, Henry Ellsworth Taintor (the family distinguished him from his father by always referring to him as "Henry E."), was born on August 29, 1844, when Delia was twenty-six years old and had been married nearly five years. George Edwin was born on December 20,

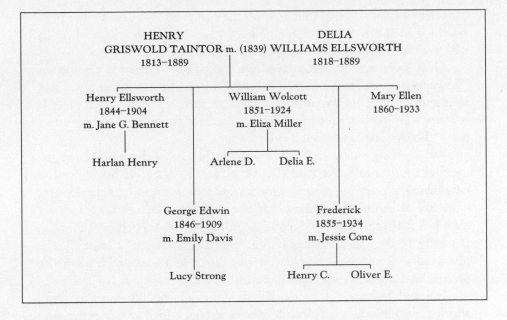

HENRY   DELIA
GRISWOLD TAINTOR m. (1839) WILLIAMS ELLSWORTH
1813–1889   1818–1889

Henry Ellsworth   William Wolcott   Mary Ellen
1844–1904   1851–1924   1860–1933
m. Jane G. Bennett   m. Eliza Miller

Harlan Henry   Arlene D.   Delia E.

George Edwin   Frederick
1846–1909   1855–1934
m. Emily Davis   m. Jessie Cone

Lucy Strong   Henry C.   Oliver E.

1846. Five years later, on July 9, 1851, came William Wolcott Taintor ("Willie" or "Will"), and four years after him Frederick ("Freddie" or "Fred") arrived on November 12, 1855. The family baby and only girl, Mary Ellen, made her appearance on October 8, 1860, when Delia was forty-two.

We know almost nothing about their births, but some cryptic notes in Henry Taintor's cash books give clues. Two weeks after little Henry E. was born, his father paid fifty cents for a "Nurse Lamp."[43] Obviously the baby was not sleeping through the night. A few months later Henry bought a "pair Cradle Blankets" and a "pair Infants Socks."[44] Henry recorded no special purchases around the times of George's or Willie's births except about a month after George was born, when his father paid a Mrs. Backus $5.25 with no notation of the reason; perhaps she was a mid-wife.[45] The month after Freddie was born his father noted, "Paid Mrs Wilcox in full $10."[46] She also could have been a midwife. The only clue when little Mary was born is a notation of two dollars to Mrs. Barrows ten days after the birth. Kate Parson was paid for five weeks' work through October of that year, so she, too, helped out.[47]

Delia's sister Abby Hall wrote her in 1856, shortly after they both had babies, pointing out to Delia that "You understand the absolute despotism of ones own baby & of other matters too that wisest mothers & house-keepers must yield our own wishes to." She wrote of her own baby that she agreed with her husband and sister-in-law that Mattie "is more promis-ing than any other baby of the house has been at so early an age & we are very happy in her. Is not a little baby—one's own baby especially the neatest thing in the world? I often think of you when I am most especially happy with mine & rejoice that you have the same pleasure."[48]

Girls learned to admire babies from the time of their own childhoods. The earliest letter Delia had ever received, when she was seven years old, mentioned "a very pretty babe" that was "growing finely" and whose little brother was "very desirous to have her baptized for fear they should lose her."[49] Sibling jealousies existed even then.

Delia's sister Abby had written of her first two children, "Ellen has improved into a talkative frolicking little child as queer & bright-eyed & bewitching as need be. Alice is pronounced a most beautiful baby, looking more like my sister Mrs. Taintor than like me!" She went on to say that her maid had taken the children out and "so many people stopped her to look at the baby & they all said 'they hardly ever saw so pretty a baby.' She is often called 'the prettiest baby in the city, beyond all compare' & I *begin* to surmise that she is something uncommon after all."[50]

But with children came danger. Caring for sick children was a mother's absolute duty. And the childhood diseases against which all babies are now immunized were all potential killers in the nineteenth century. Every illness brought fear. Abby wrote to Delia with understanding of "the heart ache watching & fatigue which consume the days & nights of the Mother of sick children."[51] A friend sympathized on the same occasion, "You must have had a Siege with a Sick husband, & three children with the whooping-cough."[52]

A terrible childhood killer was scarlet fever. Delia's sister Ellen wrote of a friend's child in 1860, "Mr. Baxter's little son, their only child is very sick indeed with scarlet fever—He was taken Saturday, and has been in a very critical state."[53] In the winter of 1860–61, just a few months after Mary was born, scarlet fever struck the Taintor household. Delia put off a visit to Windsor after Ellen warned her, "Much as we long to see you let me beg you not to come until the Dr. considers it entirely safe, as there is so much danger of after effects from Scarlet Fever."[54] At just this juncture, Henry E., who was away in Massachusetts at Monson Academy, caught the disease. Ellen went from Windsor to his bedside because Delia was still caring for those at home as well as nursing a new baby. Frantic about her eldest child, however, Delia journeyed to Monson as well. But she had to leave Ellen in charge when sickness again struck the Hampton children. Finally when Henry E. was allowed to come home, Ellen worried, "I trust he will make the journey safely, and doubt not Dr Smith is a correct judge of his ability to bear it—I cannot but tremble a little when I think how little time it is since he was so very sick."[55]

The Taintor children came safely through their childhoods, though many other children did not. Babies were the most endangered. Ellen wrote that a relative's child had died: "I hardly know what was the matter of it–Its birth was premature and it was a very puny feeble child–It was baptized the day before it died."[56]

Delia's niece Sophie Reynolds gave birth to her first child, Genevieve, in California, and her nearest relatives were in Indiana. One of her school friends wrote to Delia that she was "quite anxious to know how she and baby get along." The answer, unfortunately, was that little Genevieve died. According to Sophie's mother, who had not been able to be there to help her daughter, "The physicians think Genevieve's disease was malignant Scarlet fever but it was difficult to tell she was sick so short a time two days from the time she was taken sick she died."[57] Several years later, Sophie had "another little daughter" reported to look "a little like Genevieve."[58] When that child was three she, too, died of scarlet fever. Her mother always remembered her "dear little pale face that none of us can see again with human eyes, not even in a picture for we had never had her picture taken."[59]

Along with the care of sick children, women were expected to care for sick adults and other women in childbirth. Childbirth was, in fact, called "sickness." Sisters were the nurses of choice in childbirth: Delia's sister Ellen was with her through hers. Young Alice Hall (Abby's second daughter) wrote years later that she could not leave her sister Nelly "at all until after her sickness. . . . And she does not expect her sickness until almost the middle of this month."[60]

Women also cared for the elderly and the dying. Many of Delia's correspondents wrote to her in detail about the deathbeds they attended. The tradition of "watching"–sitting night and day with a dying person–continued throughout Delia's lifetime. A friend in Colchester wrote of her mother's last illness that she had been "a great sufferer but *very* cheerful." She met "everyone with a smile so that her room had not the usual gloomy cast of a sick room. . . . it was natural for her to make the best of everything–she felt all ready & willing to go hence." She told her daughter "about two weeks before her death & said to a friend who was watching with her the last night 'that if she did get to sleep, hoped she might never wake'–that wish was granted for she not long after fell asleep & breathed her last about 3 o'clock in the morning."[61]

Families assumed the care of the elderly and dying was part of a daughter's appointed tasks. It was Delia and Henry's task for the first ten years of their marriage, until Henry's mother (who had no daughters) died in 1849. Delia's sister Ellen lived at Elmwood for years (after she was widowed) when their mother was elderly. Delia herself visited often to help out with their mother. Out in Lafayette, Indiana, their brother Samuel's mother-in-law lived with the family for years to be cared for by her daughter. After Henry's brother Bulkeley died, his daughter cared for her mother until her death.

From the elderly, Delia and Henry turned as a matter of course to the education of their young. All their children went to the Center School in Hampton, a one-room school in those days, for their elementary education. They learned to read either at home or in school, probably at home. In school, they learned arithmetic and became familiar with the patriotic and religious stories of America that were the substance of the literacy training that most "common" or "grammar" schools offered. The boys learned some about farm life while they were at home, and Mary learned to keep house. For most of their youth there were no academies or high schools in Hampton, so after the Taintor children acquired the basics, their parents sent them away for further education.

HAMPTON AT MID-CENTURY

*"We all should be thankful that God has cast our lot
in such pleasant places."*[1]

T he names of more than 150 Hampton residents appear in Henry
Taintor's earliest accounts. That means he did business with at least
fifteen percent of Hampton's total population, many more than half
of all the families in town. The number increased from year to year.
His business and political connections embraced an ever widening circle,
both geographically and numerically.

Delia's tasks remained tied to the house and the children. She went out
of the house to church and to prayer meetings, where she met all conditions of people in town. She called on her neighbors nearly every day, and
they came to her house as often.

The Button family were the Taintors' closest neighbors. The Buttons'
houses, barns, and sheds were opposite the Taintors' on the road and green
which made up the village street. Charles C. Button, Sr., had started the
Buttons' business years before the Taintors were married, and continued to
run that business for many years after. Delia and Henry both called frequently on Charles C. Button, Jr., and his wife, Ruth, a couple about their
own age. Ruth Button took care of the Taintor children sometimes when
their parents were away.

The Buttons ran a livery stable and made and repaired harness. Of
course, they farmed as well. They provided vehicles with and without driv-
ers, teams of horses and oxen, as well as harness, repairs, and shoeing to
the Taintors as well as to everyone else in Hampton. Henry Taintor lent
the Buttons thousands of dollars over the half century of their relationship

(which may have been the working capital the Buttons required), sold them many of his own farm's products—manure, hay, potatoes, rye, and buck-wheat—and exchanged teams, farm implements, and vehicles with them. For a while in the 1840s and 1850s, the Buttons ran the tavern or inn across the street from the Taintors.

The Taintors' lives at mid-century belie some common assumptions about small-town life. While religion remained central to them, the church they went to changed. Although they lived out their lives in Hampton, they were not limited by it. Although the town was getting smaller, new people were moving in. And problems which had been ignored for years became central to the Taintors and to Hampton.

Reorienting Religion

When Henry and Delia Taintor were first married and moved into the house in Hampton, the Congregational church next door went through a significant change. In 1833, the town had built a town "hall" onto the Center School building in the village in which to hold the Town Meetings and electors' meetings that had always been held in the Meeting House.[2] There was a growing feeling that religion, and church services particularly, should be physically separated from public, governmental affairs.

In late 1839 or early 1840 the whole meetinghouse building was jacked up and turned on its axis so that its narrow end faced east toward the village street. New foundations were dug and stone put in place. The interior of the building was completely rebuilt, the existing pews and pulpit and balcony were moved and replaced, and a dais with altar table was built on the western (narrow) wall. Outside, a raised stone porch was built with steps to it, Doric fluted columns and a pediment were put on it, and a tall spire with belfry was built high above the roof. The building ceased to be the Hampton meetinghouse and became the Congregational church sanctuary. In April 1839, Henry G. Taintor, as Collector for the First Ecclesiastical Society of Hampton, paid out $500, "a part of the subscription for repairing the Meeting house," to Amos T. Kenyon for the work.[3]

The transformation of Hampton's meetinghouse into a church came as a result of changes that were taking place in Protestant Christianity all over America, affecting all churches as well as nearly every believer. Antiestablishment movements and antiorganized-church movements had grown since the 1820s. They had produced increasing efforts to separate church and religious life from political and secular life. Political rhetoric, institutions of government at every level, and the burgeoning "civil religion" in American schools gave many a sense of participation in Christian culture and ethics without the necessity of membership in or attendance at church. Many

An 1840s daguerreotype of Henry G. Taintor.

new public issues—temperance and abolition of slavery were two of increasing importance—had powerful Christian and religious connotations for most
people, but they were debated, discussed, and acted upon primarily in secular
and political spheres, not in churches and often not on the Sabbath.

Churches in general responded to this separation of organized religion
from daily and public life by emphasizing the holy and sacred character of
their buildings and of religious ritual. And they tried to create effective,
specifically religious institutions for Christian education and the promulga-
tion of Christian beliefs and morality. Local congregations, encouraged and
coordinated by national and regional church organizations, created Sabbath
schools and missionary societies to bring religious training in Christian
belief and Christian action to their own communities.

In Hampton, as in many small towns where church buildings were
already built and congregations were well established, the reorientation of
the meetinghouse and its reconstruction as a church sanctuary were both
the visible symbol and a substantive part of the separation of the church
from the fabric of a seamless community life. The new imposing building
with its gleaming white paint was a symbol of the importance of the
church's renewed, sacred activities and of church-specific societies and
organizations in the life of a modern community.

The Hampton Congregational church (officially, the First Ecclesiastical
Society of Hampton) between the 1830s and the 1850s created a Sabbath

school, formed a Ladies' Society, and created a local temperance organization. The church raised money by subscription to help members of the community in distress: for example, in 1844 William Durkee III "received . . . of Henry G. Taintor Ten Dollars in full for a subscription [a church collection] for loss of my Barn by lightning."[4] At the same time, the Hampton congregation made sizable contributions year after year—in work, in money, and in handmade (manufactured) goods—to church organizations outside town, especially the American Board of Commissioners for Foreign Missions, the Society for the Promotion of Collegiate and Theological Education at the West, and the American Tract Society. Subscriptions to periodicals published by the national church organizations—such as *The Congregationalist* and *The Messenger*—were collected from local church members and forwarded by the church treasurer (who was, in Hampton, from the late 1830s to 1889, Henry G. Taintor).[5]

Henry Taintor also helped to get instrumental music made part of the Hampton Congregational church's new style of worship in its reoriented building. Henry contracted with Denison Smith to install a tracker organ of Smith's design in the balcony of the church. The organ provided accompaniment to the choral singing of hymns and psalms which the musical Henry had encouraged in the church. Henry paid Smith for the organ in June 1841.[6] In subsequent years, Smith came back to Hampton to tune the organ and make repairs. Young men pumped the air necessary to make the pipes work—according to Henry's accounts, they were paid for "blowing organ."[7] No one mentioned that particular phraseology when the tracker organ was recently rebuilt and restored by subscription from the whole town and friends of Hampton.

A sexton was hired for the church, to keep it clean and to provide "fires" as well as lights for it. When the building was reoriented and redecorated, part of the modernization included the introduction of heating stoves to a building which had not been heated in the ninety years it had stood in Hampton village. John R. Tweedy was the sexton—although Henry Taintor never used the word. Tweedy cut and hauled the wood, too. And the church treasurer also began to pay for wine for Communion.[8]

Contact with the Cosmopolitan

The world reached into Hampton. We think of small towns as insular, but Henry and Delia Taintor's lives were not circumscribed by their home duties or Hampton's boundaries. They and their fellow townspeople traveled, subscribed to newspapers, and shared letters and news from those far away. In 1845 and 1846, for instance, former Hampton resident John Taintor and his wife, Adelia, left their Hartford home with their two daughters (Louise and Alice) and traveled for a year in Europe. John's business purpose for the trip was the purchase of animals for his growing stock-breeding enterprise. He wrote of what he saw in long letters to Henry—which were read aloud in the Taintor house and shown to friends and neighbors in Hampton.

The first letter begins on May 16, 1845: "Off Sandy Hook . . . The pilot soon leaves us, & I have only a minute to say, good bye–good bye–The sea is smooth & the wind fair & moderate. . . . On the 11th of June I think we shall dine in Liverpool. Thirty passengers & are agreeable company. 7 ladies & one little boy besides our children."[9]

In his next letter, from London, John told Henry about his voyage on a sailing ship: "When near the Banks of Newfoundland we had 4 days of calm, a dead calm, when not a ripple even, was on the face of the ocean. Then a wind sprung up, which increased into a terrible gale from the North West, & held us for 36 hours. You can judge of the force of the wind when I tell you that with only close reefd. Main & fore top sails, we made 293 miles in 24 hours [more than 12 miles per hour, a remarkable speed for a large sailing ship]. It was a hard time, & I see by the papers, many vessels were damaged by it."

The small number of passengers tested John's patience. He wrote, "We had a pleasant set of passengers except 2 from Philadelphia (Humphrey & wife). Both were frightened to death of the whole passage & gave us much trouble, by making a terrible fuss every time the ship rolled. They annoyed me & the children exceedingly, & I had a blow up with them." The blowup did not seem to prevent the Taintors from making friends with the Humphreys, because they left their children with them later in the trip.

John informed his Hampton readers that "On Sunday, June 8th at 6.P.M. we made the South West coast of Ireland . . . & I thought of you, as just going to Church in the after noon–say 1 P.M.–as there is nearly 5 hours difference, in time between London & you. Deduct 5 hours from your time, & it will give you the time here very nearly." There was no standardized time in the world.

The next adventure expressed the wonders of modern transportation and communication. John wrote, "Our signal was seen from Holly head, & by telegraph conveyed to Liverpool in 20 minutes, for a steam boat to come over for the ship and passengers. The distance was 70 miles! In the afternoon, a boat came & took us in tow, & we reached Liverpool at 12 oclock that night & went on shore after breakfast, in great spirits."

The early Victorian London of Charles Dickens impressed John by its size and panoply, not by the qualities Dickens memorialized. Perhaps John never had his pocket picked by the Artful Dodger, never saw the dinosaur-slow progress of the courts in session or the squalid interiors of the city's jails. "London is an immense place, with over 3 millions of people! Only think of what a collection!"

John knew Henry and his militia buddies would be fascinated when he wrote, "I wanted you here very much indeed, to see 2 Regiments of Horse guards & 2 of Foot, on parade at St. James Palace. The Foot, were the cele-brated Coldstream guards. The Regiments were changing quarters. The display was superb. The men were all over 6 ft 2 in., with high bear skin caps, (2 ft. high) red coats & white pants. Each Regiment had a Military band (drum & fife) of about 30, & also each, an instrumental band of 50–excel-lent performances. The latter had a boy stand in front of each man to hold the notes of the music, so accurately did they perform. It was capital."

He described the music he knew Henry would have loved. "The troops were paraded on each side of the court yard of the Palace, & the Bands in the centre. Each band played 3 pieces, for over ½ an hour in all, when the whole 160 performers struck up 'God save the Queen' & the flags were unfurld, & the order was given 'forward' & the troops wheeld. in plattoons of 16, & marchd out of the gates. It was a splendid sight & I would have given much, if you, & Cleveland had been by my side. I know you both would have enjoyed it to the life."

John's pleasure at being a spectator of such magnificence is an interest-ing counterpoint to his republicanism. "On Monday next I am invited by an Officer, to go & see the Queen review the Guards in person, & will give you a description of the affair," which he did in the same letter, delayed for the purpose. "Oh how I wanted you both at my side. Delia & the children were with me. The troops were rather over Six Thousand. 2000 horse (all blacks) except Wellington's which was white & 4000 foot. It was the most superb sight I ever saw. . . . The spectators were immense, probably over one hundred thousand. To day, I have been to Parliament & seen Sir Robert Peel, John Russell, Jos. Graham, & all the great guns of the nation & heard a long debate. Yesterday on the field, a platform, 10 feet from ours, gave way & 2 gentlemen were injured. One broke his thigh & arm & the other his leg."[10]

John next wrote to Henry from Liverpool, where he and Adelia had gone to put their children in school. English weather was "very cold here this summer. Windows are kept closed all the time, & in traveling I always wear an overcoat, & 2 blankets on the bed at night. How very strange!–& it is more strange that the crops ever ripen. The only fruit, I have yet seen, are cherries, strawberries & gooseberries, which are all of large size, & very cheap, but not sweet." He attended "an immense exhibition, covering many acres" at the Royal Agricultural Society's Annual Show, and he had

"The Great Britain Steam Ship," on a letter from
John Taintor to Henry G. Taintor, 1844.

also gone "on board the big steamer Great Britain, which sails to day at 3 oclock. She is enormous, & I think far too big—for safety—or speed. The interest she excites here is very great. She gets only a few passengers, as it is her first trip." He sent Henry a railroad map of England because, he said, "The whole country is mad on the subject."[11]

John was struck throughout his travels by the extremes of poverty as well as by the enormous standing armies of Europe, both of which he took as symbols as well as realities of the evils of monarchy. He wished Henry could "see the old World in all its splendor, & its misery. Such extremes of either, you never saw or immagined. I am more than ever satisfied with our own dear Country. This is the place to make Republicans."[12]

On the Continent, John, like the people he was writing to in Hampton, reflected both horror at the decadence of Europe ("the great mass of the people . . . are poor & the taxes are very heavy. They have a standing army of one hundred & ten thousand men, & another small army of Priests") and admiration for much of its culture. He visited the "large Cathedral" at Antwerp "with a number of paintings by Rubens & other old masters," and went to Harlem where he "heard the large organ for an hour. . . . It has five thousand pipes & the largest of them are 2 feet in diameter! The . . . Church which contains it is one of the largest in Europe. It is the wonder of the world."

John knew the readers of his letters were farmers, so he reported of Dutch cow stables that they were "as clean as ordinary houses in France, &

you will laugh when I tell you, that in every stable, hooks are placed back of each cow to tie up their tails, that no part of the animal shall be soild! This you may rely upon as a fact, strange as it may seem." He was a great admirer of the Dutch, who, he said "all work hard & live economically. No beggars are to be seen as in France & Belgium, where a miserable group of all ages in rags will follow your carriage for miles, turning somersets & playing all sorts of pranks to excite your attention or commiseration." When John and Adelia were going to see the battlefield of Waterloo, they "were followed by a group of children & girls, from 3 years old to 18, & the miserable objects would roll over like wheels, turn somersets, stand on their heads &c. &c. The larger the girls the more they seemd. to pride themselves by their indecent exhibitions. What a state of society in a Country calling itself civilized!" He contrasted Belgium with Holland, where "the common people are sober, industrious & well clad. . . . The girls are very fair & beautiful. All languages are spoken here badly, & nearly all have a few words of English at their command."

As a postscript to the same letter, after he had traveled 350 miles on the Rhine by steamboat, John commented on the backwardness of German agriculture: "There are no oxen, & nearly all the work is done by men & women, in the fields. Horses are only used for stages & coaches & they are miserable. The little work that is done (for hauling) is by cows with a piece of wood tied with ropes in front of the horns–to answer for a yoke. How very strange, they are so far behind the rest of the civilized world."[13]

Hampton had several sheep farmers, including Henry Taintor, so John's reports of Saxony sheep management would have been fascinating reading: "The rain is never allowed to fall on them & they are put under large sheds every night. This is done with all the extra fine flocks. The others are managed by a shepherd & dogs, by day & night, when he sleeps in a small straw house, which he draws on wheels. The sheep collect around it & the dogs keep all safe. It is surprising how well they have them trained."

John also admired military heroes. He wrote with pride when he visited the burial place of Frederick the Great of Prussia at Potsdam, "I put my hand on the coffin of the great warrior." And he described, in numerical detail, the masses of soldiers and armies he saw in Prussia and near Prague (then part of the Austrian Empire), and commented, "Here they think no more of soldiers by the thousands, than we do by tens."[14]

Part of the romantic and scientific interest of the age was symbolized by volcanoes and the study of them. New museums and galleries were displaying romantic paintings of the Italian volcanoes, Etna on Sicily (after which a Hartford Insurance company was named) and Vesuvius, near Naples. Engravings in schoolbooks also spread the interest. So John had a ready audience for his description of his trip to Naples and Vesuvius:

... At Naples we left the ladies & ... went to visit the crater of Mt. Vesuvius distant about 10 miles. We took 5 men for guides & to assist up the steep sides of the immense mountain.

We reached the top, about 2 P.M. & although I had a strong man to pull me along, by straps, yet I was nearly exhausted & drank nearly a bottle of wine without feeling the least effect from it. The sight was grand & awful. The crater of the volcano is round & in circumference about 2 miles. In the very centre is a place 1000 feet deep or more, from which comes the volcano. While we were there, immense masses of red hot rocks, & lava were thrown up onto the air 5 to 600 feet, & the lava would often come rolling down nearly to where we stood, so near that we could touch it with our canes, & I put 2 pieces of copper in the hot lava, & brought it off with me, which I hope one day to show you. I have also some views of the place which will interest you. We returned completely tired out by the fatigues of the day.

This is the volcano you know, which destroyd. Pompeii & Herculaneum, nearly 1800 years ago. These 2 Cities were about 6 miles from the Mountain & contained three to four hundred thousand people each. P. was covered about 15 feet & H. about 40 feet by ashes & lava & thousands were destroyed, for there was no time for them to escape.

Only a few years ago, they began to dig out the lava & now, Pompeii has been opened for five acres or more, and men are yet at work. It is astonishing in what good preservation many things are found, as I shall show you, if I ever get home. I never was more inter-ested in my life than by a visit to those 2 places. When I get home, I will (if requested,) for once, give a lecture to my Hampton friends at the Town house, on this interesting subject with an account of my visit to the volcano. It is wonderful & I could hardly believe it, if I had not seen with my own eyes. You will be astonished. . . .

He concluded his letter with a comment somewhat surprising from the man who could not wait to leave Hampton when he was younger: "I feel satisfied Hartford & Hampton are the best places in this World for me, & we all should be thankful that God has cast our lot in such pleasant places."[15]

From Naples, John and his wife traveled to Rome, and then took a ship from Italy to Marseilles, in France. On the third night they "had a terrible thunder storm which lasted for some hours. The Heavens were as bright as a furnace with lightning & the sea very rough. The vessel was loaded with figs and rolld. very hard. I got into my berth & tried to feel as if I was as well off as if at home, but I could not make it out." When they "got safe into Marseilles" they "saw 6000 men reviewed as they were going on board vessels for Algiers." The French were trying to conquer Algeria and John, typically American, saw the price of empire as excessive: "many of the men looked dejected, and well they might, for many of them will there find their graves. The French have now near 100,000 men in Africa & will eventually conquer the whole country, though with a terrible loss of lives." His Hampton audience would have echoed John's understanding of the costs of French imperialism as part of their general abhorrence of Old World empire. They would not have known that American expansion into the West, which they heartily endorsed, might be seen by later generations as very like that imperialism. (Six months after John wrote his letter, the United States went to war against Mexico and annexed all of the northern provinces of that nation.)

On his way from Marseilles to Paris, John stopped at Lyons "where we spent a day seeing the silk manufactures of the Town." We wondered if he took Adelia when he "also visited the Cemetery & saw the grave of Louisa Benedict (Mrs. Brown) daughter of old parson Benedict of Plainfield." He commented, "I knew her well in early life, & have attended many balls with her, where she was always a belle."[16]

Adelia herself wrote of their travels to Delia Taintor, but she, too, expected her letters to be read to a much wider audience. She described Pompeii in much greater detail than John, and then went on—with the prejudice against "the Roman Catholic religion in all its splendour & all its superstition" shared by most of small-town America—to describe some of the "many relics, which they showed us, which I must say, needed a larger organ of wonder than I possess to believe. What do you think of my having seen the Well where the woman of Samarium sat . . . and the table where the last supper was eaten. . . . Also the stairs from which Christ descended from the judgement hall. . . . While I was there three pilgrims went up those stairs beginning some distance back at the door & walking on their knees up the whole flight twenty four in number & kissing them as they ascended. John (our valet du place) told me they would go up for us if [we] would give them a [coin] (about 5 cents.)" The "magnificence of popery" for Adelia exceeded "any thing my eyes ever before beheld. St Peters is so large that you could put two or three churches like Dr Hawes inside of it. Thirteen congregations worship in it. It has three movable organs, & one permanent. . . . Under a superb canopy of bronze & gold reposes the head of St Peter (his body is under a similar canopy at the church of St John Lateran). Around this canopy are arranged one hundred Lamps plated with gold, which are always burning. It gave me an exalted idea of mans intellect when I reflected that this structure was the work of man. . . . Millions of dollars must have been expended on this building." Finally, she boasted, "We saw the Pope at the Vatican—& were introduced to him by our consul."

Her letter ended with real affection: "Give Aunt Taintor [Henry's mother] a great deal of love. Tell her I wish I could see her this very night. Much love to yourself & Henry & a kiss to little Henry." Yet even this expression of feeling was signed with the formal "A. C. Taintor."[17]

The descriptive language, the impressions, and the notice this American couple in the 1840s gave to soldiers, priests, the Catholic church, poverty, and the behavior of Europeans is very reminiscent of Mark Twain's *The Innocents Abroad, or The New Pilgrims' Progress,* which was not published as a book until 1869, nearly twenty-five years later. Mark Twain's book (his first) was a rewrite of a series of letters he had sent to the San Francisco *Alta California* in 1867 about a trip he took to Europe and the Holy Land. Unlike John and Adelia Taintor, Mark Twain took his trip in order to write the letters–but there is a remarkable similarity in many of the impressions of Europe seen through American eyes.[18]

Spain was the last country John visited, but most important to him because he wanted to buy merino sheep there. He left Adelia in Paris; he expected the conditions of travel in Spain to be very difficult. The reality was worse than his expectations. He wrote, "No known language can convey to you a correct idea of the misery of a Spanish Town. The inhabitants are poor, lazy & proud. The houses are generally . . . dark & comfortless. . . . Mules, hogs, dogs & family all enter at one front door, & the perfume of the stable pervades everything."

At the inns John found "the beds are miserable, with any quantity of fleas, at all seasons of the year. However, after a hard days journey, you are glad to find such a stopping place & in the morning, as glad to take your departure." In Spain John wrote there was "Such misery & poverty as I have never before seen, & I have often thought that death itself would be a welcome messenger to hundreds of them. Old, emaciated, sick, half-starved, half-clad, pitiable creatures."

John had been warned to be on the lookout for highway robbers and kidnappers. "Travelers generally carry with them a short gun, or a sword, though robbings are less frequent than formerly. My bankers inform me that they paid . . . 1000 Dollars for the return of a gentleman, who was carried off into the Mountains and kept for 5 months. Thus far," he assured Henry, "I have met with no accident." He did in fact buy "a few of the best merino sheep you ever saw," and wrote Henry that he expected to put them in the care of a Hampton farmer.[19]

John and Adelia traveled back to England after his Spanish excursion, where he reported visiting "short horn cattle breeders of Yorkshire" and hearing "of great fear of a famine in Ireland." In Liverpool he observed, "The emigration to the U. States from Europe is this year immense." He was seeing the early results of the terrible potato famine in Ireland. "It is said there are now in Liverpool 1500 waiting for a ship. At Havre and at Bremen, ships are in great demand to take passengers. The price of passage used to be $15 but it is now 25 Dolls. including water & a pound of bread a day. A far better class are going this year & many of them take along money to buy land at once. You have no idea how miserable they are, crowded into a ship, often 3 & 400, & as the ship leaves the dock, & they bid adieu to a crowd of frends who come to see them off & whom they will never see again, the sight is distressing."[20] Within five years some of the Irish emigrants whose fellows John saw in 1845 would make their way to Hampton.

John had to journey back to France to meet his "little flock" of "genuine Merino" sheep. While he was there, he saw yet another huge military review that brought the opinion "the French are surely great in Military affairs." The former student of the great scientist Benjamin Silliman and now himself an eminent scientific breeder organized a visit to the French "National veterinary College" which he knew would interest his scientific-agricultural cousin in Hampton. "There are 350 young men who spend 4 years here, studying the diseases of animals. That you may have an idea of the Establishment, you must know, that there were last year received at the College over 12,000 sick horses, of which 800 died or were killd. as incurable. The lecture & dissecting rooms are fitted up in great style, & large enough to exhibit 10 or more dead horses at a time, which are brought in on low platforms with 4 wheels. They have now on hand over 300 sick horses, 150 sick dogs, 100 sick cows, sick sheep, & even 2 cats with broken legs." John felt that young men who attended this college had an excellent education, but "The great mass of the people of France are uneducated." He was making a conscious contrast between the Old World, where there was only one "class who are educated, in the best possible manner," and America, where he felt that a rudimentary education was available to everyone. The people who read or heard his letters, he knew, were educated and literate.

Education was not the only contrast John Taintor reported. He told his Protestant Connecticut friends that "You would be surprised at the manner Sunday is kept in France. It is a sort of holly-day in which some go to church in the morning & pass the rest of the day in amusement. In Paris, all the shops are open the same as any day & the only difference I can observe is they close rather earlier in the evening, to allow the clerks to go to the Theatres or other amusements, which are always the best on Sunday evening." By the mid-1840s New England blue laws prohibited all such behavior.

On the other hand, John also commented on the presence of the military everywhere in Paris—"You scarce go out of sight of a sentinel on duty"—a chilling report to Americans who still thought of soldiers in uniform as the symbols of tyranny and oppression. Again a trip abroad had confirmed the patriotic sentiments of this cosmopolitan man. He wrote, "I have been so much with foreigners that I begin to feel half like one myself, which reminds me that I had better get home to old Connecticut. What a pleasure it will be, when far at sea, we can spy out a little spot of land, and realize that we are so near our dear Country. I have seen enough of Europe & shall be content to settle quietly down in Connecticut for the rest of my days. You must come to Europe & stay a year to know how to prize your country, and her glorious Institutions."[21]

John and Adelia's trip to Europe in 1845–46 gave Hampton people as close a firsthand look at the Old World as they would ever get. They could share in such a cosmopolitan experience and gain insight from it because it happened to one of their own, a man they knew, who, even though he had moved to the city, still spoke their language and was amazed by the things that would have amazed them. They were nourished by the big world, not isolated from it in their back-country farming town. John Taintor had left Hampton very recently. He still had much in common with the people he wrote to. And although he had left because he found Hampton dull, he nevertheless was eager to educate and enlighten those who chose to stay.

Hampton in 1850

At the middle of the nineteenth century the workplace of America was still the farm. In 1850 more than twenty-three million people lived in the United States—which had spread by then to include almost all the land of the present forty-eight contiguous states. Only about a sixth of the population lived in "urban" places of 2,500 or more people. Mills and factories were already at work, but their employees were a tiny minority of Americans. More than eighty-five percent of all the people still lived in small towns and rural places of fewer than 2,500 population, and nearly everyone came from such places.

As an older and long-established small town, Hampton was at mid-century a place many had already left behind—in the restless movement toward newer lands and better opportunities. Hampton's 1850 population was 946—a considerable decline from what had been its maximum population of 1369 in 1800. Hampton was still a farm town: 229 of its adult males—nearly all of them—did farm work as their primary occupation.[22]

At the same time the new industrial world had come directly to Hampton. Local industrial enterprises were small and short-lived, however.

The power available on the Little River was slight, and the railroads were still far away, so there was not much to encourage industrial growth. Nevertheless, the 1850 census listed a "Cotton Factory" in Hampton valued at $9,000, owned by a man who resided in Rhode Island, although it was "not in operation." The census also listed John Caulkins, a "woolen manufacturer" born in England, who had a "factory laborer" living with him. Perhaps Caulkins ran a mechanized textile operation. The census listed another man as a "mechanic," which meant he worked with machines. He might have done that work in Hampton. Newton Clark was a "tin manufacturer" and three men in his household were "tin men." Nelson Higgins, who had married Dan Bulkeley's daughter Phidelia (and in whose household Dan's widow, Phoebe, still lived), was also a "tin manufacturer." These "tin men" might well have had shops rather than factories, but they probably used machines and they were definitely a part of the industrial revolution which by 1850 reached small towns.

Most of the people in town were Connecticut-born, probably the majority in Hampton. But there were changes. In 1850, sixteen of Hampton's residents had been born in Ireland and were immigrants because of the famine, and there were four immigrants from England. There was only one Hampton household headed by an Irish couple. The rest of the Irish immigrants were young women and men, workers who lived in other people's households. The Taintors had a hired man named Martin Gannon, who was born in Rhode Island according to the census. Seven of the Irish immigrants in town were Gannons as well. Like all small towns, Hampton was the last place to attract immigrants—because the possibilities for work were few, and the land was occupied and expensive. The great majority of the millions of Irish immigrants who came because of the potato famine concentrated in big towns and cities with factories and construction work where people earned enough to pay employees. Ten percent of Connecticut's population in 1850 was immigrant, while only two percent of Hampton's was.

Unlike immigrants who went to the cities, free African-Americans tended to live in rural places. There were five households in Hampton made up of people listed as "black" or "mulatto" (of mixed black and white parentage) in the 1850 census. Neither Prince Knowles nor his wife, the African-American couple Dan Bulkeley had known, were any longer alive. Samuel Vickers, on the other hand, a sixty-year-old white farmer born in Massachusetts, headed a household in which were Sarah Vickers, his thirty-five-year-old black wife, and two mulatto children. In another part of town, a twenty-eight-year-old laborer, also named Samuel Vickers, had a wife and two children—all of them listed as mulatto. It seems likely that the older, white Samuel Vickers was the father of the younger, mulatto Samuel Vickers. Cesar Hall was another of Hampton's African-Americans. He worked for Henry Taintor on and off, and occasionally for Chauncey Cleveland. In all, there were twenty-three black or mulatto men and women in Hampton in 1850. Several of them had "Malbone" as their last name. A wealthy Tory of that name had owned a number of slaves in the town of Brooklyn through the time of the Revolution. The white Malbone had left when the British lost the war. The free black Malbones in Hampton may have been descendants of his slaves. All the African-American men in Hampton were farm laborers, except for one who was a farmer.

Although there were signs of change in Hampton's people and in the work they did, there were still a number of artisans in Hampton in 1850 who did the traditional manufacturing a small town required. There were eight carpenters, four blacksmiths, two carriage makers and three wagon makers, seven shoemakers, seven harness makers, one tailor, two masons, and two millwrights. Jonathan Clark said his occupation was "house joiner and farmer," and he was more precise than most in his insistence on "and farmer" as part of his occupation. There were five apprentices in town as well as four clerks—young men still taking the traditional ways to acquire skills. Two men peddled books for a living, three were merchants, three were clergymen, and one (Chauncey Cleveland) was an attorney. And four young Hampton men in 1850 still went "down to the sea in ships."

All these were the people Henry and Delia Taintor knew and lived with, dealing with them every day as they together were the community of Hampton.

CHAPTER 1 2

THE DOMESTIC
WORLD

෴

"In addition to the house work, I wrote letters." [1]

Delia Taintor saved most of the letters people wrote to her, so we can glimpse the way her world shaped itself around her relatives, the children in her extended family, and the wide circle of her acquaintance. The sheer numbers of the people about whose lives and deaths Delia Taintor heard, most of whom she knew intimately, is astonishing. In a sampling of letters–nearly all from women–that Delia received over the seven-year period from the beginning of 1854 to the end of 1860, for instance, 256 names are mentioned; all are people to whom she was related or with whom she was acquainted. And that is a very small sampling. The number of letters increases for the rest of her life, and so does the cast of characters.

Keeping House

Women's work in the years after Delia married, while she was bringing up her children, was mostly in the house. Women trained for housekeeping as a matter of course. They learned by doing. Daughters helped their mothers and older female relatives with all the indoor work. Some girls worked in other people's houses. If girls went away to school, as did the daughter of one Hampton neighbor of the Taintors, the school took over the training. She described her work at the Mount Holyoke Ladies' Seminary in South Hadley, Massachusetts: "After breakfast I work an hour cleaning, brushing and sweeping under six tables. It is very pleasant work. Lucy works in the evening after supper if not called to work during the day." Holidays varied the routine, as they would have at home. "Our school closed tonight for a week and the girls are doing their extra work this evening as to morrow we are to trim the Hall and prepare for Thanksgiving day. We have to do a half hour extra work on Wednesday by cleaning house."[2]

When mothers had to be away, daughters took over the housekeeping. Like the chores on the farm, household tasks had to be done every day. There was always "cleaning, brushing and sweeping." Women cleaned floors, rugs, and carpets by the vigorous application of brooms and scrub brushes. They made the beds. They washed clothes–all made of cotton, wool, linen, and sometimes silk–by hand over the modern conveniences of corrugated washboards if they were lucky, more likely simply by pounding and scrubbing each article. They heated the water for their washing and rinsing on stoves or over open fires. As often as not they hauled in the wood themselves. They used strong lye soap which most of them no longer had to make because they could buy it. They ironed all the clothing with cast-iron irons heated on stoves. Delia's sister Ellen used an already old-fashioned term one day in a letter when she spoke of "the *big* work . . . such as washing, ironing, & righting the house."[3]

Delia in fact described the work she normally did when she wrote about the tasks of a hired woman who sometimes worked in the Taintor house: "Mrs Holt has been in this morning & commenced house-cleaning. The front part, up stairs, has been manipulated, & the stairs & front hall swept, ready for window washing tomorrow. . . . The white spreads are washed, the chambers put in order, the washing & ironing out of the way, & the dining room carpet cleaned & ready to put down either tomorrow or Monday."[4]

Cleaning came in seasons. Young Susie Taintor in West Brookfield supplied more detail. "It has been a very busy spring with us, as the 'house-cleaning' was passed *over* lightly, last fall, and as of course it is all the more *terrible,* this Spring–The carpets are all pulled up 'without regard to age'–and throughout the whole, there has been 'no postponement' on account of the weather–which with painting, varnishing, and trials 'enjoyed' by water and soap, make quite a formidable program, as you can well see, and appreciate." She described her own role with humor. "The whole performance is to conclude, I guess you'll imagine with a 'solo' by the veteran in the cause, now writing you, on the miseries, and mishaps, attending such a performance."[5]

Women cooked the meals for all the people working on the farm. Dinner was in the early afternoon, the largest meal of the day. They often tended their kitchen gardens which provided the vegetables for the family. They churned cream into butter and made cheeses. They baked all the breads, pastries, and sweets the family ate. They also kept the dishes and pots and pans clean.

Delia herself described the dailiness of it all in a letter to her daughter written on a Monday. "Saturday was a busy day, pickling, baking bread, gingerbread pies, & bread cake–& when I was through my dinner & dishes I just let the floor go without sweeping, & as I wont do, Sunday, what I neglect Saturday, I have just swept it this morning, & wouldn't be one bit ashamed, now, to have any one judge of my housekeeping by the kitchen for 'tis real clean."[6]

Few women continued to spin or weave by the middle of the century. They sewed their own clothes and their children's clothes unless they could afford dressmakers, as Delia Taintor often did. They also made much of the clothing men wore. They mended all the torn or worn garments. They darned worn stockings and scarves and mittens. They did not throw anything away. Sewing was a constant occupation. Ellen wrote to Delia that she was busy with "dress making or rather turning [a dress inside out to make it last longer] & mending have filled up my time. . . ."[7] Delia was still sewing her eldest son's shirts when he went off to Yale. And like most small-town women Delia joined the Sewing Society (started by her church in the 1840s), whose job it was to provide clothing for the poor. Later, during the Civil War, she knitted and sewed for the soldiers, as did nearly every other housekeeper in the country.

Married life did not necessarily start with "housekeeping" for all young couples, although it did for Henry and Delia. Very often, if there was not money for a house or if other reasons prevented, young couples lived– sometimes separately–in boarding accommodations or with their parents. "Going to housekeeping" was a phrase for a stage of life between marriage and children. Delia's mother wrote of one young couple in a rural town, "I suppose you know Mr. Hine has left Groton has gone to Seymour and Ann [his wife] does not expect to go to housekeeping this summer."[8] In the 1860s Delia's son mentioned "a young couple who have had . . . rooms the past year & are now going to housekeeping. . . ."[9] As late as 1884, when young Mary Ellen Taintor was about to marry Fred Davis, Delia, who was helping to prepare the trousseau, wrote to her daughter, "If you do not go to housekeeping immediately after your marriage we might do some of these things afterwards–when there was nothing else to think about & when the weather was more propitious."[10] Housekeeping was hard work. "I have not taken my morning walks since we commenced house-keeping," wrote Delia's niece Sophie, "as I find running about house is exercise sufficient."[11] Delia herself, who had gone to housekeeping directly after her marriage, knew well enough what it entailed.

She did all her own housework a good deal of the time, describing a day when she was in her sixties:

I proceeded to the dining room, & in the clearing the table decided to brighten [polish] the castor & spoon holder–(and later the ladle) & then washed my dishes, & as the deep tray in which I had chopped my meat was standing on the table decided to use it in place of the dish pan, & supposing I was through (the water being discolored by the berries) emptied my bowl out of the north window, when to my utter astonishment & chagrin I saw one of our "spode" breakfast plates sailing out with the water. You may think I shut my eyes, but not, I looked to see it smash, when lo & behold! it sailed down very easily, with the falling water & struck squarely, upside down on its face, on a board & was not even cracked. I went out with a light heart to pick it up and am most sorry I did not mark it in some way, it seemed so valuable to me. After puting the kitchen in order, & brushing up & putting to rights the sitting room I sat down for a pleasant read. . . . At eleven I filled a pail with sweet apples & went over to Mrs Church's, returned soon to prepare dinner, & just as the clock was striking twelve, was seasoning my steak, having irish & sweet potatoes boild & gold puddings in the oven.[12]

A list of the women who came in to "help out" at the Taintor house in Hampton includes Mrs. Underwood, Anne Gurley, Annie Fiske, a young woman named Bridget, Mrs. Holt, girls named Jennie and Delia, Mrs. Conner "who did the washing" and many others. Bridget was paid one dollar a week. Her coming to the Taintor house (along with Henry's hiring John Gannon) marks the acceptance by the Taintors–and perhaps the townspeople of Hampton as well–of the Irish. "Irishmen" without names noted appear occasionally in Henry Taintor's accounts by the early 1850s.

Sometimes hired girls lived in the house. Sometimes women came to help with specific tasks such as washing, ironing, or spring cleaning. And there was often no help at all. Delia's sister Ellen wrote in sympathy when Delia was ill one summer, "We are sorry to hear that you have not been well. Annie sick too, & haying season in the bargain must have made it very hard for all of you –."[13] At another time, a niece hoped that "by this time . . . some *one* is helping you in the burden of house keeping."[14]

When Delia did have hired help, she sometimes had to share it with her Hampton neighbors, perhaps not always willingly. She wrote of one woman, "This is the last day I can have her services, as she goes to the Gov's [Chauncey F. Cleveland's] on Monday for the winter."[15]

The hired girl the Taintors remembered forever was Anne Gurley. She came from Nova Scotia, probably in 1849. She was so much a part of the family that Delia's nieces in West Brookfield often sent their love to her when she was still in Hampton, and hoped that she would not go west, but she did take off for California in 1855. The letter Henry and Delia obviously enjoyed most was the one Anne wrote when she first arrived in San Francisco, "safe and well . . . just one month from the time I left Hampton. Left N Y August 6th, was sick for two or three days, but soon got over it. *Picked up* a *beau* & of course had a very pleasant time." Anne described her overland journey across the Central American isthmus: "Arrived in Aspinwall on the morning of the sixteenth. Took the cars immediately after Breakfast, & reached Panama 1 P. M. I enjoyed the ride very much indeed. But I despise the natives with their blabbering of Spanish. They seem more like monkeys than anythings else there."

When Anne arrived at the Pacific, boarding the ship that would take her to San Francisco was complicated: "we had to get into a small boat, & then in a Steamboat & then in a small boat again in order to get on the John L. Stephens. It was ten oclock before I got aboard & I was among the first ones. You may be sure I was tired but I didn't think anything about it then. I saw Ladies with three & four & five children traveling alone. The children all took cold being out so late. And one Lady had a beautiful boy ten months going out to her husband. Took cold & died a few days from San F. It was her first and only. I felt very sorry for it."

Ocean voyages were the making of Anne's social life. "I forgot to say that my beau remained in Panama & of course felt very bad leaving. . . . Well got a new Spark for the Pacific Ocean & liked him just as well. left him on the Steamer & have not seen him since. . . . I like San Francisco very well so far."[16] Anne continued to write to the Taintors. Years after she had left Hampton, Henry fondly recalled some of her phrases when he wrote to Delia, who was at home while he was in Hartford, that he hoped her calls from neighbor gentlemen did not mean she "felt like Anne Gurley."[17]

Redecoration was a necessary part of keeping house. The actual labor of painting and papering seems mostly to have been done by men, with the women mopping up behind them. Delia's sister Ellen wrote from Rutland, Vermont, "we are driven into the . . . parlor by a painter & paperer–When we bought the paper for the dining room we found some remnants to match we thought would improve the library & bedroom so much that we bought them & I hope when we get 'to rights' which will be in a few days you will come & see how you like the change."[18]

Bulkeley Taintor's family in West Brookfield, Massachusetts, redecorated their house at the same time Delia was redecorating in Hampton. Susie Taintor wrote, "Is it not very tedious? We have been tried a little, in this way, for a week or two past, as the house has been painted both on the out and inside, though it does look so much better, with a lighter, and more cheerful color, that it amply repays all trouble on our part–There's a crumb of comfort for you, Auntie, if my conjectures are right as to your present condition in the 'old mansion'—though one is very apt to forget the end in the means on such occasions, I think."[19]

The houses women ran were like complex machines requiring constant care and maintenance, although it was probably not often that the house-keepers were aware of that. The large Hampton house, for instance, was subject to leaks when a sudden spring thaw caused melting of accumulated snow under the eaves. Leaks made puddles that could rot floors and ruin rugs and furniture. They could cause mildew. In 1881, when Delia was spending a great deal of time in Hartford taking care of a sick grandchild, she had to write to her daughter Mary and her visiting son Fred to shut down the machine: "The more I think of it the more I am inclined to think this is the very best time to 'let the fire go out'—leaving a key with some neighbor who may go in in case of a thaw & deluge . . . and have Mrs Holt come in & clean up the kitchen & do any sweeping that may be necessary. Remember, too, to move things in the Library where they will be safe from any innundation—the south table being in a safe situation. Fred will be will-ing to help get things into the cellar—away from frost—cranberries, eggs &c (the canned fruit safe up stairs) & the few little plants."[20] Without the woman to run it, the machine would not run.

The Single Life

Mid-nineteenth-century society still assumed that a person entered upon adulthood and full membership in the community when she or he married. There were people who married late or who did not marry. And there were widows and a very few widowers. Their lives were considered slightly peculiar by the rest of society; theirs were cautionary tales.

An old friend of Delia Taintor and of her sister Abby, who only signed her letters "Shan," did not marry. She wrote revealingly of her problems: "Children, widows, the poor—the sick, the aged, all are provided for in vari-ous institutions, but for the respectable *middle-aged single woman* no provi-sion has ever been made—a great oversight I think. What say you? We are Expected to have time to attend to every body's wants, as well as our own—to go here, go there—do this, do that, never be weary in yielding our wishes & inclinations to those of others, & conforming ourselves with unruffled amiability to all the whims & caprices of others."[21]

Women who did not marry depended for their social lives on corre-spondence and on visits. When Delia wrote inviting Shan to Hampton, she felt forced to decline, explaining, "I have been for the last two years . . . without a settled home, & wishing to find some quiet Country spot, where with kind good people, I might for the same Expense, as boarding in the city, secure for myself *more* accommodation as to room. I have, while searching for this, *my El Dorado,* been visiting my many kind friends, whose urgent invitations I could not well decline.–Now this is all very well *for a time,* but as a *life,* it is not the thing, at all."[22]

Shan's humor rebelled at being a perennial guest in other people's homes. She disliked "groping about in the cold and darkness to find a match & the screw of the gas fixture, performing my absurd toilet operations, when you feel that you *ought* to be in your bed, dreaming for two hours longer at least. I have no *Conscience* on the Subject of Early rising, (now do not laugh & say you doubt if I have any on *any* subject) but I have a great regard for my *natural instincts* in certain cases of which this is one." Shan questioned the religious pieties of her day: "I do not believe I could ever be made '*thankful* for my Earthly Existence' between the hours of six & Eight in a cold room of a Winter's morning." Hampton's new, young, unmarried minister was at this time boarding with the Taintors, and Shan suggested that they "Ask Mr Soule if the gratitude in *his* heart does not sometimes lie dormant till his shaving operations are over & his fingers & toes rejoice in the warmth of a blazing fire." Finally she declared, "Dearly do I love Winter, but I must enjoy it after my own fashion.–Winter *journeys–cold sleeping rooms & Early breakfasts* are, by no means, in the list of its peculiar pleasures."[23]

While Shan "would prefer to keep house, to all other modes of life" she did not think it advisable to do so quite alone. Her plan was "to take half a house, (or two or three rooms), furnish them, & take Care of them, myself, merely taking my meals with the family occupying the other part." She had hopes of making such an arrangement because "so many houses in the country are occupied by two families."[24] After several years' search, Shan celebrated at last when she found a place of her own in a house in Concord, Massachusetts. "My house-linen is all made, my furniture is being repaired, & put in order, & my house (or part of one) is at last *Engaged,*" she wrote.

She proceeded to tell a little of her settling in: "The parlor & *my* chamber (over it) are very good size–my guest chamber is smaller & lower, than I could wish, & having no attic, I am obliged to make a sort of baggage room of the *third* little chamber, though the bed hides some boxes, & trunks, & of two I have made a toilet table, practising what is quite foreign to my nature, a little *deception.* I have taxed my ingenuity to convert the wooden boxes I used in packing, into various useful articles of *furniture,* my means for the purchase of others, being very limited." She excused the detail of her description by remarking that "an *old maid's housekeeping* is almost Equal to a bride's *honey-moon.* If you should come into this vicinity after I am once in the successful tide of housekeeping I shall hardly forgive you if you do not turn aside to look in upon your old friend."[25] Despite her concerns, Shan seems to have found a full life in her single state.

Another of Delia's correspondents, her niece Emma Ellsworth, lived in Lafayette, Indiana. She always was close to her Connecticut relatives, particularly to Delia. Her early letters, when she was young and single, were sunny and humorous. Of one boiling Indiana summer, for instance, she wrote, "'The heated term' has been fairly inaugurated during the past week, and we are just verging on a state of fusion, now. Do you know, Aunty, that I've left off wearing my watch [pinned to her dress front], for the simple reason that I wear so little clothing that *I've no place to put it.* But, knowing as you do, my peculiar fondness for wearing my watch and my *clothes,* you can form a pretty correct idea of the intensity of the heat when I tell you that I've doffed both and wander about the house as nearly in a state of nature as a startlingly brief dressing sack will admit. Mother's dress—well never mind—we wont try to talk about things that are not."[26]

Emma became depressed in later years, when she had to yield her "wishes & inclinations to those of others, & [conform herself] . . . with unruffled amiability to all the whims & caprices of others," as Shan had put it. She was still unmarried in her late twenties, and her letters to Delia changed considerably. She lashed out to her aunt, who may have inquired one time too many about the personal. "Know that I love you very, *very* dearly my own Aunt Delia—as for my confidence, I try to believe *that is all* God's. He only *can* know *all* my life . . . Aunty mine this confidential interchange of heart emotions is not for me. Never yet have I known a heart *thoroughly* responsive to my own." This was a sad letter for Delia to receive, and Emma knew that, so she tempered her words by adding, "Dear, sympathizing friends [family] I have (God bless them all) but what I most deeply feel I cannot find words to express. And why should I wish to? *I can pray, you* and *we all* can pray for one another." Emma was a reader, so she turned for comfort to "The tender, sympathizing 'Quaker poet,'" John Greenleaf Whittier, who "has very beautifully expressed an idea which has long been a cherished one of mine, because my *heart* responded. . . .

> He prayeth best who leaves unguessed
> The mystery of another's breast.
> Why cheeks grow pale, and eyes o'erflow,
> Or heads are white—thou needs't not know.
> Enough to note, by many a sign,
> That every heart hath needs like thine.
> Pray for us."

Emma admonished "my dear Aunt Delia" not to "think that I am reading you a lecture, because you, in your dear, kind love for me, like to know all that saddens or gladdens me. I am not, I do assure you, for you have been a true friend to me when my life was very dark, and my trials made me many times peevish and unreasonable. I regret no act of confiding that has ever passed between us, but I have thus written in order to give you an insight into my nature as I myself understand it. *Reticent* I know it to be, but I hope not *distrustful*."[27] This letter is the strongest railing against the loneliness of the single life that appears in Delia's vast correspondence.

Delia Taintor's niece Fanny Hall also never married, and she, too, went through a depressed time. She wrote her aunt when she was safely past it:

> . . . I have to tell of my apparently complete restoration to health, which has been accomplished in a way which seems if not miraculous, most plainly providential in character, and I am now so contented and happy that everything is a joy, and if your visit had been made a few days later you would have had no idea of the intense melancholy from which I suffered so long. The remedy that brought me such great relief was a very simple tonic, consisting of gum guac–⅓ of an ounce, the same quantity of columbo root, three tablespoonsful of sugar and a pint of sherry wine. The drugs may be either pulverized or pounded. The lady who recommended this to me, had suffered herself just as I had, but for a much shorter time–she was entirely cured by this little tonic in the course of two weeks, and in less time than that I began to feel its effects most happily. I used it for five or six weeks I guess, & now, with the exception of a greater tendency to fatigue than formerly, I feel about as well as I ever did in my life–and oh, so delightfully at rest. It is a feeling that I had not known for nearly a year, and it seems to me now that if our good Father spares me a return of this trouble, any other possible sickness, privation or affliction I can bear with a patience or cheerfulness than I could have felt before I had learned through each bitter experience what real, deep trouble could mean. Dear Auntie, what a gain it is when we have thus learned, even in this life, to see the use and meaning of trial!
>
> I have been wondering if this medicine would do Emma Ellsworth good also. The dose is about half a small wine glassful before each meal & at bedtime. I wrote to Dr Wyckoff in regard to it, and he says that it is an excellent tonic & an old standard prescription that he used a great deal in his early practice, and that the gum guac has an excellent effect upon the menstrual secretions. I see in myself a very marked improvement in this direction, & I suppose the trouble there was the real cause of all my woe, but what gave me such exquisite relief was the clearing away of all that dreadful trouble in my head & its accompanying depression of spirits: the lady who gave me the pre-

scription suffered herself only from nervous prostration, & her idea of the matter is that this state of melancholy is dependent upon a defective circulation of the blood, which the gum guac regulates, thus removing the trouble.

I . . . will tell Emma then about this tonic, but I mentioned the matter to you that you might write to her about it, if you judged it worth while to do so.[28]

Single women often helped each other with medical advice, especially about "women's complaints." This letter is the only one we have seen that mentions "menstrual secretions."

In the years before and after the Civil War, widows were the single women with whom Delia was most acquainted. She started housekeeping with a widow–her mother-in-law–and lived the first ten years of her married life with that widow. When her father died in 1857, her own mother remained a widow until her death thirteen years later. But Delia quickly learned that widows were not necessarily old. Her younger sister Ellen's husband, George Strong, fell ill in the spring of 1858 and died that October. Their mother was with Ellen at his deathbed.

We found the letter (from his sister) that informed Delia of George Strong's death. "Your dear Mother's letter, sent to you last week, has I presume prepared you, in some measure, for the sad intelligence I have now to communicate–Our dear brother George passed calmly & peacefully away

Ellen Ellsworth Strong, Delia's sister.   Sophia Ellsworth, Delia's mother.

from us this afternoon at 10 minutes before 3 o'clock–his trust & confidence in his Savior unfaltering to the last–Dear Ellen has been wonderfully sustained–her calmness is almost surprising, but a sure & certain evidence that a covenant keeping Lord never deserts his faithful ones in their deepest extremities." She went on that "Ellen begs me to tell you that your letter, received last week, was very precious to her, & was a great comfort to George–& as she read it aloud to him, he remarked, 'it was such a letter as no one but Delia could write.'"[29]

Ellen was thirty-four years old when she was widowed, living in Rutland, Vermont. She had one child, her daughter, Kate, who was twelve. Her mother-in-law was also widowed, so Ellen and Katy lived with her for a while. Ellen wrote her sister:

> My thoughts have been exceedingly engrossed of late by trying to decide what plans it is best I should make for the coming year, and I would give anything could I *talk* the matter over with you and your good husband, still I know the responsibility of the decision must rest with myself. . . .
>
> have not been able to find anyone who will pay a rent of much more than $300 for my house and furniture and when from that I deduct the taxes a very small sum is left for our support–Katy is very desirous to go back and live in the house and take boarders. I should do so also, but I feel that it is assuming a great weight of care and responsibility for me to bear alone and fear that at the end of the year, my circumstances might be worse than now–I endeavor to . . . be led in all things temporal and spiritual in the path of duty, my own greatest pleasure would be to divide my time between Mother [in Windsor, Connecticut] and Mother Strong, but Katy must be in school, and here [in Rutland] there is an excellent one whose advantages she may enjoy without any additional expense–and it seems as if this was the home Providence has assigned for me–I shall come to a decision in a few days, if you can make any suggestions I shall be deeply obliged to you, and hope my next letter will be filled with pleasanter thoughts.[30]

Within two years of that letter, circumstances conspired to decide where Ellen would live. She was visiting her own mother at Elmwood when she wrote Delia, "Last Saturday Mother did not feel very well in the afternoon but said nothing about it & went with me over to see Cousin Mary–She sat there an hour or two & when we came home appeared unusually tired & drousy through the evening–She rested pretty well through the night, but Sunday morning could not speak with customary plainness–We called the Dr in the afternoon though she thought it unnecessary–He said her symptoms indicated paralysis, but he thought she would throw them off by a little medicine–She took it & it had the effect upon her bowels he desired, but I do not think she speaks much if any easier & she is of course weak–She was dressed yesterday & has been up this morning."[31] Her mother seems to have had a mild stroke. In a few days Ellen wrote again, "She cannot use her right hand but very little. She can open & shut it & move it without trouble, but cannot hold a knife or spoon–There seems no strength in the hand & arm."[32] Ellen spent most of the next eight years until her mother's death with her at Elmwood.

For a decade after she was widowed, Ellen lived in another person's house. The house in Windsor was "kept" by their brother Fred Ellsworth's wife, Elizabeth, known to all the family as "Aunt Libby." Running such a big place with Ellen and Katy always in residence and with constant visitors and a sick old lady must have been difficult for Libby. The hints of her difficulty are few. "Elizabeth . . . had a turn of sick headache Saturday night, but is pretty well this morning,"[33] Ellen wrote once. Another time, "Elizabeth has had a turn of sick-headache this week but is down stairs to-day & thinks she shall feel tolerably well to-morrow."[34] There were remarkably few complaints from women whose skilled and productive work was keeping house and taking care of the sick. Perhaps this was because their work was valued by the whole society, men and women alike; it was not viewed as inferior to work done outside the home.

When women were widowed, they often took in boarders in order to continue keeping house. An old friend of Delia's wrote, "I have found a great deal to occupy my time this winter in having five boarders and no help tho I have a young Irish girl to help me now–have thought of breaking up housekeeping & may do so yet."[35]

Another elderly widow, whom the family referred to as "Grandma Gleason" because she had helped care for Delia and her siblings when they were all young, wrote of her boarders in her old age to her "Del Dol," "Who and what I am to have as inmates of my low dwelling is unknown to me at present–Yet I fear not to Trust to that Wisdom & Love which is over all–even me." She referred to herself in the third person: "old grandma Gleason has no part or lot in the matter–Isolated and demented–almost thro this dark rugged way–and could the end be as tranquil as some of the . . . ones, 'gone a little while before'–I can rejoice in the event–But to dread a helpless existence, a burden to my friends, is no small cause of anxiety–A helpless, pennyless, disagreeable old woman–Oh–what can be more repelling?"[36]

The old lady kept up her correspondence as long as possible, and her elderly widow's status was a distressing warning to the young. Emma

Ellsworth told Delia, "I have had two nice pleasant letters from 'Grandma' Gleason lately. What a thoroughly lonely old age is here."[37] When Grandma Gleason finally gave up housekeeping, she wrote Delia:

> The rolling wheels, which have trundled me, hither and thither–are, I trust blocked for the present–for my life energies are exhausted–and by these oft trying changes, hopes are crushed and darkened–as to any further efforts to live, as others do, by "helping ourselves." . . .
>
> As I near the end of this rough way–and realise my true condition . . . indeed I was governed by circumstances–yet heeding the advice of friends–and this last move, to tuck my few things into as small quarters–i.e. two rooms–and be resigned to fate. . . . The . . . move . . . completely overcome and rendered me helpless to dependant on the family who rented me my two rooms–They are kind, plain worthy people. . . .
>
> The [railroad] cars pass thro the village very frequently–and if my friends would on the way to the city–"stop over" come and see me–I should be very much gratified–Tho I do not expect the favor–My little box of *faces* [photographs] afford me satisfaction I assure you–in my lonely home–they all seem to smile, as of other days. . . .
>
> my heart is as loving & craves love as when I used to say "Lullaby"–Where is our dear Ellen & Katie–I hear not from any one–They may not know where I am–I am near the meeting place of "Cousin" Frances and my old loved friend Maria Olmstead. I hope to be allowed to rest in the same cemetery. . . .[38]

Single women tried to help and comfort each other even in extreme poverty. Henry G. Taintor was aware of the depth of that poverty when, as court-appointed administrator of a poor woman's estate, he allowed a claim from a single woman, Mary Smith, who had tried to help widow Ruth Buttes with "21 scent of borrowed money I lent her the year 1847, and wone dollar in money I lent her in July, 1847." In October 1847, Mary Smith "lent 75 scent to her to get her some provision to her brother." She also let Widow Buttes have "won pound and A quater of snuf at the rate of 17 scent A pound and at a nother time I let her have A pound and A half of snuf at the rate 25 scents A pound." She also lent "won pound of brown shuggar at teen scents A pound, thirteen knotes of read singgles yearn [13 knots of red single-strand yarn] at two scent A knot."[39] Henry saw to it that Mary Smith received her full $2.90¾. He knew it was a sizable amount of money to such a poor woman.

Men, as Henry Taintor did, mostly dealt with the problems of poverty and old age in public ways. The poor were supported by the Town, and their care was in the hands of the selectmen. The men in town meeting investigated and discussed at length establishing a "poor farm," but rejected that. Women cared for widows, the elderly, and the poor more directly, in the context of their own houses and families. Delia Taintor kept track of all conditions of kin and friends, with pen and paper if she could not be with them in person. It was a pleasure as well as a duty of her Christianity, her womanliness, and her domesticity.

The Social Network

Visits and calls were the social glue of the Taintors' world. A visit–as the word was used still at mid-century–usually lasted at least a week. It involved packing and unpacking a trunk full of clothes and the attendant difficulties of transporting it. A call, on the other hand, could be accom- plished with no baggage at all in less than half an hour. People also "came in" for a few minutes in a less formal way, or "spent the evening." If they "took dinner" together it was in the middle of the day, the standard time for dinner; only later, and then in urban places, did dinner time shift to evening. And every Sunday many people simply "met" at church.

Family, especially, made visits as long as possible. In 1843, Delia's elder sister Abby Hall wrote from Washington that she intended "to secure a fortnight for Conn. if it is possible."[40] Delia met her in Windsor, and made a several-weeks' visit to their old Elmwood home on that occasion. She vis- ited there many times a year at least until her mother's death in 1870, and often went for extended visits thereafter, when her brother Frederick and his wife had taken over the place completely. She and Henry also visited Edwin Bulkeley Taintor and his family in West Brookfield, though less fre- quently. She visited her sister Ellen in Rutland. In 1860, Delia and Henry took Sophia Ellsworth (Delia's mother) to visit her brother Samuel and his family in Lafayette, Indiana.

And they certainly visited Abby in Washington, though not as fre- quently as Abby urged. Each of Abby's letters contained an invitation to some member of the Taintor family. In 1861, for instance, she wrote, "I wish dear Sister you could send your boys to see us for a while. Our house is large enough for them and it would be a great advantage to Ellsworth [her fourteen-year-old son] as well as an inexpressible pleasure to us all & there is so much in Washington to interest intelligent curiousity I believe it would be a good thing for them also. May we not have a long visit from them?"[41] Such visits could make the advantages of urban life available to Hampton people, and many undoubtedly visited kin away.

Friends of the Taintors visited in Hampton. Mrs. A. B. Dawson of Brooklyn, New York, wrote Delia recalling "the kindness and hospatality which you extended to us while in Hampton . . . For I assure you that the time we passed in your house and in your company while there, *will long be reverted too* with much pleasure by us. I feel that we are very much in your debt and hope the time is not far distant when we will have it in our power to return the compliment, hopeing therefore that you will soon come to the city again and favour us if not with a visit at least with a call."[42]

From urban Washington, Abby Hall wrote directly of the burdens placed on a household by the constant flow of visitors and their numbers: "I was seriously ill with fever & a most troublesome cough so . . . poor Alice has been so worn & busy with all the housekeeping & marketing for 12 persons always & often for more & attending both to calling company & permanent occasional guests."[43]

Calls were short and, except for the duty of making conversation and providing the occasional cup of tea, less onerous for the hosts. When Ellen visited Abby in 1861 she joined her in a call on someone with a Hampton connection. She wrote Delia about it: "Mr. [Galusha] Grow [the Speaker of the United States House of Representatives] has brought his brother's wife and children with him to Washington this winter–Mrs. Grow is a niece of Mrs. [Chauncey F.] Cleveland's she told Abby–They are housekeeping and are expecting to entertain a great deal of company in the way of weekly evening receptions–They have consulted Abby about many things, and she has interested herself very much to procure them servants &c &c–I have never seen Mrs G but shall probably call on her with Abby–I thought you might be interested to hear something about them as they were formerly from Windham County."[44] Galusha Grow was born in Eastford, on the Hampton border. Shortly after Ellen and Abby called upon him he sponsored the Homestead Act in Congress.

Men made calls as well. Henry E. and his father "called . . . on Cousin Delia Lyman last Friday evening and took tea there. We had a very pleasant evening."[45] Mrs. Lyman was married to a professor at Yale. The call lasted the whole evening, probably because this was family. They may have talked of Professor Lyman's many interests, which included astronomy, physics (his professorship at that time), volcanoes (he had been to Hawaii to study Kilauea), and scientific terminology (he had worked on revising that subject in *Webster's Dictionary*). It was a heady intellectual evening.

When young George Taintor grew up and went calling, he did not necessarily spend the time in conversation. He wrote his mother that he and his hosts "played cards until ½ past 9 oclock and then we went home."[46] Later, when George was a "drummer" (a traveling salesman), he called on family he had not seen in years, and thus made a social life for himself in faraway towns. "Friday I was in Toledo," he wrote, "& called on Cousin Dora. As it was in the afternoon, I only found she & Helen at home, but had a very pleasant call."[47]

Henry E. passed on family gossip picked up when he and George went calling:

Geo and I went out Friday to call on Cousin Delia & Alice but they did not feel well enough to see us. Cousin Delia has been sick but how sick or what was the matter I do not know. I learned it at the Williamses where we called the same evening & I was ashamed to admit that I didn't know anything about it and so pretended knowl-edge & learned all I could. She is going down to New York to try the Movement Cure which Louise has great faith in. At the Williamses we found Mary just going out with a gentleman. Gussie in New York & Cousin Oliver in his room, so we visited with Cousin Ellen & her mother. Vanderbilt is in Washington, working for a government appointment. Ellen has been sick with Lung fever but has quite recov-ered from it. . . . After leaving the W's I decided to go out and call on Emily Jackson, and did *leave my card* and also on Mr & Mrs Chas Jewell, & finally brought up at Mr Davis' where I found Geo who had left me after the call at the W's.

The Cousin Delia and Alice mentioned in this letter were Adelia Taintor (John Taintor's wife) and her daughter Alice, the Williamses were her sister's family, and Louise was John and Adelia's eldest daughter. Mary Williams was the third Williams daughter, and Gussie (Augusta) was the fourth. Ellen was the eldest Williams girl, the only one who ever married, and she had married Cornelius, the Vanderbilt who was in Washington. We do not know who Emily Jackson and Mr. and Mrs. Charles Jewell were, but the latter were probably related to the Connecticut Governor Jewell for whom Henry E. Taintor later worked. Mr. Davis was Gustavus F. Davis, who would later be George Taintor's and Mary Taintor's father-in-law.

Young unmarried ladies also went calling, as Abby reported to Delia that "Alice has just returned from making an evening call with a Mr. Smith of Pennsylvania upon his Aunt."[48] It was an acceptable way to spend time with young gentlemen. Young ladies were also called upon. When Delia's sons were growing up, they made a point of calling on single women. George wrote, "I called on Nellie Richmond who is here at school at Mr Crosby's last Friday night and had a very pleasant call."[49] And Henry E. called on single ladies even after he was engaged to be married. He men-tioned one such call in a letter home, making sure to include the fact that he had not been alone: "Al Olmsted & I went down and had a very pleas-ant call on Miss Hollister."[50]

Calls could be an obligation. When Delia's niece Sophie Reynolds came home to Indiana after some years in California, she wrote that "some time must be given to calling & visiting."[51] Another niece, Caroline Taintor, came home to West Brookfield after being a governess in Georgia for a year and found that "Since then the days have seemed to fly. Calls to receive and return, visits to make, etc. etc."[52] Her sister Susan used calls as an excuse for not writing a letter to her aunt Delia: "I had expected to pen this neglected letter yesterday, and came in from the garden for that purpose after eating cherries till I was ready to 'fight'–(you know ones intellectual faculties are so much more *active* at such a time) but Mother was very anxious I should '*make some calls*' with her that afternoon, and so donning hat and cape I *meandered* from one end of the village to the other, and if you'll believe it, every one that we called on were *at home* which of course took up the time *wonderfully* so that writing was out of the question."[53] (Not only women found themselves socially obligated to make calls. George Taintor wrote his mother at one point: "neither of us [himself or Henry E.] have been out to call at Cousin Delia's in almost a year. It is positively shameful."[54])

Women were present at all the calls the Taintor men wrote home about, even if they were not the objects of the calls. Women made calls on women and on families. Men made calls on women and on families. None of Delia Taintor's correspondents record that men made social calls on men alone. When Henry G. Taintor did make calls on men alone, there was always a business, not a social reason. As a mature man after the middle of the century, he did not any longer consider his business part of the domestic world.

CHAPTER 13

FARMING AND THE PUBLIC LIFE

༄

"... to enjoy life in the freedom of agricultural pursuits."[1]

Henry G. Taintor called himself a farmer. We saw his occupation listed that way on the Hampton manuscript censuses. But from all the rest of his papers, we know he led a double life. His public persona as a man of business and a community leader took up most of his time. Not long after he married, the farm ceased to be at the center of his work. He made a political career for himself in Hampton for which his being a farmer was essential, because he shared the work as well as the values of his neighbors. He made a statewide political career for himself which was less successful than his local career, perhaps because he was still tied to farming.

From the time he attained his majority, Henry farmed much the same way his father had. But the patterns of life in Hampton were changing in response to what everyone considered thoroughly modern innovations and progress. One sign of change in Henry's farming even before he married was a subscription to *The New England Farmer,* started in 1833. Discussions of new scientific agriculture and up-to-date farming techniques, including fertilizers and crop management, filled the magazine. Henry's accounts and cash books show that he bought seed for improved varieties of crops from seedsmen in New York City and Boston by 1839.[2] And by that time, too, he began the lifelong use of phosphate of lime and guano as fertilizers to make his land more productive. The adoption of commercial fertilizers and seeds put Henry in the company of the modern agribusiness men of his time.

Life on the Farm

Henry learned his farming from his father, Solomon, and his uncle Roger, and they had farmed in order to raise capital. There were many others who farmed, and who raised crops and animals to sell, but who did not have the same end in view as the Taintors. However, any farmer who produced goods for market in quantities was also an employer. Throughout his nearly sixty years as a farmer, Henry Taintor hired casual workers every year. Those men helped with plowing and sowing in spring, haying (several men several weeks every summer), cradling, shocking, and threshing grain, and carting or "sledding" apples, potatoes, hay, rye, buckwheat, and wood, and shearing sheep.[3] Henry also occasionally hired men and their teams of oxen or horses, along with wagons and carriages; and the same men sometimes hired Henry's teams of horses and oxen, along with his vehicles and some-times his hired man, to work for them.

Besides casual workers, Henry, like other market farmers, had a hired man who was "in residence" at least during the active farming months, and who did much of the routine farm and outdoor house work. Hired men were provided food in the household, and a place to sleep. ("Hired-men's beds" are antiques collectors' items today although they are short, narrow, and have the holes for rope "mattresses"–we found one in the attic of the house in Hampton.) The place was rarely a separate room; it was much more likely to be a space in the loft or attic of a house or barn, sometimes partitioned off, unheated in winter (but so were the bedrooms in most houses), and often windowless.[4]

Hired men did not stay many years with one employer. Their pay was low. Anson Burnham, whom Roger Taintor paid $132 per year in the late 1820s, continued to be Henry's hired man after Roger died. Henry paid him $12 per month in 1838, but it might not have been for the full year. Henry paid Henry Whitaker $90 for seven months in 1842; he paid George W. Eastman $12.50 a month for eight months in 1844, and $15 a month for eight months in 1847.

Hired men earned their wages by the month or the year, and were expected to work six full days a week *and* do essential chores on Sunday. Henry kept careful track of the time his hired men "lost," not to deduct from any month's pay, but in order to have the men "make up" the days lost at the end of their term of employment. There was no normal payday. The men seemed to draw on their employer for money as they needed it, with a reckoning and payoff when their work term ended.

On August 26, 1833, Henry recorded that Anson Burnham lost one day "at Court (Case of Miss Crandall)." Why a Burnham from Hampton needed to be at the trial of Prudence Crandall of Canterbury (the town next to Hampton on the southeast) is not clear. Miss Crandall had started a private academy for girls in Canterbury, which was not unusual, but she had encouraged African-American girls to attend, which was. And that had brought her into conflict with her neighbors, who had sufficiently influenced the state legislature to make such a school illegal and then brought Miss Crandall to trial for violating the law. It is clear that the case was of sufficient importance in Hampton so that the Taintor hired man chose to attend. Antislavery and abolitionist sentiment was growing in northeastern Connecticut, but that did not mean that the racist attitudes upon which slavery depended were dying at the same time.

Anson Burnham also "lost" days or halfdays because of a militia officers' meeting (other, later Taintor hired men also lost time because of militia training sessions). He lost time fishing and for funerals; once he lost six days because his son was sick, and once twenty-one days for his own illness. He lost a day at Thanksgiving, which was already a holiday in New England, complete with turkey dinner.

Hired man or no, a farm was a farm, and all farms worked alike. Bound by the seasons and by natural cycles, farm work proceeded inexorably. Henry Taintor did not keep a diary of his farm work. But a daily record of a farmer's work on a mid-nineteenth-century farm very close to Henry's does exist. It is Benjamin Brown, Jr.'s, journal. He farmed right on Hampton's border in the town of Brooklyn, a very few miles from the center of Hampton village.⁵ Brown probably knew Henry Taintor; they had much in common. The record Brown left of his work as a farmer illuminates the ordinary farm life of Henry Taintor's neighbors.

Brown's journal came into our hands by a circuitous route. A woman who used to live across the street from our house before we came to town (we knew her very elderly mother, who had summered in Hampton) moved west. She came upon the journal in an antiques shop in California, bought it because it mentioned placenames familiar to her, and sent it to Wendell Davis in Hampton. She hoped he might find a home for it in a local historical collection. Wendell brought it to us and we were able to figure out whose journal it was and something about Benjamin Brown, Jr., who began it in 1842.

Brown farmed his elderly father's land. His father and mother lived with him and his family, and he and his father worked the farm. The routine of farm work and the ways work was done were the same whatever the wealth or social level of the farmer. Brown's journal was not an account book, although he recorded hired hands' wages, time lost, and the weights, quantities, and prices received for the produce he sold. But he rarely made totals, even of the proceeds of a single sale.

Brown had been a schoolteacher for twelve years before he went to farming.[6] In the 1840s, he helped to manage his town's schools. He even built a schoolhouse near his house and took considerable time every year to visit schools and examine both teachers and scholars.

The succinct entries in Brown's journal made it possible to reconstruct a year of a working farm in the Hampton vicinity when Henry Taintor was farming. The journal opens on April 18, 1842, and gives a sense of the rhythm of farm life:

April 18 Albert Fuller [a hired man–Brown calls them "boys"] commenced work here. Cleaned out East stables in South barn. Cut wood in Woodhouse. Rainy day. Father went to Stonington [a whaling seaport on the coast, not easy of access from the Hampton area] as pallbearer to Mr C.

19 Young Baker cow calved [Brown "kept cows" for other farmers on his pastures]. Rainy day. Cut wood in wood house. Went to mill [to have his grain ground into meal or flour].

20 White washed kitchen. S. [another farmer named Starkweather who specialized in raising calves] took away 2 calves. Boys finished picking stones in North lot & began in 10 acre lot. Plowed in orchard & began in old house lot.

21 Sowed [by hand] hayseed in lower East lot & bushed it [dug or pulled out the brush which had grown up in the lot since it was last cleared]. Sowed 2 acres in lower lot, oats & hay seed. Took sows out hog pen.

22 Sowed North East lot east mowing. Plowed with two teams in middle lot in P.M. Boys picked stones in 10 acre lot in PM.

23 Plowed in middle lot with horses. . . . Plowed with oxen in old house lot. Boys picked stones. White faced cow calved.

24 Sunday. Went to meeting in P.M. Dr H. preached. [There were usually two services–ordinarily called "meetings"–every Sunday; Brown almost never went to both but usually wrote which, A.M. or P.M., meeting he attended.]

26 Finished plowing in middle lot. Plowed in lower lot. Plowed in orchard. Carted stones from old wall in orchard. . . .

27 Carted stones off hog pasture & made wall. First sow had five pigs last night.

28 Finished plowing in orchard. Began to plow in hog pasture. Plowed in lower lot with horses. Albert picked stones in 10 acre lot.

Second sow had 7 pigs last night. . . .

May 2 Finished plowing lower lot. Finished harrowing hog pasture. Carted manure on the garden & commenced plowing it. Albert lost today [unlike Henry Taintor, Brown never mentioned the reasons hired men lost time].

3 Finished plowing garden & planted corn, beans, potatoes, cucumbers, onions, peas, saffron, peppers, lettuce, peppergrass, cabbage, tomatoes &c. Set out cabbage stumps [cabbage stumps were kept in the cellar over the winter and replanted in spring to get early cabbages before cabbage seed grew into heads], beets & carrots. Made fence to shut up sows & pigs. Furrowed some in hog pasture. Stanton cow calved.

5 Began to plant corn in hog pasture, first this year. Drew 2 loads horse manure to S. W. corner. . . .

6 Finished planting hog pasture. Harrowed orchard lot. M. Joslin took away his cow & a small load hay. Grandfather taken sick with bowel complaint.

8 Sunday. Went to meeting. Commenced Sabbath School [devoted to the teaching and discussion of the Gospels, the Bible, and theology, primarily for adults but also for children].

9 Picked stones in 10 acre lot in A.M. . . . George Angell commenced work in P.M. for one month at 12 Dollars.

By the nineteenth of May, Brown had finished planting his corn and started planting potatoes, his largest crop. Those crops were planted by the end of May, but it rained a lot that spring, even on "Sunday. Went to meeting. Got wet coming home," so Brown had to replant several cornfields because the seed washed away or rotted. He also planted sugar beets in at least one field "back of the corn house," and he added more beans, "sweet corn, cucumbers, turnip-beets, summer savory &c in the garden." The sugar beets—a new crop in northeastern Connecticut—show that Brown was an abolitionist. Educated opponents of slavery were trying to produce sugar to avoid buying slave-grown cane sugar. Brown did not separate his work from public issues.

By June 6, he "began to hoe first time in hog pasture," and started the laborious hand work of cultivation, hoeing the rows of corn and potatoes to keep down weeds and keep the soil friable. It was not until June 9 that he and the boys "finished picking stones in 10 acre lot," the task they had begun on April 20. And after he finished all the planting in June, Brown began work on the roads in the town of Pomfret, as the way to pay his highway taxes.

The summer rhythm of work was also dutifully recorded:

June 21 Hoed in middle lot. Planted over sugar beets. Jed Baldwin commenced work. Sold 6 lambs, 1 sheep & 9 chickens for 12 dollars.

27 Hoed potatoes. Starkweather took red heifers. Abby Mason [his wife's sister] came.

28 Father went to Providence with 18 cheeses weighed 325 lbs @ 8 cts. Got oxen shod. Finished hoeing potatoes in lower lot.

30 Commenced hoeing second time in hog pasture.

July 4 Carried Father Mason [his father-in-law] & Albert to Killingly to take stage for Providence. Finished hoeing old house lot. Benj. B. Parkhurst came here.

11 Commenced mowing. Mowed door-yard, some in North lot. . . . Grass not grown enough. George Angell worked to day. Got dirt [manure] in cow yard.

13 Mowed north end Bennet meadow. Got in 1 load hay south end Bennet meadow, put on south end of west scaffold in South barn, & 1 load English hay [a newer variety of hay more productive and nutritious, but the seed was expensive] from upper side Bennet lot, put on little bay in South barn. G. A. worked to day.

Brown recorded where each load of hay was grown and where it was stored, so that when it was used to feed animals in the winter or sold, he could judge its "keeping" and nutritional qualities and maintain ongoing revision of his knowledge of his fields' productive qualities.

The mowing, stacking, and moving of hay into barns continued through July. Like all farm work, the mowing moved over all the land Brown worked. He even cut hay off "the new garden," an area he planned to devote to garden in future years. Hay was a vital crop on every farm, necessary to feed the farm animals—cattle (dairy cows, calves for veal, and oxen), horses, and sheep—and always a cash crop as well. There was increasing demand for it in every urbanizing community where there was no land on which to grow it, and hay was essential as feed for work and riding animals.

On July 22, Brown "cut the rye," and began the process of harvesting grain. The next day, he "bound & shocked the rye," which involved walking along the windrows of cut rye carrying precut lengths of twine, bending down and gathering an armful of the rye with the ripe grain kernels at the top and tying the armful into a bundle (which all farmers assumed were of an approximately standard size). A number (which would vary from farm to farm, but each farmer would learn the "right" number from his father and assume that was the "traditional" number) of the bundles were then stood on their cut ends in a cylindrical shape and one bundle was spread out in cone shape as a roof over the top of the cylinder to make a "shock." The shocks of grain were allowed to stand in the field for a while to dry. We know the details of the process of shocking grain because one of us did this farm work in just this way in the 1940s, one hundred years after Brown did it.

In Brown's case, in the summer of 1842, he "got in" his rye, "12 shocks & 4 bundles [not enough for a 13th shock]" on July 26, three days after it was shocked. He went on to "cradle" his barley. ("Cradling" was cutting the grain with a "cradle," a scythe with a large wooden rack made of several curved slats–the length of the scythe blade–which caught the cut grain and allowed the harvester to put it gently onto the ground as part of the swing-ing motion needed to cut the grain. Operating the heavy, ungainly cradle required constant, controlled, almost-balletic movement of the entire body.) Brown produced twenty-three shocks and seven bundles of barley, and seventy-six shocks of oats in one field and fifty-seven bundles in another–which he "got in" without shocking because rain threatened.

The beginning of August was wet and rainy, as it often is in southern New England, so the work of harvesting slowed. But even when five of the last seven days had been rainy, Brown "Mowed seed hay" on the eleventh. Seed hay was allowed to go to seed–for seed for the next year–unlike the hay intended for good fodder which was cut before it matured.

By the nineteenth of August, Brown had harvested all his oats–"Raised this year 152 shock & 3 bundles"–and he had started the process of threshing. But there was more hay to be mowed and stacked into barns or into outdoor stacks. On August 23, he "got in 1 load hay from middle meadow, topped off all the stacks with it. Finished haying." He had a total of fifty-two wagonloads of hay. Then he "got in red top seed hay" and fenced the haystack north of the barn. Haystacks had to be fenced to keep animals from the hay.

A few days later, Brown went to Providence on business: he sold "22 cheeses 495¾ lbs @ 8 cts [per pound and] 21 lbs sage cheese @ 9 cts [per pound]." While milking the cows did not appear in Brown's journal because it was a daily chore possibly done by the hired men, the fact that the cheesemaking very rarely appears is a sign that women made cheese in the household–Brown's wife and young women like Abby Mason who spent extended time in the household as paid or boarded workers. The women may have done the milking, too, as they did the churning of cream into butter and the processing of milk into cheeses. Throughout Brown's journal, cheese was a very important "cash crop" of his farm, always carried to Providence–by Brown or his father–and sold in the avid urban market.

As fall came on with cooler weather, the nature of Brown's work changed. He plowed a little, "drew stones and made wall," entertained several callers, and went to "camp meeting." Brown was a Baptist. Camp meetings were religious revival meetings held away from churches to generate enthusiasm. That Brown recorded camp meetings in his farm journal, as he did Sunday meeting, shows that they were central to his life as a farmer. The days he did no work he left the journal blank.

In September, Brown threshed more grain (he always wrote it "thrashed," the way it was pronounced). Threshing gets the grain kernels off the stalks. The grain was usually laid on a floor and beaten with flails or other instruments. The kernels were then picked up and "winnowed" by tossing to separate the grain from the chaff. On September 9, Brown recorded that his rye threshed out to "1¾ bushels from 31 bundles." On September 13, he began digging potatoes:

13 Cut [corn]stalks in hog pasture. Shocked stalks cut Saturday. Dug 17 bu. mercer potatoes. Put 15 in cellar & gave rest to hogs.

14 Sowed 2 acres rye & clover seed.

15 Went to Providence with load (24) cheeses. 6 sage cheeses 132½ lbs @ 9 cts & 18 others 414¼ lbs @ 8¼ cts. William Day had 1 cheese 19 lbs @ 7½ cts. Dug 20 bu. merino & blue potatoes, 16 for hogs. Got up wood. Bound stalks.

Cutting corn and shocking the stalks (with the ears of corn on them), and digging myriads of potatoes of many different varieties occupied Brown for the next month. There were mercer potatoes, merino potatoes, blue potatoes, white potatoes, yellow potatoes, and even peach blossom potatoes. There were also apples to pick and store. The potatoes went into the cellar for human consumption, into "the swill house" for animal consumption, or were fed directly to the hogs. Brown hired additional day workers to dig potatoes, so he was able to go to Providence with his wife and family for a few days, go to the cattle show in Brooklyn (at a fair which advertises itself today as the oldest continuous agricultural fair in America), and attend Town Meeting (on October 3), and still record tens of bushels of potatoes dug each day.

Early in October, he recorded that he "began to feed" several different cows "with potatoes." Within four weeks, each of those cows was slaughtered and its hide, tallow, and meat weighed and sold. Potatoes were the "fattening food" Brown used before slaughtering his animals. On October 18, he recorded:

> . . . Finished digging potatoes Saturday the 15th: 1125 bushels in all. About 580 merinoes.

> 19 Finished picking russet apples. . . . Father returned from Providence. Cheese weighed 515¾ lbs. sage 3 cheeses 63 [lbs]. Sold beans for 8 shillings bu., Turkey 9 cts lb. Anna returned from Providence to live with us till she is 18 years old.

> 25 Carried M. Juslin 26½ bu apples. Husked corn [the laborious hand-process of getting the dried kernels of corn off the cob]. Rainy P.M. . . .

> 27 . . . Made last new milk cheese [so Brown himself at least occasionally was involved in the cheesemaking].

> Nov 8 Rainy day the first for a long time. Husked in barn. . . . Began to fodder cows [to feed them hay rather than have them continue to eat pasture grass, which was by this time about gone].

> 9 Harvested sugar beets, turnips, cabbages &c. 53 bu sugar beets in all. 26 bu turnips. . . .

> 12 Finished husking middle lot corn, about 100 bu. Finished Harvesting Near 400 bu. corn [evidently Brown did not consider the harvesting finished until all the corn was husked]. . . .

> 14 Fenced [hay] stacks. Banked the house [covered the sills and lowest clapboards of the house with hay or earth to keep the cold out in the winter]. Went to Killingly. . . . Carried 13 lbs coarse wool exchanged for 9 yds overcoat cloth by paying $4.20. Rainy P.M.

> 17 Thanksgiving. Went hunting. Shot nothing. Aunt Martha Lemuel & Emmeline here . . . & Mr Stevens.

Most of November's work was "drawing" manure to the fields, bringing wood in to the house, fencing, and "thrashing." On Sunday, the twenty-seventh, Brown "did not go to meeting," and it was "cold, ground froze up." There was a snowstorm on the last day of November, and on December 1, through four inches of snow, Brown took "5 skim cheeses" to Dayville where he sold them for "2½ cts per pound."

With the advent of winter, the farm work was mostly cutting, chopping, and drawing wood, both for the Browns' use and for sale to others. On December 10, Brown slaughtered five hogs and his father took the 1,485 pounds of pork to Woonsocket, Rhode Island. On December 20, they slaughtered another hog, 346 pounds, as well as "14 Turkies weighed 108 lbs & 11 chickens weighed 31 lbs." Brown himself "set out for

Providence in evening with load & drove [his horse and wagon over more than thirty miles of narrow dirt roads] all night." He spent the day in Providence, and sold the "Turkies" for eight and one-half cents a pound, the chickens for seven cents, and the hog for five cents a pound. He came back home on the twenty-second.

Christmas and New Year's had not yet been removed from the continuing cycle of the farm year. One Christmas day entry in Brown's journal was simply "Friday. Warm & Rain. Went to mill. Carried log for sled Runners. Thrashed."

On January 24, 1843, Benjamin Brown, Jr., "went to Norwich to Liberty Convention," stayed overnight, and returned the next day. Liberty conventions were a sign of the growing political importance of the antislavery movement. Local political conventions had begun in the 1830s. They gave forums on important issues to as many citizens as possible. They so appealed to contemporary ideals of democracy that political parties started to use them in the nominating process, and by the 1840s national presidential nominating conventions began. Local (nonparty) conventions with local and national figures in attendance, with long debates and speeches, continued everywhere in America. They often resulted in the formation of political organizations around issues and the nomination of candidates who supported those issues for offices. The Liberty conventions Brown attended in the 1840s helped sharpen and give political point to the antislavery movement and brought the formation of the Liberty Party and later the Free Soil Party in national politics. In February 1844, he "went to Hampton to Liberty Convention," which probably attracted Jonathan Clark, who was a leading Free Soil Party member in Hampton a few years later, and might have attracted Henry Taintor as well. In March 1844, Brown "went to Anti-Slavery meeting in Brooklyn."

Winter returned with a vengeance to Brown's farm in February 1843. Brown recorded:

5 Sunday. Snow storm. Did not go to meeting.

6 Snowy & windy. Snow 18 inches deep or more. G A worked in P.M. Got up 4 small loads wood from swamp west road. Oxen broke through ice.

7 Windy & Cold. Snow drifting badly. . . .

8 Worked on road in breaking paths [through the snow].

Despite the winter weather, Brown took his family to Webster, Massachusetts, just across the state line to the north, on February 16. They returned on the eighteenth. At the end of the month, Brown traveled alone to Woodstock and on to Killingly where, on March 1, he "bought stove for 22 Dol. 23 cts." The next day, another "cold day," he "went after stove & carried 6 bu. corn towards paying for it." He had recently sold corn for 75 cents a bushel. He recorded that March 11 was "Last day of school," and that on the thirteenth "George Angell began work for 8 months at 12 Dollars pr month. To work 5 days in a week. . . . Snowed, hailed & rained in P.M. Chopped wood in wood house. 1 lamb died."

Lambs were being born, cows were calving, and spring was getting near. Brown "carried logs to Webbs saw mill" on March 15, suffered through a "snow storm, much drifted" on the seventeenth, and carried another "load logs to saw mill & brot back load boards" on the eighteenth. By the end of March, there was "warm rain and flood." The thaw had set in. April 3 brought "Election day" for town and state officers. Brown began to "pick up stones" in April, and on Sunday, the ninth, he recorded: "Snow melting off gradually, been on ground since 1st Feb. 2 feet deep around fences in many places." April 14 was a "Fast day [for Brown's church]. Rainy." Brown began to plow "first this year" on April 17–and the annual cycle commenced once again.

Farm years as Brown recorded them in his journal always proceeded with rock picking, plowing, animals giving birth, planting, hoeing, haying, hauling, harvesting grains, digging potatoes, feeding, slaughtering, threshing, cutting and chopping wood, hauling, and hauling. A farmer was in motion across his lots and fields with his work, and across the countryside to town centers and cities where his markets and his family and friends were.

Over the years Brown's journal recorded subtle changes embedded in the repetitious cycle of crops and animals and seasons. For instance, he "carried 1515 lbs hay to B. Wheaton in Brooklyn" in May 1843. The entry shows he was beginning to sell his hay farther away from the farm, and in weighed quantities that required the use of a sizable scale, no longer by the less precisely priced "load" or "stack."

On another occasion, he recorded that he "went to Killingly, Ballou's Factory [a new mill in what is now called "Ballouville" in the town of Killingly], Danielsonville &c," making a tour of the mills and modern industry in Killingly. The mill work done in those places attracted an increasing population of workers who were a market for his goods. Brown later recorded selling poultry, as well as quantities of turnips and potatoes, in Killingly. One December, he sold hogs by an advance contract in Danielsonville before he slaughtered them–a new method focused on the market for pork rather than on the cyclical necessities of the farm.

Farm crises, of course, were perennial: "Little Chapman heifer found & could not calve. Took calf away from her and drawed her up to barn on sled." Three days later, Brown wrote: "Little Chapman heifer likely to die. Knocked her in head and took off her hide. Hoed in N.E. lot. . . ."

Brown wrought further changes in his life when he "bought air tight stove" in December 1843, a modern convenience to provide better heat to his growing family. In January 1844, he expanded his horizons when he "went to Agricultural Society meeting." Like Henry Taintor, Brown was interested in improving his farm and his methods. He sowed and later mowed a new crop, Canada thistles, about this time. Other methods were also improving. Brown recorded one spring day that "Dr Whitcomb vacci-nated the children."

And the railroad was coming closer, bringing changes even before it arrived. Brown took his family to Webster, Massachusetts, one August day and from there "went in cars to Worcester." His world had become smaller. In January 1847, he "went to Providence with wife & 2 children," and from there the Browns "went to Boston" amidst "Snow & Rain," and returned to Providence the next day. They went by train. This ordinary farm family was able to take a ten-day vacation trip that winter, involving considerable travel as well as visits to kin, in great part "in cars." Because of the railroad, new packaged goods were also within reach. At the Killingly terminal of the railroad Brown "bought sack salt" one spring day.

In 1846, the last full year of Brown's journal, he borrowed a sizable sum of money from two widows "at 5 per cent" which provided him cash and secured them an income from the interest he paid. He bought more ani-mals and planted new crops. And he continued active political involve-ment. On April 6, 1846, he "went to Freemans meeting. John Witter cho-sen Representative [to the Connecticut Assembly] after voting five times." Windham County, in which both Brooklyn and Hampton were situated, elected the only abolitionist to the Connecticut Assembly that year. Brown himself would be elected state representative from Brooklyn as an aboli-tionist in 1849.

Brown continued to go to meetings as he farmed. On September 22, 1846, he went to Woodstock "to Liberty meeting." The next day on the farm he discharged one of his hired men, William Mosely, and the "white face cow choked. Killed her." In January 1847, he wrote that he "sent 3 Dollar to Hartford by mail in payment for Charter Oak [a scion of the famous tree near Hartford in which the Connecticut Charter had been hidden in Colonial times] for 1847 for Jacob Kimball & Francis Litchfield. Went to Liberty meeting in evening on Tatnick hill." The last entry in his journal, on March 3, 1847, was "went to Liberty Convention at Danielsonville."

Brown was in the state legislature twice—in 1849 as an abolitionist and in 1861 as a Republican. According to a commercial biographical record published in 1903, he was still alive at that time, in his nineties. He had retired from farming in 1900, and moved close to the village of Brooklyn. About Brown's life of work this record says that after twelve years of teaching "Mr. Brown resigned [in 1841] from this arduous profession to enjoy life in the freedom of agricultural pursuits."(!)

A Political Career

Henry G. Taintor became a political magnate in Hampton, one of those men automatically included in the phrase "the town fathers," still used to describe the people who manage public affairs of the town. He started out with a place in the community, which came to him from his mother and father and his uncles and aunts, who were or had recently been important figures in town. But he had to make his own career—no one could expect simply to inherit community respect or votes.[7]

From the beginning of his adult life in Hampton, Henry subscribed to periodicals in order to keep up with the rapid changes in politics and the economy of the country. He read local papers as well as the *Courant* from Hartford and a variety of New York papers. He also had subscriptions to papers published by church, Sunday school, and missionary organizations, as well as periodicals on agriculture. They came to him by mail, which meant they were held for him at the post office (probably in full view) so it was clear to townspeople that Mr. Taintor was knowledgeably up to date about the world out of town. Starting at least on August 26, 1836, when he inscribed his name in his new copy of *Col. Crocketts Exploits & Adventures in Texas . . . Written by Himself* just after Davy Crockett had died at the Alamo as part of the Texas war for independence from Mexico, he also bought and read books on current topics throughout his life.

Henry combined his knowledge of the wider world with his farming and business affairs to develop a place for himself in Hampton's public life. Once he married and had a family, he was accepted as a man to be considered in the town's political, social, and church life. His large, well-maintained, and often-modernized house in the center of the village certainly enhanced his position.

Henry was first elected to public office in Hampton in 1836 as one of the town's constables. His business dealings gave him a constantly renewed acquaintance with the town's lawyer, Chauncey F. Cleveland, and certainly with the Town Clerk, a central establishment figure. In the first decade or so of his business life, Henry was billed for recording 149 deeds and mortgages by Dyer Hughes, Jr., who was not only Town Clerk but also the town's principal physician, and one of its two licensed dealers in alcoholic beverages.[8] By the time he married in 1839, Henry was already treasurer of

Henry G. Taintor in the 1860s

the church next door. He was elected one of the "Tithingmen" who collected taxes for the church in 1840, an office he held for many years. As
church treasurer he took the moneys collected by or given to the church
into his own accounts, and paid the church's expenses out of them. It
sometimes meant handling considerable funds, which everyone knew him
capable of because of his own wealth. It often meant advancing money on
behalf of the church—particularly for the salary and needs of the minister—
which he did without hesitation. The people of the congregation evidently
trusted him, and he did the job for fifty years.

In 1842, Henry was first elected to the Hampton Board of Relief,
which reviewed complaints about assessments and taxes. He was on that
board off and on for years. Between 1842 and 1844 he was also a fence
viewer for the town and a highway surveyor. The town elected him to
state office as its representative to the Connecticut Assembly in 1843, the
second year Chauncey F. Cleveland was governor. Henry was a Whig,
while Cleveland was still a Democrat; throughout the 1840s the two parties divided the state nearly evenly.

Henry was already also an abolitionist. He had begun subscribing to
the *National Anti-Slavery Standard* in 1842. Ten years later, when Harriet
Beecher Stowe published *Uncle Tom's Cabin,* he and Delia not only read it,
but ordered the *Key* that Mrs. Stowe published within a year in order to

document her sources for the story of slavery. It is possible still, in the much-perused copy the Taintors kept, to read Stowe's opening words:

> The work which the writer here presents to the public is one which has been written with no pleasure, and with much pain.
>
> In fictitious writing, it is possible to find refuge from the hard and the terrible, by inventing scenes and characters of a more pleasing nature. No such resource is open in a work of fact; and the subject of this work is one on which the truth, if told at all, must needs be very dreadful. There is no bright side to slavery.[9]

Henry was elected as a Whig to the Connecticut State Senate from the Thirteenth District to serve in 1851–52. He ran and lost three times in the three years thereafter. Whig political power was declining by then; the 1850s saw political allegiances reorganized all over the country. Henry, for example, supported incumbent Millard Fillmore, a Whig, for the Presidency in 1852.

But by the mid-1850s, based on his effective statewide reputation, Henry helped to form the brand new Republican Party in Connecticut. He subscribed to *The Republican* from Hartford in 1852, and he started to subscribe to Horace Greeley's *New York Tribune* in 1853. Greeley, who published daily, semi-weekly, weekly, European, and California editions of his paper, gave widespread publicity to the rapid growth of the new Republican Party. Henry supported and contributed to the campaign funds of John Charles Fremont, the first Republican candidate for the Presidency, in 1856. In Hampton that year no one voted for the Whig candidate for governor, and only five voted for Fillmore—who was the Whig candidate for President. Fremont carried the town, 150 to 57 for Buchanan, the Democrat who became President. Hampton had become a Republican town. It remained Republican for presidential elections until 1988, when the majority voted for Democrat Michael S. Dukakis. Old-timers chuckled then that the town had never been particularly notorious for picking winners.

The town of Hampton kept Henry Taintor in local offices throughout his life. In 1847, he was once again on the Board of Relief and he became agent of the Town Deposit Fund. Hampton sent him, with Chauncey F. Cleveland, Philip Pearl, and Josiah Jackson, as delegate to an important meeting about railroad construction. In 1848 Henry became a justice of the peace, an office he held through 1858, and then again from 1865 at least until 1882. That made him a local magistrate. He gave initial hearings and trial to both criminal and civil cases originating in Hampton. Unlike many justices of the peace who treated their offices as merely honorific,

Henry G. Taintor gained a reputation as a considerate, hard-working judge.

Hampton made Henry one of its selectmen in 1856. He was the leader of the town Board of Relief all through the Civil War. He frequently moderated Town Meetings and was instrumental in organizing the bounties the town of Hampton paid to volunteers for the draft during the war. In July 1864, Henry moderated a Town Meeting held at the hotel across the street from his house. The Center School–Town Hall building had burned down, and shortly thereafter, the town bought three-quarters of an acre from Henry Taintor on which to build a new "school and town house."[10]

Starting when Henry was in the state legislature in 1843, he spent long times away from home on political business. He boarded in Hartford thirty-six days at the City Hotel that summer while the Assembly was in session.[11] The year he was a state senator he boarded eight weeks at the U.S. Hotel in Hartford.[12] He was also often away for his other business, nearly always without Delia. And she went away on extended visits—mostly to family—without him. We know about those times they were separated not only from Henry's accounts but because they wrote to each other and kept the letters.

Hampton elected Henry its representative in the Assembly again in 1863. He served the Republican cause, and impressed state party leaders. When the Civil War had ended, in 1866, Henry was elected state treasurer. It was his last state office. As treasurer he spent many more days in Hartford and traveled on state business. He missed his family, writing often to Delia, "Kiss Mary & Freddy for me & accept for yourself a great share of love. . . ."[13] When he intended to come home and could not, he wrote Delia, "I shall think of you to night. . . ."[14]

One night, away in New Haven, Henry shared his life with Delia, writing:

> I have just returned from a party (10 minutes of 11 oclok) . . . & perhaps ought to go to bed instead of writing you. . . . The party was composed of 23 gentelmen only. . . . At tea Small tables were brought into the parlour. Suitable for two persons to Sit at & we had Oysters, tea & Coffee, biscuit & butter, spread & three or four kinds of cake. After tea the party was entertained by remarks or an address from Revd Mr. Eustis who has spent some time recently in New Orleans. It was very interesting indeed. The individuals or Club meet again two weeks from to night with Genl Russell. . . .
>
> The College boys are singing in the Street as I am writing (I have a front room) "Stop that Knocking" & "Toll the bell for Lively Nell." I have been sitting at my window since I commenced writing, but it is

getting late & I must stop. The boys are now singing "Massa's in the Cold Cold ground" very beautifully. I wish you was here

    Good night

Aff[ectionatel]y Yours

Henry G. Taintor[15]

A Man of Judgment

As Henry established himself as a man of judicious temperament in the town, people and families called on him to help with personal problems. He managed the estates of many men and women so their heirs might not lose whatever property they had accumulated. Probate judges made him a trustee for property. And as justice of the peace, he adjudicated sometimes fierce differences among people. The earliest estate he managed was his uncle Dan Bulkeley's. Eighteen years after Dan's death he finally finished caring for and distributing what could be realized from Dan's property—first to the widow Phoebe, and then to Phidelia and her husband, Nelson Higgins, as well as to Dan's youngest child, Robert W. Bulkeley.[16]

Erastus B. Fuller, a Hampton man who had moved south and died a prosperous merchant (probably a cotton factor) in Eufaula, Alabama, in 1848, named Henry his trustee. Fuller left several thousand dollars to his nephews, his sisters, and their children—Fullers, Litchfields, and Abbotts in Hampton—and required of Henry that he invest the money for the minor children, pay the interest to the parents, and turn over the principal to the children when they reached their majorities. Henry fulfilled his trust over several years.[17]

Henry helped settle the differences between Cesar Hall (an African-American who worked occasionally for him and for Chauncey Cleveland) and Philip Pearl. Pearl sued Hall for an unpaid ten-dollar promissory note, and although Henry found Hall to be an "absent and absconding debtor," he nevertheless found a way to get Pearl and Hall to settle the case.[18]

In 1850, the probate court appointed Henry commissioner on the estate of John B. Burnett (maybe one of Dan Bulkeley's in-laws), who had died in Pittsburgh, Pennsylvania, on his way back home from the California Gold Rush. Henry allowed William Abbott to collect $320 from Burnett's estate for "cash paid for . . . board while nurseing Mr Burnett 9 weeks in Central America $45.00, . . . nurseing & taking care of Mr Burnett while sick at Central America 9 weeks at 3 dollars per day $189.00, . . . fare paid in crossing from the Pasific to the Atlantic in consequence of being detained with Mr Burnett being about 5 weeks $40.00, . . . taking care & nursing Mr Burnett on our Journey from St John to Pitsburg Penn. where he died being about 35 days and expenses, and also going to New London since I came home $46.00."[19] Henry also allowed $9.27 out of the estate for ten yards of "Bomamzine," black ribbon, and "making mantila" for the funeral dress Hannah Clark made for Burnett's widow. Mrs. Burnett herself had worked as a dressmaker and coatmaker in town while her husband was gone.[20]

Henry Taintor's decisions as justice of the peace did not always favor the leading men in town. In 1850, David Copeland, a minor, accused David Greenslit—an important man who would for several years be the Windham County sheriff—of having "appropriated" twenty-two barrels containing sixty bushels of Copeland's winter apples. Despite protests from young Copeland that the apples were his, Greenslit had sold the apples "as his own." Henry Taintor thought Copeland's evidence was good enough to find for him. Greenslit appealed to the county court. We do not know how that court decided, but we know that a horse wagon of Greenslit's, valued at the thirty-five-dollar value of the barrels and apples, was attached by Henry's order.[21]

One of the more difficult cases Henry had to deal with early in his career involved Jonathan K. Rindge (a member of a family that remained a complication for the Hampton community until early in the twentieth century) and Royal Copeland, young David's father. Henry tried to get ungarbled testimony from Rindge, but heard only a long and confused story about Rindge buying hay from Copeland that he paid for with a promissory note which he, in part, redeemed with flour and lime brought from Norwich. The point was that the hay proved foul. According to Rindge, it looked "better than it was. The cattle would not eat it." Henry could not find out whether or not Rindge returned the hay. At any rate, he refused to pay Copeland. Copeland said the flour and lime were not applied to Rindge's note, and convinced Henry that the truth lay on his side. Henry ordered Rindge to pay Copeland $20.03, including costs, and Rindge appealed to the county court.[22] Again we do not know how that court acted in the matter. What is clear is that Henry Taintor was doing his best to be fair in a very tangled case.

In 1853, Henry Taintor (who by that time was a subscriber to temperance journals) tried a case in which Francis A. Brewster, a descendant of Dr. John Brewster and a druggist, was accused of selling liquor to Solomon Shippee "to be drank in said store when sold." Brewster was not a licensed "taverner" and Shippee drank the stuff on the premises. The temperance movement in Connecticut had caused the legislature to pass laws encouraging strict town control of the sale of alcoholic spirits. Henry ordered Brewster arrested as a violator of Hampton's licensing regulations. Then he found him guilty and ordered him to pay a fine of ten dollars, and $4.60, the cost of prosecution. Brewster appealed, and Dyer Hughes, Jr., went bond of thirty dollars for him.[23] In January 1854, Brewster was again accused of selling liquor, this time to James A. Owen, "a person addicted to habits of Intoxication . . . and was known by . . . Brewster to be so addicted." Henry ordered Brewster and Owen, along with two witnesses, to be brought before him "at his dwelling house" to testify in the case. After hearing them, Henry marked the case "settled," without explanation.[24]

By the mid-1850s, drunks were being charged with breach of the peace in growing efforts to encourage temperance. When they were charged, Henry ordered them arrested and brought before him "at the Hotel" across the street (which he bought in 1854) rather than in his own parlor. One, who pled guilty, was fined twenty dollars and $8.12 in costs, and when he could not pay "was committed to the County jail to be delivered by due course of law."[25]

Sometimes Henry examined men charged with drunkenness to find out who sold them the liquor. He took testimony from Samuel Vickers (spelled "Vickus" and no doubt pronounced that way) for that purpose:

> On the 2nd day of June 1857 I went to Orrin Neff & obtained some liquor of him, a number of times during the day. I then went to Mr Loren Rockwell's & got some Rum of him. I had one drink of him, & paid him five cents for it. I did not pay Mr Neff any thing for the liquor I obtained of him. I did not on that day have any Rum of Mr L Rockwell but one. In the Evening I went to John Greeley's & obtained some Gin of him and my Son Charles took some money from me and paid for it. He paid for 2 drinks 9 cents. I saw him pay the money to Greeley.–Between 2 & 3 o'clk when I purchased the Rum of Mr L Rockwell & in the evening when I purchased the Gin of Mr John Greeley–I handed Mr Rockwell a five dollar bill for Mr Rockwell to change. I then handed him 5 cts to pay for the drink. . . .

We would probably define Vickers as an alcoholic. There is no indication that Henry convicted Vickers of anything.[26] But he certainly found out who was selling him his drinks.

Henry did not hear many cases of theft in his court. In one, the accused, Isaac N. Hendley, pled guilty to the charge that he had stolen "one ten Dollar Bank bill . . . issued by the Weybosset Bank of the State of Rhode Island Dated November 16th 1852 Signed by L Greene Cashier and by Wm Rhodes President and marked as No 32" from sixty-seven-year-old William Sweet, a hired man in town. Henry Taintor fined Hendley one dollar, plus $8.15 costs, and ordered him imprisoned in the county jail at hard labor for fifteen days.[27] In another case, a Windham man was accused of stealing sixteen geese worth twenty-five dollars from Ebenezer Griffin.

Henry issued a warrant for the man's arrest to David Greenslit, who was then deputy sheriff, and Greenslit presented the following bill to the court for his costs: "Travel in pursuit to arrest 58 miles $2.70, arrest and reading [of warrant] .59, travel with prisoner to court 10 mi 2.50, keeping prisoner by order of court to Feby 26th 3.00, Boarding prisoner 7 meals & 2 Lodgings 2.00, attending Court on the 26th .50. $11.29." The man pled guilty when he finally attended court.[28]

Later that year, Ebenezer Griffin brought another case when he accused Michael Clark of stealing his pumpkins. Griffin declared "that on the first day of Novm. 1854 he was the Lawfull owner of three Cart Loads of good sound punkins of the value of six dollars and the defendant . . . did with force & arms and without the consent of the Plaintiff take & carry away sd punkin out of the possession of the Plaintiff to some place unknown whereby the Plaintiff has wholly lost the same to his damage." Clark pled not guilty, and Henry ruled that Griffin's "declaration is not sufficient," so he found for Clark and ordered Griffin to pay costs.[29]

On Christmas day (it was not yet a holiday in the Taintor family), 1855, Henry heard one of the more serious cases he ever dealt with. He could not try major criminal cases, but he wrote a memorandum of his hearing which was forwarded to the Superior Court:

> Be it remembered that on this 25th day of December AD 1855 David Clapp Jr. of Hampton was brought before me . . . for that on or about the 28th day of May AD 1855, the said David Clapp Jr then of . . . Hampton now of Chaplin . . . did with force and arms, wickedly & artfully seduce & commit fornication with one Mary E Davis, then of . . . Hampton, & did then & there with like force and arms have carnal knowledge of the body of said Mary.
>
> And . . . that at the time of said seduction, fornication & carnal knowledge . . . Mary E Davis was & now is a female & a minor under the age of twenty one years. . . .
>
> And being required to answer to said complaint . . . David Clapp Jr (who being a minor under the age of twenty one years, by his guardian David Clapp) pleads & says that he is not guilty & puts himself on the Court for trial.
>
> I do find . . . that there are probably grounds for supporting said complaint whereupon . . . David Clapp Jr. become bound in a recognizance of Two Hundred Dollars . . . that the said David Clapp Jr appear before the Superior Court . . . then & there to answer to said complaint & abide the decision of the Court thereon. . . .[30]

In some cases of assault, Henry as a justice of the peace was competent to decide the case and order the guilty party fined and imprisoned. In other, more serious cases, the defendant, even when Justice Taintor found him guilty, was bound over to a higher court for trial and sentencing.[31]

Women were rarely involved in cases before the courts. In Henry Taintor's voluminous records of his years as justice of the peace, women were in his court occasionally as victims of crimes and occasionally as witnesses. No woman ever brought a case to Henry's court, nor was a woman ever the principal accused in a case. The public life of the courts and politics was man's place.

The power of even a justice of the peace's court to arrest, to fine, to jail, and to "attach" property (take it away from the accused owner's use until the case was tried) made it a court to be reckoned with by ordinary people. While Henry Taintor seemed, from the evidence of the case files he kept, to be an even-handed judge, and he gained a reputation in the community for fairness to all, nevertheless he did at least occasionally use his power with devastating severity. In a civil case that Lyndon T. Button brought against Edward Logan of Killingly, for twenty-five dollars of "book debt," Henry ordered an attachment which sounds like it deprived Logan—perhaps an Irish immigrant—of most of his household furniture, including his beds, as well as of a lot of food. He recorded that he "attached as the property of the . . . defendant Two Flour Barrels & contents, One Box & contents, One Pork Barrel & Contents, One Table, One saw, One Axe, one washstand, One Candle stand, Eleven Chairs, Two Bedsteds, One Tub & Contents, One Bag & Contents, One Bedquilt, Three sheets Containing Two Feather Beds and other Bedding." Henry marked the case "non suited," which might mean the case was dropped, or it might mean that Logan simply departed, leaving his food, furniture, and bedding behind.[32]

PART IV

ANOTHER REVOLUTION

The generation that came
to adulthood between the 1860s
and the 1880s in the midst of
industrialization and the Civil War

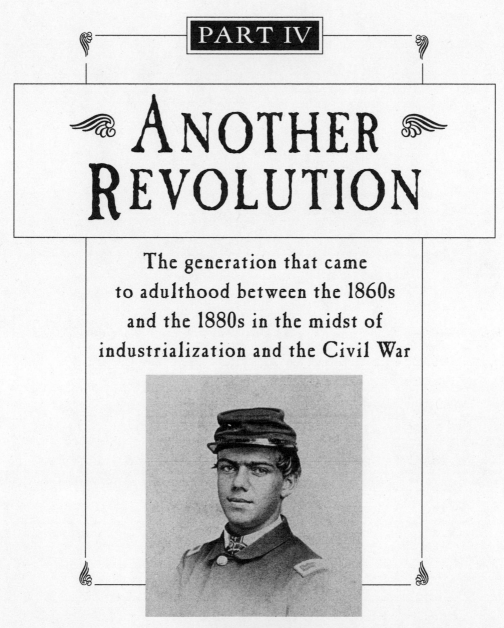

Lieutenant Henry E. Taintor
during the Civil War.

CHAPTER 14

DOWNWARD MOBILITY

"Our family is small and we can all do for each other...."

In order to pick up the story of Edwin Bulkeley Taintor, the older brother of Henry and the not-quite-twin of his cousin John, we have to move backward in time and northward in geography. Bulkeley lived in West Brookfield, Massachusetts, a small town slightly larger than Hampton, Connecticut, and about forty miles north of Hampton as the crow flies, more as the roads meander. He was twenty-six years old when he married Sally Penniman of North Braintree, Massachusetts, in 1826. Sally was eighteen.

Like his father and his uncle, Bulkeley farmed, raised sheep, and was a merchant. When his father died in 1827, he inherited several thousand dollars' worth of land in Hampton, as well as mortgages and notes. Over the next few years he bought some shares in local banks in Massachusetts and conducted his farm and mercantile business with some success. He became a justice of the peace in 1835. By that time he was a respected local leader; his Yale education and his mercantile pursuits had helped give him a place as a gentleman in community affairs. He bought a pew in the meetinghouse in West Brookfield and he and his young wife produced a family: Lucy was born in 1828, Caroline in 1830, and Susan in 1835. Bulkeley's career appeared to promise success and prosperity in about the same proportion as his younger brother Henry's.

The Vicissitudes of Fortune

While the 1840s brought Henry marriage, children, and the beginnings of lifelong financial success, they brought tragedy to Bulkeley. In 1841 his beloved wife died at the age of thirty-three. He was left with three young daughters saddened by the loss of their mother. In business, the long-term effects of the Panic of 1837 and the deep depression that followed it reached Bulkeley in Brookfield shortly after his wife died. In January 1843, he was forced to file for bankruptcy.[2] All his background and training made him regard that action as the ultimate disgrace, a public embarrassment.

His bankruptcy petition was granted, and all his property was seized and put up for auction. This meant, we realized as we read the list with horror, everything–from the pew in the meetinghouse and his sixty-six-acre home farm, another thirty-four-acre farm that he worked nearby, all his farm equipment and wagons, 112 sheep and lambs, three hogs, one cow, two yoke of oxen, and one horse–to all the furniture and pots and pans in his house (except what little the law permitted him to keep).

Bulkeley's close cousin-brother John and his real brother Henry bailed him out. John bought all his property at the bankruptcy auction. He paid a total of $8,352.46 and turned all the property back to Bulkeley; it was years before Bulkeley repaid him.[3] The whole situation strained their relationship, although they never completely lost contact with each other.

In June 1843, Bulkeley remarried. His new wife was Frances M. Prichard, the daughter of Amos and Janet Prichard of West Brookfield. Frances bore two more daughters to Bulkeley in this second marriage– Eugenia in 1845 and Clara in 1853. Her stepdaughters always referred to Frances as "Mother," and never said a direct word against her in their letters to their aunt Delia. But they did not feel in their adult lives that she was ever a reason to go home to Brookfield.

Bulkeley gradually recouped with some help from his new in-laws. His inheritance from his mother in 1849 helped him repay John and his brother Henry. In the twenty-seven years he lived after his bankruptcy, he never came near the wealth that John or Henry acquired. His experience made him dread penury. As he grew older he became stingy and much more fearful. Bulkeley's is not the story of a successful gentleman merchant-farmer.

His troubles were not only financial; they also included his lack of a son. Bulkeley's younger brother Henry had four.

The crowning tragedies for the Brookfield Taintors came during the 1850s. In 1851, when the eldest daughter Lucy–along with Caroline and Susan–inherited money from her grandfather Penniman's estate, the probate court listed Lucy Penniman Taintor as "an insane person." She was twenty-three years old. The Hampton town records show that she had witnessed a deed in Hampton three years earlier, in 1848, for her uncle Henry, apparently when she was on a visit. So her illness must have come on after that time. Lucy was confined to the new Worcester Lunatic Hospital, where she would spend the last fifty years of her life.

In February of 1853, Bulkeley and Frances' last child, Clara, was born. In the spring of 1854, one of Clara's older sisters wrote to her aunt Delia, "Little Clara is very merry, this morn and has quite a concert–or rather attempts one in opposition to the birds, very frequently–She is very lavish of her kisses–and has given me a great many, for her little cousins!!"[4] But a few short months later, she reported, "we have had *sickness* to claim all our time for the last three or four weeks–Our darling little Clara has had a very severe attack of the 'dysentery' (that numbers so many of its victims among the children)–and for days together, has hovered between life and death."[5] Then, in the late summer of 1854, little Clara died.

Six weeks passed before nineteen-year-old Susan could bring herself to write the details to her aunt Delia:

> . . . you will be waiting to hear of dear little Clara's last illness–After I wrote you, she lingered several weeks . . . but towards the last week of her life, we all, even the Dr. had strong hopes of her recovery for she seemed, and appeared really better–I remember the afternoon of the day she died. Dr. Mirick came running in, laughing–and saying to me as I stood in the hall–"Do you want anything in any line to-night?"
>
> In a few moments, he told us she was past relief and would sink away very soon–the "reaper" came very suddenly–but she fell asleep so sweetly, so gently, we could but be thankful for it. A few hours before she ceased to breathe, there was a slight spasm but after that all was perfectly peaceful–she almost *looked* a cherub, as she lay on the bed, her eyes wide opened and glancing upward, and a half smile lingering on her face–almost too lovely for earth. She was indeed a bud too delicate for the chill heath of this lower sphere; but has gone to be unfolded neath heaven's eternal sunshine–and we know that it is "well" with her.
>
> It seemed very hard, at first, to find constantly some new remembrance of the "loved and lost" in every place. A tiny plaything, it might be, or some little thing she had worn–or to start suddenly when there was a light laugh in the street (wondering as of yore if she had strayed away) and feel she was *gone*–brought a deep sadness–unlike any other. I thought so often of a song I used to sing a great deal because 'twas a favorite with us all–entitled "Resignation." The words are by Longfellow and very beautiful–They commence with
>
> > *There is no flock however watched & tender*
> > *But our dead lamb is there*
> > *There is no fire-side howsoe'er defended*
> > *But has one vacant chair. . . .*[6]

Clara's death and Lucy's insanity affected the whole family. All three of Bulkeley's other daughters lived in fear of insanity. The myth of the mad-woman in the attic, so vividly portrayed by Charlotte Brontë in *Jane Eyre* and in "The Yellow Wallpaper," by Charlotte Perkins Gilman, was a controlling image for nineteenth-century women as well as a controlling reality for Caroline and Susan and Eugenia Taintor.[7] Although in the decade after Clara's death Bulkeley was able to make a living for his family and to reestablish some of his position in West Brookfield, he, too, lived in fear of mental illness and of lurking sudden disaster for the rest of his life. And all of Solomon Taintor's descendants after Bulkeley's generation, even without knowing about Lucy, feared there was some haunting skeleton in the family closet.

The Young Ladies of West Brookfield

Caroline, Susan, and Eugenia survived together in the Taintor household in West Brookfield. Carrie and Susie were very close, despite the five years' difference in their ages. Until the end of 1853, Caroline was the eldest daughter at home, with the title of "Miss Taintor" now applied to her. It was as if Lucy no longer existed.

Brought up in this house where sadness was a commonplace, Susie retained her humor and romanticism. She wrote about rural life in West Brookfield to her "own dear Auntie" Delia one (all too typical of New England) spring, "We have had delightful weather for a week or two have we not? . . . It did seem so strange, to watch, again, the softly-falling snow flakes–and hear the boys talk of 'coasting,' when but a day or two before, the breath of the 'sweet south-west' was whispering of birds, and flowers, giving a pleasant murmuring song to the 'brooklets'! . . . And then–just think of snow-storms, in April, when we should have the flower-giving showers!"[8]

But early in 1854 came an important separation. Twenty-four-year-old Caroline left home to be a governess and teacher on a plantation called Buena Vista in Buck Eye, in very rural Laurens County in central Georgia. Dr. Tucker, the plantation owner, hired her to teach his youngest daughter, Eugenia Tucker. In January 1855 Carrie described her life "at the South" to her aunt Delia. She began with a New Englander's surprise that "The weather is very mild–and we sat with open windows today. No snow has visited us, though the first few days in December were bitterly cold for the South, and even for me who am somewhat acclimated now, to feel the cold very easily." Somewhat ruefully, the young teacher described Christmas vacation: "The children were delighted to be released from study and their teacher was scarcely less so to think of two weeks of freedom as being before her."

The South was already celebrating Christmas as a holiday by this time, and Carrie informed her aunt that she had "received a present of a gold stud from Mrs. Tucker and a bottle of cologne, and a collar from Genie– We cannot obtain anything pretty here for presents, without sending away for them, and we all neglected to do so until too late. I shall always prize the gifts I received." Caroline wrote of the holiday preparations, "Dr. T. who is a great lover of good-living sent to Savannah for a large supply of oysters, a barrel of oranges, one of N. England apples, pine-apples and banannas, with nuts etc. Mrs. Tucker had engaged an abundance of eggs, and treated us to egg-nog, and all kinds of delicacies. Mrs. Mizell [a relative] and family spent the day (Christmas) with us–and all the members of the 'Buena Vista' home circle were together, the carriages and horses having gone to the depot two days in succession to bring home Georgia, [a daughter] who is in Macon Female College, and Mr. Tucker [the son] who is now attending Medical lectures in Savannah." The preparations included greenery, but not a Christmas tree. "Saturday previous to the 25th we trimmed the drawing room with cedar, mistletoe, holly, etc–The day came at last and was very mild indeed–so much so as to render it necessary to put out the fires and open the windows!–The gardens are usually made here and peas planted before Christmas, so as to have them ready for the table in the first part of April."

The Tuckers wanted Carrie to remain with them a year longer than her original plan (or at least until spring). She wrote her aunt that "Of course the former proposition could not be thought of as Dr. Tucker wished me to teach without going home between the years but many reasons exist which influence me to stay until May. The transition from this climate to N. England's snows would be rather trying and perhaps might prevent my enjoying very much the time which would necessarily elapse before winter resigns its reign–" There was a further reason to remain, she felt, for "my salary will be proportionately increased–and certainly that is an inducement, for by remaining three months after my year expires, I shall feel as if I might indulge in a long respite before teaching again."[9] Apparently she looked on teaching as her life's work, but was not thrilled with the prospect.

In the spring Carrie looked back over her Georgia time. Her letter shows one of the effects her father's financial calamities had on the family: "The year has passed pleasantly, and profitably, and I have the pleasing testimony of my own conscience that I have been able to partially refund the money expended in my education and in so doing to relieve in a measure the burden which sometimes casts a shadow on the spirits of my father. I shall never regret the labors of the year just closed." Carrie also had an object lesson in family relations from the early experiences of her employer, which she learned about from her young pupil, who told her why he had left the North. She wrote, "He was the oldest of a large family–his parents were poor and against their wishes he ran away, obtained a situation as a clerk of a vessel bound for Dublin Ireland, and after returning taught school–Alternately teaching and studying he acquired his profession." Tucker, a proud man, had told his family that "he never asked assistance of but one human being, an Uncle, and was refused. Henceforth 'he resolved to *paddle his own canoe.*' He came South, gradually acquired property, married twice, and has now two plantations, quite a number of Negroes, and I believe [is assessed for] taxes for seventy five thousand dollars." According to Carrie's informant, Dr. Tucker "has no idea whether his relatives are living or not at the North, but presumes they are."[10] Some of them even, she thought, lived in Windham County, Connecticut, and might be known to her Hampton relatives.

Caroline returned from Georgia to West Brookfield by steamer from Savannah to New York, and then by train. She reported having "reached home safely–but almost *melted* by the heat–however a bath and the donning of a muslin dress worked wonders for me so that after tea I accompanied Father to the depot where is a Soda Fountain and took a glass."[11] For a while the doings of West Brookfield, with its modern soda fountain in the railroad depot, occupied both Carrie and Susie. The latter loved a spectacle. She wrote to Delia "of the great [militia] muster we are to have in W.B. during the month of September–There will be fifteen hundred troops here–and in all it is estimated seven thousand people from 'abroad.' . . . the encampment is on Fathers land, at a little distance."[12]

In the developing summer of 1855 she and Caroline led lives full of incident. Susie wrote a long letter after a visit to Hampton:

> My dear dear Aunty–
>   Don't think me incorrigible, that no letter has greeted you ere this, from either of the "lone, lorn creeters" with faces in a conflagration who waved an adieu from that uncomfortable depot, at Springfield, more than a week ago– . . . I promise to "wield the pen" and tell you how safely, but with what crimsoned faces, we reached home–The cars were so uncomfortable that afternoon–dear me! I can't tell you nor indeed need to, for you enjoyed trials (in a different direction) of the same kind that very day–We found father and Genie waiting for us–both panting from the walk, and were soon all gathered in the pleasant home sitting-room, with the trees nodding a most refreshing welcome–After an early tea, Father coaxed all but myself out to get a drink of soda from a new fountain, just *introduced* (that's the word, I

believe)—and said to be quite good, but I, really, this time, seemed to feel the heat more than others, and spent the time in rocking very fast, to the time of a four [in march time], almost ready (as the junkman said) to "hunt distraction"—

What a day it was, to be sure, and the rest of the week—We all suffered extremely, but Monday afternoon brought a delightful shower, and quite altered the face of things in "general"—mine in "particular"—That night after tea the young gentleman of the place (and by the by, *he* has left now) came with a "span of greys" to propose a ride to S. Brookfield to roll "ten-pins" at a private alley—We had a right nice time and came home by rather a circuitous route—

Next day we were invited to take tea, and eat strawberries, with a very pleasant family living near us. . . . —As usual, Mrs. C. made the hours pass very swiftly, and in the evening we were so patriotic (?) as to fire crackers a long time, amid the shrieks of the *bairns* and "encores" of the gentlemen—

The "glorious Fourth" found the said damsels or the patriotism in rather a sleepy state—but were up in season to see the fireman's parade in their new uniforms—There was a public dinner also that day at the "Wickaboag"-house to which Carrie and her youthful relative were invited by *the* young man and one other (here for the day) but we declined and they came to our house instead and played at backgammon and jikes till after tea when we rode a long time, and then finished the day with ice-creams, which mother is getting to make quite nicely—

. . . I should have mailed my letter this morning, too, but that from the *fright* of last night, I could not hold a pen very steadily, and you'll excuse the looks of my sheet even more I'm sure on this account— And now for the fright—Well, to commence, after the most approved style—"Once upon a time" that is to say last Friday-night, there was a burglar entered two or three houses in the village, and after taking at one place some money and jewelry found his way to the room occupied by a young-lady living there, and commenced administering chloroform—The damp cloth on her face woke her, and springing up, quickly, probably struck him in the chest with her hand, giving her time to spring over the foot of the *bed* and run down stairs—When her Father came up, the bed clothes were thrown out the window, and he [the burglar and would-be-rapist] had jumped out on them, and was off—They found the room filled with chloroform, and the cloth that had been on her face, with another saturated, and rolled up tightly, which it is supposed was intended for her mouth—Had she not started so quickly—She says, at first he pressed both hands on her face, but she seemed to have unnatural strength, and threw them off—

Such a bold attempt in our quiet village has quite excited us all as you may imagine, and when in the middle of last night I heard steps below I could scarcely breathe–In a few moments I heard Fathers voice, and ran down. He said Mother heard some one as she thought at the windows, and had started him considerably–It gave me such a *shock* that I haven't recovered from it e'en now–and of course slept no more that night–We kept lights burning, all the rest of the night, above and below [upstairs and downstairs] and of course heard no more of them–only I remember I never longed more for daylight–

But I am quite forgetting in my excitement, this will not be as inter-esting to *you*–Excuse, please, and let me fancy (as I can so easily) that I am once more seated with you in the pleasant "south-room" [in the Hampton house] with but one of the trio of little folks [Willie] to keep you company and he perhaps bringing you (as he told me at Windsor) "a little yound, yed yose picked yight by the yoad"–Dear one! How I wish I could take the "ould-place" at the tea-table and see you all there once more. . . .

I know this is "stale, flat and unprofitable" but I'm hardly myself this afternoon, and not very brilliant to say the least. Mother and Genie send love–and the latter special thanks for the orange, which pleased her very much. . . .[13]

This attractive woman probably is Caroline Taintor Buel.

By the beginning of 1856, Caroline was once again away teaching, this time out in Farm Ridge, Illinois, in the northern part of that state, west of Chicago. In this she was one of a tidal wave of New England schoolmarms, driven in part by a missionary spirit, to educate the frontier regions. In her February letter to Aunt Delia from her prairie schoolroom "With roguish boys all about me, on whom I cast an occasional glance, and one of whom I have just sent up to Mr. Williams," she made a comment about the most important issue of her time: "I am truly happy–far more so than when in Georgia for there, tho my home was a pleasant one and kind friends ministered to my wants, still the almost entire isolation and the blighting, crushing influence of slavery would at times bring unhappy thoughts. Though the labors of this situation may be greater in some respects than were mine there, I would infinitely prefer being here." It is the only direct comment Caroline ever made about slavery.

In Illinois she had been hired for a short term, but was again requested to remain, along with her fellow teacher "Sarah B.," and wrote, "How like a dream it seems! . . . Possibly we may stay one more term, tho that is not decided at all.–I have a strong desire to see the land of praries and flowers in its summer dress, and to pursue the study of Botany here." She may have been teaching drawing, because she went on to speculate, "Probably we shall stay if a large class in the ornamental branches is pledged for the coming term."[14]

In the summer of 1857, Caroline Taintor came home from Illinois to prepare for her marriage to Alexander W. Buel of Detroit, a lawyer and former Democratic congressman from Michigan. Mr. Buel was a widower with four daughters, seventeen years Carrie's senior. We do not know how she met him–probably when she was in Illinois. That summer in Brookfield, Carrie wrote to Delia declining an invitation to "the Taintor sisters" to visit Hampton "ere one of them drops her cognomen" (which is exactly what a nineteenth-century woman did when she married: she dropped her last name, but retained her middle name before her new married name).

Carrie felt that "The summer is passing away and . . . I feel that my necessary preparation for next Fall will detain me at home, and Susie (dear child) pleasantly and willingly gives up all her idea of visiting to assist me– She is a darling–as you know, I believe." She described how the two girls roomed "together in the common parlor chamber–and have such nice times."

As part of her preparation, she told her aunt, "I have engaged a dressmaker for a fortnight–a good one from Springfield–who comes the last of June and first of July. Now I wish you were here and I would ask you to pass judgment on my taste in making selections of dresses, etc. Beside, I want to sit down and talk with you a long time, as I have done in the past—and now there is so much to say, that it is useless to think of penning it. . . . Tell Uncle Henry he must be all prepared in advance to receive an invita‐tion to come to Brookfield early in October—for I want both of you to be present whoever else cannot come."

She explained that her fiancé, whom she called "My friend Mr. Buel," could not come to West Brookfield. He "is in Wisconsin just now, where he will be for some weeks—is quite well and I hear weekly. He is boarding at a hotel in Manitowoc—where he has some property needing his personal supervision. This necessary absence will make a visit East rather doubtful before October—for which I'm sorry enough—but it cannot be helped—and there will be all the more joy when he *can* come."[15]

Carrie's love seems sedate next to Susie's letter declining the Hampton invitation with her usual lighthearted effusion: "I am sure you would not blame me if you were to see all we are accomplishing during these cool delightful hours before midsummer. I need not say what—You can *imagine* the catalogue better—Suffice it to say, I am thinking seriously of writing Mr. Buel a conviction which is every‐day deepening in my own mind, viz. that it would be equally kind, and appropriate, if he were to leave his law‐cases for a little time, and assist us in the manufacture of pillow‐cases!—Don't you think it seems reasonable, Aunty?"

She hastened to assure her aunt, however, "By the way, we like this same Mr. B. very much—I am quite willing to trust Carrie to him (if I must to any one)—and it is all the highest praise and affection I could give any one—You must see him and know him dear Aunty first—but I am sure even‐tually your judgement would be the same." We found a framed lithograph portrait of Alexander Buel in our house in Hampton. So it seems Susie's "Aunty" did get to know and like him. At the time of Carrie's marriage, her sister wrote, "He is older than C. to be sure—but only in years and experi‐ence I think. He seems to enjoy young society exceedingly—and of course with such a pleasant and lovable group of daughters his *heart* could scarcely grow old." Susie lamented, "How soon he will take Carrie from us! I do not dare think of it often—how can I spare her—and still it is *her gain,* and for myself—there are always ever present sources of comfort, for *all* that life gives of sorrow." There was real sisterly regret in her realization that they were "talking of the past and present and future as we shall *never* again—You can fancy us thus, dear Aunty, and know it is indeed summer‐time to me with her dear love and presence, as a constant and unfailing blessing."[16]

When Caroline married Mr. Buel in October 1857, the young Taintor ladies of West Brookfield began to live separate lives. Luckily for us, they continued to correspond with their aunt Delia.

Bulkeley's Declining Years

The departure of Caroline from home, in the shadow of Lucy's insanity, left Bulkeley Taintor in his late fifties subject to recurring bouts of illness and depression. Susie reported on his health to her aunt Delia from time to time. "We are very well this spring–unless I except Father, who though he never acknowledges that he is sick, yet has many 'ill turns,' of a few hours–and is not as strong as usual–He is very careful, doing nothing but light work and is so much better than in the last of the winter, I am hoping to see him restored to his usual health, ere long."[17]

Bulkeley's family tried to get him to escape from home in order to improve his spirits, but "it is such a 'mountain' for him to make up his mind to leave home that we are almost discouraged in urging him to do so." Trips to Hampton seemed to do him good. Susie wrote after one such visit, "I am sure they must have had a *very* pleasant visit with you from all the recollections of it I hear daily–and it has done them all good–Father *especially*. He seems in 'extra' good spirits, and it has been worth a great deal to him to get away from his cares and forget them for even four days."[18]

Visits were only temporarily cheering to Bulkeley because his "troubles" continued, and money was a constant worry. Susie apologized to her aunt and uncle once because she did not send them six dollars she owed them. She could not send it, she explained to Delia, because her father's hired man "who has been here for *eight years,* has bought him a farm, and leaves this Fall–so he wants all his money that has been accumulating in that time–Father has to raise it this month, and as he is a little *blue* about it, he said he wished I would wait and send [the money] to Uncle Henry a few weeks later–I don't think it would make any real difference but you know just how peculiar Father is, and I can't make him think differently."[19]

Bulkeley's declining spirits were dealt a severe blow in 1862. In that year his cousin and the near twin of his youth, John Taintor, died. Susie reported, "Father received the telegram, announcing his death, Sabbath noon–and was much startled and shocked by it. He seemed for a time to feel it *very* much–said it was not *entirely* unexpected, of course–but he would have been so glad to have *seen* him, *once more*. You know, at heart, Father was much attached to him . . . altho' he says little or nothing of it. . . . They were together almost constantly till they were twenty one, you know."[20] John's death–however little contact he and Bulkeley had continued over the years–removed the last echo of a boyhood that was, by then, very long ago.

In October 1862, Bulkeley was once again (for the first time since his last commission had expired in 1849) appointed a justice of the peace in

West Brookfield. In September 1863, he became a U.S. assistant assessor for the Internal Revenue, charged with collecting the special war-time federal taxes during the Civil War.[21] But even those signs of regained respectability and those sources of additional income did not improve his state of mind. Susie wrote that "we are selling our milk" to get a little extra money and that they had "dismissed our girl this Winter." She acknowledged that "It seems a little odd–but if I am only well I shall not mind the change much–and Mother thinks it will be much more pleasant. Our family is small and we can all do for each other."[22] Bulkeley, however, continued to be "miserable–and at times very low of spirits."[23]

The situation never improved. The Taintors in Hampton continued to hear that Bulkeley "has been, and *is,* very unwell." Susie never knew "what the result may be," but she tried to "be of some assistance to Mother and Genie. . . . Father is so depressed it affects them, of course, and I feel I want to do all I can to *brighten them up* if possible." When she was home she "found Father looking feeble and *sick*–very *thin* and unable to eat anything scarcely–exceedingly weak–and depressed. It made me feel sadly–but I did not let *him* see it, and I tried to cheer him all I could. Dr. Blodgett says he *may* recover, so far as *he* can see–if he can have perfect *rest* and *patience.* I look on the bright side and still he seems *sick* to me, I confess. . . . He . . . [said] he had always wanted a son."[24] Such a sentiment cannot have cheered his third daughter.

None of the letters about Bulkeley mention a diagnosis of any particular physical illness. His physical state is described as "weak." The winters seem to have been particularly trying for him. In February 1866, Susie wrote "He is so depressed and anxious and unhappy that I don't know what the result may be."[25] Finally, Bulkeley himself wrote an appeal to Henry. He told his "Dear Brother" that he was sick "most of the time with a slow fever. I am now sick with my old compleints and never expect to be any better. I wish you would assist my wife in taking care of me, as I am completely helpless." He intended this to be the entire letter, but then went on, "I shall never get well. I was never so weak as I now am. I have no prospect of my recovery, but am almost helpless. I cannot but just walk across the room, and the slow feever & weakness continues. I have not eat anything for a month & cannot take any food. I wish I could see you again if I ever get better."[26]

By the late fall of 1866 Bulkeley's cries for help were desperate. He described his condition to Henry: "My nervous debility and nervous derangement still continue and the blindness which has so much troubled me is much worse, so that I can hardly see to get about." But this was not the worst of it. He confessed, "My mind is beginning to be seriously affected, and I cannot set myself to do anything and I cannot purchase or get what is needed for the support of my family. I am at times almost deranged, and I am at the mercy of every one who chooses to cheat me. It makes me almost crazy to think that I am doing nothing and what little property I have is wasting away."

The fear of poverty overwhelmed him. He despaired that "My money will soon be gone & then I do not know what I shall do. My farm is badly managed. The fences are all rotting down & I cannot repair them. I am completely broken down. My wife has to do all that is done to supply the family. I do not know how I am to get through the Winter. A great deal of the time I am in such great distress I do not know what I am about."

Lucy's illness was ever present in his mind. "The dread of Lucys Bills every Quarter makes me almost crazy, as they all have to come out of the principal. It is really the dread and the fear of poverty that increases my nervous distress. I have not the money now to spare but if I had I would get you to come here & talk with me." The letter continues:

I am unable to take care of myself & if my wife would be willing to sell all we have and go into a small house anywhere, I do not know but it would be the best thing that could be done. I am satisfied I shall never be any better, and while I continue in my present condition there is nothing but ruin before me.

I would at present never go out of the house if I was not obliged to, and I should never go out into the cold. To day I have groaned all day and I am in the utmost distress & am discouraged. I try to do a little work but have to give it up in despair. I had rather die than to go and mortgage my place to any body.

If you . . . could take care of me while my property lasted I would of course give you everything that I made. I do not know what my wife would be willing to do . . . but I think it would be best to be prepared for the worst whenever it comes.

I would give anything if I could see you & get you to comfort me and assure me that you would stand by me & keep me from thus being obliged to go out to manual labor or the Poor House.

I cannot explain it, but my mind is so far gone that I cannot take care of myself & the sooner I get rid of this Farm the better it will be for me, but I cannot do it myself. You will see, Dear Brother, by this letter in what a condition I am in. Almost deranged by my nervous distress, and utterly incapable of taking care of myself. I will give you everything I have in the world and everlasting thanks if you will see that I am taken care of. My wife & Eugenia can support themselves but I cannot do anything to supply myself. Yours truly E B Taintor[27]

A month later, despite Henry's best efforts, Bulkeley's "distress and despair" had deepened. The doctor had examined his eyes and pronounced one "hopelessly blind" and told him there was "great danger of loosing the other." He said that "I see no other way but I must get rid of this place and I do not see how I am to live & pay Lucys Bills. Since the discovery of my blindness, my wife has been constantly in tears & we know not what to do for our future. I cannot see to do anything with the Land, and the man who has taken it this year is ruining it. The least labor throws my head into great distress."

He wrote that he was "almost helpless," and asked Henry "to provide some way for me to live." His dream was to "get a small place, but I cannot see to take care even of a garden." His letter then simply went round and round in despair. "O the horrors of blindness. Would you be willing to assist me in my great misfortune. . . . I see that I am ruined for this world. . . . I have lived now two years and have not done a days work. . . . I want some one to take care of me. I am so blind I cannot take care of myself. . . . I cannot live in my present condition."

He signed this letter, but could not stop: "I am completely helpless I cannot see to go into the fields. I went to Church but I could not see a person there & my wife had to find the Pew for me. I must live where my wife can do all the business to take care of me." The end of the letter was a pitiful cry to Henry: "I need all the sympathy I can get and I have no one to go to to help me but you. I cannot describe in what a deplorable condition I am in. There is no other way but I must come to ruin. To be blind is the greatest misfortune. I will not annoy you any more but I am now in real distress and I shall need some one to help me. O do come at some time and see what arrangment can be made so that I can be supported. O do help me."[28]

Bulkeley's brother did go to West Brookfield and was able to help him financially. Henry undoubtedly tried to reassure the ailing man, whose property was, in fact, producing adequate income for the family. But Bulkeley's state of mind was not amenable to reassurance. Caroline wrote to Delia in August 1867, "Father's case is a sad one–I feel quite incompetent to advise what to do–and still I must say I think your remark a just one–viz–that he ought to be treated for mental disease. I am very sorry for Mother and Genie–It is hard to have so much of their lives made a period of endurance rather than anything better."[29]

Six months later, in the winter of 1868, Caroline wrote that she had shortened a visit to West Brookfield "on account of father's state," and she admitted that she was "glad to escape such depressing influences, though very sorry for them all." She was convinced at that time that her father needed "special treatment away from home." And although she was not sure that could "cure him," she did think it would "relieve Mother and Genie, and relieve also our anxiety lest he do himself personal violence."[30]

From this time on, so far as we can tell, Bulkeley remained in a total depression. Despite his daughters' wishes "to give him relief of mind and body," there was no relief. Every time they had any contact with him they were very sad. The end came in 1870. Susie came on a last visit, fearing she might not find her father alive. She was pleased actually "to receive a welcome from him and enjoy conversing with him several times during the day. His mind seemed very clear and he spoke intelligently and with something of his old manner on various subjects. This surprized us all very much (and was *so very gratifying* to me) as during all this time he was so weak, physically. He has changed, sadly in appearance—his features seem shrunken, and his flesh wasted away."

Susie reported, however, that "He often speaks of death and says he is 'not afraid to die' and that he is 'ready to go if it is God's will.' Still I think yesterday, he had a faint hope that he might recover. This morning he is much weaker, and speaks with difficulty, and I think realizes he is very low." She went on to say that she thought "he is failing rapidly," and concluded, "We have good watchers at night, but they cannot take the *anxiety* and relieve us of that constant fear of what any hour may bring."[31]

Edwin Bulkeley Taintor died on March 13, 1870. Susie wrote:

> . . . I never can forget how dreary, and terrible, it seemed to me—nor how rebellious I felt when the casket (containing what had been my dear father), was carried out in that wild storm. I can hardly bear to *think* of it now. . . .
>
> During Thursday and Friday Father remained very quiet most of the time—saying little and lying with his eyes closed. Saturday morning when I came down I found there had been a change in his appearance. He seemed so much *brighter*—wanted to talk with us constantly and his eyes were open and seemed so natural in expression. We sent for the Dr. at once, and I saw from his face that these were not favorable indications. He came into the other room shortly and said to me, "Your father is in a dying condition, but will probably live about twenty four hours from the time the change took place." This was true—He passed away very quietly the next night (about half past three Sabbath morning) at nearly the same time when he *seemed* to be better the previous morning.—
>
> When the Dr. was in, father complained of much pain, and an opiate was ordered which relieved him but *previous* to this I felt I *must* have one more conversation with him and ask him plainly of his hope in Christ and his feelings in view of death. It was a peculiarly trying

thing for me to do, but he had been *so* affectionate and kind during all the past two weeks that I *could not refrain* from speaking to him, and I shall always be so thankful that I did.

He asked me at first, what the Dr. said, and I told him as gently as I could, and tried to speak words of comfort to him–I remember he repeated after me, "going home"–"going home"–and when I spoke with him of what he had previously said of his willingness to go and asked him if it was thro' faith in Christ, he said "I hope so"–I talked still more with him, and he turned his face toward me, and seemed to lis- ten *gladly*. I spoke with him of the plan of salvation–of its simplicity and fullness–that everything was done for him there was nothing to do but accept the gracious offer–and rest in Christ by faith. When I said "You *do* trust Him," he replied with a smile "Yes I *do*."–In alluding to Christ as his best friend, to which he assented, I remembered that I had in time past heard him repeat many old hymns, *referring* to Christ and His love, and asked him if he did not feel it was of *this* hymn– "Jesus can make a dying bed"–I was unable to finish it, but *he* took it up, at once, and said, "O Yea–Feel soft as downy pillows are"–I was much affected by the manner in which he seemed to catch the spirit of the hymn and could say no more. It scarcely seemed necessary if he could rest on *that* thought–and I am glad to hope that he found com- fort in it to the last.[32]

Caroline, who lived in Detroit, could not be at her father's deathbed or his funeral. She thanked her aunt Delia for a letter of condolence and for all her aunt had done for her "in the way of excellent teaching and good influences received at a time when my own dear Mother's voice was silenced in death, and life was opening before me full of temptations." When she thought of West Brookfield she realized that "now the old homestead is again desolated and father has laid aside the burdens of life, literally and truly a *burden* to him, for so long a time."[33]

Henry G. Taintor became the administrator of his elder brother's estate and the guardian of Lucy Taintor. The estate consisted of five thousand dollars' worth of real property and ten thousand dollars' worth of invest- ments. Bulkeley had, in fact, staved off the penury he had so long feared. In an obituary printed by his alma mater, Yale, many years after his death, his first daughter, Lucy, was not even mentioned.

CHAPTER 15

WAR AND
REVOLUTION

ⱷ

". . . war even in success is dreadful."[1]

T en large leather-covered volumes of *The Congressional Globe* from
the Civil War years (1861–65) stood on bookshelves in our house
when we moved in. Their presence has made it clear to us that the
Taintors were absorbed in trying to understand that conflict from
its beginnings. As it did for all those who lived through it, the Civil War
remained a presence throughout their lives. That presence was passed on
to us with their house.

A House Divided

The United States expanded in the 1850s. The war against Mexico (which
ended in 1848) brought huge territories into U.S. control—with resources
that became sensational when gold was discovered in newly acquired
California that same year. One result of the Gold Rush was that there
were over 100,000 Americans in California by 1850, the year it entered the
Union as a new state. The population of the whole United States swelled
throughout the 1850s.

Despite growing numbers and increasing wealth, the nation was in
deepening political crisis. What national agreement there had been in the
early decades of the nineteenth century about the nature of the Republic
was fading fast. Industrialization, the railroads, and the Gold Rush itself
opened a vein of greed in the country. And the number of Americans in
slavery was a major factor weakening earlier consensus.

By 1860 more than ten percent of the population were slaves. The half
million Americans who owned them controlled the politics and the econ-

omy of at least one-third of the United States. As the effort on the part of many free Americans to abolish slavery grew, so did the push to justify and expand what its defenders called the South's "peculiar institution." The politics of slavery had been a more or less constant theme ever since the Declaration of Independence, but after the Mexican War the set of compromises that had maintained stability up to that time began to come apart.

In the national political arena in the 1850s, the question was whether the institution of slavery should expand beyond the states in which it already existed. As the expanding railroads and people by the tens of thousands moving farther and farther west made real the possible creation of a multitude of new states, the slavery question became the burning political issue. From 1854, the focus was on the creation of two new states—Kansas and Nebraska. Would they be slave or free? Who would decide? How would the decision be made?

By 1856 there was sporadic guerrilla warfare in the Kansas and Nebraska territories. John Brown and his sons clashed with those who favored slavery on the blood-soaked prairies. Senator Charles Sumner of Massachusetts gave an eloquent speech on "bleeding Kansas" and was beaten into bloody insensibility on the floor of the U.S. Senate by Congressman Preston S. Brooks of South Carolina. And in 1858 two candidates for the U.S. Senate in Illinois—incumbent Democrat Stephen Douglas and former Whig Congressman Abraham Lincoln—debated the by-then burning questions of the expansion of slavery.

In the meantime radical abolitionism grew as a political force in the northern and western parts of the country, fueled by the publication in 1852 of Harriet Beecher Stowe's popular novel *Uncle Tom's Cabin* and by newspapers like William Lloyd Garrison's *The Liberator*. One of the leading spokesmen for the abolitionist cause was Rev. Theodore Dwight Weld, who was born and grew up in Hampton, Connecticut, the son of Ludovicus Weld, Hampton's Congregational minister for thirty years at the beginning of the century.

The whole country began to come apart during the federal election campaign of 1860. The party system collapsed. There were four presidential candidates. The new Republican Party had nominated that former Whig congressman (who had lost the 1858 Illinois Senate race) Abraham Lincoln. He won a majority of the Electoral College—although he did not win a popular majority. The vote in Hampton was Lincoln 137, Breckenridge (Southern Democrat) 36, Douglas (Democrat) 9, and Bell (Constitutional Union Party) 1.[2]

Not long after the election, South Carolina seceded from the United States. By May 1861, ten southern states had seceded and formed their own nation, the Confederate States of America. The constitutional system of the United States had collapsed.

But the cultural split which divided the country was not yet complete. Susie Taintor wrote of Boston in March of that year, "The popular song of all others . . . this Winter is 'Dixie's-Land'–or as it is called 'Dixie.' You hear it in private-parlors and at the Theatre–the boys all 'whistle' it–and even the hand-organs play it! I never saw such enthusiasm for any popular song manifested as for this. It is quite lively and pretty. I actually heard *Father* trying to 'hum' the air last week!–Have you heard it in Hampton? The words are not very choice–as is the case with almost all negro-melodies, but the *music* is decidedly 'taking.'"[3]

At both inaugurations in 1861–Lincoln's and Jefferson Davis's–the bands played "Dixie." Then, within months, it became the theme song of the Confederacy.

Hampton on the Threshold of War

Hampton people still say about several houses in town that "they were stations on the Underground Railway" in the 1850s. Those stories about secret rooms and hidden closets faintly echo the horror people felt about slavery. The Underground Railway was an organized effort by abolitionists to help escaped slaves dodge the U.S. Fugitive Slave Laws. It tried to spirit them into Canada, from which no one could send them back to slavery. Because the Underground Railway was an illegal organization, there is no written evidence of its existence in Hampton.

Connecticut abolished slavery in 1848, although the number of slaves in the state had declined since the beginning of the nineteenth century. In Hampton, the last census that listed a slave was in 1820. That year there were twenty-three "Free Colored Persons" in town, and that one slave in "The Widow Sarah Howard's" household. There were twenty-nine "Colored" people in town in the 1860 census, about three percent of the population of 937. Many of them were the children or grandchildren of slaves.

By 1860 slavery was a hot issue in Hampton. Rich and poor talked about the question; nobody remained uninterested. People not only talked– they acted on their convictions. Dan Bulkeley's youngest son, Robert Worthington Bulkeley, went out to Nebraska Territory with his family, in order to help assure an antislavery majority there when Nebraska became a state. He was back in Hampton by 1860, with a two-year-old child who had been born in the Nebraska Territory. There was another Hampton baby girl, Carrie L. Fuller, who was also born in Nebraska Territory, probably of like-minded parents.

The census of 1860 showed that the population of Hampton was declining. It was also changing. There were twenty-five Irish immigrants; all were Roman Catholics. Of the seventeen adult Hampton residents who were illiterate (the largest number of illiterates Hampton had seen in half a century), thirteen were Irish and two were African-American. These statistics reflect the refusal of the English to provide public education for Irish Catholics and the refusal of the majority of whites to provide it for African Americans.

The work of Hampton families remained overwhelmingly agricultural, but the way people thought of their work on the land had changed since 1850. The majority of men in Hampton still listed themselves as farmers (115, down from the 150 in the 1850 census). But many more men in 1860 listed themselves as farm *laborers* (111) than the 79 who had listed themselves that way in 1850. The number of farms in town had stabilized, and those who no longer had any hope of owning their own farms now saw themselves as a lower class, not farmers but laborers. In 1850 young men who were in other people's households working someone else's land had still been able to see themselves as farmers; by 1860 young men in that situation knew themselves as hired hands. Some farm laborers owned some land, and no doubt grew food for their families on it, but they could not command the resources of land and capital necessary to produce the cash crops they believed defined being farmers.

Women headed ten percent of Hampton's households. Even when they headed a farm household, women did not list themselves as farmers, but simply listed no occupation. Women were, however, beginning to claim occupations for census purposes. Younger women most often listed their occupation as "Domestic." But there were also ten young women in town who were teachers and five who listed themselves as dressmakers, seamstresses, or tailoresses.

The War's Early Years

Abraham Lincoln was inaugurated President on March 4, 1861, and in April warfare began when the Confederates bombarded U.S. Fort Sumter, in Charleston, South Carolina. Henry E. Taintor, who was sixteen years old, was away at school in Monson, Massachusetts, in April of 1861. He disliked writing letters, but the war news was so exciting he wrote several. On the nineteenth he wrote to his parents asking, "Is there any excitement about war in Windham County?" He assured them that "The state of the Country is the principal topic of conversation here. We have very good facilities for obtaining news and all the important events we hear of nearly as soon as in Springfield or Boston. We heard of the taking of Fort

Sumpter on Sunday night and on Monday morning had the whole account in the Springfield Republican." Apparently communication was fast. Henry said of Monson, "We are so situated that we can obtain New York morning papers at 3 in the afternoon."

"The sound of cannon every day from Springfield as the troops come in from Boston on their way to Washington" was the unusual and constant reminder of war. Henry went to nearby Palmer, Massachusetts, "to see the 8th Regiment as it passed through on a special train. There were 17 long cars full of soldiers all dressed in their uniforms and appearing so gay that it did not seem possible that some of them would never be seen here again. Night before last a train of 18 cars with 2 engines went through Palmer making about 18 or 20 hundred men that have gone from the eastern part of the state." The entire war was fought using the new railroads, so Henry's walking to watch the troop trains go by became a commonplace experience.

Sixteen-year-old Henry concluded his letter, "It seems as if there must be many hard battles before this contest is settled, so earnest are they on both sides. Todays paper says that Virginia has seceded to take effect in two days. Are there any better facilities for obtaining news than when I came away? . . . I should think if there has been no change the news would be pretty old when it reached you."[4]

Less than a week later, he wrote that "Here in Massachusets all are excited over the death of their troops at Baltimore," in a riot by Confederate sympathizers as the Sixth Massachusetts Regiment marched through the city to change trains.[5] In Monson, Henry reported, "Last night they had a rousing union meeting here. The church was crowded. . . . A chance for volunteers to enroll their names was given and 21 came forward and enlisted, among whom were two of my classmates who have given up Greek & Latin for guns and lead." Even at his age he expressed enthusiasm about enlistment. "When I hear the news from the south and read the papers I feel sorry that I am not old enough to serve my country, even with my life if necessary. Is there any excitement in Hampton over the state of affairs?"[6]

The first man to volunteer from Hampton was Luther J. Burnham, who enlisted in Rifle Company D of the 2nd Connecticut Volunteers on April 23, 1861. More men from Hampton followed in the next few weeks, joining volunteer regiments for ninety-day enlistments. Everyone thought the war was going to be short.

Washington, D.C., quickly became an armed camp. Delia's sister Abby wrote in May, "I think with you 'there are enough northern in Washington to protect the city' & I feel perfectly safe–Our streets are almost literally filled with splendid determined looking men in military array & it is really

John A. Taintor's grave monument in Hartford's Spring Grove Cemetery.

difficult to do anything but look at the soldiers."[7] And Delia's elderly mother wrote about her eighteen-year-old granddaughter in Washington, "Alice is perfectly enthusiastic with the war movements. I don't know but she is about ready to take up arms herself."[8]

In July 1861, hundreds of people took picnics and drove wagons and carriages south from Washington to watch the battle at Bull Run. It was only after that disastrous defeat that they began to realize the war would be no picnic.

By September 1861, Henry E. Taintor, now seventeen, was at Yale. He was "quite surprised" to hear from Hampton that the Congregational minister, George Soule, had volunteered as a chaplain. He wrote home, "It will be a great loss to Hampton—but as he himself said the army needs the good and brave men of the country. I think he will be doing right and know he can but do good if he goes. It would be well if more of our good substantial christians went, men who go from pure love of country and from no selfish or mercenary motives."[9] Henry himself wanted to enlist, but his parents would not give their permission.[10]

By the summer of 1862, the people of Hampton were suffering with the war, as people were everywhere. Twenty-seven Hampton men had marched off to war in 1861, and twenty-one more went in 1862. Out of 937 men, women, and children in town, that made a large dent in the population of young working men.

The regiments they joined were in the midst of terrible battles through 1862. Nathan Lyon, who saw action with the 8th Connecticut Infantry at New Bern, North Carolina, was back home disabled by the end of the year. George Kies, Andrew J. Kimball, and William E. Ford were wounded at Antietam in September, where their regiment, the 11th Connecticut, lost 181 men and all its field officers in that "valley of death." The three Hampton men were discharged disabled. Emerson Bolton died in 1862 after three months in the army. David Card also died. The men who came out of the terrible combat of the Civil War were affected by all the disorientation and horrors that come from having participated in battle. The women and children who tried to welcome them home found them sadly changed. Delia's sister Ellen wrote in April 1862, "When we think of the thousands of sad hearts mourning for friends slain, war even in success is dreadful." Already she thought "the rebels must succumb before long"[11] because there had been so much killing.

In November 1862, when the war's carnage had been going on for a year and a half and the rebels showed little sign of succumbing, John Adams Taintor died in Hartford. He had felt strongly about the Union cause, so strongly that he left a proviso in his will, written just a month before his death: "It is my desire that neither of my children will ever marry any person who is a native or resident of any foreign country or who is a native or resident of either of the southern or slaveholding states."[12] John's daughter Louise had already married. Alice was twenty-seven when her father died; she never married. It is possible she had been courted by a southern beau before the war.

The men in the armies died of disease and infection as often as from the shooting. Delia Taintor's cousin Henry Livermore died of typhoid fever, and his mother's anguish and bewilderment appears through the stilted nineteenth-century phrases of her letter. Her son, she wrote, "never returned" after his regiment left Hartford. "He was very eager to enlist, & I have reason to think never regretted that he did. He always wrote in good spirits." His commanding officer had written to the family that "It affords me pleasure to inform you that until disabled by ill health, he did his duty in a very satisfactory manner to myself & the rest of his officers." His mother felt he was "too ambitious" and although his officers had "urged him to lay by & rest . . . he could not be persuaded to do so till he was unable to hold out any longer–& then he would not allow them to write to us . . . & we knew not how sick he was till informed of his death."

Delia surely wept at the next lines from this minister's wife: "Oh my dear cousin if I could know that he did 'die a good soldier of the cross' I believe I could cheerfully give him up. His feelings last summer & when he went away were far from what we wanted they should be. he felt that he was not a christian & ought not to belong to the church & I assure you it was a very great trial to us. . . . I can but hope that ere he left the world he was brought back to duty & to the enjoyment of that peace which the Saviour alone imparts."

The letter contained an obituary notice from a New York newspaper:

Died, at Roanoke Island, March 31st of Typhoid fever, Corporal Henry N. Livermore, of Company D. 8th Regiment Connecticut Volunteers; eldest son of Rev. A. R. Livermore, of Lebanon (Goshen Society) Conn.

Another young life, given a willing sacrifice to his Country.

Deceased was much beloved and esteemed, not only by his fellow soldiers, but also by the officers of his Regiment. Although very young–about 20–he was like a father, in his care for his companions. He was regarded as a young man of very superior abilities. His love for his country, to which he as truly gave his life as if he had fallen on the battle field, was earnest and sincere. He was exceedingly feeble at the time of the battle of Newbern; yet, so enthusiastic was he to serve his country, that it was only by the entreaties, & finally express command of Captain Ward, that he was prevented from joining in the conflict–

He was a member of the church of which his father is pastor, and we trust has only "gone before."[13]

As the war dragged on people became more and more discouraged. Every battle brought thousands of deaths. Ellen wrote, "Alas! for the many wives in our Country who can not know when if ever their husbands will return or rather I should say whose return depends upon the chances of war."[14] And Henry E. wrote to his mother, "How many lives is this atrocious rebellion costing the country & how many more I fear may be called to give up their all for the country." The war, he said, was "a terrible struggle." And he reported, "Only a week since we received news of the death of one of our classmates who was at Newberne, the first death out of our number. How many more may die in the same service God alone knows."[15]

Delia's nieces Alice and Maria Hall followed Clara Barton's lead into the hospitals the war generated. Women were new to professional nursing, but Maria's aunt reported, "Maria is now in the Naval Academy Hospital, which I supposed must be at Anapolis. Alice says it is very large, can accommodate 3000, & Maria is at the head of a third part of it."[16]

Finding men to enlist in the armies became more and more difficult as the war went on. By the summer of 1862, most of the willing volunteers had already gone. In order to get more men to volunteer, local governments all across the country offered money bonuses—bounties—to volunteers. In Hampton, a special Town Meeting voted to pay "One Hundred Dollars in favor of each and every one who shall volunteer in the Army of the United States (who are settled residents) of this town." The Town Meeting also authorized the selectmen to offer the same bounty to any volunteer who was already in the Army who would reenlist.[17] Just before the bloody battle of Antietam in September 1862, the Town Meeting raised the bounty to $150. And later in the war it was raised to $200. That was more than a hired man working on a Hampton farm could make in a year.

By 1863, as the war reached a horrible crescendo (but not an end) at Gettysburg, it was difficult to pay anyone to volunteer. Both the Union and the Confederacy introduced conscription. Hampton that year voted to donate $1,200 to a Mutual Aid Society for men who would volunteer. In 1864, the town authorized a special committee to pay whatever was necessary to get the men to fill the town's draft quota.

Hampton bore a proportion of the war's casualties even greater than the country as a whole. Of the sixty-one men whom we have been able to find who enlisted from Hampton, there were nineteen casualties—dead or wounded—nearly a third of the total. Hampton African-Americans—twenty-nine men, women, and children in the 1860 census—sent seven men to war, including three named Vickers.[18] Four of them went into Connecticut regiments in 1861, and transferred to United States Colored Regiments when those were formed in 1863.

A New Kind of Youth

Henry E. Taintor had entered Yale in 1861, and he remained there despite his desire to soldier. The college itself had altered since his uncle Bulkeley and cousin John had been there. Henry informed his parents about the new traditions: "Last Wednesday we had what is called the 'Freshman rush.' . . . In Alumni Hall the Sophomores stationed themselves in the passage way so as to prevent if possible the entrance of any Freshman who would persist in wearing his hat. The Freshmen attempted to enter and a rush of course ensues." He was proud that "the Freshmen this year got the best of it with the help of a few upper class men. I went through the rush 5 times and came out with my hat on my head. It was all in sport but it was a pretty dirty business for *men* to engage in. It would better befit little boys." In later letters he wrote about "Pow Wow" and the "Wooden Spoon Exhibition." His parents at one time or another attended both these events, and kept an invitation to the latter illustrated with flying cherubs holding wooden spoons.

Henry was a "joiner" in college, like many young Americans seeking relief from individual isolation: "I am getting somewhat acquainted in my class and now feel not quite so isolated as I did at first. I have joined . . . a Freshman society the 'Gamma Nu.' It is a non-secret but not an anti-secret society." When he was initiated, young Henry E. "took the oath" and then "quite unexpectedly (to me at least) we were called on for speeches. Now you know my bashfulness and can imagine how I felt." He said he "had a great mind to leave but I knew if I started some one would be sure to call on me as they had just before on one of my class, so I determined to stay and run the risk, hoping that I would be overlooked. But, just as I was congratulating myself on a prospect of escaping some one called out '*Taintor*.' That was enough, in 2 seconds there were 20 shouting the same and up I had to get." He assured his family that he "got through very well so some of the others said, but I assure you if I was to go through it again I should certainly think of something to say before I got up."

In this same letter Henry E. (the meticulous son of a meticulous father) accounted for every penny he had spent.

> I will put down a few things I have spent my money for that you may judge how foolishly I have expended it:

Yale Literary Magazine	2.00
Books	1.67
Cocoaine	.50
For oil, a chimney & shade	.47
Slippers	.60
Stamps	.18
Envelopes & paper	.33
Blank Book	.20
Mending Shirt Stud	.12

Henry was firm that "You will see that I have not spent a great deal on trifles. If Father has some money he can spare I should be glad of some."[19] The third item on Henry's list will surprise most readers, as it did us. Few college boys today would include it in an accounting to their families (they would also use a different spelling). Cocaine was a derivative of coca leaves, which had long been chewed by Andean peoples as a hunger suppressant and stimulant. Many educated people of scientific bent experimented with using cocaine to "enhance their mental powers" in the late nineteenth century.

In the midst of war, college students behaved much as they always had. Henry asked his parents, "Do you remember, last summer, seeing the seniors sitting each one on a post because they were forbidden 'to congregate in groups on the fence'?" He went on to describe "something of the same thing this year. The Juniors were forbidden to sit on the fence and at night after supper quite a number brought out chairs and sat down in a row just inside with their feet on the fence. It looked quite comical and of course there could be no fault found with it." The undergraduates continued their warfare against the faculty and Henry reported that "The 'powwow' has been relentlessly knocked in the head by the faculty. They told the Freshmen that if they went on with it a large portion of their class would be suspended, and the Yale faculty do not make any idle threats." On the other hand, "The seniors last night tore down all the college fence from the corner opposite the New Haven house up to the college building. . . . It was done because they had been forbidden to sit on it. The college carpenter has been at work all day and it is not finished yet."[20]

In his sophomore year, Henry—proud of his status—wrote home using envelopes embossed "Yale '65." His complaints about studies and the vagaries of the faculty, as well as his apologies for needing more money—"I am as bad as Oliver Twist, 'always wanting more'"—were pretty standard.[21] So was the fact that he fell in love.

Henry spent both Thanksgiving and Christmas of 1862 with his relatives at Windsor. His cousin Emma Ellsworth was there from Lafayette, Indiana, and she became the object of his affections. Henry was eighteen years old. Emma was a year younger, and their aunt Ellen wrote Delia that "she is a very sweet child, no one can know her without loving her dearly."[22]

By October 1863, Henry's wish to marry his cousin Emma created a family crisis. We cannot be certain that he ever spoke to Emma about his feelings. But he did talk to his parents. And he wrote to them, when they tried to change his mind, "I can not bear to say anything about my feelings is all I can say." Henry's love was the epitome of Victorian romanticism. He told his mother that he would like to know what Emma's feelings were, but he did "not see how it can be done except by your writing and that would seem strange to her." He had not heard from her and he did not quite ever resolve "to write and confess 'all my feelings and ask her, if she could not care more for me, to at least regard me as a cousin.'" He vacillated because, as he wrote, "I still love her too well not to feel a deep interest in all connected with her." Then again he "resolved to *tell* her all" when he had a vacation and thereby "come to a square understanding on the subject."

Henry's love for Emma coincided with a severe crisis in his religious life and faith, about which he wrote his parents, "I have read the hymns you spoke of but feel no desire to apply their language to myself. My heart seems hard as stone and I have no desire to love God." He told his parents he "would not try to do anything" about becoming a member of the church. He was distraught, and the war beckoned:

> . . . I have before me a N. Y. paper containing a proclamation of President Lincoln calling for 300,000 more volunteers. You know what my feelings have been and what they are. You have said "the time may come when you will be wanted."
>
> And has not the conscription shown that all the men who are *willing* to go are needed. I know it is an unpleasant subject to you and especially to father but I hope you will think of it carefully.
>
> Are *you* giving up any more than hundreds have given up during the last 2½ years, or am *I* giving up more than hundreds of other young men who have gone before.
>
> Am I any better than many who have left this very institution. Mother I wish to go! I am now 19, large enough and in my trials of strength found that I am stronger than the majority. And nothing but worldly considerations prevent my going. . . .[23]

We can imagine Henry and Delia sitting in their south parlor (the room we often write in) reading that letter on a brilliant Hampton fall day, with the maple foliage bright through the window. Their eldest child was in love, but they could not approve the match. He wanted to fight for the cause in which they believed, but in which so many young men were dying daily.

Delia wrote to Henry about Emma. She scratched out a draft in pencil on the back of a business form of her husband's. She wrote it some time after November 19, 1863; we figured that out because there is a sum scrawled over it that checks President Lincoln's arithmetic in the Gettysburg Address given on that date, beginning "Four score and seven years ago our fathers brought forth upon this continent a new nation. . . .":

$$
\begin{array}{r}
1776 \\
87 \\
\hline
1863
\end{array}
$$

We do not have the letter Delia actually sent to Henry, but her draft was clearly an effort to find words to convince her son not to marry:

> My own darling boy—
>   Sitting by the kitchen stove, with feet in the oven, I have just read for the third time your precious letter—precious as it assures me of your perfect love & confidence—an incalculable blessing to Mother & child. May it never grow less, & may your happiness my darling go on to increase—as through suffering, as a part of life's discipline you shall

grow more & more ready for those blest mansions where there is indeed true "rest for the weary."

My thoughts have been with you almost constantly. . . . I did not realize . . . how much your happiness was bound up in the hopes you had dared to cherish–I had hoped . . . it might have been a "mere fancy" & passed away harmlessly–& still hope, as Aunt Ellen [Emma's mother] said to me on Friday last, when you go into Society more & see others, you will feel differently–

She has the same feeling, I find, that I have always cherished, about relatives marrying–& says Wolcott [Emma's father] has always been extremely *opposed* to any thing of the kind–& that Emma has been brought up to regard it as something not to be thought of. . . .

Aside from the relationship, let me give you Aunt Ellen's views– that if she thought Em would ever do as well she would be perfectly satisfied–for she liked you very much–so you see eyes less partial than a Mother's see reasons for loving my darling boy.

Another cousin bearing a part of your name, has been similarly affected with yourself–Henry G. Ellsworth of California–but was vetoed by Wolcott's horror of such a union–This may not be known to Em–so do not ever allude to it. I name it that in the event of any rivalship you may know there is a prior claim–

However, my darling, I trust you may find your own heart has answered you–& that the chains may be more easily sundered than you now imagine. You know the old adage "there are better fishes in the sea than were ever caught" & who knows but your hook may draw them out? one of them at least! So cheer up, my darling, and believe all this may be for some wise reason, that you may learn to "suffer, & be strong." . . .[24]

Henry did not stand against the opposition of his parents and Emma's parents to the match. He gave her up, but insisted, "In respect to my own feelings, while I have lost that recklessness which was the first result, I still retain an *ardent* but a *governed* love for her."[25] Perhaps he never told Emma, and perhaps she never knew. But she did not marry until 1880, in her thirty-fifth year.

Henry turned to the army. He insisted to his father that "It was no sud-den impulse which caused me to ask your consent to enlist but I had thought . . . much on the subject." He said he had made his decision "under no feelings of excitement but calmly and coolly and I again write that it is my wish to enter the army if I have your own and mother's consent." His facing of realities has a distinctly nineteenth-century sound. "That I shall endure hardships and privations is but a part of a soldier's life and that con-sideration was not left out in making my decision."[26] Henry and Delia did, reluctantly, give their consent at last and immediately bent their efforts to securing a commission for their son.

Delia's cousin Dr. Skinner, who had joined up in 1861, wrote offering advice as to Henry's obtaining a commission as an officer. He said there were "two Conn. Regiments, the 1st and the 2d Artillery" in his division. He recommended the 1st Artillery Regiment "especially," but warned that new commissions had to be obtained from the governor. Still, he talked to Colonel Abbott, the commanding officer of the regiment, who said that "he wanted educated men for his officers, and he expected to find them among the Recruits now entering. But no promises would be made to any one, and merit alone would be considered." Dr. Skinner added that "if Henry was my own boy" he would recommend enlisting as a private in the 1st Connecticut Artillery over trying to get a commission in any other outfit. "The Artillery service is the *safest,* subject to the least hardships, and educated men are best fitted to succeed in it."[27] Henry did enlist as a private in the First Connecticut Artillery in January 1864. He was nineteen years old. He was soon promoted to sergeant, and it was not long before he was commissioned a lieutenant. He received four hundred dollars as a "bounty" for enlisting which his father invested for him.[28]

At the time of Henry's enlistment Delia heard from Emma's mother, who did not mention the fast-buried family secret of Henry's love for her daughter. She professed to be "very much surprised to hear that Henry had enlisted for the war—I did not know that he had ever thought seriously of doing so. It must have been a great trial for you to give him up."[29]

In was in fact a trial to both Henry's parents, as Delia wrote to him on his first full day in the Army:

Home, Jan 14th 1864.

My own, very precious boy,

   It is already ten o'clock, and dear father, with a tearful face, has gone, with little Mary [who was three years old at this time], to seek rest, while I cannot resist the feeling that impels me to tell my darling how more than ever dear he is to a Mother's heart, as with noble & holy purpose he girds himself for the fight, &

> "Evermore at 'early sun-rise'
> Evermore as day declines,
> Shall a fervent benediction
> Flow from out this soul of mine
> For each true & loyal-hearted,
> For each noble volunteer,
> For each heart from loved ones parted:

> *God himself is quick to hear....*
> *He–the Lamb of Calvary–*
> *Will sustain thy drooping soul*
> *When dark waters o'er thee roll.*
> *Ever may his counsel be*
> *All in all, my boy to thee."*

You cannot imagine how precious are the lines you sent, from which I have quoted so freely. Father could not trust himself to read them, or hear them read to night–& loves you, my darling, with an intensity of which I had no conception. He feels if he can only hear from you, & know you are any ways contented & comfortable it will be a great relief....

And now shall I tell you a little of what has occurred in the home to day? After you left my first act was to seek a blessing for you, after which I righted the dining room & commenced my labors in the kitchen. Had nearly completed the dish-washing when Mary, who was churning by the window, & standing in father's arm chair, upset the whole affair & herself with it–leaving the contents of the churn in the chair, & on the floor–covering the space from the table to the east wall of the room–some two yards in width–& herself with the cream,

Mary Ellen Taintor, about three years old, wearing the red dress on which she
spilled the cream she was churning the day her brother went off to the Civil War.

filled with particles of butter. The tray on which the churn stood, was upside down, under the table & I could but be struck with her first remark, as she stopped crying almost instantly, & surveyed the scene, "I don't know how I did it." I could but laugh, & do now, every time I think of it, as I see her little red dress, streaming with cream, & her shoes perfectly white, while she could not move for the slipping.

After working more than an hour to clean it up, I was obliged to go for Mrs Underwood to complete the job–& I know you will be glad to hear she is going to stay with me through the remainder of this, & next, week. . . .

The little boys [Willie and Freddie, who were twelve and nine years old] have been exceedingly interested in hearing all the particulars of your examination, dress &c & could hardly be persuaded to leave for bed at a quarter past nine.

And now, my darling, since I cannot put the pillow under your head, I will commit you to Him who can put underneath you his Everlasting arms, & shield you against all the evils to which flesh is heir–& bring you home to glory. . . .[30]

War's End

By that day on which Delia and Henry G. saw their eldest son depart, the Civil War had lasted nearly three ghastly, death-filled years. They were really afraid–and with reasons based on the experiences of too many young men of their acquaintance–that he would never return. Both the prayers and the rueful humor of Delia's letter to her son were typical of this mother to whom one of her boys would say, years later, "I enjoy going home & being with you both more & more as I grow older."[31]

The first report about Henry's life in the army came from Delia's sister Abby, because Henry's regiment was stationed near Washington. Abby's son-in-law, Alden, had gone "to spend the Sabbath with Capt. Gillette, the Commander of the company in which Henry enlisted, & on reaching the Camp found Henry there before him. He said Henry was very well & comfortable & in fine spirits. So far he told Alden he liked military life & did not doubt he should continue to like it, as he had always felt a desire to 'rough it' for awhile." Abby thought Henry would "exert a most powerful influence for good among his companions and he is certainly animated by a noble patriotism which must be admired & loved wherever it is known."

She assured Delia that Captain Gillette had "promised to do everything in his power" for Henry's "personal comfort and advancement. Captain Gillette & many other officers will leave the Army in the Spring–their time of service having expired–and I think there will be opportunities to advance those who prove themselves (as I doubt not Henry will) worthy of advancement." The best rumors she had heard were that "It is not at all likely that Henry's regiment will be ordered into the field this winter," and she hoped Henry would have a commission and "the protection from exposure" that went with being an officer by the time the regiment was in action. In that way, she wrote Delia, "the physical dangers you dread for him may be averted."

Abby commiserated with Delia and "brother Henry" about the interruption of young Henry's "college education & the relinquishment of the college honors that awaited him." But, she wrote, "if he had kept himself from the Army till he could graduate the war might be over and he seemed to have a special inspiration for the work with which I should not dare too long to interfere." She supported her sister and brother-in-law's decision to permit Henry to enlist. "I doubt not you & brother H. have done exactly as you ought and . . . blessing and protection will be upon you & upon your boy."[32]

In the course of 1864 both Henry G. and Delia went to Washington separately, and stayed with Abby while they visited their soldier son. In the midst of war relatives could visit the men close to the front. At the end of one of her visits Delia, a countrywoman, used to rising with the sun, departed from Washington at five in the morning, before the astonished urban Abby had imagined it possible a person could wake up. Abby wrote to apologize that she had not been up to give her sister breakfast. In the same letter she asked that Henry G. Taintor use his influence—which she thought considerable—with Connecticut's Senator Dixon to help Captain Gillette, Henry E.'s commanding officer.

The problem was that Gillette had "enlisted as a private for three years" and "that time expires next month & he did not dream till lately that he could not resign at that time." Now, wrote Abby, Secretary of War Edwin Stanton "insists that all officers enlisted in that way shall serve three years from the time of their promotion." According to Abby, that would require Gillette to spend eighteen months more in the service. But he had "made all arrangements for going into business in May and will lose much pecuniarily and probably the opportunity of establishing himself most prosperously for a life time, if he is disappointed." She pointed out that Gillette had "served his country too most bravely and skillfully & unselfishly and endured great hardship on the Penninsula—During McClellan's retreat he stood one day from 7 o'clock in the morning till 8 at night at his large gun, mowing down rebels continually and without taking food or water & he has many times exposed his life & health in the like manner."

General Burnside, from the November 29, 1862, *Harper's Weekly,*
saved by the Taintors.

Gillette's superior officers were trying to help him but, Abby wrote, "the Secretary of War will not yield to them." She wrote that "Senators (the kings of our country) are more appreciated & if Mr Dixon, out of kindness to brother Henry & from a wish to secure his farm would be willing to speak to Mr Stanton for him a worthy officer may have justice." Abby's sense of Henry G. Taintor's influence in Washington was not exaggerated, although by today's standards he was not a man of any significant power or wealth in Connecticut, much less in the nation's capital. His influence came from his leading position in Hampton. He had just been Hampton's representative in the state legislature. Under the United States Constitution state legislatures elected United States senators (they were not popularly elected until the ratification of the Seventeenth Amendment in 1913). So Senator Dixon owed a favor to Henry G. Taintor.

Abby's letters, though not frequent, were always full of news and ways to be kind to people. She also reported that a Major Rockwood had stayed with her family, and "seemed fair-spirited but we know no quarter will be shown him if he is captured & as the head of a negro regiment he is specially in danger. . . . We all feel oppressed with the apprehension that we may never see him again." The spring of 1864 had brought all the troops actively into the war. Henry E. Taintor's regiment also moved to the front. Abby's letter concluded with a description of some of those troops departing:

> Burnside's troops, 50,000 passed through Washington last Monday. We saw them as they passed the President & Burnside & other officers & their wives all standing on the Balcony over Willards porch on 14th Street. Mrs Burnside was not with the others who were gaily dressed but at a window in plain dress and weeping bitterly–uncontrollably–I felt most sympathy with her as I saw the worn, weary men, many of them marching to certain death undoubtedly–The President looked at them with the same feeling–we could see it in his face–but General Burnside smiled constantly apparently in fine spirits & health. . . .[33]

The war raged on through 1864 and half of 1865 with the continuing and terrible mixture (characteristic of modern wars of nationalism) of appalling mass slaughter of human beings with ardent patriotism and eager enthusiasm among many of those not directly caught up in killing. Henry E. Taintor was sent this astonishing poem, composed for him by a female admirer in Hampton, probably his neighbor across the street, Delia Button, in May 1864:

> In my quiet home I'm thinking,
>   Of the soldiers, loyal, true.
> Who still love our dear old banner,
>   With its stars, and field of blue.
> With its stripes so proudly floating,
>   On each gentle wave of air.
> Ah! you cannot find another,
>   That can with this one compare.
> Long upheld by noble heroes,
>   Who have dared to fight and fall.
> And who left this pledge of Freedom
>   To wave o'er us each and all.
> Shall they from their home in Heaven
>   Look to see it trampled . . .
> See it rent and soiled forever.
>   Neath the heel of Southern foe?
> No! we must and will protect it.
>   Guarded safe it still shall be.
> Traitor hands shall never win it,
>   This dear emblem of the free. . . .

Henry, you have left your Parents
  'Neath the pleasant homestead roof,
Bade adieu to Sister, Brothers,
  And the friends you prized in youth!
All the glad associations
  Mingled with your College life,
Left the scenes of early childhood.
  To meet, perhaps, in deadly strife
Those who would destroy our banner.
  And raise high their hateful flag.
Shall they prosper? God forbid it!
  Go, lay low that Southern rag.
Fight as brave men fight, nor falter,
  When the battle rages high. . . .

Upward, Onward, be your motto.
From these may you never stray.
  When this cruel war is ended.
May you meet your friends once more.
  If not here, then pray to meet them.
On a brighter happier shore.

D. E. B.[34]

    Henry's younger brother George, who was boarding and clerking in a retail store in Hartford, did his bit for the cause by helping to provide music for public rallies in support of the Union presidential ticket of 1864. Republican President Lincoln was running on that ticket, with former Democrat Andrew Johnson of Tennessee as his running mate. They were opposed by the Democratic ticket headed by the popular General George B. McClellan. Young George Taintor found "it is a pretty good thing to be a member of the 'Union Campaign Glee Club' for besides the benefit I get to my singing power I get always a good seat on the stage at all the Meetings, and although we can not see the speaker quite as well, we can hear every thing that is said."[35] (This was a distinct advantage since there were no electronic means of amplifying a speaker's voice.) Perhaps George's musical efforts during that bitter campaign helped bring about Lincoln's reelection.

    Some of Delia's correspondents in those years did not write about the war because they were very far from it. Her niece, Sophie Reynolds, wrote from a new mining town in California that "Business needs close watching, to be successful, & with the best care & attention many men fail because property is so unstable in value here." The view Sophie gave of small towns in the mountain West was a great contrast to New England.

"Mines, of course, are more or less uncertain, & in these mountain towns it is the mines more than any thing else that gives value to other property. One year a town is full of people, a busy, restless anxious crowd–stores are open–houses all inhabited–rents high–streets noisy with business day & night. Next year there is a new excitement somewhere else, & the busy town is deserted, the stores are closed, dwellings are empty & property worthless. One year more may make it worse or better than ever. The wisest cannot tell. And so the years go on."

The Civil War did not impinge on the life Sophie described. "Every body is overworked, every faculty of body & brain is at its utmost tension, & there is no time for rest, till Death comes & says, to the young, & to those in their prime 'Your life-work is finished you *must* rest now.'" While she thought "it sad to see so many young people lie down in the long sleep," she believed Christianity would redeem them "if amid all the hurrying excitements they have found time for the great work of the Soul's salvation, & in all their haste to lay up earthly treasures they have not forgotten the true riches–the treasure in Heaven."[36]

From the very center of the war, on the other hand, another of Delia's nieces, Maria Hall, wrote of the new purpose she had found in her work at the naval hospital in Annapolis. "Oh," she wrote, "if all the mothers who are pining for their boys could get them back again from the horrible prison pens of the South! The sights we have brought to us lately are not to be described–this morning we assembled to pay the last tribute to 30 of our dead soldiers! 40 at one time last week–& many times since we have buried 9–or 10–sometimes 16." Delia may well have shuddered, knowing as she did that one Hampton man, Thomas J. Holt, died in the prison camp at Andersonville.

Maria wrote that the entire hospital rejoiced at the news of Sherman's army's successful March to the Sea through Georgia: "No cheers are more glad & hearty than the broken feeble–'bully for Sherman' that the poor skeletons of soldiers send up from their sick beds–I wished . . . to tell them the news–& every where the same response 'bully for our side' went up." She speculated that "Perhaps we grow unlady like–& unrefined in our intercourse with such men? But we get something better than so called refinement–& outside polish–Every thing that is *good* in a person–whatever of earnestness & truth & sympathy for good & right is brought into exercise–and the heart is kept alive & awake to good impulses, & *real* life."[37]

One of the most agonizing of the war's many problems was locating and hearing about loved ones who were at war, despite the widespread use of the telegraph and the detailed reporting available in newspapers everywhere through the new "wire services" of the Associated Press. The casualties in combat and in hospitals were often not identified or identifiable (the military had no identification "tags"), and families tried every means available to them to discover the fate and location of their soldiers. Delia forwarded one request from Hampton for news about a sailor to Maria, who replied that she "gave the name to our Chaplain who attends to those matters more than any other person here." He in turn gave her "the unwelcome answer that he finds no trace of the name among the list of those buried here." Maria concluded that he must have been "buried at sea." She wished she could give her aunt Delia "something more positive in regard to the boy–but how many hundreds of friends have not even this slight clue of certainty to rest upon! Suspense, the hardest of all to bear is constantly the lot of so many dear ones."[38] We have not been able to find out who that sailor from Hampton was.

Organized support of the war came in many forms in small towns both North and South. The American Sanitary Commission, for example, was a Union organization with many local chapters and supporting groups that tried to supply military hospitals and nurses with the clothes, sheets, cloth, and bandages essential to the care of the tens of thousands of wounded and diseased soldiers. There were soldiers' aid organizations, there were organizations devoted to supplying the needs of refugees–most of them newly freed slaves, and there were organizations that tried to help the growing numbers of widows and orphans. Established fraternal lodges, female groups, and church societies devoted their efforts to the war. In Hampton, Henry G. Taintor, as treasurer of the First Ecclesiastical Society, collected and shipped clothing for the wounded and the refugees sewn by Hampton women. Sanitary Commission officials expressed their gratitude with what was perhaps an early form letter:

> The contribution of clothing from the Ladies of your place was received in good condition for which please accept our sincere thanks.
>
> We are continually receiving urgent appeals for aid from the destitute and suffering that are daily increasing as our armies advance. We have dispatched an agent to Nashville to distribute clothing and other articles as he finds they are needed and expect to send more as soon as we can make arrangements.
>
> We feel encouraged by the interest that has been manifested in various societies but still labor under the necessity for additional donations and trust your kind liberality will not cease. . . .
>
> We earnestly solicit your sincere prayers for the prosperity of the Cause we have undertaken. . . .[39]

The Hampton Soldiers' Aid Society, led by Mrs. David Greenslit, made contributions throughout the war.[40] The Congregational church made special collections for Refugees, for Disabled Soldiers, and for the Soldiers' Thanksgiving. Henry Taintor sent the money to the proper national organizations.

The Taintor family "kept up" with the war through its newspaper subscriptions. War news was shared with townspeople by passing on newspapers and by word of mouth. Henry Taintor had the *Congressional Globe* sent to him so that he could read the debates in Congress at leisure and get more detailed news. He also bought the publications of the Congressional Committee on the Conduct of the War. And he recorded buying from peddlers two popular books during the war, one a *History of the Rebellion* and the other a war "thriller" called *Nurse and Spy*.[41]

There had never been a federal income tax and indeed the Constitution prohibited direct federal taxation of individuals (not changed until the Sixteenth Amendment in 1913). The war nevertheless brought special taxes on incomes (five percent on incomes below $5,000, and ten percent on incomes over $5,000), as well as taxes on personal "luxury" items. Henry had to pay some of the new taxes: $201.45 on his 1864 income of $4,029, as well as one dollar for his carriage worth less than $100, two dollars for his piano worth no more than $200, and two dollars for his two gold watches valued at not more than $100 each. He did not have to pay the ten-dollar tax for owning a billiard table, the ten-dollar tax on carriages worth over $500, the fifty-cents-per-ounce tax on gold plate "kept for use" or the five-cents-per-ounce tax on silver plate. Nor did he have to pay the tax on yachts. But the income tax brought a connection with the federal government that the "middling sort" of Americans, like the Taintors, had never before had.

Early in 1865, Delia Taintor went to Washington in order to discover the whereabouts of young Henry—who had by then been promoted to lieutenant—and to stay with Abby. But Henry's artillery regiment was involved in the siege of Petersburg, so Delia did not see him. Not long after, her sister Ellen wrote, "I am right sorry you should have been so disappointed about seeing Henry, it is a disappointment in which we all share." She was able to report, however, that she had just seen a man who "had recently been down to Petersburgh or as near there as the army has gone & . . . spent an evening with Mr. Taintor & Cornelius Gillett–Said he (Henry) was very well & appeared very finely–that he was a very fine Officer & much respected–I knew it all before but it is pleasant to hear our dear ones spoken of with appreciation."[42]

The beginning of April, 1865, brought the horrific final assault on Petersburg, the taking of Richmond, and the surrender of the Confederate Army of Northern Virginia at Appomattox Court House. A Hampton man, George W. Tracy, was in Company F of the Tenth Connecticut Regiment of Infantry at Appomattox Court House that day. A few days later President Lincoln was assassinated. And not long after that, the *last* Confederate Army surrendered. Still no one could be sure the fighting and the dying had stopped. Delia's sister Ellen wrote anxiously, "Have you heard from Henry since the taking of Petersburgh & Richmond? I have hoped each day would bring us some news of him through you." She tried to be reassuring by telling Delia that a friend of hers "did not hear from her husband for a long time but received letters a few days since from him saying he was well and unhurt–I trust you have the same news from Henry before this." But, she wrote, "oh! what tragical scenes our country has passed through since we have heard from each other. The terrible death of our good President has engrossed every one's thoughts and words. It is hard to realize that God's hand is over the assassin's."[43]

Young Henry did soon communicate with his parents. In early June, his father mailed him $100 to *Richmond*–the federal mails were again going there, and perhaps Henry was celebrating. The Taintor family also bought an engraving of a portrait of Lincoln (which was still in the house when we moved in). Soon Delia was beginning to hope "Henry will not be disappointed in his expectation of a furlough,"[44] and by summer the war was over and Henry was home. In July he had his photograph taken in Lowell, Massachusetts, probably with army buddies.[45] Alice Hall wrote from Washington that she was "very glad you are all able to have Henry again with you. *Ex* Capt Gillette says he saw him in Hartford & he was looking *very* well–Please give him my love & tell him I am *very* sorry I have never seen *Lieut* Taintor–especially as he was so long near Washington."[46]

None of the men who came home were unscathed. Nearly twenty years after it was over, one thrice-wounded veteran of that terrible War, Oliver Wendell Holmes, Jr., eloquently summed up what the survivors may have felt:

> . . . the generation that carried on the war has been set apart by its experience. Through our great good fortune, in our youth our hearts were touched with fire. It was given to us to learn . . . that life is a profound and passionate thing. . . . We have seen with our own eyes . . . the snowy heights of honor, and it is for us to bear the report to those who come after us. . . . Our dead brothers still live for us, and bid us think of life, not death. . . .[47]

Like most of the men who fought in the Civil War, Henry E. Taintor kept his dress uniform and his sword. He wore them to meetings, encampments, and parades of the Grand Army of the Republic (the Union veterans' organization). They are still kept by his great-nephew in Hampton.

CHAPTER 16

DISAPPOINTED DAUGHTERS OF ASPIRATION

ぴ

*"... commendable faithfulness in the fulfillment
of an oldest daughter's duties."[1]*

Their **T**he Taintor young ladies of West Brookfield, Massachusetts, weathered the early misfortunes of their family with optimism intact. Despite the death of their mother and the deterioration of their father's health and fortune, they were cheerful young women. They all left West Brookfield and made their adult lives in cities during and after the Civil War. Theirs were the Victorian domestic expectations that gentlewomen could only find their life's work fulfilled within marriage. Carrie married west, Susie married up, and Genia did not marry. As we pieced together their stories from their correspondence with their aunt Delia, we wished them well. But none of them found the lives for which they hoped.

A Ready-Made Family

Caroline's marriage to Alexander W. Buel took place in 1857. Buel was a widower with four young daughters—Mary, Julia, Clara, and Delia. The family lived in Detroit, Michigan, and included Mr. Buel's first wife's sister, the spinster aunt who had taken care of the girls between his marriages. Caroline's earnest effort to fit herself into the city life of Detroit, communicated to her aunt Delia in small-town Hampton, included the transfer into a new setting of many of the rural values with which she had grown up.

Detroit was a booming center for trade and commerce, and a jumping-off place for new settlement in upper Michigan and Wisconsin. There were over 40,000 inhabitants when Caroline arrived. By the time she had been there two years, she could describe her "new sphere of duties" to her aunt Delia. "There is no longer the stranger-like feeling, the fear lest I might not do what it would be right for me to do." She wrote about her stepdaughters that "I never knew such a band of sisters before. Sometimes when I think of their kindness and delicate appreciation of the peculiar and trying position I occupied on first coming here, I feel that I owe them a great deal."

Caroline had grown up a Congregationalist, but attended the Episcopal church after her marriage. Church life was important to her and she wrote at length and often to her aunt about it. "The Episcopal church now seems quite like home to me, tho I am not at all of the opinion that having once made a profession of my faith, it is necessary to have the hands of the Bishop laid on my head to make me a member of the 'true fold.'" She made it clear that she still retained her "connection with the church in Brookfield," and thought of her attendance in Detroit as something she did for her new family. "I always go to their communion. Mary, Julia, and Clara also go, having been confirmed since I came here."

She and her stepdaughters taught in the "Sabbath school." Her class was "girls sixteen and eighteen years old." She had a German immigrant girl in it who could not read English "very well," whom she also taught at home. Proud of her eldest stepdaughter, Julia, she wrote Delia, "Julia has a class of twenty or thirty poor German children, and takes them away by themselves into the rector's study. She can instruct them easily as she speaks the German language readily. Mary and Clara have classes of very small children, and Delia is still a pupil–It is very pleasant for us all to go together, and I never enjoyed a Sunday school so much in my life."

She reported that they had a new rector in the Episcopal church who came from Norwich, Connecticut, and she remembered meeting his father at "Cousin John Taintor's" nearly twenty years before. The rector's wife, "a most lovely lady we hear, was often thought of by us all and we were thinking how very pleasant it would be to receive her as our pastor's wife, when the sad intelligence came that she was dead. She died one week ago yesterday, leaving an infant a few days old. [The Rector] Mr. Paddock was in Norwich making preparations to leave for his new Detroit home the first of February. The Society of Christ ch. were going to build him a rectory, and many plans were formed for the future. Now alas, how changed!"

Not quite thirty years old, Carrie had settled into her matronly role in her new household. She reported "having a very quiet winter, there being very little gaiety here, except among a class who are fond of merely dancing parties. But I have enjoyed the smaller social companies exceedingly.

One evening in the week we set apart for reading aloud–Our family and that of one of our neighbors, where there are several young ladies, meet weekly at each other's houses alternately, and we find it very pleasant."[2]

When she visited West Brookfield in the summer of 1860 Carrie returned briefly to her girlhood. She enjoyed seeing Susie and wrote, "We sleep together and are enjoying every moment." But she had moved beyond that life and was happy to find "a pile of letters waiting for me" from her husband, from two of her stepdaughters, and from her former pupil "Miss Tucker of Georgia." She quoted her stepdaughter Julia in her letter to Delia: "'Father gave us particular instructions not to hurry you home, but I imagine he would have given more selfish orders if he had not been going to be absent.' She says it seems months instead of weeks that I have been absent. It does me so much good to read all her kind words, and I long to see all the dear ones again."

Although Carrie protested that she was not political, she sent along for her uncle Henry's perusal a copy of a political "address" her husband had given in Detroit. She proudly described how he had come to write it. Buel was an active Democrat who had ended up supporting Breckinridge and Lane on the Southern Democrat ticket for the Presidency in 1860 because, as he had told Caroline, "I must be *somewhere* at the election, and so upon urgent solicitation consented to write the address." But the writing itself had nearly daunted him. He wrote, "I waked up the next morning oppressed with the burden I had assumed, for how to write the address as I was to start in a day or two for Macinac I knew not. But the mind works hard sometimes when it is pressed. So I shut myself up in our room, in a hot day, wrote and wrote till ten o'clock P.M., when I was happy to find my address nearly finished. It was in fact a twelve hour's production."[3]

The beginning of the Civil War did not at first affect Caroline's life in Detroit. But by 1863, when she wrote Delia a letter with news of her two stepdaughters (Mary and Julia) who were now married, the war had touched at least one of them: "Julia [who had married her father's partner, Mr. Trowbridge] is in Washington boarding in the family of a very pleasant widow lady, who takes her, and a gentleman and lady from Detroit as boarders, more for company than profit. . . . The 'fifth cavalry' of which Mr. Trowbridge is first major, is stationed on East Capitol Hill, a mile and a half from the Capitol so that until the regiment is ordered away into service, he can see Julia frequently. When that occurs, she will probably leave and take her route homeward." Julia "could not find words to express her disgust with Washington mud–the army wagons having so cut up the soil as to make it very bad, especially since the snow and rain storms we have had lately."

Even though Caroline was very close to her aunt Delia, she referred to one piece of news in the veiled language of a Victorian gentlewoman: "Mary . . . goes out very little now and anticipates a very important *event* quite late in the spring." A further elliptical allusion to Mary's pregnancy was in Caroline's news about "Auntie" (the first Mrs. Buel's maiden sister who lived with the family): "She is at present all engaged in manufacturing diminutive garments of all sorts. With a view to their *prospective* usefulness."

Of "Auntie" herself, Caroline wrote that she was "just as devoted as ever to *her four children*." Caroline's emphasis was a signal to Delia of the irony whereby the spinster aunt claimed the children, whereas she, a married woman, saw herself childless on the sidelines. She wrote of this ever-present aunt, "Age does show itself, as the years pass by but we hope she will live many more. She has always been kind and considerate with me–a great thing as I was situated, when I came to take the head place in the family–a place she had held since her sister's death." One wonders how much, in fact, Auntie had given up.

Carrie proudly said that the third daughter, Clara, "now rejoices in the name of 'Miss Buel,' which the course of events has bestowed on her, and practically steps in to her sisters' place with much ease, and commendable faithfulness in the fulfillment of an oldest daughter's duties. She is a lovely young lady, I think, and I only hope some of the young beaux won't think so too for sometime to come. Next April she will be twenty years old. Julia was engaged at eighteen!–Delia will be eighteen next September. It does not seem possible." Carrie herself had not married until she was twenty-seven, but the implication of her comments was that younger marriages were more common.

One unusual occurrence of that winter of 1863, according to Carrie, was that "My good husband is at home this winter, engaged in the practice of his profession–and since Mr. Trowbridge left, he has been very busy, as he took no new partner." She was, however, "afraid next Spring will take him away again up the lakes for another term of Court."[4]

Mr. Buel was away in the Lake Superior region for twelve weeks in the summer at court. Carrie insisted to Delia that "it is a great benefit to his health to get away from these hot streets, and the treadmill life of the office, and fish, and row, between the hours of business in those fine large lakes, so attractive to fishermen. And then the business there is very profitable, most of it being from persons at the East who are largely interested in the mines there, and in the heavy lawsuits involved, are able to pay quite handsomely for legal services."

The lawsuits on which Mr. Buel worked involved big money battles over the rights to huge iron and copper deposits in the region around Lake

Superior. Caroline reported that one was "between the National and Minnesota Mining Co.s. Mr. Buel being employed for the National Co. A very large property is involved—and the case has been decided over and over again in favor of the National—till finally the other side took it up to the Supreme Court of the U. S. and Mr. Buel argued it in Washington two or three years before I ever met him—Since that time (the National beating in Supreme Ct.) it has been tried on some other points here in Detroit, and two days before Mr. Buel left for L. Superior the last time, the attorney for the Minnesota served him with a notice of another trial before the Supreme Court."

Caroline herself "immediately gave my notice that I was to go too, and have a sight at Washington—a place I've always wanted to see but my ardor was somewhat dampened by finding that the trial will come off a year from next winter!! No one knows where we will all be then." The "all" of whom she spoke was increasing in number. Her stepdaughter Julia was back living with the family, anticipating "her confinement in the fall—and is very busy with sewing at present. . . . Mary has a dear little baby named 'Alice.' . . . Last week we had a musical evening, and Mary sang quite as well and as strongly as she used to do, to her father's great delight. . . . We were afraid she might not retain her voice after so very severe an illness [childbirth]—She suffered terribly when her child was born."

Caroline, who was not having any children, continued to look young. She told Delia a story about the visit of "A very nice old gentleman from Hartford." The man was "an old friend of the girls' mother (Mrs. Buel)" who "knew her when she was music teacher in an Academy at Middlebury Vt." The man had never seen any of the girls. "We were all at church Sunday evening when he called—and Auntie had him all to herself—She had told him all about the girls—and that the youngest resembled her mother strikingly—As we came in about ½ past nine o'clock, I happened to go into the parlor first, and was introduced as Mrs. Buel." The gentleman was obviously a little deaf, and thought Auntie had said "Miss Buel." He came up to Carrie "with the most benevolent smile on his face—and almost with tears in his eyes—he took my hand in both of his, and said 'Yes, you do look exactly like your mother'! I supposed he was some one who used to know my own mother—and when Auntie hastened to explain that I was not the youngest daughter, I could not keep my face straight. He did not like to give up the idea—but said 'Well you do look like the family.'"[5]

In 1864, major illness struck the Buel household for the first time. Carrie's letter to Delia made vivid for us what a nineteenth-century sickroom was like without any of modern medicine's diagnostic or palliative tools. She had a "physician in daily attendance" for two weeks. "My first trouble was a very severe cold–which finally terminated in a local inflama-tion in the forehead directly over the eyes." She reported that "The pain came on periodically–every morning at about nine o'clock it would com-mence, gradually increasing in severity until it seemed as if I could not endure it–and did not leave me until four or five o'clock in the afternoon." Her first medication was "large quantities of quinine, enough the Dr. said to break up any but a very obstinate case–Then morphine, which only gave a temporary relief." She did get some help "from constant applications of hot hops, as a poultice over my forehead and eyes." But she could still "bear no light, nor heavy stepping in the room." After "eight or nine days, and as a last resort I took chloroform, inhaling it for hours together, as fast as the effect passed off–But the effects of this narcotic, in the way of extreme nausea were terrible–I was deathly sick, and lame from constant retching and vomiting." Finally she "was able to keep one teaspoonful of beef tea down at a time," and "this inflammation passed away."

Before she was able to leave her bed her husband "was taken very sick . . . with an alarming attack of congestion of the lungs," which sounds like pneumonia. "He was delirious, and seemed to be in a lethargy a great deal of the time, raising with a great deal of pain much dark bloody matter from the lungs. His law business was constantly in his mind, and he showed how he had overstayed [overworked] himself lately." Caroline was moved out of their bedroom "into the sitting room on a cot bed, but I heard him groan all night, and could not sleep for anxiety–I could not keep my tears back when the thought of his danger would come over me. By prompt and severe remedies and the sparing mercy of God, we were spared a great and overwhelming sorrow."

The experience had been terrifying for Caroline. "I have felt so differ-ently about almost everything since those days of anxious suspense–as though I was, and ought to be thankful and content with any and all of life's experiences." She appreciated the calls her "good rector" made during this time, and told Delia that "when he knew how anxious I was, he reminded me of the opportunity for 'casting all my case on God'–but O, Aunt Delia, is it not hard sometimes to do this? hard to say *sincerely,* 'Not as I will but as Thou wilt'?" All illness took a long time. Mr. Buel was "con-fined to the house" for nearly three weeks before Carrie felt "that if we could have a sunshiny pleasant day he would go down to his office."[6]

Carrie gradually became a city person. "I never care very much about leaving Detroit," she wrote to Delia, "for the sake of going into the *country* in the summer, we are so comfortable here."[7] Carrie reviewed her urban life–a contrast to small-town Hampton in many ways–to Delia after nearly ten years of marriage. She wrote that there had, at the beginning, been "years of economy and self-denial." But now, "as a result of unremitting and very laborious professional labors, we have a delightful home, *unencumbered* and can read the Apostle's injunction, 'Owe no man' etc. without compunction."

She wished her aunt Delia "could look in on the garden now. It is all laid out in gravelled walks–the white gravel having been brought down from Mackinac in barrels–Now the fountain is in good working order again–and gives us much pleasure. A large strawberry bed is beginning to supply our table nicely. A new asparagus bed made last year is doing well, and the tomatos are climbing on the new trellis built for them. We have indulged in a new grape arbor and the vines set out are flourishing well." This in the middle of Detroit! The whole family took care of the garden. "Three beds for flowers cut out in figures among the turf are consigned respectively to Clara's Delia's and my care–and we try which shall look the prettiest. My husband is working there morning noon and night–coat off–and using the rubber hose in the evening to freshen up everything. We can just attach the hose to the fountain and thus are almost independent of rain." This was the impressive result of having a city water supply, something Henry and Delia never had, and which still does not exist in Hampton.

The Buels had at least one person to help them. Carrie wrote, "An old German woman is raking the hay into large mounds, she having cut it yesterday with her sickle–from the grass plot which serves us for a clothes yard" where washed clothes were hung on a line to dry. There was also "a new wood house–with lattice work outside which is quite ornamental–and on which we are training ivy."

The indoor facilities were much improved as well, Carrie reported. "We have a nice new iron sink–new kitchen floor etc. etc. with two good water closets [flush toilets], one in the basement and one in our bath room next to my room." She explained the financing of all this work by telling Delia, "One of our neighbors bought ten feet of our lot to build an addition to his house–paying $1500.00 for it–so most of our improvements are the result of that sale and I do not believe you would miss the ten feet from our lot."

As usual Caroline reported on her family. All but the youngest stepdaughter had left home, and Mr. Buel was spending considerable time near Lake Superior, with which "His legal business is pretty well identified." So Caroline was home in Detroit with young Delia and "Auntie," about whom she reported that she was "well–and almost distracted between her four nieces and their four babies. She is cutting out work–sewing etc. from one week to another–with no cessation. I can see that she grows old, but she is very lively and in good spirits."[8]

Carrie accompanied her husband north on one of his summer business trips to the upper peninsula of Michigan in the 1860s. Her letter to Delia describes a summer resort at that time:

... I am ... writing in a pleasant room of the "Chipperman House" with the roar of St. Mary's Falls [Sault Ste. Marie, Michigan] in my ears, and many other reminders all about me that I am away from home, and in a very isolate spot. I had not been very well during the last month ... So my husband insisted on my accompanying him on this upper Lake trip for a little change from home cares and duties. We had a delightful ride here on the Steamer Meteor–though it would have been still more agreeable if there had been more passen-gers on board–and of just the right kind–But there was no rough weather and I enjoyed it extremely. Sunday morning the steamer stopped two hours at a small place to take on freight and I went on shore and to a church near the wharf where service had just com-menced–but I had to keep close watch of the time and leave before the sermon–or else run the risk of being left. It is not agreeable to travel thus on the Sabbath–but it is unavoidable in these lake trips, as matters are arranged at present.

... This hotel is generally filled during the hot season with visitors from all parts of the Union–and there were a good many here the first day we came. The cool weather is now sending them all home [she wrote in late August]. ... A party of military people from Fort Wayne in Detroit–most of whom I knew were at this house when we arrived, and the evening we came they had a party–a gay dancing affair in the dining-room. We were invited and went for a little while–but as I do not dance I felt rather in the way, and retired early. There is little to do here after seeing the Rapids and the St. Mary's Canal–looking in at the Indian wigwams–and walking over Fort Brady. ... I am to take a steamer for home, while my husband goes up to L. Superior on other business–I regret very much that ... he is obliged to ... remain until the latter part of October–Navigation as late in the season as that is invariably attended with much risk–and violent storms frequently call forth all the skill available to guide the vessels.[9]

After Thanksgiving and Christmas in 1867, Carrie thanked Delia for her letter "written from the old homestead at Windsor." She remembered Elmwood and reminisced that "it scarcely seems possible that it is twenty-five years since I was present" at a family Thanksgiving there. She went on to describe Christmas in Detroit, where the large number of German immi-grants had introduced Christmas tree rituals. "We saw the Tree lighted for the children–heard them all sing together, and then the little folks had their supper. Afterwards the older people all sat down to theirs–and two long tables were quite filled." She reported that one of her stepgranddaughters "has an unwavering faith in Santa Claus."[10]

Widowhood

In the late winter of 1868 Carrie went east, stopping in West Brookfield and going on to Boston to visit Susie and her husband. While there she heard Charles Dickens read. Mr. Buel planned to pick her up in Boston after he visited his daughter Julia in Knoxville, Tennessee. And she was "delightfully surprised with the prospect of his company on the way home."[11] It was their last trip together. Alexander Buel died shortly thereafter. About a month afterward Caroline wrote her aunt that "This sore bereavement which God has sent upon me has shadowed my life. Its sudden coming, just when we were full of plans for the future—the sad circumstances of my dear husband's illness, (I refer especially to the delirium which continued almost to its close) and his leaving us at last without one long interchange of thoughts about the future, such as would have been so pleasant to remember if we must miss him here,—all these sad remembrances seep over me at times with overwhelming power, and I feel as if years instead of weeks had been added to my life."

In her grief Caroline tried desperately to count her mercies: "I have had a very happy married life. Present or absent from my dearly loved husband, his approval of anything in which I have been engaged, has always been something I especially desired and my sure confidence in *his* affection, and sometimes in his pride in my efforts to fill my sphere of duty here, has given life all its zest." Now she was alone and began to "realize what it would be to go to the silent room at night, alone—to hear no kindly words of encouragement, or confidence given about matters equally concerning us both, but instead, the memory of pain and delirium, of days and nights of watching and prayers that the cup of agony might pass from me—of the sad parting scene—the rigidity of death—the burial—the going with faltering steps in widow's weeds to my seat in church." She told her aunt, "When I closed his eyes in death, one wish was uppermost in my heart—*to go too*." But she tried to believe that if she "willingly and cheerfully" waited, her God would show her "some path of usefulness."

Her stepdaughters made immediate plans. Julia and her husband, Mr. Trowbridge, came back to Detroit. Caroline wrote that "in view of the fact that the *care* of keeping up such a place as this would be a great one for a lady, and as we are now so deprived of the income coming from the labors of that busy brain and those unwearied hands now stilled forever, it is thought best by all of us that Mr. Trowbridge should take this house as his for a year at least.—Julia to be the housekeeper and our family including Auntie, Clara, Delia and myself to be boarders with them."

Carrie's central place in the household was over and she admitted to Delia that "this is, as you can readily understand, attended with trials to me, who have for eleven years had the care of the house, but it seems best, and certainly I could not yield my place to a more lovely, considerate daughter than is Julia." She protested that all her stepdaughters were "very kind and affectionate to me, and I love them for their own sake and because *he* loved them so devotedly–to the last hour of life." She was allowed, for the time being, to retain her "old room where we have enjoyed so much together, and which is full of precious memories." And she closed her letter to Delia by asking her, "Remember me in my loneliness, will you not, Aunt Delia."[12]

Caroline was only thirty-seven when her husband died. Shortly the home they had shared went to her stepdaughter Mary and her husband, and Carrie had to move to the new home of Julia and Mr. Trowbridge because it was the eldest daughter's responsibility to take charge of her father's remaining family. The night before she left her old home she wrote to Delia Taintor for the last time from her "own sleeping room–that room which was all newly fitted up for me, and to which I came as a bride eleven years ago. This is the last Sabbath night I ever expect to spend in it. Before another week we shall probably be settled in another house." She had spent the day feeling "it is the last time," memories had been "thronging of past joys and sorrows," and it seemed to her "as if a distinct portion of my life was being closed up, and finished. And though it is no small trial to leave this precious room, this garden, and all the familiar places, I can but feel that the enduring of the severer sorrow has made all lighter ones seem very light in comparison."

She tried to find comfort in the thought of living with Julia's family, and particularly with her stepgranddaughter, Clara, who was to be her roommate: "The pleasantest and largest chamber is assigned me, where I shall have my little Clara, as now, to love and care for–She slept with me the first night here, after our precious dead was removed from the room– and has done so ever since."[13] When we read that letter we remembered that Carrie's little sister who had died had been named Clara.

Caroline lived only five years after her husband died. During her widowhood she made several extended visits to West Brookfield, Hampton, and her sister Susie in New York. She also visited her married stepdaughter who lived for a while at West Point. When she went home to Detroit after spending several months with Susie in 1872, Julia's family had moved yet again, but she still had a room in their house, still shared with her stepgrandchild Clara. She reported to Delia that when she arrived "at Julia's the entire family were assembled, and as the carriage stopped the demonstrations of the children could have been heard for a block or farther–It was indeed 'good' to receive so pleasant a welcome, and we chatted together, opened the trunks, distributed toys, candy, books–etc, until the little people were running over with happiness."

She wrote, "My room is cheerful, and with its fresh new matting seems very cool and comfortable. There are two windows in it looking out on Jeff. Avenue and the large trees about the house and yard keep out the bright sun-light." Clara was "growing very pretty," according to Caroline, and was becoming "quite womanly, and amiable." Her old friends had been "very prompt in calling." And she said that she was "especially touched by the kindness of Mrs. Ford whose husband took our family pew in Christ Ch. when we gave it up–She came early one Sunday morning to ask me to take my old seat at the head of the pew, as long as I remained in the city."[14]

A year later, in the fall of 1873, Caroline fell ill while on an extended visit to her sister Susie in New York. Distressed at her sister's condition, Susie wrote to her aunt Delia, "When I see you, I can tell you some things that retarded her recovery in Detroit," then crossed out a sentence in which she had written, "I do not feel quite right about the *care*–or the lack of it, she has there." Carrie was constantly in bed, with her meals brought upstairs to her.[15]

After a month Carrie was a little better, and Susie continued hopeful. She read to her daily from the Episcopal Book of Common Prayer. She assured Delia that "dear Carrie really seems much better" but "that does not mean as much as I wish it did." Susie tried to be cheerful. "She is *very* happy here, and enjoys so much the care and nursing, I am only too happy to give her. Everything that love and skill can suggest will be done for her, and I *now* hope she may be *much* better, tho' Dr. Minor says he fears she may never be *well* again." Not well herself, Susie had hired "an excellent nurse (*not* a '*professional*') but a very pleasant young lady, and we *share* the care of Carrie–as it is impossible for me to be with her at *night* and retain my own strength."[16]

Barely forty-three years old, Caroline Taintor Buel died at the end of 1873. She had, of course, no children of her own. Her stepdaughter Julia Trowbridge wrote to Delia Taintor in February 1874 that the arrangements Delia and Susie had made about Caroline's few things were "perfectly satis-factory." Julia sympathized that "the duty must have been a sad one for you both, and you may imagine how hard it has been for me, and is still, the putting away, and caring for things which mother will never more have any use for." She found it "almost impossible to realize that she will never come back to us." She remembered that Caroline always spoke of Delia "in terms of deepest affection," and told her that young George Taintor's visits to Detroit had given Caroline great pleasure, "She enjoyed them not only on his own account, but because he was Aunt Delia's child."[17] At the end of her life, Caroline's only family by right was her Taintor family.

Lucy's Yearnings

In the last half of 1874, after her father had died, Lucy Taintor wrote a letter to him from the Worcester Lunatic Hospital. We do not know if anyone had told her he was dead. We do not know if this letter was one of a series or was singular. She addressed the letter to him in Hampton where he had never lived in her lifetime (and where he had not lived for nearly fifty years). She did not address it to West Brookfield, her childhood home, and that address says something about the place she—and perhaps her father?—thought was "home." Hopelessly confined in Worcester, she yearned for her small-town family. We print the whole letter because it shows so well Lucy's "derangement." She journeys in and out of reality and time, writing much about her desire to return home and about "Mis Prichard" whom her father had married before Lucy went to the Worcester Lunatic Hospital.

My dear Fathier

As you are apt to be rathier older & somewhat diferent from the rest of us & I not forgetting wheir you live and your age besides others in the home circle. as I am a very little older than I used to be & as I wanted to write to you very much indeed I took the liberty to say what I was a mind to for onse more to see what you would think about my going away from that Collage. I have been their some time and getting a little tired of being thier I wanted to go home but Mothier being a little the oldest wasn't very wiling that I should be thier & for that reason I thought best, wouldt you think best to let me. Lucy Goodnight.

To write what I have done. As their is a reason in all things I never forget who it is that makes the diference which this medicine as well as the world that we live in whetheir they think I do or not do we seem to be rathier diferent from each otheir and will the medicine alter my minde some what more than I like the Idea of quite as well. Isnt just the thing always to have Mothier a little to gard for something with me to have me know her about when she is apt to be some what diferent. I have been to get berries with the rest have I wasnt very wiling to dont you live wheir you used to are you a little older than I am and dont your general health be exactly the thing for Mis Prichard to know you to well about. has Mis Prichard been thier and did she say she would like to have me live in London with her very much indeed to repeat her talk to you. and she sayes to wanted be you to let me live in London would it you could let me know could

you be sure & let her come because she thinks it would do her good
& she would like the Change and be better for her than to live where
you do now becourse her sister was quite as diferent have the girls
been married & do they do a little diferent than they used to ain't
they me exactly. Isnt it very pleasant while we live in the world to
have those diferent frome oureselves for them to know us better than
we would like to have them little to much to have the care of to have
to think of, away from the rest & not only that mis you a very little
should you think best to let me live in London to please me a very little alter a litle does sister Colly live in London & would it rathier suit
my mind a very litle to go thier a first time for every thing need
Mothier be quite as good for something when I am not at home rathier
diferent from her. *Connectian.* Colly apt to be rathier diferent if you
was willing that I should would like to have me arrange. The Idea so
that I could little something else to do than to know me to well makes
cheese & Confecary will this weatheir & this liveing to & this haveing fathier to pay for every thing and any thing that we want will it
alter oure minds so that home wasnt just the place for us. If we have
any home on this earth. cant I always have fathiers Company just
when I want it & have home to live in besides I hear that your teeth
have been makeing you not feel quite as well. Does the world alter a
little from what you would think for fathier Tainter since I lived their
did your little affairs alter a very litle from others that I know of. are
your worth a very litle something of that place isnt very civile or right
or proper eithier to have wife expect to much litle money from
Husband. That is to have Clothes cost to much ount my teeth very
well. as I am thinking of closeing this letter let me just say to you that
Mis Prichard a very little when you get this letter if you will tell me
about these affairs I will take the nine or else the eleven oclock
rathier thank you with a great deal of love train to leave Worcester
for London from Lucy P. Taintor

[slightly below the above] not the Hosptal not just the place for
you. my talk rather to nervous me to bear from. alterd a *littled* pleas to
astonish me

Henry G. and Delia read that letter; they saved it. The next month
came a letter from Lucy addressed to her sister Caroline in Hampton.
Caroline, too, was dead by 1874, and she of course had never lived in
Hampton.

My Dear Sister Caroline,
    haveing been some time since I have heard or seen from you &
thinking that I wanted to hear from you very much indeed I thought
best to address a few lines to you to see if you couldnt come & see me
& have me at home. It seems some time for me to be away from home

not with the rest for us girls to be quite as diferent for you to be married & have a home of your own. is Mr. Howland your Company is it rathier pleasantier to live by yourself & does it suit your mind rathier better were you apt to be Sister to me & do I. Rathier miss you a very little every day isnt very pleasant to have this medicine make us feel or act just as it does when we are apt to be quite as different getting nearly time for Thanksgiveing time miss me any play a great many new tunes does fathier ever come to see you his teeth havent been very well have they heard your Mothier mis Sally Penniman was going to live with you after it a little how many pairs of stockings have you knit lately. not quite so natural for you to do so. do alter a little & will this wealthier & will our work alter us a very little what we dont like quite as well. Like to do as your are a mind to & have you way it makes you feel rathier different & I should think by the actians that Mothier needt do as she has she has a child like fathier so I heard. astonish me a little. is fathier worth a little something & did he alter a little. raises sweet Potatoes doesnt he. & then not only that for him to make leathier. & farm it beside not so pleasant to be wheir I am. doesnt fathier live wheir he used to had a piece of custard pie for dinner do such things costs something. the trustees called here today Mr. Nasan & Mr. Washburn ride up to meeting once in a while dress a little diferent. heard from Susan lately are we a little older grown went over to Worcester awhile ago had rathier of a pleasant time with Miss Hubbared. Mr. Patch carried us down their & we walked back. would like to come & stay with you. & help you a little heard Mothier say Cally thought Lucy might have written to you. Pleas excuse me for not doing it I have written home & they seem to be pretty well. as I shall send this in the morning as I generally do or as we have to do when Mr. Patch comes down in the morning with bread for diner I have written this tonight because I could send it in the morning I hope you will excuse all mistakes & except a great deal of love from your affectianate Sister Lucy P. Tainter

The condition of the sad and sick woman who wrote those letters troubled her family. The modern sister of a schizophrenic has characterized the precautions a family can take even when the ill person is hospitalized: "I decided to have one small lamp burning near my closet, where [he] could be hiding, ready to spring,"[18] she wrote. The Taintor family could perhaps have written the same about Lucy.

Lucy lived another quarter century in the Worcester Lunatic Hospital. Like her younger sister Caroline, she stayed connected to her small-town past. Her uncle Henry G. Taintor was her official guardian until he died in 1889. Lucy's stepmother, Frances Prichard Taintor, and her half-sister Genia visited her regularly after her father and sisters died. After Frances

Eugenia Taintor in old age.

died, Genia made clothes for Lucy and visited her for all the years in which the two of them were the only surviving members of Bulkeley Taintor's family. Lucy died in 1901. Genia died in 1931. They were buried with their father and their mothers in West Brookfield, Massachusetts. When the descendants of the Taintors asked us if there were any skeletons in the family closet, no one seemed to remember Lucy had ever existed.

CHAPTER 17

SMALL-TOWN FORTUNES

⌒⌒

"He has much confidence in it, knowing the management well."[1]

A lmost all of Henry G. Taintor's business records are small note-books in which he recorded his daily income and spending, and carefully packeted bunches of receipts for each year of his business life. When we untied the "red tape" from the packets or unpinned the thicker packages, we found raw material for tracing the expenditures and the income of a small-town banker/capitalist tied to his rural roots and trying to make his way through the increasingly industrial, urban, consumer world. Henry's records run for more than fifty years—from the 1830s to the 1880s. The brief notes he made in his cashbooks were not as clear to us as they were to him, and many are still opaque. What follows is our effort to make sense out of some very dense material and to reconstruct, as much as we can from this evidence, how Henry thought and how he viewed the world he lived in.

Henry G. Taintor tried to meet the modern world head-on in his business life. But the modern world changed as a result of the Civil War, which itself brought together the economic transformations that had been coming in the years before 1860. With all deliberate speed, Henry changed his businesses and moved his investments to profit from the industrialization he saw all around him. He made money for himself (although by the end of his life he had lost much of it). The values he grew up with in Hampton did not stretch to making and *keeping* a fortune in the industrial world.

As the son of Solomon Taintor, Henry's inheritance had not simply been land and the tools to work it. He also inherited secured (usually by mortgages) notes from farmers and merchants, most but not all resident in the vicinity of Hampton, worth a total of nearly $15,000. And he received shares of stock in four banks—the Hampshire Mechanics Bank in Ware, Massachusetts, the Windham County Bank in Brooklyn, Connecticut, and the Hartford and the Phoenix Banks in Hartford—which were worth over $6,000.[2] From the beginning, Henry's income came from three sources: the products of his farm—mostly hay and wool and animals, the interest on the notes and mortgages he held, and the dividends from his stocks. Although he called himself a farmer all his life, his farm income was the least of what he earned.

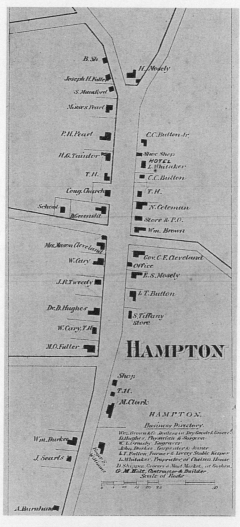

Hampton Village, from an 1869 atlas.

Becoming a Capitalist

Henry gradually transformed his inherited property from active proprietor-exploitation to income-producing investment. He took the first step in that process immediately after he received his inheritance. He started renting out rooms in the store building on the southeast corner of his property to other merchants and artisans. William Fuller rented "the North room" at twelve dollars per year in 1833 and 1834. Fuller was a tailor and clothing maker. William Clark, another tailor, also rented a room in 1834. In May 1834, Brown & Bennett "commenced business in the Store"–and in 1836 it was Brown who succeeded Dan Bulkeley as postmaster of Hampton. Brown & Bennett occupied the store building until 1841.

During the 1840s, J. K. Dorrance & Co. rented the store, and so did Joel Searls, a local shoemaker. Newton Holt rented the "Store Chambers" in 1851. The last time the "store" appears in Henry's accounts was in 1862, when he paid Joel Fox two dollars for "taking out chimney of Store building."

As the "store" disappears from Henry Taintor's accounts, a "house" appears. It was first rented to Dr. William Soule and George Soule (the new Hampton minister) in 1853 and 1854. In 1855, the house was divided and the upstairs rented to one set of tenants, the downstairs (sometimes with "garden" and sometimes without) to another set. The tenants were nearly all local people, and by the 1860s tended to be widows living alone. Henry had changed the building from a place in which he worked to an investment from which he received income. The house remained a tenant house until 1902, when Henry's children tore it down, and a "chapel" for the Congregational church was built on the site.

Without ever calling himself a banker, Henry functioned as a private banker for nearly half a century. He had learned the private banking business, as he learned the farming business, from his father and his uncle Roger, from his teachers in school and from the merchant he clerked for in Brooklyn, from his uncle Dan Bulkeley, from his older brother Bulkeley, and from his cousin John. And while he was establishing his family and his place in the community, he changed very little of what he did and how he did it. He lent to local people. He became treasurer of the church next door, and the church's money contributed to his own "cash flow"–he never in any of his accounts made any distinction between his own and the money he collected from the church and paid out on the church's behalf. The bank stocks he owned produced a steady cash income with which to pay the $400 per year his father's will had provided for his mother, until she died in 1849. From the beginning of his business career, he maintained bank accounts—the first at the Windham County Bank, in which he was a stockholder—upon which he drew by check.

Henry trained himself to record all of his business transactions. At the beginning of his adult life, he kept the standard kind of daybook/account book that farmers, merchants, and artisans had kept in his father's day. But it became clear that, for his purposes, the big leather-bound volumes would not do. He did much of his business, buying, selling, lending, and collecting, on a cash basis, and cash transactions were not recorded in the standard accounts. So he began to record his transactions in a small cash book he could carry in his pocket.

Henry Taintor's cash books record his daily transactions—although some books are missing, making hiatuses in the record which are a year or more long—from the early 1840s to the late 1880s. Taken in combination with his bank books, canceled checks, and the voluminous packets of receipts he kept all his life, they provide a detailed record of the changes in small-town business throughout the core of the nineteenth century, as those changes gradually occurred in the busy, daily life of a small-town farmer, banker, investor. And they show, in the lively detail of one person's experience, the capital sources that enabled him to participate in the development of the industrialized, productive national market.

The cashbooks Henry Taintor used are a certain indicator of important changes in the pattern of small-town business. Cash was increasingly available, and in demand for all transactions. Small-merchant and retail credit was declining, as Dan Bulkeley's changing experience indicated. As book credit declined, so did small-scale exchanges of goods and services without cash.

If a farmer or a local manufacturer wanted to participate in the new cash economy, he had to produce goods in large-enough quantities to reach the urbanizing cash marketplaces. For most, that meant increasing production and hiring help. As the century wore on, those who could not produce cash crops were relegated to subsistence farming and barter exchanges. They were out of the mainstream that moved goods into the cities.

Henry lent money, long- and short-term, secured and unsecured, to local farmers and small-scale manufacturers who needed working capital to reach the cash marketplace; and he received money from such people for investment. He transferred money for others to banks in Windham County, Hartford, New York, and Boston. He paid interest, sometimes over very long term, on his own notes, held by others, which were like today's interest-bearing certificates of deposit. He bought and held bonds for others, and collected and paid over to them the interest due on coupons.

He also became an investor in stocks and bonds, mostly on his own behalf, but since he–like everyone else–made little distinction between funds he received from his own work and investments and funds received from others, it is not possible from his records to make a distinction between investment on his own behalf and investment of the funds of others. Throughout his adult life, an increasingly large part of his income came from the dividends collected from his "portfolio" of investment (the interest paid on bond coupons was called a "dividend" as were the payments made on shares of stock, which were very often calculated as a percentage of the "par" or "face" value of the stock share).

Henry's views on stock purchases, like his views on all investment, came from his training and background. A careful businessman risked his capital only when he could control its use and management or when he had direct, trustworthy connections (preferably family connections) to the people who were in charge. Investment in ventures one did not manage or to which one had no family connections was made, like lending money, only when one had considerable, trustworthy (and what we would today consider "insider") knowledge of the people and the firm.

In the midst of his older brother Bulkeley's bankruptcy, for instance, Henry asked Bulkeley to find out how the stock in Massachusetts's Western Railroad that Bulkeley had held in trust for their mother could be transferred to him. Bulkeley had lost the stock certificates, but he asked a Mr. Quincy, who was an officer of the company, and Quincy told him "to get a vote of the Directors to grant a new certificate of stock" and there would be no problem.[3] It was Henry's first involvement with the stock of the new, expanding railroads. He was very curious about railroads, as was everyone at the time. But he preferred to invest in what he knew, and two months later he bought stock in another bank through his cousin John.[4]

Henry Taintor's first purchase of stock without reference to family or connections came in 1846, when he bought fifteen shares of Bank of America stock (at 96¼ for $1443.75) through Ketcham & Olcott, New York brokers at 1 Hanover Street ("near Wall Street").[5] At the same time he "took a flier" in printed textiles–which did not net him much–and he did not repeat it. Bank of America, however, paid him substantial dividends for years before he sold the stock. Early in 1847, he bought five more shares of Bank of America at 97½ and five more the next day at 98½, through Howard Williams, "his man" at Ketcham & Olcott (who could have been a relative). When his mother died in 1849, he became the owner of many of the bank shares he and John Taintor had been holding in trust for her.[6] And in early 1850, on a trip to Boston, he bought forty shares of Merchants Bank stock at 108½ for $4,340.[7] Thus very gradually he moved some of the money he had earlier invested in local notes and mortgages into bank stocks—which for him were longer-term investments but had the advantages of paying higher dividends and of liquidity.

In the fall of 1850, Henry bought his first railroad stock on his own—forty shares of the Erie Railroad at 72¾. His broker was William Searls (a relation of a Hampton Searls?) in New York. Henry bought the stock on a trip to New York, a sign that he had not yet developed the kind of trust of brokers necessary to purchase by mail. The Erie stock purchase marked the beginning of Henry's lifelong investment of more and more of his capital in railroads.

The Erie Railroad was a very long line (483 miles when it was completed in 1851) that ran through New York State from New York City to Lake Erie well south of the Erie Canal. It was already doing a large business carrying dairy products, fruit, and fresh produce from the farms of New York State to New York City. By that year, the United States had nine thousand miles of railroad (more than there was in all the rest of the world), nearly fifteen percent of it in the state of New York. And Americans, from state governments to small stockholders like Henry Taintor, had already invested more than a combined $300 million to build them. There seemed no end to the possibilities of building and running—and profiting from—more of them.[8]

By the 1850s, the railroads had come very close to Hampton. Henry Taintor used the railroad depot in Willimantic to ship hundreds of barrels of apples to Hartford and beyond, and to receive goods from as far away as New York City. It required three separate railroads to ship goods from New York to Willimantic: the New York & New Haven Railroad Company from New York to New Haven, the Hartford & New Haven Railroad Company from New Haven to Hartford, and the Hartford, Providence & Fishkill Railroad Company from Hartford to Willimantic.[9] In New Haven and in Hartford each company had its own depot, located on the side of the city from which its railroad operated. Goods arriving on one railroad were carted by horse and wagon from one depot to the other, and then loaded onto the other company's cars.

The railroads not only shipped and brought goods, they also made travel to cities and markets quick and easy. By the 1850s, day trips to Hartford were simple matters for all the Taintors, and Henry went frequently on political as well as financial and family business. New York City, too, became possible to get to in less than a day—even when the trip required a combination of train and ship travel. It meant that the pleasures and the goods of America's largest city were easily available to the Taintors. And to Henry Taintor, private banker and investor, the railroads meant easier and quicker access to brokers and exchanges as he grew more interested in trading the stocks and bonds of banks, railroads, and insurance companies.

In July 1854, Henry recorded receiving $160 as a Home Insurance Company dividend from an investment made despite the opinion of his much-admired cousin John—"I never would own a dollar of Insurance stock. It is gambling."[10] The Home Insurance Company paid substantial dividends to Henry over several years, and within two years of buying that stock, he began selling insurance and collecting premiums for, and lending substantial sums to, the Windham County Mutual Fire Insurance Company.[11] He continued to be an agent for and investor in fire insurance companies for the rest of his life.

In 1860, Henry recorded first doing large-scale business with G. P. Bissell & Co., a private bank in Hartford, which became an important part of his career as an investor.[12] The Bissell bank bought and sold stocks and bonds for him, collected his dividends and clipped his coupons, and collected on many of his note investments as well. He had used the Windham County Bank to collect on his local notes, especially those held against men in Hampton, for a number of years. He had inherited his connection to that bank from his father and uncle Roger, and it served very well so long as his primary financial interests were local. But by 1860, he wanted a larger bank in an urban center which was easily accessible to him *and* had access to the growing financial markets of the nation. Henry was by then transferring more and more of his capital from local to national investment (as the railroads and telegraph were creating a national marketplace). He found in Bissell & Company a bank to which he could still feel a personal connection and which provided the kind of market exposure his investment business required.

The War's Changes

The Civil War brought great economic stimulation to the Union and considerably increased Henry Taintor's investment. One of Bissell & Company's first transactions for him was to buy him shares in the Hartford & New Haven Railroad. They also helped in sizable purchases of gold that Henry carried out on behalf of some Hampton residents during the war.[13] The war threatened the stability, and the very existence, of the U.S. government and its currency. Gold—relatively plentiful since the California Gold Rush—seemed a safe hedge in wartime to some investors who were just getting accustomed to a cash economy. Henry bought gold for several people in Hampton—he made sizable purchases on behalf of his cousin, Edward S. Moseley—although there is no evidence he bought any for himself.[14]

Henry's Connecticut railroads—he added stock in the New York &
New Haven Railroad in 1862—earned him sizable dividends throughout the
Civil War.[15] He also moved his railroad investment further afield. In
August 1862, he recorded receipt of a $500 dividend from the Cleveland
Columbus & Cincinnati Railroad. John Taintor also owned stock in that
road—which he left as part of his estate when he died that year. He and
Henry may have discussed investment possibilities. Certainly Henry fol-
lowed his lead in railroad investing. In the months following John's death,
Henry bought shares in all three railroads John had invested in—as well as
in several of the banks in which John had owned stock.[16]

During the war, Henry bought and sold with greater frequency. He
often carried stock and bond certificates to Hartford or to New York, as
well as considerable (for him) sums of cash. He began to use the telegraph
to his bankers and to his brokers. He bought Aetna Bank stock, and sold
some of his railroad stocks. He invested on behalf of Edward S. Moseley,
Roger S. Williams, and William Durkee—all leading Hampton men.[17] He
bought large quantities of U.S. government bonds.[18] And his broker wrote
him that his practice of buying and selling odd lots cost money:

> . . . Your telegram of this day is received (½ past 2 Oclock PM)
>
> I could not buy the 75 shares Chicago & Toledo [Railroad] as no
> one would break a hundred lot. As it is only $50 per share Stocks.
> Had you not better take a whole hundred? They are so much easier
> bought, and got rid of when you wish to sell. Besides that amt. cannot
> be bought without paying a higher price then the regular market, and
> when you come to sell you will have to sell under the price for even
> lots.
>
> I shall buy the 75 shs if I can in the morning, unless I hear further
> from you.
>
> The price for [lots of] hundreds this PM was 116½ asked and I
> offered 117 for the 75 shs & 118 was offered for a lot of 12 shs by
> another party.[19]

So Henry learned some of the more esoteric business of stock exchanges.

After the war ended, Henry bought some "Oil Stock"—he did not
record which company—an unusual and risky investment (he did not buy
much, five hundred and thirty dollars' worth at 17½).[20] The business of
manufacturing kerosene (called "oil") from petroleum had started just before
the Civil War, but was already booming.

Six years later, in 1872, Henry recorded receiving dividends from
"Stan Oil," presumably the Standard Oil Company, which John D.
Rockefeller and his associates had incorporated in Ohio in 1870.[21] In the
1860s, it was unusual for a small Connecticut investor to buy a manufac-

turing stock if he was not actively in that business himself. Standard Oil's headquarters and refining center in Cleveland were far from Hampton. Although Henry did own stock in a Cleveland bank and a Cleveland railroad, Standard Oil was chancier as far as he was concerned and he did not hold it long. He sold it to invest more in railroads. (It became for Henry Taintor one of those "missed opportunities" for great wealth that nearly everyone who has invested in stocks has to tell: before Henry's death in 1889, Standard Oil had become the producer and seller of a majority of petroleum products throughout the world, and its major stockholders had become multimillionaires. Not long ago, John E. Holt, a Hampton businessman, told us similar stories of "missed opportunities" involving IBM and Xerox stocks.)

After the Civil War ended, Henry Taintor began to treat his farm itself as an investment. He started "share-farming" with Henry Jackson, with each man taking fifty percent of the selling price of at least some of the animals, wool, and hay produced on Henry Taintor's land. In 1867, he made a similar arrangement with Cyril Whitaker—they had the livestock they owned jointly surveyed that year—and they built a "Milk Room" at a joint cost of more than fifty dollars. Henry had long since stopped working the land himself, and he now transferred the decisions and work of farm management to his tenant, "share" farmers. In return for the use of his land, buildings, tools, and animals, he received half the income Jackson and Whitaker produced. Farm tenancy was increasing all over the country; Henry's system was part of the trend of increased investment farming. In the South, white landowners introduced share-cropping tenancy to replace slavery. In the North and West other forms of tenancy (Henry's arrangements were only one kind) grew, as large landowners sought to maximize cash return from the exploitation of their land; they, like Henry, had recognized that land was capital.

Capitalist Politics

In 1866, the year after the war ended, Henry G. Taintor was elected treasurer of the state of Connecticut. His term of office lasted one year. His job was to supervise the payments made by the state government, enforce the state banking and insurance laws, and receive the tax monies of the state and hold them safe. Connecticut, like most state governments, invested in the stocks and bonds of corporations chartered to provide needed economic services—canals, turnpikes and roads, railroads, banks, insurance, and manufacturing. The state treasurer in Connecticut was the official responsible for the state's investments. Henry kept a copy of a letter he sent as state treasurer giving notice "of the desire of the State to become Stockholder in the Hartford National Bank" among his own letters.[22] Henry himself later became a stockholder in the bank.

While he was treasurer, Henry also bought shares in the Chicago & Alton Railroad Company, whose offices were in New York City.[23] The Chicago & Alton was one of the new railroads being built in every part of the country, supported by hundreds of millions of dollars of new investment, by state governments, and by the federal government's land-grant and loan program which had been instituted at the beginning of the Civil War. Most of those new roads became "counters"–as the Boston, Hartford and Erie did, and the Chicago & Alton–in the great railroad "game" played out in the latter part of the nineteenth century on Wall Street by men who became known as "bulls" and "bears" and "robber barons" and whose names have become American legends–Adams, Cooke, Crocker, Dodge, Drew, Field, Fisk, Forbes, Gould, Harriman, Hill, Huntington, Morgan, Sage, Vanderbilt, and Villard.[24]

As treasurer, Henry received twenty-five-dollar payments from each of the life insurance companies in the state, quite probably as fees required by law. His only records of the payments are in his own cash books, which means that the accompanying letters and the receipts were part of the files of the treasurer's office.

During his term as treasurer he also asked for and received information about investment possibilities that were not public knowledge. Lines about "insider" information and its use had not yet been drawn. Large-scale corporations with enormous financial requisites had just come into existence. The management of some of the larger railroad companies, the direction of armies of more than a million soldiers, and the financing of the Civil War were the very largest and most complex economic experiences anyone had ever had. No one had yet learned how to run the large-scale industrial world or *any* of its institutions. Nor did anyone yet know what the implications (social, economic, legal, or ethical) or ramifications of that world might be. For a merchant-banker who was temporarily in a state office to make inquiries among his acquaintances about investment possibilities they were close to would certainly not have seemed improper to Solomon or Roger Taintor, nor did it seem so to Henry.

For example, Henry inquired about the stock of a bank in Norwich. The son-in-law of the banker wrote with information only insiders could know, that his father-in-law wished him "to say that the Stock can be bought for about 110 or 112 and that he believes it by the books of the Bank to be worth 130–he has much confidence in it, knowing the management well. The last dividend was in July–paid on the 1st."[25] It was the letter of a man who had grown up when mercantile and financial affairs were managed and controlled as personal property by family connections and personal acquaintance. That world was fast being replaced by large-scale corporate management of investment of fortunes collected from hundreds or thousands of different, unrelated merchants, bankers, businessmen, and property owners. For some time after the Civil War, that change from the private to the public world was not yet obvious to the people involved.

In November 1866, in another instance, Henry received a letter from Gabriel W. Coite, who had been state treasurer before him and was now in New York State. Coite must have kept some stationery because he wrote on the state treasurer's letterhead that he had "an opportunity to offer you one lot of the Stock of our Bank," the Bowery National Bank of New York, "of twenty four shares at five per cent, and one of ten shares at six per cent." Coite wrote Henry that "One of our Directors" had "just left an order with our Cashier to buy for a friend of his fifteen shares at five per cent." He also wanted Henry to know that the bank would pay "a dividend of five per cent on the first of January and have a surplus of from ten to twelve per cent—and probably more." And Coite concluded by pressing Henry to let him know immediately whether he wanted "any part" of the available shares.[26] Five days later, Coite acknowledged "receipt of check for $2520 in payment for Twenty four Shares of Stock in our Bank,"[27] so we know Henry bought the stock.

In the meantime, Henry sold twenty shares of a Michigan railroad through William Searls (who sent a check for the $1,826.55 proceeds), and after some looking, Searls bought him twenty-five shares of Central National Bank stock he requested, at 112½ (for which Henry sent him a check for $2,808.62).[28] In another transaction Henry as treasurer received a note from the president of the New York & New Haven Railroad—in response to questions—who said that although he was "unwilling to assume to state" what the next dividend would be, he would "presume to guess that we shall pay a 5 pr ct Divd on the whole amount of Stock issued ($6,000,000) on or about the 1st Jany 1867. We are doing very well and I see no reason why the stock of the N Y & N H RR Co shall not be among the best stocks of the country. I fear nothing but unfriendly Legislation. If let alone we can do well enough."[29] Henry promptly bought for his personal use thirty-five more shares of the company's stock for $4,099.62.[30]

He received a second letter from the same man (E. C. Scranton), this time as president of the Second National Bank of New Haven, announcing the declaration of a five percent dividend at the bank, and reminding Henry that "we are doing a good business & if we can avoid unfriendly Legislation we can do rightly. I trust you will have an eye to this in the Election of your next Members to the Legislature, especially Senators. We must look to our friends for help in case of need."[31] Ten days later, Henry's broker reported that he had bought forty more shares of New York & New Haven stock for him, at 119, for $4,765.25.[32] Two months later, in February 1867, Henry sold forty of his New York & New Haven shares for $4,600, a somewhat lower price than he had recently paid.[33] And in March that year, he sold all the rest of that stock, seventy-three shares, for another $8,600. (He immediately reinvested some of the proceeds in shares of the Cleveland & Toledo Railroad.[34]) The men writing to him about all these business opportunities assumed he was an important political figure. They believed government and legislation affected their business, and they wanted to be on the good side of men like Henry.

Henry Taintor was a cautious investor throughout his life. Except for this brief flurry at the beginning of 1867 while he was treasurer, there is no evidence that he speculated, and very little basis to assume that he bought stock or bonds for the potential appreciation in their value rather than for income. He seems to have preferred the fixed percentages and fixed amounts paid on his investment which bonds offered. For the twenty-two years of life that remained to him after 1867, he was a constant investor in banks and railroads both on his own behalf and on behalf of smaller investors in Hampton for whom he bought, sold, and collected on coupons.

His cash books contain evidence of investments made and managed for George M. Holt, Russell Tweedy, George Soule, William Brown, William Bennett, Roger S. Williams, Jacob H. Fuller, A. Woodruff, L. H. Jewett, A. B. Clark, E. H. Newton–all of them from Hampton, and several of them men who were regularly among the holders of the most important governmental offices in town. He also invested on behalf of his brother Bulkeley, for Frances, Bulkeley's wife, and for Eugenia, their daughter, as well as for Lucy in the Worcester Lunatic Hospital. He made investments for other relatives, including his sister-in-law Ellen Strong, his brother-in-law Frederick Ellsworth, and his Hampton cousin Edward S. Moseley.

The ungrateful Moseley ran against him for the treasurer's office in 1867–as a Copperhead. And it was in the midst of this crisis in Henry's own life that the desperate letters from his older brother Bulkeley came. He turned to Delia for comfort as he always had, venting his feelings about the world in a tirade against the Hampton people who had betrayed him. He wrote her that he had "accidentally met [Edward] Moseley & had a Conversation with him" in a Hartford street. Moseley had told him "that he brought a document with him from Hampton signed by Durkee, the two Tiffanys H. Hughes the *two Perkins*, Horace Jackson &c &c expressing very strong opposition to my being retained in the Treasury office." Moseley planned to see Chauncey F. Cleveland about the election. Henry wrote

Delia "you know my opinion of" Cleveland. "He is a snake in the grass." He complained that "Moseley has used me very meanly & I shall tell him so before I leave." He thought Moseley would "see the time when he will regret the course he has taken."[35]

Henry's close family was distressed when he lost the 1867 election to his "traitor" cousin. Delia's sister Ellen wrote her that she had gone "into your good husband's office a while, and it made me feel worse about the election I believe than any thing else. It seems as if it could not be that a Copperhead Treasurer would have that place in a month more."[36]

Henry remained furious. He wrote Delia as he prepared to leave Hartford, "I know it will be seen that it was better for me to leave than to stay. Were I here I should have to see & hear Copperheads in great abundance." His state political friends "did all they could for me, but Chauncey Cleveland put his foot down and would not allow me to stay." His son Henry E., who was his assistant, "is very indignant & says if he (Cleveland) ever *speaks* to him he will give him a piece of his mind." For himself, Henry G. hoped Cleveland "will never darken my doors. I can say with Mr Cary [of Hampton] 'if he will keep his side of the Street I will keep mine.'"[37] (This series of letters is strongly reminiscent of Dan Bulkeley's furies at Cleveland thirty years earlier.)

At home in Hampton and still actively investing in the 1870s, Henry G. Taintor continued to make money. At one time or another, he held bonds of the federal government, the state of Connecticut, the Central Pacific Railroad, the Lake Shore Railroad, the Union Pacific Railroad, the New York, New Haven & Hartford Railroad, the Rochester and Saratoga Railroad, the Albany & Susquehanna, and, one of the few manufacturing companies he was interested in at all, Fairbanks & Company of St. Johnsbury, Vermont.

In the quarter-century of his active investment in stocks, Henry recorded the receipt of dividends from an even more impressive list of stocks, in the Phoenix Bank, Adams Express Company, the Hartford & New Haven Railroad, the Chicago & Fort Wayne Railroad, a Norwich bank, the Continental Life Insurance Company, the Hartford Trust Company, the Windham County Bank, the Home Insurance Company, the Charter Oak Bank, the Bank of America, the Pennsylvania Railroad (which was the largest corporation in America), the Chicago, Burlington & Quincy Railroad, the Pittsburgh & Fort Wayne Railroad, the Union Bank, the Alton & Terre Haute Railroad, the Mechanics Bank, the Little Miami Railroad, the Merchants Loan & Trust Company, the U.S. Trust Company, the Chicago & Pittsburgh Railroad, the Bowery Bank, the Rock Island Railroad, the Illinois Central Railroad, the Michigan Central Railroad, and the Second National Bank of Cleveland. He made himself a considerable fortune through his investments.

He was an investor who did not buck many trends in the developing securities markets. All the big banks and big investors poured their money, from Europe as well as America, into American land development, banks, and railroads, from the Civil War's beginning to the early 1890s. Manufacturing industries drew much less investment, depending on local commercial banks and local investors who expected to play some active part in their management. In 1870 Henry took a flyer in manufacturing. He bought several thousand dollars' worth of the commercial paper of a number of New York firms and emerged from that investment with his capital intact, though not augmented.[38]

In the midst of his business and investing success Henry suffered from depression. His son George felt his trouble was not physical but "simply & only . . . nervous, & that he will be able soon to conquer & throw it off." The Taintor sons were distressed. George never hesitated to express his concern and affection, writing, "I love you both so dearly, more & more it seems to me every year, that I can not bear to think of you as being in any respect unhappy or uncomfortable."[39] Willie cautioned that his father should "not give up to his bad feelings but . . . fight them off as much as possible, as a person can make themselves really sick by constant imagination."[40] Other relatives also wrote with like suggestions. Avoiding bad feelings and too much imagination seem to have been the standard psychological therapy of the day. Perhaps for Henry the specter of insanity loomed in the years after his depressed brother Bulkeley died, and when he had taken over paying for the care of Lucy.

In his long life Henry much augmented the wealth he had inherited from his and Bulkeley's father. He built his fortune by slowly and shrewdly moving his capital out of Hampton. As his life neared its end he claimed still to be a small-town farmer, but his fortune was utterly dependent on the life and industry of cities.

PART V

UPROOTING AMERICA

The generations in the
diminishing small-town world
from the 1880s to the 1920s

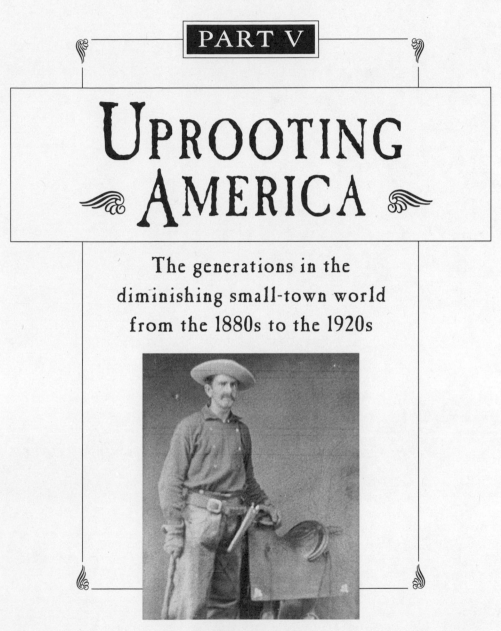

Fred Taintor as a cowboy
in Kansas about 1880.

CHAPTER 18

GROWING AWAY

"I hope you will excuse mistakes for you are not here to correct them...."[1]

The four sons of Henry and Delia Taintor came of age in the 1860s and 1870s. Mary, who was born just before the Civil War began, grew up as the adored pet of brothers who were shaped by those years. Her mature life would begin in the 1880s, some part of a generation behind her siblings.

None of the young Taintor men chose to make his livelihood in Hampton. Perhaps this predilection for other places began because, after the local schools had taught them reading, writing, and arithmetic, the boys were all sent away from their small town for further education. They went to school for a while in neighboring Brooklyn, Connecticut, then to Woodstock, Connecticut; Easthampton, Massachusetts; and Monson, Massachusetts.

Henry and George

Henry E. was, even before he went off to Yale and to war, the scholar, the responsible son, the dutiful eldest. In 1861, when he and George were at Monson Academy in Massachusetts, he wrote revealingly of their relationship: "George is doing nicely this term. He seems to feel that he must improve his time and advance himself as much as possible. He is much more sober than I expected before I came from home and seems willing to do what is best and to give up anything which I tell him I think is not just the thing so that we have not had the least sign of a quarrel and hope that we may not have for the entire term." As Henry explained, the boys studied very different subjects in school. Henry, as we know, was preparing for

Yale, studying Latin and Greek. George, on the other hand, was preparing for a mercantile career. He studied some Latin, but concentrated on subjects like arithmetic and bookkeeping.[2]

In 1863 seventeen-year-old George was finished with the academy and was teaching school. He was not happy. He wrote his family from his school house that he would "never . . . teach school again if I can get a decent living without."[3] He lasted only until the beginning of March, and then found a position in a store in Hartford. George seems never to have thought of working in Hampton, of making his home anywhere but the city. For the next thirteen years he worked for Collins Brothers, later Collins & Fenn, dry goods merchants in Hartford.

George's handwriting was always beautiful, perfect for a clerk in those pre-typewriter days. He boasted of other skills as well, mentioning to his parents in a letter, "I have just been called off to multiply with the Book-keeper which I have been doing for the last half or ¾ of an Hour. By the way–He gave me quite a compliment the other day 'viz.' That I could multiply quicker and more accurate than any new boy who has ever been here since he came which was nine years ago."[4] Grammar was never George's long suit, but with charm like his, perhaps it was not necessary.

He always loved the advantages of city life, going to lectures "at the Institute," some of which he found "not quite as interesting as I had anticipated," but others were "quite a treat."[5] He heard Henry Ward Beecher, George S. Hilliard, John B. Gough, and others. The musical son of a musical father, he sang in glee clubs whenever he could. His social life was a round of calls, and he relished his evenings out.

After a year on the job George's pay jumped to two hundred dollars a year. His father had been sending him money to eke out the earlier pay, but he anticipated then that on his new pay he would be pretty much on his own. His letters did not include particular accountings to his father of his expenditures.

When Henry E. had left Yale to soldier in the war, his parents had worried that his education and hopes for a profession were over. After the war, he found work in a store in Boston. So the next Taintor to launch a career never considered beginning in Hampton either. Opportunity lay in cities–but only opportunity, not a living wage. Henry agonized over his expenditure of every penny to his father, who subsidized his start:

> I have tried this month but my cash acc't I find does not come under $50.00 which is not as well as last month. I subjoin it so you will see "where the money goes" though I know you do not think that I mean to be extravigant.

Board & Room Rent	28.00
Boots	5.65
Concert (with Susie)	1.50
Theatre (alone)	.50
Fare (from Home)	3.25
H. Cars	.78
Dinner (at Danielsonville)	.50
Cocoaine	1.00
Blacking & Brush	.75
Washing	1.00
Indelible Inc	.35
Exhibition (at home)	.25
Shaving &c	.40
Boat down the harbor (Fast-day)	.40
Horse Hire (at Buttons)	.50
" (at Winchester)	2.00
Books Papers &c	3.80
Fare (to Winchester & back)	.45
Cigars	.50
Tobacco	1.82
Maple Sugar, Candy & Pop-corn	.35
	$53.75

The "books & paper" item includes a subscription to the "Boston journal" in company with a friend and one volume of poems which I had particular reason for buying. The other items all speak for themselves and I think only the last three can be called "foolish" and you know I will not admit *that*.

In looking it over I find some things that I did not *positively need* but felt that I could afford it. These are as follows and if you see others please write me.

Theatre (alone). Boat. Horse Hire. Books. Fare & Tobacco &c. With these exceptions I could not have spent much less than I have.

Of course under the circumstances I have to ask for another remittance and am going to "try again" this month to live on less.[6]

Again, there is that interestingly spelled "cocoaine," which he characterizes as something he "positively needs." Lest we jump to a modern conclusion that he was an addict, however, it must be pointed out that the subject faded utterly from his correspondence after this period, and no one even hinted in any way in his later life that he ever had a problem with addiction. They did hint at such things in other cases, so the absence of evidence points to Henry's having given up usage of cocaine.

By August 1866, Henry left his Boston job. Although still on the family payroll it was now in another capacity. His father had been elected state treasurer of Connecticut, and Henry E. went to Hartford to be his assistant. And the necessary requisite for a professional career was now in his possession, as he proudly wrote his parents: "You may have seen by the papers that I have *got my degree as* BA and in a letter recd from Pres Woolsey he says I can receive my diploma on application to the College Treasurer."[7] Yale awarded degrees to the men who had left college to fight in the Civil War. Now Henry could study law, which he proceeded to do by an apprenticeship in Hartford.

He was sanguine about his new life in the city: "I am going to like very well I think in Hartford. The work with father is almost nothing, and the hardest duty I have is breaking into studious habits after having been so long free from them." He sent for his uniform so he could have "a large picture taken 'en militaire.'" He also did ask for his "bottle of cocoaine" in the same letter, and gave the only indication in his whole correspondence that there were ever harsh words in the family: "I ask pardon for the way I spoke the night before I left but can only say that I felt tired and cross anyway and did not stop to think."[8]

Henry E. had found a girl, and although she was from a Hampton family, she, too, did not live in town. Her parents had moved to Amsterdam, New York. Perhaps the son had words with his parents on that subject. But Jane G. Bennett (Jennie) was always a favorite with the Taintors. She

Henry E. Taintor and his wife, Jennie.

must have been visiting in Hampton when Henry saw her that summer of 1866 on a visit home.

George, too, had found a girl, named Emily Davis. She lived in Hartford. The first time her name came up in one of his letters, he justified the friendship to his mother: "I can assure you Mother Emily Davis is a very different girl from what you took her to be . . . & in fact very different from what I supposed her to be. She is a real *good* girl which is a *great deal* in my estimation & although she is very lively I never knew her to do the first thing which was inconsistent with her professions as a Christian. She is very smart & bright & the most sensible young lady I have ever met."

He couched this in a letter in which he told how he was reading the Bible with Emily: "In regard to reading one chapter from the New Testament each day commencing with Mathew I would say that I commenced on the 27 Oct. with Miss Emily D. at the 1st Chapter of John, to read one chapter each day until she returned. which I have kept up thus far." Delia had suggested that she and her son read the Bible together, but George replied, "I don't suppose it would injure me to read two Chapters each day but ofttimes in the morning when I happen to sleep rather late my time is somewhat limited, and I think it will do me more good to read one chapter carefully than to try & read two & have to hurry over it. I thank you kindly for the invitation & would gladly accept it if I was not already reading with Emily."[9]

Delia and Henry had a lot to get used to in this next stage of their elder sons' lives. Whether the parents liked it or not, Henry E. and George had found their future wives. Delia and Henry G. wisely decided to like it. With Jennie that appears to have been easy; perhaps it was less so with Emily. One of the strange aspects of charming young men like George is their innocence in the face of women with a purpose, and Emily Davis's purpose seems to have been to marry George E. Taintor. Once she married him, it is not clear that she thought her purposes should include either his further happiness or her own.

Willie and Freddie

The third Taintor son to leave the nest was Willie. When he was twelve he went to Brooklyn to school. When he was fifteen, in 1866, he went to Hartford High School, studying Latin, philosophy, and geometry. He boarded with his two older brothers. Later he studied Greek, as Henry had, but he does not seem to have been scholar enough to have chosen a professional career, or to have gone to college. Perhaps Henry and Delia did not think him sufficiently able.

As we read the Taintor correspondence we wondered when it happened that Willie fell through the family cracks. He was the middle child of

Young Willie Taintor.

the Taintor five, and he was the neglected one, especially after the long-awaited girl, Mary, was born in 1860. His corresponding relatives rarely asked about him after that, even when they carefully inquired for all the rest.

In the fall before Mary's birth the older boys were away at school, and Freddie was not quite five years old. Willie was nine. He was sent to Windsor for several months. His aunt Ellen wrote to Delia praising him:

I have as usual a very good account to give of Willie, he is very well and has behaved beautifully about not going home to the fair–He really wanted to be there very much indeed, and felt at first as if he must go. The Hartford County Fair is given up this year, on account of the apprehensions in regard to the Cattle disease and we could not offer him that as an equivalent. When I did not get a letter from you Saturday, he concluded he could not get home in time, and that he had better make the best of it, and has given it all up without one single tear–He thinks he should like very much to go home, but says he is willing to stay a week or two longer if we all think it is best, and seems perfectly happy about it. I told him I should tell you just what a good boy he had been. When you wish him to come home if you or his father will write whether he shall go so as to meet the stage, or whether one of the boys will meet him at Willimantic I think he would be much pleased and better satisfied.[10]

He sounds already like a brave and lonely little boy.

Delia's letters that fall of 1860 to her middle child are cautionary and a bit surprising. She wrote to Willie when she was eight months pregnant, printing carefully so he would be able to read it himself:

> We are all very happy to know you are a good boy & not making trouble. I hope you will be able to do something for the kind friends who are doing so much for you.
>
> We are all very well & often speak of you. I think Freddy will have a good hearty snuggle for you when you come home. He thinks he should like to go & live at Uncle Freddy's too. Oscar Holt is quite sick with typhoid fever. All the other neighbors are as well as usual. Frank Malbone struck John Hall [both were African-American] Saturday with an axe, cutting a bad gash in his head, & yesterday Frank run away, fearing he should be taken up.
>
> Freddy says give my love to Willie, & to his I will add that of all the rest of the family, & hope there will soon be a letter from Willie to his
>
> affectionate Mother[11]

Delia was an "affectionate Mother" to all her children. But Willie's share of the family's affections seems to have become smaller than the shares of his siblings after his little sister was born.

By 1869 Willie, then eighteen, was living and working in Williamsburg, New York, just across the East River from the big city. He, too, had not gone back to Hampton after he finished school. That summer the family was going to Watch Hill, Rhode Island, on a vacation, but Willie was not going with them. He wrote that he "did not feel bad about Father's descision about my trip as I thought very likely he would think it best for me not to go and I had not got my heart set upon it."[12] Much of his correspondence sounds like he was responding to criticism from his parents. He constantly felt it necessary to justify himself: "About my doing well my position in the store speaks for itself without my saying anything about it. I think that I have begun well and I intend to continue doing so."[13]

Willie drank. It is impossible to know, more than one hundred years later, whether he drank to excess in his early days in New York. But if the definition of an alcoholic is someone who cannot give up alcohol, perhaps Willie Taintor was an alcoholic. His family certainly worried about his drinking. The first hint of it we have is in a letter he wrote to his mother when he was not yet twenty. "You wrote to know where I was last

Sunday. in the morning I went to St John's Church with a friend and in the afternoon as it snowed quite hard I sat in his room and read a temperance tale and after tea I came to my room and smoked and read untill about nine oclock when I retired and slept soundly untill morning." His mother pressed him to take "the temperance pledge," but he wrote, "I cannot promise not to touch a drop but if I do not do that I have no desire to abuse it."[14]

Delia was concerned enough to write to relatives in New York, urging them to ask Willie to visit. They were not eager the way they always were to see Henry E. and George, but did their duty. Delia also kept suggesting church activities and organizations to her son, and Willie dutifully assured her that "The papers you sent me I read with a great deal of pleasure and I have given my name to one of the members of the Y.M.C.A and he is to propose me the next meeting and I hope to spend many pleasant & profitable hours there."[15]

He was rooming with young Arthur Bulkley, perhaps a relative. Apparently Delia thought Arthur was a bad influence. Willie wrote, "I *know* you have an *entirely* wrong opinion of him and should like very much to bring him home with me for a day or two in the summer so you could see him. We have lived together so long that we know every kink of each other and to separate would be like brothers parting as I think almost as much of him as of a brother." His comments are interesting from a young man who had three brothers–from whom he had separated. It seems to imply that he had little feeling of closeness to his own brothers. In this case he also had Arthur Bulkley write to Delia, who told her, "I too have a *dear Mother* that would not close her eyes in sleep this night, if she knew that there was one person in this world that thought her Son not a fit companion for any young man."[16] As Willie grew older and his companions changed, his drinking remained a problem.

His parents continued to ignore him in important ways. When he met his future wife and fell in love, they did not pay attention. Perhaps they did not like Elizabeth Miller, his intended, who was a woman from a background very different from their own–she was a city woman, not well-educated, and she had been earning her own living (we do not know at what) when she met Willie. Willie brought home his news about her one summer, and yet he wrote his parents in some discouragement in January of the following winter, "You speak of my engagement being announced, and think it may be so from my letter to Father. I was engaged when I was home in the Summer and thought you all knew it."[17] They never seemed to know what was important in his life.

His brother Freddie's progress away from Hampton, which would be the farthest, began last, because he was the youngest boy. When he was a small child he was always referred to by Delia's sister Ellen and others—in contrast to Willie—as "dear little Freddy." When Delia went west to Indiana in the spring of 1860, Ellen had advised her, "I think you will have more care and less anxiety about him if he is with you." She thought "the fatigue and restraint" of the train trip "would be the greatest trouble with him. I am sure he will be a most welcome visitor wherever you stop." She wrote that she would "be delighted to have the dear little fellow come and stay with me" if Delia decided to leave him behind.[18] Willie, who was older than Freddie, was sent to Windsor, while Freddie accompanied his parents on their trip.

When Freddie was not quite eleven, he stayed behind in Hampton with the Taintors' friends the Buttons while Delia was in Windsor. He wrote his mother, "I am very well and you can stay as long as you want to," and Mrs. Button wrote that "Freddie seems very happy and contented."[19] The next summer Delia and Henry went to Boston to visit, leaving him behind again. They kept his letter to his mother, written on a hot June afternoon:

> My dear Mother I am writing this letter in the schoolhouse. I am all alone. The teacher sayes send my love and tell your mother that you have been a very good boy. I have got up 2 today. This morning I made a dam and put some pollywogs in to it. I have lamed my right foot and hurt my left one. My lessons to-day have been as follows arithmetic 20 geography 20. How are you and father and cousin Susy and cousin henry. I have been at the head 7 times. The folkes are all well. Pleas write when yous shal come home so that I shal know when to expect you. I am so sweaty I can not write any more. Please excuse mistakes. From your little boy Freddie.[20]

One year later, at Woodstock Academy, he still signed himself "Freddie" but no longer as a "little boy." By the time he went to Hartford to school in 1870 he could stay with his married brother Henry E. But when he wrote home he was yearning for country life. It was not a sentiment any of his brothers ever expressed. As he grew up more, Freddie became Fred to all his family and began to be different from them all.

In his late teens he took time off from school because of his health. We do not know how much time, nor is it clear what his problem was. He went briefly to an academy in Massachusetts when he was eighteen, and finally to the new Sheffield Scientific School of Yale College in the fall of 1874. It was ten years after Henry E. had left Yale, and Fred saw the new form of Freshman Rush as a chance for fun:

. . . I passed through the "rush" safely, with the loss of my coat only. As you perhaps do not know what a "rush" is and it might interest you to know I will try and tell you a little about it. We (the Freshmen) all met at the "Grammar School Lot" at 2 oclock, from there we proceeded in a procession to the "Grange St Lot" where the "rush" was to take place. The Juniors reached the lot about half an hour after us, and then we had a series of games of foot ball in which we '77 were victorious.

Next we formed for the "rush" which was as follows. First five or six of the largest men lock arms and behind these are placed another row with arms locked, and clasped around those in front of them, behind these was another line arranged in the same manner, and so on until all the members of the class were arranged. The Juniors were arranged the same as we were. We slowly advance towards each other, the front ranks come together breast to breast and those behind push and crowd as hard as they are able. Which ever side gives way first is beaten. We won the first rush and the Juniors the second.

No one seemed to want to rush any more so we formed a ring and had some wrestling, in which we were decidedly the victors. When this was finished we started for home and there the *fun* commenced. The struggle was to see who should have the walk. First a Junior would seize a Freshman and yank him into the street or visa versa and

Fred Taintor at Yale, about 1877.

then they would clinch and see who could throw. I had five wrestles comeing home. I threw my man three times and twice my man floored me. Such a looking crowd you never saw, hatless, coatless and many shirtless. So ended the "rush" which was pronounced a success. . . ."[21]

Despite his obvious pleasure in (and strength for) these hijinks, Fred Taintor never completed his course of study at Yale. His family referred over the years to his "health" as the reason he left college; his parents seemed to feel his interest in farming was also a cause.

He went back to Hampton to do farm work. Was he trying to follow a family pattern? Although his father had started life farming, by the time Fred returned home in the mid-1870s, Henry was an investor and banker. Fred's brothers were "city men." But he raised chickens and sold eggs, he split wood, carted hay, and trimmed trees (for which his father paid him).[22] Henry and Delia must have felt that the family continuity in the next generation in town was safely in Fred's hands—until 1878, when at the age of twenty-two he decided to go west.

After a few gasps, the extended family tried to help. His aunt Libby, Frederick Ellsworth's wife, "received papers from her nephew Mr. Frederick Halsey who is in Atchison Kansas" which contained "glowing accounts of the Kansas and Nebraska lands—Growth and improvements have been very rapid, and Mr. Halsey, who is a practical business man, seems to consider that country well adapted to repay the wise farmer. Stock-raising is a prominent industry there." Whatever Fred decided to do, his aunt Libby wanted to see him, but "*particularly* if he has *serious* thoughts of going West. She says again—she wouldn't dare to take the responsibility of *advising* him *at all,* but simply feels that she would like to throw all the light on his way she can, and so wishes him to have the benefit of what she has heard and read."[23]

Fred set out to go west visiting family—another pattern from the past, when so many had traveled with kin into the unknown. Seventeen-year-old Mary summed up her family's feeling when she wrote, "It is dreadful to think Fred is going away and I dont like to think of it but I suppose it is all for the best."[24] She reported to her mother about the night Fred actually left Hartford that the train had departed at 1:20 A.M., "and we all sat around talking until twelve o'clock." Fred's brother "Henry went down to the depot with him and they *carried* his trunk as it was impossible to get an expressman at that time and he did not pack his trunk until evening."[25]

Fred's journey west took him first to Fort Wayne, Indiana, where his cousin Wolcott Ellsworth was in business, then to Lafayette, Indiana, where his cousin Sophia Ellsworth Reynolds and her husband Jimmy welcomed him. Sophie wrote to a worrying Delia that the "very pleasant visit" had seemed too short to her. She "wanted him to see more of Indiana & its resources." Fred visited with her and her family–Delia's brother Samuel– over one weekend and then "went into the country to see a stock man whom Father knew, & who could tell him much about the business. Wednesday & Thursday he said he rode on horseback about 20 miles each day, & he came back Wednesday afternoon. He felt that he must reach Kansas City by Tuesday of the following week to meet a man whom he saw in Fort Wayne, & who would introduce him to some one who had just gone out there on a stock farm." Fred "seemed to change his mind a little about going to Texas, as most who know about stock raising here told him Colorado was a much better place, & likely to be a better grazing country for a longer time than either Texas or Kansas."

When Sophie wrote, her father had already heard from Fred, who was in Atchison, Kansas, working for the Fred Halsey of whom Aunt Libby had told him. Sophie thought "that will be a good thing for him so it will give him an opportunity to see western country & men, & their mode of business. He writes that he likes it 'first-rate as far as he's got.'" Her opinion was that "Fred is a fine frank, manly fellow. He has a mind & will of his own is not afraid of work & does not seem to be extravagant. I think he will succeed. I am sorry he could not see something in Indiana that looked attractive. He thinks it an unhealthy state, & perhaps he is right."[26]

The railroads of the modern world had taken Fred away from his native town not to Hartford or Boston or New York, but out west to Kansas. At the end of April, 1878, he was there, working in his aunt Libby's relative's office. He stayed awhile, but it was too much like the cities he had wanted to avoid. He settled on a ranch at a place in the Oklahoma panhandle that became known as Taintor Creek. As far as the letters indicate, he never had "health" problems again.

Mary Grows Up

Mary Ellen, the child who grew up into Delia and Henry Taintor's old age, was a little girl during the Civil War. Born in late 1860, she lived her growing-up conscious life in a world already revolutionized by the changes the war had wrought. The year she was five, after the war ended, was the year her two eldest brothers, Henry E. and George, fell in love with the women they would marry. The chasm of a generation yawned between her world and theirs.

We do not know much about Mary's babyhood. When she was only four months old, in the winter of 1861, her brothers were sick with scarlet fever, and then her mother also fell sick, so sick that her grandmother wrote from Windsor with concern: "Have you been obliged to take little Mary from the breast dear little precious one?"[27] We do not know the answer to that question, but Mary did survive, and many children who had to be weaned suddenly in like circumstances died unless a wet nurse was quickly found.

Mary was an immediate family favorite. Her aunt Abby wrote from Washington, "From sister Ellen's account of her I think she gives entire satisfaction to all family friends as well as to her Father, Mother & brothers."[28] Her Ellsworth grandmother knitted her stockings, and so did her aunt Ellen. Her brother Henry E. wrote from school of another baby he had seen that "though it is very pretty I do not think she is quite equal to little Mary, (the darling how I wish I might see her), she is very fat and her cheeks hang down on each side they are so full."[29] Mary's little sayings–she called Windsor "Winny" and one day "thought she saw Aunt Ellen 'down to tore in a wanggry'" [down to store in a wagon]–were passed from aunt to aunt.[30]

The little girl learned to do her chores early. The day her brother left home to go to war, when she was only three years old, she was already churning butter. But Mary not only did chores. Later–we do not know exactly when–she began school in Hampton. And before she was nine years old she was taking music lessons.[31] She went to Elmwood with her mother, and put a red ribbon around the kitten's neck. Ellen wrote Delia, "Please tell Mary that Kitt still wears her red velvet neck ribbon–I saw her try to wash it off the other day, but it was fastened too tight. The poetry she copied so nicely for Grandma is very pretty indeed She thanks her very much indeed for doing it–It was a sweet thought from her dear little heart."[32] (We wonder how her grandmother read it–Mary's handwriting was never very neat.)

By the time she was ten, however, her handwriting was good enough for her to send her mother a letter. Delia was visiting in Hartford and Mary wrote from Hampton:

Dear Mother.
    I now take my pen to answer your letter. I was very glad to receive it. Last night I went over to Johnnie Clevelands to spend the evening. I staid till half after eight I had a very pleasant time. Lillie Varian was going up to his house (her Mother had promised her she might) and while I had come home to ask Father if I might go her Father came out and told her that she could not come up and then she cried like everything. I took tea at the Govornors yesterday and so did Johnnie. I got a new arithmetic to day and Miss Lydia covered it for me with cloth. she sent her best love to you. My blue shoes that I had blacked look

very nicely indeed. I get along very nicely in school. In arithmetic we have got way over most to Decimal Fractions the examples are pretty hard. I have been playing with my paper dolls this morning and have had a very pleasant time. I have been practicing a little this morning. I hope you will excuse mistakes for you are not here to correct them. Give my love to George and Emily and to Henry and Jennie and Harlie when you see them and accept a large share for yourself I remain your aff daughter.

Mary E Taintor.

P S Please write to me again if you stay long enough. Mary.[33]

All her life Mary kept her friends in Hampton. Her letter shows that she was not as anxious a child as Willie had been. And she blacked her shoes and played with paper dolls; she did not put polliwogs in a pool or sweat like Freddie.

Delia and Henry picked Miss Williams' School in Windsor for Mary, and she went away to school by the time she was twelve. Fred was in school at Hartford by that time, so for the first time in the twenty-eight years since Henry E. was born, Delia and Henry G. were home without any children in the house in Hampton. They had never been home there alone before; Henry's mother, Judith, had been there when they married, and she had lived until 1849. Now came the years when Delia's correspondence nearly doubled, and when Henry's business concerns occupied more and more of his attention.

They heard a lot from their daughter; Mary's experiences with clothes and money—retailed in a constant flow of letters—were very different from those of her brothers. When Henry E. started at Yale, he had sent home to his mother for the making of most of his clothes. Mary had dressmakers in Hartford to make her clothes from the time she was a schoolgirl. And when they took their time about getting her clothes ready she announced herself "dreadfully provoked."[34]

All four boys had accounted strictly for their spending money. Mary just asked, and her accounting was sketchy at best. In 1874 she wrote from school, "will you please send me some money. I owe Miss Williams a dollar and twenty cents ($1.20) for something she bought for me the first of the term, and I have only a dollar and thirty cents ($1.30) to my name."[35] Henry or George in such circumstances would have paid the $1.20 and then thought long and hard about asking for more with ten cents still in hand. The subject was not fraught with anxiety for Mary.

Later that year she asked whether Miss Williams had sent her school bill yet. "If she has I guess she would be glad of the pay as soon as she could get it for she told the day scholars that she was disappointed about some money in August and she should be glad if they could pay their bills soon if it did not inconvenience their parents."[36] Mary also asked without compunction for the things that money could buy: "I should like one of these blue plaid [wrappers] (like Emily had when she was on her wedding trip.) I should like black velvet cuffs and collar on it. When can you get it?"[37]

Later, when she was living with her brother and his wife in Hartford, she was miffed that Henry E.'s attitude about money was not like her own. She had grown a little more careful, she wrote her parents, and kept "a cash account so that you can see what I spend my money for." But she reported, "I asked Henry for some money this afternoon to get some writing paper as I had not any to write on & he said he didn't know about beginning to do that. I told him you probably forgot to send it and he laughed."[38] Nearly every letter Mary wrote asked for money. Perhaps Delia and Henry were old-fashioned in the amounts they handed out, but it is certainly always the case that when she asked, they sent. She seems never to have lacked for luxuries.

The young ladies' seminary which Mary attended in Windsor was less and less to her taste. She liked her friends, but she wrote home in July 1874:

> . . . I *hope* [this letter] . . . will be the last I shall ever write you from *this* school. There are plenty of other schools that are just as good as this that are not as expensive and I should like to go to some school where I could lern a *little* politeness, and that Misses W–and F–have not. Do you think you should like to have me take my breastpin off and pick my teeth with it before a good many people. Well! *that* is what Miss Francis does and if you want me to learn such manners as those, why, just send me here to this school a little longer, and I think I shall have the art *perfect.*
> Lizzie Browne has written nearly the same thing to her Mama as I have to you and *every* girl in the house agrees with us. . . .[39]

Despite her protests, Mary returned to Miss Williams' School the next term. For the time being she even found compensations. For instance she liked "Mollie Starkey for a room-mate very well" because "She has got a great box of toffies and three tumblers of coffee jelly and we have feasts."[40]

However, when she went to Hartford High School the next spring, she was much happier. She studied arithmetic, botany, and French, and often signed her letters, "Your petite fille." Later that year she added algebra and history. Over the years, history was her best subject. She "hated" geometry, liked philosophy "*very much.*"

Mary roomed with a girl named Bessie in her boardinghouse, and had new city friends and a life of excitement. She also began to have a social life based on visits extending at least over weekends. She wrote her parents of one such visit she made to her friend Mamie Hatch in Meriden:

> . . . A little while after tea Jessie Lindsley (one of Mamie's friends) came around to have us go down street with her so we went. Sunday morning we went to the 1st Cong. Church and then to Sunday School. We were going to another Cong. Church in the afternoon where Lizzie Hatch plays the organ but did not get through dinner in time so we stayed at home and read and talked. We went to church in the evening. Oh! I have skipped over Saturday so I guess I will go back. Saturday morning Carrie & Mamie Hatch and myself went over to the Brittania works and went all through the Show Rooms. There are some elegant things there. Enjoyed myself very much. In the afternoon we went to a little dancing sociable. Had a splendid time. Mamie & I made an engagement to go skating in the evening with Emmet Williams and Charlie Dodd (two Meriden boys) but it commenced to snow about six o'clock so it spoiled the skating.[41]

Her descriptions of her social encounters show her a pert little miss. Less than a month after her Meriden trip she paid a visit to the young ladies' seminary she had attended in Windsor. She went "sleighing with Charlie Marvin," a friend of her brother Fred's and "We went to the Seminary to see Emma Pratt. I also saw Miss Williams, Bertha, Sadie Hakes, Belle Jex and Lou Brownback. Miss Williams was just as sweet as honey to me because I was to her. Of course I had to be. Miss Frances did not come in to see me at all. She was right in the sitting room & I stood in the hall talking fully five minutes. Emma told her I was there but she didn't come to see me. I knew she was there because I heard her speak to someone and I said to Miss W. so that Miss F. could hear me, 'Is Miss Frances well?' Miss W. said 'Yes, very well.' I then said 'Please give my love to her and all the rest that I know.'"[42]

Another day Mary went boating on the Connecticut. She reported to her mother that "Mr. Hungerford asked me to go rowing and ask some one else to go. I asked May Loomis. We went down at two o'clock and got home about quarter of six. I guess it was about half past two before we got out on the water and about five when we got off." She wrote that they went "away down to Wethersfield Cove (four miles) and coming home a tug came along that was towing two schooners and the last schooner threw us a line and towed us up home. It was quite a help for the wind was blowing some and it would have been quite a hard row up to Hartford."[43]

She continued to see the young men she met in her high school years, and in the spring of 1877 wrote that she was going to the high school "Reception" with Charlie Dodd. "Mamie Hatch is going to stay up with me and going with Emmet Williams. E. W. and C. Dodd—are great friends so that makes it very nice." Mary was not quite seventeen that spring.

In Hartford Mary had a glimpse of the larger world of politics. She wrote in the fall of 1876 that she "went to a political meeting" at which "Mr. H. C. Robinson, Gen. Hawley and Mr. Walker spoke. I had never seen Hawley before and I think he is splendid." The scene was somewhat foreign to her: "It was an audience composed almost entirely of men and boys except in a part of the gallery there were some ladies. A great many of the men had their hats on and before the speakers commenced there were a great many news-papers to be seen which looked very funny."[44]

Her boardinghouse and the churches also supplied a political forum, and she heard and held opinions about that year's long-undecided contest for the Presidency between Samuel Tilden, Democrat of New York, and Rutherford B. Hayes, Republican of Ohio. "I do hope the Republicans will get it. One day when we were talking politics at the table Mr. Catlin said he heard that Mr Gage (the minister at Pearl St. church) prayed last Sunday or Sunday before I guess it was, that the Republicans might be successful in this campaign."[45] Being a woman, and therefore not a voter, she would have no say in elections until she was sixty years old and could finally vote in 1920. Her aunt Abby's granddaughter, as a matter of fact, was an important organizer and lecturer for the passage of the woman suffrage amendment to the Constitution that made that vote possible.

Mary channeled more and more of her energies into religious interests which provided "fit activities" for young women of her age and station. She went to church every Sunday morning unless she was sick, except for one morning when she "had quite a funny time":

I was all ready for church, had my gloves on and all and started to go in to Henry's as I always do to walk to church with them. I usually go the back way so as to save their coming to the door. When I got down in the kitchen I found Statia [the maid] was just going out to church & Maggie [Henry and Jennie's maid] was in here to go with her. I asked Maggie if I could get in their back door and she said Yes so Statia let me out this door & locked it after me & went right off to church. I started to go into Aunties [her aunt Ellen Ellsworth Strong, who was at that time living in one of the three houses involved in Mary's morning search] but found that Bridget [Aunt Ellen's maid] had gone up stairs and locked the door so I hurried right back here, but I was too late. Statia had gone. I pounded & rapped & screamed. I

Mary Ellen Taintor as a young woman.

knew Mr. & Mrs. Williams were up in the parlor and I thought they would hear me. I got up on a bord in the back yard and took a stick and tried to reach the parlor windows to rap on them but I couldn't quite reach the glass but I pounded on the side of the house & screamed Mrs. Williams & Lou & Hal but could not make any one hear. I kept running from house to house to see if perhaps Bridget hadn't come down. After a long time Mr. Bennett [Jennie's father] happened to come down to get some water and he let me in. Of course by that time they had all gone to church as it was just about time to start when I first tried to get in there. . . .[46]

In the afternoons on Sundays Mary went to Sunday school. Soon there was a sewing society on Wednesdays and Saturdays that she and her friends could join, and she enjoyed the social occasions it provided; she also sewed for the poor. But when Mary decided to join a church, she wanted to go home to Hampton to do so. She wrote Delia in 1877 that she wanted "to unite with the church this summer." She requested her mother to "see if Hattie Utley and Mary Rawson are expecting to, too." She supposed that the church would not have the "next communion until August and so I can be examined before my name is read in church as when I was home you said it might have to be read before I came home but I should much rather be examined first. I *shall* be, and *am* dreadfully afraid I cannot answer the committees questions and what would I do then, but I shall pray that right words may be put into my mouth." Even though it was not the much more Puritan church of Samuel Moseley's ministry one hundred years before, the Hampton congregation still asked formidable questions of those who wished to join. Mary insisted that she wished "to unite with the church even if no one else does."[47] That summer she did pass the gauntlet of questions posed by the committee, and the whole family learned of her joining the church. Her cousin Emma sent her "tenderest love, and most hearty congratulations,"[48] as did many other happy Ellsworths and Taintors.

Mary Taintor graduated from high school in Hartford in 1879. By that time she had grown used to city life, so that her mother's complaint, "You only give us your vacations,"[49] had a ring of truth. Hampton would see her every summer from then on, but rarely at any other season.

Seeing the Past and the Future

Henry G. and Delia Taintor made an excursion with their family to the United States Centennial Exhibition in Philadelphia in 1876. The Taintors were not alone. Fully one-fourth of the whole population of the country—more than ten million people—went to Philadelphia. And it was a watershed time; looking backward at the American past was the height of fashion. Centennial Reproduction furniture—copies of the fashions of early republican forebears—was all the rage. Architects built Colonial and Federal Reproduction houses in cities and suburbs. Families collected their histories and proudly pointed to illustrious ancestors. And at the top of this hill of time there were optimistic visions, despite the economic depression in which the country was foundering in 1876. The horizons, according to the country's enthusiasts that year, were still the limitless American dream. The dreamers did not look at the growing slums and squalor of the cities or see the emaciated faces of the children working in mines or at machines.

The Centennial Exhibition opened on May 10, 1876, in Fairmont Park across the Schuykill River from downtown Philadelphia. The millions of visitors to it saw sights on scales nearly impossible to imagine from the small towns in which most of them lived. The iron and glass Main Building covered twenty acres. The exhibit hall inside was 1,880 feet—about six football fields—long. There were 250 other buildings. Emperor Dom Pedro II of Brazil and the Empress Theresa, the first reigning monarchs ever to visit the United States, joined President Ulysses S. Grant and Mrs. Grant for the opening ceremonies. Bands played a Centennial inauguration march by Richard Wagner. A choral group sang the "Centennial Hymn," by John

Greenleaf Whittier, and a Centennial cantata by Sidney Lanier. Eight hundred singers blared forth the "Hallelujah Chorus" at the very moment when the President ceased speaking, as a chime of thirteen large bells sounded and the artillery fired a 100-gun salute. Then the President and the Emperor marched at the head of a parade to Machinery Hall where they started the huge single-cylinder steam engine, designed by George H. Corliss of Providence, Rhode Island, that drove all the machinery in the hall and produced the electricity that illuminated the whole exhibition.[50]

No small town could compete with such an extravaganza; only one of the nation's burgeoning cities could offer a Centennial. The exhibition demonstrated to Americans and the rest of the world that the United States was by then the leading industrial nation on earth. The 31,000 exhibits gave promise of the country's technological power and unlimited production for the glorious future.

Henry and Delia went to see the wonders a month after the opening. They took Henry E. and George and Fred and Mary, and their niece Kate Strong. They may have also taken Henry E.'s wife, Jennie, and son, Harlie, and George's wife, Emily, and daughter Lucy; there is no evidence. And their son Willie's name does not crop up in any receipts. They went down to Philadelphia on the train in sleeping cars. They stayed at the Grand Villa Hotel, took an excursion boat on the Schuykill, went to the zoo, and of course they went to the exhibition. Admission was fifty cents for a day.[51]

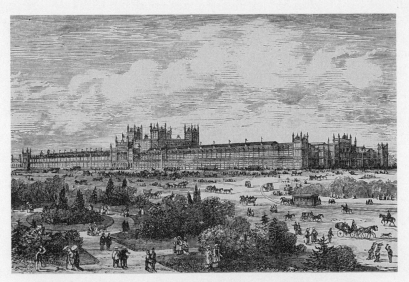

The main building of the Centennial Exhibition in Philadelphia, 1876.

The Centennial took place at a time of economic depression and political turmoil. On June 25, 1876, George Armstrong Custer got himself and 272 of his officers and men killed "with their boots on" at the Little Big Horn. The presidential election that year–election day was just before the exhibition's closing day of November 10, 1876–produced no clear result. In fact the outcome hung in the balance nearly until Rutherford B. Hayes's inauguration in March 1877. Among those out of work that year was George Taintor. His cousin Wolcott Ellsworth wrote of the bad times, "The financial conditions in the west are far from satisfactory and my own affairs require my constant supervision. I have given up my house and taken lodgings and day board from economical considerations." Frederick and Elizabeth Ellsworth had invited him for Thanksgiving to Elmwood, but Wolcott replied, "if I should make the trip to Connecticut at this time I fear I should go shoeless and ill clad this winter. . . ." He assured his uncle that Republicans in Indiana did not "talk bullets and blood so alarmingly as the democrats do," but he wondered whether "the bitterness" of the election was "eradicating . . . the old confidence in an electoral government."[52]

What Henry and Delia Taintor saw at the Centennial Exhibition and what Wolcott Ellsworth wrote about were part of the same phenomenon. The scale of all of life had changed. The railroads had made it possible for the Taintors–young and old–to be on the move. The country itself had grown larger and the cities that promised work and wealth held burgeoning populations. A small town like shrinking Hampton was separated from a Centennial Exhibition city like Philadelphia by more than a railroad journey. The imaginations of Henry and Delia's children were different from those of their parents. Industry had brought wealth to very few, poverty to very many, and goods on a scale beyond the elder Taintors' dreamings. The Gilded Age glimmered already. The country had moved far from the republican sentiments of Henry and Delia's youth.

Henry was sixty-three years old the year they went to the Centennial; Delia was fifty-eight. By the standards of their times they were old folks looking at the past; their children had moved away.

CHAPTER 19

EMIGRANTS TO THE GILDED AGE

&

"I have so few to love much, you know, here...."[1]

Some of the Taintors bridged the gap of customs and mores between antebellum small-town America and the conspicuous consumption of the Gilded Age at the end of the nineteenth century. Henry and Delia lived until 1889, and Henry ventured an important investment in the 1880s which did not turn out to be gilded. Their niece Susan Taintor, too, lived her adult life very much a participant in the Gilded Age–although she died before Henry and Delia.

We have come to know much of Susie Taintor's story because she wrote letters all her life to her "Dear Aunty" Delia in Hampton. Through her letters and the people she made connections with, the Hampton Taintors were touched by the high life of the late nineteenth century. As we read Susie's correspondence, we realized that the cheerful hopes of this small-town girl did not equip her to survive the modern, urban life she had to lead.

Forced into the Mold

Susie's early correspondence described her family life in West Brookfield in cheerful terms. As she became an adult, she continued to welcome the changes brought by the modern world. One change she wrote about with enthusiasm was the celebration of Christmas by the Bulkeley Taintor family. By the mid-1850s, the family not only celebrated the holiday, but had introduced a Christmas tree. Susie wrote her aunt Delia wishing her a "'Merry merry Christmas' and 'happy New-Year.'–Rather late, say you, for such greetings. I know it, but they were in my heart, and would have utterance–I must tell you, too, of our famous 'Christmas-Tree' which we prepared with the assistance of one or two other families at our house. 'Twas a cosy home gathering, of course, but the 'Tree' really did look beautifully and the happy hearts and faces clustered around it did honor to Santa-Claus' advent with a right good will–I wean we would all fain have claimed him as our patron saint. The presents have been very handsome." Susie's language shows she had been reading the popular novels of Sir Walter Scott. She sparkled on: "Though there is many a hill and dale separating us from those we love on earth, yet there's a golden chain which the breath of time may not dim linking the true-hearted together. . . . I was . . . wishing there were some 'telegraphic-heart-wires'–(don't laugh), to reach the slower and more incomplete medium of pen and paper."[2]

After Caroline had married in 1857, Susie's young life rolled on in West Brookfield, interspersed with visits to Hampton and to her friends elsewhere. But there was always the shadow of Lucy. Susie wrote her aunt, "You know perhaps that Mother or myself are obliged to go to Worcester twice during the year to see to poor Lucy's clothes." But being Susie she combined this obligation with a visit to friends in Worcester. She enjoyed "the exciting pleasures of City life." When she returned to West Brookfield it seemed "quiet to me just now after my Worcester sleigh-rides and parties and dancing–but I usually am happy wherever I am and find the most good possible in all things (or try to)–every day."[3]

Susie had suitors. One of them in the summer of 1860 was Mr. Henry L. Clapp of Boston. He called at the Taintor household and "gave Susie a ride to North Brookfield, stopping afterwards to tea."[4] She met other suitors on visits to Boston and Worcester. Her detailed description of two months in Boston in the winter of 1860–61 gave Delia a vivid picture of the gaiety and intellectual stimulation Susie found:

I visited a former school-mate of mine . . . who commensed house-keeping last-Spring. She has a delightful home on W. Cedar St. quite near Beacon St. and lives in very pleasant style. Her husband is quite wealthy and as they have no children, Mary gives all her time to her friends when they are with her and makes it very pleasant for them. We enjoyed the sleighing many times–for it has been good all Winter long–and tho' I do not skate, yet I enjoyed *seeing others* very much. The Boston ladies are quite famous for their superior grace on skates– and I noted the other day that the Empress Eugenia had complimented a Boston lady, now in Paris, on her skill in skating there. . . .

I have quite a number of friends in Boston who were all very kind to me, so that my invitations came sometimes faster than I knew how to dispose of them. Then Mary and her husband are very fond of company and amusement—so I went almost everywhere with them—to Lectures Concert-Parties and to the Museum and "Athaneum." I heard Geo. W. Curtis of N. York give a very fine lecture on the "Policy of Honesty" at Tremont-Temple. The building was packed full for half an hour before Mr. C. appeared. He is very popular in Boston, and indeed most anywhere as a Lecturer I think.

I heard any quantity of good music while I was in B—which you know is a great treat to me and I remember one night waking to find the Germania-band serenading Gov. Andrew who lived very near us. They played beautifully—and the effect in the stillness and quiet of midnight was delightful. I heard them play "Gentle Annie" (which Uncle Henry likes so much) one night and wished he was there. They gave a new beauty and sweetness to the melody which is one of the prettiest we have so everyone seems to think. . . . I went with a friend to hear Rev. E. E. Hale, who is *quite* popular in Boston also. Perhaps you have noticed that his society are about building an elegant church for him at the South-End. . . .

The Winter at home [in West Brookfield] seemed really short. We have had a very pleasant course of lectures in our Town-Hall this season, which has given more enjoyment to people than anything else. Geo. Sumner, Josiah Quincy Jr. Rev. Mr. Manning and Dr. Holland are some of those who have given the best satisfaction tho *all* were very interesting. The hall is so near us, we find it very conveniant indeed—and in stormy evenings especially it is so nice to have only a few steps to go if there is anything at the hall we are anxious to attend. . . .[5]

The comparison Susie made between Boston and her own small town makes clear that she did not find the differences in culture enormous.

In 1861 Susie fell in love with a young man named Frank Holt and even brought him to meet her relatives in Hampton. Then fifteen-year-old George Taintor, a perennial favorite in his family, came to visit in Brookfield for Thanksgiving. The Thanksgiving feast took the family "an hour and a half to dispose of" and they "had quite a pleasant time over the nuts and wine." They all "took a walk afterward and in the evening played whist." When George left, Susie hated to see her young cousin go and assured her "dear Aunty, that others beside his 'partial' Cousin Susie will miss him sadly." She wrote that he seemed "quite brother-like to me—or as I can imagine one *would* seem—and I do believe I love him as well as if he were." It was, Susie wrote, "a Thanksgiving day to *me*, truly—At least I seemed to feel I had *more to be thankful for* than ever before. I am *very* happy, dear Aunty, both in the Present and anticipations of the Future. Frank is all I could wish—and more dear to me than I can tell you with lips or pen. I believe mine is decidedly a 'love-match'! but fancy those *wear as well* as any, do they not? I always had a horror of any other, tho they are so common in 'our best society.'"

Susie overflowed with love, and told her "dear dear Aunty–I love to be with you, and I know it *does me good*–Do be sure dear Aunty that I love you with all my heart! and that you seem very near to me, since my last visit. I have so few to love *much,* you know, *here*–Carrie is far away, and there is scarcely any one that *knows* me as well as you."[6]

Some time between Thanksgiving and the end of the year something happened which made Susie break off her engagement to the young man she loved so dearly. We have searched and searched through all the family correspondence and have not been able to determine exactly what it was. The following is all Susie was able to say on paper to her aunt Delia:

> . . . The events of the past few weeks have so changed everything connected with my happiness that I could hardly pass through them without feeling the change in myself–and tho' I try always to be cheerful, yet my *heart* is so sad I know I must, sometimes, betray it.
>
> It is now six weeks since I first knew of this trouble, and yet *now* it seems like a dream to me–that I must wake and find it was only a dream. O, dear Aunty, can you realize it?–How can I live on, day after day, without him? I say it every night and think of it when I first wake–but I am trying to learn to–tho for a long time, life seemed too great a burden to endure.–
>
> I suppose Mother wrote you all the particulars of our knowledge of his character. [Unfortunately, Delia did not save the letter to which Susie here refers.] He denied everything so far as "intentional wrong" was concerned to the last. The great trouble was, that what *we* justly considered great evils, *he* thought were nothing–or that they were what many young men in cities are practising constantly, and that they would not harm him.
>
> I know, many young men, whose position should make them care-ful, for the sake of their influence on others, often lead lives which are a daily reproach to them–but it does not make *wrong, right.* I need not say more of this. It is enough to write that with all my best friends, whose judgement in the matter I had reason to respect, I finally con-cluded I must give him up–tho' we felt then (and it is *the bitterness* of the sorrow *now*) that he *might be* all we could wish.
>
> You know how we all loved him–and I think dear Aunt you did, a little, didn't you? I know he was very much attached to all your family often speaking of you all, and especially of little Mary, who he was so fond of. He spoke many times of writing you, too, and when your last letter came, I remember so well his saying, "Now Susie, we must *both* write 'Aunt Delia'–will you?" and that afterward he said, laughing,

that he should tell you to scold me for his not writing before, for I was the "sole cause" of it, etc.

These memories come to me every day suggested by everything I see–or say–or hear–and sometimes I can hardly endure the thought of them. It is harder for me to bear, too, because to myself he was always the same. When the first tidings of it came, it made me sick–I was confined to my room and unable to see him. I saw him but twice afterward, and then, if he said anything in any way unpleasant–he addressed his conversation to Mother–never to me.

I do not say this to defend him at all–but I think he loved me very dearly. I know he did–I remember writing Carrie that I really thought I had enjoyed more during the six months I was engaged to him, than many did, in a life-time. You know his manner–how gentle and winning he was always to those he loved and I just idolized him. I believe I would have done *anything* for him.

I must not write of this–It is not wise or best, but O, my heart *will cry out for him* sometimes!–

Just now, he is bearing a great grief, which it would seem *must* affect him very much. His Mother who was especially near and dear to him died on the 17th of this month, and was buried on the following Sabbath-day. He was telegraphed to, to come home *immediately* and went down on the night-express Thursday. She died Friday, and whether he saw her alive or not I do not know. He has not returned from Lowell as yet.

I don't know but I am writing too much of this. I shall not again, but I could scarcely help it in this letter. It is so hard for me to *unlearn* loving him, when he was my very *life* that I cannot *entirely*, at once–and I *must* speak of him, sometimes. Life seems dreary and *unspeakably* lonely to me, but I am trying, for the sake of others, to rise above it, and do good to every one as far as I can. I have no desire to sadden the lives of my friends by my grief–and I try to be myself when with them–but my *heart aches* sometimes. . . . Every one is so *very* kind to me! I could scarcely have borne this otherwise, it seems to me. . . . Do not think of me as unhappy, dear Aunty. I try not to be–I am only a little more quiet now–outwardly–and I find so much love coming to me from all my friends, that I should be ungrateful if I did not appreciate it.

. . . Do not think, dear Aunty, I care too much for him now. We are every *way separated*. I do not allow myself to dwell upon it often. . . . I felt I must write you *once* about it, and then I had better not say much more of him–I cannot bear to think how happy I *have been,* and it is *best* for me to keep my mind from it, as much as I can.[7]

Try as she clearly did, Susie could not keep her mind from her trouble. The unnamed specter of Lucy's insanity loomed, and her asthma flared, as it did with increasing frequency for the rest of her life. She was "so miserable in health and spirits at home, that it was thought best" to send her away to Worcester for several months in the spring of 1862. She wrote Delia that "I came from associations that made every day hard to endure into such an atmosphere of love and kindness that I could not resist its genial influence, and in trying to express my appreciation of it to others, was *myself* strengthened, and made better. I hope I am more like *myself* now, and shall return home in a few days ready to be to the friends there what I used to, as far as possible." She did not look forward to the summer when "every day will be an anniversary of some past joy." She promised to "try and let no one perceive this from my face or manner for all have been so kind to me and so patient with me, that I *ought* to be cheerful for their sakes. I can never forget how much I owe to my Worcester friends for all their kindness this winter." She had a severe asthma attack in Worcester and hoped the warm weather would keep her "free from it till next Fall."[8]

All the women of Susie's extended family were concerned about her. Delia's sister Ellen wrote, "I am sorry indeed for Susie Taintor, in her delicate health it seems as if her trial would be too much for her."[9] And when Susie went back to West Brookfield, she tried to be "Susie Taintor again," and hoped "to forget the Past enough to enjoy the Summer." She wrote Delia that although "The sorrow through which I have passed is so near that I can not quite put it aside, entirely–and its shadows fall on my life every day," nevertheless she was very happy "to feel I am taking my old place once more."

She reported that she had "not seen Mr. H. *at all,* except at quite a distance, since our engagement was broken. He was all ready to leave town, and probably would have done so, this week–but on Tuesday morning was taken *very* ill with a dreadful *hemorrhage of the lungs.*" Her half-sister Genie had an errand to his landlady's, and the landlady told her "she 'didn't know but Mr. Holt was bleeding to death.'" Susie was terrified, but reported that "He is more comfortable now, and if it does not occur again, he will probably get up from it." She piously hoped this brush with death would "do him good, but I do not know. He is so young–only twenty four!"[10]

She did manage to get through the summer, but the wound seemed still open in November 1862, when news came that Cousin John Taintor had died. Even that death in the family reminded her of her own grief, and she wrote her aunt Delia "I have tasted a more bitter sorrow than that. It is hard to give up our loved ones to death–but it is *harder* to know them *living,* and still *dead* to ones-*self.*" She had seen Delia in the fall and not said much of her own sorrow, "for I could not bear to sadden any of the hours." She said she had "dreaded to lose my self-control which it was sometimes difficult to maintain—for the sight of your familiar faces awoke such pleasant memories of enjoyment with him, in Hampton and in Brookfield, when we were together, that I could scarcely refrain from speaking of it, sometimes—With George, especially, I longed to talk, but I *dared* not—He reminds me more than *any one ever can* of Mr. H—for I used to see them together day after day—riding and walking—and chess-playing—till they are associated very closely in my mind. . . ."[11] By the end of her letter, however, Susie made an effort to turn away from remembering: "So I go on with new courage—and 'take up the burden of Life again'—saying only 'It *might* have been'!—I think Whittier never wrote a sweeter poem than the one from which these two lines are taken." The lines she thought of are from the ending of Whittier's "Maud Muller" (a poem about a dreamed-of marriage that never happened):

> *Then she took up her burden of life again,*
> *Saying only, "It might have been."*

The two final couplets of the poem are:

> *Ah, well! for us all some sweet hope lies*
> *Deeply buried from human eyes;*
> *And, in the hereafter, angels may*
> *Roll the stone from its grave away![12]*

As the winter a year after her tragedy wore on, Susie began to hope for recovery—but she still had to write, at least to her aunt Delia, of her lost love: "Father and Mother, and Genie too, are in good health and spirits—and for me, too, dear Aunty, there comes much quiet home sunshine during these long winter days. Not the *former* brightness (which touched my life with such a radiance that I forgot anything else, in the great joy)—but a more quiet pleasant happiness—more than I thought would come to my life again." She wrote Delia that "Sometimes, at night, I think of what has been—but I find I cannot *bear* it, even now. Of this I never *speak*." She requested that Delia "not allude to it, please." Her social life in Brookfield, while no longer the setting for her own "great joy," was nevertheless busy, with "our singing-schools and Lyceum—and Fairs that have been frequent and pleasant during the season. Our Reading-Circle too was never more prosperous, and we have just purchased a collection of new-books that are very *enjoyable*. Last week we all ventured out in the worst *mud* you can imagine to attend a little party—at Mrs. Carews. It is such a pleasant place to go that all made an effort to be there. We had a right nice time—acted *charades* and had a good time till 11 o'clock."[13]

Susie did not pine away, because that was not her personality, but asthma continued a constant battering of her body, and never completely

Henry L. Clapp, husband of Susie Taintor.

let up after this time. By the next summer she experienced a personal reli-gious conversion that gave her some comfort.[14] From that time on she never mentioned Frank Holt or her engagement to him again. She was no longer the free spirit who had tripped off with her sister to bowling alleys on a July Fourth weekend years before, nor was she the young woman who thought that only a love match could make a marriage. She was learning to conform.

Moving Up in the World

One of Susie's earlier suitors, Henry L. Clapp, proposed to her in the fall of 1864 and she accepted him. After they were engaged, not before, she spent time getting to know Mr. Clapp better. She and her half-sister Genie went to Boston in October, where "Henry was with us *considerably* you can imagine, and his partner told me he considered *himself* the *working* partner for two weeks, and that Henry could go 'scot free' for that time. He (Mr. Brown) is a very gentlemanly pleasant man–genial and sunny, always, and an active *Christian* also–which is such a recommendation to me, now. I am so glad that Henry *has such* a partner."

Henry Clapp and his partner had a "large store on Milk St." that impressed Susie as one of the "handsomest stores on the street." She "went with my good friends Mrs. Leach and Mrs. Harding (formerly my old school mates 'Mary Bellows' and 'Carrie Lawrence') and Henry–(other-wise Mr. Clapp) and engaged rooms at the 'United States,'" a hotel in which she and Henry planned to begin their married lives. They "went out riding, and walking, and to evening entertainments, and to *church* together and had a *very* pleasant time. Mary and Carrie adopted Mr. C—as friend most cordially, as did their husbands, so that we had an unusually large and pleasant circle of friends to enjoy the bright October days together." The dinners and teas her friends gave were the setting in which Susie felt that she and Henry Clapp "became quite *well acquainted.*"

After the sisters came back to West Brookfield they were "*very* busy in preparing for the 'wedding.'" Susie was pleased to report to her aunt "'*entre nous*' strictly, that I think Father is learning to *like* Henry *very much.* He seems to enjoy his coming here and talks with him by the hour together, so that you can *imagine* it makes me very happy. He (Father) consented, at last, to the wedding day being fixed this Winter, tho' I think I may say, without self praise, that he did dislike to have me go so soon."

Sewing was an important part of the preparation. Susie and her stepmother "worked on *cotton cloth* very busily for some weeks," probably making and embroidering underwear as well as sheets and pillowcases. Then they went to Boston together "to do my shopping." Henry Clapp "very kindly made an arrangement with friends of his, so that we had goods at wholesale prices. Wasn't it kind in him?—Mrs. Leach sent an invitation to Mother and myself to come right there and make it our home, and she and Carrie Harding went with us *every day* and helped select everything. They were just like *sisters* to me and I can never forget their kindness." Susie wanted her aunt Delia to see her "pretty things" and noted "Of course I did not have or need so rich a wardrobe as Carrie's, but everything is pretty and *just what I want*—and my two best silks are *handsome* I think tho' plain."

The wedding was to take place very soon, on January 25, 1865. Susie explained, "It is a *little* earlier than was intended, but Mr. and Mrs. Frank Fairbanks are going to Washington the first of March to attend the 'inauguration' and so desired to make the Brookfield trip as early as possible—as *we* are going home with them to St. Johnsbury *from* the Wedding! You know Mrs. Fairbanks is Henry's only sister and they live very handsomely in St. Johnsbury. I have had several boxes of flowers from their greenhouse this Winter."[15] Frank Fairbanks was the wealthy owner of the Fairbanks Scale Company of St. Johnsbury, Vermont. He and his wife were on their way to attend Abraham Lincoln's second inauguration.

Susie Taintor entered the post—Civil War world of the newly rich after her marriage. Henry Clapp's connection to the Fairbanks family and company connected Susie to money that came from industry. The aspiration and the desire for consumer goods she expressed were characteristic of her new society. These were the very rich whom Mark Twain and

Charles Dudley Warner later satirized in *The Gilded Age,* and whose behavior Thorstein Veblen later called "conspicuous consumption." Although the *roots* of our present-day consumer society are visible in the behavior of this new class, nevertheless no one in 1865 dreamed that such a society would ever be possible or ever affect the lives of the majority.

Susie's parents and their siblings had been married without fanfare. Even Caroline's wedding had been a low-key celebration. Susie's was less so—presaging a style that would become more and more elaborate as the century wore on. And railroad timetables played their part in the planning. It was a "*day wedding*" in order "to accommodate Boston friends who wish to return in the 3 o'clock train." On the one hand Susie wrote that she was inviting only relatives; on the other there seem to have been numerous exceptions, and "I may invite a few friends, like the Carews and Mrs. Mirick to come in *after* the ceremony and say 'good-bye' and take a taste of 'cake and wine' but this is undecided–I hope we shall have a right pleasant social time, and you and Uncle Henry are certainly *two good assistants* to that end!"

As to the bridal party, she wrote Delia, "I expect now, Genie will be first bridesmaid, with her Cousin Ed Mirick for groomsman–(who by the way is studying Theology at East Windsor)–and Mr. Clapp's particular friend, a young lawyer, of Boston, with the lady to whom he is engaged will take the *second* place in the bridal party."[16] Caroline was to come as a guest, perhaps because according to custom only unmarried people were part of the bridal party.

Caroline herself wrote to Delia about her high hopes for Susie's future in her marriage. But she also recalled that she had "had a world of anxiety about Susie during the last few years." She was especially concerned about Susie's "cruel experience of misplaced confidence and affection. O, Aunt Delia, that was so very bitter a trial to happen to one so sensitive as Susie is– . . . I wonder she ever lived to endure so much." Caroline alluded obliquely to Lucy, writing that when Susie "told me about thinking her mind was failing her at one time, and wanting to have me sent for to see her once more before all trace of Susie Taintor was gone, I could not listen for grief, nor can I think of it now, and all she was called to suffer in wasting sickness, and worse *heart desolation* without blinding tears."[17]

Susie's own reports after the wedding about her marriage were models of sentimental propriety. The reader looks in vain for the lighthearted enthusiasms of her youth. "Here am I way up among these Berkshire-hills which I have often heard of, as famed for beauty and picturesque scenery, and find 'the half has not been told me!'" Her asthma attacks were continuing, and the doctors "told Henry it would do me good to have a little change from Boston when I recovered." The doting Henry "had some business in the country so we combine that with pleasure and have a splendid time together. It seems to me sometimes (as I just wrote Carrie) that we are like two children off having a 'good time' and pleased and delighted with what every day brings us. I enjoy Henry's company so much that it is *half* my pleasure to have him with me constantly, as he is so closely confined to the store in Boston. He is a good husband Aunty, and I love him more and more, I believe, as the weeks and months pass along."[18] Each month brought further protestations of gratitude on Susie's part. "I can but choose to love him very dearly–I am sure you will be glad to know I am so happy."

By the time the young couple celebrated their first anniversary in their own home on Springfield Street in Boston, Susie wrote that "we can certainly ask for no more happiness in the Future than we have had constantly in the Past, and the new year opens as brightly as anyone could desire for us both." She reported that Henry gave her "a beautiful porcelain photograph of himself and a silver vase lined with gold" on the occasion. And she wrote of their busy social life. "During this last sleighing season every one has seemed to have an *especial* good time, in enjoying it. Henry took us out on the 'Brighton-road' one day, and I never saw even there, before, so fine a display of fine 'establishments' with great elegance of dress, also. It was like a fairy-land scene. Another day, we all went off with a party of *thirty nine* in a mammoth sleigh, drawn by eight horses, thro' Roxbury, Brookline, Newton, and Watertown to Waltham, where we had a nice supper, and dance, reaching home sometime among the 'small hours.'" The scenes are reminiscent of William Dean Howells's later descriptions of the new rich in *The Rise of Silas Lapham.*[19]

Susie was particularly happy once she and Henry had moved into their own home. "We find our calling list increases, too, as we are able to *receive* calls and I find one *must needs* live a busy life in the City, always.–I enjoy it very much, however–and more than ever now that I have a home for a 'center.'"[20] Caroline, too, wrote that "It is wonderful what a cheerful home– freedom from special care, and a good and watchful husband have done" for Susie. Carrie went on to say, "I verily believe she would have been in her grave long before this time, if necessity had kept her in the Brookfield home."[21] The Brookfield home was the scene of "necessity" but Susie's married home in Boston was the scene of "freedom."

Carrie later reported, on a visit to Boston, about the busy social life her sister Susie led despite her having become a kind of semi-invalid because of her asthma. While Carrie was there, Susie's sister-in-law "Mrs. Fairbanks came to be in season for Mr. Dickens' reading this week." Carrie assured Delia that "Susie entered into all the visiting very heartily, but

Sunday morning she was troubled with the old symptoms of derangement of the stomach, which so often succeed her severe colds. The Dr. was sent for, and though she has not been and is not now very sick, yet she does not sit up, and yesterday and today has taken a little morphine–when getting too nervous, and too much nauseated by raising such quantities of phlegm from her lungs."

Susie had been looking forward to "Mr. Dickens' readings" and had "wanted very much to feel equal to" making calls with Carrie. "But it is all for the best," Carrie wrote to Delia, "and I am only delighted to be able to sit with her and play the nurse a little (as long as some *one* must take that role.) Henry says she is not as sick as he has often seen her after asthmatic attacks, and we all hope Saturday of this week will see her a very comfort-able convalescent."[22]

One of Susie's greatest comforts was the relationship she and Henry Clapp had with Henry's sister Fanny and her husband, Frank Fairbanks. But Susie was always the "country mouse" in her sister-in-law's elegant house in St. Johnsbury. In the autumn of 1866 the Fairbankses were "just home from Europe, and full of enthusiasm in describing their year of travel." Susie "found Fanny's supply of souvenirs from the 'old world' almost inexhaustible. She had the most lovely jewelry, and her wardrobe fresh from Paris was *something* to see. Then the engravings photographs and stereoscopic views were very enjoyable, with *their comments* and the specimens of Swiss work, guns for Frank's cabinet–and various things from Paris and Venice were charming." The couple had brought back a "'cuckoo clock' and music box from Geneva, and many other things which seemed to bring the old-world very near."[23]

Susie had been a small-town farm girl, who milked her own cow the years there was not a hired girl. Here she was related by marriage to people who had a greenhouse in northern Vermont! Her wonder was that of a person who had grown up in a house without a furnace to heat the people, let alone one to heat plants and trees. Her envy was palpable. "Sister Fanny receives me so cordially *as* a Sister, that I can but love her very much–and she is so highly educated, and having just had the benefit of a year's travel in Europe, I think it is improving as well as enjoyable to be with her–Since brother Frank's return from abroad, they have newly carpeted and fur-nished drawing-room, parlor, and library, and with the addition of the vari-ous pictures–vases–statuettes, and works of art they brought with them from Europe, the house is very elegant and attractive." The routine in St. Johnsbury appealed to Susie. "Every morning Fanny adds the 'crowning ornament' in the shape of five or six vases of fresh flowers from the green-house–She takes great pleasure in arranging them herself, and I almost always go with her for the flowers. The greenhouse is beautiful just now. The plants are tastefully arranged, and the whole effect is fine—the rare colors and the air filled with fragrance—As you look up it seems one mass of bloom, and I cannot realize that I am away up in northern Vermont."

The Fairbanks brothers competed in their conspicuous consumption. Susie reported, "Yesterday, we saw something quite new to me, and that was an 'orchard house.' It belongs to Mr. Horace Fairbanks, but brother Frank is going to build one this year." In the orchard house Susie saw "plums, peaches apricots, nectarines, cherries, oranges, and strawberries all growing (even the strawberries) in large pots, and the fruit already quite large and abundant. On one little peach tree there were *one hundred peaches.* When we went in to the house to call on Mrs. Fairbanks she gave us some *ripe strawberries* which were as sweet, ripe, and luscious as those we gather in July. Isn't it a luxury to have ripe fruit up here (as Fanny says) 'near the North Pole' right at your door. Mr. Fairbanks gardner has charge of both orchard and green houses."[24]

In another letter about her new life of wealth, Susie described her activities at a summer resort in Auburndale, Massachusetts, in 1867. The Clapps made friends there, and "Every pleasant day we are out riding, and then sit in the parlor, or in each other's rooms—(occupying the bed for a sofa when the chairs are filled!)" The ladies ate dinner in the afternoon before their husbands came from work. "After dinner, we rest or read, and dress for tea, when the gentlemen come; and in the evening there is always *something* for a good time—Indeed the other evening we all played 'Puss in the Corner' and 'Fox and Geese'!" Susie seemed unaware of the infantilization such childlike activity produced in the rich women of her society. When her husband was there on weekends they sometimes had "a two or three days excursion to the beach, for my benefit; and once a party of six from the house accompanied us. We went to Rye Beach, and had a *delightful* trip—enjoying all the pleasures of sea-side life; bathing, riding—watching the surf—and going out in a row-boat away off on the ocean. This last exploit Henry did not share, and was a little anxious to have me *out of sight,* on the water, but I came back in safety."[25]

Back at her house in Boston, she wrote Delia about one of the ordinary hazards of nineteenth-century life, "a severe accident. . . . I was sitting by our little grate in the Sitting room, one Monday morning most four weeks since, and in *some way* dropped a large bottle of camphor I was holding. Of course my clothes were saturated with it, and as it ignited at once I was almost encircled with flames." Luckily there were servants in the house. Susie "screamed to Eliza, and tried to put it out, but failed—I thought I *certainly* was face to face with death. When with a desperate effort I pressed all my clothes on to one limb, and held it there–thus finally suffocating the flames." "Limb" is Victorian for "leg," an unmentionable body part.

Her burns were serious and she had them "dressed twice a day, and thought they were doing nicely. Then came Thanksgiving week and I was tempted to do more than usual and so irritated one of the largest burns so that it became inflamed, and I had to call Dr. Buckingham, and lie on the lounge again, for some time. I am better now–and go down to my meals, tho' I do not walk about the house at all."[26] Again she was an invalid. There was nothing to prevent or cure infection.

Susie lived much of her life upstairs in her rooms, and seemed to find her pleasures more and more in money and consumption. She wrote her "dear Aunty" that day "Henry came up, at dinnertime," and said, "'Susie you have had a present' and went on to say that brother Frank had just sent him word to take a check for $50.00 which he enclosed, and buy me a present (something that I should enjoy) and give it to me with his love. Don't you believe I felt happy Aunty? Not so much because of the fifty dollars (for I haven't yet thought of anything I really want–) but as an expression of kindness and affection. I think it was very 'good' of him. My life has so much of sunshine that I wonder every day if I am truly grateful enough for it. I *try* to be."[27] The difficulty of reading such letters in the late twentieth century is that we see all too clearly that, despite her efforts, Susie was not very happy.

Some newfangled inventions brought out Susie's Yankee conservatism, expressed in her Yankee twang. She asked Delia about bicycles (called "velocipedes"): "Do you have any in Hampton yet? With us they are very popular–but I can't think they will ever be of much use, except in a hall– where a young man can enjoy them as he would exercise in a gymnasium. Still, many think they will be very generally used, I believe. I must confess that they seemed very '*onsartin*' affairs to me!"[28]

Life in the Gilded Cage

In 1870, the Clapps moved from Boston to New York City.[29] They first rented and then bought a house on Fortyfirst Street between Madison and Fifth avenues in New York.[30] Susie took to life in the big city with enthusiasm: "We have been to the Park to the picturestores engaged with shopping–and with receiving and returning calls, beside attending last evening a Reception of the Union League Club. This was *very elegant*. The display of diamonds–lace, and velvet something to remember!"[31]

Susie soon had a companion living with her in her New York house, a woman named Anna C. Stone, who often took over writing to Delia when

Susie was not well: "My sweet little Mrs. Clapp was taken sick on Sunday last with that distressing of all troubles. Asthma."[32] The "trouble" for which Susie and Henry hoped, the birth of a child, continued to be in the future. Asthma distressed her more and more. She managed a busy social life around it, even visiting back in Boston. She wrote Delia herself, "Out of the ten evenings we were there, we were invited out to eight evening companies, beside twice to dinner, and once to an elaborate lunch party. This with our forty calls received was extremely trying to the 'flesh' tho' the 'spirit' appreciated and enjoyed all the attention and kindness received . . . but Tuesday night my old enemy the asthma, appeared."[33]

Back in New York she became involved in church affairs and "opened my house for those who came to attend the meetings of the Evangelical-Alliance. I had *four* here, constantly, and from eight to thirteen to dinner every day—often *five* ministers!" It was a busy schedule, and she asked Delia, "Don't you think I did my share in entertaining?" The "class of men" attending the meetings impressed Susie: "It was something to *see* that great body of deligates from so many distant countries—and among them the white turban of Rev. Mr. Sheshadrai, the converted Bhramin, from Bombay. One truly realized that . . . the 'communion of saints' was a blessed thing."[34]

The clergymen had barely left in the fall of 1873 when Susie's sister Carrie arrived. It was Carrie's last visit. After her death, by the spring of 1874, Susie was continually bedridden. When Henry went away to Europe on business, he instituted complicated arrangements for her care. She had "Mr. Wells (from the store) and his room-mate (Mr. Carpenter) to occupy the blue-room" until Henry returned. An old friend "Miss Billings is making me a good visit, and shares my room, so you see I am well supplied with friends." Still, she wrote Delia, "at 6 o'clock, I *do* want so *very* much to see Henry's face, every night."[35]

After a few weeks of this Susie wrote, "Mr. Wells and Mr. Carpenter have done everything to brighten the days, and their cheerful, bright faces have brought much sunshine into the house. Their consistent Christian life has been a help to me too." She promised, "*Sometime* I must tell you more of this," but she never did.[36]

Susie's semi-invalid life became a round of travel. She and Henry took a summer house in Tarrytown, New York, the parsonage of a church, while the minister was on vacation. She more and more frequently went to resorts, seeking relief from her asthma. She wrote in detail about life at Saratoga Springs:

> I never enjoyed a visit there more—and we met so many friends that it was just delightful! The weather was wonderfully cool and pleasant,

so that we almost *lived* out of doors, and the days were only too short, for all we desired to accomplish.

In the morning, came the visit to Congress Spring–then breakfast at 9 o'clock–afterward, reading the morning mail on the piazza, then a stroll up and down the street looking at the windows and making some purchases–(for there are many dainty and lovely souvenirs of Saratoga to tempt one!)–then a little rest, before dinner at 2:30–and immediately *following* this, a concert on the piazza (which was unusually good, this season)–Next in order, a drive for two hours, generally to the "Lake" and over the *new* and charming road on its shores–watching the College boys practicing for the regatta–and stopping on our way homeward . . . for a sip of lemonade, and a taste of [the] famous "fried potatoes" on the broad piazza.–Tea at 7.30, and then a long evening, generally on the piazza.–When the lamps were lighted there–(i.e. on the piazza, over the hanging-baskets)–and the promenading began–with the charm of fine music and flowers in abundance–gay toilettes, happy voices–and dancing in the broad parlors, it was like a scene in fairy land! *With* all this, however came *some* quiet hours for *rest* and I think the trip did us both good.

Henry's great anxiety–lest he should not select the *best Spring* for his needs, amused our party very much–the fact being so evident that he didn't *need any!* . . . *My dear husband is just the same merry, sunny body that you always find at "No. 21."* He enjoys *everything,* I believe, and makes me laugh, as usual, half of the time![37]

In New York Susie and Henry continued to hobnob with the rich and famous. They "attended an elegant dinner party, at Mr. Cha's Adams, given in honor of his brother (a West Point officer) and his *bride.* The dinner was formal, and elaborate–but we had a very good time, meeting agreeable people among the guests." She also reported to Delia, "Henry is going, on Saturday, by invitation, to a *gentlemans'* dinner given for 'Lord Houghton.' I dare say you may have seen some notice of his being in this country."[38]

At last, in the summer of 1877, Anna Stone wrote to Delia from Tarrytown that after twelve years of marriage, at the age of forty-two, Susie was pregnant. She prefaced her confirmation of this fact with the observation that "No doubt you think my letters are always harbingers of ill news. and you have reason to think so. For it is only when Mrs C–is sick and unable to write that I do it for her." And indeed there was worrying news mixed in with the good. "You of course *read* of the fearful thunder-storm of Tuesday the fury of which seems to have spent itself in our neighborhood. The church steeple was struck by lightning and burned down but the church saved. . . . The church being higher than the parsonage was all that saved us. It was a fearful shock to Mrs Clapp as you may know (for she intimated her *condition* to you in her last letter.)" The doctor came at once, "fearing a miscarriage" and "has been here ever since." By the time Anna Stone wrote, Susie was "past the danger we so much feared. but has suffered much. Mr. Clapp was at Niagara Falls at the time but Dr. M— telegraphed him and he reached home Thursday eve." Susie was "more comfortable today. being out of pain–but very weak and under the influence of morphine." No one seemed to worry about the danger of drugs for mother or child. Susie was six months pregnant, "hopes to be sick the last of October. We expect great things of her," wrote Mrs. Stone, "as she has been so well all along until this shock."[39]

Susie herself wrote to Delia a few weeks before she was due to deliver and thanked her for the news of a mutual friend's easy labor, commenting, "How often and *often* the Lord is better than our fears!" She thanked Delia also for her "affectionate and kindly wishes," and went on, "I *trust* they may all be realized, tho' I do not quite dare expect it–remembering the past [miscarriages?]. I am *very* well however,–have had *no* asthma since the middle of July–go out every day,–have a good appetite and am *told* that I *look very well!* So you see with so many *present* blessings, it would be ungrateful not to expect every good thing in the future. I trust *all* to the loving Father who is giving me *so much* daily, *sure* that 'I cannot drift/Beyond His love and care!'" Just before the baby was due, Susie redecorated her New York house. She wrote in detail, "Maria and I have been cleaning *all* the closets, and drawers," and reported that "now we are in '*apple pie order*' I believe!"[40]

On November 8, 1877, Mrs. Stone wrote Delia "The little *10. lb. daughter* arrived this morn at 7- oclock." Susie "had a very hard time. She was sick about nine hours," but Mrs. Stone reported "is now as comfortable as can be expected. The little lady as far as we can judge is more like Mr Clapp–having his fair skin and hair–She is a splendid big healthy baby."[41] Three weeks later, Mrs. Stone wrote Delia that Susie's recovery was "slow." Her care after childbirth was very different from today's practice. "She has not sat up as yet–but hopes to this week. She is doing quite as well as could be expected having been such a sufferer." Mrs. Stone sympathized with Susie's condition: "Poor little woman is getting weary of her many aches and pains. and I do not wonder. Yesterday she was placed on a lounge and taken in the sitting-room. She was almost beside herself with joy at seeing another room and having a little change."

About the baby, who was named Caroline, Mrs. Stone reported, "Little Carrie is growing every day and is the prettiest *little baby* I ever saw. I wish you could see her many and lovely presents–Yesterday she received a floral cradle. it was simply *magnificent.*"[42]

Ten days later, in the middle of December, Mrs. Stone sent news that was not good. Susie had "found her way back to bed again. with an abscess in her left breast." She described the treatment and its result: "On Saturday Dr. Miner gave her chloroform and lanced it. She is relieved from pain but is much exhausted. She seems brighter this morning and hopes soon to be up again. She was setting up when the abscess made its appearance. The Dr thinks by the last of the week she will be able to ride out." Of the baby Mrs. Stone said, "'Dumplings' as Mr. C. calls the baby is doing splendidly– never has had a sick day and good as a little Pet."[43]

But on the day after Christmas Susie's younger sister Genie began a letter to Delia with the news that "Susie wrote baby had not been well for a week, as she said drooping, but they have a wet nurse now, and they think will be all right. I do hope nothing will happen to her, for it would most kill Susie." Genie did not finish that letter, but continued a week later, on January second, "I have not been able to finish this before, and write now with a very sad heart. You may have heard too. I cannot realize that Susie will have to give up her little Carrie but they write Dr. Minor says she cannot live. Poor Susie my heart aches for her, and we can only leave her and her little one with the kind Father who never makes mistakes. Susie is sick and I fear what this will do for her."[44]

Indeed, on New Year's Eve, Henry Clapp had written to Henry Taintor:

My dear Mr. Taintor
    Our little Carrie is so ill that the Dr. gives us no occasion to expect her recovery. Susie is quite calm–though almost heart broken–[45]

The short note Henry Clapp wrote on January 3, 1878, told it all:

My dear Mr. and Mrs. Taintor
    Our little Carrie died last night and the funeral service is to morrow noon–Susie is quite heartbroken–and I am very anxious for her health as she has not yet recovered her strength since the baby's birth–
    Excuse a short note as I have much to occupy my time today–
    We know we have your love and sympathy and such friendship lightened these burdens–though the Arm only of Him, who has promised to be our refuge in every time of trouble–can sustain us in such trying hours–Our love to all the friends
                                            Affectionately,
                                            H. L. Clapp[46]

It was not until late February, nearly two months later, that Susie herself could at last write to Delia:

I am indebted to you for many loving words of remembrance, but I have hardly used my pen at all, for the past four months–so you will be patient, and pardon me.

During that time I have tasted the sweetest joy my life has known– and drank deeply of its most bitter sorrow. Untill my dear little girl was taken, I was gaining, wonderfully, day by day.–*Then,* I sank very low, from exhaustion, and I *thought* I should go to her. I suppose the dear Lord had something more for me to do *here*–for I came back, very slowly, from the valley of shadows–and with hardly a thank offering on my lips, for the new gift of life–for I did want to go to my darling.– *Now* I am trying, daily, to regain my strength, and vigor! Not easy, always, with a sad heart–but grace is given for every day–and all is peace, and trust, *now,* tho' the "*why*" is sometimes a thought that brings back "the clouds after the rain"!

My dear little daughter was a very beautiful child. Her features were almost perfect and she was *so* fair,–like a lily! Always gentle and sweet in all her ways, she won the love of everyone who saw her, and when the little life ceased, you would scarcely believe how sad a house this was. The servants idolized her, and mourn for her, now, every day. She was too lovely for earth, and so the dear Saviour took

Photograph of Susie Taintor Clapp that was copied by the painter of the posthumous portrait that hung in the Taintor parlor.

her. *Some* day, I shall claim her, again. Meanwhile the *memory* of her lovely face, and her dear self, is more to me than anything in the world, save my husband's love.

I need not say I have had constant care, and love, and tenderness, day by day. I am responding to it, now, and improving slowly–tho' I see no callers, yet–and have not been able to breakfast down stairs–tho' I take my lunch and dinner there. Mrs. King, who was with Sister Fanny for eight months, when little Ellen came, and was with me when my baby was born, is still here, and will be a little longer. She is kind and tender, and is bringing me back to confirmed strength, by every care, and help, one can give another.[47]

Henry Clapp left on an extended business trip to Europe in April, to be gone nearly three months. Susie went up to Tarrytown early in the summer with Mrs. Stone. For the next few years she dutifully grasped at possibilities for health, trying to find comfort in religion and good works. The Clapps continued their busy social lives, but perusal of Susie's letters to Delia shows that her heart was not in remaining on this earth. She died in 1881 in Colorado, whither she had gone gasping for the air that had eluded her for so long. She had lived for just forty-six years. Her death was no surprise to her aunt and uncle who had continued to love her all her life, but who knew that material wealth never brought her back the happiness of her youth. A portrait of Susan Taintor Clapp hung in Henry and Delia's south parlor the rest of their lives.

In a memorial volume published privately after Susie's death, the Reverend John A. Todd (from whom the Clapps had rented their summer home in Tarrytown) wrote, "To all her traits she added a uniform cheerfulness, so that to me she seemed to be always standing in the sun." It is a quality any reader of Susie's letters from her youth can recognize. It is her triumph that people still saw it in the wealthy Victorian woman who had been molded, infantilized, and invalided by the Gilded Age.

Losing One's Fortune

From the time Susie and Henry Clapp were married, Susie's uncle Henry G. Taintor used the services of and depended on the advice of his niece's husband. An important reason was that Henry Clapp was related–by his sister's marriage–to the Fairbanks family, who had made a fortune in the first part of the century manufacturing scales. Henry Clapp went to work for the Fairbanks firms in 1870, when he and Susie moved to New York. The Fairbankses invested largely in railroads and textile manufacturing in New England as well as in the constant expansion of their own scales business and its associated machine tool manufacturing. After the Civil War,

E. & T. Fairbanks letterhead, on a letter from Henry L. Clapp to Henry G. Taintor, March 11, 1867.

they expanded nationally by the establishment of their own sales and ware-housing units all over the United States, and by investment in the new western and transcontinental railroads.

Henry Clapp was a younger man than Henry G. Taintor, knowledge-able, well-traveled, and evidently in the "main stream" of the new develop-ments in the economy.[48] Using his advice, Henry Taintor invested heavily (possibly more than $150,000) in the bonds of the Portland & Ogdensburg Railroad. He did so because Henry Clapp had told him that the Fairbanks family had invested in the railroad and would back their investment. So a shrewd, independent investor like Henry Taintor felt he could put his money in the same company with some security.[49]

As a family member, Henry Clapp felt it legitimate to give his "uncle" Henry Taintor and the rest of the Taintor family some very "inside" infor-mation about the Fairbanks interest in the railroad. He corresponded pri-marily with young Henry E. Taintor, who was closer to being a contempo-rary in age and generation, who was an attorney in Hartford, and who helped his father with this particularly difficult investment problem. Clapp wrote to young Henry E. and enclosed a letter of "Governor Fairbanks" which was "a confidential one and I have no right to send it to you. So please consider it as most thoroughly confidential and make no reference to it to anyone. I wanted you to see it, and you must not betray me in letting it pass out of my hands—as I am doing. Return it to me by next mail." That letter and others contained information about the Fairbanks family's and company's bond holdings in the railroad. Henry Clapp assured the Taintors, "I can write you confidentially from time to time and you can count on my keeping you posted, but you . . . must not quote me at all." He went on to tell them that he would "sound" the Fairbankses and their banks about making further market for the railroad's bonds.[50]

But problems with the Portland & Ogdensburg grew acute, and the bondholders, who received none of their promised interest payments, grew restive. Committees of bondholders formed, and legal battles over first mortgages, trusteeships, and new bond issues ensued over several years. In 1879, Henry G. Taintor was assessed nearly $1,000 as his share of the expenses of the Bondholders' Committee.[51]

Despite such committees the problems of the railroad were not solved, and the records Henry kept show that the value of his investment declined radically. At one point, perhaps in 1882, he drafted a letter to one of the railroad company's officers, A. B. Jewett, which shows him close to rage:

> . . . You cannot I think expect me to accept of your offer of $16,000 for $160,000 being the interest which I have in the . . . railroad. I cannot make so great Sacrifice. I have . . . believed, what has always been represented to me, when asked to loan my money to the Company in which the Messrs Fairbanks have so great an interest, that it was safe for me to put my money there and that the Stock or Bonds would be a good dividend paying investment.
>
> I still think the future of the road is very promising ["Through the influence of Mr H L Clapp I loaned the Company a large amount of money &" is crossed out here] & feel that when I part with the Stock I now hold it must be at a much larger figure than you offer.
>
> I had partly made my arrangements to go to St. Johnsbury and talk the matter over with you, but it is so very severe cold I do not wish to be on trains at this time.
>
> Will you have the goodness to have your Treasurer send to me at Hampton the gross monthly earnings of the Road from July last together with the net monthly earnings.[52]

Young Henry E. Taintor was deputized to go to a meeting in St. Johnsbury in March 1884, where he was the only stockholder "outside of the Fairbanks interest" there. "The Fairbanks (except William P., the Treasurer) were not present in person but their stock was voted by Jewett." Henry E. said he "learned some facts of interest . . . which seem to give promise of better days by & by" about a new bond issue to keep the company solvent, about construction in progress, and about plans to lease sections of the railroad to others. He talked to Jewett, who wanted to buy the Taintors' stock, "but don't want to pay much for it. . . . He finally told me he would give 2.50 per share for the common stock. I think he might go 25c or 50c per share above that." He told Jewett he would write to him. He also said he came home "by way of Boston," with a thirty-one-year-old man named Harris, who had been at the meeting as an adviser to bondholders and who was the "son of D. L. Harris formerly of Springfield." Harris was "interested" in the Connecticut River Railroad, and he was, Henry E. wrote, "President of the 'Vermont Valley,' 'Cheshire' and 'Sullivan County' railroads and is a good deal of a man. His ideas have a practical ring about them and the plan that has been adopted was his suggestion." (When we read that, we wondered if the young Taintor had just been taken in by one more railroad man.)

Finally, Henry E. reported to his father about the complexities of train travel to and from northern Vermont that he had had "a rather hard trip." He left Hartford at 7:21 P.M. on a Wednesday, expecting to reach St. Johnsbury at 2:41 A.M., "but the trains were delayed and it was nearly 5 oclock AM before we reached there. There was only an ordinary coach on the train (no sleeper runs north of White River Junction) and the ride was tiresome and tedious." His trip home was via Boston. It took him six hours and a quarter from St. Johnsbury to Boston, and four hours from Boston to Hartford. He "took sleeper from Boston and had a good rest."[53]

Two months later, in April 1884, Henry E. reported to his father that their Portland & Ogdensburg stock had indeed been sold to Jewett. They sold 1864 shares for $5,000 ($2.68 a share), and the proceeds were divided five-eighths to Henry G. Taintor, and one-eighth to each of his three older sons.[54] There is no further mention of this railroad in any of the Taintor records. The heavy investment in the railroad's bonds had simply disappeared. And after this debacle there is no further mention of contact with Henry L. Clapp in the Taintor papers. He had ceased to be a member of the family after Susie's death, and his advice and connections had brought great investment loss to Henry G. Taintor. The number of banks and railroads from which Henry G. recorded dividend payments after 1884 was much smaller—and his income much lower—than in the years before.

Henry left his money to his children when he died in 1889, almost all of it still invested in railroads or banks dependent on railroads. The massive upheaval in the stock markets (and the permanent decline in the value of railroad stocks) which came with the deep depression of the 1890s shortly after Henry's death severely reduced the value of his estate. The next generation of Taintors—the estate was divided among all five children—did not inherit any fortunes from their investor father.

CHAPTER 20

HOMETOWN

"Mother says the neighbors were very kind,
and she had abundant help from them. It is a pleasant feature
of Country life I think."[1]

Delia was canning peaches at the beginning of September 1870. Earlier in her life she had dried perishable fruits like peaches or pickled them–sometimes with brandy–to keep them beyond their season. (Apples could be stored in a cool place to keep for months.) Now Delia bought the peaches, she sent out of town to Brooklyn to buy sugar, and she bought "fruit jars" for the finished product which she boiled up on the kitchen range. Hampton and its kitchens were rapidly modernizing.[2] The picture of a small-town mother canning at the kitchen range was an image her children carried with them to the cities and the West when they left home. And their visions of what "home" meant were transformed–by the permanence of that departure and by nostalgia for the dream of what was left behind.

"Nostalgia" was a word created just before the beginning of the nineteenth century to define a disease, "a form of melancholia" caused by absence from home.[3] "Home-sickness" by the end of the nineteenth century had become a recognized problem for young people (the ones who most frequently left home). The younger Taintors had already started to cope with the disease at mid-century when Henry E. proudly wrote his mother that "I think of you every day but do not have any homesick feelings."[4] When he was sixteen he comforted Willie to help him avoid homesickness,[5] and later wrote to his mother "I hope to be soon at home. *Home!* How sweet the word sounds."[6]

Home was the center of the family's life. It was a place–a house and the community in which the house was–to which the family was connected and familiar. The whole family–or at least parents, husband, or wife–had to be there in order to make it home. In their expanding, impermanent world, *home* was where Americans expected the family, at least, to be permanent.

"We reached home safely" is a recurring phrase from travelers. "Down home" began to have a comfortable ring of easy access to security by the end of the century.[7] Everyone came to use the phrase "at home" to indicate a willingness to have people call. "At home" meant you were on your own territory, your home ground, and ready to grant hospitality to those who were not members of the "home circle" or the "family circle." Delia always referred to her parents and siblings at Elmwood in Windsor as "my dear home friends,"[8] and at the same time thought of her husband and children in Hampton, too, as "dear home friends."[9]

As the Taintors' children permanently moved away from home and into city life, they began the process of *remembering* home. When Willie was first in New York, for example, he wrote his mother, "I purchased with the dollar which you sent me 'Poems of Home Life' and think it a very pretty collection."[10] Seven years later, his sister Mary reported that she, too, had been given "a little book called 'Poems of Home Life'" which she liked and thought her mother would like as well.[11] Delia, and many parents like her, reinforced her children's nostalgia. From the time Henry went off to the Civil War to the end of her life, when she wrote to her adult children she datelined her letters "Home."

The Sons Who Moved to the City

Henry E. Taintor and his wife, Jennie, in Hartford had their baby, Harlie, that September shortly after Delia was canning her peaches. Jennie's was a modern, city experience of childbirth–with a doctor and a nurse in attendance–as Henry wrote to his mother:

> . . . Through the P.M. yesterday Jennie complained that her back ached but this has been so common that we did not think much of it and too the ache was continuous. Before bed time the ache had all gone and Jennie went to sleep feeling the same as usual. Just before midnight she waked me up and said she had a severe pain in her back. It passed off in a minute or two and presently came again. I then got up and lit the gas at 5 minutes before 12, by no means sure that the pain meant anything. However I dressed, called Mrs Bennett [Jennie's mother who must have been with them], and then roused the Doctor. He said I had better go for the nurse who lives but a short distance up church St.

The pains grew more frequent & severe till the Doctor thought it advisable to give chloroform and from that time Jennie knew nothing of what was done till the matter was all over. The chloroform was first given about 2.45 and the baby was born at 3.30 A.M.

The whole time from the first pain was less than four hours, and a part of the time Jennie was unconscious. After things were quiet Jennie went to sleep and slept most of the time till daylight.

She is feeling of course very tired & somewhat sore but not so much as if she had not taken chloroform. The nurse we have seems very good & competent and with a Doctor in the family we feel pretty safe.[12]

Within three years Henry E. and Jennie, established in the city, were building a new house for themselves on Spring Street in Hartford. It was part of a "development" group of houses, and was to have all modern urban conveniences. Henry E. described the plans to his parents:

. . . We have at last got figures on our houses. They will cost a little more than we anticipated but the extra cost gives us a better house by far than we talked of when we began–The fact is that in the plans the architect put in so far as he could any pet ideas that were advanced by any member of the seven and also any of his own, expecting that many things would be cut off; but when we came to open the bids we found so little difference between the house as drawn and the pro- posed modifications that it was the unanimous feeling that the best house was the cheapest.

We have our brown-stone steps our hot and cold water (marble basins), in the Hall, the bathroom and each of the four large sleeping rooms, Registers, with separate pipes, in the dining room, library, each parlor & the four large chambers besides both halls–Marble mantels in every room i.e. dining room, both parlors, library & four chambers– Speaking tubes from kitchen to each story & all modern conveniences in the Kitchen including small zink sink in china closet for washing china–and set soap stone tubs–The front windows have but four panes of glass each. In fact the appointments are those of a $12 or $15000 house. We hope to be in it by next fall or early winter though the contract not yet being signed we cant talk definitely about the time–

I figure now that my house will cost between $7500 & $8000 probably pretty close on the latter sum though it may come in $200 or $300 under it–We don't say what our contract is, but guess its safe to tell you in Hampton–We pay the contractor $4997 per house–My land costs $1800; then there is to be added, the expense of mantels, grates, furnace, range, grading & fencing the rear yards and architects fees & commission for all of which I deem $1200 a more than liberal allowance. There is no question in my own mind that when complete the houses would sell readily for $10,000. The location adds a $1000 to its value easily–I hope we may enjoy it together next winter. . . .[13]

Although Henry E.'s house was an obvious contrast to old-fashioned country houses like his parents', his attitude about his house–that it would "sell readily" for more than he would have to pay for it–was an urban contrast to the unpurchasable permanence of "home."

Henry's life in the big city was an even greater contrast with small-town life. He spent two years early in his legal career as secretary to Connecticut's Governor Jewell. He and Jennie thus participated in the glitter that city wealth and power brought when they went to New York one summer to a dinner given by Jewell for the ambassador from the Czar of All the Russias. Henry E. wrote to his parents that they went from Hartford "Tuesday morning at 8 o'clk to New Haven and then took the boat for New York." They stayed at the Fifth Avenue Hotel. Then at six o'clock Henry "went to the Hoffman house where the supper was given leaving Jennie with the other ladies." Most such dinners were all-male functions. Henry said for Jennie that "she had a fine time that evening as Lyman Jewell (brother of the Gov.) invited the ladies to a ride and took them over Central Park and Thomas' Gardens getting back to the hotel about 10 o'clock."

The dinner to which Henry went "was said to be the finest thing of its kind that has ever been in N.Y. The Hoffman House has the name of the finest cooking &c in the City and on this occasion had *carte blanche* to do the best they could–Plates were laid for 25 people." He reported that they "went through the bill of fare *tasting* of everything & eating much and after hunger was satisfied, speeches were in order." He tried to describe "the table and room" to give his parents an idea of the elaborate meal. "From the central chandelier strips of red & white bunting with gilt stars extended to the sides & on the walls were the U.S. and Russian Flags draped together." He wrote that "The table was very handsome. In the center was a large silver fruit & boquet holder with a smaller one on each side i.e. one towards the head & the other towards the foot of the table. On each end of table was an immense boquet of rare and beautiful flowers, and between several piles of fruit, ornamental candy work &c &c." The dinner, he said, "was a success throughout–and one thing I was glad of–with seven different wines, no one was noticeable affected by them–Two of the Company did not take any." All of Delia and Henry's children were very temperance conscious.

The next day, Henry wrote that the whole party had gone "aboard the revenue cutter 'Grant'" and sailed "from foot of 23rd St to Jersey City–

where the Minister left us and went aboard the Cunard steamship 'Java'–
We started down the bay and were soon followed by the 'Java'–She over-
took us and we ran together nearly down to Sandy Hook, where we
turned around." He wrote, "The whole sail was very delightful and the
heat of the morning made the sea-breeze doubly refreshing."

Henry ended his letter trying to excuse his conspicuous consumption to
his parents. "The expense of the trip was heavier than I feel really able to
afford–but I felt *compelled* to go and we made it as economical as possible–
As I said once before, I must save somewhere else if possible."[14] The "com-
pulsion" Henry felt to keep up with the Jewells was part of his urban life,
not something he had brought from home. He and Jennie were among the
rapidly increasing middle classes in the cities, possessed of comfortable
incomes but with few clues to proper behavior in urban circumstances and
with no familiar classes of leaders upon whom they could model themselves.

Their life was not the same as that led by George and Emily. When
Henry and Jennie's house was finished, George wrote to their parents that
"I expect you will have to go before a great while & make Henry a visit in
his new home. I was out to see them one week ago to-day & was delighted
with the house. It is just as pretty & cozy as can be." He longed "for the
time to come when I can be at home so that we can again go to housekeeping–Not but what we are *very very* pleasantly situated where we are, &
shall probably never have any more comfort, but yet it is pleasant to feel
that one's home is their own."[15] He and Emily were living with Mr. and
Mrs. Gustavus Davis, Emily's parents.

George spoke from considerable experience. When he and Emily had
first married they rented a house but did not move in because Emily's
mother would not let her go. Emily wrote to Delia six months after her
wedding that she was "still at my old home." Her mother, she said, was
"*absolutely unwilling* to let me go to my new home. You would not for one
minute suppose that my going so short a distance from her would afflict
her." It was an impossible situation. The young bride wrote, "You don't
know how hard it is for me–My dear Mother holding me fast . . . and my
dear husband thinking on the other hand that we ought to begin housekeeping." She said she sometimes felt "that it would have been best, & easier for Mother if I had left home as soon as I was married, but she couldn't
hear *one word* of *that*. So here I am now. Mother says I can have my new
house to store my things in & to visit *sometimes* but I better *live here*."[16] Mrs.
Davis was rich and spoiled, and all her life long petulant about letting
Emily go.

George and Emily's married life included constant struggles over having their own home. When they did take up housekeeping, Emily wrote

Delia that she nearly had to promise to bring the piano back to the Davis home, and herself with it, because her mother was so unhappy that she had left.[17] At various times throughout her married life she did go home. For instance, she moved back for a while after her daughter Lucy was born. Her parents were wealthy city folk; her father was president of the Hartford Bank, and Emily's own expectations about housekeeping were very high; they certainly included her piano, fashionable clothing, and servants.

Most of the servants she hired were recent immigrants from Europe. Emily Taintor found them a trial. In fact at one point she found Irish servants so difficult that she wrote Delia she had again decided to board in a hotel rather than keep house. "Do you know that the Priests have demanded a strike from the servants, saying they must *each one raise her wages one dollar* a week and the extra dollar must be given to build their new cathedral. In *this way,* they think to make the Protestants build their *old Cathedral!*" Here was raw anti-Catholicism. Emily planned to be among the "very many ladies" who "have already said they will *not* raise their servants wages one cent," and she insisted it was dreadful that others felt they must raise wages "rather than be left alone" without servants. Emily asserted that "if *Every* lady would say *never! go* if you like–the terrible servant question of rights & privileges would for once & all be settled–and the lady would be mistress of her own home, which is not the case now by any means."[18]

Emily was a complainer. She "bemoaned greatly her temporary widowhood"[19] whenever George was not at home. George was a commercial traveler, not at home much. There are no letters that describe Emily as happy or even contented. It must have been hard to have her husband away so much in the first years of their married life, and little Lucy seems to have been a sickly child. Also, Mrs. Davis's constant demands wore on Emily.

George and Willie (from now on called "Will") both lived their lives on a level different from their brother Henry's. They were salesmen, traveling men through the 1870s and the 1880s. The occupation of "commercial traveler" had first become possible when the railroad network spread after the Civil War so that most of the country's growing cities were connected to each other. Nowadays commercial travelers travel by car or plane. Those old enough to remember preplane days still recall groups of traveling salesmen playing cards and smoking on passenger trains. The mid-twentieth-century musical *The Music Man* used cheerful imagery of the commercial travelers of George and Will Taintor's days.

But George's adventures in his traveling years were not always pleasant. He once wrote his mother from Urbana, Ohio:

I arrived here this A.M. about half past five o'clock, having passed the worst night I ever experienced. I will give you a little description of it, although I am well aware of my inability to do it anything like justice.

Well! I passed yesterday in Tiffin [Ohio], about 100 miles north of here [Urbana], and when I had finished my business, & begun to think about getting down here I found much to my disappointment that the only train that would get me to this point before Monday afternoon was a local freight train, leaving Tiffin about 7 o'clock in the evening. I knew that on a passenger train, one could make the distance in four or five hours, and supposed that I could get here on the freight by about two or three o'clock sure, so rather than lose pretty much the whole of the day Monday, a drummer [salesman] from N.Y. who I have been traveling a few days with, & myself concluded to try this freight train.

The freight trains west run what they call a caboose, on the rear of the train. This Caboose, is a common freight car with a row of benches running around the car on the inside. On this bench we managed to get a *little* sleep, using our sachels . . . for pillows & our overcoats for bed-clothes. I took a fearful cold it being a cold night, & the door which is on the side, having in some manner got stuck so that we could not shove it, remained open all night. The stove which we kept full of wood, warmed about a foot around it, & although we could by standing pretty close to it keep our fronts very comfortable, our backs were like Icicles. For a while we would be pretty jolly & think it a pretty good joke, then we would get cross & disgusted & vow that we would get off at the next station, if we had to sleep in a bar, but finally after the longest night I ever knew we arrived here. . . .

I am feeling pretty well this afternoon, but when you get me on to a freight train again to ride 100 miles it will be when I am some older than I am now. I laugh now to think of it, but of all the joltings, jerkings, and sudden halts which I *ever* got, last nights experiences go far ahead.

He ended his letter by saying, "This travelling about the country for a business is getting to be pretty well played out with me."[20] He would be at it for many years more.

One time on his travels George heard a report of his brother Will that reminds us today of Arthur Miller's *Death of a Salesman*. It was from another commercial traveler who knew Will and said that he "is very popular at the store & is very much liked." George wished, he told his mother, that he could travel with Will, but "as he stops at the smaller places" he would not be able to.[21] Indeed, after his very earliest traveling years George did not stop at smaller places; he went to the big cities. His itinerary for Collins & Fenn included cities in New York, Pennsylvania, Michigan, Ohio, Indiana, Illinois, and points west. And he moved fast.

 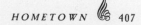

He wrote from Louisville, Kentucky, in 1874, of one anticipated break when he would "be in St Louis on the 4th [of July]. They are to have a Monster celebration there, over the formal opening of their big bridge across the Mississippi [the Eads Bridge], & I suppose I shall Enjoy it as much as such crowds are ever Enjoyed." He then appended his itinerary for the next few weeks, with dates:

> St. Louis, July 3 & 4–La Clede Hotel
> Kansas City Mo. 6–Pacific Hotel
> St Joseph Mo. 7–Pacific House
> Keokuk Iowa 8–Paterson House
> Burlington Iowa 9–Barret House
> St Paul Minn 11–Merchants Hotel
> La Cross Wis 13–International Hotel
> Milwaukee Wis 14–Newhall House
> Chicago Ill 15–Grand Pacific Hotel
> Detroit Mich 16–Merchants Exchange
> Cleveland O. 17–Kennard House
> Rochester N.Y. 18–Osburn House
> Syracuse N.Y. 20–Globe Hotel
> Albany N.Y. 21–Delavan House[22]

Later George wrote from Alliance, Ohio, with another account of his travels that shows how important railroad schedules were to him:

I am very well but pretty tired having done a good deal of work & riding in the past 4 days.–as follows–Left Hfd at 8 oclock Tuesday A.M. Left N.Y. at 7 oclock that evening arriving at Binghamton at 7 oclock Wednesday morning. Left B. at 2 oclock that afternoon–& was delayed on the road so that we did not reach Buffalo until 3 oclock Thursday (yesterday) morning–Left there for Rochester at 2 oclock yesterday P.M. arrived at R. at 5 & left again at 6 going back to Buffalo. Left Buffalo at 1:35 this A.M. & arrived in Cleveland at 7 oclock. Left there at 3 oclock this P.M. & arrived here between 6 & 7 this Evening. I leave for Pittsburgh at 11 tonight. Now if that isn't a pretty good record with all the work I have done in the different cities I'll give it up. . . .[23]

George must have asked himself why he was working at such a break-neck pace. At any rate he answered the question for his mother: "There is at least one consolation, & comfort viz We are doing a fine business, and I am accumulating that which if I am fortunate enough not to lose will give me pleasure and comfort bye & bye."[24] Years later, after George lost his traveling job, he found work (possibly through the good offices of his father-in-law) managing real estate in Hartford. He and Emily then made a home of their own, but Emily's mother's demands continued, and Emily herself remained ill at ease.

Will and his wife, Lizzie, lived in flats in New York tenements in their early married years. The contrast between Will's country upbringing and Lizzie's city expectations was often considerable. Once when Will was sick, Lizzie thought he should go home to Hampton to get well. She wrote Delia that she thought Will would "be tended better, than I can do here." But she felt his country ways had brought on his illness in the first place: "I *know* he has slept for years with both windows" open, "all the way some-times," she wrote, and in the past his landlady "has shoveled up the *snow* from the floor. Now you know that even an *Iron constitution*" cannot "stand that always."[25] The couple lived in small quarters, as Will wrote Delia: "You spoke in one of your letters about our changing our appartments, we shall not do so any way before the first of the month and then . . . we shall have both the front & back rooms on our floor." He and Lizzie did not have a piano to move in and out of fancy lodgings as George and Emily did. Instead Will planned "to put the carpet that is now on our room, on the other room, the other side up, and get a good serviceable carpet of a bright pretty pattern for our sleeping room." In order to take even this modest step it was necessary to economize. "We have been very quiet lately spending most of our evenings at home and I think I enjoy it as well as run-ning around and I know it is better for us both."[26]

George and Emily, Henry and Jennie, and Will and Lizzie all lived and worked in cities. Because all the Taintors had grown up in a small town, they focused much of their city lives on domestic arrangements, houses, and making homes. But city life offered other possibilities. Theater seems to have been a favorite activity with this Taintor generation as it had been with their "Cousin John Taintor" in the generation before. When Henry E. had spent his storekeeping time in Boston just after the Civil War, he had gone to the theater. We know how much it cost (fifty cents) for a ticket, but we do not know what he saw. Within a few years he took his intended bride to hear Dickens read in Albany. He wrote that they heard "A Christmas Carol" and "Trial from Pickwick."[27] Susie and Caroline heard Dickens that same year in Boston.[28]

And the last year Carrie Taintor Buel was alive she wrote about run-ning into George and Will together at the theater in New York.[29] They were seeing Edwin Booth in *Julius Caesar*. A few years later Will saw it again with another actor and commented, "I do not think Davenport took the part of Brutus as well as Booth did."[30] One time Emily went to the the-ater alone in Hartford–leaving a sick baby Lucy at home and earning some disapproval from her brother-in-law Henry E.[31] Another time, when Kate Strong went down to New York to visit her cousin Susie Taintor Clapp, she too went to the theater.[32] And Mary wrote her mother from school about the family's theater-going in Hartford: "Henry and Jennie went to hear Booth in 'Merchant of Venice' last night and Kate went to here him in 'Hamlet' Friday night. . . . Thursday evening about seven o'clock Mr Gross came over and gave Henry two tickets for 'Aimee' (a play at the Opera House that night). He bought them for himself and when he reached home found his wife sick and gone to bed so he could not use them. Henry & Jennie went so you see they have been quite dissipated the last three nights."[33]

Delia and Henry G. also went to the theater when they were in the city. Henry recorded frequent attendance at the theater and at minstrel shows in New York and in Hartford.[34] The music in minstrel shows may have particularly appealed to him. And in Hartford on at least one occasion they heard Mark Twain read.[35]

A Wedding at Home

When Henry Taintor's and Delia Ellsworth's parents were married—in the 1790s—a wedding ceremony had been a simple ritual performed in a few minutes by a minister or a justice of the peace, at home with few attending. There was sometimes celebratory food for family. The newly wedded couple often took up residence with parents, and "went to housekeeping" later when they could afford it. Among the very wealthy, there might have been an occasional wedding trip, but it was far from ordinary.

When Henry and Delia were married in 1839, there had probably been a more elaborate ritual and celebration than for their parents, at Elmwood. They had moved in with Henry's mother, and gone to housekeeping in that house. There had been no honeymoon, although they had done some traveling after their wedding.

By the time Henry and Delia's children married, the wedding and celebratory reception (always with ritual foods—cake—and often with a meal) was becoming an elaborate, lengthy, decorated rite of passage focused on the dream/ideal of home and family. A wedding trip or honeymoon tour was expected—symbolic of the departure of the new couple from the old home. And the ordinary expectation grew that the wedding marked the creation of a new home.

The first of the Taintor children to marry was the eldest, Henry E., who married Jennie Bennett at her parents' home in Amsterdam, New York. The family preserved no descriptions of that wedding, but Henry E. did write to his parents describing some weddings he attended. He mentioned some of the things weddings included. For instance, at the wedding of Miss Henrietta Cone, "There were five grooms & maids, among them [Cousin] Gussie Williams who had the handsomest partner and the honor of leading the procession up the aisle." He and George went "out to the house after supper, getting through about ½ past 6. The newly-married couple left at 7.30 and many of the party came away soon after. I came about 8 but George with other young folk staid & danced till after 10."[36] While that couple left on a wedding trip the evening of their wedding, young William Coite, who had worked for Henry G. when he was state treasurer, waited several days before "going away with his bride on their wedding tour."[37]

Not long after his own wedding, Henry E. described his wife's sister's wedding, also in Amsterdam, New York, "which was postponed from Wednesday to Thursday on account of the freshets & consequent delay of travel." Mr. Quick, "a young minister from the other side of the river," performed the ceremony and "did it very finely." The bride and groom gave their responses "with full clear voices." Henry E. was pleased that "there was no hitch in any of the arrangements and we saw them safely started on the train for the West." The wedding presents "were very handsome, most of them being silver articles for housekeeping. Mr & Mrs Kline gave her an elegant tea service of seven pieces." The groom's "present was a watch and chain. The whole affair was perfect and left nothing to be desired."[38]

When it was George's turn to marry, Emily's wealthy family had social aspirations. The preparations for the wedding were elaborate and expensive. Emily wrote to Delia about shopping for the wedding, for clothes for Delia and her younger children: "I sent for your samples of black silks. They arrived a few days since, with some samples of my own." She was "going to New York on Saturday of next week, at which time I shall be happy to get your sash and either of the *silks* you desire, *if* you wish me to. We think them very nice, at the prices marked, don't you?" She also offered to meet her future mother-in-law in New York for a shopping expedition: "I am going down alone on Saturday of next week. I wish you were going the same day. I should enjoy shopping with you so much in N. Y. If you are there when I am, if you will send me word at Aunt Warner's I will go to see you immediately and try to be of service to you if possible." She offered to consult her dressmaker in New York "about pretty dresses for children and give you the benefit of her good taste." Delia had asked her about a particular sash, and Emily replied, "In regard to the other sash being proper for an "*old* lady" I can not say, but for a lady of your age, it was *made*."[39]

Henry and Delia Taintor did make a buying trip to New York City in preparation for George and Emily's wedding. They took Mary with them (she was ten), and bought some quite expensive clothes for her from James McCreery & Co., on Broadway at Eleventh Street. The major purchase on that trip was a "black silk twill—with train" which Delia bought for herself from M. Sullivan, at 1199 Broadway (some distance uptown from McCreery's), for what was—as compared to all the other clothes she bought during her life—an enormous price: $175. (From notes Henry Taintor made at the time, we know Delia's hoop skirt to have been thirty-eight inches long, with a twenty-six-inch waist.) The Taintors also stopped in at Tiffany & Co. (at 550–552 Broadway) and purchased an elegant black marble "shelf or mantel clock" for $50. (It seems they bought the clock for themselves, because it was part of the furniture we bought with the house. It still runs well and has a delicate chime.)[40]

There were details about George and Emily's wedding that Delia and Henry did not like. We know this because Delia's niece Sophie Reynolds wrote to her that "I do not like a day wedding with the beautiful sunlight shut out any more than you do—but it is fashionable & stylish, & these young people think more of that now than they will when they are a few years older."[41] The parents of the groom hired a carriage to take them to Mr. Davis's house in Hartford, and Sophie when she wrote again was sure "it must hve been a very handsome affair, & I . . . am sure our dear Aunty looked well in her handsome black silk, & though I do not love her any better in that than in calico still I feel proud to see her look the lady that she is when the occasion demands & I hope to see her in that same black silk before it goes out of fashion."[42]

Not every wedding was so elegant, as Sophie Reynolds wrote about her brother Wolcott Ellsworth's wedding in Michigan City, Michigan. The bride "wore the traveling dress of dark green cashmere trimmed with velvet of the same shade—& looked less like a bride than most of her guests, but she & Wolcott were both very anxious not to be recognized as newly married people." She suspected "however that the indescribable something betrayed them before they had gone far. They only went to Chicago for a day or two, & then to Ft Wayne" to go to housekeeping. She reported that "Wolcott was very nervous during the wedding ceremony, but he seems very happy & very well now, & Kate too has been well since her marriage which is an unusually long time for her to be well, for she has been quite an invalid. I told Wolcott that her ill health was the one thing in their future which I regarded with apprehension, for Kate seems a very pleasant sensible woman, & she & Wolcott very much in love with each other."[43]

Delia's wedding silk was useful again when her niece Alice Hall married. Mary wrote, "Auntie told me to tell you that at Alice's wedding you with your black silk dress and camels hair shawl with a nice bonnet would be the queen (or she supposed Alice would be *the* queen) but you would be one of the queens of the feast." The groom, Mary reported, "is very particular about being married in an Episcopal Church and as Alice attends the Congregational in Springfield she did not want to be married there and so they will probably be married at the Episcopal church in Windsor and have the reception at 'Elmwood.'"[44] Alice's sister Mattie thought "there never was a more beautiful and fitting old home from which to be married." Alice added a note that the food was to be brought from elsewhere by caterers and that there were problems marrying a man from a different church. "This difference in our church views has been the only one that has risen between us & altho it is a matter of real regret, I know the Dr [the groom] is very desirous that . . . we have the same spiritual Home–His letters & whole character show such deep Christian faith & dependence that I am sure we will be entirely harmonious in the more essential matter of Christian living."[45]

At last, in October 1884, Delia and Henry's youngest child, their daughter, Mary, married Frederick Wendell Davis. Frederick Davis was George's wife Emily's brother and the younger son of Gustavus Davis of Hartford. He had gone to Yale (class of '76) where he had known Fred Taintor and been a member of Yale's first football team. He had been married before, and had a young son. His first wife had died in New Orleans, possibly of yellow fever, after which he came back to Hartford to live. He

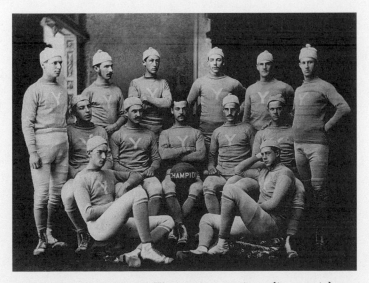

Yale's first football squad. The young man reclining (lower right) is
Frederick W. Davis.

and Mary met through George and Emily. Mary may have even attended a party Emily gave for forty family members in honor of Fred's first engagement.[46] One evening before he was married, Fred Davis had walked Mary home from George and Emily's house, and Mary noted in a letter to her parents that "Fred Davis came home with me on his way to see Lucy Smith."[47] Perhaps Fred Davis as a young widower remembered the sprightly Mary who had walked home with him one June evening not too many years before.

The preparations for Mary's wedding, which was to be at home in Hampton, were long and elaborate. It was the first wedding the house witnessed. Delia wrote to Mary, in June 1884, "I have been thinking Miss Scarborough might be a real good person to secure for a few weeks" to do housework and "help about your quilt, the bolsters &c." She suggested that "If you do not go to housekeeping immediately after your marriage we might do some of these things afterwards—when there was nothing else to think about & when the weather was more propitious. You will have enough to commence with & can give directions about what you want." Delia was a little hesitant about interfering with her headstrong daughter and assured her "I only throw out these hints."

She went on to tell Mary that the hired girl "has the silver out & I think it is going to look very fine. Not the tea set, but spoons & forks. If you can find some more of Scoville's powder for [polishing] silver it will be wise to get a bag." Delia also told her to "do as you choose about curtains" for the south parlor of the Hampton house. "The length from the cornice to the floor is about two inches over two & a half yards,"[48] which is about the right measurement. The walnut cornices are still on those windows.

We first heard stories of Mary's wedding from her grandson, and from her daughter Dorothy's account of the "ancestral home." We were told that the wallpaper in the northeast front parlor—one of the rooms in which this book was written—was put on for Mary's wedding (we took it off slightly more than a century later). When our daughter was married at the house in 1986, we had to rebuild the small rose arbor on the crest of the terrace southwest of the house to be an arbor over the bride and groom. We do not know if the arbor was built for Mary and Fred Davis's reception.

The most detailed information we have about Mary Taintor's wedding comes from the receipts her father kept. They make it clear that Emily Davis Taintor and her parents—also Frederick Davis's parents—were very much involved in the preparations for the wedding. Emily shopped with Mary and the Taintors in New York City, and the bills for much of Mary's trousseau from B. Altman & Co. (at 19th Street and 6th Avenue) and James McCreery & Co. were sent first to Gustavus Davis, who forwarded

The 1884 wedding photographs of Mary and Fred Davis.

them to Henry G. Taintor. Mary bought much of her lingerie at B. Altman, as well as three soaps, two brushes, one powder, one comb, one box, twenty-five handkerchiefs, four quires of paper and envelopes, four and one-half dozen collars (three varieties), six pairs of hose, twelve (different) gowns, twelve (different) corset covers, twelve drawers, two skirts, three sacques, and one monogramed bag, for a total of $99.86.[49] McCreery's provided the material for Mary's wedding dress (twenty yards of white silk, four yards of illusion, and nine and one-half yards of lace), as well as some other items for her trousseau, including eleven and one-half yards of velvet, a robe, ten yards of "cloth," four pairs of hose, eight and one-half dozen buttons (five dozen were identical), and lesser quantities and qualities of twist, silk, canvas, satin, and cambric. The total bill was $332.57.[50]

The Taintors also paid for engraved notes, cards, stationery, and envelopes from Tiffany's (in Union Square) for Mary. And they bought one dozen monogramed teaspoons and one dozen tablespoons from Whiting Silversmiths for her.[51]

In Hampton, Mary hired Angie G. Lyon to make dresses for her, and possibly to work on her wedding veil. Angie Lyon had not made clothes for Mary before this, although she made dresses for both Mary and Delia in the years after Mary's wedding. The bill she presented, dated on Mary's wedding day, was large for a small-town dressmaker—but not out of line for the number of dresses made. It is a written list on a sheet of paper with no heading, receipted on the back, and dated by Henry G. Taintor:

```
To making silk & veiling–················· $8.00
To balance due on veiling················     .45
To work on silk waist·····················     .50
To making skirt ····························   2.75
To work on white muslin················      1.25
To work on sack·····················         2.50
To making morning dress ·················    7.00
To making white sack ····················    3.50
To making black silk···················     15.00
To two pieces braid ······················     .16
To brown cloth dress ····················    9.00
To cloth coat·····························      5.00
To making gray cashmere ················     9.00
To making over black skirt···············    4.50
To work on night dress ··················      .25
To work on dresses ·····················     2.00
            [total]                      $70.86
Credit by $5.00 [cash] paid ·············    5.00
      By 2 yds lining ··············          .40
      By 3 yds Wiggan·············             .30
      By 1 yd Crinoline ···········            .10
      [credit total] ··········            $5.80
      Due ····················            $65.06
      2 doz Eggs ·············                .50
                                         ————
                                         $65.56⁵²
```

Angie Lyon also sold eggs to the Taintors, among her other accomplishments.

On the day Mary was wed in the Congregational church next door to the family house, Henry received a routine letter from his niece Eugenia Taintor. On this happy day it was a sad reminder of Lucy Taintor, still in the Lunatic Hospital in Worcester. Genie had bought ten yards of dress flannel, six of cotton flannel, and some lining material, thread, buttons, and some hair ribbons, to make new dresses for Lucy. Henry sent the $10.50 it all cost to Genie.[53]

The reception for the bride and groom at the house was serenaded by Colt's Armory Band from Hartford (which charged twenty-five dollars to come and play).[54] And the collation was provided by Edward Habenstein of Hartford, an "Ornamental Confectioner and Fancy Baker" who ran a "Ladies' and Gents' Restaurant" in Hartford, the "Cottage Restaurant" at Watch Hill, Rhode Island, "from July 1st to September 1st" each year (where the Taintors may have found him when they were there on vacation), and the "Capitol Restaurant" in Hartford "during sessions" of the legislature. It is not clear from the receipt how many people the caterer served at the reception, but the charge, which included the "expenses of railroad and express charges" as well as a "Brides Loaf," was $188.65.[55]

Mr. A. Perkins presented a bill to Henry Taintor the day after the wedding for hauling packages, people, and trunks back and forth from Hampton's depot to the Taintor house. Between September 25 and October 2, he brought a total of twenty-eight express packages to the house. On September 25, six days before the wedding, he brought Mary and a trunk "down" home. On the twenty-ninth, he brought two more trunks. On the thirtieth, he had to send two teams to the depot for four passengers and four loads of baggage. On October 1, the day of the wedding, he carried five passengers "down," and then five passengers "up" along with a load of baggage. And on the second, he brought a final load of baggage "up" to the depot.[56] The Taintors themselves transported the newlyweds—and the elder Davises—to the depot after the reception.

In 1917, when Mary's husband, Frederick Wendell Davis, died, thirty-three years after their wedding, she received a sympathy note from one of the people who had been there, who wrote, "It does not seem long to me since that day when You and Mr. Davis were married. It seemed to me then the most beautiful sight which I had ever seen and I have never attended any more beautiful one since."[57]

Mary Taintor's wedding in Hampton set the seal on her firm intention to remain a part of the town in which she grew up. Just the year before she married, her mother bought an engraving in New York called "Coming Home" which hung in the house.[58] Mary always considered Hampton home, although she lived most of every year thereafter in Hartford.

The Town as Family

There were two important aspects of the town Mary Taintor Davis knew in the last decades of the nineteenth century—one had been there since Hampton's earliest days, the other was part of its changing face. The first was the sense of extended family pulling together despite the hazards of wind and weather. The second was the actual people moving in and out, living and dying, who formed that extended family.

And the climate of a place determines more than its agricultural productivity. It sometimes determines whether people live or die:

> Edwd. Wadsworth was drowned last Sunday morning in Mount Hope River near Mansfield Hollow. The water over flowed the Road near the bridge & he either drove off or the current swept him off into deep water & himself & horse were drowned. The horse &

wagon were found a mile & a half or two miles below the bridge, lodged against a tree, but his body is not yet found. About thirty men went from Hampton on Tuesday and searched both sides of the stream for two or three miles after the water had subsided, but without success. Under all the circumstances . . . it was a most shocking affair and as you may suppose creates a great deal of talk about town.[59]

This was the report of Patrick Pearl to Henry G. Taintor. The news as one woman reported it to another had a different emphasis:

It is indeed sad to think of the death of Edwin Wadsworth. I suppose he once thought himself a christian & if he was truly converted & his heart changed, even if he had *strayed*–it may be that the Lord had mercy on him in those last moments when he clung so closely to the *Alder* until he was so chilled that he could hold on no longer and was obliged to let go & sink, so that his body has not yet been found. His father . . . came on last Sunday & Monday it being the *ninth* day they were in hopes of finding it & *they* with *twenty or more* went over & searched for it again, but could not find it. It would be such a comfort for the friends to have the body so as to bury it. It seems all the ag- (I was going to say all the more aggravating as every thing else was found even his *Hat* & Buffalo robe & blanket) when . . . Mr. Avery brought the news that the body was seen this morning to go over the dam . . . and it was taken out of the water & so it will probably be got home today & I *am so* glad it will be such a comfort to the friends.[60]

Ruth Button, who wrote the letter, cared most particularly for the comfort of the dead man's relatives through the rituals of burial and mourning. She was not related to Wadsworth, but he was part of the extended family that was Hampton. Her matter-of-fact assumptions that neighbors cared for and would help each other were not only for times of crisis; they were a part of a kind of everyday life that Mary Taintor Davis valued and tried to remain connected to.

The kind care of neighbors was part of West Brookfield's life as well as Hampton's. Susie Clapp wrote of a time of family illness there that her stepmother had told her that "the neighbors were very kind, and she had abundant help from them. It is a pleasant feature of Country life I think, that in sickness, all ones friends are *so* ready and willing to give help and comfort."[61] While Susie thought her city friends were also willing to help in crises, she recognized the isolation of city dwellers and the unwillingness of city folk to make "much personal sacrifice" in order to provide neighborly help.

The people of Hampton did not understand that. For instance, when they read in their newspapers about the great Chicago fire in 1871, the

Congregational church collected $70.84 and sent it to Chicago. Henry G. Taintor kept the letter of receipt thanking the "generous citizens of your place," asking him to "convey to the kind hearted donors the grateful thanks of our distressed people and say to the givers that their donation is truley appreciated. We are now taking care of 14000 families, feeding, clothing & sheltering & warming them, and we are enabled to do this through the great charity our fellow men have shown."[62] (In 1992, Hampton people still thought they should help a city in crisis. In one small evening meeting, a few of them collected seventy dollars and sent it to the First A.M.E. Church in Los Angeles to help rebuild after the riots there.)

"Friends" had become a word with a modern meaning by the last part of the nineteenth century. The word no longer meant "family" or "extended family" in cities. But it still carried its older connotation in small towns.

On one occasion when Ruth Button was away for several weeks she asked her neighbors the Taintors "if you would look my *house over* & see if things will take any hurt if I stay. I think of my feather bed at home, . . . & the carpets, especially the parlor one for fear of the *moths* & the front room stove, will you, if you have time look at them . . . & let me know, & some-times I will try to do as much for you. . . . How is brother *Taintor* your good husband. I hope he is well will he please tell me if ther are any apples on my trees."[63] Maybe this casual–and warranted–assumption that neigh-bors could be counted on was what Mary Taintor Davis remembered and wanted to retain in her life. It was the good side of the coin which had as its other face knowing all the details of those neighbors' lives.

George M. Holt went from house to house in the warm June of 1880 asking questions about some of the details of people's lives and laboriously filling out big report sheets for the Tenth Decennial Census of the United States. He was recording the changing populace who were Mary Taintor Davis's neighbors in Hampton. He found a population smaller than it had been at any time since the first census, 827 people in 207 families.

The composition of the population had also changed. There were fewer "colored" in Hampton than there had been for more than half a cen-tury. And twenty-five percent of all the people were either born in Ireland or born of Irish parents. Illiteracy among those who were Irish-born was still endemic. The Roman Catholic Irish community had a church by 1880. A priest, John F. Murphy, boarded at the hotel across the street from the Taintor house, according to the census. The Congregational minister, Alfred Goldsmith, was the only other clergyman.

Our Lady of Lourdes Roman Catholic Church stood–and still stands–on Cedar Swamp Road, not far west of the combined Center School/Town Hall (built in 1864). It was not built on the Main Street as was the Congregational church. According to stories told to us, the Catholic church was off Main Street because the "Town Fathers" did not want it there. "They" gave the land on Cedar Swamp Road—and trees to hide the church building—so that the Irish Catholic presence would not be visible. We were even told that "they" replaced those screening trees after the 1938 hurricane blew them down. The Protestant Congregationalists took a long time to adjust to the Roman Catholic community in their midst. For years the political party division in town followed the lines of religious division: Protestants who became Republicans as a result of the Civil War and Catholics who became Democrats because the Protestant "establish-ment" excluded them.

The political structure of Hampton had by 1880 achieved its modern shape. A fixed two-party system had become the core of local government, imposed by the state in the years after the Civil War. The town was required to elect two registrars of voters, where one registrar had done in the past. One registrar was from the Republican Party, one from the Democratic Party. Each was allowed to appoint an assistant or deputy. All four of these officials were required to take an oath of office, and the town clerk had to administer the oaths.[64] (No former Confederate would be allowed to slip in!) A new election system for justices of the peace was also in place, requiring that an equal number of justices of the peace be elected from each party.

Most of the men voted in every election. In 1880, there were 140 men listed on the census as farmers and another 100 who were laborers. But the largest single occupation was that of the 200 women who listed them-selves as "housekeepers," and who could not vote. Keeping house or, as many of them would have called it, "making a home," was the largest occu-pation of Hampton.

The number of those with a specialized occupation was much reduced from such listings in earlier censuses. There were but two blacksmiths left in town in 1880, only one harness maker, only two shoemakers, one tailor, and two dressmakers. Most of these artisans did repair work rather than manufacturing. There was only one miller left—almost all of America's flour was being ground in Minneapolis by 1880 and shipped everywhere else on the railroads. Three men were "engineers" or "firemen," the first Hampton residents who were railroaders.

The general impact of the modern world restricted the diversity of work available in all small towns; those railroaders did not work in Hampton. Cities were the centers for opportunities, and the rate at which people flocked to them was increasing. The new small towns in the West either expanded into cities, or in a single generation (not the two or three or four of the long-established towns) reproduced the pattern of declining opportunity that was evident in Hampton. Hampton's population continued to decline from 1880 to 1920.

The census reports did not list the wandering homeless men called "tramps," who had started to appear in Hampton after the Civil War. The problem of tramps had become so prevalent by the 1880s that by state law five constables were elected in each town specifically to deal with them.[65] Henry Taintor as justice of the peace had to commit them to the county workhouse.[66] The Town Meeting had empowered the selectmen to "furnish a suitable place for the Keeping of Tramps,"[67] and even authorized them "to pay not more than Fifty cents per head."[68] Homelessness had already become endemic in modern life, and tramps became a permanent feature of the American rural landscape until at least the 1940s. A folklore of tramps developed–the source for James Whitcomb Riley's poem "The Raggedy Man."[69] That lore was epitomized in Connecticut by stories about "The Leatherman," a homeless wanderer who made a yearly circuit in the state.

The nonwandering, countable 207 families of Hampton lived in 191 households. Of those, thirty-two households had more than six people in them–the largest had fourteen. More than a third of those large households included boarders. For instance, James Wooley boarded five laboring men– one Irish, one Canadian, and three American-born. Juni Evans boarded four Canadian laborers. (The Canadians were part of a large migration from Quebec, most of them French speakers who came to New England to work in textile mills.) The Chelsea Inn across the street from the Taintors had six boarders in the summer of 1880, among them Charles Gardiner, the town's only practicing physician; Elizabeth Parker, a disabled teacher from out of town who was recuperating from illness; William Brown, a retired Hampton farmer; Father Murphy; and two laboring men. Most of the people who boarded in Hampton worked out of town.

The census was the official listing of the Taintors' friends and neighbors, the people with whom Mary Taintor Davis wanted to maintain her connection. Her mother had kept that connection by seeing them daily. A few years before she died she wrote Mary, "I was out all the afternoon with Mrs Williams making calls (on Mrs Gates, Mrs Durkee, Mrs Geo. Holt, Mrs Mason Fuller, Mrs Cocking & 'Aunt Rena'–and Mrs Newton) & winding up by stopping at Mr Tweedy's door, but finding them at tea did not enter."[70]

If Mary Taintor Davis wanted to keep her parents by keeping connected to Hampton, of course she could not succeed. They died in the winter of 1889, Delia in January, Henry in March.

The last photographs of Delia and Henry G. Taintor, probably from the 1880s.

Henry G. Taintor was born in the house in Hampton, but he died in Hartford. Delia Williams Ellsworth was also born in a small town–Windsor–but she too died in Hartford. Delia did not rate a separate obituary in the *Windham County Transcript,* but Henry did:

Windham county loses still another of her distinguished citizens by the death of Hon. Henry G. Taintor, of Hampton, which occurred at the residence of his son in Hartford, on the 11th inst, at the age of 76. Mr. Taintor was a man of such courteous and kindly bearing to all, without respect to social conditions, that he quickly won the confidence and esteem of any one who came within the circle of his acquaintance and influence. He was well known throughout the state, having held official positions that brought him in contact with our leading public men. He had been a member of the House several times, we think, and State Treasurer, State Senator, Assistant Commissioner of the School Fund, and had often been called upon by his townsmen to hold local offices of trust and honor. Mr. Taintor's wife preceded him to the better land only a few weeks ago. He leaves five children, Henry E., George E., William W., and Mary E., wife of Frederick W. Davis, all of Hartford, and Frederick, who is in business in Kansas.[71]

It is interesting that this obituary begins and ends with the private Henry G. Taintor, framing his public life. He and Delia would have enjoyed the account of a turkey supper in Dayville that appears in the newspaper next to his obituary:

The turkey supper given by the ladies of the Congregational society was a success notwithstanding the disagreeable weather; the "turks," being greatly outnumbered, would doubtless have surrendered at discretion, but they were surrounded and literally cut to pieces before they could offer any resistance. Proceeds of the slaughter about $40.[72]

Henry lived to the age of seventy-six, Delia only to seventy. Both had been ill on and off in their last years; there are many doctor bills among Henry's last cash accounts. He even tried a "complete metaphysical treatment" in Hartford in 1885, and on at least one occasion traveled to New York for treatment by a doctor without an M.D. His incoming correspondence refers often to unnamed health problems as well as to many bouts of depression. But there is every indication that he functioned as a caring father, a loving husband, and a diligent man of business until the end of his life. He adored his wife and he did not outlive her by more than a few weeks.

Throughout their lives together Delia had always been a very strong woman. She was a believing Christian, a loving wife, a caring mother, and a great communicator. She had become the powerful kin-keeper of a widely scattered combined family of Taintors and Ellsworths. Henry may well have simply turned his face to the wall after she died; we do not know. It was six months before the fiftieth anniversary of their wedding. They were buried next to each other, in the plot with Roger, Nabby, Solomon, and Judith, in Hampton's South Cemetery.

CHAPTER 21

THE DEATH OF AN ERA

෯

"It seems to me that four weeks will be all I can stand of that exceedingly quiet life..."[1]

F or the thirty years after Henry and Delia died until the 1920s, Hampton was in decline. All over America people were leaving small towns in droves, just as Henry and Delia's children had done. The rural places they left behind became ghost towns or empty crossroads. Some of them became summer resorts. Many began to turn up on maps as suburbs or exurbs, the bedroom towns of cities. But the days when small towns were centers of productivity were over. What happened to the Taintor house and to Hampton are instances of the way small-town homes were relegated to the periphery of life in the twentieth century. They were relics of a past that was dead.

The Inheritors

Henry and Delia left five children, none of whom made their homes in Hampton. Four Taintor families lived in the city of Hartford by 1889: Henry E.'s, George's, Will's, and Mary's. Fred lived in the West.

Henry E. Taintor was a lawyer and later a probate judge. He and Jennie had only one child–their son, Harlie. Harlan Henry Taintor attended the Hartford Public High School in the 1880s and graduated from Yale College in the class of 1892. He began to study law in his father's office, opting for an apprenticeship as his father had, rather than attending a law school. Late in the winter after his graduation from Yale he caught pneumonia, and died on April 17, 1893, when he was twenty-two years old. We have been told the family story that Henry and

Jennie's grief at the loss of this promising young man colored the rest of their lives.

Henry E. himself died of a heart attack in his sixtieth year, in 1904. Known always as "Judge Taintor" in his later years, he had combined his busy law practice with the management of the family property until his death. He spent much of his time in the last few years of his life arranging the transfer of the ownership of Elmwood, the Ellsworth family home which Oliver Ellsworth, Delia's grandfather, had built in Windsor, to the Daughters of the American Revolution for preservation as a museum. As a descendant of Ellsworth himself, and as executor of his aunt Libby's and his uncle Fred Ellsworth's estates, he corresponded with all his Ellsworth cousins, arranging some reunions, in order to orchestrate the successful assignment of all of the ownership rights of all of the Ellsworth heirs. Throughout his life, he remained active in the Grand Army of the Republic, the Union Civil War veterans' association. Jennie outlived Henry for many years. She died in Amsterdam, New York (her hometown), in 1925.

George Taintor went into the business of managing real estate for several large Hartford landowners—among them the Goodwin family. He also became a director of the State Bank and of the Hartford Street Railway Company in his later years. George died in 1909, and Emily lived until 1920.

George and Emily had one child, their daughter, Lucy, named after Emily's mother. She never married. Lucy Taintor's younger Davis cousins remembered "Cousin Lucy" as an eccentric delight and told stories about her. One was of how in the latter years of her life she lived in the Heublein Hotel in Hartford. One night she called down to the desk to complain of noise. "They're holding the Elks' Ball," the desk clerk explained. "Well," said Lucy, "tell them to let go." Her family thought of her as a jolly and amusing relic of the nineteenth century. She died in Hartford in 1940.

By the 1890s, Will Taintor and his wife, Lizzie, had left New York for Hartford. Will worked for the Hartford Ice Company. They had two daughters born in Hartford, neither of whom had children. Lizzie died of cancer in 1908. Will himself was declared "incompetent" in 1913 on petition of his elder daughter, Arline. He was resident at that time in the Hartford Retreat. He fought the incompetency ruling on and off for the next ten years. When he died in the Norwich State Hospital in 1924, a Hartford judge said he was "a victim to his intemperate habits."[2] All three of the elder Taintor brothers and their wives—Henry and Jenny, George and Emily, Will and Lizzie—are buried in the same Taintor plot at the Cedar Hill Cemetery in Hartford.

Left: Judge Henry E. Taintor.
Right: Hartford businessman George E. Taintor.

Lucy Strong Taintor, daughter of George and Emily.

The fourth Taintor brother, Fred, was the only member of his generation of the family who lived out his life in small towns far from Hampton.
Fred obviously modeled himself on his father, although he became a
rancher instead of a farmer, and he founded a small-town bank.

When he went west, Fred first settled in Atchison, Kansas, where he
clerked for an acquaintance of a relative. Late in 1878, he lost that job and
fell on pretty hard times. According to a story told a century later by his
son, Fred "had a big silver watch that he hocked, for some reason," and
worked "in an elevator [a grain elevator] for a while to make a little
money."[3] He wrote his parents just after Christmas that he "was out of
work for the greater part of the month of December, and with my board,
and other bills to pay, I found myself quite short." He found a job as a
freight billing clerk for the Union Pacific Railroad at forty dollars a month,
but payday was not until the twentieth of the month, he explained, so he
would "get no money until February 20th when I will draw my January
pay." With his board paid up until January 1, he had just four dollars left,
"so you see I have got to figure pretty close to get along until the 20th of
February." His parents had sent a "present of money for Christmas" which
Fred admitted was "quite opportune." He found life in Kansas different
from Connecticut: "We have had magnificent sleighing here for the last
three weeks, and it has been so cold that the Missouri River has frozen
hard enough for teams [of horses] to cross on the ice. Good sleighing for so
long time is something unknown in the history of Kansas."[4]

Fred did not spend long being a clerk. At some point, he drove "a six-
mule freighter out of Topeka carrying supplies down to what at that time
was Osage Indian territory," according to his sons.[5] And, according to a
long story written about him after he died–by Milton Wallace "Doc"
Anshutz who worked for him in the 1880s as a ranch hand "cowboy"–by
the end of the 1870s Fred went "to the Comanche Pool country" in Kansas
"where he learned the rudiments of cattle ranching as practiced at that
time."[6] In 1881 he went into partnership with his cousin Jimmy Reynolds of
Lafayette, Indiana, and bought a herd of 1,500 Texas longhorn cattle and a
"ranch site." The ranch was "located on a small nameless creek on the
south side of the Cimarron River, near where Crooked Creek empties into
the river" in what was then called "No Mans Land" but is now Beaver
County, Oklahoma (in the present Oklahoma panhandle). Fred's cattle and
horses were valued at $5,500 when he started the partnership, and he put
another $1,500 into the ranch that year; Jimmy Reynolds matched his
$7,000 total investment. It seems likely–although there is no record, since
Henry G. recorded none of his capital contributions to his children–that
Fred's father helped him get started. Fred's brand was "G.G." according to

"Doc" Anshutz, who went to work as a cowboy for him that year; and the creek on which his ranch was located came to be known as "Tainter Creek."

According to Anshutz's story, "Tainter Creek at that time was a remote and beautiful place. It gave the effect of being tucked away out of sight from the rest of the great open world. Fed by springs, the little creek of clear, sweet water flowed about three miles between rather narrow canyon walls never reaching the river toward which it flowed, but sinking away in the sand." The ranch site is north of the present tiny towns of Gate and Knowles in Beaver County, Oklahoma, and southwest of the tiny town of Englewood, Kansas. These were the only "wide places in the road" anywhere near the Taintor ranch.

When Fred went to live there, the "ranch house" was "a small dwelling that was part dugout and part logs, windowless, with a fireplace in the end opposite the entrance." The corral and the stable were "both made of poles lashed together with rawhide," and "the stable roof was brush covered." In the years following his start on the ranch, Fred "soon replaced" the dugout with "a two room house made of rock laid up in gypsum and sand. Later another large room was added," according to Anshutz, and the house was improved "until it was one of the most comfortable and homelike ranch houses to be found in the country."

Fred Taintor "was a great reader" all his life, according to his cowhand chronicler, and at the ranch there was always "plenty of good reading matter, periodicals, newspapers, stock publications," and "a small, well chosen library of works by standard authors" as well. His sons remembered him as an "avid reader," and they had vivid memories of his sitting in his woven hickory rocking chair "puffing his pipe and reading."

Fred bought out other, smaller ranchers to increase his herds. And he brought in "registered Hereford" cattle to improve the meat quality. According to one Kansas legend, he was the first rancher to bring white-faced Herefords west of the Mississippi. He bought them in Indiana, fifty head, according to Anshutz, with two or three bulls worth five hundred dollars each. John A. Taintor would have been pleased to have had such a young cousin. Fred crossbred his Herefords with "range" cattle—"about one-eighth Hereford and about seven-eighths range cow," according to his son—and produced calves which were "fifty to one hundred pounds heavier than those sold by other ranchers." The Taintor G.G.-brand herds grazed over 200,000 acres of open rangeland, according to a 1934 interview of Fred Taintor by Victor Murdock, the editor of the *Wichita Eagle*.[7]

"In the first few years of the limitless open range, life on the ranches was free and easy," according to Anshutz. No one had to buy the grass-

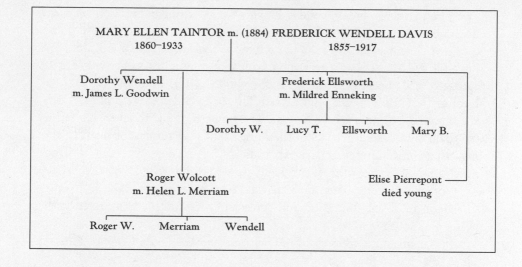

MARY ELLEN TAINTOR m. (1884) FREDERICK WENDELL DAVIS
1860–1933   1855–1917

Dorothy Wendell   Frederick Ellsworth
m. James L. Goodwin   m. Mildred Enneking

Dorothy W.   Lucy T.   Ellsworth   Mary B.

Roger Wolcott   Elise Pierrepont
m. Helen L. Merriam   died young

Roger W.   Merriam   Wendell

lands the cattle grazed, and if there was a good "home ranch" with water the cattle could roam with little care much of the year. Ranch owners, according to Anshutz, "spent the Winter months in town–Dodge City, Kansas City, or 'back home.' Mr. Taintor made several trips to his Connecticut home during this time. The boys on the ranches, with little work to do, just a few horses to grain and keep in good condition, a little desultory range riding to do, to see how the cattle were faring, found much idle time on their hands."

Among the stories told about Fred Taintor were an unusual number of tales of kindness and generosity. "Doc" Anshutz wrote that the Taintor ranch "was a most hospitable place" to which Fred often "brought out from Dodge City some young fellow fresh from the East, who was eager to learn something of ranch life." Several of those were young men "who had come West to find, if possible, healing for lung trouble, consumption, we called it then." Some of them died, but all enjoyed room and board and care at Fred's ranch. Fred's sons thought he himself went west in order to recover from tuberculosis.

The winters of 1885–86 and 1886–87 were terrible on the plains, combining drought with great blizzards. The combination destroyed the open-range cattle business. And it threatened human lives, especially of settlers and farmers who had been pushing in great numbers into the grasslands. Because of the influx of settlers (called "sodbusters" by the cattlemen because the act of plowing the plains for crop-growing busted the grass's sod and destroyed the grazing) many ranchers, Fred Taintor among them, contemplated leaving the territory for greener pastures. But while he was away in Nebraska and Wyoming looking for new range, Fred left instructions with his ranch hands "to supply the needy ones with beef, flour, potatoes, coffee and sugar" through the winter. According to George Rainey, in his book *No Man's Land,* the Taintor hands killed and dressed twenty-three cattle to feed the hungry one of those winters.[8] The following spring the local settlers made a "deal" with Fred Taintor in order to help him stay in the ranching business where he was. The farmers agreed to allow his cattle to "roam unmolested over all of their grass lands" in return for his furnishing "them material for fencing their fields." And so, according to Doc Anshutz, "the Tainter ranch survived, grew and flourished." By the beginning of the twentieth century it was two spreads, one north of the Cimarron of about four thousand acres and one south of the river with about six thousand acres.

It was not until 1898 that Fred married—to Miss Jessie Cone of Kansas City. "She had a good job at the Midland Hotel in Kansas City," according to her sons; "she was a bookkeeper. That's where she acquired that beautiful Spencerian writing of hers." They met because Fred Taintor stayed at the Midland Hotel. He was forty-two and she was thirty. They lived in Kansas City the first five years of their marriage, although Fred traveled back and forth to the ranch to supervise its operation. After their two sons, Henry and Oliver, were born, the family moved to the ranch so the boys could be raised on Tainter Creek.

The house they lived in was a long one-story, three-room house, with a kitchen, a dining room in which there was also a bed and a big wardrobe, and a parlor bedroom which was also Fred's office, with a big roll-top desk. The middle room was "kind of a family room," according to Fred's sons; "they did a lot of sewing in there, and had an early Edison phonograph in there." Each of the rooms had a door outside to the "sidewalk," and they were connected by interior doors as well. In the area around the ranch house, there was a one-room stone bunkhouse with four beds, a big stove, and windows that were pivoted to tilt open; there was also a two-story barn for grain storage with a long row of stables, a smoke- and butcher house for meat, a buggy shed, a stone chicken coop, a stone cow barn for the milk cows, and a machinery shed, where the manure-spreader, mowing machine, plows, and a binder were kept; and in the midst of all this there was a corral.

By 1909, Fred moved his family to Englewood, Kansas, so his sons could attend school. Both boys had learned to read from their parents, and the elder, Henry, remembered learning from the Montgomery Ward catalogue. The boys earned a tiny candy bead for each new word they learned. Englewood was the rail center from which Fred shipped the cattle he sold each year (he invariably sold them as yearlings). Fred founded the Home State Bank there and was its president. His farmer-banker grandfather Solomon and great-uncle Roger would no doubt have approved his investment of capital earned from the sale of cattle in loans on land.

The end of World War I brought upheaval to Fred Taintor and his family. It marked the end of the boom in farming and ranching which had accompanied the war since 1914. Sometime between 1918 when the war ended and 1921 (the sources we have are in conflict), the bank in Englewood failed, Fred sold the ranch, and the whole family moved to Wichita. Rather than have the bank depositors lose money, Fred sold the ranch in order to pay them one hundred percent on the dollar.[9] Fred's elder son, Henry, graduated from the Massachusetts Institute of Technology in 1921 as an engineer. His younger brother, Oliver, went to the Kansas State Agricultural College in Manhattan because he thought he would be running the ranch. He left there when his father sold the ranch, "free to do what he wanted to."

Fred and his sons made several visits to Hampton and the Taintor home there. Fred's son Henry visited there last in 1986, after attending his sixty-fifth class reunion at MIT. He remembered his father as "a really large man," about five feet eleven inches tall, who astounded his tailor because he had "about a fifty-four inch chest and a thirty-four inch waist." He wore a seven and seven-eighths hat, a Stetson. And he "always wore a vest, no matter what the weather was, because that was where he carried his pipe, tobacco, cigars, matches, little notes—it was his filing cabinet."[10]

Fred survived all his siblings. He died in Wichita in 1934 at the age of seventy-eight, and was buried in the Old Mission cemetery there. The Wichita newspaper headline was "Cattle King Dies at Wichita Home . . . Fred Taintor Widely Known as Cattleman in 'No Man's Land' and in Kansas." The article said he "was a native of Hampton, Conn. His forefathers had lived there for many generations." Despite his permanent move West, Fred had stayed very close to the life of those forefathers.

The Inheritance

The four Taintor children who lived in Hartford and their families used the Hampton house by turns in the summers after Henry and Delia died. They had, after all, been summer visitors for years when their parents were still alive. All five children shared ownership for twenty years after 1889. Sometimes one of the families had the house for an entire summer; sometimes they shared it for part of the summer, overlapping each other's visits. One of Mary's children, Dorothy Davis Goodwin, remembered that "they took turns using it for a summer home, and I spent many happy weeks there from the time I was a small child, visiting an Aunt for a week or two the summers that my family did not go."[11]

During those twenty years that Henry and Delia's children used it as a summer residence, not much about the house itself changed. Mary and Fred Davis's children were the youngest in all the family. Mary's stepson, Carl, had been born in 1880, the child of Fred Davis's first wife, who had died when the baby was barely three months old. The eldest of her own children, Dorothy, was born in 1886, followed by Roger in 1890, Ellsworth in 1892, and Elise in 1897 (who died while still a child). The house was "made safe" for Mary's little children by squaring off the corner of the porch between the front and side piazzas. Attitudes about children had changed. Henry and Delia had not built that porch corner for Harlie or Lucy when they were small.

It was after Henry's and Delia's deaths that the house came to be called "Maple Terrace"–a name that was its address until we bought it. There was a social cachet for middle-class city folks like the Taintors and Davises of Hartford who owned a country house with a name–"the country" in the early twentieth century was fast becoming an acceptable place to visit and take recreation in as people aspiring to upward social mobility formed or participated in exclusive and expensive "country clubs."

During the time the house was owned by the whole family, "the building that had been the store" on the southeast corner of the house's lot next to the Congregational church was torn down. Under Henry G. Taintor's management that building had been used as a store and then as a tenant house rented out as a residence, a shop, a store, or some combination. Bertha Bennett Burnham, a Hampton contemporary of Mary's children, remembered that "there was a store in the basement of that" house and a family "the Chandlers lived upstairs."[12] The house was torn down by 1902, because in that year a chapel was built for the Congregational church on the land where Roger and Solomon's store had once stood. (The chapel was, in its turn, torn down in 1948, and replaced, after a complicated land exchange with Roger Davis, by a parish hall added to the church building itself.)

In 1909, after her brother George died, Mary Taintor Davis bought– from Jennie, Henry's widow, from Emily, George's widow, from Will, and from Fred (who moved from the ranch to Englewood that year)–all the "shares" of the house and became its sole owner. Her attachment to the "old home place" was very strong. Her brothers' families continued to visit, but they visited Mary and her family in *her* house.

Once she owned the house, Mary began to add some modern conveniences. Until that time there had been no plumbing. A hand pump in the kitchen was the only water supply (there was still a hand pump in the kitchen sink when we bought the house). Mary put in a bathroom, supplied, according to her daughter Dorothy's recollection, "by water from a well in the field pumped into a compressed air tank by *hand*."[13] In fact, three "dug" wells were ultimately used to supply the house with water. Mary also enlarged (by extending the room into an existing shed ell) the downstairs southwest room for a dining room. It was the first time a room was set aside as a dining room in the house. Delia and Henry had eaten most of their meals in their kitchen, although they took tea, which was a meal, at small tables in one of the parlors. A large "picture window" (which was an openable sash) was installed at the west end of the new room, and a rose arbor built west of it to give it a lovely prospect. Candles and kerosene lamps still lit all the rooms in the long summer evenings; electricity did not come to Hampton until 1922.

Outdoors, Mary's great project was the terracing of the lawn to the south and west of the house into three great tiers. The fences were all removed, and big boulders from the hay field west of the house were brought down to make a retaining wall for the lowest terrace. The large maples Mary's great-uncle Roger had planted in 1829 were incorporated into the modern landscaping scheme, making "Maple Terrace" an appropriate name. Dorothy Davis remembered that "the inhabitants of the village including the mason who laid the wall said it would never stand–that the weight of the earth would push it out. My 19-year old brother thought it would stand and he had to take the responsibility. 'Well, Roger,' the mason said, 'You tell me where each stone is to go and I'll put it there.' And it has never budged an inch."[14] The boulders are still, more than eighty years later, securely in place although the earth behind them has heaved and moved.

A Place in the Country

As the house became "Maple Terrace," a summer residence for city folk, the town around it had also become something of a summer resort. Henry and Delia's home became a twentieth-century place in the country, and Hampton became a nostalgically depicted hometown that was home to fewer and fewer people.

The tradition of taking in boarders in Hampton was long-standing. Even Henry and Delia had occasionally had boarders. As early as the 1850s, George Soule, before he became the Congregational minister and married Caroline Litchfield, had boarded with them. And young Henry E., when he was away at school, heard that his parents had "a boarder this winter. How came Miss Bacon to leave Mrs Buttons? I was surprized when I heard she was at our house."[15]

Temporary populations of boarders in small towns grew in the years after the Civil War because the expanding railroad network made it easier to travel to and from "the country." Newly affluent city dwellers began to take "summer vacations," as Henry and Susie Clapp started to do in the 1860s. Susie's sister Genie wrote to Delia about one of those vacations that they had "a very nice boarding place, & very pleasant circle of travelers." They were vacationing on the seashore, and Genie had "never been near the ocean before, & like it so much. Susie's windows look out on the water, & I love so much to watch the huge waves as they break on the rocks."[16]

Hampton's appeal to city vacationers was cool hill-country air and fishing in the large mill pond near Bigelow on the Little River. After the Civil War, the town's reputation as a place to spend the summer began to spread, and some people looked for long-term boarding there. Delia's old friend Lucretia Hayden spoke to her "about a boarding place in Hampton" in case she did not find one in Branford, another country town but nearer the coast. She thought that "if there were good boarding places in Hampton it would be patronised if they ever get the R. R. near, the air there is so pure & delightful, I have been healthier ever since I breathed it & enjoyed the felicity of your companions."[17] Many of the towns in Hampton's area began to cater to summer residents. When Fred Taintor had gone to Woodstock to the academy there, he lived at Elmwood Hall, "A. Chandler, Proprietor. A pleasant and commodious home for school and city boarders," and one term when he went back to school he "found a Miss Cumstock a city boarder had my old room so three other boys besides myself had to go into a room together." The whole house, he reported to his parents, "is full of city boarders."[18]

Henry G. Taintor had helped Hampton become a summer resort by getting a group of men to invest in "the hotel" across the street from the Taintors just before the Civil War. He had supervised its remodeling and enlargement—two houses were put together into one large building complete with a ballroom on the second floor. It had become a meeting place and residence for a regular and transient clientele. Local justices of the peace, including Henry, held court there from the 1850s on. The selectmen and Town Meeting met there in the 1860s when the Town House burned down. The Board of (Tax) Relief of which Henry was a member met there for much of the last third of the nineteenth century.[19] Late in the 1860s, Henry wrote Delia about a "party at the Hotel" which "was a success." He said that "About 70 took Supper at the Hotel." He "took Mrs Underwood with me to the supper. The tables were very handsomely arranged & were loaded with good things Turkeys, Oysters, various kinds of pies & cakes &c &c made up the 'Bill of Fare.' I wish you could have been present."[20]

After the Civil War, Lucius Whittaker and his wife took over the operation of the hotel. The Whittakers raised the food and meat for the hotel on their own farm.[21] Under their aegis it developed into a popular resort for summer people. There were also regular boarders, known to all and considered part of the Whittakers' and the town's extended family. Delia wrote to Mary in 1880 the intimate details reserved for family about the people at the hotel: "The Doctor reports Miss Parker better for the present, as she can retain milk on her stomach, but for a day or two has been obliged to take nourishment only by Enemas as her stomach rejected every thing & she went down very very low. Lida is quite ill, too, with a lame knee, & has had a good deal of fever, so she needs waiting on." Delia continued that "a catholic priest & a book agent are added to Mrs. W's boarders & she nurse & only Sarah Lathrop for help. I am sorry for them all, especially for the sick ones & Mrs W, but think she ought not to have taken extra boarders while trying to wait on Miss Parker."[22] And as was true in most of Hampton's family, Delia did not tell "Mrs. W" what "she ought not" to have done; rather, she visited the sick Miss Parker and tried to help Mrs. Whittaker cope. And there were many times in the last two decades of their lives when Henry and Delia took their "dinners & teas at the hotel."[23]

Stories about the Whittakers' days at the inn still were told nearly a century after the Whittakers had left. One was about how Mrs. Whittaker "had a colored woman worked there. It seems that she was an awful swearer, the colored woman was, and Mrs. Whittaker was getting after her for her swearing. She said 'There's no harm in swearing when you're so god-damned mad you can't help it!'"[24]

The hotel across the street from the Taintors was not the only boarding place for summer visitors. A different "social condition" boarded farther south on Main Street, in the house now owned by the Hampton Antiquarian and Historical Society. "Mary Estelle Burnham acquired the house in 1897," according to the guidebook to the house. "Miss Estella (as she was called) . . . boarded transients from time to time. Among her boarders were chauffeurs of families coming for weekends and holidays, from nearby cities young women wanting country vacations, School teachers, road workers, and Gypsy-moth workers. Her Sunday morning breakfast was codfish balls and maple syrup."[25] By the early twentieth century, several families in town regularly took in summer boarders. At the old parsonage which the Reverend Samuel Moseley had built at the end of Main Street, Jewish boarders were accommodated.

While Delia and Henry were still alive, when their city children and families came to visit, they often stayed at the hotel. The visits were sometimes a matter of painful duty for the daughters-in-law. George's always outspoken wife Emily wrote to Delia about one summer's plans that she was "much obliged to you for your Enquiries in regard to the family who are to be at the Hotel with us next summer—I don't know Exactly why I wanted to know about them—But I did." She went on to say that "there was one part of Mr. Whittaker's letter which said 'we shall be very happy to have you spend the summer here.' I have said from the first that I do not expect to be in Hampton but four weeks—July—But something might happen which would decide me to remain longer." She thought Mr. Whittaker should have understood since she had told him "many times." She made clear to Delia that "We have friends who desire us to be near them in several, more attractive places than Hampton. It seems to me that four weeks will be all I can stand of that exceedingly quiet life but so I felt last season. and yet I managed to stay seven or nine weeks there."[26] When all the members of the large Taintor family were visiting, they took their meals at the hotel, even those who were staying in the house.

At the beginning of the twentieth century, Charles Burnham owned the hotel and Mr. and Mrs. Frank Starkey ran it for him. One woman who worked there when she was a young girl (Bertha Burnham) remembered "all the long porches along the front, upstairs and down, and the barn in the back and the little building next to the inn called 'The Nutshell' and then of course the large Prospect House which was the annex." Built in the first years of the twentieth century, the "Prospect House" annex to the north of the hotel was larger, and had more rooms than the hotel—"the inn"—itself. "People came from all over—Hartford, Rhode Island, New York—and sometimes they'd stay a month," according to Bertha Burnham. "They'd sit out there on the porches rocking, enjoy the air that was supposed to be cooler and healthier than Hartford and those places. They came on the train and I used to drive up to Hampton Station and get them lots of times. I'd drive the canopy-top surrey or—we had a buckboard and smaller buggies. The guests could play golf at the golf course down in Bigelow Valley or go boating on Bigelow Pond."[27]

Run by Annah Burnham, the hotel continued to operate until the 1940s. Bertha Burnham's daughter Ethel said that "people stayed quite a while. There were two ladies who came over from Sag Harbor and my grandfather'd meet them at the boat in New London and then they'd spend several weeks there." The hotel was often full to overflowing. Ethel did not "know how many rooms there were," but she said "one time Annah Burnham gave up her own room and slept on the ironing board. I don't imagine she slept very much but she rested her bones for a bit." The inn's doors closed, she said, "during the years of World War II."[28]

The hotel had become an "inn" to conform to more countrylike parlance long before it closed. Going to the "country" for its old-fashioned qualities was part of the appeal of small-town resorts. In the 1880s for the first time a Hampton store used a printed billhead (such things had long been used in cities). It announced "James S. Baldwin. Choice Family Groceries. A Complete Stock of all Goods Usually Found in a First-Class *Country* Store."[29] No one would have boasted about being a "country" store in earlier days. By the twentieth century, part of the appeal for summer visitors was the chance to view the natives, with their quaint accents and peculiar speech, at play on July Fourth, at Reunions, and at Old Home Days. Robert Fitts, when he was an old man, told about how "there used to be dances down in what was once the Curtis Tavern in Howard Valley. . . . I was only a little fella then. . . . We went down in horse and buggies, that's about all you could get over them roads." The people who went to such dances "paid for it," he said, "about a half a buck or so to get in and they paid the players—somebody played the piano and somebody else the fiddle and they'd have somebody come in and do the callin'. As I say, they used to hold dances upstairs theyah. Boy what a crowd used to pile in there—on that spring floor. Oh, my, you'd get six or eight sets of people on that floor there and boy that thing would hop right up and down!"[30]

As towns like Hampton ceased to be part of the experience of most people, they became increasingly exotic. Even those who had family there considered visiting and learning from such natives out of the ordinary: Edward Martin Fuller, for instance, whose family had always lived in Hampton, thought of his own "experiences of that life on the farm and in Grandfather's workshop" as only "vacation" experiences.[31] Hicks and hayseeds, cracker-barrel philosophers, "naturals" both male and female, swamp Yankees came to be the assumed denizens of rural towns. It was not long before Edgar Lee Masters would apotheosize them in *Spoon River Anthology,* and Clarence Webster would write, in Hampton, about the peculiar but quintessentially American goings-on in *Town Meeting Country.*[32]

It was not only boarders who came for the summer. More affluent city dwellers or those who had more than a few weeks to spend wanted to "take" houses in the country—as Henry and Susie Clapp had rented a vicarage in Tarrytown, New York, for eight summers, for "the rest and refreshment it gives us, year by year."[33] Delia's sister Ellen had told, back in the 1880s, of city folk who came to Vermont small towns in the summer—one "who spends her winters at St Louis & opens her home in Castleton every Summer" and another for whom "this is the only place that seems like home to her & yet she cannot feel it best to live in it."[34] The Taintors were not alone in Hampton in making the big house on the main street into a summer residence. Many of the town's old houses became summer houses, some for "old families" that had moved away, and some were sold to "summer people."

The real citizens of Hampton were not always like the Taintors "up on the hill." One such, Andrew Rindge, had been party to a complicated case that he lost before Henry G. Taintor as justice of the peace in 1882.[35] Henry and Delia's children knew him, as did some of their grandchildren. He was remembered still long years after his death by an old lady who had known of him when she was young. As she told Andrew Rindge's story, "his wife was only twenty-six when she died—she got tuberculosis. But evidently it had been a love match and they were very much in love and when she died it was something he never recovered from. That's why he began to drink. Then he married again and lost the second wife, too. That was probably the straw that broke the camel's back and he went on and became an alcoholic."

After that, Andrew let his "house go to rack and ruin. And he brought the animals in. He lived in that one room and had a fire in the fireplace—in the fall of the year he'd open the window and put a big log into the room coming through the window and just saw off pieces as he needed them." The animals became his companions. "The chickens roosted on the bottom of his bed and the pig lived in the little room off the hall there. He would cook potatoes in one of those iron pots—he would fill that with potatoes and cook them over the fire on the hearthstone and then when they were done and cooled off he'd open the door and call the pigs. They'd come in and eat out of the pot and he'd reach down and get a potato and eat right along with the pigs."

Rindge gained quite a reputation, not only because he was a drunk, but because "he wrote poetry. When anything happened he'd put it into a poem and put it on the town bulletin board at the store." Everything was grist for his poetic mill: "One time he wrote about a certain lady who was very nice to all the gentlemen. Then she decided she'd settle for just one, and all the others weren't welcome so all the others caught her lover and tarred and feathered him. Well when this poem came out, there were the names of all the men who patronized this lady, you see, and they didn't want to be there at all—it was all very hush-hush, of course—and to have it come out and tell who they were—'cause most of them were married men—a scandal in Hampton! He must have had a lot of fun!"[36]

It is not clear that life for Andrew Rindge was a lot of fun. He drowned in a brook on his own property into which he had fallen when drunk. There were not many ways to sanitize that story for the summer-time nostalgia buffs, so most of them did not hear it. It was the sort of truth about small-town life that played well for Edith Wharton,[37] as for Edgar Lee Masters, but it belied Emily Taintor's complaints about the quiet.

A Very Small Place

Hampton's population dropped by almost twenty-five percent between 1880 and 1900. (The 1890 manuscript censuses burned in the National Archives, and are lost.) At the turn of the century there were only 629 people living in 164 households. The enumeration was made by the beginning of June, before many summer people were in town, but twenty-seven people were listed as boarders.

Only half the heads of households were farmers by 1900. Nearly a fifth of the households were headed by women—three of them farmers, two of them nurses (there were three other nurses, two of whom were men). Nursing was a modern, urban occupation, as were the jobs of most of the rest of the men who were employed. They included ten railroad laborers, twenty-nine day laborers, who were distinguished from forty-eight farm laborers, two machinists, two telegraph operators, three teamsters, two railroad station agents, a water man (also for the railroad), a coffee merchant, a peddler of novelties, a sawyer in a steam mill, as well as one "capitalist."

The 1900 census no longer listed occupations for most women, a sign of the triumph of the Victorian domestic ideal (that woman's place was in the home), at least at the Census Bureau, after the 1880s. Not one of the 108 Hampton women listed as "wives" had an "occupation" recorded by the census taker. Twenty-three of the women who were heads of households were listed without an occupation. Since there were several one-room schools, it is peculiar that only one person, a woman, is listed as a schoolteacher.

While the population was declining radically, the resident population was *changing.* Not only young people, but whole families left—and new families replaced some of them. Fifteen percent of Hampton's population in 1900 was born outside of Connecticut, while immigrants to the United States accounted for ten percent, and the children of immigrants yet another ten percent.

Fifteen residents were listed as "black" on the census. (The classification of "mulatto" was no longer available to the census taker, a sign of the crystallization of racism.) There were four families that included blacks, one of which had a white head of household married to a black woman—their two daughters were unclassified as to color. Two black men boarded in town, one with a black family, the other with a white family.

There were thirty-three Irish immigrants in 1900, and forty others whose parents were Irish immigrants. There were seven English immigrants and eleven others whose parents were English. There was a family of five that had migrated from Sweden. There were seven Canadian immigrants. And there were nine Italian immigrant men resident, all of them railroad laborers. Sixteen people were illiterate—eight Irish immigrants, five Italian immigrants, and three adult native-born Americans (one of whom was also listed as an "imbecile").

Twenty years later, the 1920 census showed that for the first time a majority of all Americans lived in cities, in urban places of greater than 2,500 population. Small towns had ceased to be the center of the reality of American life. The population of Hampton had dropped further to 475 people—barely one-third its population in the first census in 1790. The population continued to change. Twenty percent were now born in other states, and another twenty percent were immigrants or the children of immigrants.

While half of the heads of households still listed themselves as farmers, more than fifteen percent of the adults in Hampton held jobs and earned their incomes out of town. At the end of the first decade of the twentieth century renters had occupied more than a quarter of the inhabited houses, and there were several that were not inhabited at the time the census was taken—including Mary Taintor Davis's house. Fewer than half of Hampton's farmers owned the land they worked. With few exceptions, theirs were subsistence farms whose few acres and animals produced food for the families on them. There were some specialized stock and dairy farms that produced some cash income, but most of the money that came into farm families now came from wages for labor or services performed elsewhere.

People who did not live in Hampton owned more and more of the houses on the main street of the village as well as more and more of the land in town. A Hartford gun club bought some acreage to hunt over. Four women kept boardinghouses or hotels.

In 1885, the Grange—formally called the Patrons of Husbandry—had come to Hampton. The Grange Hall was built in 1906, and has seen continuous use ever since. George Fuller, a descendant of the founder of the local Grange, was sitting in his house on Bigelow Road, when he said, "It was started by my great-grandfather George Holt in this room and the sofa that they set on is upstairs." Hampton's lodge was "named Little River Grange after the river goin' by in back here. Great-grandfather was first master and I guess Grandmother was an officer." He remembered that "the purpose of the Grange was learning, agriculture."[38]

The national Grange had started in 1867, and was instrumental in organizing farmers as a political force all over the country, serving as a voice for rural Americans in the rapidly industrializing society as well as providing a small-town institution for sustaining rural social life. It was the first nationwide organization to treat women as equals in all aspects and offices. The weekly meetings of local granges provided ritual and singing, educational lectures, information about up-to-date farming and housekeeping techniques, amateur entertainments, and social get-togethers for small, declining farm communities in settled parts of the country as well as for the scattered and isolated newer farms and farm families in the booming agricultural regions of the West. In Hampton, the Grange, and the Junior Grange started in 1905 to involve children, helped everyone learn modern farm and household techniques and skills. It also fostered a sense of Hampton as part of a region, because "we neighbored around with Granges in other towns,"[39] as one member recalled. The Grange gave Hampton's dwindling population ways to be less isolated in the rural world.

Lessening population or not, Hampton continued to need government in the twentieth century. Its governmental institutions mostly survived the vicissitudes of population decline, but some local government services ceased to be necessary. The town pound fell into disrepair. And haywards, who had been in charge of supervising fences, were no longer among the town's necessary officers. There were many fewer wandering animals, and more to the point, animals were no longer the hazard to people's very livelihood they had been before railroads made out-of-town supplies available to rural householders. In the twentieth century, if an animal broke into a farmer's field and ate some of his grain the farmer could buy flour and bread to eat in a store.

Town meetings still legislated for the community, and elected boards of education, tax assessors, and selectmen carried out the responsibilities of government. The fixing of the two-party system that had come after the Civil War meant in Hampton that the Republican Party dominated local politics. And each town clerk–the pivotal and often most powerful town official–stayed in office for many years. The town continued to send representatives to the state legislature, and voted Republican in congressional and presidential elections. The drift away from the republican virtues and community values of the generation that had voted the Connecticut Constitution of 1818 a century before was still gradual.

Since the 1870s, Hampton had direct rail connections to the outside, urban world. There were two railroad stations (often called depots), one at Clark's Corner on the southwestern edge of town, and the other at "Rawson" on Station Road northwest of the village. As street railways, trolleys, and inter-city railroads provided ever-more-elaborate transportation networks by the beginning of the twentieth century, people could and did live farther and farther from their jobs, their food supplies, and the manufacturers of the goods they needed. In twentieth-century Hampton, "the milk train" went through "at twelve minutes of seven in the morning, that went east, the ha' past eight went west–and most of the kids went to high school, went on that, to Willimantic. Ten o'clock there was one went to Putnam, went east. Eleven o'clock there was another one went west." That was the list of morning trains. "Then there was the ha' past three train come up from Willimantic, brought the kids back from school, the ha' past six down to Willimantic, eight o'clock it came back. The mail come" to Hampton four times "in the mornin' and two at night."[40] Milk trains picked up cans of fresh milk and took them as far away as Boston.

Before the 1920s, most people in town still used horses and horse-drawn transport for local travel. To get the eleven miles to Willimantic by road, Harold Stone said for his family "it must have taken two hours, two and a half. Nellie was a good horse when it come on a buggy. You didn't have to prod 'er, she'd take that steady jog and keep right on goin'." But the Stones, like most modern Hampton families, "mostly took the train to Willimantic."[41]

The automobile changed not only the way people traveled in America, but where and how they lived. The first car came to Hampton in 1904. It belonged to Dr. Amos Avery. John Hammond remembered "it was made like a buckboard with the dashboard up in front and one seat, with the engine under it, and all open in back. You steered it with a lever the way a kid pulls back the handle of his wagon towards him and steers with it."[42] Only after the Ford Motor Company started unlimited mass production of automobiles in 1912 did Americans in great numbers take to the idea of having their own wheels. By the 1920s there were several million cars on roads that had been made for horses and wagons. From 1916 throughout the rest of the twentieth century a *minimum* of a million new cars every year traveled the roads. The automobile made it even more possible than railroads for people to get out of small towns, and they did leave; it also made rural places much more accessible to city people, and they did go to the country, vacation in the country, and even live in the country more than ever before.

State governments and local governments began the never-ending process of paving and maintaining roads for the horseless buggies. The federal government began its automobile-highway construction program in 1916. The changes those highways brought were not always obvious. Hampton, according to Gertrude Pearl, beat the Feds by one year into the highway construction business. "About 1915, I think it was," she said about the construction of the new highway through the green in the center of the

Hampton's railroad station at Rawson.

village. There had been "two roads" through the village, "both of them muddy and a grass strip in the center." When the town "voted to build the road," she said, "they had an awful time–they didn't know where they were going to put a stone crusher to crush rocks" to make the macadam surface of the highway. "Finally they put it right out here" nearly in the middle of the village, "and they used all our stone walls. Used to be y'know, you had a field . . . and there was a stone wall . . . and then there was another stone wall taking up all the space. And they said if they could put their stone grinder out here that they would use all of those stone walls, clear our lots just perfectly clear." Echoes of generations of New England farmers hoping and praying for a "fair field," one "just perfectly clear" of rocks, are in her complaint that "those stone walls" took up all the space, and in her pleasure at having clear lots. Not everyone there was that loved a wall, not even in Robert Frost's New England. But, Mrs. Pearl pointed out, "when they got these rocks all crushed and ready for the road that Green disappeared."[43] The new highway ran (and still runs) through the village between the two rows of houses, and its surface covered what had been the green.

In the years after 1920, the population shift to cities accelerated. All over America, small towns followed the pattern of depopulation Hampton had already known. At the same time, and especially since the middle of the twentieth century, the national population grew explosively. As a result, some places have repopulated and then grown much larger than ever before. That has happened to Hampton. Its 1990 population is larger than it has ever been, a few more than 1,500 people. But the new population has come from cities–not from other rural places. And it is oriented to urban life. In 1950, the census definition of a small town changed: it is now a place of 5,000 or fewer inhabitants. In modern terms, Hampton is an anachronism, an inconceivably small place where people live but almost none of them work. It can no longer claim to be a productive community.

The Death of Dear

One of the reasons the "old homestead" may have become such an important part of early-twentieth-century nostalgia, and such an important part of the lives of families like the Taintors, was because people lived longer. Having grandparents alive when one was adult was becoming a common experience. Some, but not all, of Henry and Delia's grandchildren were *born* while they were still alive. *All* of Mary Taintor Davis's grandchildren knew her well and for a number of years before she died. And, as Sophie Reynolds had written long before about her own grandmother (Sophia Ellsworth), "while she lives I am sure we all feel that Elmwood is our home, no matter how long our absence or how far our wandering."[44] Grandmother's house became a fabled place for several living generations—something which had never before been common human experience.

Then, too, in the half century after the Centennial, interest in American history, and in genealogy and family history, grew and spread, accompanied by fascination with antique furniture and objects, old houses, and even old cemeteries. That, in turn, was a part of the nostalgia for the old home. Families deliberately held reunions to reminisce, the "old folks" were encouraged to tell what they knew of their ancestors, and some people even began to write down what they knew of their family's history.[45]

Home had also become, for many, a metaphor for heavenly paradise and life after death. As Susie once wrote to Delia after they had each had a sister die, "'in a moment–in the twinkling of an eye' comes the summons 'home' and *we* are left weeping and wondering at the strange mystery of death."[46] Of Delia's mother's death, Emma wrote, "I love to think of the flight of the freed spirit, from the poor, worn body, to the better home, where waited many that were dear to her in life, but who had gone before."[47] Much later, when Susie was near death, Delia wrote to Mary, "I wish she might be spared this terrible suffering in her translation to the 'beautiful home' for which she seems so meet."[48] And Sophie Reynolds wrote of her continuing search for home that "I cannot tell when we can go home, or whether we shall stay here, or find a new home, but I *know* that through *God's infinite love & mercy* we *may* all come to our happy home at last–that 'house not made with hands, eternal in the Heavens.'"[49] Mary Taintor Davis took care that her earthly home in Hampton remained a gathering place for all those who were dear to her in life.

Mary's husband, Frederick Wendell Davis, died in June 1917, shortly after their daughter Dorothy married James L. Goodwin. Their elder son, Roger Wolcott Davis, had gone to Yale and become an attorney in Hartford, and their younger son, Ellsworth Davis, was making a career as an

---

A Fourth of July picnic and baseball game in the field behind the Taintor house, the church, and the Center School.

officer in the U.S. Navy. It was not long after her husband's death that Mary began letting Dorothy and Jim Goodwin "have the house for July while she visited" them, rather than have the young couple visit her. In the 1920s, Mary made more changes in the house in order to accommodate joint occupancy with the Goodwins. According to Dorothy, she "made another maid's room by building out a big dormer window in the north ell" over the kitchen. "A second bath room" on the second floor "was made later of the little room" that had been Dorothy's bedroom when she was a child. "The north parlor on the ground floor was used as a guest room, and finally a bathroom was made out of part of the room behind, so that bathroom has a fireplace in it." (That fireplace was removed when the Goodwins later installed a furnace to heat the house.) In order to give the Goodwins a spacious bedroom complete with fireplace for themselves, "a second story was put over the *south* ell," over the big dining room, and another chimney built.[50]

Mary's son Roger bought the next house north on Main Street for a summer home for his growing family of three sons. Those boys well remember their grandmother, whom they all called "Dear," in the big house next door. They often visited her, and had rather formal meals with her, and with Aunt Dorothy and Uncle Jim Goodwin. Ellsworth Davis, Mary's younger son, many years later, bought the old, closed inn across the street, intending to retire there from the navy. Mary's house, owned for many years by the strong only daughter of Henry and Delia Taintor, was passed on not to a son but in turn to her only surviving daughter, Dorothy.

Mary Taintor Davis as "Dear."

Mary Ellen Taintor Davis died at seventy-three on September 18, 1933, not in Hartford where she had lived all her adult life, but in Hampton. Her son Roger said at the time, and his children have always remembered it of her, lying in the big sleigh bed in the southeast bedroom, "It is not often a person has the privilege of dying in the bed in which she was born."

That big sleigh bed still stood in the southeast bedroom of the house when we moved in. If Mary Ellen Taintor was born in that bed, it was Henry and Delia's bed. The south side of the house, then, must have been the side occupied by Roger and Nabby Taintor, and taken over by Henry G. after his uncle Roger's death. He brought his bride, Delia, to that southeast bedroom and to their new sleigh bed. His mother (Mary's grandmother) Judith lived out her life on the north side of the house where she and Solomon had lived.

Mary had never known her grandparents, who had died long before she was born. Perhaps her oldest brother, Henry E., had told her stories of Grandmother Judith Bulkeley Taintor, whom he had known until he was five. But Mary's grandchildren, very much alive as this book was written, knew and loved "Dear." They remember well this granddaughter of men and women born before the American Revolution. One of her grandsons lives in Hampton. One of her granddaughters still wears the necklace Mary's mother wore in her wedding portrait. Some of Mary's grandchildren still visit the house in which she was born and died. And *their* grandchildren are learning the stories of the world she came from.

WHOSE YESTERDAYS?

❧

*"I often visit the place in imagination, and O what changes and
desolations do I behold! Some have sold their possessions and
strangers now occupy them...."*[1]

We have a picture of our house, taken about a hundred years ago.
The maples out front were younger then. There was a white
picket fence behind them. A horse was munching peacefully in
the yard. The porch across the front of the house had the same
slender Victorian columns we have carefully painted and repainted. In the
picture are a group of ladies in the same rockers we still have, hot in their
bombazine dresses, sitting on the porch. We sit and rock on that porch
sometimes with our friends now, a hundred years later.

The Taintor house late in the nineteenth century.

A hundred years ago our great-grandparents were sitting on that porch. No. They really weren't. They were young in those days, but not in Connecticut. They were young in North Dakota and Wisconsin and Michigan in homesteads they were carving out from a hostile land, they were young in Hungary and Russia in the little *shtetls*—the Fiddler-on-the-Roof villages of eastern Europe. They were not sitting on porches. We don't come from old New England.

The United States is a diverse country. The particular story of the Taintors and their neighbors is not by any means the story of us all. The families of many Americans have come to these shores since the Taintors left Hampton. Many of us have lived in cities for generations. Most who came from Asia to a less-than-hospitable America did not live in its small towns. Those whose families came from south of the border into the United States have also had little direct experience with small-town America.

How can we honestly call the story of the Taintors in Hampton, Connecticut, "all our yesterdays"?

One of the greatest values we can see in America's multicultural beginnings and present multicultural mix is that we all have—whatever our ethnic and cultural origins and identities—many pasts and their cultures available to us. If the price of becoming American is tearing oneself loose from one's ethnic and cultural origins, the benefit of acquiring an American identity is that it makes a surprising diversity of cultures and identities available to each of us.

We can learn vital lessons for our survival as a people if we pay attention to what Native Americans, who were here before most of us invaded, knew about care for the land, or learned about cultural survival. We can learn about the triumph of spirit in the face of nearly unbelievable oppression if we pay attention to the past of African Americans. We can learn from the experience of each new wave of migrants about the painfully achieved dignity and the sacrifice of generations who worked for far too little so that their children could participate in more and better.

The particular variety of rural society from which the nation started and made its political, social, and economic way through the nineteenth and into the twentieth century is also an American past available to us all. For the great majority of those who *were* American in the nineteenth century, small-town family life was the common experience. The Taintors were there, in Hampton, and their neighbors, too, were there and in other small towns spreading across the continent. Their story is a real part of the national past.

～

A few days after we moved into our house, we had a visitor. For some reason the dog did not bark, and suddenly Dorothy Holt was in our living room.

"Whooooeee! Yooohooo!" was what we heard.

One of us flushed the upstairs toilet, one of us flushed the downstairs toilet, and we headed for the voice. It came from an elegantly dressed lady replete with stockings and high-heeled shoes. Her gray hair was coiffed in a style popular in the 1930s. This was the 1960s, and we were in blue jeans.

"I'm so glad to meet you!" She greeted our red faces and went on in a rapid-fire rush that was nearly too much for us to take in. What was clear was that she was being friendly, interested, kind, and bossy, all at the same moment. She was there, it developed, to get our names, our children's names, and our birthdays to include in the town-wide Grange birthday calendar for the next year, and to sell us copies of that calendar.

We bought. No one could resist Dorothy Holt. We did not even know what the Grange was yet, but it would not be long before we became members. She also suggested membership in the Congregational church and the Republican Party, but we did not join *everything*.

Twenty-five years later, we were among the sizable chunk of the whole town's population to attend a farewell party for Dorothy Holt at the Congregational church parish hall, which was named "Holt Hall." Dorothy and her husband John E. Holt had moved to Hampton in 1942. They had bought the old Curtis tavern south of the village in Howard's Valley, moved it a few hundred yards to a better site, completely renovated it, and called their place "Still Pond." Dorothy and Jack had plunged into active leadership of the town's social, political, and religious life–they held town offices, Grange offices, Congregational church offices, Republican Party offices, helped consolidate all the one-room schools into a new multigrade elementary school, participated in everything, gave their time, money, and work to making the community operate. When we moved to town, we were invited to dinner at the Holts' to meet some of our neighbors. Jack and Dorothy both spent time showing us around town, showing us "the ropes," and telling us stories of all the people who lived in town. We learned from them that in a small town, everybody may know every secret of your life, and everybody may talk about your secrets, but only very rarely and only when extremely provoked will people confront you or judge you. Since we were not given any special treatment by the Holts, there were by 1991 very few people in Hampton whose lives had not been touched and changed by Jack and Dorothy. In the later years of his life, Jack had made it a point to drive every bride in town to church in his 1920s Brewster-body Rolls-Royce.

Roger W. Davis, Mary and Fred's eldest son.

Jack was no longer alive in 1991 when Dorothy decided she had to move somewhere where she and her lifelong Swiss friend Margitte could get live-in care. So in her always-practical, straight-shooting way, she bought a place in Manchester, about twenty miles away, sold the house she and Jack had built not long before for their old age, and prepared to move. And the whole town turned out to say a tearful good-bye and Godspeed to her. As Wendell Davis–the Taintor descendant who lives in town–said at that farewell party, "The Hampton town sign says 'Settled in 1712 and made a town in 1786.' We should add to it 'organized in 1942,' when the Holts came to town." Dorothy's departure left a very large hole in the fabric of the community.

We learned from Jack and Dorothy Holt not only how our small town worked, but how to cherish it. And we also learned that families still come to town, put down deep roots, and then depart.

Roger Wolcott Davis wrote in his will in March 1950 that it was his "earnest desire that my ancestral home in Hampton known as 'Maple Terrace' and a suitably sized lot therefor shall continue in the ownership of descendants of my mother, Mary Taintor Davis." When Roger's sister Dorothy Goodwin had died, childless, in 1945, he had inherited the house. His son Wendell, with his wife, Alison, and their young family, had lived in the house three years in the late 1940s. Except for that time, it was not lived in for twenty-five years after Dorothy died. None of Roger's children found it possible to live in it, and they had little time to spend in Hampton at all. Nevertheless, in view of his father's will, Roger's lawyer-son Merriam had an agonizing task when he and his brothers reluctantly concluded that if the house was to have a hope of preservation it must be sold.

We did not know as we finally brought the year-and-a-half-long adventure of buying it to a successful conclusion on July 3, 1967, that we had just rammed into the tip of the submerged mountain which was the Taintor-Davis family's history. We thought, as do most people, that when we bought a house we were finished with its previous owners. We have learned in the twenty-five years since then that old houses in small towns sometimes preserve some of the character of people who have lived in and shaped them. We have learned, much more importantly, that one can acquire roots and flourish in places where others have lived—by trying to understand and respect their lives.

We have continued the long Taintor tradition of changing the house to suit those who live in it. We have built bookcases into almost all the rooms in the house (when our daughter applied to college she wrote in one application that only the bathrooms did not have bookcases). We made what had been Henry and Delia's southeast parlor into Jim's study, and after some years as a dining room, the northeast parlor was made into Janet's study. The southwest room that Mary had extended and made a big dining room has become our living room—as close as we come to a "parlor." The greatest change we have so far made was to expand the old kitchen into a very large family-dining-kitchen room with modern windows to the west (as well as the north windows Mary had installed) and a big wood stove on a tiled hearth.

Not long after we moved in, we tried to insulate the house to make it more livable in these modern times. We found we could only insulate in the attic, because the outside walls were made of wood slabs (no air space into which to put insulation). We took up some floorboards in order to blow in the insulation, and found a small old-fashioned square glass bottle between the attic floor and the ceiling below. It must have been blown into a mold because there are letters on one side that say "O M Ballard New York" and on the other "Permanent Liquid Hair Dye." "Who do you suppose," we said to ourselves, "might have used hair dye? Maybe a servant, who dropped the bottle in the attic?" We too easily assumed it would have been a woman.

Years later, when we went through Henry G. Taintor's meticulously kept cashbooks, we found frequent entries for hair dye. Henry, according to family tradition his great-grandsons repeated to us, had a "remarkable head of hair." He was evidently pretty vain about it. He went all the way to

Hartford to get his hair cut. And he used hair dye. Even when we didn't know it, those Taintors were impinging on our lives.

Outside the house, we have taken off the large dark-green shutters ("blinds") Henry and Delia had added—because here in "do-it-yourself-or-it-doesn't-get-done" Yankeeland the work of caring for, scraping, and painting seventy large, working wooden shutters has proved more than we are willing to do. (The shutters are all carefully stacked in the barn—also in good Taintor tradition—so they can be used by some future generation or owner, or so they can be sold for someone else to use on some other house.)

During the last year this book was being written, the upstairs south side of the house (which includes Henry and Delia's bedroom, which was then Mary's room, and the rooms which had been fixed up and added on for the Goodwins, along with the first bathroom in the house) has been lived in by our daughter, son-in-law, and our first grandson. In some sense, then, we have brought the house back full circle—two closely related families have been living here as they did when Roger and Nabby and Solomon and Judith moved in.

People who do not live in small towns are often nostalgic about them. They talk about America's lost rural values. They visit the scenes of an often made-up small-town past. Migrants to cities from small agricultural towns, along with their children and grandchildren, often institutionalize their nostalgia. They make a point of going to "old home days" and family reunions. And they sometimes get together in clubs of people who are migrants from the same town.

Nicholas Lemann, in his recent book, *The Promised Land,* which deals with the great African-American migration from the rural South to the cities of the North, writes of one such club of migrants from Clarksdale, Mississippi, in Chicago that they "started the Clarksdalians Club, which was one of hundreds of associations for people from a shared Southern hometown that sprang up in Chicago in the 1970s, as the people who had made the great migration became middle-aged and nostalgic." One such club in Chicago owns a clubhouse building, Lemann wrote, but "the Clarksdalians Club" did not. Nevertheless "it holds regular meetings, puts on large dinner dances, gives scholarships and community service awards, and rents a fleet of buses once a year to take its members back to Clarksdale for a reunion."[2]

The people who joined that club had escaped to Chicago from the near-peonage of sharecropping in the South. The Clarksdale they visit in their meetings and on their buses has nothing to do with the life they abandoned when they left. The community and the families they are homesick for no longer exist. But they still go back.

~

The constant in small-town life has been change. Towns have grown and declined, houses have burned or been torn down, the people and families in them have come and gone. The Reverend Ludovicus Weld, who was Hampton's Congregational minister for more than thirty years, summed up the town's vicissitudes in his eloquent 1827 letter to Roger Taintor:

> Death has indeed made distressing ravages and materially changed the condition of families, if not of society, in Hampton. . . . I often visit the place in imagination, and O what changes and desolations do I behold! Some have sold their possessions and strangers now occupy them; some have withdrawn from the Society who were once among the pillars by which it was supported. Some are shaken in property who once, to appearance, were approaching independence. Some have sunk into insignificance and contempt, who were once respectable. Some who merit detestation still hold a decent standing through the criminal partiality of friends, and their own duplicity and hypocritical pretensions.[3]

We find ourselves among the "strangers" who "now occupy" Hampton. And Weld's description of the nature of a changing small town still applies.

We moved from a city to Hampton, and it changed our lives. We were slowly and cautiously invited into the life of the town, and we gradually found out that it was very like becoming part of a sprawling family where everyone had very long memories, everyone was very sensitive, and everyone knew a lot about everyone else. We never knew who was related to whom, who hated someone else for something done twenty-five or fifty years before, which part of whose family was on which side in feuds about everything from lovers to tax assessments. We still have not been in town long enough to know everything we need to know in order to understand. But we quickly learned that such personal, familial concerns were what *mattered* in making the community work, because they were the ways in which the independent individuality of each actual person in town was recognized and incorporated.

We were invited to take part. We were asked to join the Grange—and the woman who asked us also taught our seven-year-old daughter to knit. The parent-teacher organization of the Hampton Consolidated School roped us in, and we soon were officers. The volunteer fire company hesitantly asked Jim if he wanted to join and he did. Our two children in school found that the local enrichment program consisted of being taken to the town library and taught how to use it, and being taught by neighbors in town, individually and in Scouts and 4-H clubs, to sew, cook, camp, ride horses, hike in the woods, and twirl a baton. Jim was asked to become a member of the library board (which he continues to be) and Janet was elected to the school board. Not many years after we moved to town, Jim started being elected moderator of Town Meeting, and he has been moderator for a majority of the Town Meetings ever since. (In the most recent meeting, he had to rule Janet out of order for trying to get a last word in after the question had been called, which brought a roar of laughter from the 150 people there, and offers of a refuge for the night for Jim from several townspeople after the meeting adjourned.)

Our children grew up in Hampton, went through the Hampton School and graduated from the regional high school that opened the year we moved to town. We have made many close friends in town, because the town has really become "family." And we have made some enemies, too, for the same reason.

Since our Hampton—in contrast to the Taintors' Hampton—is part of an urban world, and so are we, we do not spend all our time in town. Jim is a "perfesser" (as some of our friends in Hampton like to call him) at the University of Connecticut, which is fifteen miles away in the town of Mansfield. And both of us travel, frequently, to Boston and New York, as well as to Providence, Worcester, Hartford, and New Haven, for friends, lectures, meetings, theater, museums, collections, and libraries. It means very high mileage on our cars, but that, we figure, is just one of the necessary expenses of living in Hampton. Where else, we ask ourselves, could we live in the midst of a community that really cares about us and belongs to us—and still see our other friends and have the advantages of all those cities? Where else could we afford to own an old fourteen-room (or more, depending on the rooms you "count") house on more than seven acres of land in the middle of a picture-postcard New England village?

Quite aside from all such considerations, Hampton is home. It is our hometown. It is not only the place we go back to, to visit; it is where we live. And where we hope to be buried.

"Scribble, scribble, scribble, eh Mr. Gibbon?" is what King George III said to that author when Edward Gibbon presented to the king the second volume of his great *The Decline and Fall of the Roman Empire.* And while we know we have not written such a work as Gibbon's, we also know it has portrayed—through the voices of the Taintors, their friends and neighbors—the decline and fall of the agrarian small-town and family life upon which the United States was based at its formation. In the century and a quarter or so spanned by this book, Americans everywhere decided to pay—and, as we have seen, worked hard to pay—what modern urban and industrial life cost: the abandonment of the communities and families of small towns with their economic, social, political, and religious networks, cultures, and values. We have tried to paint a portrait of the decline even to terminal hanging-on of one of the *places* from which the American nation and the American people came.

We decided to write this book because we had come to live, twenty-five years ago, in an altogether remarkable survival from another age. We have completed the book surrounded by every evidence that our small town, too, is turning into an urban bedroom filled with people who remain strangers to one another, just as if they lived in a city. More people now reside in Hampton than it ever before contained. For most of the twentieth century, people in town have maintained *some* of the community concern for the common welfare that had been the staple of nineteenth-century small towns. But its old institutions—the Town Meeting, the Board of Selectmen, the churches, the Grange, the schools, the volunteer fire company, and the volunteer ambulance corps—now look for services and for values, very often for leadership, from "out of town." The two-parent families that used to live and work in single-family homes in small towns are becoming quaint anachronisms in Hampton, as they are everywhere. Like home, hometowns are not any longer where many of us live. They may be all our yesterdays, but they are not our todays or our tomorrows.

Part of the myth of the small town is that it is wonderful because it is like an extended family. But we have seen that if it is like an extended family, it is not necessarily wonderful. It is not always open or welcoming to those who are new or those who are different. Towns and families often are closed systems, opposed to allying themselves to those not born in their small circle. The Taintors found that out, and all the generations of the family have experienced some exclusion from the Hampton community. The efforts of the town to maintain its exclusivity brought discomfort and pain to others—to Indians, to African Americans, to Irish Americans, to Roman Catholics, and to other immigrants. In a small town there is always the potential for oppression of those who are part of the family-community but who dare to differ or to stray. While the ideal of the town as an extended family is that it cares and it does not judge, and there have been many who render more than lip service to that ideal, it was nevertheless not achieved in any real past. Is it worth being nostalgic for a myth?

When we finished writing the body of this book, we decided to try to find Taintor Creek and the site of Fred Taintor's ranch. The creek wasn't on any map.

We made our way first to Englewood, Kansas; a town that is mostly gone. Some folks in the Senior Center there, though, directed us to the patch of weeds which is all that is now left on a ghost of a main street of Fred's Home State Bank, which they remembered even though it had failed when the oldest of them could not have been more than a child. One of them remembered the Taintor family and knew where they had lived in town although they had moved away seventy years ago.

In Gate, Oklahoma, south of Englewood and the Cimarron, one older lady, the mainstay of a tiny historical museum, knew Fred Taintor's name. Her father had worked for him, and when she was a little girl she'd picnicked by Taintor Creek. She remembered it as a lovely place, but she hadn't been out there in years because the ranchers who own the area had closed it to the public.

Between Gate and Knowles was a historical marker explaining that "No Man's Land" had been the label for the area left off of maps when the southern border of Kansas, northern border of Texas, eastern border of New Mexico, and western border of what was then "Indian Territory" had been established. It is now the panhandle of the state of Oklahoma. Fred Taintor picked a perfect place for using range land without having title to it.

Our search ended in Knowles, Oklahoma, where, over burritos in the Country Store/Cafe, we found more memories of Fred. The formica-covered tables were nearly all filled by large, weathered men wearing brimmed caps. We met Knowles's postmistress, and she said that indeed she knew where Taintor Creek was and that the ranch had been a cool oasis in a mostly hot and treeless country. She had often picnicked there. The county had dammed the creek and made a small lake some years back, and everybody used to go there. The whole area, however, was now closed to the public.

"I can draw you a map to get you there," said a man who came to sit at our table. We were to take dirt roads out of Knowles, cross several cattle guards (it is still ranch country), and following his map we'd find the Taintor ranch site. We'd pass an ancient lake bed, he said, which used to be Fred Taintor's horse pasture.

Another big man stopped by to tell us he "just couldn't stand it any longer" not to speak to us because his grandmother "worked on the Taintor ranch from the time she was ten until she was twenty-two when she married Granddad." He had been told it was a beautiful ranch and the Taintors were good people to work for.

Because we lived in the house where he grew up, the people we spoke to who had memories of Fred Taintor seemed to feel we had a connection to their lives. We found good, pleasant memories in these small towns of a man and a family who had left before most of the people remembering were born. In a country where ranchers and farmers were and often are bitter enemies, Fred Taintor was special. Shakespeare's Mark Antony had it wrong. People have remembered the good Fred Taintor did for a long time.

When Iris Origo wrote a biography of an unimportant fifteenth-century Florentine merchant, from his preserved letters and business documents, she justified it by writing that "it is the smaller men, who belong almost completely to the climate of their times, who can tell us most."[4] So we have tried to allow, as much as we could in the space of this book, the voices of all the people we have found in the stacks of letters and records and documents of the Taintor-Davis Collection to be heard. They were, after all, the men and the women who were *there*.

There are still hundreds of letters in that collection that we have done no more than read. There are stories of people's lives in cities near and far that we have had no room to tell here. And there are letters, scrapbooks, diaries, journals, and account books of many in the family, and more in the town, that we have not read or even found. The treasure of that collection, and the excitement of opening old letters and reading them for the first time, and the delights of finding yet more stories of real people are unending.

It is, nevertheless, difficult to stop telling about people we have not only come to know but come to love, as we read their letters, pored over their accounts, and looked at their pictures. While it has been a great pleasure to try to piece together the evidence and write about their lives, it has been terrible each time we have been forced to recognize and write about their deaths: Roger and Solomon, Nabby and Judith; Nathaniel F. Martin, painter and furniture maker; crotchety Ludovicus Weld; deaf-mute John Brewster, Jr. (when we first came upon his portrait of his half-sister Betsey Avery Brewster at the Museum of Fine Arts in Boston, we turned to each other and said, "Hey, we know her! She married lawyer Joseph Prentis and lived just down Main Street!"); John A. Taintor, and Adelia and their daughters; Edwin Bulkeley Taintor, and his daughters Lucy, Caroline, Susie, and Genie; Dan Bulkeley and Phoebe, along with Andrew J. and Phidelia; Henry G. and Delia; the Ellsworth sisters Abby and Ellen, their brother Frederick, and all their cousins, aunts, and uncles; Henry E. and Jennie, George and Emily, and "Cousin" Lucy, Willie and Lizzie, and Fred with his life as a rancher on the high plains; strong, lively Mary–"Dear"– and Fred Davis; and finally, their children, especially Dorothy, whose story of her ancestral home was our real beginning of the Taintor story, and Roger, who did not want to have his mother's house leave the family.

We have sought roots in a past that did not seem to belong to us. Can you buy into history when you buy a house? Only in America, perhaps. We would like to feel that we have provided the next best thing to Roger Davis's desire that the house continue in the hands of Mary Taintor Davis's descendants. We have given the house good care and an active life. We have done our bit to keep the community that is Hampton going. And we have endeavored to tell the stories that made Mary Taintor Davis's house so important to her.

We have tried, with respect for the realities of their lives, to find our own roots in the Taintors and in Hampton and to understand that other people's pasts can be all our yesterdays.

ACKNOWLEDGMENTS

⌘

More than we can adequately express, we are grateful to Wendell Davis and Alison Davis, who not only have been good friends for a quarter century but who also actually brought us all the boxes and bags and cartons full of what has become the Taintor-Davis Collection. They have told us stories, and collected other information, and given us introductions to most of what we know about their family and about Hampton as well. We are also grateful to Wendell and his brothers, Roger W. Davis and Merriam Davis, for having decided to sell us their grandmother's house twenty-five years ago, for helping us to find out about their family, and for granting us permission to use and publish material from the Taintor-Davis Collection. And we thank Merriam for the portrait of Henry E. Taintor that he gave us to "watch over our work" on this book.

We appreciate that we were able to spend an afternoon in our living room with the late Henry C. Taintor. We thank his nieces, Leanne Taintor Souzis and Eleanor (Laurie) Taintor Stevens, for the material they lent us, for permission to publish from that material, and for the information they provided about their grandfather, Fred Taintor.

We thank Mark Davis and Beth Davis Powning for their cheerful friendship and for the stories they told us about the house.

There are letters in the Taintor-Davis Collection, the great majority of them written more than a century ago, from hundreds of different people. We have not been able, with the time and resources available to us, to search out the descendants of all those correspondents, who could by now number in the thousands. In these pages we have treated the letter-writers with respect, and we sincerely acknowledge our gratitude to their descendants for their ancestors' written expressions.

We gratefully acknowledge:

The University of Connecticut Research Foundation for support which enabled James Oliver Robertson to begin the organization of the Taintor-Davis Collection and start the research process;

The Fannie S. Cohen "Foundation" which has given generous support over the whole term of this project, as it has to so many others;

The Rockefeller Foundation for granting us residencies at the Rockefeller Study Center in the Villa Serbelloni, Bellagio, Italy, for five luxurious weeks of uninterrupted writing combined with intelligent and critical audiences for our ideas;

The MacDowell Colony, in Peterborough, New Hampshire, for making us Chubb LifeAmerica Fellows at the Colony, and giving us precious writing time in the most favorable circumstances, along with the support and friendship of artists and writers and composers; and we want especially to thank Mary Carswell.

Another group which has given us both support and encouragement in the writing of this book consists of Bernice Buresh, Phyllis Karas, Diana Korzenik, Caroline Toll Oppenheim, and Caryl Rivers. In the same context, we are grateful to Sally Steinberg and Diane Cox.

Neither of us separately, nor both of us together, could have brought this project to successful completion without the constant support of E. Diane Kirkman.

This project involved research in collections other than the Taintor-Davis. We are much indebted to the librarians and staffs of the Connecticut State Library and the Connecticut Historical Society, both in Hartford, for access to their collections, help in finding the materials we

Roger W. Davis, Jr., Merriam Davis, and Wendell Davis, about 1925. Forty-two years later, they sold their grandmother's house to the authors.

needed, and guidance through some of them. We are particularly grateful
to Christopher Bickford, director of the Connecticut Historical Society, for
all his help and for permission to publish from several of the Society's manuscript documents. We also wish to acknowledge the staffs and collections
of the Stirling Library at Yale University; the Homer Babbidge Library at
the University of Connecticut; the American Antiquarian Society in Worcester, Massachusetts; the Massachusetts Historical Society in Boston; Old
Sturbridge Village in Sturbridge, Massachusetts; the Illinois State Library
in Springfield, Illinois; the New-York Historical Society in New York City;
and the Archives of the University of Connecticut Library in Storrs,
Connecticut.

Our research has not only been in libraries and other formal collections. There are many individuals and families who have helped over a
number of years with the many tasks of research and have provided us
with appropriate materials for this project: Burr Harrison (who, with
Nicholas Maxwell, did the initial cemetery research); Ethan and Pamela
Tolman (who helped with newspapers, local history, and small-town life);
Andrew Leinhoff (who gave us copies of Bennett letters he found in his
house); June Pawlikowski Miller (who lent us C. C. Button's journals);
Charles and Marian Halbach (who lent us a Jewett scrapbook); Bea and
Bill Utley (for letters to Patrick Pearl–and a lot more); Austin and Marian
Emmons (for a stream of information about Hampton people); Bruce Stark
and Doris Sherow (for material ideas); and Bruce Daniels (whose work
started our interest in Connecticut history).

We wish to express our gratitude to Lance Mayer and Gay Myers,
conservators, who involved us with the Devotion family, the Lyman Allyn
Museum, and American portraits of the late eighteenth and nineteenth centuries. We are also grateful to Henry Bowers of Scotland, Connecticut,
who introduced us to Taintor materials in the Windham Free Library and
to the social studies program at Parish Hill High School.

Rosemary Ballard, when she directed the restoration project at
Elmwood, the Ellsworth Homestead, was a valuable source of information,
as was Donna Holt Siemiatkoski.

People of the town of Hampton gave us direct help and generous
encouragement in becoming part of the town and in the writing of this
book. Rather than risk forgetting the many who deserve mention, we want
to acknowledge with deep gratitude every single person in Hampton who
over the past twenty-five years has enriched our lives. We also wish to
thank all those with whom we have served on the Hampton School Board,
the Regional District Eleven School Board, the Hampton Planning and
Zoning Commission, and the Hampton Conservation Commission, as well

as all our fellow members of the Hampton P.T.O., Little River Grange #36, the Hampton Volunteer Fire Company, the Board of the Fletcher Memorial Library, the Couples Club, the Hampton Community Players, the Board of the *Hampton Gazette,* and, most recently, the Hampton Seniors Club. And it would have been difficult to produce this book without the inspiration and sustenance, as well as the photocopying and fax services, provided by Quentin Woodward and The Hampton General Store.

None of this could have happened if Lib Norris had not been the real estate agent who helped us buy our house. Or if we had not had the advice of Michael S. Dukakis and the help of Barclay Robinson, Jr.

Many read or listened to draft portions of the text and gave us invaluable suggestions and criticism. Foremost among them are our son, Jonathan Marc Robertson, our daughter, Rachel Molly Robertson Maxwell, and her husband, Nicholas Peter Pomp Maxwell, who gave editorial help, advice, and comfort we could not have done without. Our good friends and colleagues Joel and Karen Kupperman, and Dick and Irene Brown, carefully read and gave us critical help on several chapters. So have Fritz and Sara Freer, and Chuck Zink.

We are grateful for the appreciative audiences at the Mansfield Historical Society, the Columbia Historical Society, and the Hampton Antiquarian and Historical Society. We thank the Old Sturbridge Village Symposium, "Art, Popular Culture, and Society in Rural New England, 1780–1850," and Caroline Sloat and Jessica Nicoll for the opportunity to present some of the material used in this book.

We wish to thank Florence Wisenhunt of Gate, Oklahoma, and Idell Green and Charles Bond of Knowles, Oklahoma, who helped us find Taintor Creek, and who told us more, perhaps, than they knew about Fred Taintor.

Professional-historian colleagues at the University of Connecticut have been particularly helpful and encouraging. So, too, were Arthur W. Wang, Elaine Markson, and Joanna Coles. Jeremy Tarcher was, as usual, very supportive.

We still do not quite believe the extent of the help and encouragement we have received from Aaron Asher and Joy Johannessen. All of it was aided and abetted by Carol Leach. Joel Avirom's design has shown us what a beautiful book can be.

Finally, there is a special category of our extended family who must be thanked because we could not have done this book without them. Those we have not already mentioned include Judy Zink, Aleza Beauvais, Rad and Leila Ostby, Bill Homan, Bonnet and Frank Sornberger, Susan McCurdy, Bill and Frances Ackerly, Richard F. Samson, Betty and Charlie

Gregg, Miranda Marvin, Mimi Brien, Helen and Ed Samson, Dorothy and Paul Homan, Shirley Roe, Molly Samson and Michael Blackmun, our mothers who are still with us, Fannie S. Cohen and Frances E. C. H. Robertson, and our fathers who are not, D. Leonard Cohen and Haney M. Robertson.

J.O.R.
J.C.R.

NOTES

In the following Notes, the Taintor-Davis Collection is referred to by abbreviations for each of its sub-sections:

> rst = Roger & Solomon Taintor papers
> jat = John A. Taintor papers
> ebt = Edwin Bulkeley Taintor papers
> db = Dan Bulkeley papers
> hgt = Henry G. Taintor papers
> det = Delia Ellsworth Taintor papers
> het = Henry E. Taintor papers
> get = George E. Taintor papers
> wt = William Taintor papers
> ft = Frederick Taintor papers
> mtd = Mary Taintor Davis papers
> tdmisc = Taintor Davis miscellaneous papers

All references to "Hampton" are to Hampton, Connecticut, unless otherwise specified. The Town Records of Hampton are referred to by the series title (Hampton Deeds or Hampton Town Records), the book letter, and a page number. The secondary works cited in the notes are only those from which we quote or on which we have depended for insight and interpretation. We have tried to cite the latter only once.

PROLOGUE

[1]See Susan Allport, *Sermons in Stone: The Stone Walls of New England and New York* (New York, 1990). 1871 U.S. Department of Agriculture *Statistics of Fences in the United States* said there were 20,505 miles of wall in Connecticut, and that it would have taken a thousand men working 365 days per year fifty-nine years to build those walls.

[2]Dorothy Davis Goodwin, "My Ancestral Home" (1943). Photocopy of handwritten manuscript, given to us by Merriam Davis on 3 July 1967 when we bought the house.

[3]We wish to express our deep gratitude to Wendell and Alison Davis for the loan of the Taintor-Davis Collection which belonged to Wendell Davis's ancestors, and for permission to use and publish its contents. We also wish to thank Roger W. Davis and Merriam Davis for their permission to use the collection and for all their help. The Davis family has been an important part of our personal, familial, and professional lives since 1967, and we are very grateful to them all.

[4]Ludovicus Weld, Fabius, New York, to Roger Taintor, Hampton, 27 January 1829, rst.

[5]George Sisson, Abington (Luzerne County, Pennsylvania–Wallsville, Pennsylvania, postmark), to Dan Bulkeley and Rodman Sisson, Hampton, 3 February 1835, db.

⁶Ann Gurley, San Francisco, California, to Delia E. Taintor, Hampton, 4 September 1855, tdmisc.

[7]Delia E. Taintor, Hampton, to Henry E. Taintor, New Haven, Connecticut, pencil draft, undated, c. 1863, det.

[8]H. L. Clapp, New York City, to Mr. and Mrs. Henry G. Taintor, Hampton, 3 January 1878, det.

[9]The underlying scholarship on which our study is based was pioneered by Fernand Braudel and the Annales school in Paris. Our models include: Emmanuel LeRoy Ladurie's *Montaillou: The Promised Land of Error* (New York, 1978), a brilliant study of a thirteenth-century village in the French Pyrenees, based on analysis of Inquisition documents; Robert Darnton, *The Great Cat Massacre and Other Episodes in French Cultural History* (New York, 1984), about eighteenth-century French artisans and policemen; Carlo Ginzburg, *The Cheese and the Worms: The Cosmos of a Sixteenth-Century Miller* (Baltimore, 1980); Iris Origo, *The Merchant of Prato: Francesco di Marco Datini, 1335–1410* (Boston, 1986), about an Italian Renaissance merchant, of whom Origo wrote that "it is the smaller men, who belong almost completely to the climate of their times, who can tell us most"; and Jonathan Spence, *The Death of Woman Wang* (New York, 1978), about peasant life and death in a sixteenth-century Chinese village, written as an antidote to "local studies [which] have tended to focus not on rural areas for their own sakes but rather on areas that had some prior claim to fame."

Among professional American historians, the works important to us for the problems they pose include: Hal S. Barron's *Those Who Stayed Behind: Rural Society in Nineteenth-Century New England* (Cambridge, 1984), about a late-nineteenth-century Vermont village; Jonathan Prude's *The Coming of Industrial Order: Town and Factory Life in Rural Massachusetts, 1810–1860* (Cambridge, 1983), about Massachusetts towns very near Hampton as they were affected by Samuel Slater and his mills; John Mack Faragher's *Sugar Creek: Life on the Illinois Prairie* (New Haven, 1986), a model of community history; and Steven Hahn and Jonathan Prude's edition of recent essays, *The Countryside in the Age of Capitalist Transformation* (Chapel Hill, 1985).

[10]Clifford Geertz, *Local Knowledge: Further Essays in Interpretive Anthropology* (New York, 1983); recent American social histories which use the local and particular as the basis for general interpretations include: Richard D. Brown, *Knowledge Is Power: The Diffusion of Information in Early America, 1700–1865* (New York, 1989); Joy Day Buel and Richard Buel, Jr., *The Way of Duty: A Woman and Her Family in Revolutionary America* (New York, 1984); John Putnam Demos, *Entertaining Satan: Witchcraft and the Culture of Early New England* (New York, 1982); Robert A. Gross, *The Minutemen and Their World* (New York, 1976); and Christopher M. Jedrey, *The World of John Cleaveland: Family and Community in Eighteenth-Century New England* (New York, 1979).

[11]Peter Laslett, in *The World We Have Lost* (New York, 1965) and *The World We Have Lost—Further Explored* (London, 1983), explores family and community life before industrialization.

[12]Sinclair Lewis, *Main Street* (New York, 1920); Shirley Jackson, "The Lottery," from *The Lottery,* by Shirley Jackson (New York, 1948, 1949); Grace Metalious, *Peyton Place* (New York, 1959).

[13]The original deed to the Taintors is in our possession. The story about the house being built for Thomas Stedman, Jr., is in Ellen D. Larned, *History of Windham County, Connecticut* (Bicentennial Edition, Chester, Connecticut, 1976. First published 1880), II 240–41, 245.

CHAPTER 1

[1]Larned, *History,* I 289.

[2]Larned, *History,* I 99.

[3]Hampton, Connecticut, First Congregational Church Records 1723–1897 (Connecticut State Library), I 92; Larned, *History,* I 91–8.

[4]Hampton Church Records, I 137; Larned, *History,* I 282.

[5]Perry Miller, "Jonathan Edwards and the Great Awakening," in *America in Crisis,* ed. Daniel Aaron (New York, 1952) 7; Alan Heimert, *Religion and the American Mind: From the Great Awakening to the Revolution* (Cambridge, Mass., 1966); Robert G. Pope, *The Half-Way Covenant: Church Membership in Puritan New England* (Princeton, 1969); Larned, *History,* I 283, 434; Hampton Church Records I 11–12, 65–73.

[6]Jean Hankins has worked on Ebenezer Moseley and kindly shared some of her research with the authors; *New England Historical Genealogical Register,* III 195, IV 277, V 257–8, 402; Larned, *History,* II 68.

[7]Larned, *History,* II 241–2.

[8]Hampton Baptist Church Records (Micro-film 496, Connecticut State Library), I 1–5; Larned, *History,* II 193, 283–4; Hampton Deeds C316.

[9]Gravestone of Mrs. Mary, consort of the Reverend Samuel Moseley in Hampton's North Cemetery.

[10]Hampton Church Records, I 139; Robert H. Abzug, *Passionate Liberator; Theodore Dwight Weld and the Dilemma of Reform* (New York, 1980); Charles Roy Keller, *The Second Great Awakening in Connecticut* (New Haven, 1942); Richard D. Shiels, "The Second Great Awakening in Connecticut: Critique of the Traditional Interpretation," *Church History* 49 (Winter 1980) 401–16; Richard D. Shiels, "The Feminization of American Congregationalism, 1730–1835," *American Quarterly* 33 (Spring 1981), 46–62.

[11]Larned, *History,* II 143.

[12]*Ibid.* 124–5.

[13]*Ibid.* 145–54.

[14]*Ibid.* 190.

[15]*Ibid.* 163, 174, 179.

[16]*Ibid.* 181.

[17]Ellen D. Larned, *Historic Gleanings in Wind-ham County, Connecticut* (Providence, R.I., Pres-ton & Rounds Company, 1899), 127.

[18]*The Bulkeley Genealogy,* compiled by Daniel Lines Jacobus (New Haven, Connecticut, 1933), 722.

[19]The authors are grateful to Richard D. Brown for his comments on this section.

[20]Larned, *History,* II 238–40. See also Richard L. Bushman, *From Puritan to Yankee: Character and the Social Order in Connecticut, 1690–1765* (Cambridge, Mass., 1967); Bruce C. Daniels, *The Connecticut Town* (Middletown, Conn., 1979); Charles S. Grant, *Democracy in the Connecticut Frontier Town of Kent* (New York, 1961); Sumner C. Powell, *Puritan Village: The Formation of a New England Town* (Middletown, Conn., 1963).

[21]Hampton Town Records A20–21.

[22]Hampton Deeds C52, C85, C97, C149, C152, C260.

[23]*Ibid.* C141.

[24]*Ibid.* C189, C196.

[25]Hampton Town Records A10–11.

[26]*Ibid.* A11.

[27]*Ibid.* A24.

[28]*Ibid.* A68, A104.

[29]*Ibid.* A60, 66, 72, 92, A114, *passim.*

[30]*Ibid.* A115.

[31]*Ibid.* A56.

[32]*Ibid.* A39–40.

[33]*Ibid.* A73, A31, A97, A117.

[34]*Ibid.* A77.

[35]*Ibid.* A123. Also see Robert E. Cray, *Pau-pers and Poor Relief in New York City and Its Rural Environs, 1700–1830* (Philadelphia, 1988).

[36]Hampton Town Records A93.

[37]Larned, *History,* II 244; Hampton Town Records A140.

[38]Hampton Town Records A29, A31–3, A48–50.

[39]Hampton Deeds B232.

[40]Hampton Town Records A50.

[41]*Ibid.* A48.

[42]*Ibid.* A34.

[43]*Ibid.* A130.

[44]*Ibid.* A103, A108–9.

[45]Hampton Deeds C335.

[46]Hampton Town Records A39–40.

[47]Hampton Deeds B57, B106, B349, C56, C91, C93, C104, C312, C330, C368, C472, D32, D204, D205, D220, D221; Hampton Town Records A11–14, A42–45, A58; Larned, *His-tory,* II 240, 245.

[48]Hampton Deeds. B57, B206, B309, B349, C436, C495; Account Book of Nathaniel F. Martin (Connecticut Historical Society), *passim.*

[49]Hampton Deeds D8, C550; Larned, *History,* II 240.

[50]Larned, *History,* I 288–9 contains Elizabeth Shaw's story. See also David E. Philips, *Leg-endary Connecticut* (Hartford, 1984).

CHAPTER 2

[1]Dorothy Davis Goodwin, "My Ancestral Home" (1943).

[2]Hampton Deeds B213, B246, and B317.

[3]Dorothy Davis Goodwin, "My Ancestral Home" (1943).

[4]Hampton Town Records A232.

[5]Hampton Deeds C103 and C383, Hampton Town Records A90, Hampton Deeds C159.

[6]Hampton Town Records A103, A108–9.

[7]The execution was registered November 17, 1800: Hampton Deeds C494. Also see Hampton Deeds C550.

[8]Account Books of John and Charles Tain-tor of Windham, Connecticut (76 Volumes, The Connecticut State Library, Hartford, Connecti-cut); Nathan Deans mortgage to Roger and Solomon Taintor, 11 January 1802, rst; Early accounts . . . before 1815, rst.

[9]Hampton Town Records A143.

[10]Nathaniel F. Martin Account Book (The Connecticut Historical Society, Hartford, Connecticut). See the valuable work on account books in: Winifred B. Rothenberg, "Farm Account Books: Problems and Possibilities," *Agricultural History* 58 (1984) 106–112; Jack Larkin, "The World of the Account Book: Some Perspectives on Economic Life in Rural New England in the Early 19th Century," a paper presented October 13, 1984, at the TARS Symposium on Social History: Locality and Mentality, Keene State College, Keene, New Hampshire; and Christopher Clark, *The Roots of Rural Capitalism: Western Massachusetts, 1780–1860* (Ithaca, New York, 1990), 21–83.

[11]All material about Nathaniel F. Martin's accounts is from his Account Book. See also Faye E. Dudden, *Sewing Women: Household Service in Nineteenth-Century America* (Middletown, Conn., 1983); Claudia Goldin, "The Economic Status of Women in the Early Republic: Quantitative Evidence," *Journal of Interdisciplinary History* 16 (1986), 375–404; Brooke Hindle, ed., *Material Culture of the Wooden Age* (Tarrytown, N.Y., 1981).

[12]Larned, *History,* II 245.

[13]Nina Fletcher Little, "John Brewster, Jr., 1766–1854," *Connecticut Historical Society Bulletin* 25 (October 1960); William L. Warren, "John Brewster, Jr.; A Critique," *ibid.* 26 (November 1960); Nina Fletcher Little, "John Brewster, Jr.," in *American Folk Painters of Three Centuries,* Jean Lipman and Tom Armstrong, eds. (New York, 1980).

[14]Charles M. Taintor Papers (Connecticut Historical Society, Hartford, Connecticut).

[15]William C. Young Account Book. Hampton 1806–1817. Blacksmith. (4 volumes, Connecticut Historical Society, Hartford, Connecticut).

[16]All material about Ebenezer Jewett's accounts is from Ebenezer Jewett Account Book, 1792–1814 (Connecticut Historical Society, Hartford, Connecticut).

[17]Lease between John Hovey and Ezekiel Holt, March 29, 1799 (Hampton Antiquarian and Historical Society collection in the University of Connecticut Archives). See also Toby L. Ditz, *Property and Kinship: Inheritance in Early Connecticut, 1750–1820* (Princeton, N.J., 1986).

[18]Hampton Deeds C338–40.

[19]Deed from Ezekiel Holt to John Hovey, March 29, 1799 (Hampton Antiquarian and Historical Society collection in the University of Connecticut Archives). See also Sarah F. McMahon, "Provisions Laid Up for the Family: Toward a History of Diet in New England," *Historical Methods* 14 (1981), 4–21.

[20]Recent historical interpretation has made it possible to set the few documents about Hampton and Taintor women into a wider context. See particularly: Nancy F. Cott, *The Bonds of Womanhood: "Woman's Sphere" in New England, 1780–1835* (New Haven, 1977); Jill K. Conway with the assistance of Linda Kealey and Janet E. Schulte, *The Female Experience in Eighteenth- and Nineteenth-Century America: A Guide to the History of American Women* (New York, 1982); Philip Greven, *The Protestant Temperament: Patterns of Child-Rearing, Religious Experience, and the Self in Early America* (New York, 1977); Joy Day Buel and Richard Buel, Jr., *The Way of Duty: A Woman and Her Family in Revolutionary America* (New York, 1984); James Oliver Robertson, *American Myth, American Reality* (New York, 1980); Mary Beth Norton, *Liberty's Daughters: The Revolutionary Experience of American Women, 1750–1800* (Boston, 1980); John Mack Faragher, "History from the Inside-Out: Writing the History of Women in Rural America," *American Quarterly* 33 (1981), 537–57; Mary P. Ryan, *Cradle of the Middle Class: The Family in Oneida County, New York, 1790–1865* (Cambridge, 1981); and see William Lyman, *A Virtuous Woman the Bond of Domestic Union, and the Source of Domestic Happiness* (New London, Conn., 1802), and Nancy Maria Hyde, *The Writings of Nancy Maria Hyde of Norwich, Connecticut. . . .* (1816).

[21]Hampton Deeds D215; Hezekiah Hammond deed to Roger Taintor, 7 April 1829, rst. See also William J. Gilmore, "Elementary Literacy on the Eve of the Industrial Revolution: Trends in Rural New England, 1760–1830," *Proceedings of the American Antiquarian Society* 92 (1982), 87–178.

[22]Hampton Deeds C449.

[23]*Ibid.* C421. See also Lee Virginia Chambers-Schiller, *Liberty, A Better Husband: Single Women in America: The Generations of 1780–1840* (New Haven, Conn., 1984).

[24]*Ibid.* C196.

[25]*Ibid.* C466.

[26]*Ibid.* D130.

²⁷James M. Goodwin and Roxana his wife deed to Roger and Solomon Taintor, 16 May 1810, rst.

²⁸Hampton Deeds C503.

²⁹*Ibid.* D57.

³⁰Asa Smith mortgage to Roger and Solomon Taintor 24 August 1810, rst. The mortgage was due in 1812.

³¹Estate of Benjamin Martin deed to Roger and Solomon Taintor, 28 April 1807, rst.

³²Hampton Deeds D34, D203, D385, D470.

³³Hampton Town Records A199–200.

³⁴Hampton Deeds D119.

³⁵Hampton Town Records A196.

³⁶The lives of rural women and midwives are vividly reconstructed in Laurel Thatcher Ulrich, *A Midwife's Tale: The Life of Martha Ballard, Based on Her Diary, 1785–1812* (New York, 1991). See also Judith Walzer Leavitt, *Brought to Bed: Child-Bearing in America, 1750–1950* (New York, 1986); Linda Gordon, *Woman's Body, Woman's Right: A Social History of Birth Control in America* (New York, 1976); Michael Grossberg, *Governing the Hearth: Law and the Family in Nineteenth-Century America* (Chapel Hill, N.C., 1985).

³⁷Nathaniel F. Martin Account Book.

CHAPTER 3

¹Parrum Palmer note on Samuel Dorrance, R & S Taintor, Early accounts . . . Before c. 1815, rst.

²Discussions of these general issues can be found in: Richard L. Bushman, *From Puritan to Yankee: Character and the Social Order in Connecticut, 1690–1765* (Cambridge, Mass., 1967); Christopher Clark, "Economics and Culture: Opening Up the Rural History of the Early American Northeast," *American Quarterly* 43 (June 1991), 279–301; Allan Kulikoff, "The Transition to Capitalism in Rural America," *William and Mary Quarterly* 46 (January 1989), 120–44; Michael Merrill, "Cash Is Good to Eat: Self-Sufficiency and Exchange in the Rural Economy of the United States," *Radical History* 3 (Spring 1977), 42–71; Daniel Vickers, "Competency and Competition: Economic Culture in Early America," *William and Mary Quarterly* 47 (January 1990), 3–29; Joyce Appleby, *Capitalism and a New Social Order: The Republican Vision of the 1790s* (New York, 1984), and "Commercial Farming and the 'Agrarian Myth' in the Early Republic," *Journal of American History* 68 (1982), 833–49;

Rowland Berthoff, "Independence and Attachment, Virtue and Interest: From Republican Citizen to Free Enterpriser, 1787–1837," in *Uprooted Americans: Essays to Honor Oscar Handlin,* Richard L. Bushman et al., eds. (New York, 1979), 99–124; Andrew R. L. Cayton, "The Fragmentation of 'A Great Family': The Panic of 1819 and the Rise of the Middling Interest in Boston, 1818–1822," *Journal of the Early Republic* 2 (1982), 143–67.

³Gordon S. Wood, *The Radicalism of the American Revolution* (New York, 1991), 24, and *passim* for his illuminating discussions of hierarchy and social status in America after the Revolution. See also Steven Watts, "Masks, Morals, and the Market: American Literature and Early Capitalist Culture, 1790–1820," *Journal of the Early Republic* 6 (1986), 127–49; and Paul C. Bourcier, "'In Excellent Order': The Gentleman Farmer Views His Fences, 1790–1860," *Agricultural History* 58 (1984), 546–64.

⁴Kneeland Townsend, New Haven, to Roger Taintor, Hampton, 16 April 1810, rst. See also Percy W. Bidwell, "Rural Economy in New England at the Beginning of the Nineteenth Century," *Transactions of the Connecticut Academy of Arts and Sciences* 20 (1916), 319–53, and "The Agricultural Revolution in New England," *American Historical Review* 25 (1921), 685–702; Percy W. Bidwell and John I. Falconer, *History of Agriculture in the Northern United States, 1620–1860* (Washington, D.C., 1925); John D. Black, *The Rural Economy of New England* (Cambridge, Mass., 1950); Howard S. Russell, *A Long, Deep Furrow: Three Centuries of Farming in New England* (Hanover, N.H., 1976).

⁵Undated receipt, "Sales of Wool," R & S Taintor, Misc. Bills and Accounts, Post 1815, rst. See also David C. Smith and Anne E. Bridges, "The Brighton Market: Feeding Nineteenth-Century Boston," *Agricultural History* 56 (1982), 3–21.

⁶Archibald Williams Bill, Hampton, 11 September 1826, R & S Taintor, Misc. Bills and Accounts, Post 1815, rst.

⁷Accounts with Mr. Jesse Brown and Jesse Brown & Son, R & S Taintor Early Accounts . . . before 1815, rst; R & S Taintor Accounts–Samuel Dorrance, rst. See also Christopher Clark, "The Household Economy, Market Exchange and the Rise of Capitalism in the Connecticut Valley, 1800–1860," *Journal of Social History* 13 (1979), 169–89; S. A. Mann and J. M.

Dickinson, "Obstacles to the Development of a Capitalist Agriculture," *Journal of Peasant Studies* 5 (1978), 466–81.

[8] Jacob Hovey and John Tweedy deed to Roger and Solomon Taintor, 12 June 1804, rst; Nathaniel F. Martin Account Book.

[9] R & S Taintor–Estate of Benj. Martin, rst; Amasa Flint and Hannah Flint deed to Roger and Solomon Taintor, 31 October 1808, rst; Nathan Clark deed to Roger and Solomon Taintor, 22 November 1808, rst; Hampton Deeds D26, D257.

[10] Origen Augustus Perkins deed to Roger and Solomon Taintor, 30 May 1810, rst.

[11] William Allworth deed to Ebenezer Moseley, Roger and Solomon Taintor, and John Brewster, 28 July 1810, rst; Hampton Deeds D73.

[12] William Allworth deed to Roger and Solomon Taintor, 27 September 1810, rst; Receipt from Eliezer Baker, R & S Taintor–Early accounts, notes, orders, etc. before c. 1815, rst.

[13] R & S Taintor from Rufus Pearl–Goods & notes taken over 1818, rst.

[14] Terminology used in these ways from end of eighteenth century, according to *Oxford English Dictionary*.

[15] Acct. of James Howard, R & S Taintor Early Accounts . . . before 1815, rst. See also Michael A. Bernstein and Sean Wilentz, "Marketing, Commerce, and Capitalism in Rural Massachusetts," *Journal of Economic History* 44 (1984), 171–3.

[16] R & S Taintor–Leicester Academy, rst.

[17] R & S Taintor–Early Accounts . . . Before 1815, rst. See also Allan G. Bogue, *Money at Interest* (Ithaca, N.Y., 1955); Stuart W. Bruchey, *Robert Oliver and Mercantile Bookkeeping in the Early Nineteenth Century* (New York, 1976).

[18] See also the Day Books of John and Charles Taintor (Connecticut State Library, Hartford, Connecticut).

[19] Two documents in Hampton Antiquarian and Historical Society Collection (University of Connecticut Archives, Storrs, Connecticut). The execution was registered 17 November 1800: Hampton Deeds C494.

[20] R & S Taintor–I. Baldwin, rst.

[21] R & S Taintor to Joseph Prentis, Notes for collection, rst.

[22] Small blue-gray bound notebook, Roger Taintor, Misc. Notes, rst.

[23] P. P. Tyler, Bill of Board, 15 Sept 1826, and H. Strong, Esq., Receipt, 22 Mar 1827,

R & S Taintor, Receipts, rst.

[24] R & S Taintor, Early accounts . . . Before c. 1815, rst.

[25] *Ibid.*

[26] Acct. of James Howard, R & S Taintor Early Accounts . . . before 1815, rst.

[27] R & S Taintor Agreement–Samuel S. Moseley, rst.

[28] Taintors and Bulkeley Store, rst; Taintors and Bulkeley, Geo. Hopkins to John & Chas. Taintor, rst; Zaccheus Ami mortgage to Taintors & Bulkeley, 7 November 1809, rst; and R & S Taintor from John and Chas. Taintor and Gad Bulkeley, rst.

[29] Account in Taintors & Bulkeley Store, rst.

[30] Elijah Bulkeley and Gad Bulkeley, Administrators of the Estate of John Bulkeley deed to Roger and Solomon Taintor, 26 April 1809, rst; Gad Bulkeley deed to Roger and Solomon Taintor, 14 May 1810, rst; James M. Goodwin and Roxanna deed to Roger and Solomon Taintor, 16 May 1810; Dan Bulkeley deed to Roger and Solomon Taintor, 23 May 1810, rst; Harriet Bulkeley deed to Roger and Solomon Taintor, 30 October 1810, rst.

[31] R & S Taintor–Receipts, rst.

[32] Nathan Daines (Deans) mortgage to Roger and Solomon Taintor, 11 January 1802, rst.

[33] Hampton Deeds D123, D166, D207, D224, D237.

[34] Hampton Deeds D44, D50, D62, D72, and D80.

[35] R & S Taintor–Thomas Stedman, rst; R & S Taintor–estate of Benj. Martin, rst; R & S Taintor from Oliver Barret, rst; Rufus Pearl & Co. from Lester Kingsbury, rst; R & S Taintor from Asa Smith, rst; James Spaulding mortgage to Roger and Solomon Taintor, 21 November 1810, rst; John Hunt mortgage to Roger and Solomon Taintor, 21 November 1810, rst; John Robbins mortgages to Roger and Solomon Taintor, 12 December 1810 and 23 October 1811, rst; R & S Taintor from William Snow, rst; R & S Taintor–Anna Rindge, rst; Hampton Deeds D126, D134. See also Robert F. Severson, Jr., "The Source of Mortgage Credit for Champaign County, 1865–1880," *Agricultural History* 36 (1962), 150–5.

[36] Rufus Pearl & Co. Accounts, rst.

[37] R & S Taintor from Rufus Pearl–Goods and Notes taken over 1818, rst.

[38] Rufus Pearl & Company Accounts, R & S Taintor from Rufus Pearl–Goods and Notes

taken over 1818, rst; Loomises & Barker Gun Co. Ashford, rst.

[39]R & S Taintor–Moses White from Laban Bates, rst; R & S Taintor–Rufus Pearl & Co. notes, rst; R & S Taintor from Rufus Pearl–Goods & notes taken over 1818, rst.

[40]R & S Taintor from Rufus Pearl–Goods & notes taken over 1818, rst.

[41]Donald R. Hickey, *The War of 1812: A Forgotten Conflict* (Urbana, Ill., 1989); J. C. A. Stagg, *Mr. Madison's War: Politics, Diplomacy, and Warfare in the Early American Republic, 1783–1830* (Princeton, N.J., 1983); John K. Mahon, *The War of 1812* (Gainesville, Fla., 1972).

[42]Loomises & Barker Gun Co. Ashford, rst.

[43]Rufus Pearl & Company Accounts, rst.

[44]Undated memo, "Call on White . . ." R & S Taintor, Misc. Bills and Accounts, Post 1815, rst.

[45]Oliver E. Williams, Hartford, to Roger and Solomon Taintor, Hampton, 20 Oct 1824, rst.

[46]Petition to the Superior Court at Brooklyn, dated Mansfield, 18 November 1822, Willimantic Cotton Mfg. Co.–Roger Taintor, Trustee, rst.

[47]For all the quotations and the narrative outline of Roger Taintor's trusteeship, see the contents of four files of Willimantic Cotton Mfg. Co.–Roger Taintor, Trustee, rst. See also Gary Kulik, Roger Parks, and Theodore Z. Penn, *The New England Mill Village: 1790–1860* (Cambridge, Mass., 1982).

[48]L. Woodworth & Co. Account, 1824. Willimantic Cotton Mfg. Co. #2–Receipts, Roger Taintor, Trustee, rst.

[49]See William F. Willingham, "Grass Root Politics in Windham, Connecticut during The Jeffersonian Era," *Journal of The Early Republic* 1 (1981) 127–48. See also Lance Banning, *The Jeffersonian Persuasion: Evolution of a Party Ideology* (Ithaca, N.Y., 1978); Ronald Formisano, "Deferential-Participant Politics: The Early Republic's Political Culture, 1789–1840," *American Political Science Review* 57 (1974), 473–87; Drew R. McCoy, *The Elusive Republic: Political Economy in Jeffersonian America* (Chapel Hill, N.C., 1980); Richard J. Purcell, *Connecticut in Transition 1775–1818* (Washington, D.C., 1918); William A. Robinson, *Jeffersonian Democracy in New England* (New Haven, Conn., 1916).

[50]Hampton Town Records, Book A, Town Meeting minutes, *passim.*

[51]Hampton Town Records A144, A150.

[52]James M. Banner, Jr., *To the Hartford Convention: The Federalists and the Origins of Party Politics in Massachusetts, 1789–1815* (New York, 1970), 348–50; Theodore Dwight [Secretary of the Convention], *History of the Hartford Convention . . .* (New York, 1833); Steven Watts, *The Republic Reborn: War and the Making of Liberal America, 1790–1820* (Baltimore, 1987).

[53]Hampton Town Records B16.

CHAPTER 4

[1]Edmund Badger, Philadelphia, to John A. Taintor, Hampton, 28 March 1822, jat.

[2]Hampton Town Records A26, A31, A48–50; Recorded Accounts by Hampton residents, Hampton Antiquarian and Historical Society meeting, 5 October 1988, on "Schools and Schooling in Hampton"; Alison Davis, *Hampton Remembers: A Small Town in New England, 1885–1950* (Hampton, Conn., 1976), 55–70; Pearl Scarpino, "South Bigelow School," *Willimantic Chronicle* (Willimantic, Conn., undated). See also Patricia Cline Cohen, *A Calculating People: The Spread of Numeracy in Early America* (Chicago, 1982); Carl F. Kaestle, *Pillars of the Republic: Common Schools and American Society, 1780–1860* (New York, 1983).

[3]John A. Taintor. School Work, jat. See also Barry Schwartz, "The Character of Washington: A Study in Republican Culture," *American Quarterly* 38 (1986), 202–22.

[4]Ezekiel Terry, "The Rose, A Moral and Pleasing Collection of Pieces" (Palmer, [Mass.?], March 1812), jat.

[5]Three notebooks belonging to John Taintor are inscribed Phillips Academy, Andover, October 13th, 15th, and 20th, 1814, and both John and Edwin Bulkeley Taintor are listed in the "Catalogue of the Officers and Students of Phillips Academy, Andover," August 1814, jat.

[6]Jesse Flint, Andover, Mass., to Roger and Solomon Taintor, Hampton, 26 August 1814, rst.

[7]New England Tract Society Pamphlets Nos. 5, 7, 10, 12, 13, 18, 22, 57, 64, 69, 73, and 74 (Andover, Massachusetts, 1817–19); Alexander Proudfit, D.D., "Sermon . . . Before the American Board of Commissioners for Foreign Missions . . ." (Boston, 1822); *The National Preacher,* Vol. 2, Nos. 1–12 (New York, June 1827–May 1828); *The Missionary Herald,* Vol. 25, #6 (Boston, June 1829); Ten *Hartford Evangelical Tract Society* Pamphlets (Hartford, 1820–21), including eleven pristine copies of an anonymous pamphlet, "A Letter from a Mother to Her Only Son" (1821)

[It is interesting to note that Nabby Taintor was the mother of an only son]; "Solemn Review of the Custom of War; Showing, That War Is the Effect of Popular Delusion, and Proposing a Remedy," by Philo Pacificus (Providence, 1818).

8Isaac Clark, Phillips Academy, Andover, to Isaac Bennet, Hampton, 23 April 1816, photocopy in our possession of letter found in the "old Bennet house" by Andrew Leinhoff. See also Whitney Cross, The Burned-Over District: The Social and Intellectual History of Enthusiastic Religion in Western New York, 1800–1850 (New York, 1965); Paul Johnson, A Shopkeeper's Millenium: Society and Revivals in Rochester, New York, 1815–1837 (New York, 1978); Charles Roy Keller, The Second Great Awakening in Connecticut (New Haven, Conn., 1942); Donald G. Mathews, "The Second Great Awakening as an Organizing Process, 1780–1830," American Quarterly 21 (1969), 23–43; William G. McLoughlin, Revivals, Awakenings, and Reform: An Essay on Religion and Social Change in America, 1607–1977 (Chicago, 1978); Richard D. Shiels, "The Second Great Awakening in Connecticut: Critique of the Traditional Interpretation," Church History 49 (1980), 401–16; Sandra Sizer, Gospel Hymns and Social Religion: The Rhetoric of Nineteenth Century Revivalism (Philadelphia, 1978).

9Receipts in John A. Taintor, Bills at Plainfield, 1815, jat.

10John A. Taintor, Colchester, to Roger Taintor, Hampton, 28 January 1817, rst; Donald Lines Jacobus, compiler, The Bulkeley Genealogy: Rev. Peter Bulkeley (New Haven, 1933), 722–3.

11John A. Taintor School Work, Bacon Academy 1816–17, Play Parts #1, Play Parts #2, jat.

12Notebook, "John Taintor, Hampton, Bacon Academy, 1817, Bacon Academy Colchester, Yale College, June 21st, 1818." Play Parts #2, jat.

13Ibid.

14The Laws of Yale College, in New-Haven, in Connecticut: Enacted by the President and Fellows (New Haven, 1817), jat. See also Stephen Berk, Calvinism versus Democracy: Timothy Dwight and the Origins of American Evangelical Orthodoxy (Hamden, Conn., 1974).

15John A. Taintor, New Haven (Yale College), to Roger Taintor, Hampton, 10 February 1818, rst.

16John A. Taintor, New Haven (Yale College), to Roger Taintor, Hampton, 3 March 1818, rst.

17John A. Taintor, New Haven, to Roger Taintor, Hampton, 25 March 1818, rst.

18John A. Taintor, New Haven, to Roger Taintor, Hampton, 3 August 1818, rst.

19The Laws of Yale College, op. cit., 12.

20"Extract of a letter to the author of the 'Examiner,'" Independent Chronicle & Boston Patriot, Saturday Morning, 13 November 1819. See also John S. Whitehead, The Separation of College and State: Columbia, Dartmouth, Harvard and Yale, 1776–1876 (New Haven, Conn., 1973).

21John A. Taintor, New Haven, to Roger Taintor, Hampton, 22 February 1819, rst.

22John A. Taintor, New Haven, to Roger Taintor, Hampton, 6 April 1819, rst. John included a list of all the candidates for treasurer and for senators and a careful count of the votes cast for each.

23John A. Taintor, New Haven, to Roger Taintor, Hampton, 27 June 1820, rst.

24John A. Taintor, New Haven, to Roger Taintor, Hampton, 17 March 1821, rst.

25John A. Taintor, New Haven, to Roger Taintor, Hampton, 29 November 1818, rst.

26John A. Taintor, New Haven, to Roger Taintor, Hampton, 19 July 1819, rst. John listed the names of all the commencement speakers.

27John A. Taintor, New Haven, to Roger Taintor, Hampton, 31 October 1819, rst.

28John A. Taintor, New Haven, to Roger Taintor, Hampton, 16 December 1820, rst.

29John A. Taintor, New Haven, to Roger Taintor, Hampton, 24 March 1821, rst.

30John A. Taintor, New Haven, to Roger Taintor, Hampton, 16 June 1821, rst.

31Leonard G. Wilson, ed., Benjamin Silliman and His Circle: Studies on the Influence of Benjamin Silliman on Science in America (New York, 1979), especially John C. Greene, "Protestantism, Science and American Enterprise: Benjamin Silliman's Moral Universe," 11–28; Chandos M. Brown, Benjamin Silliman: A Life in the Young Republic (Princeton, N.J., 1989).

32Laws of Yale College, op. cit., 5; Notebooks, John A. Taintor, Yale College 1819, and Yale College 1820, in John A. Taintor, Yale College Notebooks, jat; Notebook, Edwin Bulkeley Taintor, Yale College, 1820–21, ebt.

33Isaac Clark, Hampton, to John Taintor, Hampton, 2 February 1818, jat.

34John A. Taintor, New Haven, to Roger Taintor, Hampton, 22 February 1819, rst; John

A. Taintor, New Haven, to Roger Taintor, Hampton, 23 August 1819, rst.

[35]*Laws of Yale College, op. cit.,* 29. See also David Grimsted, *Melodrama Unveiled: American Theater and Culture, 1800–1850* (Chicago, 1968); Francis Hodge, *Yankee Theatre: The Image of America on the Stage, 1825–1850* (Austin, Tex., 1964); Winfred A. Morgan, "An American Icon: Brother Jonathan in the Popular Media Between the Revolutionary and the Civil Wars," Ph.D. Dissertation, University of Iowa, 1982; Arthur Hobson Quinn, *A History of the American Drama from the Beginning to the Civil War* (New York, 1943).

[36]Published in New York by D. Longworth, October 1813.

[37]Published in New York by D. Longworth, March 1819.

[38]No author listed. Published in New York by David Longworth, 1817.

[39]Published in New York by D. Longworth, December 1817.

[40]Published in New York by David Longworth, 1818.

[41]Published in New York at Longworth's Dramatic Repository, 1819.

[42]Published in New York by E. Murden, January 1822.

[43]No author listed. Published in New York by C. S. Van Winkle, 1820.

[44]Published in New York by E. M. Murden, 1822.

[45]John A. Taintor. Playbill, jat.

[46]John A. Taintor. Bills While at Yale, jat.

[47]John A. Taintor, New Haven, to Roger Taintor, Hampton, 14 August 1820, rst.

[48]John A. Taintor, Utica, New York, to Roger Taintor, Hampton, 2 August 1821, rst.

[49]John A. Taintor, Niagara Falls, to Roger Taintor, Hampton, 8 August 1821, rst.

[50]John A. Taintor, New Haven, to Edwin B. Taintor, Hampton, 25 August 1821, rst.

CHAPTER 5

[1]Mary A. and Sarah Bulkeley, Williamstown, Mass., to Roger Taintor, Hampton, 13 March 1824, rst.

[2]John A. Taintor, New York, to Roger Taintor, Hampton, 19 March 1825, rst.

[3]Mary A. and Sarah Bulkeley, Williamstown, Mass., to Roger Taintor, Hampton, 13 March 1824, rst. See also Peter Benes, ed., *House and Home,* Vol. 13 *Annual Proceedings of the Dublin Seminar for New England Folklife* (Boston, 1988); Thomas C. Hubka, *Big House, Little House, Back House, Barn: The Connected Farm Buildings of New England* (Hanover, N.H., 1984); Nina Fletcher Little, *Country Arts in Early American Homes* (New York, 1975); Sally McMurry, "Progressive Farm Families and Their Houses, 1830–1855: A Study in Independent Design," *Agricultural History* 58 (1984), 330–46; Rexford B. Sherman, "Daniel Webster, Gentleman Farmer," *Agricultural History* 53 (1979), 475–87.

[4]John A. Taintor, Hartford, to Roger Taintor, Hampton, 8 August 1822, rst.

[5]John A. Taintor, Hartford, to Roger Taintor, Hampton, 8 September 1822, rst.

[6]Roger Taintor, Hampton, to John A. Taintor, Hartford, 9 September 1822, jat.

[7]Edwin B. Taintor, Hampton, to John A. Taintor, Hartford, 19 September 1822, jat.

[8]*Oxford English Dictionary.* Dysentery had been known in Europe since the fourteenth century.

[9] T. D. Stewart, Hartford, to John A. Taintor, Hampton, 14 January 1823, jat.

[10]John A. Taintor, New York, to Roger Taintor, Hampton, 12 March 1825, rst.

[11]John A. Taintor, New York, to Roger Taintor, Hampton, 19 March 1825, rst.

[12]*Catalogue of Paintings, Sculptures, and Engravings, Exhibited by the American Academy of The Fine Arts . . . The Tenth Exhibition, Third Part* (New York, 1825). See also Neil Harris, *The Artist in American Society: The Formative Years, 1790–1860* (New York, 1966).

[13]John A. Taintor, New York, to Roger Taintor, Hampton, 26 March 1825, rst.

[14]John A. Taintor, New York, to Roger Taintor, Hampton, 28 March 1825, rst.

[15]John A. Taintor, New York, to Roger Taintor, Hampton, 1 April 1825, rst.

[16]John A. Taintor, Hartford, to Roger Taintor, Hampton, 5 April 1825, rst.

[17]Edwin B. Taintor, West Brookfield, Mass., to John A. Taintor, London, 14 July 1828, jat.

[18]George Sisson, Abington [Luzerne County, Pennsylvania] (Wallsville, Pennsylvania postmark), to Dan Bulkeley and Rodman Sisson, Hampton, 3 February 1835, db.

[19]In Untitled Medical Treatise, Chapter 50, "Of Surgery," p. 404, "Of Inflammations and Abscesses."

[20]Estate of Solomon Taintor, 1827. Windham Probate Records #3662 (Connecticut State Library, Hartford, Conn.).

[21]Edmund Badger, Philadelphia, to Dan Bulkeley, Hampton, 17 December 1830, db.

[22]Ludovicus Weld, Fabius, New York, to Roger Taintor, Hampton, 24 September 1827, rst.

[23]Roger Taintor's last Account Book, rst.

[24]Jonathan Clark's accounts, Hampton Antiquarian and Historical Society Collection (University of Connecticut Archives). Understanding Roger and Solomon Taintor and their world is made easier by Robert F. Dalzell, Jr., *Enterprising Elite: The Boston Associates and the World They Made* (Cambridge, Mass., 1987).

CHAPTER 6

[1]Frank Rotch, New Bedford, to John A. Taintor, Hartford, 9 November 1828, jat.

[2]Edwin B. Taintor, Hampton, to John A. Taintor, Hartford, 21 July 1822, jat. See Susan Geib, "'Changing Works': Agriculture and Society in Brookfield, Massachusetts, 1785–1820," Ph.D. Dissertation, Boston University, 1981.

[3]John Cleveland, Scotland, to John A. Taintor, Hartford, 13 and 18 March 1823, jat. See Ellen K. Rothman, "Sex and Self-Control: Middle-Class Courtship in America, 1770–1870," *Journal of Social History* 15 (1982), 409–25.

[4]John Cleveland, Scotland, to John A. Taintor, Hartford, 25 February 1822, jat.

[5]John A. Taintor, Misc. Invitations, jat.

[6]T. D. Stewart, Lansingburgh, New York, to John A. Taintor, Hampton, 15 July 1823, jat.

[7]"Rose," Hartford, to John A. Taintor, Hampton, 20 July 1823, jat.

[8]Anne Frior Scott, "The Ever-Widening Circle: The Diffusion of Feminist Values from the Troy Female Seminary, 1822–72," in *Making the Invisible Woman Visible* (Urbana, Illinois, 1984), 64–88.

[9]T. D. Stewart, Lansingburgh, New York, to John A. Taintor, Hampton, 27 August 1823, jat.

[10]Erastus Lester, Col. 5th Regiment, Plainfield, Connecticut, to John A. Taintor, Hampton, 3 September 1823, John A. Taintor Militia Orders, jat.

[11]Edwin B. Taintor, Brookfield, Massachusetts, to John A. Taintor, Hampton, 3 October 1823, jat.

[12]"Rose," Hartford, to John A. Taintor, Hampton, 15 November 1823, jat.

[13]"Rose," Hartford, to John A. Taintor, Hampton, 13 December 1823, jat.

[14]"Rose," Hartford, to John A. Taintor, Hampton, 30 December 1823, jat.

[15]"Rose," New York, to John A. Taintor, Hampton, 24 June 1825, jat.

[16]"Rose," New York, to John A. Taintor, Hampton, 9 July 1825, jat.

[17]H. Huntington, Jr., Hartford, to John A. Taintor, Hampton, 17 October 1825, jat.

[18]H. Huntington, Jr., Boston, to John A. Taintor, Hampton, 21 October 1825, jat.

[19]John A. Taintor, New York, to Roger Taintor, Hampton, 5 November 1825, rst.

[20]Edwin B. Taintor, Hampton, to John A. Taintor, Hartford, 13 May 1822, jat.

[21]Edwin B. Taintor, Hampton, to John A. Taintor, Hartford, 21 July 1822, jat.

[22]John A. Taintor, Hartford, to Roger Taintor, Hampton, 8 September 1822, rst.

[23]E. H. Clark, Hartford, to John A. Taintor, Hampton, 21 December 1822, 5 January 1823, 11 February 1823, and 5 March 1823, jat; B. Hudson, Jr., Hartford, to John A. Taintor, Hampton, 25 February 1823, jat; B. M. Binge, Hartford, to John A. Taintor, Hampton, 24 March 1823, John A. Taintor Letters Unattributed, jat; John A. Taintor, Hartford, to Roger Taintor, Hampton, 29 September 1822 and 6 October 1822, rst.

[24]O. E. Williams, Hartford, to John A. Taintor, Hampton, 15 April 1823, jat.

[25]"Rose," Hartford, to John A. Taintor, Hampton, 24 January 1824, jat.

[26]Peter Hall, Pomfret, to John A. Taintor, Hartford, 17 December 1826, jat.

[27]George W. Stanley, Middletown, to John A. Taintor, Hartford, 12 July 1827, jat.

[28]"Mathews' Trip to Paris; or The Dramatic Tourist; As Performed by Mr. Mathews at the English Opera House," first American, from the twelfth London edition (New York, published by E. M. Murden Circulating Library and Dramatic Repository, No. 4 Chamber St., 1822), jat.

[29]R. I. Ingersoll, Washington, D.C., to John A. Taintor, Hampton, 18 January 1827, jat.

[30]R. I. Ingersoll, Washington, D.C., to John A. Taintor, Hampton, 9 March 1828, jat.

[31]Henry Huntington, Jr., Paris, to John A. Taintor, Hartford, 27 April 1828, jat.

[32]R. I. Ingersoll, Washington, D.C., to John A. Taintor, Hartford, 13 May 1828, jat.

[33]Edmund Badger, Philadelphia, to John A. Taintor, Hampton, 22 March 1828, jat.

[34]Fisk, Grinell, and Company, New York, to John A. Taintor, Hampton, 3 April 1828; John kept a receipt for his passage in a letter from

O. E. Williams, Hartford, to John A. Taintor, Hampton, 3 September 1829, and he also kept an empty sheet of paper folded as an envelope, addressed, "Mr. Taintor, Passenger on board ship York," jat.

[35]Benjamin Rodman, New Bedford, to John A. Taintor, Hampton, 14 April 1828, jat.

[36]American cities held less than ten percent of the total population. There were only ninety places in America in 1830 with a population of more than 2,500 people, enough to be considered urban. In thirty-four of those places there were only 2,500–5,000 people. In another thirty-three there were between 5,000 and 10,000 people. There were sixteen cities with between 10,000 and 25,000 people, and seven of more than 25,000. The largest cities were: New York (202,000), Philadelphia (161,000), Baltimore (80,000), Boston (61,000), New Orleans (46,000), Charleston (30,000), and Cincinnati (25,000).

[37]Augustus J.C. Hare, *Walks in London* (fifth edition, revised, London, 1883, 2 vols.), II, 214.

[38]Edwin Bulkeley Taintor, Brookfield, to John A. Taintor, London, 14 July 1828, jat.

[39]Frank Rotch, Harrow, to John A. Taintor, London, 1828, jat.

[40]Frank Rotch, New Bedford, to John A. Taintor, Hartford, 9 November 1828, jat.

[41]Frank Rotch, New Bedford, to John A. Taintor, Hartford, 27 November 1828, jat.

[42]Caroline Gilmour, Giles Taintor, and Hannah Gibbons, New York, to John A. Taintor, Hampton, 2 April 1829, jat. See also Harriet Martineau, *Society in America* (London, 1837); Sean Wilentz, *Chants Democratic: New York City and the Rise of the American Working Class, 1788–1850* (New York, 1984).

[43]Ellen and Hugh Kirkman, Nashville, to John A. Taintor, Hampton, 18 May 1829, jat. Contains Hugh Kirkman's card.

[44]See particularly Washington Irving, *Letters of Jonathan Oldstyle, Gent.,* originally published in 1802–3, and *Salmagundi,* originally published in 1807–8, in the Library of America's *Washington Irving* (New York, 1983).

[45]Hannah Gibbons, New York, to John A. Taintor, Hartford, 27 May 1829, jat.

[46]Ellen and Elizabeth Williams, Hartford, to John A. Taintor, Hampton, 27 May 1829, jat.

[47]Hannah Gibbons, New York (completely crossed), to John A. Taintor, Hartford, 13 June 1829, jat.

[48]Ellen Kirkman, New York, to John A. Taintor, Hampton, 16 July and 19 August 1829, jat.

[49]John A. Taintor, Hartford, to Roger Taintor, Hampton, 15 November 1830, rst.

[50]John A. Taintor and Adelia Croade, Hartford, to Roger Taintor, Hampton, 1 February 1831, rst. See also Richard H. Abbott, "The Agricultural Press Views the Yeoman: 1819–1859," *Agricultural History* 42 (1968); Richard D. Bushman, "Family Security in the Transition from Farm to City, 1750–1850," *Journal of Family History* 6 (1981), 238–56; Elizabeth Johns, "The Farmer in the Works of William Sidney Mount," *Journal of Interdisciplinary History* 17 (1986), 257–81.

[51]Frank Rotch, New Bedford, to John A. Taintor, Hampton, 27 November 1828, jat.

[52]Henry W. Terry, Hartford, to John A. Taintor, Hampton, 24 December 1824, jat.

[53]William Gibbons, New York, to John A. Taintor, Hampton, 8 August 1829, jat.

[54]O. E. Williams, Hartford, to John A. Taintor, Hampton, 3 September 1829, jat.

CHAPTER 7

[1]Ebenezer Williams, New London, to Dan Bulkeley, Hampton, 21 December 1831, db.

[2]Account with Joseph H. Strong, beginning 4 October 1817, account with William Williams, beginning 9 November 1817, in Accounts–Taintors & Bulkeley, 1819, db. Hampton Deeds D106.

[3]Joseph Prentis to Dan Bulkeley, 13 February 1821, Hampton Deeds E 237.

[4]Clark Barnett, Coventry, to Dan Bulkeley, Hampton, 22 May 1830, db. See also Lewis L. Atherton, *Main Street on the Middle Border* (Bloomington, Ind., 1954) for numerous suggestive descriptions of later small-town stores and cultures; Caroline Fuller Sloat, "The Center of Local Commerce: The Asa Knight Store of Dummerston, Vermont, 1827–1851," *Vermont History* (1979) 205–19; Jack Larkin, *The Reshaping of Everyday Life 1790–1840* (New York, 1988).

[5]Accounts–Taintors & Bulkeley, 1819, db. Charles Taintor, Windham, to Dan Bulkeley, Hampton, 20 January 1828; Rapelye & Purdy, New York, to Dan Bulkeley, Hampton, 13 October 1829; E. A. Bill, Norwich, to Dan Bulkeley, Hampton [9 items], db.

[6]Rapelye & Purdy, New York, to Dan Bulkeley, Hampton, 2 June 1829, db.

[7]Peregrine Terry, Enfield, Connecticut, to Dan Bulkeley, Hampton, 24 January 1829 and 6 November 1829 [not in Terry's hand], db.

[8]Rapelye & Purdy, New York, to Dan Bulkeley, Hampton, 7 June 1839, db.

[9]J. Weston, Willington, to Dan Bulkeley, Hampton, 16 July 1832, 23 January 1833, and 6 February 1833, db.

[10]Robert L. Stuart, New York, to Dan Bulkeley, Hampton, 24 February 1836, 9 February 1830, 27 August 1836, and 8 September 1832, db.

[11]Henry Whitman, Providence, R.I., to Dan Bulkeley, Hampton, 9 January 1835, db.

[12]George W. Webb, Windham, to Dan Bulkeley, Hampton, 15 December 1830, 2 March 1831, db.

[13]Lesters & Co, Norwich, to Dan Bulkeley, Hampton, 26 January 1831, and 20 April 1831; Henry Whitman, Providence, R.I., to Dan Bulkeley, Hampton, 9 January 1835, 25 July 1835, 7 September 1835, and 14 September 1835, db.

[14]Taintors & Bulkeley–Accounts Misc. (7 August 1821), rst.

[15]John Williams, Abington, to Dan Bulkeley, Hampton, 11 March 1830; Jacob Wood, Enfield, Connecticut, to Dan Bulkeley, Hampton, 24 January 1831; Adams White, Jr., Brooklyn, Connecticut, to Dan Bulkeley, Hampton, 4 May 1840, and 10 March 18??, db.

[16]John A. Smith, Windham, to Dan Bulkeley, Hampton, 3 September 1833, db.

[17]Shubael Morgan, Norwich, to Dan Bulkeley, Hampton, 25 November 1834, db.

[18]E. A. Bill, Norwich, to Dan Bulkeley, Hampton, 27 December 1831, db.

[19]See the two Dan Bulkeley account books, one opening 1834, November 25, the other 1836, July 11, db.

[20]Ebenezer Williams, New London, to Dan Bulkeley, Hampton, 21 December 1831, db.

[21]George Martin, Brooklyn, to Dan Bulkeley, Hampton, 17 October 1831, db. See also Richard D. Brown, "The Emergence of Voluntary Associations in Massachusetts, 1760–1830," *Journal of Voluntary Action Research* 2 (1973); Don H. Doyle, "The Social Functions of Voluntary Associations in a Nineteenth-Century Town," *Social Science History* 1 (1977), 333–56.

[22]J. W. Bulkeley, Norwich, to Dan Bulkeley, Hampton, 4 February 1835, db.

[23]J. B. Simmons, Ashford, to Dan Bulkeley, Hampton, 23 January 1832; I. Bulkeley, Ashford, to Dan Bulkeley, Hampton, 15 February 1832, db.

[24]D. C. Robinson, Brooklyn, Connecticut, to Dan Bulkeley, Hampton, 30 January 1834, db.

[25]Raynolds & Morris, Springfield, Massachusetts, to Bulkeley & Grosvenor, Hampton, 11 November 1828 and 15 November 1828; John B. Kirkham, Springfield, to Dan Bulkeley, Hampton, 31 October 1831, db. See Glenn Porter and Harold C. Livesay, *Merchants and Manufacturers: Studies in the Changing Structure of Nineteenth-Century Marketing* (Baltimore, 1971).

[26]Clark Barnett, Coventry, to Dan Bulkeley, Hampton, 22 May 1830, db.

[27]Jonathan Hovey, Hampton, to Dan Bulkeley, Hampton, 22 December 1830, and 8 July 1831, db.

[28]Jacob Corlies & Sons, New York, to Dan Bulkeley, Hampton, 13 May 1829, 5 October 1830, 10 March 1831, and 12 December 1831, db.

[29]H. P. Wright, Philadelphia, to Dan Bulkeley, Hampton, 7 October 1831, db.

[30]Jacob Corlies & Sons, New York, to Dan Bulkeley, Hampton, 8 September 1832, 16 March 1833, and 18 September 1833; J. W. Bulkeley, Norwich, to Dan Bulkeley, Hampton, 19 February 1834, db.

[31]U.S. 20 Cong. 1 Sess. HR Doc. 159. *Memorial of Sundry Inhabitants of the Counties of Windham and Tolland . . . Praying for the Aid of Government in the Cultivation of the Mulberry Tree and of Silk.* February 25, 1828. Washington, Gales & Seaton. 1828.

[32]U.S. 20 Cong. 1 Sess. HR Doc. 158. *Letter from the Secretary of the Treasury . . . Being a Manual in Relation to the Growth and Manufacture of Silk Adapted to the Different Parts of the Union.* 7 February 1828. Washington, Gales & Seaton, 1828. Dan Bulkeley's part is on pp. 213–14.

[33]Edmund Badger, Philadelphia, to Dan Bulkeley, Hampton, March 1831, db. See also Gregory H. Nobles, "Commerce and Community: A Case Study of the Rural Broommaking Business in Antebellum Massachusetts," *Journal of the Early Republic* 4 (1984), 287–308; James W. Wessman, "The Household Mode of Production–Another Comment," *Radical History Review* 22 (1979–80), 129–46.

[34]Paul Ware, Warren, R.I., to Dan Bulkeley, Hampton, 15 January 1831, db.

[35]P. K. Hubbs, Philadelphia, to Dan Bulkeley, Hampton, 8 October 1828, db.

[36]L. P. Brockett, *The Silk Industry in America: A History Prepared for the Centennial Exposition* (Washington, 1876), *passim.*

[37]O. E. Huntington, Norwich, to Dan Bulkeley, Hampton, 10 January 1832, db.

[38]Wm. A. Budd, Philadelphia, to Dan Bulkeley, Hampton, 29 January 1829, db.

[39]George Hill, Hawley, Franklin County, Mass., to Dan Bulkeley, Hampton, 24 May 1830, db.

[40]James Mease, Philadelphia, to Dan Bulkeley, Hampton, 23 April 1830; Aaron B. and William Jones, Bucklands Corners, Conn., to Dan Bulkeley, Hampton, 26 July 1838; S. N. Richmond, Providence, to Dan Bulkeley, Hampton, 23 November 1830 and 2 April 1831, db.

[41]Justus A. Blanchard, Catskill Plains, New York, to Dan Bulkeley, Hampton, 25 June 1832; Aaron B. Jones, Hartford, to Dan Bulkeley, Hampton, 27 March 1837 and 25 July 1837; Ebenezer Moseley, Newburyport, Mass., to Dan Bulkeley, Hampton, 3 May 1838, db.

[42]Godfrey Cady, to Dan Bulkeley, Hampton, 19 December 1834; William Jones, Buckland's Corners, Connecticut, to Dan Bulkeley, Hampton, 22 April 1837; Aaron B. and William Jones, Buckland's Corners, Connecticut, to Dan Bulkeley, Hampton, 1 September 1838, db.

[43]Brockett, *The Silk Industry,* 44.

[44]Daniel Wardwell, Mannsville, Jeff. County, New York, to Dan Bulkeley, Hampton, 3 April 1829; G. Thorburn & Sons, New York, to Dan Bulkeley, Hampton, 27 July 1832; Godfrey Cady, Boston, to Dan Bulkeley, Hampton, 19 December 1834; E. W. Bull, Hartford, to Dan Bulkeley, Hampton, 14 August 1835 and 22 July 1836; William Thorburn, Albany, to Dan Bulkeley, Hampton, 27 February 1836 (G. Thorburn & Sons), db.

[45]Charles Dubouchet, Paris, France, to Dan Bulkeley, Hampton, 31 May 1831, db.

[46]Henry Clark, Brooklyn, to Dan Bulkeley, Hampton, 7 June 1830, and from Pittsburgh 25 April 1830; Edmund Badger, Philadelphia, to Dan Bulkeley, Hampton, 17 December 1830, db.

[47]Edmund Badger, Philadelphia, to Dan Bulkeley, Hampton, 2 August 1833, db.

[48]Thomas Gibson, Conneaut, Ohio, to Dan Bulkeley, Hampton, 1 June 1834, db.

[49]S. N. Richmond, Providence, to Dan Bulkeley, Hampton, 11 January 1834, db.

[50]Receipts from William Tyler, 30 April 1824 and 5 March 1824, in Receipts–Taintors & Bulkeley, db.

[51]Gordon Dorrance, Windsor, Mass., to Dan Bulkeley, Hampton, 30 October 1832; J. T. Benton, Pulteney, to Dan Bulkeley, Hampton, 3 February 1830; Dan Bulkeley, Hampton, to Willard Crafts, Bridgewater, N.Y., 28 December 1829, db.

[52]Samuel Preston, Lockport, Pennsylvania, to Dan Bulkeley, Hampton, 27 December 1827; Jonathan Burnett, Jacksonville, New York, to Dan Bulkeley, Hampton, 21 July 1828, db.

[53]Calvin Manning, Coventry, Conn., to Dan Bulkeley, Hampton, 11 January 1830; James Manning, Bethany, Pennsylvania, to Dan Bulkeley, Hampton, 2 June 1831; Rapelye & Purdy, New York, to Dan Bulkeley, Hampton, 8 July 1831, db.

[54]James Manning, Bethany, Wayne County, Pennsylvania, to Dan Bulkeley, Hampton, 12 September 1837, db.

[55]James Lincoln, Windham, to Dan Bulkeley, Hampton, 6 September 1834, db.

[56]Enoch Pond, Chaplin, to Dan Bulkeley, Hampton, 4 March 1835, db.

[57]Lyman Foster, Hiramsville, Pa., to Dan Bulkeley, Hampton, 27 July 1834, db.

[58]*Ibid.*

[59]Dan Bulkeley–Agreements to Sell Door Guards, db.

[60]Robert W. Robinson, Urbana, Ohio, to Dan Bulkeley, Hampton, 7 October 1834, db.

[61]William Ashley, Portland, Maine, to Dan Bulkeley, Hampton, 4 April 1835, db.

[62]George Sisson, Abington [Wallsville, Pennsylvania postmark], to Dan Bulkeley, Hampton, 3 February 1835; Robert W. Robinson, Urbana, Ohio, to Dan Bulkeley, Hampton, 7 February 1835; Jonathan A. Hovey, Suffield, Conn., to Dan Bulkeley, Hampton, 9 March 1835, db.

[63]Additional Inventory of the Estate of D. Bulkeley Decd. 27 September 1843. Dan Bulkeley Estate–Inventories, db.

[64]Richard R. John, Jr., "Managing the Mails: The U.S. Postal System in National Politics, 1823–1836," Ph.D. dissertation, Harvard University, 1989; Richard B. Kielbowicz, "The Press, Post Office, and Flow of News in the Early Republic," *Journal of the Early Republic* 3 (1983) 255–80; James R. Rohrer, "Sunday Mails and the Church-State Theme in Jacksonian America," *Journal of the Early Republic* 7 (1987), 53–74.

65 N. T. Fairfield, Pomfret, to Dan Bulkeley, Hampton, 27 April 1833, db.

66 Joseph Barber, New Haven, to Dan Bulkeley, Hampton, 12 April 1828, db.

67 Paul Goodman, "The Social Basis of New England Politics in Jacksonian America," *Journal of the Early Republic* 6 (1986) 23–58; Ronald P. Formisano, *The Transformation of Political Culture: Massachusetts Parties, 1790s–1840s* (New York, 1983); John Ashworth, "The Democratic-Republicans before the Civil War: Political Ideology and Economic Change," *Journal of American Studies* 20 (1986), 375–90; Lee Benson, *The Concept of Jacksonian Democracy* (New York, 1967); Marvin Meyers, *The Jacksonian Persuasion: Politics and Belief* (Stanford, Cal., 1960); Edward Pessen, *Jacksonian America: Society, Personality, and Politics* (Homewood, Ill., 1978).

68 Joseph Barber, New Haven, to Dan Bulkeley, Hampton, 12 April 1823, 16 April 1825, and 4 October 1825, db.

69 F. P. Blair, Washington, D.C., March 1832, enclosed in Isaac Hill, Washington, D.C., to Dan Bulkeley, Hampton, 27 April 1832, db.

70 Andrew T. Judson, New Haven, to Dan Bulkeley, Hampton, 5 May 1830, db.

71 I. Bulkeley, Ashford, Conn., to Dan Bulkeley, Hampton, 20 October 1832, db.

72 Hiram W. Bulkeley [sp. "Bulkley"], Williamstown, Massachusetts, to Dan Bulkeley, Hampton, 18 May 1829, in Dan Bulkeley from Albert R. Bulkeley, db.

73 Edwin A. Cooley, Lockport, New York, to Dan Bulkeley, Hampton, 7 July 1829, 11 May 1831, and 9 January 1833, db. See also Paul Goodman, *Towards a Christian Republic: Antimasonry and the Great Transition in New England, 1826–1836* (New York, 1988); Kathleen S. Kutolowski, "Freemasonry and Community in the Early Republic: The Case for Antimasonic Anxieties," *American Quarterly* 34 (1982), 543–61; Dorothy A. Lipson, *Freemasonry in Federalist Connecticut* (Princeton, N.J., 1977); William Preston Vaughn, *The Antimasonic Party in the United States, 1826–1843* (Lexington, Ky., 1983); James Turner, *Without God, Without Creed: The Origins of Unbelief in America* (Baltimore, 1985).

74 William Ashley, Portland, Maine, to Dan Bulkeley, Hampton, 4 April 1835; David M. Durkee, Westfield, New York, to Dan Bulkeley, Hampton, 31 January 1835; Silas Spencer, Westfield, New York, to Dan Bulkeley, Hampton, 13 September 18??, db.

75 Silas Spencer, Westfield, New York, to Dan Bulkeley, Hampton, 28 June 1829; John Spencer, Gouverneur, New York, to Dan Bulkeley, Hampton, 6 August 1829; Silas Spencer, Westfield, to Dan Bulkeley, Hampton, 2 January 1830, 13 September 18?? (between 1830 and 1836), and 12 September 1836, db.

76 (Dr.) Thomas Fuller, Cooperstown, New York, to Dan Bulkeley, Hampton, 23 April 1832, db.

77 Abigail Farnham Durkee, Salem, Ohio, to Dan Bulkeley, Hampton, 3 March 1833, db.

78 David L. Dodge, New York, to Dan Bulkeley, Hampton, 12 December 1835, db.

79 Solomon Wait, Preston, Chenango County, New York, to Dan Bulkeley, Hampton, 10 August 1836, db.

80 G. Dunworth, Westford, Conn., to Dan Bulkeley, Hampton, 10 May 1836, db.

81 Joseph Prentis, Douglas, Mass., to Dan Bulkeley, Hampton, 30 January 1835, db.

82 Thomas Clark, Mansfield, to Dan Bulkeley, Hampton, 16 March 1835, db.

83 Thomas Martin, Hartford, to Dan Bulkeley, Hampton, 22 May 1835; Thomas Clark, Mansfield, to Dan Bulkeley, Hampton, 22 August 1835, and 29 August 1835, db.

84 David Clark, Hartford, to Dan Bulkeley, Hampton, 21 January 1836, db.

85 Dan Bulkeley, New York, to Gideon Tomlinson, 5 May 1836, in Dan Bulkeley–Copies and Drafts of Letters, db.

86 Charles L. Franklin, Brooklyn, N.Y., to Dan Bulkeley, Hampton, 2 May 1836, db.

87 Dan Bulkeley, Hampton, to Charles N. Gardiner, Auditor, P.O. Department, 15 May 18??, in Dan Bulkeley–Copies and Drafts of Letters, db.

88 Dan Bulkeley, Hampton, to Orrin Holt, Washington, D.C., 15 January 1838, in Dan Bulkeley–Copies and Drafts of Letters, db.

89 Orrin Holt, Washington, D.C., to Dan Bulkeley, Hampton, 8 January 1838, db.

90 Philip Pearl, Jr., Hampton, to Dan Bulkeley, Hampton, 9 April 1836, db.

CHAPTER 8

1 Robert Thurston, Livonia, New York, to Dan Bulkeley, Hampton, 21 August 1831, db.

2 Lyman Foster, Hiramsville, Pennsylvania, to Dan Bulkeley, Hampton, 27 July 1834, db. See also Merle Curti et al., *The Making of an American Community: A Case Study of Democracy in a*

Frontier Community (Stanford, Cal., 1959), the classic study of the kind of community the people who went west from Hampton tried to build; Lois Kimball Mathews, *The Expansion of New England: The Spread of New England Settlements and Institutions to the Mississippi River, 1620–1865* (New York, 1909); Anthony F. C. Wallace, *Rockdale: The Growth of an American Village in the Early Industrial Revolution* (New York, 1978); William Wyckoff, *The Developer's Frontier: The Making of the Western New York Landscape* (New Haven, Conn., 1988).

[3]Lyman Foster, Farrandsville, Pennsylvania, to Dan Bulkeley, Hampton, 14 September 1834, db.

[4]W. B. Moneypenny, Eaton, Pennsylvania, to Dan Bulkeley, Hampton, 9 August 1828, db.

[5]Ichabod Thurston, Mount Morris, Pennsylvania, to Dan Bulkeley, Hampton, 20 November 1831, db.

[6]Robert Thurston, Livonia, New York, to Dan Bulkeley, Hampton, 21 August 1831, db.

[7]Robert Thurston, Livonia, New York, to Dan Bulkeley, Hampton, 23 December 1832, db.

[8]Lucy Leach, Cazenovia, New York, to Dan Bulkeley, Hampton, 25 July 1833, db.

[9]Lyman Foster, Farrandsville, Pennsylvania, to Dan Bulkeley, Hampton, 4 January 1835, db.

[10]Silas Spencer, Westfield, New York, to Dan Bulkeley, Hampton, 12 September 1836, db.

[11]Robert D. Dorrance, South Oxford, Massachusetts, to Dan Bulkeley, Hampton, 10 July 1829, db. See also Thomas Dublin, *Women at Work: The Transformation of Work and Community in Lowell, Massachusetts, 1826–1860* (New York, 1979), and "Women Workers and the Study of Social Mobility," *Journal of Interdisciplinary History* 9 (1979), 647–65; Philip S. Foner, ed., *The Factory Girls: A Collection of Writings on Life and Struggles in the New England Factories of the 1840s . . .* (Urbana, Ill., 1977); Susan Hirsch, *The Roots of the American Working Class: The Industrialization of Crafts in Newark, 1800–1860* (New York, 1978); John Karson, *Civilizing the Machine: Technology and Republican Values in America, 1776–1900* (New York, 1976); Gerda Lerner, "The Lady and the Mill Girl: Changes in the Status of Women in the Age of Jackson," *Midcontinental American Studies Journal* 10 (1969), 5–15; Barbara M. Tucker, *Samuel Slater and the Origins of the American Textile Industry, 1790–1860* (Ithaca, N.Y., 1984), and "The Merchant, the Manufacturer and the Factory Manager: The

Case of Samuel Slater," *Business History Review* 55 (1981) 297–313.

[12]Robert Thurston, Livonia, New York, to Dan Bulkeley, Hampton, 21 August 1831, db.

[13]Edmund Badger, Philadelphia, to Dan Bulkeley, Hampton, 22 May 1832, db.

[14]Edmund Badger, Philadelphia, to Dan Bulkeley, Hampton, 9 June 1832, db.

[15]Edmund Badger, Philadelphia, to Dan Bulkeley, Hampton, 27 October 1832, db.

[16]Harriet Fuller, Oxford, to Dan Bulkeley, Hampton, 30 September 1833, db.

[17]David Spencer Jr., Pomfret, to Dan Bulkeley, Hampton, 2 November 1832, db.

[18]Lucy Leach, Uncasville, to Dan Bulkeley, Hampton, 13 March 1836, db.

[19]Lucy Leach, Cherry Valley, New York, to Dan Bulkeley, Hampton, 17 August 1834, db.

[20]Lucy Leach, Cherry Valley, New York, to Dan Bulkeley, Hampton, 17 August 1834, db.

[21]Jonathan Burnett, Jacksonville, New York, to Dan Bulkeley, Hampton, 21 July 1828, db.

[22]Robert W. Robinson, Urbana, Ohio, to Dan Bulkeley, Hampton, 7 October 1834, db.

[23]Anson Howard, Milford Center, Ohio, to Dan Bulkeley, Hampton, 30 December 1830, db.

[24]Mary B. Eaton, Douglas, Massachusetts, to Dan Bulkeley, Hampton, 17 August 1831, db.

[25]Mary B. Eaton, New Brunswick, N.J., to Dan Bulkeley, Hampton, 25 October 1831, db. [year date on internal evidence]

[26]Mary B. Eaton, New Brunswick, N.J., to Dan Bulkeley, Hampton, 22 November 1831, db. [year date from death of Nabby Taintor]

[27]Mary B. Eaton, New Brunswick, N.J., to Dan Bulkeley, Hampton, 12 February 1832, db. [year date on internal evidence]

[28]Mary B. Eaton, New Brunswick, N.J., to Dan Bulkeley, Hampton, 6 August 1832, db. [dated on internal evidence, and cholera epidemic]

[29]Mary B. Eaton, New Brunswick, N.J., to Dan Bulkeley, Hampton, 17 March 1833, db.

[30]Asa M. Martin, Albany/Enfield/Longmeadows, Massachusetts, to Dan Bulkeley, Hampton, 3 February 1834, db.

[31]Asa M. Martin, Enfield, to Dan Bulkeley, Hampton, 23 February 1834, db.

[32]Asa M. Martin, Enfield, to Dan Bulkeley, Hampton, 30 June 1834, db.

[33]Asa M. Martin, Enfield, to Dan Bulkeley, Hampton, 27 July 1834, db.

[34]Asa M. Martin, Thompsonville, to Dan Bulkeley, Hampton, 1 February 18??, db. [The

1835 date is conjecture based on the whole series of letters.]

[35]Anson Fox, Lima, New York, to Dan Bulkeley, Hampton, 2 March 1835, db.

[36]Anson Fox, Lima, New York, to Dan Bulkeley, Hampton, 26 April 1835, db.

[37]Anson Fox, Bethany, New York, to Dan Bulkeley, Hampton, 8 December 1835, db.

[38]Anson Fox, Bethany, to Dan Bulkeley, Hampton, 1 January 1836, db.

[39]Anson Fox, Buffalo, New York, to Dan Bulkeley, Hampton, 10 April 1836, db. See Elliott J. Gorn, "'Gouge and Bite, Pull Hair and Scratch': The Social Significance of Fighting in the Southern Backcountry," *American Historical Review* 90 (1985), 18–43, for a perceptive discussion of the kind of culture Fox and many others carried with them into new settlements.

[40]Anson Howard, Milford Center, Ohio, to Dan Bulkeley, Hampton, 25 April 1829, db.

[41]Abigail Durkee, Salem, Ohio, to Dan Bulkeley, Hampton, 3 March 1833, db.

[42]Jonathan Burnett, Jacksonville, New York, to Dan Bulkeley, Hampton, 21 July 1828, db.

[43]W. B. Moneypenny, Eaton, Pennsylvania, to Dan Bulkeley, Hampton, 9 August 1828, db.

[44]Abigail Durkee, Salem, Ohio, to Dan Bulkeley, Hampton, 3 March 1833, db.

[45]Robert Thurston, Livonia, New York, to Dan Bulkeley, Hampton, 23 December 1832, db.

[46]Robert W. Robinson, Urbana, Ohio, to Dan Bulkeley, Hampton, 7 October 1834, db.

[47]Elisha Farnham, Cazenovia, to Dan Bulkeley, Hampton, 23 February 1837, db.

[48]Charles Moulton, Jefferson (Madison County) Ohio, to Dan Bulkeley, Hampton, 6 January 1840, db.

[49]Lucy Leach, Cazenovia, New York, to Dan Bulkeley, Hampton, 25 July 1833, db.

[50]Lyman Foster, Hiramsville, Pennsylvania, to Dan Bulkeley, Hampton, 27 July 1834, *op. cit.*

[51]Ebenezer Jewett, Vernal, New York, to Dan Bulkeley, Hampton, 16 March 1835, db.

[52]Ebenezer Jewett, Bethany, to Dan Bulkeley, Hampton, 3 March 1836, db.

[53]Ebenezer Jewett, Bethany, Genesee County, Linden post office, New York, to Dan Bulkeley, Hampton, 24 April 1836, db.

[54]Abigail Durkee, Salem, Ohio, to Dan Bulkeley, Hampton, 3 March 1833, *op. cit.*

[55]Albert R. Bulkeley [sp. "Bulkley"], Williamstown, Massachusetts, to Dan Bulkeley, Hampton, 31 January 1827, db; "Home, Sweet Home," by John Howard Payne and Henry Bishop; see Russel Nye, *The Unembarrassed Muse: The Popular Arts in America* (New York, 1970), 308.

CHAPTER 9

[1]J. W. Bulkeley, Norwich, to Dan Bulkeley, Hampton, 15 June 1835, db.

[2]Lucy Leach, Cherry Valley, New York, to Dan Bulkeley, Hampton, 9 November 1830, db.

[3]Phidelia Bulkeley, Norwich, to Dan Bulkeley, Hampton, 6 May 1835, db.

[4]J. W. Bulkeley, Norwich, to Dan Bulkeley, Hampton, 15 June 1835, db.

[5]Phidelia Bulkeley, Norwich, to Dan Bulkeley, Hampton, 23 June 1835, db.

[6]G. S. Moseley, New York, to Dan Bulkeley, Hampton, 27 June 1835, db.

[7]J. W. McKee & Co., Middletown, to Henry G. Taintor, Hampton, 15 September 1838, in Dan Bulkeley from Andrew J. Bulkeley, db.

[8]Stephen A. Johnson, Pearl Street, New York, to Dan Bulkeley, Hampton, 30 October 1838, db.

[9]Andrew J. Bulkeley, Hartford, to Dan Bulkeley, Hampton, 12 December 1838, db.

[10]Stephen A. Johnson, Hartford, to Dan Bulkeley, Hampton, 5 February 1839, db.

[11]Andrew J. Bulkeley, Hartford, to Dan Bulkeley, Hampton, 12 February 1839, db.

[12]Andrew J. Bulkeley, Hartford, to Dan Bulkeley, Hampton, 25 March 1839, db.

[13]Andrew J. Bulkeley, Hartford, to Dan Bulkeley, Hampton, 20 April 1839, db.

[14]Andrew J. Bulkeley, New York, to Dan Bulkeley, Hampton, 9 May 1839, db.

[15]William Jones, Bucklands Corners, to Dan Bulkeley, Hampton, 14 May 1839, db.

[16]Charles Curtis & Co., Hartford, to Dan Bulkeley, Hampton, 16 July 1839, db.

[17]Charles Curtis & Co., Hartford, to Dan Bulkeley, Hampton, 20 August 1839, db.

[18]Winchester & Johnson, Hartford, to Dan Bulkeley, Hampton, 20 August 1839, db.

[19]Andrew J. Bulkeley to Dan Bulkeley, Hampton, 3 September 1839, db.

[20]Charles Curtis & Co., Hartford, to Dan Bulkeley, Hampton, 5 September 1839, db.

[21]Winchester & Johnson, Hartford, to Dan Bulkeley, Hampton, 7 October 1839, db.

[22]Andrew J. Bulkeley, New York, to Dan Bulkeley, Hampton, 8 October 1839, db.

[23]Andrew J. Bulkeley, New York, to Dan Bulkeley, Hampton, 14 October 1839, db.

[24]Benning Mann, Hartford, to Dan Bulkeley, Hampton, 5 February 1840, db.

[25]Andrew J. Bulkeley, Greenville, Illinois, to Dan Bulkeley, Hampton, 9 October 1840, db. See Don Harrison Doyle, *The Social Order of a Frontier Community: Jacksonville, Illinois, 1825–1870* (Urbana, Ill., 1978) for the life of a community near Greenville.

[26]Andrew J. Bulkeley, Greenville, Illinois, to Dan Bulkeley, Hampton, 23 November 1840, db.

[27]Andrew J. Bulkeley, Greenville, Illinois, to Dan Bulkeley, Hampton, 24 January 1841, db.

[28]Dan Bulkeley, Hampton, 30 December 1839, in Dan Bulkeley–Copies and Drafts of Letters, db.

[29]Papers, Accounts–Bulkeley Estate; Dan Bulkeley Estate–Mrs. Bulkeley's Bills, db.

CHAPTER 10

[1]Abigail E. Hall, Washington, D.C., to Delia E. Taintor, Hampton, 27 January 1856, det.

[2]Henry G. Taintor, Plainfield, Connecticut, Penmanship Book, 1824, hgt.

[3]Henry G. Taintor, Plainfield, Connecticut, Penmanship Book, 1828, hgt.

[4]First published in Keene, N.H., in 1814. Henry had the ninth edition, published in 1828, the year he used it.

[5]Letter from ? to Delia W. Ellsworth, det.

[6]Clarissa ?, Hartford to Delia W. Ellsworth, Windsor, 9 July 1832, in Delia E. Taintor from Misc., det.

[7]From C. S. Watson, Greenfield, Massachusetts, to Delia W. Ellsworth, undated, det. See also Patricia A. Dean, "The Meek Get in Their Licks: Temperance Literature of the Early Nineteenth Century As an Expression of Private Feminism," Ph.D. Dissertation, University of Minnesota, 1981; Carroll Smith-Rosenberg, "The Female World of Love and Ritual: Relations Between Women in Nineteenth-Century America," *Signs: A Journal of Women in Culture and Society* 1 (1975), and *Disorderly Conduct: Visions of Gender in Victorian America* (New York, 1985); Barbara Welter, "The Cult of True Womanhood, 1820–1860," *American Quarterly* 18 (1966), 151–74.

[8]Elisa Pickett, to Delia W. Ellsworth, 2 October 1834, det.

[9]Elisa Pickett, to Delia W. Ellsworth, May 1839, det.

[10]Letter from an aunt to a nephew named Thomas, 12 October 1838, in Four Unattributed Letters on Religious Subjects., hgt.

[11]Goodwin & Avery, Hartford, to Henry G. Taintor, Hampton, 11 February 1839 and 20 September 1839, in Receipts, Travel, 1840s., hgt.

[12]The riddle ended: "Let x equal his age; then from the conditions of the question $x/3 =$ her age at time of marriage. $x/3 + 15 = (x + 15)/2$. $x + 45 + (3x + 45)/2$. $2x + 90 = 3x + 45$. $x = 45 =$ his age. $45/3 =$ her age $= 15$." In Receipts for Setting Up Housekeeping, c. 1840., hgt.

[13]A. M. Litchfield, Hampton, to Henry G. Taintor, Hampton, 20 November 1838, in Receipts, Household, 1840s; and A. M. Litchfield, Hampton, to Henry G. Taintor, Hampton, 18 April 1839, in Lumber and Paint Receipts 1830s, hgt.

[14]Henry G. Taintor, Hampton, to ?, New York, 1 May 1840, in Receipts for Setting up Housekeeping, c.1840., hgt.

[15]George W. Corning, Hartford, to Henry G. Taintor, Hampton, 1 July 1834, in Receipts for Clothes, Tailors, 1830s, hgt.

[16]Henry Oakes, Hartford, to Henry G. Taintor, Hampton, 20 December 1836, in Receipts for Furniture, 1830s, hgt.

[17]On reverse of "Receipt for Knives & Forks," 1 Set Ivory Cutlery–$14.50, Watson & Brown, Boston, to Henry G. Taintor, Hampton, 26 August 1830, in Receipts for Furniture, 1830s, hgt.

[18]Tremont House, Boston, to Henry G. Taintor, Hampton, 18 October 1833, in Receipts Re: Travel, 1830s, hgt.

[19]"1 Fowling piece $12.00, 1 Box caps .42," Allen & Barber, Springfield, Massachusetts, to Henry G. Taintor, Hampton, 17 September 1832, in Receipts for Furniture, 1830s, hgt.

[20]Samuel Grundy, Washington, D.C., to Henry G. Taintor, Hampton, 25 May 1834, hgt.

[21]Pencil notes on reverse of Samuel Frost, 63 Maiden Lane, New York, to Henry G. Taintor, Hampton, 30 September 1835, in Receipts for Clothes, Tailors, 1830s, hgt.

[22]G. K. Hurlburt, Hartford, to Henry G. Taintor, Hampton, 5 February 1836, in Receipts for Furniture, 1830s, hgt.

[23]Robbins & Winship, Hartford, to Henry G. Taintor, Hampton, 2 June and 25 July 1840, in Receipts for Setting Up Housekeeping, c. 1840., hgt.

24Clark & Tomblin, Hampton, to Henry G. Taintor, Hampton, 15 September 1835, and Daniel Dewry, Hartford, to Henry G. Taintor, Hampton, 5 February 1836, in Receipts for Furniture, 1830s, hgt.

25Smith & Williams, Windham, to Henry G. Taintor, Hampton, 25 July 1833, and Brewster & Co., New York, to Henry G. Taintor, Hampton, 28 June 1839, in Receipts for Horses, Vehicles, 1830s, hgt.

26Knowles & Thayer, Brookfield, Massachusetts, to Edwin B. Taintor, Brookfield, October 1833, in Receipts for Horses, Vehicles, 1830s, hgt: apparently Bulkeley passed this on to Henry; Erastus Lumbard, Hampton, to Henry G. Taintor, Hampton, 20 March 1836, in Receipts for Horses, Vehicles, 1830s, hgt.

27Gen'l John O. Howard, Howards Valley, to Henry G. Taintor, Hampton, 25 July 1833, hgt.

28"Inventory of property received of J. A. Taintor Apr. 1 1833," hgt, lists the name of the borrower, initial amount of note, date borrowed, any endorsements, and the present value.

29Hezekiah Hammond, Hampton, to Henry G. Taintor, Hampton, 14 December 1830, hgt.

30Prince Knowles, Hampton, to Henry G. Taintor, Hampton, 28 March 1829, hgt.

31Henry G. Taintor, Hampton, to Delia E. Taintor, Windsor, 10 July 1843, det.

32Henry G. Taintor, Account Book "Hampton August 20th 1833," 2 April 1841, hgt.

33Herman J. Viola, The Indian Legacy of Charles Bird King (Washington and New York, 1976); Andrew J. Cosentino, The Paintings of Charles Bird King, 1785–1862 (Washington, D.C., 1977); Caroline F. Sloat, ed., Meet Your Neighbors: New England Portraits and Society, 1790–1850 (Sturbridge, Mass., 1992).

34Ralph D. Snow, Hampton, to Henry G. Taintor, Hampton, 6 November 1845, in Receipts, Household, 1840s., hgt.

35Harvey Smith, Hampton, to Henry G. Taintor, Hampton, February 1844, in Receipts, Farming, 1840s., hgt.

36Lewis Fuller, Hampton, to Henry G. Taintor, Hampton, 20 July 1854, in Receipts, Farming, 1850s., hgt.

37Andrew M. Litchfield, Hampton, to Henry G. Taintor, Hampton, 15 March 1855, and H. L. Danielson, to Henry G. Taintor, Hampton, 1 April 1854, in Receipts, House, 1850s., hgt.

38Susan Taintor (Clapp), West Brookfield, Massachusetts, to Delia E. Taintor, Hampton, 19 May 1854, det; Elwin B. Day, Danielsonville, Connecticut, to Henry G. Taintor, Hampton, 7 June 1854, in Receipts, House, 1850s., hgt.

39Henry G. Taintor, Hampton, entries between 10 July 1854 and 13 December 1855, in Cash Books (2), 1850s, hgt.

40Dorothy Davis Goodwin, "My Ancestral Home" (1943).

41Charles Ashley, Hampton, to Henry G. Taintor, Hampton, 17 July 1857; D. F. Johnson, Willimantic, to Henry G. Taintor, Hampton, 20 July 1857; John Breed & Co, Norwich, to Henry G. Taintor, Hampton, 9 July 1857; Estate of S. W. Meech, Norwich, to Henry G. Taintor, Hampton, 27 July 1857; Henry W. Birge, Norwich, to Henry G. Taintor, Hampton, 27 July 1857; and George C. Snow, Hampton, to Henry G. Taintor, Hampton, 28 August 1857, in Receipts, House, 1850s., hgt.

42Delia E. Taintor, Hampton, to William W. Taintor, Windsor, 30 September 1860, wt. See also Elisabeth Donaghy Garrett, At Home (New York, 1990).

43Newton Clark & Co., Hampton, to Henry G. Taintor, Hampton, 12 February 1845, hgt.

44Joseph Langdon, Hartford, to Henry G. Taintor, Hampton, 12 October 1844, in Receipts, Clothes, 1840s., hgt.

4518 January 1847, Henry G. Taintor Cash Book, 44/10/01–47/04/11, hgt.

46Henry G. Taintor, Cash Book, 55/12/14–57/03/19, in Cash Books, 1850s, hgt.

4719 October 1860, Henry G. Taintor, Cash Books 60/07/30–62/09/10, Paperbound dark red leather-covered, 1860 in ink at top center, hgt.

48Abigail E. Hall, Washington, D.C., to Delia E. Taintor, Hampton, 27 January 1856, det. See also Horace Bushnell, Views of Christian Nurture (Hartford, Conn., 1847); Carl Degler, At Odds: Women and the Family in America from the Revolution to the Present (New York, 1980); Mary Kelley, Private Woman, Public State: Literary Domesticity in Nineteenth-Century America (New York, 1984); Anne L. Kuhn, The Mother's Role in Childhood Education: New England Concepts 1830–1860 (New Haven, Conn., 1947); Mary P. Ryan, The Empire of the Mother: American Writing about Domesticity, 1830–1860 (New York, 1982).

49Delia E. Williams, Hartford, to Delia W. Ellsworth, Windsor, 24 January 1826, det.

50Abigail E. Hall, Washington, D.C., to Delia E. Taintor, Hampton, 11 May 1843, det.

[51]Abigail E. Hall, Washington, D.C., to Delia E. Taintor, Hampton, 9 January 1855, det.

[52]"Shan," Fitchburg, Massachusetts, to Delia E. Taintor, Hampton, 27 March 1855, det.

[53]Ellen Ellsworth (Strong), Rutland, Vermont, to Delia E. Taintor, Hampton, 13 March 1860, det.

[54]Ellen Ellsworth (Strong), Windsor, to Delia E. Taintor, Hampton, 21 January 1861, det.

[55]Ellen Ellsworth (Strong), Monson, Massachusetts, to Delia E. Taintor, Hampton, 13 February 1861, det.

[56]Ellen Ellsworth (Strong), Rutland, Vermont, to Delia E. Taintor, Hampton, 29 April 1855, det.

[57]Eleanor D. Ellsworth, Lafayette, Indiana, to Delia E. Taintor, Hampton, 27 January 1864, det.

[58]Ellen Ellsworth (Strong), Windsor, to Delia E. Taintor, Hampton, 29 March 1865, det.

[59]Sophie W. Reynolds, Lafayette, Indiana, to Delia E. Taintor, Hampton, 25 April 1869, det.

[60]Alice Hall (Wycoff), Springfield, Massachusetts, to Delia E. Taintor, Hampton, 3 November 1865, det.

[61]Leonora H. Dolbeane, Colchester, Connecticut, to Delia E. Taintor, Hampton, 26 February 1868, det.

CHAPTER 11

[1]John A. Taintor, Rome, Italy, to Henry G. Taintor, Hampton, 5 November 1845, hgt.

[2]Hampton Town Records B78, B79, B99.

[3]Amos T. Kenyon, Hampton, to Henry G. Taintor, Hampton, 2 April 1839. Receipt for Church Repair, 1839, hgt. See also Peter Benes, ed., *New England Meeting House and Church: 1630–1850* (Boston, 1979); Charles A. Place, "From Meeting House to Church in New England," *Old-Time New England* 13–14 (1923); Edmund W. Sinnott, *Meetinghouse and Church in Early New England* (New York, 1963).

[4]William Durkee 3rd, Hampton, to Henry G. Taintor, Hampton, 6 December 1844, in Receipts Re: Church, 1840s, hgt.

[5]For some examples see Receipts, Hampton Church, 1850s, and Receipts, Periodicals, 1850s, hgt.

[6]Denison Smith, Hampton, to Henry G. Taintor, Hampton, 27 June 1841, hgt.

[7]See entries 14 March 1859 "1 Eccl Society blowing organ 2.50" and 20 March 1860 "Andrew Fuller blowing organ 2.50," in Henry G. Taintor, Hampton, Cash Book 58/06/02– 60/07/28; and the entries 15 March 1856 "pd Edward Button blowing organ 1.75," and 26 May 1856, "pd Luther tuning Organ 4.50, and pd Henry blowing ditto .25" in Henry G. Taintor, Hampton, Cash Book 55/12/14–57/03/19; in Cash Books, 1850s, hgt.

[8]John R. Tweedy, Hampton, to Congregational Church, 1 April 1859, in Receipts, Hampton Church, 1850s; J. R. Tweedy, Hampton, to Henry G. Taintor, 1 November 1860, Bills & Receipts, 1860–1864, hgt. Also see entry for 25 June 1861 "Smith Wine for Church 6.00" in Henry G. Taintor, Cash Book 60/07/30– 62/09/10, in Cash Books (2), 1860s., hgt.

[9]John A. Taintor, off Sandy Hook, to Henry G. Taintor, Hampton, 16 May 1845, hgt.

[10]John A. Taintor, London, to Henry G. Taintor, Hampton, 28 June 1845, hgt.

[11]John A. Taintor, Liverpool, to Henry G. Taintor, Hampton, 26 July 1845, hgt.

[12]John A. Taintor, Liverpool, to Henry G. Taintor, Hampton, 18 August 1845, hgt.

[13]John A. Taintor, Amsterdam, to Henry G. Taintor, Hampton, 1 September 1845, hgt.

[14]John A. Taintor, Leipzig, to Henry G. Taintor, Hampton, 12 September 1845, hgt.

[15]John A. Taintor, Rome, Italy, to Henry G. Taintor, Hampton, 5 November 1845, hgt.

[16]John A. Taintor, Paris, to Henry G. Taintor, Hampton, 20 December 1845, hgt.

[17]Adelia C. Taintor, Paris, to Delia E. Taintor, Hampton, 25 December 1845, in Henry G. Taintor from John A. Taintor, European Trip 1845–46, hgt.

[18]See the Library of America edition of Mark Twain, *Innocents Abroad Roughing It* (New York, 1984) for an excellent text, and an informative "Chronology," 987–94.

[19]John A. Taintor, Madrid, to Henry G. Taintor, Hampton, 4 February 1846, hgt.

[20]John A. Taintor, Liverpool, to Henry G. Taintor, Hampton, 28 April 1846, hgt.

[21]John A. Taintor, Paris, to Henry G. Taintor, Hampton, 12 May 1846, hgt. See also Peter Dobkin Hall, *The Organization of American Culture, 1700–1900: Private Institutions, Elites, and the Origins of American Nationality* (New York, 1982).

[22]All the names and information are from the manuscript census reports for Hampton, 1850 U.S. Census, National Archives. See also Clyde and Sally Griffen, *Natives and Newcomers:*

The Ordering of Opportunity in Mid-Nineteenth-Century Poughkeepsie (Cambridge, Mass., 1978); Michael B. Katz, Michael B. Doucet, and Mark J. Stern, "Migration and the Social Order in Erie County, New York: 1855," *Journal of Interdisciplinary History* 8 (1978), 699–701; Wilbur Zelinsky, "Changes in Geographic Patterns of Rural Population in the United States, 1790–1960," *Geographical Review* 52 (1962), 492–524.

CHAPTER 12

¹Delia E. Taintor, Hampton, to Mary E. Taintor, Windsor, 7 October 1880, mtd.

²Delia ?, South Hadley, Massachusetts, to Delia E. Taintor, Hampton, 16 November 1858, det. See also Lewis Perry, *Childhood, Marriage, and Reform* (Chicago, 1980).

³Ellen Ellsworth (Strong), Windsor, to Delia E. Taintor, Hampton, 22 July 1863, det.

⁴Delia E. Taintor, Hampton, to Mary E. Taintor, Hartford, 13 October 1881 and 16 November 1882, mtd.

⁵Susan P. Taintor (Clapp), West Brookfield, Massachusetts, to Delia E. Taintor, Hampton, 24 May 1855, det.

⁶Delia E. Taintor, Hampton, to Mary E. Taintor, Rutland, Vermont, 8 October 1880, mtd.

⁷Ellen Ellsworth (Strong), Windsor, to Delia E. Taintor, Hampton, 24 October 1869, det.

⁸Sophia Ellsworth, Windsor, to Delia E. Taintor, Hampton, 16 June 1861, det.

⁹Henry E. Taintor, Hartford, to Delia E. Taintor, Hampton, 22 March 1869, det.

¹⁰Delia E. Taintor, Hampton, to Mary E. Taintor, Hartford, 26 June 1884, mtd.

¹¹Sophie W. Reynolds, Lafayette, Indiana, to Delia E. Taintor, Hampton, 16 July 1855, det.

¹²Delia E. Taintor, Hampton, to Mary E. Taintor, Windsor, 4 October 1880, mtd.

¹³Ellen Ellsworth (Strong), Windsor, to Delia E. Taintor, Hampton, 22 July 1863, det.

¹⁴Caroline Taintor (Buel), Detroit, to Delia E. Taintor, Hampton, 15 August 1872, det.

¹⁵Delia E. Taintor, Hampton, to Mary E. Taintor, Rutland, Vermont, 29 October 1880, mtd. See also Faye E. Dudden, *Serving Women: Household Service in Nineteenth-Century America* (Middletown, Conn., 1983); David Katzman, *Seven Days a Week: Women and Domestic Service in Industrializing America* (New York, 1978); Carol F. Lasser, "Mistress, Maid and Market: The Transformation of Domestic Service in

New England, 1790–1870," Ph.D. Dissertation, Harvard University, 1982; Daniel E. Sutherland, *Americans and Their Servants: Domestic Service in the United States from 1800 to 1920* (Baton Rouge, La., 1981).

¹⁶Anne Gurley, San Francisco, to Henry G. Taintor, Hampton, 4 September 1855, in Letters from "A. G.," San Francisco, tdmisc.

¹⁷Henry G. Taintor, Hartford, to Delia E. Taintor, Hampton, 9 January 1867, det.

¹⁸Ellen Ellsworth (Strong), Windsor, to Delia E. Taintor, Hampton, 1 May 1867, det.

¹⁹Susan P. Taintor (Clapp), West Brookfield, Massachusetts, to Delia E. Taintor, Hampton, 19 May 1854, det.

²⁰Delia E. Taintor, Hartford, to Mary E. Taintor, Hampton, 4 February 1881, mtd: date conjectural, from context.

²¹"Shan," Fitchburg (Maple Hill), Massachusetts, to Delia E. Taintor, Hampton, 28 May 1854, det.

²²"Shan," Fitchburg (Maple Hill), Massachusetts, to Delia E. Taintor, Hampton, 28 May 1854, det.

²³"Shan," Bridgeport, Connecticut, to Delia E. Taintor, Hampton, 8 December 1854, det.

²⁴"Shan," Fitchburg (Maple Hill), Massachusetts, to Delia E. Taintor, Hampton, 28 May 1854, det.

²⁵"Shan," Concord, Massachusetts, to Delia E. Taintor, Hampton, 22 July 1855, det.

²⁶Emma Ellsworth, Lafayette, Indiana, to Delia E. Taintor, Hampton, 26 June 1870, det.

²⁷Emma Ellsworth, Lafayette, Indiana, to Delia E. Taintor, Hampton, 15 October 1873, det.

²⁸Fannie E. Hall, Springfield, Massachusetts, to Delia E. Taintor, Hampton, 3 March 1878, det.

²⁹Lucy Jane W. Strong, Rutland, Vermont, to Delia E. Taintor, Hampton, 25 October 1858, det.

³⁰Ellen Ellsworth (Strong), Rutland, Vermont, to Delia E. Taintor, Hampton, 13 March 1860, det.

³¹Ellen Ellsworth (Strong), Windsor, to Delia E. Taintor, Hampton, 2 April 1862, det.

³²Ellen Ellsworth (Strong), Windsor, to Delia E. Taintor, Hampton, 4 April 1862, det.

³³Ellen Ellsworth (Strong), Windsor, to Delia E. Taintor, Hampton, 21 January 1861, det.

³⁴Ellen Ellsworth (Strong), Windsor, to Delia E. Taintor, Hampton, 2 April 1862, det.

[35]Leonora H. Dolbeane, Colchester, Connecticut, to Delia E. Taintor, Hampton, 26 February 1868, det.

[36]Laura Gleason, Windsor, to Delia E. Taintor, Windsor, 28 September 1871, det.

[37]Emma Ellsworth, Lafayette, Indiana, to Delia E. Taintor, Hampton, 26 March 1873, det.

[38]Laura Gleason, East Hartford, to Delia E. Taintor, Hampton, 20 May 1873, det.

[39]Miss Mary Smith Account, 1 October 1848, in Estate of Ruth Butts, hgt.

[40]Abigail Ellsworth (Hall), Washington, D.C., to Delia E. Taintor, Hampton, 11 May 1843, det. See also Karen Halttunen, *Confidence Men and Painted Women: A Study of Middle Class Culture in America, 1830-1870* (New Haven, Conn., 1982); John F. Kasson, *Rudeness and Civility: Manners in Nineteenth-Century Urban America* (New York, 1990).

[41]Abigail Ellsworth (Hall), Washington, D.C., to Delia E. Taintor, Hampton, 29 March 1861, det.

[42]A. B. Dawson, Brooklyn, New York, to Delia E. Taintor, Hampton, 26 February 1854, det.

[43]Abigail Ellsworth (Hall), Washington, D.C., to Delia E. Taintor, Hampton, 25 January 1864, det.

[44]Ellen Ellsworth (Strong), Washington, D.C., to Delia E. Taintor, Hampton, 25 December 1861, det.

[45]Henry E. Taintor, New Haven, to Delia E. Taintor, Hampton, 16 December 1862, det.

[46]George E. Taintor, Hartford, to Delia E. Taintor, Hampton, 20 May 1863, det.

[47]George E. Taintor, Urbana, Ohio, to Delia E. Taintor, Hampton, 1 November 1868, det.

[48]Abigail Ellsworth (Hall), Washington, D.C., to Delia E. Taintor, Hampton, 25 January 1864, det.

[49]George E. Taintor, Hartford, to Delia E. Taintor, Hampton, 6 October 1864, det.

[50]Henry E. Taintor (and George E. Taintor), Hartford, to Delia E. Taintor, Hampton, 1 September 1867, det.

[51]Sophie W. Reynolds, Lafayette, Indiana, to Ellen E. Strong, Windsor, 7 June 1868, in Delia E. Taintor from Sophie W. Reynolds, det.

[52]Caroline Taintor (Buel), West Brookfield, Massachusetts, to Delia E. Taintor, Hampton, 5 May 1855, det.

[53]Susan P. Taintor (Clapp), West Brookfield, Massachusetts, to Delia E. Taintor, Hampton, 10 July 1855, det.

[54]George E. Taintor, Hartford, to Delia E. Taintor, Hampton, 14 December 1868, det.

CHAPTER 13

[1]Entry for Deacon Benjamin Brown in *Commemorative Biographical Record of Tolland and Windham Counties Connecticut* (Chicago, 1903).

[2]George C. Thorburn, New York, to Henry G. Taintor, Hampton, 7 May 1839; George C. Barrett, Boston, to Henry G. Taintor, Hampton, 7 October 1839, in Receipts Re: Farming, 1830s, hgt.

[3]For example, see payments for work in 1833 and 1834 to William Durkee, 3rd, Hampton, from Henry G. Taintor, February 1834, in Receipts Re: Farming, 1830s, hgt.

[4]The information cited in the paragraphs above is all gleaned from two account books of Henry G. Taintor, the first dated "Hampton. August 20th, 1833," hgt; Also see Sally McMurry, "Progressive Farm Families and Their Houses, 1830-1855: A Study in Independent Design," *Agricultural History* 58 (1984), 330-46.

[5]Benjamin Brown, Jr., Farm Journal. (Our thanks to Wendell Davis for bringing it to our attention and lending it to us.) See also *Report of the Commissioner of Patents for the Year 1851, Part II, Agriculture* (Washington, D.C., 1852), 170-73, report from Brooklyn, Connecticut, signed by Albert Day, John Gallup, 2d, Edwin Scarborough; Holly Izard Paterson, "A Small Farmer's World: The Economic and Social Networks of Philemon Shepard of Sturbridge, Massachusetts," Unpublished Paper, presented to TARS Symposium on Social History, Locality, and Mentalité (Keene, N.H., 1984); Richard D. Brown, Ross W. Beales, Jr., Richard B. Lyman, Jr., and Jack Larkin, *Farm Labor in Southern New England during the Agricultural-Industrial Transition* (Worcester, Mass., 1989); Clarence Danhoff, *Change in Agriculture: The Northern States, 1820-1870* (Cambridge, Mass., 1969).

[6]Entry for Deacon Benjamin Brown in *Commemorative Biographical Record of Tolland and Windham Counties Connecticut* (Chicago, 1903). See also Frederick J. Blue, *The Free Soilers, Third Party Politics 1848-1854* (Urbana, Ill., 1973); Lawrence J. Freedman, *Gregarious Saints: Self and Community in American Abolitionism* (Cambridge, 1982).

[7]All of the discussion of Henry G. Taintor's political career is based on our analysis of the mass of his detailed receipts, cash books,

accounts, and correspondence in the Taintor-Davis Collection, supplemented by the Hampton Town Records, and State Records in the Connecticut State Library. See also Albert L. Demaree, *The American Agricultural Press, 1819–1860* (New York, 1941); Donald B. Marti, "Agricultural Journalism and the Diffusion of Knowledge: The First Half-Century in America," *Agricultural History* 54 (1980), 28–37; Wayne C. Neely, *The Agricultural Fair* (New York, 1935).

8Dyer Hughes, Jr., Hampton, to Henry G. Taintor, Hampton, 7 September 1848, hgt.

9Harriet Beecher Stowe, *A Key to Uncle Tom's Cabin* . . . (Boston, John P. Jewett & Co., 1853), iii. See also Angelina Grimke, *Letters to Catherine Beecher, in Reply to an Essay on Slavery and Abolitionism*. . . . (Boston, 1838).

10Hampton Town Records, C116–21.

11City Hotel, Hartford, to Henry G. Taintor, Hampton, 8 June 1843, in Receipts, Travel, 1840s, hgt.

12U.S. Hotel, Hartford, to Henry G. Taintor, Hampton, 2 July 1851, in Receipts, Travel, 1850s., hgt.

13Henry G. Taintor, Hartford, to Delia E. Taintor, Hampton, 18 July 1866, det.

14Henry G. Taintor, Hartford, to Delia E. Taintor, Hampton, 5 January 1867, det.

15Henry G. Taintor, New Haven, to Delia E. Taintor, Hampton, undated, det. See also Eric Foner, *Free Soil, Free Labor, Free Men: The Ideology of the Republican Party Before the Civil War* (New York, 1970).

16John A. Taintor, Hartford, to Henry G. Taintor, Hampton, 17 February 1842, in Robert Bulkeley file; Andrew J. Bulkeley, Hampton, to Henry G. Taintor, Hampton, 14 June 1842, in Andrew J. Bulkeley Notes; I. Gordon Smith, Hartford, to Phoebe Bulkeley, Hampton, 15 June 1842, in Dan Bulkeley Estate; Spicer & Curtis, Hampton, to Henry G. Taintor, Hampton, 29 June 1842, in Mary Bulkeley file; J. T. Carpenter, Hampton, to Henry G. Taintor, Hampton, 1 July 1842, in Dan Bulkeley Estate; Robert W. Bulkeley, Hampton, to Henry G. Taintor, Hampton, 11 October 1842; Daniel S. Dewey, Hartford, to Henry G. Taintor, Hampton, 25 October 1842, in Andrew J. Bulkeley Notes; Harriet H. Avery, Hampton, to Robert W. Bulkeley, Hampton, 16 April 1857, in Henry G. Taintor Bills & Receipts, 1860–1864, hgt. The final receipt is "Recd . . . of Henry G. Taintor One dollar in full of all demands up to this date. Hampton June 24,

1860. [signed] R. W. Bulkeley," Robert W. Bulkeley, Hampton, to Henry G. Taintor, Hampton, 24 June 1860, in Henry G. Taintor Bills & Receipts, 1860–1864, hgt.

17Erastus B. Fuller Estate, Eufaula, Alabama, 5 March 1848, hgt.

18Philip Pearl, Hampton, v. Cesar Hall, Hampton, 20 August 1849, JP Case, hgt.

19William Abbott, to John B. Burnett, 29 August 1850, in Estate of John B. Burnett, hgt.

20(Mrs) William Clark, Hampton, to John B. Burnett, 29 June 1850; D. L. Fuller, Hampton, to (Mrs) John Burnett, Hampton, 14 June 1851, in Estate of John B. Burnett, hgt.

21David Copeland, Hampton, v. David Greenslit, Hampton, 20 December 1850, JP Case, hgt.

22Royal Copeland, Hampton, v. Jonathan K. Rindge, Hampton, 21 March 1851, JP Case, hgt.

23Edward S. Moseley, Hampton, to Francis A. Brewster, Hampton, 18 July 1853, Francis A. Brewster JP Case, hgt.

24Edward S. Moseley, Hampton, to Francis A. Brewster, Hampton, 18 January 1854, Francis A. Brewster JP Case, hgt.

25Edward S. Moseley, Hampton, to David Avery, Hampton, 22 January 1855, David Avery JP Case, hgt; Edward S. Moseley, Hampton, to John Peaster, Chaplin, 22 January 1855, John Peaster JP Case, hgt.

26John R. Tweedy, Hampton, to Samuel Vickers, Hampton, 6 June 1857, Samuel Vickers JP Case, hgt.

27Edward S. Moseley, Hampton, to Isaac N. Hendley, Hampton, 26 August 1853, Isaac Hendley JP Case, hgt.

28Edward S. Moseley, Hampton, to Ebenezer Hutchins, Windham, 23 February 1855, Ebenezer Hutchins JP Case, hgt.

29Ebenezer Griffin, Hampton, v. Michael Clark, Hampton, 23 July 1855, JP Case, hgt.

30John R. Tweedy, Hampton, to David Clapp, Jr., Chaplin, 24 December 1855, David Clapp, Jr. JP Case, hgt. John R. Tweedy was the Grand Juror who formally brought the charges.

31Asa Weeks JP Case, 26 May 1857; William Card JP Case, 12 June 1857, hgt.

32Lyndon T. Button, Hampton, v. Edward Logan, Killingly, 1 April 1858, JP Case, hgt.

CHAPTER 14

1Susan P. Taintor (Clapp), to Delia E. Taintor, Hampton, 22 November 1863, det.

[2]Petition for Bankruptcy, 23 January 1843, in Bankruptcy, 1843, ebt.

[3]In Bankruptcy, 1843, ebt. For a discussion of the questions of solvency, shame, and honor among American gentlemen, see T. H. Breen, *Tobacco Culture: The Mentality of the Great Tidewater Planters on the Eve of Revolution* (Princeton, N.J., 1985). One of those planters, George Washington, was a great model and hero to all early nineteenth-century Americans who thought of themselves as gentlemen. Also see Michael B. Katz, *In the Shadow of the Poorhouse: A Social History of Welfare in America* (New York, 1986).

[4]Susan P. Taintor (Clapp), West Brookfield, Massachusetts, to Delia E. Taintor, Hampton, 19 May 1854, det.

[5]Susan P. Taintor (Clapp), West Brookfield, Massachusetts, to Delia E. Taintor, Hampton, 31 July 1854, det.

[6]Susan P. Taintor (Clapp), West Brookfield, Massachusetts, to Delia E. Taintor, Hampton, 7 October 1854, det.

[7]See Sandra M. Gilbert and Susan Gubar, *The Madwoman in the Attic: The Woman Writer and the Nineteenth-Century Literary Imagination* (New Haven, Yale University Press, 1979). See also Norman Dain, *Concepts of Insanity in the United States, 1789–1865* (New Brunswick, N.J., 1964); Gerald Grob, *The State and the Mentally Ill* (Chapel Hill, N.C., 1966), and *Mental Illness and American Society, 1875–1940* (Princeton, N.J., 1985); David Rothman, *The Discovery of the Asylum* (Boston, 1971).

[8]Susan P. Taintor (Clapp), West Brookfield, Massachusetts, to Delia E. Taintor, Hampton, 19 May 1854, det.

[9]Caroline Taintor (Buel), Buck Eye, Georgia, to Delia E. Taintor, Hampton, 3 January 1855, det.

[10]Caroline Taintor (Buel), Buck Eye, Georgia, to Delia E. Taintor, Hampton, 10 February 1855, det.

[11]Caroline Taintor (Buel), West Brookfield, Massachusetts, to Delia E. Taintor, Hampton, 9 July 1855, det.

[12]Susan P. Taintor (Clapp), West Brookfield, Massachusetts, to Delia E. Taintor, Hampton, 9 July 1855 [missing the beginning], det.

[13]Susan P. Taintor (Clapp), West Brookfield, Massachusetts, to Delia E. Taintor, Hampton, 10 July 1855, det.

[14]Caroline Taintor (Buel), Farm Ridge, Illinois, to Delia E. Taintor, Hampton, 7 February 1856, det.

[15]Caroline Taintor (Buel), West Brookfield, Massachusetts, to Delia E. Taintor, Hampton, 13 June 1857, det.

[16]Susan P. Taintor (Clapp), West Brookfield, Massachusetts, to Delia E. Taintor, Hampton, 15 June 1857, det.

[17]Susan P. Taintor (Clapp), West Brookfield, Massachusetts, to Delia E. Taintor, Hampton, 19 May 1854, det.

[18]Susan P. Taintor (Clapp), West Brookfield, Massachusetts, to Delia E. Taintor, Hampton, 28 September 1860, det.

[19]Susan P. Taintor (Clapp), West Brookfield, Massachusetts, to Delia E. Taintor, Hampton, 22 November 1861, det.

[20]Susan P. Taintor (Clapp), West Brookfield, Massachusetts, to Delia E. Taintor, Hampton, 17 November 1862, det.

[21]Commissions as justice of the peace, dated 14 October 1862, and as assistant assessor, Division 5 of the 8th Collection District of Massachusetts, U.S. Treasury, 30 September 1863. In Commissions, ebt.

[22]Susan P. Taintor (Clapp), West Brookfield, Massachusetts, to Delia E. Taintor, Hampton, 22 November 1863, det.

[23]Caroline Taintor (Buel), Detroit, to Delia E. Taintor, Hampton, 1 May 1865, det.

[24]Susan P. Taintor (Clapp), Stockbridge, Massachusetts, to Delia E. Taintor, Hampton, 5 June 1865, det.

[25]Susan P. Taintor (Clapp), Boston, to Delia E. Taintor, Hampton, 15 February 1866, det.

[26]Edwin Bulkeley Taintor, West Brookfield, Massachusetts, to Henry G. Taintor, Hampton, 24 February 1866, hgt.

[27]Edwin Bulkeley Taintor, West Brookfield, Massachusetts, to Henry G. Taintor, Hampton, 26 October 1866, hgt.

[28]Edwin Bulkeley Taintor, West Brookfield, Massachusetts, to Henry G. Taintor, Hartford, 6 November 1866, hgt.

[29]Caroline Taintor (Buel), Sault St. Marie, Michigan, to Delia E. Taintor, Hampton, 28 August 1867, det.

[30]Caroline Taintor (Buel), Boston, to Delia E. Taintor, Hampton, 22 February 1868, det.

[31]Susan P. Taintor (Clapp), West Brookfield, Massachusetts to Henry G. Taintor, Hampton, 2 March 1870, det.

[32]Susan P. Taintor (Clapp), Boston, to Delia E. Taintor, Hampton, 20 March 1870, det.

33Caroline Taintor (Buel), Detroit, to Delia E. Taintor, Hampton, 7 April 1870, det.

CHAPTER 15

1Ellen Ellsworth (Strong), Windsor, to Delia E. Taintor, Hampton, 11 April 1862, det.

2The Connecticut popular vote was 43,800 for Lincoln, 16,100 for Breckenridge, 15,300 for Douglas, and 2,300 for Bell.

3Susan P. Taintor (Clapp), West Brookfield, Massachusetts, to Delia E. Taintor, Hampton, 25 March 1861, det. The outstanding works which give particular color to the Civil War experience of Americans at home are C. Vann Woodward, ed., *Mary Chesnut's Civil War* (New Haven, Conn., 1981) and Robert Manson Myers, ed., *The Children of Pride* (New Haven, Conn., 1972). Also see David Donald, *Lincoln Reconsidered: Essays on the Civil War Era* (New York, 1956).

4Henry E. Taintor, Monson, Massachusetts, to Henry G. Taintor, Hampton, 19 April 1861, in Delia E. Taintor from Henry E. Taintor, det.

5Henry E. Taintor, Monson, Massachusetts, to Delia E. Taintor, Hampton, 25 April 1861, det.

6Henry E. Taintor, Monson, Massachusetts, to Delia E. Taintor, Hampton, 27 April 1861, det.

7Abigail Ellsworth (Hall), Washington, D.C., to Frederick Ellsworth, Hampton, 7 May 1861, in Delia E. Taintor from Abby E. Hall, det. See also Margaret Leech, *Reveille in Washington, 1860–1865* (New York, 1941).

8Sophia Ellsworth, Windsor, to Delia E. Taintor, Hampton, 16 June 1861, det.

9Henry E. Taintor, New Haven, to Delia E. Taintor, Hampton, 12 September 1861, det.

10Henry E. Taintor, New Haven, to Delia E. Taintor, Hampton, 5 December 1861, det.

11Ellen Ellsworth (Strong), Windsor, to Delia E. Taintor, Hampton, 11 April 1862, det.

12John A. Taintor's will, October 2, 1862, Hartford Probate Records, Connecticut State Library.

13Mary Livermore, Lebanon, Connecticut, to Delia E. Taintor, Hampton, 19 May 1862, det.

14Ellen Ellsworth (Strong), Hartford, to Delia E. Taintor, Hampton, 18 November 1862, det.

15Henry E. Taintor, New Haven, to Delia E. Taintor, Hampton, 16 December 1862, det.

16Ellen Ellsworth (Strong), Windsor, to Delia E. Taintor, Hampton, 22 July 1863, det.

17Hampton Town Records C-91.

18Henry C. Davis, Cesar Hall, William W. Hazzard, James Roberts, Charles C. Vickers, Henry Vickers, and Samuel Vickers.

19Henry E. Taintor, New Haven, to Delia E. Taintor, Hampton, 23 September 1861, det. See "Coca" and "Cocaine," *The Encyclopaedia Brittanica,* 11th Edition (New York, 1910) VI, 614–15.

20Henry E. Taintor, New Haven, to Henry G. Taintor, Hampton, 26 May 1863, hgt.

21Henry E. Taintor, New Haven, to Henry G. Taintor, Hampton, 1 June 1863, hgt.

22Ellen Ellsworth (Strong), Windsor, to Delia E. Taintor, Hampton, 3 December 1862, det.

23Henry E. Taintor, New Haven, to Delia E. Taintor, Hampton, 18 October 1863, det.

24Delia E. Taintor, Hampton, to Henry E. Taintor, New Haven, undated pencil draft., det.

25Henry E. Taintor, New Haven, to Delia E. Taintor, Hampton, 9 November 1863, det.

26Henry E. Taintor, New Haven, to Henry G. Taintor, Hampton, 3 November 1863, in Delia E. Taintor from Henry E. Taintor, det.

27S. W. and Dora F. Skinner, Arlington, Virginia, to Delia E. Taintor, Hampton, 4 January 1864, det.

28Entries for 8 February and 29 February 1864, in Cash Book of Henry G. Taintor, 10 September 1862–14 March 1868, hgt.

29Eleanor D. Ellsworth, Lafayette, Indiana, to Delia E. Taintor, Hampton, 27 January 1864, det.

30Delia E. Taintor, Hampton, to Henry E. Taintor, 4 January 1864, het.

31George E. Taintor, Alliance, Ohio, to Delia E. Taintor, Hampton, 18 September 1874, det.

32Abigail Ellsworth (Hall), Washington, D.C., to Delia E. Taintor, Hampton, 25 January 1864, det.

33Abigail Ellsworth (Hall), Washington, D.C., to Delia E. Taintor, Hampton, 28 April 1864, det.

34D. E. B., Hampton, to Henry E. Taintor, 7 May 1864, in Delia E. Taintor from Henry E. Taintor, det.

35George E. Taintor, Hartford, to Delia E. Taintor, Hampton, 21 October 1864, det.

36Sophie W. Reynolds, California, to Delia E. Taintor, Hampton, 3 October 1864, det.

37Maria M. C. Hall, Annapolis, Maryland, to Delia E. Taintor, Hampton, 16 December 1864, det.

[38]Maria M. C. Hall, Annapolis, Maryland, to Delia E. Taintor, Hampton, 14 February 1865, det.

[39]B. L. Martin, for the American Sanitary Commission, New York, to Henry G. Taintor, Hampton, 19 January 1865, in Delia E. Taintor from Soldiers Aid Society, det.

[40]Ellen Collins, of Soldiers Aid Society, New York, to Mrs. David Greenslit, Hampton, 14 February 1865, in Delia E. Taintor from Soldiers Aid Society, det.

[41]Entries for 23 January, 18 November, and 25 November 1864, and 4 January 1865; and for the books bought from "pedlar" see 11 March 1863 and 13 March 1865, in Cash Book of Henry G. Taintor, 10 September 1862–14 March 1868, hgt.

[42]Ellen Ellsworth (Strong), Windsor, to Delia E. Taintor, Hampton, 29 March 1865, det.

[43]Ellen Ellsworth (Strong), Windsor, to Delia E. Taintor, Hampton, 25 April 1865, det.

[44]Delia E. Taintor, Windsor, to Henry G. Taintor, Hampton, 22 May 1865, hgt.

[45]Receipt from N. C. Sanborn, Lowell, Massachusetts, to Henry E. Taintor, 21 July 1865 (for $22.50, which seems more than most portraits cost) in Bills & Receipts, 1865–1869 (3 Packets), hgt.

[46]Alice Hall (Wycoff), Springfield, Massachusetts, to Delia E. Taintor, Hampton, 3 November 1865, det.

[47]Oliver Wendell Holmes, Jr., "Memorial Day," an Address Delivered May 30, 1884, at Keene, N.H., Before John Sedgwick Post No. 4, Grand Army of the Republic, in *The Occasional Speeches of Justice Oliver Wendell Holmes,* Mark DeWolfe Howe, comp. (Cambridge, Mass., Harvard University Press, 1962), 15–16.

CHAPTER 16

[1]Caroline Taintor (Buel), Detroit, to Delia E. Taintor, Hampton, 2 March 1863, det.

[2]Caroline Taintor (Buel), Detroit, to Delia E. Taintor, Hampton, 22 January 1860, det.

[3]Caroline Taintor (Buel), West Brookfield, Massachusetts, to Delia E. Taintor, Hampton, 17 August 1860, det.

[4]Caroline Taintor (Buel), Detroit, to Delia E. Taintor, Hampton, 2 March 1863, det.

[5]Caroline Taintor (Buel), Detroit, to Delia E. Taintor, Hampton, 4 August 1863, det.

[6]Caroline Taintor (Buel), Detroit, to Delia E. Taintor, Hampton, 30 March 1864, det.

[7]Caroline Taintor (Buel), Detroit, to Delia E. Taintor, Hampton, 30 March 1864, det.

[8]Caroline Taintor (Buel), Detroit, to Delia E. Taintor, Hampton, 21 June 1867, det.

[9]Caroline Taintor (Buel), Sault St. Marie, Michigan, to Delia E. Taintor, Hampton, 28 August 1867, det.

[10]Caroline Taintor (Buel), Detroit, to Delia E. Taintor, Hampton, 27 December 1867, det.

[11]Caroline Taintor (Buel), Boston, to Delia E. Taintor, Hampton, 22 February 1868, det.

[12]Caroline Taintor (Buel), Detroit, to Delia E. Taintor, Hampton, 18 May 1868, det.

[13]Caroline Taintor (Buel), Detroit, to Delia E. Taintor, Hampton, 7 February 1869, det.

[14]Caroline Taintor (Buel), Detroit, to Delia E. Taintor, Hampton, 24 June 1872, det.

[15]Susan Taintor (Clapp), New York, to Delia E. Taintor, Hampton, 25 October 1873, det.

[16]Susan Taintor (Clapp), New York, to Delia E. Taintor, Hampton, 23 November 1873, det.

[17]Julia (Buel) Trowbridge, Detroit, to Delia E. Taintor, Hampton, 27 February 1874, in Delia E. Taintor from Caroline Taintor (Buel), det.

[18]Elizabeth Swados, "The Story of a Street Person," *The New York Times Magazine,* August 18, 1991, 47.

CHAPTER 17

[1]Calvin G. Child, Norwich, to Henry G. Taintor, Hampton, 8 August 1866, hgt.

[2]John A. Taintor, Hampton, to Henry G. Taintor, Hampton, 1 April 1833, in Inventory of Property, 1833, hgt; that "Inventory of Property received of J. A. Taintor Apr. 1 1833" lists the name of the borrower, initial amount of note, date borrowed, any endorsements, and the present value.

[3]Edwin Bulkeley Taintor, West Brookfield, Massachusetts, to Henry G. Taintor, Hampton, 25 April 1844, hgt.

[4]He bought ten shares of Bank of Commerce stock, and it might have been for his mother; John A. Taintor, Hartford, to Henry G. Taintor, Hampton, 14 June 1844, hgt.

[5]Ketcham & Olcott, New York, to Henry G. Taintor, Hampton, 2 December 1846, in Receipts, Stocks, 1840s, hgt.

[6]Inventory of Judith Taintor's Estate, 5 September 1849, hgt; also see Judith Taintor, Hartford, to Henry G. Taintor, Hampton, 29 September 1849, in Judith Taintor Estate, hgt; the Trust contained: just under $7,000 total, with five

shares of Phoenix Bank Stock valued at $577.50, seven shares of Windham County Bank Stock for $770, thirty-seven shares of Hampshire Manufactures Bank stock at $3,700, seventeen shares of Bank of Commerce (New York) stock at $1,700, and cash mostly in dividends on those stocks. Henry took the five shares of Phoenix, twenty shares of Hampshire, the seven shares of Windham County, and some of the cash, for his half.

[7]Matthew Bolles, Boston, to Henry G. Taintor, Hampton, 28 February 1850, in Receipts, Stocks, 1840s, hgt.

[8]John F. Stover, *American Railroads* (Chicago, 1961), 26–35.

[9]Hartford, Providence & Fishkill Railroad Co., Willimantic, to Henry G. Taintor, Hampton, 4 April 1859, in Receipts, Misc., 1850s, hgt. See also Edward C. Kirkland, *Men, Cities, and Transportation: A Study of New England History, 1820–1900,* 2 vols. (Cambridge, Mass., 1948); Leo Marx, *The Machine in the Garden: Technology and the Pastoral Ideal in America* (London, 1964); George R. Taylor, *The Transportation Revolution* (New York, 1951).

[10]Entry for 27 July 1854 in Henry G. Taintor Cash Book 10 July 1854–13 December 1855, in Cash Books (2), 1850s, hgt; John A. Taintor, Liverpool, to Henry G. Taintor, Hampton, 18 August 1845, hgt.

[11]Entries for 14 June 1858 and after in Henry G. Taintor Cash Book 2 June 1858–28 July 1860, in Cash Books (2), 1850s, hgt.

[12]Henry G. Taintor Cash Book 2 June 1858–28 July 1860, in Cash Books (2), 1850s, hgt; the first entries which specify payments in connection with Bissell & Co. are 6 January ($2,194) and 17 February 1860 ($1,900).

[13]Entries for 4 September 1861 and 3 January 1862 in Henry G. Taintor Cash Book 30 July 1860–10 September 1862, in Cash Books (2), 1860s, hgt.

[14]Entries for 31 January, 5 and 6 February, 6 March, and 17 October 1863 in Henry G. Taintor Cash Book 10 September 1862–14 March 1868, in Cash Books (2), 1860s, hgt.

[15]Entry for income 24 November 1862 in Henry G. Taintor Cash Book 10 September 1862–14 March 1868, in Cash Books (2), 1860s, hgt.

[16]Inventory of John A. Taintor's Estate, 5 February 1863, Hartford Probate Records, Connecticut State Library.

[17]Entries for 3 August, 25 and 27 September, 23 November 1864, and 17 and 27 February, 24 March, 3 and 15 April, 16 August, and 14 October 1865 in Henry G. Taintor Cash Book 10 September 1862–14 March 1868, in Cash Books (2), 1860s, hgt.

[18]Receipt from George P. Bissell & Co., Hartford, to Henry G. Taintor, Hampton, 29 September 1864, in Bills & Receipts, 1860–1864, hgt.

[19]William Searls, New York, to Henry G. Taintor, Hampton, 7 March 1866, hgt.

[20]Entry for 24 January 1866 in Henry G. Taintor Cash Book 10 September 1862–14 March 1868, in Cash Books (2), 1860s, hgt.

[21]Entries for 2 March and 24 May 1872 in Henry G. Taintor Cash Book 14 March 1868–10 October 1872, in Cash Books (4), 1870s, hgt. See also LaWanda C. Cox, "Tenancy in the United States, 1865–1900," *Agricultural History* 18 (1944), 97–105; Earl W. Hayter, *The Troubled Farmer, 1850–1900: Rural Adjustment to Industrialism* (DeKalb, Ill., 1968).

[22]Henry G. Taintor, Hartford, to Hartford National Bank, Hartford, 18 July 1866, in Misc. Receipts, 1860s, hgt.

[23]Chicago and Alton Rail-Road Company, New York, to Henry G. Taintor, Hartford, 26 July 1866, in Misc. Receipts, 1860s, hgt; M. K. Jesup & Co, New York, to Henry G. Taintor, Hartford, 15 September 1866, hgt.

[24]See Maury Klein, *The Life and Legend of Jay Gould* (Baltimore, 1986), for one of the more recent, detailed, and careful histories of the nineteenth-century "railroad game."

[25]Calvin G. Child, Norwich, to Henry G. Taintor, Hampton, 8 August 1866, hgt.

[26]Gabriel W. Coite, Hartford, to Henry G. Taintor, Hartford, 10 November 1866, hgt.

[27]Gabriel W. Coite, New York, to Henry G. Taintor, Hartford, 15 November 1866, hgt. See Alan Dawley, *Class and Community: The Industrial Revolution in Lynn* (Cambridge, Mass., 1976); Michael H. Frisch, *Town into City: Springfield, Massachusetts, and the Meaning of Community, 1840–1880* (Cambridge, Mass., 1972).

[28]William Searls, New York, to Henry G. Taintor, Hampton 10, 13, and 16 November 1866, hgt.

[29]E. C. Scranton, New York, to Henry G. Taintor, Hampton, 15 November 1866, hgt.

[30]William Searls, New York, to Henry G. Taintor, Hampton, 24 November 1866, hgt.

[31]E. C. Scranton, New Haven, to Henry G. Taintor, Hampton, 6 December 1866, hgt.

[32]William Searls, New York, to Henry G. Taintor, Hampton, 8, 10, and 20 December 1866, hgt.

[33]William Searls, New York, to Henry G. Taintor, Hampton, 9 February 1867, hgt.

[34]William Searls, New York, to Henry G. Taintor, Hampton, 8 and 13 March 1867, hgt.

[35]Henry G. Taintor, Hartford, to Delia E. Taintor, Hampton, 30 April 1867, det.

[36]Ellen Ellsworth (Strong), Windsor, to Delia E. Taintor, Hampton, 4 April 1867, det.

[37]Henry G. Taintor, Hartford, to Delia E. Taintor, Hampton, 1 May 1867, det.

[38]Cash Book of Henry G. Taintor, 14 March 1868–10 October 1872, in Cash Books (4), 1870s, hgt; On the last written-on pages the following is all X'ed over:

1871, *A/c Notes Purchased in New York:*

Carhart Ellis Clark & Co., 8/11 Mch, $2081.17, Left at Htfd BK; Carhart Ellis Clark & Co., 1/4 Apl, $980.74, ditto–disc; G. W. Da Canha, 6/9 May, $385.42; Dawes Finke & Fanning, 5/8 June, $1786.43; Carhart Ellis Clark & Co, 28/31 July, $1285.43.

[39]George E. Taintor, Chicago, to Delia E. Taintor, Hampton, 3 October 1875, det.

[40]William W. Taintor, New York, to Delia E. Taintor, Hampton, 19 April 1877, det.

CHAPTER 18

[1]Mary E. Taintor (Davis), Hampton, to Delia E. Taintor, Hartford, 9 September 1871, det.

[2]Henry E. Taintor, Monson, to Delia E. Taintor, Hampton, 25 April 1861, det.

[3]George E. Taintor, Hartford, to Delia E. Taintor, Hampton, 6 January 1863, det.

[4]George E. Taintor, Hartford, to Delia E. Taintor, Hampton, 6 November 1863, det.

[5]George E. Taintor, Hartford, to Delia E. Taintor, Hampton, 18 November 1863, det. See Donald Scott, "The Popular Lecture and the Creation of a Public in Mid-Nineteenth-Century America," *Journal of American History* 66 (1980), 791–801.

[6]Henry E. Taintor, Boston, to Delia E. Taintor, Hampton, 30 April 1866, det.

[7]Henry E. Taintor, Hartford, to Delia E. Taintor, Hampton, 1 August 1866, det.

[8]Henry E. Taintor, Hartford, to Delia E. Taintor, Hampton, 1 August 1866, det.

[9]George E. Taintor, Hartford, to Delia E. Taintor, Hampton, 4 January 1866, det.

[10]Ellen Ellsworth (Strong), Windsor, to Delia E. Taintor, Hampton, 27 September 1860, det.

[11]Delia E. Taintor, Hampton, to William W. Taintor, Windsor, 3 September 1860, wt.

[12]William W. Taintor, Williamsburg, New York, to Delia E. Taintor, Hampton, 26 August 1869, det.

[13]William W. Taintor, New York, to Delia E. Taintor, Hampton, 30 January 1870, det.

[14]William W. Taintor, Williamsburg, New York, to Delia E. Taintor, Hartford, 15 January 1871, det. See Ian R. Tyrrell, *Sobering Up: From Temperance to Prohibitionism in Antebellum America, 1800–1860* (Westport, Conn., 1979).

[15]William W. Taintor, New York, to Delia E. Taintor, Hampton, 5 February 1871, det.

[16]William W. Taintor and Arthur C. Bulkley, Williamsburg, New York, to Delia E. Taintor, Windsor, 4 April 1871, det.

[17]William W. Taintor, New York, to Delia E. Taintor, Hampton, 12 January 1875, det.

[18]Ellen Ellsworth (Strong), Rutland, Vermont, to Delia E. Taintor, Hampton, 13 March 1860, det.

[19]Frederick Taintor and R. H. Button, Hampton, to Delia E. Taintor, Windsor, 8 October 1866, det.

[20]Frederick Taintor, Hampton, to Delia E. Taintor, Boston, 7 June 1867, det.

[21]Frederick Taintor, New Haven, to Delia E. Taintor, Hampton, 27 September 1874, det.

[22]Cash Book of Henry G. Taintor, 1 September 1876–28 August 1878 (a black-scored leather-bound notebook with "Cash Book Commencing Dec 3rd 1877" on the first leaf with, crossed out below, "Fred Taintor, Hartford, Conn, Sep 1st 1876") in Cash Books (4), 1870s, hgt.

[23]Emma Ellsworth, Windsor, to Delia E. and Henry G. Taintor, Hampton, 5 March 1878, det.

[24]Mary E. Taintor (Davis), Hartford, to Delia E. Taintor, Hampton, 21 March 1878, det.

[25]Mary E. Taintor (Davis), Hartford, to Delia E. Taintor, Hampton, 31 March 1878, det.

[26]Sophie W. Reynolds, Lafayette, Indiana, to Delia E. Taintor, Hampton, 21 April 1878, det.

[27]Sophia Ellsworth, Windsor, to Henry G. Taintor, Hampton, 15 March 1861, in Mrs. Sophia Ellsworth Letters, det.

[28]Abigail Ellsworth (Hall), Washington, D.C., to Delia E. Taintor, Hampton, 29 March 1861, det.

[29]Henry E. Taintor, Monson, Massachusetts, to Delia E. Taintor, Hampton, 25 April 1861, det.

[30]Ellen Ellsworth (Strong), Windsor, to Delia E. Taintor, Hampton, undated 1862, det; Eleanor D. Ellsworth, Lafayette, Indiana, to Delia E. Taintor, Hampton, 27 January 1864, det.

[31]Emma Ellsworth, Windsor, to Delia E. Taintor, Hampton, 26 August 1869, det.

[32]Ellen Ellsworth (Strong), Windsor, to Delia E. Taintor, Hampton, 22 November 1869, det.

[33]Mary E. Taintor (Davis), Hampton to Delia E. Taintor, Hartford, 9 September 1871, det.

[34]Mary E. Taintor (Davis), Hartford, to Delia E. Taintor, Hampton, 30 May 1875, det.

[35]Mary E. Taintor (Davis), Windsor, to Delia E. Taintor, Hampton, 18 June 1874, det.

[36]Mary E. Taintor (Davis), Windsor, to Henry G. Taintor, Hampton, 24 September 1874, in Delia E. Taintor from Mary Taintor, thru 1875, det.

[37]Mary E. Taintor (Davis), Windsor, to Delia E. Taintor, Hampton, 27 September 1874, det.

[38]Mary E. Taintor (Davis), Hartford, to Delia E. Taintor, Hampton, 4 June 1875, det.

[39]Mary E. Taintor (Davis), Windsor, to Delia E. Taintor, Hampton, 5 July 1874, det.

[40]Mary E. Taintor (Davis), Windsor, to Delia E. Taintor, Hampton, 13 September 1874, det.

[41]Mary E. Taintor (Davis), Hartford, to Delia E. Taintor, Hampton, 30 January 1876, det.

[42]Mary E. Taintor (Davis), Hartford, to Delia E. Taintor, Hampton, 6 February 1876, det.

[43]Mary E. Taintor (Davis), Hartford, to Delia E. Taintor, Hampton, 5 November 1876, det.

[44]Mary E. Taintor (Davis), Hartford, to Delia E. Taintor, Hampton, 2 April 1876, det.

[45]Mary E. Taintor (Davis), Hartford, to Delia E. Taintor, Hampton, 19 November 1876, det.

[46]Mary E. Taintor (Davis), Hartford, to Delia E. Taintor, Hampton, 16 January 1876, det.

[47]Mary E. Taintor (Davis), Hartford, to Delia E. Taintor, Hampton, 24 June 1877, det.

[48]Emma Ellsworth, Lafayette, Indiana, to Delia E. Taintor, Hampton, 11 July 1877, det.

[49]Delia E. Taintor, Hampton, to Mary E. Taintor (Davis), Hartford, 2 April 1878, mtd.

[50]1876, A Centennial Exhibition, Robert C. Post, ed. (Washington, D.C., The Smithsonian Institution, 1976), 11–13. See also Fred A. Shannon, The Centennial Years (New York, 1967);

Lally Weymouth, America in 1876: The Way We Were (New York, 1976).

[51]Receipt from Grand Villa Hotel, Philadelphia, to Henry G. Taintor, 14 June 1876, and receipt from Henry E. Taintor, Hartford, to Henry G. Taintor, Hampton, 29 June 1876 in Bills & Receipts (2 Packets), 1874–1876, hgt.

[52]S. Wolcott Ellsworth, Fort Wayne, Indiana, to Frederick Ellsworth, Windsor, 15 November 1876, det. See also Robert V. Bruce, 1877: Year of Violence (Indianapolis, 1959).

CHAPTER 19

[1]Susan Taintor (Clapp), West Brookfield, Massachusetts, to Delia E. Taintor, Hampton, 22 November 1861, det. See also Ronald T. Takaki, Iron Cages: Race and Culture in Nineteenth-Century America (New York, 1979); Mark Twain and Charles Dudley Warner, The Gilded Age (Hartford, 1873); Edith Wharton, The House of Mirth (New York, 1905), and The Age of Innocence (New York, 1920).

[2]Susan Taintor (Clapp), West Brookfield, Massachusetts, to Delia E. Taintor, Hampton, 22 January 1855, det.

[3]Susan Taintor (Clapp), West Brookfield, Massachusetts, to Delia E. Taintor, Hampton, 1 February 1860, det.

[4]Caroline Taintor (Buel), West Brookfield, Massachusetts, to Delia E. Taintor, Hampton, 17 August 1860, det.

[5]Susan Taintor (Clapp), West Brookfield, Massachusetts, to Delia E. Taintor, Hampton, 25 March 1861, det.

[6]Susan Taintor (Clapp), West Brookfield, Massachusetts, to Delia E. Taintor, Hampton, 22 November 1861, det.

[7]Susan Taintor (Clapp), West Brookfield, Massachusetts, to Delia E. Taintor, Hampton, 28 January 1862, det.

[8]Susan Taintor (Clapp), Worcester, Massachusetts, to Delia E. Taintor, Hampton, 6 April 1862, det.

[9]Ellen Ellsworth (Strong), Rutland, Vermont, to Sophia Ellsworth, Windsor, 16 February 1862, in Delia E. Taintor from Ellen Ellsworth Strong, det.

[10]Susan Taintor (Clapp), West Brookfield, Massachusetts, to Delia E. Taintor, Hampton, 9 May 1862, det.

[11]Susan Taintor (Clapp), West Brookfield, Massachusetts, to Delia E. Taintor, Hampton, 17 November 1862, det.

[12]John Greenleaf Whittier, "Maud Muller" (1854).

[13]Susan Taintor (Clapp), West Brookfield, Massachusetts, to Delia E. Taintor, Hampton, 23 February 1863, det.

[14]Eugenia Taintor, West Brookfield, Massachusetts, to Delia E. Taintor, Hampton, 24 June 1864, in Delia E. Taintor from Susan P. (Taintor) Clapp, 1850s & 1860s, det.

[15]Susan Taintor (Clapp), West Brookfield, Massachusetts, to Delia E. Taintor, Hampton, 25 December 1864, det.

[16]Susan Taintor (Clapp), West Brookfield, Massachusetts, to Delia E. Taintor, Hampton, 25 December 1864, det.

[17]Caroline Taintor (Buel), Detroit, to Delia E. Taintor, Hampton, 1 May 1865, det.

[18]Susan Taintor (Clapp), Stockbridge, Massachusetts, to Delia E. Taintor, Hampton, 5 June 1865, det.

[19]William Dean Howells, *The Rise of Silas Lapham* (New York, 1885).

[20]Susan Taintor (Clapp), Boston, to Delia E. Taintor, Hampton, 15 February 1866, det.

[21]Caroline Taintor (Buel), Sault St. Marie, Michigan, to Delia E. Taintor, Hampton, 28 August 1867, det.

[22]Caroline Taintor (Buel), Boston, to Delia E. Taintor, Hampton, 22 February 1868, det.

[23]Susan Taintor (Clapp), Boston, to Delia E. Taintor, Windsor, c/o Mr. Frederick Ellsworth, 4 October 1866, det.

[24]Susan Taintor (Clapp), St. Johnsbury, Vermont, to Delia E. Taintor, Hampton, 16 April 1867, det.

[25]Susan Taintor (Clapp), Auburndale, Massachusetts, to Delia E. Taintor, Hampton, 22 August 1867, det.

[26]Susan Taintor (Clapp), Boston, to Delia E. Taintor, Hampton, 10 December 1867, det.

[27]Susan Taintor (Clapp), Boston, to Delia E. Taintor, Windsor, 30 January 1868, det.

[28]Susan Taintor (Clapp), Boston, to Delia E. Taintor, Hampton, 10 March 1869, det.

[29]Susan Taintor (Clapp), Boston, to Delia E. Taintor, Hampton, 28 May 1870, det.

[30]Susan Taintor (Clapp), Boston, to Delia E. Taintor, Hampton, 16 June 1870, det.

[31]Susan Taintor (Clapp), New York, to Delia E. Taintor, Hampton, 31 January 1873, det.

[32]Anna C. Stone, New York, to Delia E. Taintor, Hampton, 25 February 1873, det.

[33]Susan Taintor (Clapp), New York, to Delia E. Taintor, Hampton, 22 March 1873, det.

[34]Susan Taintor (Clapp), New York, to Delia E. Taintor, Hampton, 25 October 1873, det.

[35]Susan Taintor (Clapp), New York, to Delia E. Taintor, Hampton, 8 May 1874, det.

[36]Susan Taintor (Clapp), New York, to Delia E. Taintor, Hampton, 22 June 1874, det.

[37]Susan Taintor (Clapp), Tarrytown, New York, to Delia E. Taintor, Hampton, 23 July 1875, det.

[38]Susan Taintor (Clapp), New York, to Delia E. Taintor, Hampton, 17 November 1875, det.

[39]Anna C. Stone, Tarrytown-on-Hudson, New York, to Delia E. Taintor, Hampton, 21 July 1877, det.

[40]Susan Taintor (Clapp), New York, to Delia E. Taintor, Hampton, 4 October 1877, det.

[41]Anna C. Stone, New York, to Delia E. Taintor, Hampton, 8 November 1877, det.

[42]Anna C. Stone, New York, to Delia E. Taintor, Hampton, 30 November 1877, det.

[43]Anna C. Stone, New York, to Delia E. Taintor, Hampton, 10 December 1877, det.

[44]Eugenia Taintor, West Brookfield, Massachusetts, to Delia E. Taintor, Hampton, 26 December 1877, det.

[45]Henry L. Clapp, New York, to Henry G. Taintor, Hampton, 31 December 1877, in Delia E. Taintor from Susan P. (Taintor) Clapp, 1870s, det.

[46]Henry L. Clapp, New York, to Delia E. and Henry G. Taintor, Hampton, 3 January 1878, in Delia E. Taintor from Susan P. (Taintor) Clapp, 1870s, det.

[47]Susan Taintor (Clapp), New York, to Delia E. Taintor, Hampton, 21 February 1878, det.

[48]See for example Henry L. Clapp, Boston, to Henry G. Taintor, Hartford, 11 March 1867, hgt.

[49]Henry L. Clapp, New York, to Henry E. Taintor, Hartford, 2 November 1877, enclosed in a letter of Henry E. Taintor to Henry G. Taintor, 19 November 1877, hgt; the letterhead was for Fairbanks Scale Warehouse, 311 Broadway, and listed warehouses run by Fairbanks & Co. in New York, Baltimore, Buffalo, New Orleans, St. Louis, Albany, Montreal, and London, as well as those run by Fairbanks, Brown & Co. in Boston, Fairbanks & Ewing in Philadelphia, Fairbanks, Morse & Co. in Chicago, Cincinnati, Cleveland, Pittsburgh, and Louisville, Fairbanks & Hutchinson in San Francisco. E. & T. Fairbanks & Co., St. Johnsbury, are listed as manufacturers.

[50]Henry L. Clapp, New York, to Henry E. Taintor, Hartford, 14, 15, and 16 November 1877, hgt.

[51]Receipt from Louis Fitzgerald, New York, to Henry G. Taintor, Hampton, 2 September 1879, in Bills & Receipts (3 Large Packets), 1878–1883, hgt.

[52]Henry G. Taintor, Hampton, to A. B. Jewett, St. Johnsbury, Vermont, 18 February 1882 (date uncertain), in Cash Books (8), 1880s, hgt.

[53]Henry E. Taintor, Hartford, to Henry G. Taintor, Hampton, 23 March 1884, hgt.

[54]Henry E. Taintor, Hartford, to Henry G. Taintor, Hampton, 29 April 1884 and 2 May 1884, hgt.

CHAPTER 20

[1]Susan Taintor (Clapp), Boston, to Delia E. Taintor, Hampton, 19 February 1869, det.

[2]Entries for 9 September 1870 and 15 August 1870 in Cash Book of Henry G. Taintor 14 March 1868–10 October 1872, in Cash Books (4), 1870s, hgt.

[3]See the entry in the *Oxford English Dictionary*.

[4]Henry E. Taintor, New Haven, to Delia E. Taintor, Hampton, 23 September 1861, det.

[5]Delia E. Taintor, Hampton, to William W. Taintor, Windsor, 30 September 1860, wt, starts with letter from Henry E. Taintor.

[6]Henry E. Taintor, New Haven, to Delia E. Taintor, Hampton, 9 November 1863, det.

[7]Delia E. Taintor, Hampton, to Mary E. Taintor (Davis), Hartford, 26 June 1884, mtd.

[8]Ellen Ellsworth (Strong), Windsor, to Delia E. Taintor, Hampton, 14 February 1864, det.

[9]Delia E. Taintor, Hartford, to Mary E. Taintor (Davis), Hampton, 9 January 1881, mtd.

[10]William W. Taintor, New York, to Delia E. Taintor, Hampton, 5 February 1871, det.

[11]Mary E. Taintor (Davis), Hartford, to Delia E. Taintor, Hampton, 14 April 1878, det.

[12]Henry E. Taintor, Hartford, to Delia E. Taintor, Hampton, 19 September 1870, det.

[13]Henry E. Taintor, Hartford, to Delia E. Taintor, Hampton, 27 April 1873, det.

[14]Henry E. Taintor, Hartford, to Delia E. Taintor, Hampton, 6 July 1873, det.

[15]George E. Taintor, Columbus, Ohio, to Delia E. Taintor, Hampton, 26 April 1874, det.

[16]Emily Davis Taintor, Hartford, to Delia E. Taintor, Hampton, 27 April 1871, det.

[17]Emily Davis Taintor, Hartford, to Delia E. Taintor, Hampton, 27 April 1871, det.

[18]Emily Davis Taintor, Hartford, to Delia E. Taintor, Hampton, 15 March 1873, det.

[19]Abigail Ellsworth (Hall), Windsor, to Delia E. Taintor, Hampton, 17 September 1873, det.

[20]George E. Taintor, Urbana, Ohio, to Delia E. Taintor, Hampton, 1 November 1868, det. See also Daniel T. Rodgers, *The Work Ethic in Industrial America, 1850–1920* (Chicago, 1974).

[21]George E. Taintor, Columbus, Ohio to Delia E. Taintor, Hampton, 26 April 1874, det.

[22]George E. Taintor, Louisville, Kentucky, to Delia E. Taintor, Hampton, 30 June 1874, det.

[23]George E. Taintor, Alliance, Ohio, to Delia E. Taintor, Hampton, 18 September 1874, det.

[24]George E. Taintor, Quincy, Illinois, to Henry G. Taintor, Hampton, 10 May 1874, in Delia E. Taintor from George Taintor, det.

[25]Elizabeth (Mrs. William) Taintor, Brooklyn, New York, to Delia E. Taintor, Hampton, 8 April 1875, det.

[26]William W. Taintor, New York, to Delia E. Taintor, Hampton, 19 April 1877, det. See also R. Richard Wohl, "The 'Country Boy' Myth and Its Place in American Urban Culture: The Nineteenth-Century Contribution," *Perspectives in American History* 3 (1969), 77–156.

[27]Henry E. Taintor, Hartford, to Delia E. Taintor, Hampton, 22 March 1868, det.

[28]Caroline Taintor (Buel), Boston, to Delia E. Taintor, Hampton, 22 February 1868, det.

[29]Caroline Taintor (Buel), New York, to Delia E. Taintor, Hampton, 26 May 1872, det.

[30]William W. Taintor, New York, to Delia E. Taintor, Hampton, 15 January 1876, det.

[31]Henry E. Taintor, Hartford, to Delia E. Taintor, Hampton, 3 December 1872, det.

[32]Susan Taintor (Clapp), New York, to Delia E. Taintor, Hampton, 11 January 1876, det.

[33]Mary E. Taintor (Davis), Hartford, to Delia E. Taintor, Hampton, 8 April 1877, det.

[34]Cash Book of Henry G. Taintor, 14 March 1868–10 October 1872, in Cash Books (4), 1870s, hgt.

[35]Cash Book of Henry G. Taintor, 16 October 1872–8 December 1873, in Cash Books (4), 1870s, hgt.

[36]Henry E. Taintor and George E. Taintor, Hartford, to Delia E. Taintor, Hampton, 1 September 1867, det.

[37]Henry G. Taintor, Hartford, to Delia E. Taintor, Hampton, 30 April 1867, det.

[38]Henry E. Taintor, Hartford, to Delia E. Taintor, Hampton, 9 October 1869, det.

[39]Emily Davis Taintor, Hartford, to Delia E. Taintor, Hampton, 3 September 1870, det.

[40]Cash Book of Henry G. Taintor, 14 March 1868-10 October 1872, in Cash Books (4), 1870s, hgt. Receipt from James McCreery & Co., New York, to (Mrs.) Henry G. Taintor, Hampton, 11 October 1870, receipt from M. Sullivan, New York, to (Mrs.) Henry G. Taintor, Hampton, 10 October 1870, and receipt from Tiffany & Co., New York, to Henry G. Taintor, Hampton, 17 October 1870, in Bills & Receipts (4 Packets) 1870-1874, hgt.

[41]Sophie W. Reynolds, Lafayette, Indiana, to Delia E. Taintor, Hampton, 11 October 1870, det.

[42]Sophie W. Reynolds, Lafayette, Indiana, to Delia E. Taintor, Hampton, 1 May 1871, det.

[43]Sophie W. Reynolds, Lafayette, Indiana, to Delia E. Taintor, Hampton, 12 January 1874, det.

[44]Mary E. Taintor (Davis), Hartford, to Delia E. Taintor, Hampton, 8 April 1877, det.

[45]Martha B. Hall & Alice Hall (Wycoff), Springfield, Massachusetts, to Delia E. Taintor, Hampton, 30 April 1877, det.

[46]Emily Davis Taintor, Hartford, to Delia E. Taintor, Hampton, 28 May 1878, det.

[47]Mary E. Taintor (Davis), Hartford, to Delia E. Taintor, Hampton, 23 June 1878, det.

[48]Delia E. Taintor, Hampton, to Mary E. Taintor (Davis), Hartford, 26 June 1884, mtd.

[49]Receipt from B. Altman & Co., New York, to Henry G. Taintor, Hampton, 3 September 1884 in Bills & Receipts (2 Large Packets), 1884-1888, hgt.

[50]Receipt from James McCreery & Co., New York, to Henry G. Taintor, Hampton, 3 September 1884 in Bills & Receipts (2 Large Packets), 1884-1888, hgt.

[51]Receipt from Tiffany & Co., New York, to Henry G. Taintor, Hampton, 5 September 1884, and receipt from Whiting Manufacturing Company, New York, to Henry G. Taintor, Hampton, 27 September 1884 in Bills & Receipts (2 Large Packets), 1884-1888, hgt.

[52]Receipt from Angie G. Lyon, Hampton, to Henry G. Taintor, Hampton, 1 October 1884 in Bills & Receipts (2 Large Packets), 1884-1888, hgt.

[53]Receipt from Eugenia Taintor, West Brookfield, Massachusetts, to Henry G. Taintor, Hampton, 1 October 1884 in Bills & Receipts (2 Large Packets), 1884-1888, hgt.

[54]Receipt from Colt's Armory Band, Hartford, to Henry G. Taintor, Hampton, 1 October 1884 in Bills & Receipts (2 Large Packets), 1884-1888, hgt.

[55]Receipt from Edward Habenstein, Hartford, to Henry G. Taintor, Hampton, 2 October 1884 in Bills & Receipts (2 Large Packets), 1884-1888, hgt.

[56]Receipt from A. Perkins, Hampton, to Henry G. Taintor, Hampton, 2 October 1884 in Bills & Receipts (2 Large Packets), 1884-1888, hgt.

[57]Mary C. Soule, Naugatuck, Connecticut, to Mary Taintor Davis, Hartford, 27 June 1917, mtd.

[58]Receipt from M. Knoedler & Co., New York, to (Mrs) Henry G. Taintor, Hampton, 14 May 1883 in Bills & Receipts (3 Large Packets), 1878-1883, hgt.

[59]Patrick H. Pearl, Hampton, to Henry G. Taintor, Hartford, 14 February 1867, hgt.

[60]Ruth H. Button, Hampton, to Delia E. Taintor, Windsor, 22 February 1867, det.

[61]Susan Taintor (Clapp), Boston, to Delia E. Taintor, Hampton, 19 February 1869, det.

[62]Receipt from Dexter Wirt, Chicago, to Henry G. Taintor, Hampton, 7 November 1871 in Bills & Receipts (4 packets), 1870-1874, hgt.

[63]R. H. Button, Philadelphia, to Delia E. Taintor, Hampton, 21 June 1878, det.

[64]Hampton Town Records, Book C, 5 October 1868.

[65]Hampton Town Records, Book C, 19 April 1879.

[66]John Holander (Alias John Smith), JP case, 9 December 1869, hgt.

[67]Hampton Town Records, Book C, 4 October 1875.

[68]Hampton Town Records, Book C, 4 October 1875.

[69]Paul T. Ringenbach, *Tramps and Reformers, 1873-1916: The Discovery of Unemployment in New York* (Westport, Connecticut, 1973). See also LaWanda C. Cox, "The American Agricultural Wage Earner, 1865-1900: The Emergence of a Modern Labor Problem," *Agricultural History* 22 (1948), 95-114; Amos N. Currier, "The Decline of Rural New England," *Popular Science Monthly* 38 (1891), 384-89; Henry U. Fletcher, "The Doom of the Small Town," *Forum* 19 (1895), 214-23.

[70]Delia E. Taintor, Hampton, to Mary E. Taintor, Hartford, 16 November 1882, mtd.

[71]*Windham County Transcript,* Danielsonville, Connecticut, March 20, 1889.

[72]*Ibid.*

CHAPTER 21

[1]Emily Davis Taintor, Hartford, to Delia E. Taintor, Hampton, 8 April 1875, det.

[2]Letter dated September 26, 1924 in William W. Taintor Estate, Hartford Probate District, 1913. Connecticut State Library, Hartford.

[3]From a taped interview of Henry and Oliver Taintor, Fred Taintor's sons, made by Leanne Taintor Souzis and Laurie Taintor Stevens (Oliver's daughters) in the early 1980s. We are very grateful to Mrs. Souzis and Mrs. Stevens for providing us with much material and information about Fred Taintor and his family.

[4]Frederick Taintor, Atchison Station, Kansas, to Henry G. Taintor, Hampton, 31 December 1878, in possession of Leanne Taintor Souzis, who provided us a copy.

[5]Taped interview of Henry and Oliver Taintor.

[6]"Fred Tainter," by Milton Wallace (Doc) Anshutz, *The Clark County Clipper,* Ashland, Clark County, Kansas, 28 November 1940 (copy provided by Leanne Taintor Souzis).

[7]Copy of typescript by Victor Murdock (provided by Leanne Taintor Souzis).

[8]George Rainey, *No Man's Land* (1937), 101.

[9]Leanne Taintor Souzis told the story this way, and it does not contradict the information in "Doc" Anshutz's and Henry and Oliver's memories.

[10]Taped interview of Henry and Oliver Taintor.

[11]Dorothy Davis Goodwin, "My Ancestral Home" (1943).

[12]Alison Davis, *Hampton Remembers; A Small Town in New England 1885–1950* (Hampton, Connecticut, 1976), 93. Alison Davis's book is based on oral history interviews she did with elderly Hampton residents for the Hampton Antiquarian and Historical Society, and extensively quotes the interviews. In this chapter, we have quoted some of those interviews as Davis transcribed and used them.

[13]Goodwin, "My Ancestral Home."

[14]*Ibid.*

[15]Henry E. Taintor, New Haven, to Delia E. Taintor, Hampton, 17 November 1862, det.

[16]Eugenia Taintor, Rockport, Massachusetts, to Delia E. Taintor, Hampton, 22 August 1865, det.

[17]Lucretia L. Hayden, Hartford, to Delia E. Taintor, Hampton, 17 January 1867, det.

[18]Frederick Taintor, Woodstock, to Delia E. Taintor, Hampton, 29 August 1868, det.

[19]Delia E. Taintor, Hampton, to Mary E. Taintor, Hartford, 1 January 1882, mtd.

[20]Henry G. Taintor, Hampton, to Delia E. Taintor, Windsor, 28 January 1868, det.

[21]Ethel Edwards, quoted in Davis, *Hampton Remembers,* 105.

[22]Delia E. Taintor, Hampton, to Mary E. Taintor, Hartford, 19 February 1880, mtd.

[23]Delia E. Taintor, Hampton, to George E. Taintor, Hartford, 24 January 1874, gt.

[24]Harold Stone, quoted in Davis, *Hampton Remembers,* 105.

[25]Ethel B. Jaworski, Janet C. Robertson, and Beatrice S. Utley, *The Burnham-Hibbard House Guide* (Hampton, Connecticut, 1989).

[26]Emily Davis Taintor, Hartford, to Delia E. Taintor, Hampton, 8 April 1875, det.

[27]Bertha Burnham, quoted in Davis, *Hampton Remembers,* 103, 104.

[28]Ethel Jaworski, quoted in Davis, *Hampton Remembers,* 105, 106.

[29][italics ours] Receipt from James S. Baldwin, Hampton, to Henry G. Taintor, Hampton, 2 January 1882 in Bills & Receipts (3 Large Packets), 1878–1883, hgt.

[30]Robert Fitts, quoted in Davis, *Hampton Remembers,* 124, 125.

[31]*Hampton and the Fullers* (typescript), as related piecemeal in 1936 by Edward Martin Fuller to his friend George Miner, 9.

[32]Edgar Lee Masters, *Spoon River Anthology* (New York, 1915), and Clarence M. Webster, *Town Meeting Country* (New York, 1945).

[33]Susan Taintor (Clapp), Tarrytown, New York, to Delia E. Taintor, Hampton, 23 July 1875, det.

[34]Ellen Ellsworth (Strong), Rutland, Vermont, to Delia E. Taintor, Hampton, 16 May 1878, det.

[35]Andrew J. Rindge, Hampton, v. William H. Hammond, Hampton, 3 April 1882, JP Case, hgt.

[36]Margaret Marcus, quoted in Davis, *Hampton Remembers,* 142.

[37]Edith Wharton, *Ethan Frome* (New York, 1911).

[38]George Fuller, quoted in Davis, *Hampton Remembers,* 126–27.

[39]Margaret Marcus, quoted in Davis, *Hampton Remembers,* 131.

[40]Russell Thompson, quoted in Davis, *Hampton Remembers,* 90. See also Peter J. Schmitt, *Back to Nature: The Arcadian Myth in Urban America* (New York, 1969); John L. Shover, *First Majority–Last Minority: The Transformation of Rural Life in America* (DeKalb, Ill., 1976); Page Smith, *As a City Upon a Hill: The Town in American History* (New York, 1966).

[41]Harold Stone, quoted in Davis, *Hampton Remembers,* 85.

[42]John Hammond, quoted in Davis, *Hampton Remembers,* 86.

[43]Gertrude Pearl, quoted in Davis, *Hampton Remembers,* 109–10.

[44]Sophie W. Reynolds, Lafayette, Indiana, to Delia E. Taintor, Hampton, 5 February 1868, det.

[45]The process started early in the Taintor family, see Ellen Ellsworth (Strong), Rutland, Vermont, to Delia E. Taintor, Hampton, 14 September 1874, det, and Celinda Chapman, Colchester, Connecticut, to Delia E. Taintor, Hampton, 2 July 1867 in Henry G. Taintor from Celinda Chapman, hgt.

[46]Susan Taintor (Clapp), New York, to Delia E. Taintor, Hampton, 13 April 1874, det.

[47]Emma Ellsworth, Lafayette, Indiana, to Delia E. Taintor, Hampton, 26 June 1870, det.

[48]Delia E. Taintor, Hampton, to Mary E. Taintor (Davis), Hartford, 23 January 1880, mtd.

[49]Sophie W. Reynolds, California, to Delia E. Taintor, Hampton, 3 October 1864. det, with notation "Extract from Sophie's letter to her Mother, Copied at Elmwood Sabbath eve. Dec 4th 1864."

[50]Goodwin, "My Ancestral Home."

EPILOGUE

[1]Ludovicus Weld, Fabius, New York, to Roger Taintor, Esq., Hampton, 24 September 1827, rst.

[2]Nicholas Lemann, *The Promised Land: The Great Black Migration and How It Changed America* (New York, 1991), 276.

[3]Ludovicus Weld, Fabius, New York, to Roger Taintor, Esq., Hampton, 24 September 1827, rst. See also Edwin Way Teale, *A Naturalist Buys an Old Farm* (New York, 1974), which is about the Teales moving into Andrew Rindge's house some years before we moved to Hampton.

[4]Iris Origo, *The Merchant of Prato: Francesco di Marco Datini, 1335–1410* (Boston, 1986), xxviii.

INDEX

Ginzburg, Carlo (*The Cheese and the Worms*), 466
Gleason, "Grandma," 255–6
Gold, 346
Gold Rush (to California), 277–8, 301, 320–1
Goldsmith, (Rev.) Alfred, 419
Goodman, Paul, 478
Goodwin, Dorothy Davis, 429, 431–3, 445–6
  account of her ancestral home, 4, 11
Goodwin, James L., 429
Goodwin, James M., 53
Goodwin, Roxana. *See* Bulkeley, Roxana
Gorn, Elliott J., 480
Grand Army of the Republic, 324, 425
Grange. *See* Patrons of Husbandry
Great Awakening, 17
"Great Britain Steam Ship," 235
Greenfield High School, 212, 215–16
Greeley, Horace, 275
Greeley, John, 279
Greene, John C., 472
Greenslit, David, 278, 280
Greenslit, Mrs. David, 322–3
Greenville, Illinois, 203–6
Greven, Philip (*The Protestant Temperament*), 468
Griffin, Ebenezer, 24, 39
Griffin, Ebenezer, Jr., 24, 39, 279–80
Gross, Robert A. (*The Minutemen and Their World*), 466
Grosvenor, Charles, 152–3
Grow, Galusha, 8, 258
Grow, Thomas and Thomas, Jr., 76
Grow, William and James, 18
Grundy, Samuel, 219
Gurley, Anne, 6–7, 247–8
Gurley, (Capt.) Artemas, 44–5

Habenstein, Edward, 416–17
Hahn, Steven (*The Countryside in the Age of Capitalist Transformation*), 466
Hall, A. C., 201
Hall, Abigail E., 225–7, 257–8, 316–19. *See also:* Ellsworth, Abigail Wolcott
Hall, Alice, 227, 259, 306, 308, 412–13
Hall, Cesar, 243, 277
Hall, David Aiken, 216, 222
Hall, Ellen, 222, 226
Hall, Fanny, 252–3
Hall, John, 361
Hall, Maria, 308, 321–2
Hall, Peter, 125
Halsey, Frederick, 367–8
Hammond, Abigail and Marcy, 53
Hammond, Hezekiah, 54, 221

Hampton
  Catholics in, 304, 419–20
  in Civil War, 305, 306–7, 309, 319–20, 321–3
  Congregational church of, 2, 15–19, 81, 230–2, 274, 342, 374–5, 432
  depots in, 417, 443
  description of, 2
  early families of, 28
  education in, 26–7
  immigrants in, 242, 247, 304, 419–20, 421, 439–40
  incorporation of, 22
  inn/hotel in, 230, 276, 279, 434–7
  location of, 1
  migration from, 68, 176–94, 200–1, 203–6, 241
  maps of, 3, 341
  modern institutions of, 454–5
  politics, 73–7, 171–4, 272–6, 302–3, 351–2, 420, 441
  population of, 421
    (1800), 2
    (1850), 241–3
    (1860), 303–4
    (1880), 417–18, 419
    (1900), 439
    (1920), 440
    (1990), 443
  and railroads, 345, 434, 441–2
  as a resort town, 436–7
  schools in, 123, 183–4, 228, 230, 276, 455
  settlement of, 1
  silk manufacturing in, 155–9
Hampton General Store, 146
Hankins, Jean, 466
Harding, Carrie Lawrence, 385, 386
Hare, Augustus J. C. (*Walks in London*), 475
Harris, D. L., 400
Harrison, William Henry, 222
Hartford Asylum for the Deaf, 41
Hartford, Connecticut, 105, 124, 198–9, 211, 219, 371–5, 403–4, 424–5
Hartford Convention, 75
Hartford High School, 361, 371–3, 424
Hatch, Mamie, 372–3
Hayden, Lucretia, 434
Hayes, Rutherford B., 373, 377
Health care, 25
Heimert, Alan (*Religion and the American Mind*), 466
Hendley, Isaac N., 279
Hickey, Donald R. (*The War of 1812*), 471
Hierarchy, 56–7, 86

PHOTOGRAPHY CREDITS